Handbook of Climate Change and India

How do policymakers, businesses and civil society in India approach the challenge of climate change? What do they believe global climate negotiations will achieve and how? And how are Indian political and policy debates internalizing climate change? Relatively little is known globally about internal climate debate in emerging industrializing countries, but what happens in rapidly growing economies like India's will increasingly shape global climate change outcomes.

This handbook brings together prominent voices from India, including policymakers, politicians, business leaders, civil society activists and academics, to build a composite picture of contemporary Indian climate politics and policy. One section lays out the range of positions and substantive issues that shape Indian views on global climate negotiations. Another delves into national politics around climate change. A third looks at how climate change is beginning to be internalized in sectoral policy discussions over energy, urbanization, water, and forests. This volume is introduced by a chapter that sets out the critical issues shaping climate politics in India, and its implications for global politics.

The chapters show that, within India, climate change is approached primarily as a developmental challenge and is marked by efforts to explore how multiple objectives of development, equity, and climate mitigation can simultaneously be met. In addition, Indian perspectives on climate negotiations are in a state of flux. Considerations of equity across countries and a focus on the primary responsibility for the action of wealthy countries continue to be central, but there are growing voices of concern on the impacts of climate change on India. How domestic debates over climate governance are resolved in the coming years, and the evolution of India's global negotiation stance are likely to be important inputs toward creating shared understandings across countries in the years ahead, and to identify ways forward. This volume on the Indian experience with climate change and development is a valuable contribution to both purposes.

Navroz K. Dubash is a Senior Fellow at the Centre for Policy Research, New Delhi, India.

Handbook of Climate Change and India

Development, Politics and Governance

Edited by Navroz K. Dubash

LONDON AND NEW YORK

First published 2012
by Earthscan
2 Park Square, Milton Park, Abingdon, Oxfordshire OX14 4RN

Simultaneously published in the USA and Canada
by Earthscan
711 Third Avenue, New York, NY 10017

First issued in paperback 2015

Earthscan is an imprint of the Taylor & Francis Group, an informa business

© 2012 Selection and editorial material, Navroz K. Dubash; individual chapters to their authors

The right of Navroz K. Dubash to be identified as the author of the editorial material, and of the authors for their individual chapters, has been asserted in accordance with sections 77 and 78 of the Copyright, Designs and Patents Act 1988.

All rights reserved. No part of this book may be reprinted or reproduced or utilised in any form or by any electronic, mechanical, or other means, now known or hereafter invented, including photocopying and recording, or in any information storage or retrieval system, without permission in writing from the publishers.

Trademark notice: Product or corporate names may be trademarks or registered trademarks, and are used only for identification and explanation without intent to infringe.

British Library Cataloguing in Publication Data
A catalogue record for this book is available from the British Library

Library of Congress Cataloging in Publication Data
A handbook of climate change and India : development, politics, and governance / edited by Navroz K. Dubash.
p. cm.
Includes bibliographical references and index.
1. Climatic changes–India. I. Dubash, Navroz K.
QC903.2.I4H36 2011
363.738'740954–dc23
2011023209

ISBN 13: 978-1-138-92401-7 (pbk)
ISBN 13: 978-1-84971-358-0 (hbk)

Typeset in Sabon
by Keystroke, Station Road, Codsall, Wolverhampton

Contents

List of figures	ix
List of tables	xiii
Notes on contributors	xv
Foreword by Jairam Ramesh	xix
Preface and acknowledgements	xxiii

Introduction   1

NAVROZ K. DUBASH

PART I
Climate science and potential impacts   27

1 Impacts of climate change on India   29

   J. SRINIVASAN

2 Sea level rise: impact on major infrastructure, ecosystems and land
along the Tamil Nadu coast   41

   SUJATHA BYRAVAN, SUDHIR CHELLA RAJAN AND
   RAJESH RANGARAJAN

3 The impact of climate change on a shift of the apple belt in Himachal
Pradesh   51

   RANBIR SINGH RANA, R.M. BHAGAT, VAIBHAV KALIA AND
   HARBANS LAL

4 India in the Intergovernmental Panel on Climate Change   63

   R. RAMACHANDRAN

PART II
Past as prologue: early Indian perspectives on climate change   79

5 Global warming in an unequal world: a case of environmental
colonialism (selected excerpts)   81

   ANIL AGARWAL AND SUNITA NARAIN

vi *Contents*

6 Present at the creation: the making of the UN Framework
   Convention on Climate Change   89
   CHANDRASHEKHAR DASGUPTA

PART III
The international climate negotiations: stakes, debates and dilemmas   99

7 International climate negotiations and India's role   101
   SANDEEP SENGUPTA

8 The reach and limits of the principle of common but differentiated
   responsibilities and respective capabilities in the climate change regime   118
   LAVANYA RAJAMANI

9 Equity and burden sharing in emission scenarios: a carbon budget
   approach   130
   T. JAYARAMAN, TEJAL KANITKAR AND MARIO D'SOUZA

10 Equity in climate change: the range of metrics and views   147
    NARASIMHA RAO

11 Climate change debate: the rationale of India's position   157
    PRODIPTO GHOSH

12 India's official position: a critical view based on science   170
    D. RAGHUNANDAN

13 Views from the outside: international perspectives on India's climate
    positions   180
    EUROPEAN UNION, BERT METZ
    BANGLADESH, SALEEMUL HUQ
    PHILIPPINES, VICENTE PAOLO YU III
    CHINA, YING CHEN
    USA, MICHAEL LEVI

PART IV
Domestic politics of climate change   195

14 Climate politics in India: three narratives   197
    NAVROZ K. DUBASH

15 Climate change and the Indian environmental movement   208
    SHARACHCHANDRA LELE

16 The Hiding Behind the Poor debate: a synthetic overview   218
    SHOIBAL CHAKRAVARTY AND M.V. RAMANA

Contents vii

17 Climate change and parliament 230
COMMENTARY: SURESH PRABHU
EXCERPTS FROM LOK SABHA DEBATES
EXCERPTS FROM RAJYA SABHA DEBATES

18 Climate change and the private sector 246
TARUN DAS

19 Corporate responses to climate change in India 254
SIMONE PULVER

20 A change in climate? Trends in climate change reportage in the
Indian print media 266
ANU JOGESH

PART V
Integrating climate change and development: a sectoral view 287

21 Energy, development and climate change 289
GIRISH SANT AND ASHWIN GAMBHIR

22 Climate change and urbanization in India 303
PARTHA MUKHOPADHYAY AND AROMAR REVI

23 Agriculture in the environment: Are sustainable climate friendly
systems possible in India? 317
RAJESWARI RAINA

24 Framework for India's strategic water resource management under
a changing climate 328
HIMANSHU KULKARNI AND HIMANSHU THAKKAR

25 Mitigation or exploitation? The climate talks, REDD and forest areas 341
SHANKAR GOPALAKRISHNAN

26 The technology agenda 352
ANAND PATWARDHAN AND NEHA UMARJI

PART VI
Looking to the future 367

27 Mainstreaming climate change 369
SHYAM SARAN

28 The geopolitics of climate change 373
NITIN DESAI

Index 385

Figures

1.1	Increase in global mean temperature for various scenarios	30
1.2	The increase in global mean sea level, past and future	31
1.3	The simulation of seasonal variation of rainfall over India by different climate models in the IPCC Fourth Assessment Report	36
1.4	The prediction of changes in rainfall over India by different climate models in the IPCC Fourth Assessment Report	36
1.5	The prediction of changes in rainfall over India by MRI climate model in the future compared to the 20th century	37
2.1	Global mean temperatures and sea levels	42
2.2	Probable maximum storm surge (PMSS) above tide level in Tamil Nadu	46
3.1	Apple growing regions of Himachal Pradesh	53
3.2	Cumulative chill unit trends (Utah model) at Bajaura in the Kullu Valley, 1986–2003	57
3.3	Cumulative chill units (Utah model) of Shimla, 1990–2003	58
3.4	Cumulative chill units (Utah model) at Bhang, Kullu, 1983–2001	58
3.5	Cumulative chill units (Utah model) at Dhundi, Kullu (2700 msl), 1989–2001	59
3.6	Annual average snowfall trends in Satluj catchment, 1984–2005	60
4.1	IPCC structure	64
4.2	IPCC review procedure	65
5.1	Permissible emissions vs total emissions of carbon dioxide of select countries on the basis of population (in million tonnes of carbon equivalent) as calculated by CSE	83
5.2	Permissible emissions vs total emissions of methane of select countries on the basis of population (in million tonnes of carbon equivalent) as calculated by CSE	86
5.3	Percentage distribution of net emissions of greenhouse gases by industrialized and developing countries	87
9.1	Development of emissions for Annex-I countries under three effort-sharing approaches	134
9.2	Development of emissions for non-Annex-I countries under three effort-sharing approaches	135
9.3	Correlation between cumulative emissions and cumulative GDP for all countries	141
11.1	An international comparison between Human Development Index and per-capita energy consumption	158

x *Figures*

11.2	Annual central government expenditures to address climate variability, 1997–2000	159
11.3	Components of adaptation expenditure, 2006–7	160
11.4	CO_2 emissions from the food sector – from field (production) to table (processed food) excluding cooking	161
11.5	Recycling of solid waste and waste-related emissions	161
11.6	CO_2 emissions from passenger transport	162
11.7	Illustration of the concept of Environmental Kuznets Curve (EKC)	163
16.1	A comparison of the estimated emissions of various rural and urban income classes in 2004 with the average emissions of select countries of the world	223
16.2	Projected evolution of the emission distribution of India, assuming that inequality in emissions stays the same as in 2003–4	225
19.1	Carbon dioxide emissions from the consumption and flaring of fossil fuels per thousand dollars of gross domestic product (using PPP), 1992–2006	255
19.2	Share of total global Clean Development Mechanism projects by region, 2004–2011	257
19.3	Number of Clean Development Mechanism projects in India by type	258
19.4	Financial and reputational drivers of corporate Clean Development Mechanism investment in the Indian and Brazilian sugar and cement industries	262
20.1	Timeline of climate-related events, September 2009–March 2010	267
20.2	Indian newspaper coverage of climate change, January 2004–December 2009	269
20.3	Frequency of climate news coverage across nine newspapers, September 2009–March 2010	271
20.4	Distribution of content across nine newspapers, September 2009–March 2010	272
20.5	Frequency and geographical distribution of the coverage of climate impacts. Distribution of impacts across nine newspapers, September 2009–March 2010	273
20.6	Media coverage of climate controversies. Distribution of coverage across nine newspapers, September 2009–March 2010	274
20.7	Domestic climate policies versus domestic climate politics. Distribution of coverage across nine newspapers, September 2009–March 2010	276
20.8	Narratives pertaining to responsibility for climate change impacts	277
20.9	Narratives pertaining to action on climate change mitigation	279
20.10	Articles supportive of the Indian government's shift in negotiating position on climate action versus articles critical of the government's negotiating stance	281
21.1	HDI – electricity consumption per capita	291
21.2	Emissions (CO_2) intensity of the economies of five major countries using Purshcasing Power Parities, 1990–2009	292
21.3	India's elasticity of electricity production to GDP, 1981–2010	293
21.4	Balancing between climate and development objectives	298

Figures xi

22.1	Ratio of rural to urban share of households with specific consumer durables	306
24.1	Relative share of surface and groundwater to India's net irrigated area, 1950–2000	330
24.2	Trends in gross irrigated area, net irrigated area, irrigation by canals and irrigation by groundwater, 1990–2008	331
24.3	Groundwater resources: availability, demand and supply – business-as-usual approach	333
24.4	Groundwater resources: availability, demand and supply – managed resource approach	334
24.5	Springs – increasing demand, climate change and decreased discharges	335
24.6	Springs – spring recharge, managed demand and sustainable discharges	336
26.1	Transformation from Baseline to Blue Map scenario	354
26.2	Power generation mix	355
26.3	Transitions in transportation sector	355
26.4	Technology development cycle and its main driving forces	357
26.5	Effect of progress ratios on break-even point and learning investments	358
26.6	Global expense on R&D (GERD) as a % of the GDP for various countries	360

Tables

2.1	Land area inundated by a 1 metre rise in sea levels along the Tamil Nadu coast	45
2.2	Future storm surge heights and corresponding areas at risk for different districts	46
2.3	Summary results with replacement value for infrastructure, present value of ecosystem services for wetlands, and market value for land in different coastal districts of Tamil Nadu with a 1 metre sea level rise	47
3.1	Farmers' perceptions regarding climate change and its impact	55
3.2	Change in land-use pattern, apple area and income from fruits per farmer in apple-growing regions of Himachal Pradesh	56
3.3	Cumulative chill unit trends (mean monthly model) equations for different winter months at Kullu (Bajaura) and Shimla (CPRI, Shimla)	59
3.4	Cumulative chill unit trend equations for different sites and at different elevations (Utah model)	61
4.1	Number of authors from selected regions contributing to the Fourth Assessment Report, 2007	68
4.2	Comparison of numbers of authors from India and China for the five IPCC Assessment Reports	68
4.3	The distribution of Indian IPCC authors by subject area	71
7.1	Timeline of key events in climate change negotiations	105
9.1	Entitlements to carbon space: 1850 basis	139
9.2	Entitlements to carbon space: 1970 basis	139
9.3	Entitlements and potentially realizable carbon space: 1850 basis	143
9.4	Comparison of budgets allocated by various economic models	144
10.1a	Comparison of resource sharing proposals – Indian perspective	152
10.1b	Comparison of burden sharing proposals – Indian perspective	152
11.1	EKC estimates of turning points of India and a set of 32 countries (developed and developing) for wastewater treatment	163
11.2	Air quality: comparisons of EKC turning points for India and several other country groups	164
11.3	Energy intensity of GDP: EKC turning points for India and several other countries	165
14.1	Diversity of opinion on domestic and international climate policy engagement with global climate regime	201
14.2	Three strategic Indian perspectives on climate change	202
16.1	Distribution of emissions in 1989–90 by household expenditure	222

xiv *Tables*

16.2	Distribution of emissions in 2003–4 by household expenditure	222
16.3	Distribution of emissions in 2007 by income	222
16.4	Distribution of emissions in 2009 by income	223
16.5	Projection of 2003–4 emission distribution to 2030	225
18.1	Responses for Carbon Disclosure Project (CDP), 2010	250
20.1	Frequency and distribution of news coverage across nine newspapers	285
20.2	Frequency and distribution of the nature of news content	285
20.3	Source of news content	285
20.4	Frequency and geographical distribution of climate-related impacts	285
20.5	Frequency of climate scepticism	285
20.6	Impact of climate controversies	286
20.7	Coverage during the Copenhagen Summit (7–18 Dec. 2009)	286
20.8	Narratives on responsibility for climate change impacts	286
20.9	Narratives on responsibility for climate change mitigation	286
20.10	Domestic politics versus domestic policies	286
21.1	Share of Indian electricity generation by source (2010)	294
22.1	Capital cities and public transport availability	308
24.1	Comparative status of level of groundwater development, 1996 and 2004	332
24.2	Impact of impacts – water resources and climate change	338
26.1	Science and technology-related aspects of some NAPCC missions	361

Notes on contributors

Editor

Navroz K. Dubash is a Senior Fellow at the Centre for Policy Research, New Delhi. His current work examines climate change as a problem of multi-level governance by focusing on domestic regulatory changes in environmentally sensitive sectors. He also works on the political economy of energy in India and Asia, international climate change negotiations, the role of civil society in global environmental governance, and water governance. He is currently a member of India's Expert Group on Low Carbon Strategies for Inclusive Growth, a lead author for the Fifth Assessment Report of the Intergovernmental Panel on Climate Change, and also serves on the editorial boards of several international journals.

His recent publications include a co-edited special issue of *Climate Policy* entitled 'Beyond Copenhagen' and a co-edited special issue on Global Energy Governance for the journal *Global Policy*. He has a long history of engagement with civil society organizations, including as the first international coordinator of the Climate Action Network, from 1990 to 1992.

Navroz holds PhD and MA degrees in Energy and Resources from the University of California, Berkeley, and an AB in Public and International Affairs from Princeton University.

Contributors

Anil Agarwal (1947–2001). Article reproduced with permission of Centre for Science and Environment.

R.M. Bhagat, Research and Development Coordinator TRA Jorhat, Assam.

Sujatha Byravan, Senior Fellow, Centre for Development Finance, IFMR.

Shoibal Chakravarty, Research Associate, Princeton Environmental Institute, Princeton University.

Ying Chen, Deputy Director and Senior Research Fellow of Research Centre for Sustainable Development (RCSD), Chinese Academy of Social Sciences (CASS), China.

Tarun Das, Former Chief Mentor, Confederation of Indian Industries.

Chandrashekhar Dasgupta, Distinguished Fellow, The Energy and Resources Institute and Former Lead Negotiator on Climate Change, Government of India.

Mario D'Souza, Research Officer, Centre for Science, Technology and Society, Tata Institute of Social Sciences.

xvi *Notes on contributors*

Nitin Desai, Distinguished Fellow, TERI, and Former Under-Secretary General for Economic and Social Affairs, United Nations.

Ashwin Gambhir, Researcher, Prayas Energy Group.

Prodipto Ghosh, Distinguished Fellow, The Energy and Resources Institute, Former Secretary, Environment and Forests and Member, Prime Minister's Council on Climate Change.

Shankar Gopalakrishnan, Campaign for Survival and Dignity.

Saleemul Huq, Director, International Centre for Climate Change and Development, Independent University, Bangladesh.

T. Jayaraman, Professor and Chairperson, Centre for Science, Technology and Society, Tata Institute of Social Sciences.

Anu Jogesh, Deputy Special Features Editor, CNN-IBN.

Vaibhav Kalia, Centre for Geo-Informatics Research and Training, CSK Himachal Pradesh Agricultural University, Palampur.

Tejal Kanitkar, Program Officer, Centre for Science, Technology and Society, Tata Institute of Social Sciences.

Himanshu Kulkarni, Executive Director, Advanced Centre for Water Resources Development and Management.

Harbans Lal, Directorate of Extension Education, CSKHPKV, Palampur.

Sharachchandra Lele, Senior Fellow, Centre for Environment and Development, Ashoka Trust for Research in Ecology and the Environment.

Michael Levi, Senior Fellow, Council on Foreign Relations, New York.

Bert Metz, Fellow, European Climate Foundation.

Partha Mukhopadhyay, Senior Fellow, Centre for Policy Research.

Sunita Narain. Article reproduced with permission of Centre for Science and Environment.

Anand Patwardhan, Professor, Indian Institute of Technology, Mumbai.

Suresh Prabhu, Member of Parliament, and Former Minister of Environment and Forests.

Simone Pulver, Assistant Professor, University of California, Santa Barbara, USA.

D. Raghunandan, President, All India Peoples Science Network.

Rajeswari Raina, Scientist, National Institute for Science, Technology and Development Studies.

Lavanya Rajamani, Professor, Centre for Policy Research, New Delhi.

Sudhir Chella Rajan, Professor, Department of Humanities and Social Sciences, IIT. Madras.

R. Ramachandran, Associate Editor (Science), Frontline, New Delhi.

M.V. Ramana, Associate Research Scholar, Program on Science and Global Security, Princeton University, USA.

Ranbir Singh Rana, Centre for Geo-Informatics Research and Training, CSK Himachal Pradesh Agricultural University, Palampur.

Rajesh Rangarajan, Senior Researcher, Centre for Development Finance, IFMR.

Narasimha Rao, Postdoctoral scholar at the International Institute for Applied Systems Analysis (IIASA).

Aromar Revi, Director, Indian Institute for Human Settlement.

Girish Sant, Convenor, Prayas Energy Group.

Shyam Saran, Senior Fellow, Centre for Policy Research, and Former Prime Minister's Special Envoy on Climate Change.

Notes on contributors xvii

Sandeep Sengupta, DPhil. Candidate in International Relations, Oxford University, UK.

J. Srinivasan, Chairman, Divecha Centre for Climate Change, Indian Institute of Science.

Himanshu Thakkar, Convenor, South Asia Network on Dams, Rivers and People.

Neha Umarji , Researcher, Indian Institute of Technology, Mumbai.

Vicente Paolo Yu III, Head of Administration and Programme Coordinator for Global Governance and Development, South Centre, Geneva, Switzerland.

Foreword

Shri Jairam Ramesh, Minister, Rural Development, Former Minister, Environment and Forests, Government of India

When Navroz Dubash approached me to write the foreword for this handbook, I readily accepted – it is not often that one gets asked to introduce a tome that attempts the daunting task of capturing such a wide range of viewpoints on climate change. At several of the climate change-related events that I have been part of, the heated debates have often raised the temperature by 1.5 degrees, sometimes even more than 2 degrees above normal, so Navroz's efforts are particularly admirable! More seriously, Navroz and his team's extensive research on international negotiations and Indian policies, governance and laws means he is especially well-placed to bring together such a wide selection of Indian and other voices on the debate.

In introducing this book, I will trace broadly India's recent approach and actions on climate change. I hope this will serve to set the context for the perspectives, debates and analyses that follow.

I

As I argued during my tenure in the Ministry of Environment and Forests, *I think there is no country more vulnerable to climate change than India, on so many fronts.* There are four points of vulnerability that are particularly worth mentioning.

The first major point of vulnerability arises from our heavy dependence on the monsoons: our economic and agricultural systems are closely tied to it. Two in three Indians – either directly or indirectly – depend on agriculture for employment. An indifferent monsoon brings down our economic performance, but more importantly, affects low-income groups the most. An analysis of data over the last 50 years shows that nearly half of our fluctuations in GDP are related to variations in the monsoon. To my mind, what happens to the monsoon is the single largest determinant of prosperity in India.

The second point of vulnerability is our long coastline – one of the longest in the world; plus with one of the highest concentrations of people. 250–300 million people live along the coast, and a large proportion of them are dependent on climate-sensitive livelihoods such as agriculture and fishing. A sea level rise of even one metre would have serious implications, and on an index of vulnerability therefore, we rank high.

The third vulnerability arises from the threat to the health of our Himalayan glaciers. While glacial movement is a highly complex phenomenon – some glaciers in India are retreating, while others are advancing or staying steady – it is unequivocal that in general, the health of our glaciers is threatened. Melting glaciers will have a

xx *Foreword*

direct impact on water availability to hundreds of millions people across our Gangetic belt, disrupt crop production, and affect rainfall patterns.

Our fourth major point of vulnerability is our dependence on natural resource extraction: most of our core mining areas are in the heart of our densest forests. This simply means that the more mining we do, the more forests we destroy, the more we add to our GHG emissions, and the more we lose our biodiversity.

Therefore, I am convinced that acting on climate change is a national priority – we need to act, for our own sake, not because of or for the sake of anyone else. We need an aggressive domestic agenda that addresses these vulnerabilities – an agenda that produces substantive policy action in the short as well as medium term and an agenda that is delinked from progress in international negotiations. The traditional Indian approach of (i) we will not do anything substantive because we have not caused the problem of global warming; and (ii) we will not do anything unless there is an international agreement, makes for good polemics but does nothing for advancing our national interest. Saying that our per capita emissions will not cross the per capita emissions of developed countries is an excellent starting point but cannot be the sole element of our approach. It has to be per capita *plus.*

II

It is with this in mind that we have worked tirelessly over the last few years to strengthen our domestic actions and ensure a more robust response to climate change – both on adaptation and mitigation.

As described in several chapters in this handbook, the National Action Plan on Climate Change (NAPCC) released in 2008 has accelerated our response to climate change, and provided an opportunity to integrate related sectoral issues of poverty and vulnerability, energy efficiency, sustainable development, and forestry into the development rubric.

As part of the NAPCC, the National Mission for Enhanced Energy Efficiency is scaling-up energy efficiency actions at every level. Most notably, the Perform Achieve and Trade (PAT) mechanism under this mission will get 700 of the most energy intensive industries to become more energy efficient and help reduce India's CO_2e emissions by 25 million tons per year by 2014–15. The Green India Mission will provide a bottom-up participatory approach to improve the quality of our forests, and will also help us sequester 43 million tons of CO_2e annually. The Jawaharlal Nehru Solar Mission will target generating 20,000 MW of solar power by 2022. Other Missions have begun working as well on equally ambitious goals.

An Expert Group on Low Carbon Strategies for Inclusive Growth established in 2010 has been charged with developing sectoral roadmaps which will firmly integrate low-carbon growth into the mainstream of our planning process. These roadmaps will be a central part of our Twelfth Five-Year Plan, the avowed motto of which is faster, inclusive, and *more sustainable* growth. Indian states are also doing their part. Many have initiated state-specific action plans, and the exercise will be completed in the next few months across all states.

While strengthening domestic policy actions, we are also enhancing our capabilities of rigorous scientific work, and taking major steps in bridging the gaps in Indian climate science. The Indian Network for Comprehensive Climate Change Assessment (INCCCA), a network of over 125 national scientific institutions has been formed to undertake scientific assessments of different aspects of climate change and published a '4 × 4 assessment' of climate change in India in 2010. This study involved a comprehensive, long-term assessment of the impacts of climate change on four key sectors – agriculture, water, natural ecosystems and biodiversity, and health, across four climate-sensitive regions of India.

III

While we have stepped up our domestic actions, we have also engaged constructively and meaningfully in the international climate change negotiations. Our efforts in recent negotiation sessions have constantly been to ensure that while India has not been part of the problem, India will be part of the solution and be seen to be a constructive part of the solution. Debates are all very well but when India is refashioning its place in the world community based largely on its economic performance (and not just potential) its climate change negotiating strategy – both in terms of substance and style – has to be nuanced, flexible and responsive to changing circumstances and challenges. We have already announced our voluntary domestic commitment of reducing the emissions intensity of our GDP by 20–25% by the year 2020 on a 2005 reference level.

We are intent on building trust and furthering collective multilateral action at global and regional levels. Since Copenhagen, and even more so since Cancun, India has taken on a very proactive role in international negotiations. India's contributions at Cancun were critical in the drafting of the 'Cancun agreements' at various places – for example, on the design of the technology mechanism, on introducing the phrase 'equitable access to sustainable development' and developing the concepts of 'international consultation and analysis' and 'international assessment and review'. Furthermore, India's contributions went well beyond the negotiating text. India spoke up for its developing country partners, showcased its proactive voluntary actions, pushed the envelope on the intellectual debate, and helped bridge the gaps between parties. In my opinion India will continue this proactive engagement in international negotiations, bringing parties together, while safeguarding our national economic interests. We must also demonstrate greater sensitivity to the special needs of the small island states, LDCs and Africa.

IV

Even as we have contributed proactively to international negotiations, India has also given a new impetus to regional cooperation in climate change. The South Asian Association for Regional Cooperation (SAARC) has adopted cooperation on climate change as a major defining theme of its partnership. Regional initiatives through SAARC and individually with Nepal, Bhutan, Bangladesh and Maldives have begun to show results. India has made grants of US$1 million each to the SAARC Forestry Centre, Thimpu, Bhutan and SAARC Coastal Management Centre, Male, Maldives. Our partnership as part of the BASIC group of countries, comprising Brazil, South Africa, India and China, is now also extending well beyond international negotiations, to include areas of collective action.

The message as far as I am concerned is very clear: *while India will continue to proactively engage in international negotiations, even playing the role of 'deal-maker'* xxii *Foreword*

where appropriate, we will not wait to act. We will continue to aggressively pursue domestic and collaborative actions to combat climate change.

I take this opportunity to once again congratulate Navroz and his editorial team for producing such an excellent handbook, which brings together so many views and perspectives from India; providing for an accessible information base on the issue of climate change in India. Importantly, it adds Indian voices to the global discussion, which has so far, seen only a smattering of voices from the South. I am sure the handbook will play an important role in bridging some of the gaps in understanding that exist both within India and within the international community.

Preface and acknowledgements

The seed for this book was sown while I was teaching a course on environmental politics at Jawaharlal Nehru University. As an intermittent participant in Indian and global climate debates, I was aware that there was a vibrant and often contentious public discourse on climate change, certainly in the seminar rooms of Delhi, but increasingly so in universities, government offices, and NGO hallways across India. Yet, the contending perspectives, and the unanswered questions they threw up, were all too seldom systematically written down and, therefore, hard to organize, contextualize, and learn from. As a further result, our international interlocutors also had access to only a limited slice of the rich discussions on climate change in India, leading to very sketchy and limited global impressions of Indian climate debates and politics. This handbook is, therefore, an effort to systematically pull together the various strands of climate debates in and about India, in order to deepen and enrich the national and global conversations on climate change.

In many ways, the handbook is also a testimony to the growing community of scholars, activists, and professionals seeking to make sense of climate change from the vantage point of deep engagement with development debates. In my opinion, the most exciting and creative part of the Indian climate debate are the efforts to re-envision the challenge of climate change within the larger objective of sustainable and inclusive development. Continuing a long legacy, another strain of thinking has sought to deepen engagement with concerns of equity in the ongoing global negotiation process. Senior officials, long steeped in the minutiae of climate negotiations, have increasingly brought their knowledge into the public domain. Activists are forcing these often abstract debates into conversation with the realities of local politics and implementation challenges. And a generation of younger scholars and activists are bringing the insights of legal, historical and political analysis to bear on Indian climate politics and its role in global debates.

This volume is, then, in large part a collective enterprise, and owes its existence and any impact it might have to the cumulative knowledge and wisdom of the contributors. I thank each of them for their contributions. The overall product has been considerably enriched by a two-day contributors' workshop, during which participants provided each other detailed feedback on their work, prior to producing final chapter drafts, and by the comments of two anonymous referees.

Of the broader community of participants in India's climate debate, my own thinking and efforts to structure this handbook owe a great deal to rich individual and collective conversations with a small group of peers. Without burdening them with any responsibility for the final outcome, I wish to particularly thank Girish Sant,

xxiv *Preface and acknowledgements*

MV Ramana, Sharachchandra Lele, Shantanu Dixit, Lavanya Rajamani, Ambuj Sagar, D. Raghunandan and T. Jayaraman. Several senior participants in the Indian climate debate, who combine within themselves the personae of both scholars and practitioners have been particularly generous with their time and insights. I am grateful to C. Dasgupta, Nitin Desai, Suresh Prabhu, and Shyam Saran, all of whom contributed to this volume and shared their advice. The Minister of Environment and Forests from mid-2009 to mid 2011, Shri Jairam Ramesh, has unarguably stirred the pot of Indian climate politics and thereby greatly enlivened and enriched the debate, and I am grateful to him for agreeing to write a foreword to this handbook.

Katha Kartiki at the Centre for Policy Research (CPR) has been absolutely central to every aspect of this volume. She effortlessly juggled coordination with authors, publishers and funders, managed an authors' workshop, and single-handedly edited and proof-read all the chapters. Most important, she has been an important intellectual sounding board for editorial decisions, and a constructively critical reviewer of the volume introduction. She is emblematic of the new generation of enthusiastic and creative Indian climate scholars who give hope for the future.

The Centre for Policy Research (CPR) has provided a congenial and stimulating intellectual home. Pratap Bhanu Mehta, President of CPR, is not only the chief architect of this happy institutional context, but also continues to display the intellectual breadth and proclivity to engage substantively on an enormous array of topics. I particularly valued his key inputs in the early period of structuring this volume. I am also grateful to CPR's administration and staff, who provided seamless support for all the detailed but critical tasks that go into producing an edited volume.

I am thankful to the Ford Foundation for providing generous support for CPR's Climate Initiative and thereby for this volume. The Ford Foundation has been particularly supportive of our efforts to broaden and deepen deliberative politics on climate change in India.

The contributors and I also appreciate the interest and support of Nick Bellorini and Mikey Jones at Taylor & Francis, who are publishing this book as part of their Earthscan imprint, and Nitasha Devasar and Neha Kohli at Oxford University Press, India, who are publishing the book in South Asia. I am further grateful to the publication staff at Taylor & Francis, who have rapidly and smoothly brought this book to press.

Finally, my spouse, Rinku Murgai, and children Ela and Rustom, ensured that climate change received at most passing mention at the dinner table. For this ongoing reality check, too, I am grateful.

Introduction

Navroz K. Dubash

Why a handbook on climate change and India?

In India, as in many other countries, the climate change debate has firmly been joined. In the years since 2007 the Indian Parliament has witnessed several, and heated, debates over what India's role should be in the global climate negotiations. The government has set up major policy and expert processes, notably a Prime Minister's Advisory Council to prepare a national action plan on climate change. Media attention, too, has ballooned. A rough-and-ready internet search for media articles on climate change reveals that from tens of hits a year in each major newspaper between 2000 and 2006, this number had increased to tens of hits a day by 2009–2010.[1] A reading of opinion and editorial pages shows that opinions on climate change have become part of the necessary repertoire of the economic and political commentariat (for example Shourie, 2009; Subramanian, 2009). And civil society groups active on a range of environment and development issues – water, forests, and energy in particular – have scrambled to identify substantive and political linkages between the issues they work on and national and global climate debates.

The increase in intensity of the debate, however, conceals other shortcomings of India's national climate conversation. The information and analysis base for debate on climate change is relatively limited (with the possible exception of India's stance on the global negotiations process), and the material that does exist is relatively inaccessible and not in wide circulation. Indeed, the limited range of materials available with which to teach a course on climate change to Indian students was an initial impetus for this volume.

One reason for this shortcoming is the relatively narrow range of participants in India's climate debate. There is a small core of deeply knowledgeable people working on climate change in India, many of whom are represented in this volume, whose knowledge rests on direct and sustained participation in global climate negotiations and discussions. But their perspectives, and the knowledge that has informed them, have only partially filtered out into the public domain. In part, this is because for much of the past two decades, climate change debates were closely tied to global negotiations, and, as such, a relatively inaccessible area of deep specialization.

In the past few years, climate change concerns have become more mainstream, in part driven by the growing attention to national policies in the global negotiations. Accordingly, interest in climate change has broadened, as policymakers, journalists, business leaders, and civil society activists all seek to understand what climate change means for their areas of focus. The result is growing demand both for accessible information on the global negotiations process, as well as new forms of information

2 Dubash

and analysis that bridge the gap between climate change and domestic policy concerns, and new voices providing a broader range of perspectives on these linkages. In many ways, the debate has shifted from whether to engage with climate change, to how to do so in a manner that is consistent with India's development needs and foreign policy concerns.

The primary objective of this handbook is to respond to a growing demand for informed and knowledgeable perspectives and analysis on climate change from within India, so as to inform and contribute to India's expanding debate on climate change. In so doing, by means of this introductory chapter, and through the selection of chapters that follows, the aim is also to provide a comprehensive framework for thinking through the implications of climate change for India, in a manner that covers both global negotiations and the linkages to domestic policy concerns. The voices expressed within this handbook are diverse, and include policymakers, scholars and activists, including seasoned observers and relatively new entrants to the discussion. To further stimulate internal reflection, one chapter also collates perspectives on Indian climate debates as viewed from other parts of the world.

This handbook is also aimed at achieving a second important objective. The limited availability of information and perspectives from within India on climate change has had the effect of limiting global understanding of India's policy and political debate on climate change. International interlocutors have too often been presented with a caricature of Indian views that obscures both the thought process and the robustness of internal debate. That these views are filtered through the global media does not help deepen understanding of Indian climate politics and policies. The second objective, therefore, is to provide global audiences with ready access to the full range of perspectives on climate change within India, along with some reflection of the internal debate, so as to promote a more productive and better informed global conversation.

Informing interested parties of such a conversation is important in at least two ways. First, given the predominance of scholarship and advocacy on climate change from the industrialized world, having access to perspectives from at least one part of the global South may contribute to a richer global discussion. And India is playing an ever-increasing role in the global climate debate, not least through participation in climate-specific coalitions such as the newly formed BASIC bloc (Brazil, South Africa, India, and China), as well as through the climate negotiations and the G20. At the same time, India has memorably been described as a 'premature power' by the country's former foreign secretary and chief climate negotiator, capturing the disconnect between India's relative global power and measures of domestic well-being (Saran, 2010). This twin identity is nowhere more true than in climate change, where India is both among the largest emitters in absolute terms, but also among the smallest of major economies in per capita terms, reflecting the enormous share of the world's poor that continues to reside in India. Understanding the tensions introduced by this duality would considerably assist global interlocutors who seek to engage India on climate change.

Second, and closely related, Indian domestic climate politics is strongly shaped by the need to simultaneously address growth, distribution and environmental objectives, using the rubric of 'co-benefits'. This is a challenge that many other developing countries, and particularly large emerging economies, also face in varying degrees. India's ongoing efforts to operationalize a co-benefits framework for climate mitigation and adaptation could fruitfully inform similar discussions elsewhere, and provide a basis for learning from the experience of other countries.

Approach to the handbook

Climate change is an enormous political and policy problem, but it is also a conceptual and deliberative challenge. Different frames for climate change can lead to different political and policy solutions. Notably, environmental versus developmental frames of the problem, which often map to northern versus southern perspectives, provide very different political and policy entry points. Similarly, narratives of technological fixes, which assume positive sum outcomes, suggest very different ways forward than do equity narratives, which emphasize equitable access to atmospheric space, in what is predominantly a zero-sum context. Many of these polarities are oriented along North–South lines, creating long-standing fissures in the negotiation process (Dubash, 2009b; Dubash and Rajamani, 2010).

Perhaps as a reflection of the repeated setbacks at the global negotiation level to forge common political and policy approaches, there is growing scholarly attention to the conceptual underpinnings of climate debates. Thus for Hulme (2009), climate change is an idea to which we bring differing, and often competing cultural, social, and political assumptions and approaches – a challenge to the imagination and not only to the intellect. Malone (2009) argues that understanding climate change is inevitably a social process and that we should embrace that process rather than looking to science alone to cut through the thicket for us. Pettenger's (2007) edited volume emphasizes, among other themes, the role of power relations in the social construction of climate change, emphasizing that power can also flow from control over ideas.

This volume is designed to take seriously the process through which alternative frames for climate change are constructed, and the socio-cultural context and power relations that shape their construction. By better understanding how we think about climate change, the hope is that we will be better able to forge a common national understanding and contribute to a better global understanding. In other words, alongside its analytic intent, there is an unabashedly normative aspiration underpinning this volume.

Collectively the chapters are designed to encapsulate a very wide range of positions in the Indian climate debate, with opposing views clearly laid out. Some chapters are written by active participants in the debate, who forcefully argue one position or other. Others are more synthetic and analytic, seeking to understand the context within which perspectives emerge and evolve. As this approach suggests, there is certainly no intent to paper over disagreement or seek premature consensus, but rather to promote dialogue by deepening understanding within India, and with international interlocutors.

As a result of this approach, the contributors are eclectic in background and their contributions diverse in style. Several chapters are written by active participants in the climate debate: policymakers, activists, businesspeople and media. Others are written by academics who are in a position to pull back the lens and take a broader view. Given the nature of the topic, a wide range of disciplines are represented: historians, political scientists, lawyers, scientists and self-declared interdisciplinary scholars. While almost all the chapters are original contributions, in a very few cases important documents have been reproduced, for example, the transcripts of India's parliamentary debates prior to and after the Copenhagen negotiations.

In terms of scope, the volume covers both the international negotiation process and domestic policy and politics. The global negotiations process has dominated the past

4 *Dubash*

decade and a half of climate debate. Following the Copenhagen (2009) and then Cancun (2010) climate negotiations, the global regime appears to be shifting inexorably toward finding ways of recognizing, sanctifying and accounting for national actions, rather than driving national change through global agreement (Rajamani, 2011; Grubb, 2011), although there is fierce disagreement in the global debate on whether this is a good or bad outcome.[2] However, paying attention to domestic policy goes beyond a reading of the tea leaves on the direction of the global regime. Ultimately policies addressing climate change have to be internalized within national political economies and institutionalized within national laws, policies and regulations, in a manner consistent with domestic politics and aspirations. It is with attention to this latter point that this volume focuses on domestic policy arenas.

As the subtitle of the handbook indicates – development, politics, governance – three broad themes cut across and inform the chapters. A view that development objectives must be the starting point for a discussion of climate change in India informs many of the perspectives expressed here, even while there is broad, if not unanimous, recognition that the two cannot and should not be separated. The chapters in this volume seek to stimulate discussion on how exactly development and climate objectives are to be usefully brought into conversation, with considerable emphasis on the concept of 'co-benefits'.

This handbook is also informed by an understanding of climate change as a deeply political problem, one that has the potential to generate winners and losers at local, national and global levels. The chapters engage a wide-ranging set of politically laden issues: whether climate-related policies will weaken local populations' control over natural resources; the shifting alliances among interest groups in national climate politics; allocation (implicit or explicit) of atmospheric space through climate negotiations, and the larger canvas of climate change and geopolitics.

To internalize climate change within development in a manner consistent with national and global political constraints is ultimately a challenge of governance – the third common theme. Much of the literature on climate governance focuses on global level processes – the climate negotiations, transnational advocacy networks, and private governance (Bulkeley and Newell, 2010). When juxtaposed against national development policy, however, climate governance takes on additional levels of complexity. Here an emergent literature on climate change as a problem of 'multi-level governance' becomes relevant (Dubash, 2009b; Selin and vanDeever, 2009; Ostrom, 2010; Bulkeley and Betsill, 2005; Gupta, 2007). The broad thrust of this idea is that climate governance will invariably have to operate at a wide variety of scales (global, national and sub-national) guided by multiple institutions communicating across scales, and working toward complex and multiple objectives. This handbook begins the process of making explicit these linkages in an Indian context.

Finally, it is important to stress what this volume explicitly does not attempt to accomplish. Since the emphasis is on longer-term conceptual issues, this volume should not be read as a primer on the current state of the debate. For example, there is no update on the specific outcomes at the Copenhagen and Cancun climate negotiations, nor on specific negotiation issue areas such as technology or finance. In addition, the chapters in this volume are not prescriptive policy analysis on the basis of which decisions can be taken. Instead, the emphasis is on providing frameworks that allow the reader to engage more completely with contemporary debates. Where necessary, the chapters provide citations to additional material that helps set the context or provides background material necessary for relative newcomers to the climate debate to enter the discussion.

The remainder of this introduction provides a substantive entry point to the rest of the handbook. Each of the six parts of the volume provides a relatively self-contained set of chapters that explores one of the volume's themes: climate science and impacts; early debates; international negotiations; the domestic politics of climate change; integrating climate change and development; and a concluding section. This introduction is meant to provide context for each of the parts that follows, as well as to lay out the intellectual rationale for the choice and organization of chapters in each part.

Climate science and potential impacts

At the core of the global public policy challenge of climate change lie substantial scientific complexity and uncertainties. The underlying theory of the greenhouse effect – the idea that changes in the composition of the earth's atmosphere can cause a long-term trend towards a warming earth – is well known and relatively undisputed. However, to justify and enable a global public policy response requires engagement with several more questions: To what extent does theory translate into observed warming trends? What is the net result of complex interactions between the climate system and several negative and positive feedbacks that could either accelerate or slow down warming? How are global trends manifested at the regional level, and with what implications for climate impacts at national and sub-national scales? What is the range of adjustment possibilities – mitigation and adaptation – available to humanity, and what will they cost?

While the science of climate change is not the focus of this handbook, an understanding of the basic science, the nature of possible impacts on India, and some discussion of the global process charged with collating climate-related knowledge – the Intergovernmental Panel on Climate Change (IPCC) – is necessary to fully engage in subsequent discussions. Part I covers these issues.

An appropriate starting point for discussion of climate science is an understanding of the IPCC itself, which was rocked by controversy in recent years. As the chapter by Ramachandran describes, the IPCC is an elaborate and complex process of developing a scientific assessment of climate change, involving hundreds of scientists globally, and backed by a complex architecture of review and commentary by governments and independent experts. The key overarching conclusion of the Fourth Assessment Report (AR4) released in 2007 states: 'warming of the climate system is unequivocal'. It goes on to add that 'most of the observed increase in globally averaged temperatures since the mid-20th century is *very likely* (emphasis in original) due to the observed increase in anthropogenic GHG concentrations' (IPCC, 2007). The terms 'unequivocal' and 'very likely' are precisely defined and calibrated indications of the IPCC's level of confidence in its findings, and these qualifiers have been getting increasingly definitive over the various assessment reports.

The IPCC is not, of course, without its critics. Over the course of 2009 and 2010, the entire process has been subject to severe criticism based on some serious errors contained in the Fourth Assessment Report, notably on the rate of melting of Himalayan glaciers (see Ramachandran, this volume; Raina, 2009). These errors certainly do call for improvements in the IPCC process, examinations of how the IPCC treats uncertainty (Malnes, 2008) and reflection on the role of the IPCC itself, given the

6   *Dubash*

complex nature of the relationship between science and public policy (Grundmann, 2007). However, it is hard to argue, as some have done (Schiermeier, 2010) that these errors undermine the overarching conclusions of the IPCC with regard to the reality of human-induced climate change and the imperative to address this challenge.

Readers interested in further understanding climate science would be well served by starting with the Synthesis document of the IPCC Fourth Assessment Report, followed by the summaries of the working groups on climate science, impacts and adaptation and response strategies (IPCC, 2007).[3] An additional useful source of contemporary debate about climate science by practising climate scientists for the public is the website www.realclimate.org. Those interested in understanding the views of those scientists who, in their self-description, are 'not predisposed to believe that climate change is caused by human greenhouse gas emissions' may wish to visit a website documenting material contesting the IPCC views.[4]

The approach taken in this handbook is based on a view that while it is indeed necessary to progressively reduce uncertainties in climate science and the implications of mitigation actions, the accumulation of evidence on human-induced climate change merits precautionary action. This requires serious policy consideration at global, national and sub-national levels on how to manage and structure a suitable response to the threat of global climate change. The question remains open as to whether and how India should respond to this challenge, which is the subject for much of the rest of the handbook.

Since an Indian policy response must first be informed by an understanding of what climate science suggests are India's stakes in this debate, the first three chapters assess the likely impacts of climate change on India from three different perspectives. J. Srinivasan provides a careful review of the state of scientific understanding on regional impacts of climate change on India from a macro perspective. He carefully distinguishes between likely impacts on rainfall, temperature and other climate variables based on available observations and what future model-based projections suggest is likely to occur. He cautions against attributing all local and regional environmental changes to global climate change drivers and argues for separating ongoing environmental degradation in India that may have regional impacts from impacts caused by global drivers.

To complement this macro perspective, two chapters examine specific impacts of potential climate change at a more micro scale. Rana, Bhagat, Kalia and Lal carefully examine the impact of climate change on apple cultivation in Himachal Pradesh. Significantly, their work seeks to assess the impact already observed, rather than speculating on future projections. Building on both a survey of farmer perceptions and impressions as well as on quantitative trends over the last two decades, they are able to show discernable impacts on the important apple cultivation sector for Himachal Pradesh. While they do not attempt to separate out whether this is due to local or global drivers, their chapter provides a careful attempt to signal livelihood impacts due to a changing climate that are already visible.

Byravan, Chella Rajan and Rangarajan provide insight into the future costs of sea level rise in the state of Tamil Nadu. Based on a careful mapping of the Tamil Nadu coast, they estimate likely sea level rise and the present value of consequent economic costs through 2050 due to loss of land, loss of coastal infrastructure and destruction of coastal ecosystems. While this is necessarily a speculative exercise, it does illustrate that the economic costs of even one dimension of climate impacts – sea level rise –

Introduction 7

could be of considerable economic and political importance. These chapters illustrate the need for more detailed micro case studies of the impact of climate change on India, complemented by better regional scale models of future impact.

Since the advancement of science, particularly on large-scale multidisciplinary issues such as climate change, is inevitably a function of the context within which scientific exploration proceeds, the final article in this part locates the IPCC within the context of Indian climate science. R. Ramachandran summarizes the IPCC process and explores the role of Indian scientists in the IPCC. He further provides texture and nuance to the debate over the IPCC's credibility by exploring a few high profile debates that have been particularly relevant to India, including the Himalayan glacier controversy, and early discussions over the accuracy of methane emission estimates from rice fields. These and other such examples illustrate how the scientific process, through choice of research topics and the disparity in capacity for research, reflect the political contexts within which science is generated.

Understanding the IPCC is critical, since it provides the scientific backbone to support the global political process of climate negotiations. Indeed, negotiations toward a UN Framework Convention on Climate Change (UNFCCC) were launched only after release of the First Assessment Report of the IPCC in 1990, which declared sufficient scientific consensus on climate change to justify efforts toward a global climate change convention. Part II of the handbook turns to an understanding of the early days of those negotiations.

Past as prologue: early Indian perspectives on climate change

Few policy reports can boast a more attention grabbing opening line than Agarwal and Narain's (this volume) chapter 'Global warming in an unequal world': 'The idea that India and China must share the blame for heating up the earth and destabilising its climate . . . is an excellent example of environmental colonialism'. In this one sentence, the article lays the ground for the central plank of what would become India's negotiating approach to climate change – differentiation between north and south – and emotively packages the stakes as 'environmental colonialism'. It also illustrates vividly how the past history of climate negotiations continues to shape current climate politics – hence the importance of Part II (which examines the early days of climate negotiations through an Indian lens) to the current debate on climate in the overall handbook. As a range of literature suggests, the tussle over affixing responsibility among nations for climate change and the underlying North–South fault lines continue to be central themes of climate negotiations (Dubash, 2009a; Grubb, 2010).

The two chapters in Part II provide an entry point to the early years of climate negotiations. They address the initial phase of climate negotiations from 1990 to 1992, during which the UNFCCC was negotiated by parties and opened for signature at the 1992 Rio Earth Summit. The first chapter, authored in 1991 by Agarwal and Narain from the Centre for Science and Environment, disputes the approach to understanding responsibility for climate change espoused by a leading American think-tank, and in so doing, lays out the rationale for India's long-standing approach to negotiations. The second is a retrospective analysis by India's leading climate negotiator of the early years of negotiations.

In order to appreciate these chapters, it is necessary to keep in mind the broader context within which the climate negotiations of 1990–92 occurred. The years leading

8 Dubash

up to the 1992 Earth Summit were a time of considerable intellectual ferment and political energy on questions of environment and development. The Brundtland Commission's (1987) formulation of 'sustainable development' provided a political hook around which to operationalize the integration of environment and development concerns (Brundtland Commission, 1987). By bringing together values encouraging the conservation of resources, focusing attention on equity and human needs, reviving but re-directing growth toward less materials and energy intensity, and signalling restraints on population growth, the Brundtland Commission successfully erected a large and encompassing tent.

The sustainable development concept provided a common base of understanding on which several specific efforts at global cooperation were built. In the years prior to Rio, the successful negotiation of the Montreal Protocol (1987) on Substances that Deplete the Ozone Layer provided confidence in the ability of nations to come to collective agreement on global environmental problems (Benedick, 1998). The first assessment report of the Intergovernmental Panel on Climate Change (IPCC), released in 1990, provided both a model for global cooperation on science and the initial scientific basis for global negotiations, although the conclusions were certainly couched within cautious language (IPCC, 1990). All these factors combined to generate considerable political tail-winds on global environmental problems such as climate change and biodiversity. At the Earth Summit, a globally agreed framework to encourage domestic action toward sustainable development also emerged in the form of 'Agenda 21'.

At the same time, undercurrents of dissonance, both intellectual and political, were insistently expressed during this period. Critics noted that the seeming consensus around the Brundtland formulation of sustainable development – 'development that meets the needs of the present without compromising the ability of future generations to meet their own needs', appeared just a little too intellectually neat and politically convenient (Lele, 1991; Lohmann, 1990). Who was to define what constituted 'needs', particularly in a context of wide global disparities? What exactly was to be sustained? What definition of development was proposed? If needs were to be met by sustaining economic growth, how convincing was the rejection of a trade-off between continued growth and biophysical or ecological limits, which an earlier generation of environmental scholars had forcefully articulated? (Meadows et al., 1972). Did sustainable development provide a means to address the core causes of global environmental crises, or was it a palliative that avoided the hardest questions?

A second dissonant note emerged out of two decades of contentious global conversation around economic disparities between North and South. Through the 1970s, developing countries charged the North with perpetuating an unequal global order that systematically disadvantaged the developing world. A series of global commissions, notably the Brandt Commission and the South Commission, sought to provide a basis for global economic cooperation, and forge a more fair economic order (Dubash et al., 2001). In the 1980s, these efforts were eclipsed by a decade of 'structural adjustment' as developing countries, particularly in Latin America and Africa, reeled under macroeconomic shocks and subsequent efforts to re-make their economies in the mould of a new 'Washington Consensus' around open markets, promotion of exports, and an expanded role for the private sector (Williamson, 1994). Internationally, these national transformations were complemented by global trade negotiations that sought to create a framework for progressively more open economies, and which then had a far greater political profile than did global environmental negotiations. The North–South tensions running through discussions on the global economic order could not but spill over into global environmental arenas, including the climate change negotiations.

In the early 1990s, India was particularly concerned about sustaining economic growth. Emerging from a serious balance of payments crisis, and a resultant IMF economic stabilisation programme, concerns over ensuring autonomy over economic policy, and ensuring revitalized economic growth were paramount (Mukherji, 2007). Despite these other preoccupations, and perhaps because of this insecurity, India played an important role in the early years of the climate negotiations, primarily as a voice arguing for a distinct and collective Southern position in the response to climate change.

The first chapter in Part II is excerpted from a seminal 1991 report by Agarwal and Narain, then one of the few Southern non-governmental organizations active in climate negotiations. In addition to the strong rhetorical invocation of a colonial climate politics, *Global Warming in an Unequal World* made three lasting substantive points. First, Agarwal and Narain contested a framing of climate responsibility based on annual national emissions or emissions *flows*, and argued instead for allocating responsibility based on each nation's cumulative contribution to emission *stocks* in the atmosphere. This distinction between flows and stocks of emissions is critical, and underpins India's argument for differentiation between North and South. As Jayaraman et al. show, this distinction is central to present discussions as well. Second, Agarwal and Narain argued that each individual should have access to the atmosphere's resources, reinforcing the notion of a *per capita* allocation principle in the negotiations. While others had made this point before and have done so since (Rao, this volume), this early and cogent intervention firmly enshrined the principle within the climate debate. Third, the chapter introduced a distinction between 'survival' and 'luxury' emissions, particularly relating to methane emissions from agriculture and livestock. While hard to operationalize in practice, this distinction has also been internalized within several subsequent efforts at sharing the burden of climate change adjustment (Baer et al., 2008; Chakravarty et al., 2009).

This article was influential at the global level, but even more important has defined Indian civil society and media perceptions of what constitutes fairness in the climate debate. It also introduced a measure of wariness and cynicism within India about the global debate and the good faith of industrialized countries, which has persisted. Finally, this article shows the enduring importance of framing in the climate debate, illustrating how different representations of emissions numbers can carry widely divergent political implications.

The second chapter is a retrospective of the early days of the climate negotiations written by Ambassador C. Dasgupta, India's lead negotiator for much of the two decades of climate talks. Drawing on early submissions of text by India and other countries backed by his personal recollections, Dasgupta traces the roots of contemporary North–South differences. He convincingly argues that the 1990–92 period saw the emergence of several ideas and debates that are still central to climate negotiations: the concept of 'pledge and review' of national commitments, as opposed to binding national commitments by industrialized countries; the importance and political sensitivity of review mechanisms; and the linkage between action by developing countries and provision of financing by developed countries and the basis of this linkage in the concepts of responsibility and capability.

10 *Dubash*

Dasgupta's reflections provoke a sobering realisation that two decades after they began negotiating, countries are still divided over fundamental issues that first emerged while negotiating the framework convention. They also suggest that an appreciation of history is extremely important to this process, and current proposals and ideas must contend with this sedimented negotiating past. Collectively, the two articles in this part provide an accessible entry point to global climate politics in 1992, which in turn is an essential prerequisite to understanding contemporary climate negotiations and India's role in this process.

The international climate negotiations: stakes, debates and dilemmas

While the first two years of climate negotiations were deeply contentious, they were also remarkably productive, in that a relatively brief two-year period of negotiations successfully resulted in the UNFCCC. The two decades since have lost none of the contention, but have devolved into a grinding, nearly two-decade long process of filling in implementation details, incrementally increasing effectiveness, and, most important, rehashing disagreements that were never fully resolved.

In his review of this period, Sengupta provides an essential bridge between 1992 and the present, including the negotiation and adoption of the Kyoto Protocol in 1997. He traces through the key contributions of Indian negotiators to the process, emphasizing their role in forging and holding together a 'Southern' coalition built largely around the idea of ensuring differentiation between the responsibilities, and therefore actions, of industrialized and developing countries (see Rajamani, this volume for a detailed legal treatment of this concept). He notes both the considerable continuity in India's position and role in climate negotiations from 1992 to 2007, as well as strong indications of some change in strategy and approach which he dates to 2009.

Many of the chapters that follow in Part III debate the wisdom, meaning and drivers of India's perceived shifting role in the global climate negotiations. The focus of these chapters is on the underlying concepts – differentiation, equity, stock versus flow measures of emissions – that constitute many of the differences in perspectives. Hence I discuss here the immediate negotiating context within which global and national discussions took place between 2007 and 2010 to set the stage for the detailed chapters.

In the build-up to the high profile 2009 climate change negotiations held in Copenhagen, the global media often portrayed India as the problem child of the international process. That bellwether of mainstream global opinion, *The Economist* (2009), labelled India 'obdurate' and clubbed India with America and Russia as obstacles to a global deal. However, what was obduracy to some in the international media was principled steadfastness to many in India. Through Indian eyes, that India ended up in this diplomatic *cul de sac* was deeply ironic; India is on the frontline of climate impacts, has a substantial proportion of the world's poor, and has a much better than average track record of energy efficiency and carbon intensity (Dubash, 2009c).

In many ways, the tagging of India as a problem case had a great deal to do with India's continued championing of the idea of 'differentiated responsibility' and its salience for a possible deal at Copenhagen. In the build-up to Copenhagen, whether or not to continue the 'two track' process of negotiations established at the Bali negotiations in 2007 – one track for the Kyoto Protocol and the second for 'Long-term Cooperative Action' for actions by countries not committed to mitigation actions

Introduction 11

under the Kyoto Protocol – became the central issue of contention. The argument for bridging the two tracks was largely one of political expediency. This approach, it was thought, would allow the US political space to get on board. Continued advocacy of differentiated responsibility came in the way of this bridging and was constructed as obduracy by those who favoured political pragmatism. In practice, however, even though the Copenhagen Accord and the subsequent Cancun Agreements were lauded by American commentators as providing this bridge and facilitating US inclusion,[5] the US has moved further from, rather than closer to accepting commitments under a global agreement due to its own domestic political compulsions.

While this sequence of events suggests the limits of re-thinking India's climate strategy based on accommodating US politics alone, another set of drivers nonetheless prompted a re-evaluation of India's long-held negotiating position. As Sengupta's and Raghunandan's chapters discuss, these include shifting the strategic interests and geopolitical aspirations of an ascendant India; new global alliances with other large industrializing countries that complicate positions of South solidarity; fractures in domestic public opinion due to rising concern with climate change impacts; and the influence of new policymakers that have opened the door to revisiting past positions. As many chapters in this handbook show, there is considerable debate and discussion within India on a way forward that combines principle with strategic savvy and realism. A shifting Indian position has yet, however, to coalesce into a cogent vision for climate change negotiations that both protects Indian interests and enables a robust global response to climate change.

Key to understanding both continuity and change in India's climate negotiating position is the UNFCC principle of 'common but differentiated responsibilities and respective capabilities' (CBDRRC). Rajamani provides a close reading of CBDRRC, and a historical contextualization of the contestation over interpretation of the principle. She explores, for example, the tussle over interpreting differentiation based on historical responsibility for contributing to the problem, as India has argued, versus that based on capabilities to act. The latter, of course, would expose India and other large industrialized countries to increasingly more insistent demands to play an expanded role in climate mitigation commensurate with rapid economic growth, while the former would provide a defence against these demands. Her chapter not only illuminates the substantive debate over differentiation, but also illustrates the political importance of historically laden and complex legal concepts in the negotiation process.

If it is immediately intuitive that legal concepts will be politically significant, it is perhaps somewhat less so that the science also affects political interpretations. Jayaraman, Kanitkar and D'Souza illustrate how shifting understandings of climate science can also shape understandings of the relative burden that should be borne for climate mitigation by different countries. They draw an important distinction between tracking annual levels of emissions by each country, or emission flows, versus tracking the cumulative emissions by each country from an agreed starting point, or stocks of emissions. They argue that climate science makes a compelling case for the latter, which, they suggest, then tips the policy discussion towards consideration of carbon budgets rather than formulations of peaking years for emission flows. This distinction also has critical implications for how equity objectives across countries might be formulated, and therefore operationalization of differentiation, echoing arguments made by Agarwal and Narain (this volume) early in the debate. The chapter also usefully provides a set of projected emission trajectories, which provides a sober reality

12 *Dubash*

check on the adjustment challenge ahead, including that for developing countries. Heightened appreciation of this challenge, in part informed by analyses such as this one, has contributed to recent revisions in India's negotiating position

Whether based on stocks or flows, discussions over burden-sharing stem from the UNFCCC injunction that Parties' actions should be 'on the basis of equity' as well as in accordance with common but differentiated responsibilities and respective capacities (UNFCCC, 1992). However, there is little agreement on what constitutes a fair but also implementable basis for operationalizing equity, let alone one that is politically viable across the broad range of interests in the climate debate. Narasimha Rao's chapter clearly surveys the substantial literature on equity in climate change broadly under two categories: 'resource sharing' that treats the earth's absorptive capacity as a resource; and 'burden sharing' that leaves scope to factor in different national capacities for action. While per capita based formulations dominate the literature, Rao shows that there remain, nonetheless, several different ways of articulating sharing, with widely different political implications across countries. Significantly, the chapter also raises challenging questions for an Indian stance on equity. Should intra-country equity matter? Should developing countries be obliged to pursue 'no-lose' strategies for mitigation? Again, the growing engagement with questions such as these has been part of explaining India's revisionist stance.

However, whether or not India should be revising its stance is still the subject of heated debate. Prodipto Ghosh, who served for many years as a leading member of India's negotiating team, provides a robust defence of India's long-standing negotiating position. He argues for maintaining the focus of negotiations on unsustainable emission levels in the North, thereby ensuring that India is able to focus on much-needed growth and poverty eradication objectives. He makes this case by looking at the burden of India's development challenge going forward, but also by noting that India is doing rather well on the emissions front despite the development burden. In the latter half of the chapter, he turns to an issue-by-issue articulation and defence of India's long-standing negotiating position, particularly in the period leading up to Copenhagen.

By way of counterpoint, D. Raghunandan provides a critical view on India's long-standing positions, even while arguing that the strategic focus should remain on pressurizing industrialized countries to act. The starting point for this critique is that India has paid insufficient attention to the growing scientific evidence of substantial climate impacts, including for India. The scale of change then required globally also implies that large developing countries cannot expect a 'free pass'. However, the challenge is to create an international regime, appropriately cognizant of shifting geopolitics, that ramps up the pressure on industrialized countries to take the lead, while also enabling developing countries to play a larger role. The first step toward articulating a strategy, however, is to acknowledge that the objective needs to shift, to encourage more serious global action by all, although consistent with differentiated responsibility between North and South.

Finally the diversity of views by observers from other countries comes through forcefully in a compilation of different international perspectives on India's position on climate change, from the EU, Bangladesh, the Philippines, China and the USA. Read together, they provide a fascinating diversity of views that, naturally enough, tend to mirror the national interests of the countries within which the writers are located. But the diversity, in itself, is instructive, as it provides a snapshot of the range of interests and pressures Indian policy is seeking to balance.

Collectively, the chapters suggest that India's approach to climate negotiations is at an inflection point, but one with no easy resolution. India has long been an effective champion of North–South differentiation. This approach has couched the problem largely in economic terms, with the over-riding concern one of ensuring sufficient environmental leeway or 'development space' to pursue economic growth and poverty eradication, with climate outcomes only as a secondary objective subject to the first being met.

India has been by no means the only country to subsume environmental objectives to economic ones. Many industrialized countries increasingly voice concern that the climate regime should not erode their competitiveness. Levi (this volume), suggests that an economic frame still trumps environmental objectives. If, however, India is to take seriously climate science, and place greater weight on climate outcomes as an additional objective that is not easily separated from development objectives, the conceptual challenge to framing an effective negotiation strategy becomes much harder. Such a strategy would require keeping pressure on industrialized countries to take aggressive mitigation measures, while also keeping one eye on the emissions trajectory of BASIC partners, notably China. It would also require making the complex calculus on whether to shift India's own development trajectory in a low carbon direction and by how much, which it turn requires balancing whether doing so helps keep pressure on others or whether it is a futile strategy of appeasement. And since this latter consideration carries implications for domestic development outcomes, it involves taking seriously the domestic politics of climate change, which is the subject of Part IV of this handbook.

Domestic politics of climate change

Climate has, historically, been a political non-issue in India. Despite, or perhaps even because of, two decades of heated global negotiations, climate change has been considered a distant foreign policy issue, the preserve of a few specialized diplomats and technocrats, and a handful of activists and academics. While climate change is still a non-issue in electoral politics, the issue has begun to seep into elements of national political discourse, and into formulations of national policies and priorities.

That climate politics has long been confined to global diplomacy and foreign policy follows directly from Indian adherence to the idea of differentiated responsibility across North and South. If exclusive responsibility for the problem is understood to lie with industrialized countries, then it follows that the primary, and indeed, exclusive concern of India should be to hold those countries to account. However, as discussed in the previous section, growing evidence from climate science and the dynamics of the international process have had their echoes at the domestic level. Part IV explores these domestic discussions, illustrating how climate politics in India is gradually becoming broader and deeper, with particular attention to perspectives from the environmental movement, parliamentary politics, business and the media.

The starting point for shifts in domestic politics on climate change has been a questioning of the critical shared understandings that inform Indian views on climate change. In his chapter, Dubash suggests three such points of conventional wisdom on which debate has been joined within India: whether India is a 'major emitter' or a disadvantaged newcomer when it comes to greenhouse gas emissions; consideration of internal equity alongside equity across countries; and burden-sharing versus

14 *Dubash*

opportunity-seeking perspectives on climate change. On each of these, he suggests, there has been a blurring of views, creating space for new alliances and shifting politics. In particular, he outlines three distinct strategic perspectives on climate change that have emerged, each with different implications for national and global climate policies.

Domestic environmental movements are a natural constituency for support of robust global and national climate mitigation. However, as Lele shows, the relationship between Indian environmentalism and climate change is complex, and strongly shaped by a larger idea of Southern environmentalism as one closely informed by concerns of equity and justice; what Guha (2007) has called an 'environmentalism of the poor'. Lele describes how Indian environmentalists, basing their arguments on climate justice, have long been leery of any re-thinking of domestic policy on climate grounds, and focused instead on calls for more action in the north. However, he also observes that the Indian environmental movement has made a slow progression from this stance to one that integrates climate change into a broader environmentalism in an open and plural manner. This shift, albeit a nuanced one, matters a great deal to climate politics and the politics of environment and development in India. If climate change is likely to play any role in influencing discourses around environment and development in India, the environmental movement is likely to have a significant role in bringing about this change.

While North–South aspects of climate equity have dominated the Indian discourse, as several chapters have already brought out (Agarwal and Narain; Rao; Jayaraman et al., this volume), Chakravarty and Ramana's chapter discusses the introduction of intra-country equity across income classes – the 'Hiding behind the Poor' debate – as a significant new development in Indian climate politics. Taking their chapter title from a widely discussed and criticized report of this name by Greenpeace-India, they lay out the methodology and results and discuss the alternative readings of a range of studies that explore intra-country equity. Making clear political choices and presuppositions, they conclude, is central to understanding this debate. However, they also point out that beyond the truism that there are wide disparities in emission levels in India as a function of differing access to energy, they note that the hiding behind the poor debate feeds into larger, long-standing, and necessary debates on the distributional consequences of different development choices.

An intriguing aspect of shifting climate politics within India is the increased engagement of the formal political system with climate change and its implications, although attention to the international negotiation process continues to dominate the discussion. Introducing a set of two transcripts of Indian parliamentary debates on climate change, former Minister of Environment and Forests Suresh Prabhu reflects on the role of Parliament in climate debates. He draws attention to the importance of the executive and more recently the judiciary in setting environmental policy, to the relative exclusion of the Parliament. However, he notes approvingly the creation of a Parliamentary forum for climate change.

A debate in the Lok Sabha, immediately prior to the Copenhagen negotiation illustrates the breadth of perspectives on climate change within Parliament. Among the themes that emerge is a broad acceptance of the seriousness of the problem (although there is at least one voice of scepticism on climate science), a focus on developed country responsibility, discussion of local impacts in Members' constituencies, elaboration of the National Action Plan, an emphasis on equity and lifestyle issues, and clear articulation of developed country responsibilities.

Introduction 15

A Rajya Sabha debate, coming as it does immediately after Copenhagen, focuses much more closely on India's negotiating stand. This debate illustrates powerfully that any Indian government is going to be held tightly to account on firmly drawn 'red lines' the primary objectives of which are to ensure that India does not subject itself to obligations that limit the country's growth and development. Notably, in the entire course of the debate, there is no discussion of whether the Copenhagen Accord sufficiently addresses the challenge of global climate change. In this debate, India's interests are constructed around protecting growth and not at all around avoiding climate change.

Collectively, the two debates reflect a mixed picture. The first suggests a broad and diverse interest beginning to emerge on climate change, with parliamentarians making links to local environmental issues that affect their constituencies. The second is far more reminiscent of the historical tenor of Indian climate discussions, focused on the international negotiations and preservation of India's interest, defined around protecting space for growth. The debates suggest Parliamentarians are getting the signal from their constituents that they will be held accountable, if at all, to protecting development space rather than to pressing for more robust global action. While both dimensions are present simultaneously in India's Parliament, the negotiations aspect continues to dominate..

As in any other sphere of politics, the business community is a potentially important player. However, as Tarun Das, a former Chairman of the Confederation of Indian Industries (CII) suggests, Indian business has arrived rather late to the table. He attributes Indian business' relatively passive early approach to the Government's 'defensive' negotiation strategy that signalled to industry that 'they would be insulated from climate measures'. The significant exception to this passivity was Indian industry's mobilization in support of the Clean Development Mechanism (CDM). Drawing on evidence from the Carbon Disclosure Project, he suggests that at least a section of Indian industry has more recently embraced a proactive climate agenda by, for example, welcoming India's voluntary commitment to a carbon-intensity target. This includes company measures to aggressively promote energy efficiency and initiatives at the level of the CII to engage fully in consultations around policy-making.

However, it is important to realize that CII represents only a portion of the voice of Indian industry.[6] Another industry association, the Federation of Indian Chambers of Commerce and Industry (FICCI), for example, objected to India's energy intensity target announced prior to Copenhagen, arguing it would impose undue costs on Indian business, and suggesting the pledge should have been linked to access to technology and supporting finance (Thakur and Seal, 2009; *The Times of India*, 2009). Readers interested in further exploring this view may choose to read a FICCI report with detailed sectoral recommendations, which provides a more detailed insight into their perspective (FICCI, 2007). Finally, both CII and FICCI are associations formed by large businesses. Small- and medium-scale enterprises (SMEs) may have very different perceptions, but are not represented in this volume because they are difficult to assess. The perspectives and role of SMEs in climate policy and politics requires further exploration and study.

Pulver provides another, more academic, perspective on Indian business, with a particular focus on its role in the CDM. She suggests that awareness of climate change is high among developing country industries, although lower than that for industrialized countries, and that high awareness frequently translates into additional

16 *Dubash*

action. She presents detailed data on India's CDM projects, comparing them to projects in other countries, and also disaggregating them by sector. Politically, she finds Indian business has been relatively quiet at the international level, while domestically their advocacy has been focused largely on carbon market opportunities. Finally, she presents evidence that climate change is beginning to be factored into Indian industry's corporate governance.

The cumulative picture of Indian industry suggests an important constituency that has been relatively quiet thus far, limiting its intervention to policy around the carbon market. However, there are indications of mobilization for more substantial political engagement on climate change, most apparent in Das's chapter, even though Indian industry by no means speaks with one voice on this issue.

One of the more remarkable, if indirect indicators of the growing engagement with climate change and its politics is the rise in attention to the subject in the Indian English-language press. Based on an analysis of coverage over nine newspapers for the seven months centred on the Copenhagen negotiations, Jogesh maps trends in climate coverage. She finds a remarkable average rate of an article a day in each newspaper across this period, much of which is predictably focused on global politics and processes, with Indian domestic debates a distant second. The chapter points to the need for systematic analysis of media coverage, given its important role in shaping politics, as also the need to extend this analysis to Hindi and local-language papers.

The chapters in this Part suggest a modest shift in India's climate politics, to provide support for more active engagement with climate change – both mitigation and adaptation – but only in the context of a co-benefits agenda. Much of the formal politics is still bound up with concern over a failure to adequately address equity in the global negotiations, and differentiated responsibility continues to be a bedrock principle with wide support from environmentalists and politicians and some sections of business, and one that looms large in media reports. Climate change is still indisputably an elite issue, and this is only likely to change if the topic is better connected to livelihood concerns and the importance of a robust resource base for the well-being of India's less advantaged citizens.

Integrating climate change and development

In what ways and how should India begin grappling with climate change in its domestic policy? Until about 2008, and following directly from India's international negotiating position, this question was almost never considered in policy circles. However, since then climate change is often invoked as a factor, even if often tangentially and without much clarity, in considerations of domestic policy. For example, the Planning Commission, along with the Ministry of Environment and Forests has constituted an Expert Group to report on 'Low Carbon Strategies for Inclusive Growth' as an input to the 12th five-year plan (Planning Commission, 2011). Whether or not such reports and plans lead to changes on the ground remains to be seen, but certainly there has been a shift in the articulation of priorities.

The most important facilitator of this shift is the framing of India's domestic climate policy within the framework of 'co-benefits'. First introduced into policy discourse through the National Action Plan on Climate Change, co-benefits are 'measures that promote our development objectives while also yielding co-benefits for addressing climate change effectively' (Prime Minister's Council on Climate Change, Government

Introduction   17

of India, 2009). The prioritization is deliberate and explicit: development objectives are primary and climate change is a secondary co-benefit. The idea of co-benefits – for example between improvements in health from cleaner burning cook-stoves and climate change – is not new and has a long history in the academic literature (Smith and Haigler, 2008). However, the formal adoption of co-benefits as the overarching approach of India's Action Plan unlocked important political doors.

Most important, a co-benefits approach is consistent with India's core negotiation principle of 'common but differentiated responsibility and respective capabilities'. It allows exploration of domestic policy changes, but in a manner that is driven by domestic development objectives. The co-benefits frame guards against any implicit acceptance of responsibility for global climate change and hence responsibility for action, and leaves open the door to demanding international financial support for policies that are primarily driven by climate mitigation or adaptation. Even if in practice this line between policies driven by domestic objectives and climate change objectives is hard to define on a policy-by-policy basis, the conceptual line between the two, which is paramount for negotiation purposes, is maintained.

It is important to note that maintenance of this line does not mean that the NAPCC introduced only cosmetic changes. The co-benefits logic could encompass a very wide swathe of India's economic activity. For example, decisions about urban planning, future energy choices, and forest policies can all potentially be re-considered within this framework. In this sense, the perspective and process introduced by the NAPCC provides a political opportunity and institutional vehicle to re-frame existing development debates. For example, creation of a separate energy efficiency mission under the NAPCC has provided both a higher political profile, and a tangible process through which to develop and implement far reaching energy efficiency measures, in a manner that arguably would not have been possible without the NAPCC (Dubash, 2010).

At the same time the NAPCC and its motivating approach of co-benefits does not guarantee integration of climate change and development concerns. The NAPCC itself was born out of growing international pressure to demonstrate seriousness on climate change, even while satisfying domestic constituencies that India's long-standing position was not being compromised.[7] The Plan itself received mixed reviews, with one critique dubbing it 'not vision, not plan' since it neither provided a clear future vision, nor a detailed framework for action (*Economic and Political Weekly*, 2008). Another suggested the Plan lacked adequate diagnosis of both the problem and lack of a clear articulation of solutions (Bidwai, 2010). In format it introduced eight 'missions', each of which was charged with formulating a way forward on areas as diverse as solar energy, habitats, and water. In most cases, line ministries were put in charge of elaborating missions, leading to concern that the outcome would be simply a re-packaging of existing plans and proposals (*Economic and Political Weekly*, 2008). In other words, the tangible impact of the co-benefits approach to climate mitigation is deeply contingent on the uses to which this approach is put, and, in any given sector, could result in outcomes ranging from window-dressing to deeply transformative change. In any specific case, the outcome will likely depend on how different institutional actors – ministries, other units of governance such as municipalities and sector regulators, advocacy groups and NGOs, industry associations and professional networks – interact to shape outcomes. In this context, the exploration of co-benefits in the context of development policy becomes an intriguing political moment, one that potentially acts as a tipping factor pushing the domestic debate in one direction or other.

18 *Dubash*

These dynamics play out at the level of the individual sector, since co-benefits requires starting with development objectives, which tend to get defined along the lines of existing governance structures. The benefits of this approach are that the connections to mechanisms of implementation are tighter; the costs are that the scope for new thinking and linkages across issues are weaker. Notably, this approach also requires discarding the conventional organization of national policies into mitigation and adaptation measures. If the unit of analysis is the sector, and the starting point is development objectives, then each sector needs to be examined for the relevant mix of mitigation and adaptation objectives, to the extent they overlap with development concerns. For example, while energy discussions focus predominantly on mitigation and water on adaptation, agriculture and urban issues require addressing both mitigation and adaptation.

The chapters in Part V explore the scope for integrating climate change into development objectives in the spirit of the co-benefits approach. Each chapter takes as its starting point existing development concerns. However, the authors do not take as given conventional wisdoms on development objectives and approaches, and instead take seriously critiques of existing policies and approaches on purely developmental grounds. These are challenging chapters to write, since each chapter must necessarily cover vast terrain about which there are widely conflicting views. Instead of aiming for bland reviews, each author has sought to forcefully articulate a point of view, while acknowledging and gesturing to other perspectives. Collectively, the chapters in this part are intended to take seriously the potential for the co-benefits approach to actually shape India's domestic development approach in a range of key sectors.

Sant and Gambhir initiate the discussion with a panoramic study of the energy sector, along with a brief treatment of the transport sector. Since, as they note, energy-linked emissions make up 64 per cent of India's greenhouse gas emissions, the sector is central to any discussions of India's contribution to climate change mitigation. The chapter explains why energy policy must be treated as a multiple criteria optimization problem, which admits of no easy solutions. They suggest a framework for analysis that prioritizes low-cost options, including those that have a development benefit but with a climate penalty, allowing for strategic investment in climate friendly options, such as solar power. Energy efficiency emerges as a clear high-priority area of focus from this analysis. It is also clear, however, that substantial increases in capacity, likely led by coal and hydro power, are inescapable in the next decade, or even two.[8] Even within existing availability, more could be done to target energy access; supply constraints are only a partial reason. The co-benefits story in energy, therefore, is partial and complex. Interestingly, the co-benefits logic operates far more powerfully in the transport sector, where measures necessary to avoid fuel insecurity and urban congestion are also those needed to mitigate climate change.

Mukhopadhyay and Revi review both the impact of climate change on urbanization and that of urbanization on climate change, or both the adaptation and mitigation dimensions. They catalogue a vast array of linkages, including migration, building, transport, water supply and so on. They identify the challenge of forging links between multiple institutional levels as a key factor in productively engaging the urban–climate interface in the future. They also note that addressing urban challenges will require addressing several broader governance challenges, such as levels of decentralization, the patterns of federal finance for urban areas, and policies toward home-ownership. Perhaps more than any other sector, urban issues expose the extent to which integrating climate change with development is a governance challenge.

Introduction   19

In her chapter on agriculture, Raina argues for a reorientation of agriculture to embed agricultural practices in the environment. By this she means re-thinking conventional approaches of energy- and irrigation-intensive industrial agriculture in favour of more diverse and robust methods. This would require building on existing practices in small farms in rain-fed agriculture that are more robust to shocks, and relying on techniques such as integrated pest management and traditional water harvesting in place of industrial inputs. She argues that this would be a far more effective adaptation strategy than those currently espoused in the NAPCC, which tend to focus on interventions to tame the environment, rather than work with it. She also suggests that this approach would also result in mitigation gains. Her chapter, therefore, positions climate change as an opportunity to re-focus the Indian agriculture agenda on a more diverse, less industrialized model, building on and strengthening both existing practice and an existing movement calling for such a shift for domestic policy reasons.

Declining availability and greater variability of water is perhaps the greatest adaptation challenge India will face due to climate change. Kulkarni and Thakkar argue that the best way to maximize co-benefits is to re-orient water policy to emphasize demand-orientation, instead of the historical focus on the supply side of water, complemented by appropriate forms of resource augmentation. One important element in doing so is greater attention to India's groundwater resources, which have historically been orphaned by water policy. Kulkarni and Thakkar build on a long and contentious debate in Indian water policy, particularly focused on the appropriate role of large dams and large water diversion structures.[9] Echoes of this debate may be found in the National Water Mission under the NAPCC, which comes under scrutiny in the chapter. Finally, the authors note the linkages between adaptation in water and forests, wetlands, and different categories of water use, highlighting, again, the governance challenge in managing water under the threat of climate change.

In his chapter on the forest sector, Gopalakrishnan focuses more directly on the proposed mechanism that directly links the global climate regime and national forests, including India's, which is called 'Reducing Emissions for Deforestation and Degradation' (REDD). Locating his argument in a historical understanding of forest debates, Gopalakrishnan forcefully argues that REDD, which creates a financial incentive for developing countries to preserve forests (and with the addition of REDD+ to promote afforestation), is unviable in the poor governance environment of India's forests. He suggests that creating carbon value for forests will only lead to a renewed resource grab that will hurt India's poorest the most, in a manner inconsistent with the co-benefits framing.[10] He briefly discusses the various safeguards proposed in the international process and finds them wanting, not least because existing power holders in India's forest sector will stand between the poor and the effective use of these mechanisms.

The final chapter deviates from the sectoral template to look at one critical cross-cutting issue: technology. While a technological approach by itself is unlikely to address India's concerns with climate change – the other chapters have stressed the centrality of governance concerns of all sorts – technological progress is likely to be instrumental in at least some key areas, particularly energy. Consequently, Umarji and Patwardhan explore the nature of the technological challenge, and then explore the challenge ahead for India's technology infrastructure and institutions.[11] However, to explicitly incorporate climate concerns, they argue, the international community will have to assist in overcoming three obstacles: financial; access to intellectual property rights; and capacity constraints.

20 *Dubash*

Taken collectively, the chapters demonstrate that there is a rich conversation to be had to explore how a co-benefits framing of climate change can be brought to bear on domestic policy debates in critical sectors. However, they also show that this conversation is just beginning. In energy, for example, opening the door to a strategic focus on solar power still begs the question of whether India should deploy scarce resources on promoting solar technologies and how much, or whether these are better deployed on energy inclusion agendas. In water and agriculture, how powerful is climate change in providing additional arguments for re-directing policy in directions that domestic critics have long argued it should be taken? And if these arguments have not taken hold, will climate change be a sufficiently powerful driver to propel them in that direction? How will the multiple connections – with building design, transport policy, water use – that need to be made for urbanization to become climate-smart actually be forged? Should climate change become a factor driving a fundamental re-orientation of sectoral policy, or is it at best a consideration indicating change at the margin? These are the sorts of questions that will likely engage future policy-makers grappling to integrate climate change with development.

Looking to the future

The chapters in this handbook present a complex and often contradictory picture of India's engagement with the climate change debate. India's climate negotiation stance is shifting, but where it has come from is far clearer than where it is going. The domestic debate over climate change, while still limited to the elite, is rapidly broadening, with ever more constituencies seeking to figure out their stakes and interests in this debate. The results of this broadening are yet to be fully realized, but it seems clear that emergent climate politics in India supports enhanced domestic action, even while there remains considerable cynicism about global climate politics. And while the discussion on how to integrate climate change with development under the rubric of co-benefits has begun, what this integration might mean in practice is very much a work in progress.

In the final part of this handbook, Shyam Saran and Nitin Desai, both distinguished veterans of the Indian policy scene, provide their reflections looking forward. Here, I draw on their observations and those of other authors in the volume to suggest three broad future trends in the climate debate.

First, as several authors note (most directly Raghunandan, but also Dasgupta, Rajamani, and Sengupta, all this volume) the trajectory from the Copenhagen Accord to Cancun Agreements points toward a global climate regime built around bottom-up country pledges (see also Bodansky, 2011; Khor, 2010). If this trend is realized – and there is considerable dispute about whether it will be, also its implications – the global climate regime will likely move increasingly in a procedure-heavy direction. Rather than a focus on *ex ante* negotiated commitments, the driving mechanism of the global regime is likely to be *ex post* review mechanisms – the 'measurement, reporting and verification' of emission pledges and financing, and 'international consultation and analysis' of developing country reports (UNFCCC, 2011). This procedural turn will require re-orienting historical areas of emphasis for Indian climate negotiators in interesting ways. Concerns of differentiated responsibility, for example, are likely to shift toward examining whether the procedures for scrutiny and review are adequately differentiated to maintain greater responsibility for industrialized countries (Rajamani,

2011). Considerations of equity may have to be creatively internalized through the metrics against which procedures for scrutiny are pegged (Dubash and Rajamani, 2010). More broadly, a procedurally focused climate regime requires a re-orientation of intellectual work towards understanding the role of global 'soft law' mechanisms – those that are not based on legal obligation, are less than fully precise, or are not backed by adequate delegation of authority for implementation purposes (Abbot and Snidal, 2000). For those interested in the formal global climate negotiation process, these are all likely to be significant themes for the future.

Second, there is a substantial unfinished intellectual, political and policy agenda ahead to 'mainstream' climate change in India, as in other countries. As Saran puts it, even while working toward an equitable climate regime, India must independently chalk out a path to sustainable growth. However, going beyond asserting the need for this transition to designing and managing it remains a complex task. There is active national debate on how to manage the balance between environmental protection and growth (Ramesh, 2010). To further complicate matters, the relationship between climate change and other environmental agendas remains a subject of negotiation (Lele, this volume). The discussion on domestic politics of climate change suggests that so far, at least, addressing climate change is a political agenda 'from above' primarily in reaction to global rather than domestic pressures, although there is a growing domestic base calling for action. This form of environmental action stands in uneasy relationship to livelihood-based environment struggles 'from below'. To the extent the two agendas are congruent, climate change could provide both institutional opportunities (such as the NAPCC) and political opportunities. If, however, climate change becomes an agenda for special interests, a concern expressed by Gopalakrishnan (this volume) in the context of forests, climate change concerns can work against the entrenchment of environmental objectives as a core objective of domestic policy, along with growth and social inclusion.

Even if the political will to internalize environmental concerns is generated in a manner that is consistent with both agendas from above and below, there still remain complex questions about how to institutionally manage trade-offs across multiple objectives of growth, inclusion and environmental sustainability. The sectoral chapters in Part V on integrating climate change and development signal very clearly that climate change can be, at best, one of these multiple objectives of development policy in India. But they provide only preliminary indications of how to govern toward multiple objectives. Exploring how best to institutionalize co-benefits as an active framework for climate governance in India is a rich area for future work.

Finally, at the global level, too, the time may have come to re-conceptualize how we imagine climate change. Desai broadens the canvas beyond climate negotiations to explore the geopolitical implications of climate change for energy markets and, through climate impacts, other aspects of human security such as water scarcity, environmentally induced displacement and the like. He provides a double conclusion: climate diplomacy, mitigation action, and impacts are unlikely to change geopolitical balances; but if an effective climate regime is not secured in short order then we enter the world of tipping points in which, as Desai says, 'all bets are off'.

Given this sober scenario, it may be useful to also turn around Desai's question and explore not only how climate change may affect geopolitics, but also whether and how global politics is creating the conditions for internalizing climate change in diverse non-climatic arenas. Over the last two decades, global climate change discussions have,

22 Dubash

in a sense, been restricted within the climate negotiations, while important decisions relevant to climate futures were made elsewhere. In particular, broader debates on global governance of energy, including regulating energy markets, stimulating technology development, managing joint data collection, and coordinating the work of diverse agencies such as the International Energy Agency and World Bank are all salient to climate change (Bazilian et al., 2011; Dubash and Florini, 2011). On the adaptation side, global coordination of health, food and water security could fruitfully internalize the implications of climate change for each of these arenas. It is unrealistic, and inconsistent with past experience, to expect this internalization to be driven entirely by the climate negotiation process alone. A broader agenda of internalizing climate concerns within the full range of global institutional arenas should become a growing part of a global governance agenda to complement climate negotiations if effective global coordination on climate change is to be realized.

At the risk of over-simplification, these three themes coalesce into an overarching message: addressing climate change at both national and global levels will require complex mechanisms of governance that stimulate and manage interactions across institutions and trade-offs across objectives. This messy reality belies the neat imagery that has informed much of the last two decades of climate negotiations and which now seems remote: an overarching global climate negotiation that allocates responsibilities across countries, which drives change through national systems via carbon markets. To manage the integration and mainstreaming climate considerations into other arenas – energy, health, water, food – at national and global scales, will require much broader engagement by policy-makers and citizens with the substantive issues at stake and their politics. This volume seeks to provide a basis for understanding alternative conceptual underpinnings of the climate debate, particularly within India, to facilitate this broadening of deliberation and engagement.

Notes

1 This search was limited to two English language papers – *The Times of India* and *The Hindu*, using trends over time for 'climate change' in Google.
2 For an example of the former, see Stavins (2010). For the latter, see Raghunandan (2010). For a glass half full position, see Jayaraman (2010).
3 Available at www.ipcc.ch
4 See http://www.nipccreport.org/index.html
5 See, for example, comments by American commentators on Copenhagen (Bodansky, 2010; Doniger, 2009) and Cancun (Stavins, 2010). For additional and different perspectives on the Copenhagen Accord see Dubash (2009a); and Rajamani (2010), and Grubb (2011). For a detailed reading of the Cancun Agreements, see Rajamani (2011).
6 An additional perspective is available from an industry survey conducted by KPMG in India (2008).
7 While there is no direct evidence for this view, it is a perspective corroborated by informal conversations, and also by the timing of the NAPCC, which was released shortly before the G8 meeting in 2009.
8 Particularly on the energy sector, there are a wide variety of contending views on India's future to which readers could refer, among them the Government's landmark Integrated Energy Policy (GoI, 2006) that projects massive capacity expansion in the near future. By contrast, others are optimistic about and strongly advocate an early transition to renewable energy, including for rural access (Greenpeace and EREC, 2008; Global Wind Energy Council, 2009; Vasudha Foundation, 2010.)
9 For a historical treatment broadly sympathetic to the view espoused here, see Iyer (2007). For a different perspective that is more open to a continued, even renewed role for surface

water projects and enhanced use of market mechanisms, while recognizing the importance of groundwater and better governance, see Briscoe and Malik (2006).

10 For views more supportive of REDD+ see India Carbon Outlook (2010) and MoEF (2010). For a generally positive assessment of whether India is capable of implementing REDD plus see Aggarwal, Das and Paul (2009).

11 For an additional perspective on what developing countries can expect in the climate and technology arena, see United Nations Department of Economic and Social Affairs (2009).

References

Abbott, K. and Snidal, D. (2000) 'Hard and Soft Law in International Governance', *International Organization* 54(3) Summer 2000: 421–456.

Aggarwal, A., Das, S. and Paul, V. (2009) 'Is India Ready to Implement REDD Plus: A Preliminary Assessment', The Energy and Resources Institute, New Delhi.

Baer, P., Fieldman, G., Kartha, S., Athanasiou, T. (2008) 'The Greenhouse Development Rights: Towards an Equitable Framework for Global Climate Policy', *Cambridge Review of International Affairs* 21(4): 649–669.

Bazilian, M., Hobbs, B., Blyth, W., MacGill, I., Howells, M. (2011) 'Interactions Between Energy Security and Climate Change: A Focus on Developing Countries', *Energy Policy* (in press).

Benedick, R.E. (1998) *Ozone Diplomacy: New Directions in Safeguarding the Planet*, Harvard University Press.

Bidwai, P. (2010) *An India That Can Say Yes*, Heinrich Boell Stiftung, New Delhi.

Bodansky, D. (2011) 'A Tale of Two Architectures: The Once and Future U.N. Climate Change Regime', SSRN: http://ssrn.com/abstract=1773865, accessed 13 May 2011.

—— (2010) 'The Copenhagen Climate Change Conference: A Post-mortem', *American Journal of International Law* 104(2): 230–240.

Briscoe, J. and Malik, R.P.S. (2006) 'India's Water Economy: Bracing for a Turbulent Future', World Bank.

Brundtland Commission (1987) 'Our Common Future', *Report of the World Commission on Environment and Development*, Oxford University Press, Oxford.

Bulkeley, H. and Betsill, M. (2005) 'Rethinking Sustainable Cities: Multilevel Governance and the "Urban" Politics of Climate Change', *Environmental Politics* 14(1): 42–63.

Bulkeley, H. and Newell, P. (2010) *Governing Climate Change*, Routledge, Abingdon.

Chakravarty, S., Chikkatur, A., De Coninck, H., Pacala, S., Socolow, R. and Tavoni, M. (2009) 'Sharing Global CO_2 Emissions Reductions among One Billion High Emitters', *Proceedings of the National Academy of Sciences* 106(29): 11884–11888.

Chauhan, C. (2010) 'Link states' green quotient with resources', 10 September, *Hindustan Times*.

Doniger, D. (2009) 'Copenhagen Accord: A Big Step Forward', *The Huffington Post*, 23 December.

Dubash, N.K. (2010) 'From Norm Taker to Norm Maker? Indian Energy Governance in Global Context', under review with *Global Policy*.

—— (2009a) 'Climate of Mistrust', *Economic and Political Weekly* 44(52): 8–11.

—— (2009b) 'Environmentalism in the Age of Climate Change', Seminar 601, pp. 63–66.

—— (2009c) 'Toward a Progressive Indian and Global Climate Politics', Working Paper 2009/1 (September), Centre for Policy Research.

Dubash, N.K. and Florini, A. (2011) 'Conceptualizing Energy Governance', *Global Policy*, vol. 2, S.1.

Dubash, N.K. and Rajamani, L. (2010) 'Beyond Copenhagen: Next Steps', *Climate Policy* 10 (6): 593–599.

Dubash, N.K., Dupar, M., Kothari, S. and Lissu, T. (2001) 'A Watershed in Global Governance: An Independent Assessment of the World Commission on Dams', World Resources Institute, Lokayan and LEAT.

24   *Dubash*

Economist, The (2008) 'China, India and Climate Change: Melting Asia', 5 June.

Economic and Political Weekly (2008) 'Climate Change: Not Vision, Not Plan', 12 July, pp. 5–6.

FICCI (2007) 'Climate Change Task Force Report', New Delhi.

Global Wind Energy Council (2009) 'Indian Wind Energy Outlook', GWEC and Indian Wind Turbine Manufacturers Association.

Government of India (2006) 'Integrated Energy Policy', Report of the Expert Group, Planning Commission, http://planningcommission.nic.in/reports/genrep/intengpol.pdf, accessed 13 May 2011.

Greenpeace and EREC (2008) 'Energy Revolution: A Sustainable India Energy Outlook', Greenpeace International and European Renewable Energy Council (EREC).

Grubb, M. (2011) 'Cancun: The Art of the Possible', *Climate Policy* 11(2): 847–850.

—— (2010) 'Copenhagen: Back to the Future?', *Climate Policy* 10(2): 127–130.

Grundmann, R. (2007) 'Climate Change and Knowledge Politics', *Environmental Politics*, 16(3): 414–432.

Guha R. (1997) 'The Environmentalism of the Poor', in R. Guha and J. Martinez-Alier (eds.) *Varieties of Environmentalism: Essays North and South*, Earthscan, London.

Gupta, J. (2007) 'The Multi-Level Governance Challenge of Climate Change', *Environmental Sciences*, 4(3): 131–137.

Hulme, M. (2009) *Why We Disagree about Climate Change*, Cambridge University Press, Cambridge.

India Carbon Outlook (2010) 'A REDD dawn in India', http://india.carbon-outlook.com/content/redd-dawn-india, accessed 9 March 2011.

IPCC (1990) *Climate Change: The IPCC Scientific Assessment*, J.T. Houghton, G.J. Jenkins and J.J. Ephraums (eds.), Cambridge University Press, Cambridge.

—— (2001) *Climate Change 2001: Synthesis Report, A Contribution of Working Groups I, II, and III to the Third Assessment Report of the Intergovernmental Panel on Climate Change*, R.T. Watson, and the Core Writing Team (eds.), Cambridge University Press, Cambridge.

—— (2007) *Climate Change 2007, A Contribution of Working Groups I, II and III to the Fourth Assessment Report of the Intergovernmental Panel on Climate Change*, R. K. Pachauri and A. Reisinger (eds), IPCC, Geneva, Switzerland.

Iyer, R. (2007) *Towards Water Wisdom: Limits, Justice, Harmony*, Sage, New Delhi.

Jayaraman, T. (2010) 'Taking Stock of Cancun', *The Hindu*, 13 December.

Khor, M. (2010) 'Complex Implications of the Cancun Climate Conference', *Economic and Political Weekly*, 25 December, vol. xlv, no. 52.

KPMG (2008) 'Climate Change: Is Indian Inc. Prepared?', http://www.kpmg.com/IN/en/ThoughtLedership/Climate%20Change-%20Is%20India%20Inc.%20Prepared.pdf, accessed on 10 March 2011.

Lele, S. (1991) 'Sustainable Development: A Critical Review', *World Development* 19(6): 607–621.

Lohmann, L. (1990) 'Whose Common Future?', *The Ecologist* 20(3): 82–84.

Malnes, R. (2008) 'Climate Science and the Way We Ought to Think about Danger', *Environmental Politics* 17(4): 660–672.

Malone, E. (2009) *Debating Climate Change: Pathways through Argument to Agreement*, Earthscan, London.

Meadows, D., Meadows, D., Randers, J. and Behrens, W. (1972) *The Limits to Growth*, Universe Books, New York.

Ministry of Environment and Forests (2010) 'India's Forests and Redd+', Government of India, http://moef.nic.in/downloads/public-information/REDD-report.pdf, accessed 9 March 2011.

Mukherji, R. (ed.) (2007) *India's Economic Transition: The Politics of Reforms*, Oxford University Press, New Delhi.

Ostrom, E. (2010) 'Polycentric Systems for Coping with Collective Action and Global Environmental Change', *Global Environmental Change*, 20, pp. 550–557.

Pettenger, M. (2007) *The Social Construction of Climate Change: Power, Knowledge, Norms, Discourses*, Ashgate, UK.

Planning Commission, GoI (2011) 'Low Carbon Strategies for Inclusive Growth: An Interim Report of the Expert Group', http://moef.nic.in/downloads/public-information/Interim%20Report%20of%20the%20Expert%20Group.pdf, accessed 16 May 2011.

Prime Minister's Council on Climate Change (2009) *National Action Plan on Climate Change*, Government of India.

Raghunandan, D. (2010) 'Kyoto Is Dead, Long Live Durban?', *Economic and Political Weekly*, vol. xlv, no. 52, 25 December, New Delhi.

Raina, V. K. (2009) 'Himalayan Glaciers A State-of-Art Review of Glacial Studies, Glacial Retreat and Climate Change', Discussion Paper, Ministry of Environment and Forests, Government of India.

Rajamani L. (2011) 'The Cancun Climate Agreements: Reading the Text, Subtext and Tealeaves,' *International and Comparative Law Quarterly* 60(2).

—— (2010) 'The Making and Unmaking of the Copenhagen Accord', *International and Comparative Law Quarterly* 59(3): 22–41.

Ramesh, J. (2010) 'The Two Cultures Revisited: The Environment–Development Debate in India', *Economic and Political Weekly*, 16 October, vol. xlv, no. 42.

Saran, S. (2010) 'Premature power', *Business Standard*, 17 March 2010.

Schiermeier, Q. (2010) 'IPCC Flooded by criticism', *Nature* 463: 596–597.

Selin, H. and vanDeever, S. (eds.) (2009) *Changing Climates in North American Politics: Institutions, Policymaking and Multilevel Governance*, MIT Press, London.

Shourie, A. (2009) 'Changing course on climate', *The Indian Express*, 2 July 2009.

Smith K. R. and Haigler, E. (2008) 'Co-Benefits of Climate Mitigation and Health Protection in Energy Systems: Scoping Methods', Annual Review of Public Health, 29: 11–25.

Stavins, R. (2010) 'What Happened (and Why): An Assessment of the Cancun Agreements', http://belfercenter.ksg.harvard.edu/analysis/stavins/?p=876, accessed 28 February 2011.

Subramanian, A. (2009) 'Climate Change – Winning the Narrative', *Business Standard*, 29 July 2009.

Thakur, N. and Seal, V. (2009) 'Industry Frets at Emission Cut, Move Likely to Burden Economy', http://www.dnaindia.com/money/report_industry-frets-at-emission-cut-move-likely-to-burden-economy_1326166, accessed 6 March 2011.

The Times of India (2009) 'Jairam Persuades Negotiators to Join Climate Talks', 7 December.

UNFCCC (2011) Cancun Agreements, Decision 1/CP.16, FCCC/CP/2010/7/Add.1 and Decision 1/CMP.6, FCCC/KP/CMP/2010/ 12/Add.1

UNFCCC (1992) *United Nations Framework Convention on Climate Change*, Bonn.

United Nations Department of Economic and Social Affairs (2009) 'Climate Change: Technology Development and Transfer', Background Paper prepared for the Delhi High Level Conference on Climate Change: Technology Development and Transfer, New Delhi, India, 22–23 October 2009.

Vasudha Foundation (2010) 'Indian Civil Society Perspective on World Bank Energy Strategy', http://www.christianaid.org.uk/images/energybriefingindia.pdf, accessed 13 May 2011.

Williamson, J. (ed.) (1994) *The Political Economy of Policy Reform*, Institute for International Economics, Washington DC.

Part I

Climate science and potential impacts

1 Impacts of climate change on India

J. Srinivasan

Introduction

In this chapter we will look at changes in climate that have occurred in India during the 20th century. We will examine both local and global factors that have influenced our climate. The predictions for climate change in India in the 21st century made by climate models will be discussed. The major challenges that we will face in order to adapt to impacts of climate change in the 21st century will be delineated.

One may be tempted to attribute all the changes that have occurred in India to global climate change and blame every adverse change that occurs in the environment on it. It is important to recognize that climate change is part of a larger problem of environmental degradation that is occurring in India. There are other local issues equally important such as the increase in air pollution and water pollution. These issues can be tackled without linking them to factors that cause global climate change.

The term climate change refers to long-term changes in temperature, humidity, clouds and rainfall and not to day-to-day variations (IPCC, 2007). Regional climate change is caused by both local and global factors. This difference is very important because if a regional climate change occurs on account of local factors then these changes can be mitigated by local actions. If a city is getting warmer because of too many concrete buildings, then this can be altered by local laws that require some greenery between buildings. On the other hand, if a city is warming because of global increase in carbon dioxide then the action to reduce CO_2 emission has to be initiated through global negotiations.

The Intergovernmental Panel of Climate Change (IPCC) was created by the United Nations to enable scientists from all parts of the world to provide an authentic summary of our present understanding of the climate change induced by human beings and indicate the ways to mitigate this climate change or adapt to it. More than 500 scientists from different nations were involved in writing the fourth assessment report published by IPCC in 2007. This report was reviewed by more than 2,000 experts from all over the world (IPCC, 2007). The report is an excellent summary of our present state of understanding of the changes in the earth's climate during the past 100 years. The report states that during the past 100 years the global mean temperature has increased by 0.74°C (Figure 1.1) (IPCC, 2007). This large increase cannot be attributed to natural causes such as the variation in radiation emitted by the sun. Complex climate models have shown that this increase is primarily triggered by a 33 per cent increase in CO_2 in the atmosphere during the past hundred years (see

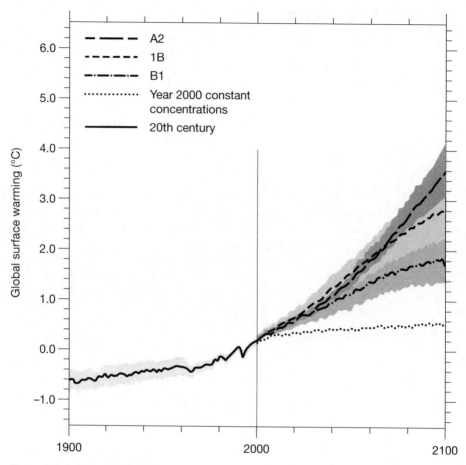

Figure 1.1 Increase in global mean temperature for various scenarios

Source: IPCC, 2007

Box 1.1). The IPCC report has highlighted that the increase in global mean temperature has caused a rapid decrease in Arctic sea ice and an increase in sea level by around 17 cm during the past 100 years (Figure 1.2). The frequency of heavy rainfall events has increased in most land areas of the world during the past 50 years. These conclusions regarding global climate change are robust.

However, observed changes in regional climate cannot be attributed confidently to one cause. This is because regional climate change is caused by both local and global factors. There have been large changes in air pollution and land-use pattern in India. This can cause changes in temperature that can be as important as those caused by an increase in CO_2 in the atmosphere. The IPCC report does not provide many examples of regional climate change that can be attributed confidently solely to the increase in CO_2 in the atmosphere.

Impacts of climate change on India 31

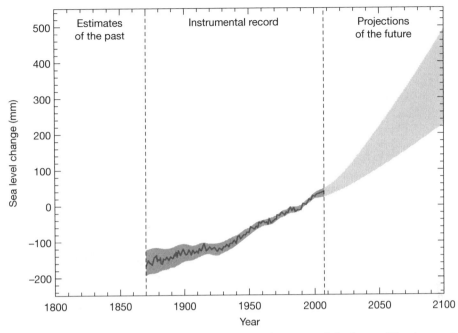

Figure 1.2 The increase in global mean sea level in the past and the future. The changes in sea level are with reference to the 1960–1990 mean

Source: IPCC, 2007

BOX 1.1

The earth would have been about 33°C colder if minor gases like CO_2, methane, ozone and water vapor were absent (Srinivasan, 2008). Although the amount of these gases in the earth's atmosphere is very small they have a profound impact on earth's climate because of their ability to absorb radiation emitted by the earth's surface (like the glass in a greenhouse). During the ice ages, which have occurred many times in the past, CO_2 and methane in the earth's atmosphere was much lower than the present. The amount of CO_2 in the earth's atmosphere has increased by more than 33 per cent during the past hundred and fifty years on account of the burning of fossil fuels (coal, oil and natural gas) (IPCC, 2007). An increase in CO_2 in the atmosphere causes an increase in global mean temperature which in turn leads to increase in water vapour. Water vapour in the earth's atmosphere causes more trapping of the thermal radiation emitted by earth. This ability of water vapour to amplify the initial warming caused by CO_2 is called a positive feedback. Another factor that can cause positive feedback is the change in cloud type and amount. In addition to changes induced by human beings there are also natural factors such as volcanic eruption and variation in the sun's energy output that can also cause changes in the earth's climate. In the 21st century, the changes induced by human beings will have a much greater impact on earth's climate than natural causes.

32 *Srinivasan*

Climate change in the 20th century in India

Temperature

Regional climate is influenced not only by the global increase in CO_2 but also by regional change in land use and particulates (like sulphate and soot) (Marshall et al., 2004). Hence it is not easy to attribute regional climate change to a single factor such as the monotonic increase in CO_2.

The all-India annual-mean surface air temperature was the highest in 2010 (IMD, 2010). On 26 May 2010, a maximum temperature of 53.5°C recorded in Pakistan was the highest temperature ever recorded in Asia. The All-India annual-mean surface air temperature has increased by 0.51°C in the past 106 years. Most of the increase was seen during the past 30 years during the pre-monsoon season and in winter (Rupa Kumar et al., 2002). The change in mean temperature was primarily on account of an increase in daily maximum temperature since the daily minimum temperature does not show any trend. In contrast the increase in global mean temperature is primarily on account of an increase in daily minimum temperature. The increase in maximum temperature in north India was found to be less than that in south India (Dash et al., 2007). This may be on account of a higher amount of particulates in the atmosphere in north India. The presence of particulates in the atmosphere reduces the surface temperature. The surface air temperature in Rajasthan has, however, decreased. This could be on account of an increase in area under irrigation in Rajasthan. The sea surface temperatures in the oceans around India have also warmed by 0.6°C during the past 50 years with the largest increase seen around the equatorial Indian Ocean (Rajeevan et al., 2008). The number of heat waves during the pre-monsoon period has shown an increasing trend. During the period 1970–2005, the number of hot days has increased from 2 days to 20 days in the west coast of India. The number of cold days has decreased by 10 days during the same period (Dash et al., 2007). In Nepal, the surface air temperature has increased 1° per decade during the past 30 years in some high altitude stations (Shreshta et al., 1999). This is much higher than that observed in most stations in India. The increase in surface temperature has been higher in some urban areas than in the rural areas. This is because of the storage of heat in concrete buildings and roads in urban areas. The increase in temperature in many urban areas during the past 100 years is both on account of urbanization and the increase in CO_2.

Rainfall

Most of the rainfall in India occurs during summer (June to September). This is known as the summer monsoon. The All India summer monsoon rainfall has not shown any significant trend during the last 140 years (Rajendran and Kitoh, 2008). In most years, the All India summer monsoon rainfall is within 10 per cent of the long-term mean. The Indian summer monsoon rainfall can be much lower than normal when the sea surface temperatures in the equatorial central and eastern Pacific Ocean are warmer than normal. These are called El Niño years. The Indian rainfall can also be below normal if the sea surface temperatures in the eastern equatorial Indian Ocean are above normal. Changes in sea surface temperatures in the tropical oceans thus exert a strong influence on the Indian summer monsoon. The increase in CO_2 in the

Impacts of climate change on India   33

earth's atmosphere during the past hundred years has warmed the tropical oceans but this warming has not been uniform. The warming of the equatorial Indian Ocean has been much greater than that of the northern Indian Ocean.

Although the seasonal mean monsoon rainfall has not shown any trend, the extreme rainfall events have increased. During the past 50 years the heavy rainfall events (rainfall greater than 100 mm/day) has increased by 50 per cent in Central India (Goswami et al., 2006) This rapid increase in heavy rainfall events may be on account of global warming or increase in aerosols. The seasonal mean monsoon rainfall over India does not show any long-term trend because the increase in extreme rainfall events has been compensated by a decrease in moderate rainfall events (rainfall below 100 mm/day). The number of cyclonic disturbances has decreased from 7 per year 60 years ago to below 2 per year in the last decade (Dash et al., 2007). There has been a decrease in winter snowfall in Western Himalayas during the past 20 years (Shekhar et al., 2010). There is, however, no clinching evidence to prove that rainfall patterns have changed on account of the global increase in CO_2.

Glaciers

There is a lot of concern about the impact of global warming on glaciers. In most parts of the world glaciers are retreating. Some glaciers are retreating rapidly (more than 20 metres per year) while other are retreating slowly. Glaciers can retreat or advance due to natural climate fluctuations. During the past 50 years, many Himalayan glaciers have retreated more than 10 metres per year (Kulkarni et al., 2007) This is much faster than the gradual retreat of glaciers due to natural causes. During the past 25 years the Gangotri glacier has retreated by around 500 metres. The glaciers can retreat rapidly both on account of warmer air above it and lesser snow falling on it. In addition to change in temperature and snowfall, the rate of retreat of the glacier depends also upon the altitude of glacier. High altitude glaciers will not melt easily since the temperatures at high altitudes are below the temperatures at which ice melts. In many high altitude stations, the air temperatures have, however, increased more rapidly than in stations at lower altitudes. In the Indian Himalayas, small glaciers (area less than 1 square kilometre) have been retreating rapidly. In the Chenab basin in Himachal Pradesh the area of small glaciers has decreased by 38 per cent in the last 42 years while the area of large glaciers (area greater than 10 square kilometres) has decreased by 12 per cent in 42 years (Kulkarni et al., 2007). Hence many small glaciers in the Himalayas may disappear completely in the next 50 years. This is not true of large glaciers and the distinction between small and large glaciers was not made in Chapter 10 of the IPCC Fourth Assessment Report (Working Group II). This led to a lot of controversy which could have been avoided if this distinction had been made. Our knowledge about glacier retreat is limited because less than 0.2 per cent of the glaciers on the earth are monitored regularly.

Sea level

An increase in sea surface temperature will lead to an expansion of sea water and hence an increase in sea level. In addition, ice melting from land glaciers will lead to further increase in sea level. During the past 100 years, the global sea level has increased by around 170 mm. The melting of glaciers has contributed about 45 mm to sea level rise

34 *Srinivasan*

during the past 100 years. The rate of sea level was 1 mm/yr in early 20th century and 3.3 mm/yr during the last decades of the 20th century (IPCC, 2007)

In addition to global factors, local factors (such as subsidence) also contribute to sea level rise. In Mumbai sea level has increased by 0.77 mm/yr during the past 100 years while in Kolkotta the sea level has increased by 5.22 mm/yr during the past 50 years (Unnikrishnan and Shankar, 2007). Sea level rise is a major concern since a large fraction of the human population resides within 50 km of the sea coast (McGranahan et al., 2007). Since the last ice age 20,000 years ago, the global mean temperature has increased by about 5 degree Celsius while the sea level has risen by about 125 metres (Vermeer and Rahmstorf, 2009). This indicates that the sea level will rise by 25 metres when global mean temperature increase by 1°C. Most of the contribution will be from the melting of glaciers but this will not occur immediately but we do not know if it will occur within the next hundred years.

In India, West Bengal and Gujarat are most vulnerable to sea level rise. An increase of one metre in sea level will inundate almost 6000 km^2 of land in India. A sea level rise of one metre will cause 17 per cent of the land in Bangladesh to be inundated (Ali and Huq, 1989). The increase in sea level will cause enhanced damage during storm surges that occur during cyclone land-fall. IPCC 4th assessment report indicated that the maximum rise in sea level in 2100 will be 0.5 metres (IPCC, 2007). The work done subsequently indicates that sea level rise in 2100 may be above one metre (Vermeer and Rahmstorf, 2009). There is a large uncertainty in the estimate of sea level rise because it is difficult to simulate how rapidly the glaciers in Greenland and Antarctica will melt. The models that are used to simulate the melting of glaciers do not account for all the complex interactions that occur during the melting of the glaciers.

Aerosols and the Indian climate

Small solid or liquid particles suspended in the atmosphere are called aerosols and these can also influence our climate (Chung and Ramanathan, 2006). The emissions from thermal power plants (that burn coal or oil) contain large emissions of sulphur dioxide which later become sulphate aerosols. Sulphate aerosols cool the earth surface and the atmosphere and hence lead to a decrease in surface temperature and rainfall. On the other hand, soot emitted from incomplete combustion (diesel engine exhaust or burning of firewood for cooking) heat the atmosphere and cool the surface. The amount of cooling of the Indian land surface by sulphate aerosols and soot is much larger than the warming caused by CO_2. This indicates that the impact of higher aerosols on local climate is much larger than the impact of higher CO_2.

This is not true of global mean temperature. The increase in global mean temperature is primarily on account of increase in CO_2 but the changes in local surface temperature are both on account of aerosols and CO_2. The impact of aerosols on global mean temperature is not clear but it could have reduced the warming caused by CO_2.

In India, aerosols are present in the atmosphere from November to June. During the period November to March soot aerosols dominate while dust is dominant during April to June. The impact of these aerosols on the Indian monsoon is not clear. Since all aerosols cool the land surface, the land-sea contrast in surface temperature will be lower during the pre-monsoon season. Some investigators have argued that this can

Impacts of climate change on India 35

lead to a weaker monsoon (Chung and Ramanathan, 2006). An alternate view is that the heating of the atmosphere by soot aerosols will lead to a stronger monsoon (Lau, Kim and Kim, 2006). We do not have sufficient observations to show whether the surface cooling or the atmospheric warming has a dominant influence on the Indian monsoon.

The most important effect of aerosols is in the formation of clouds. The presence of aerosols decreases the diameter of cloud droplets. Smaller cloud droplets reflect more solar radiation and evaporate more easily and hence this can reduce the rainfall falling on the ground. The effect of aerosols on clouds is not represented accurately in most climate models and hence one cannot predict confidently how aerosols will influence clouds and rainfall. Since the understanding of the impact of aerosols on clouds and climate is poor, scientists cannot provide robust recommendation with regard to how reducing aerosols will influence either global climate change or local climate.

Although our understanding of the impact of aerosols on climate is poor, the impact of aerosols on our health is documented well (Kagawa, 2002). Hence it is quite obvious that we must reduce the amount of soot and sulphate in the atmosphere in order to reduce the adverse impact of these particulates on our health. In the developed world the impact of reducing aerosols on respiratory and cardiac problems has been demonstrated (Pope et al., 2002). We should, therefore, embark on a mission to reduce soot and sulphate aerosols in view of the benefits with regard to the health of the population although the impact of aerosols on Indian climate is not well understood.

Impact of climate change in the 21st century

To predict climate change in India in the 21st century we need to use climate models. The different climate models used in IPCC AR4 show that the global mean temperature will increase between 2 and 4° C (Figure 1.1). The actual increase in temperature will depend upon the rate of increase of CO_2 emissions. If the increase in emissions is high (A2 scenario) the global mean temperature can increase by as much as 4°C. On the other hand if the increase in emissions is low (B1 scenario) the increase in global mean temperature can be restricted to 2°C. All models indicate that the surface air temperature over India will increase but the magnitude of the increase varies between 2 to 4° C (by the end of the 21st century). Battisti and Naylor (2009) have shown that there is a 90 per cent chance that the average summer temperature during the period 2080–2100 will be higher than the highest summer temperature observed so far. This will pose a serious challenge for agriculture and industry since the efficiency at the work place will drop dramatically under these conditions. Takahashi et al. (2007) have indicated that such an increase in temperature will cause a large increase in mortality due to heat waves in Asia. In Figure 1.3, the change in rainfall predicted by these models is shown. We see that about half the models predict an increase in monsoon rainfall while others predict a decrease in monsoon rainfall. The models differ a lot in their ability to simulate summer monsoon precipitation over India in 20th century (see Figure 1.4). We find that among the 18 models shown only a few simulate the seasonal variation of monsoon rainfall in the 20th century. This implies that we cannot trust the predictions of these models with regard to rainfall in India in the future.

The results obtained from high resolution models (spatial resolution around 20 km) have more credibility. Rajendran and Kitoh (2008) have shown that a high resolution climate model simulates the spatial structure of Indian monsoon rainfall very well. This

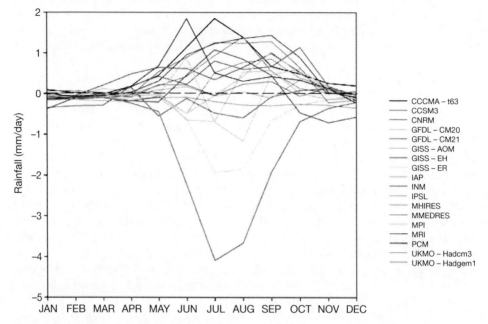

Figure 1.3 The simulation of seasonal variation of rainfall over India by different climate models in the IPCC Fourth Assessment Report

Source: IPCC, 2007

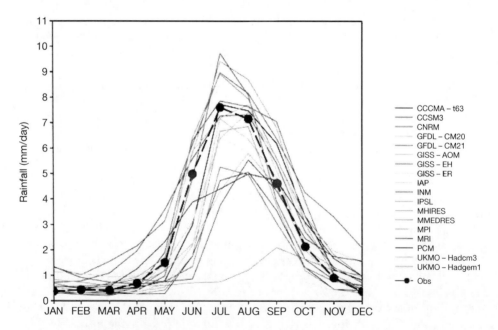

Figure 1.4 The prediction of changes in rainfall over India by different climate models in the IPCC Fourth Assessment Report

Source: IPCC, 2007

Impacts of climate change on India 37

model predicts that Indian monsoon rainfall will increase in most regions of India in the 21st century on account of the increase in carbon dioxide but there will be a decrease in rainfall over Kerala. During the past 50 years there has been a decrease in rainfall over Kerala (Figure 1.5). Hence we may be witnessing the impact of global warming already. Bollasina and Nigam (2009) have stated that current models cannot provide durable insights on regional climate feedbacks nor credible projections of regional hydroclimatic variability.

The impact of increase in temperature and rainfall on agriculture has been discussed by many investigators (Panda, 2009). Aggarwal (2003) has estimated a 2 to 5 per cent

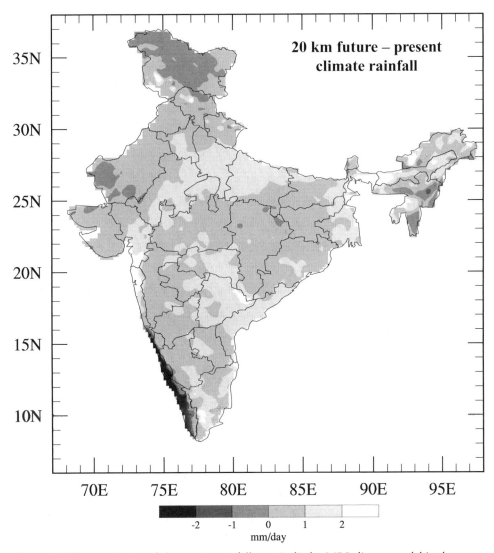

Figure 1.5 The prediction of changes in rainfall over India by MRI climate model in the future compared to the 20th century

Source: Rajendran and Kitoh, 2008
Note: 20 km future – present climate rainfall

38 *Srinivasan*

decrease in yield potential of wheat and maize for a temperature rise of 0.5 to 1.5°C in India. Note that an increase in rainfall and carbon dioxide may not completely offset the adverse impact of increase in temperature. The impact of climate change on fisheries is complex since it depends upon both changes in ocean temperature, ocean circulation and oxygen content and hence no reliable predictions are available.

The increase in surface temperature and changes in rainfall patterns may have an impact on vector-borne diseases. There has been a large increase in malaria and dengue in India during the past 40 years (Bhattacharya et al., 2006). The increase in surface temperature over land will make more areas conducive for the spread of malaria and dengue (Bhattacharya et al., 2006). We do not have sufficient evidence to demonstrate that the increase in malaria and dengue during the past 40 years is linked in any way to global warming. Reiter (2001) has stated that 'The natural history of mosquito-borne diseases is complex, and the interplay of climate, ecology, vector biology, and many other factors defies simplistic analysis. The recent resurgence of many of these diseases is a major cause for concern, but it is facile to attribute this resurgence to climate change.'

Conclusions

There is clear evidence of global warming in India in the 20th century and this will accelerate in the 21st century. The climate models used to predict climate change in the 21st century are not agreed on the nature of regional climate change. This is caused both by poor spatial resolution of the climate models and our incomplete understanding of the impact of aerosols and clouds on climate. This uncertain future has made it difficult to plan strategies for adaptation and mitigation. In the Indian context, if we adopt strategies to adapt to climate variability (i.e. year-to-year climate changes) then we will be able to tackle long-term climate change more confidently. One can expect more heavy rainfall events, higher sea level and more severe heat waves in the future. Agricultural production will be hampered by the increase in heavy rainfall events and heat waves. Thus climate change will add one more dimension to the problems created by uncontrolled population growth and inappropriate development policies in India.

References

Aggarwal, P.K. (2003) 'Impact of climate change on Indian agriculture', *Journal of Plant Biology*, 30, pp. 189–198.

Ali, S.I. and Huq, S. (1989) 'International Sea Level Rise: National Assessment of Effects and Possible Response for Bangladesh', College Park, University of Maryland Center for Global Change.

Battisti, D.S. and Naylor, R.L. (2009) 'Historical warnings of future food insecurity with unprecedented seasonal heat', *Science*, 323, pp. 240–244.

Bhattacharya, S., Sharma, C., Dhiman, R.C., and Mitra, A.P. (2006) 'Climate change and malaria in India', *Current Science*, 90, pp. 369–375.

Bollasina, M. and Nigam, S. (2009) 'Indian Ocean SST, evaporation, and precipitation during the South Asian summer monsoon in IPCC-AR4 coupled simulations', *Climate Dynamics*, DOI 10.1007/s00382-008-0477-4.

Chung, C.E. and Ramanathan, V. (2006) 'Weakening of Northern Indian SST gradients and the monsoon rainfall in India and the Sahel', *Journal of Climate*, 19, pp. 2036–2045.

Cruz, R.V., Harasawa, H., Lal, M., Wu, S., Anokhin, Y., Punsalmaa, B., Honda, Y., Jafari, M., Li, C. and Huu Ninh N. (2007) *Asia: Climate Change 2007: Impacts, Adaptation and*

Vulnerability. Contribution of Working Group II to the *Fourth Assessment Report of the Intergovernmental Panel on Climate Change*, Parry, M.L., Canziani, O.F., Palutikof, J.P., van der Linden, P.J. and Hanson, C.E. (eds). Cambridge University Press. Cambridge, UK, pp. 469–506.

Dash, S.K., Jenamani, R.K., Kalsi, S.R. and Panda, S.K. (2007) 'Some evidence of climate change in twentieth-century India', *Climatic Change*, 85, pp. 299–321.

Goswami, B.N., Venugopal, V., Sengupta, D., Madhusoodanan, M. and. Xavier, P.K. (2006) 'Increasing trend of extreme rain events over India in a warming environment', *Science*, 314.

India Meteorological Department (IMD) (2010) 'Annual Climate Summary', National Climate Centre, Pune.

IPCC (2007) *Climate Change (2007) Scientific Basis*, Inter-governmental Panel on Climate Change, Cambridge University Press, 2007.

Kagawa, J. (2002) 'Health effects of diesel exhaust emissions – a mixture of air pollutants of worldwide concern', *Toxicology*, pp. 181–182, 349–353.

Kripalani, R.H., Oh, J.H., Kulkarni, A., Sabade, S.S., and Chaudhari, H.S. (2007) 'South Asian summer monsoon precipitation variability: Coupled climate model simulations and projections under IPCC AR4', *Theoretical and Applied Climatology*, 90, pp. 133–159.

Kulkarni, A.V., Bahuguna, I.M., Rathore, B.P., Singh, S.K., Randhawa, S.S., Sood, R.K. and Dhar, S. (2007) 'Glacial retreat in Himalaya using Indian Remote Sensing Satellite Data', *Current Science*, 92, pp. 69–74.

Lau, K.M., Kim, M.K., and Kim, K.M. (2006) 'Asian monsoon anomalies induced by aerosol direct effects', *Climate Dynamics*, 26, pp. 855–864.

Li, C., and Huu Ninh, N. (2007) 'Asia', *Climate Change 2007: Impacts, Adaptation and Vulnerability*, Contribution of Working Group II to the *Fourth Assessment Report of the Intergovernmental Panel on Climate Change*, edited by M.L. Parry, O.F. Canziani, J.P. Palutikof, P.J. van der Linden and C.E. Hanson, Cambridge University Press, Cambridge, UK, pp. 469–506.

Marshall, C.H. Jr., Pielke Sr., R.A., Steyaert, L.T. and Willard, D.A. (2004) 'The impact of anthropogenic land cover change on warm season sensible weather and sea-breeze convection over the Florida peninsula', *Monthly. Weather Review*, 132, pp. 28–52.

McGranahan, G., Balk, D. and Anderson, B. (2007) 'The Rising Tide: Assessing the risk of climate change and human settlements in low elevation coastal zones', *Environment and Urbanization*, 19, pp. 17–37.

Panda, A. (2009) 'Assessing Vulnerability to Climate Change in India', *Economic and Political Weekly* 44, pp. 105–117.

Pope III, C.A., Burnett, R.T., Thun, M.J., Calle, E.E., Krewski, D., Ito, K. and Thurston, G.D. (2002) 'Lung cancer, cardiopulmonary mortality and long-term exposure to fine particulate air pollution', *Journal of American Medical Association*, 287, pp. 1132–1141.

Rajeevan, M., Bhate, J., and Jaswal, A.K. (2008) 'Analysis of variability and trends of extreme rainfall events over India using 104 years of gridded daily rainfall data', *Geophysical Research Letters*, 35, L18707.

Rajendran, K. and Kitoh, A. (2008) 'Indian summer monsoon in future climate projection by a super high-resolution global model', *Current Science*, 95, pp. 1560–1569.

Reiter, P. (2001) 'Climate change and mosquito-borne disease', *Environmental Health Perspectives*, 109, pp. 141–161.

Rupa Kumar, K., Krishna Kumar K., Ashrit, R.G., Patwardhan, S.K., and Pant, G.B. (2002) 'Climate change in India: observations and model projections', in *Climate Change and India: Issues, Concerns and Opportunities*, P.R. Shukla et al. (eds.), Tata McGraw-Hill Publishing Co. Ltd, New Delhi.

Rupa Kumar, K., Krishna Kumar, K., and Pant, G.B. (1994) 'Diurnal asymmetry of surface temperature trends over India', *Geophysical Research Letters*, 21, pp. 677–680.

Shekhar, M.S., Chand, H., Kumar, S., Srinivasan, K., Ganju, A. (2010) 'Climate-change studies in the western Himalaya', *Annals of Glaciology* 51, pp. 105–112.

40 *Srinivasan*

Shrestha, A.B., Wake, C.P., Mayewski, P.A., and Dibb, J.E. (1999) 'Maximum temperature trends in the Himalaya and its vicinity: an analysis based on temperature records from Nepal for the period 1971–94', *Journal of Climate*, 12, pp. 2775–2787.

Srinivasan, J. (2008) 'Climate change, greenhouse gases and aerosols', *Resonance 89*, pp. 1147–1155.

Stephenson, D.B., Douville, H. and Rupa Kumar, K. (2001) 'Searching for a fingerprint of global warming in the Asian summer monsoon', *Mausam*, 52, pp. 213–220.

Takahashi, K., Honda, Y. and Emori, S. (2007) 'Estimation of changes in mortality due to heat stress under changed climate', *Journal of Risk Research*, 10, pp. 339–354.

Unnikrishnan, A.S. and Shankar, D. (2007) 'Are sea-level-rise trends along the coasts of the north Indian Ocean consistent with global estimates?', *Global and Planetary Change*, 57, pp. 301–307.

Vermeer, M. and Rahmstorf, S. (2009) 'Global sea level linked to global temperature', *Proceedings of the National Academy of Sciences*, 106, pp. 21527–21532.

2 Sea level rise

Impact on major infrastructure, ecosystems and land along the Tamil Nadu coast[1]

Sujatha Byravan, Sudhir Chella Rajan and Rajesh Rangarajan

Background and rationale

Sea level rise (SLR), due to climate change, will affect the coastline in India in a variety of ways, including inundation, flood and storm damage associated with severe cyclones and surges, erosion, saltwater intrusion, and wetland loss. Nevertheless, there are major, existing and proposed, economic and infrastructure developments, including ports, power plants, highways and even airports, which are being proposed very close to the shoreline along India's coast. Thousands of crores of new investment are being considered along the coast in cities such as Mumbai, Chennai, and Kolkata in addition to the substantial existing infrastructure. Clearly, we are not preparing to integrate our coastal development plans with the potential impacts of climate change.

How much SLR can we expect? The IPCC estimate of a maximum SLR of 59 cm by 2100 is widely acknowledged as being conservative since it excludes future dynamical changes in ice flow, including some very important ice sheet processes that speed up the movement of glaciers, particularly in the polar ice caps (IPCC, 2007). Most estimates also assume that the West Antarctic ice sheet will stay stable, but sub-surface warming, thinning of ice, changes in wind patterns and the effect of feedbacks altering the speed at which warming takes place are not well understood. The Scientific Committee on Antarctic Research suggests a rise in mean sea levels of up to 1.4 m by 2100 and other scientists anticipate SLR of one to several metres (Rignot and Kanagaratnam, 2006; Ivins, 2009; SCAR, 2009) in the same period. The seas, of course, will continue to rise even beyond 2100 if warming is not stabilized. The German Advisory Council on Global Change (WBGU) expects around a metre rise by 2100 and several metres by 2300 (WBGU, 2006).

James Hansen (2007) and others (e.g., Oppenheimer et al., 2007) believe that the low end of these expectations is a serious underestimate and that under 'a business as usual' scenario, climate change can result in SLR measured in metres within a century. Paleoclimatic data appear to support these claims. The Plio–Pleistocene records tell us that with a global warming of only 2–3°C, the planet was a dramatically different place with average sea level about 25 metres higher than it is today (see Figure 2.1). Moreover, there is also evidence for at least three separate events involving catastrophic rises in sea level between about 6,500 and 14,500 years ago, when the rate of SLR exceeded 45 mm/year (Blanchon and Shaw, 1995).

For the purposes of this study, we assumed that average SLR of 1 metre may be expected as early as 2050, a somewhat conservative estimate especially if large portions

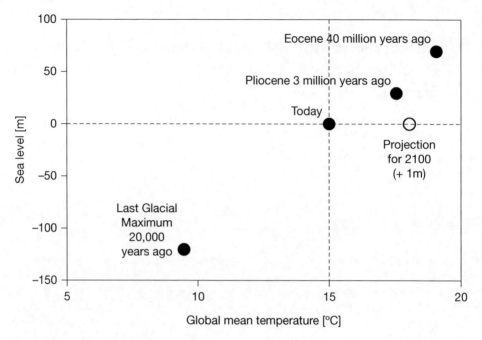

Figure 2.1 Global mean temperatures and sea levels
Reprinted with permission from WBGU, 2006

of the West Antarctic ice sheet were to break off or if ice streams from Greenland were to accelerate, both of which being widely believed as likely occurrences in this century.

This study concentrated on the impacts of a 1-metre sea level rise on coastal infrastructure, ecosystems and land using the state of Tamil Nadu, India, as a case study. It estimated the replacement value of infrastructure, the present value of the foregone ecosystem services associated with the loss of wetlands, and the market value of property losses associated with damage to usable coastal land.

It highlights the financial implications of sea level rise on *existing and proposed* infrastructure along the Tamil Nadu coast and provides thereby an 'early warning' of the implications of indiscriminate development close to the shoreline. This study does not evaluate the impact on human populations along the coast from SLR, which will likely be devastating, as recent experience from cyclones and the tsunami indicates. The intent has been to focus on the financial implications of infrastructure, ecosystem and land loss. The analysis performed here is indicative rather than comprehensive, primarily because of data constraints, but it is hoped that its findings will provide the basis for conducting more detailed studies covering larger portions of the Indian peninsula.

The Tamil Nadu coast and vulnerability from SLR

The Tamil Nadu coastline is about 1,076 km, with thirteen coastal districts, and it forms a fairly large, contiguous and narrow coastal strip dotted with fragile ecological features. The coast here, as elsewhere in India, faces severe development pressures which lead to problems such as pollution, coastal erosion, damage to the coast and so on. In addition to these there is erosion and accretion that test the vulnerability of the coast. As part of natural processes, sediment movement northward and southward (called littoral drift) is a unique feature of the east coast, which ties in with the activity pattern of the Indian monsoons. Any hindrance to this process alters the coastline rendering it vulnerable to storm surges, cyclones and consequent inundation of low-lying areas. The Tamil Nadu coast has already undergone such alterations and is also witness to frequent cyclonic storms. The 2004 tsunami demonstrated the level of vulnerability that the coast faces and triggered many studies that have only heightened the concerns.

SLR will affect the coastal zone in multiple ways. Warmer waters will lead to *more intense storms* accompanied by *storm surges* with coastal structures having to withstand the force and impact of higher winds and water (Emanuel, 2005; Bengtsson et al., 2006; Landsea et al., 2006). The physical changes associated with SLR may take place in abrupt nonlinear ways as thresholds are crossed. For example, rising sea levels will result in the increased frequency of coastal flooding due to storm-surge events, even in the absence of increased storm intensities. Similarly, dramatic *retreat of sandy beaches* is expected; beach *erosion* typically takes place at tens to hundreds of times the rate of sea-level rise and will degrade or remove protective coastal features such as sand dunes and vegetation, further increasing the risk of *coastal flooding* (Church et al., 2008). In addition, *ecosystem changes* and *saltwater intrusion* into groundwater are expected to take place. As a result of all these effects, the *area at risk* from SLR is much larger than the area that is actually inundated.

Intense storms accompanied by surges and flooding along with the SLR will also result in adverse impacts on coastal wetlands and ecosystems. In addition, SLR will likely transform coastal morphology and soil characteristics. Human activities along the coast such as the building of ports, ground water extraction, shrimp farming and agriculture will all simultaneously play a role in shaping the coastal changes that take place along with global warming. Built-up areas tend to be more vulnerable than those protected by mangroves, and deltas, low-lying coastal plains, coral islands, beaches and barrier islands. Degradation of coastal ecosystems by human activity will generally aggravate the problems caused by SLR, increasing shoreline retreat and coastal flooding in cities. For example, it is estimated that the area of the Tamil Nadu shore north of Ennore port will have an erosion rate of 20 m/year if no intervention is planned (ENVIS, 2008) and there is already silting in Ennore Creek due to accretion.

Data and methods

The analysis carried out in this study was based on publicly available information on infrastructure location and investments. GIS baseline information was taken from sources such as LandSat 7 and OpenStreetMaps as well as government agency websites. In some cases, this information was obtained through Right to Information requests. Market values for coastal land were estimated on the basis of interviews with real estate agents, after collecting around 80 data samples of agricultural, commercial and residential price estimates all along the Tamil Nadu coast for property at about one kilometre from the coast.

Existing and proposed ports, power plants, the East Coast Road (including its possible extension along the coast), wetlands and land were considered in the analysis.

44 Byravan, Rajan and Rangarajan

Other private and public investments, such as hotels and resorts, housing developments, shrimp farms and other commercial establishments were not included, in part because of the lack of available data, but also because the details needed for the analysis would have been overwhelming.

Project costs, obtained or estimated using methods described above were taken to be replacement costs for major infrastructure. The economic value of mangroves was estimated on a per hectare basis by estimating the lost ecosystem services till 2050 for a 1 metre SLR. We reviewed a number of studies and then used methods described in two international studies in the region (Sathirathai and Barbier, 2001; UNEP/GPA, 2003). Given the long-term social benefits of mangroves, a social discount rate of 1.4 per cent is used, following the recommendations of the Stern Review (Stern, 2007) and others (e.g. Gunawardena and Rowan, 2005).

Detailed geomorphological analysis and modelling of the coastline would need to be carried out in order to provide precise estimates for the land area at risk of inundation, storm surges and erosion as a result of SLR. Such techniques were well beyond the scope of this preliminary study. Instead, an important simplification in this analysis is that district-level Probable Maximum Storm Surge heights obtained from Kalsi et al. (2007) have been used as the basis on which to estimate the land areas in each district that would be at risk from *future* storm surges, flooding and erosion associated with SLR.

Area at risk from SLR

Future storm surge heights along the Tamil Nadu coast will be influenced by several factors, including increased storm intensity, higher mean sea levels, and continental uplift and subsidence, particularly in delta areas. Dasgupta et al. (2009) and Nicholls (2008) provide a simple approach to estimate future storm surge heights:

Future storm surge = S100 + SLR + (UPLIFT * 100 yr) / 1000 + SUB + S100 * x

Where:

S100 = current 1 in 100 year surge height (m);

SLR = 1 m;

UPLIFT = continental uplift/subsidence in mm/yr;

SUB = total subsidence 0.5 m (applies to deltas only);

x = 0.1, or increase of 10%, in coastal areas prone to cyclones.

In this analysis, we have ignored the uplift and subsidence values, primarily because of the lack of reliable data for this purpose. Kalsi et al. (2007) report that the probable maximum storm surge (PMSS) heights along the Tamil Nadu coast vary from about 3 to 9.8 m, with a median of about 4.5 m along the coast. For the purposes of this report, we have assumed the district level PMSS levels to be equivalent to the S100 value and calculated future storm surge heights on that basis. Furthermore we have defined an 'area at risk' that roughly corresponds to the land area vulnerable to future storm surges. Flooding associated with storm surges is also a major cause of coastal erosion, causing damage to buildings and other structures by direct wave impact, hydraulic lift of waves and sub-surface water beneath buildings and wave energy reflected from protruding structures such as ports and battering from floating debris (Coch, 1995).

Further information on the data and methods used for the analysis are provided in Appendix 1 in the full report of the study. Details on the valuation are provided in Appendix 2 of the full report.[1]

Results of the study

Examining the area under each contour level in coastal Tamil Nadu, we estimated that about 1,000 sq. km would be inundated with a 1 metre rise in mean sea levels. Table 2.1 provides details for area under each contour level.

The area at risk from a 1 metre SLR was estimated on the basis of district-level analyses of the likely impacts from storm surges and is about six times as much as the area inundated.

For five coastal districts: Nagapattinam, Thiruvarur, Thanjavur, Pudukottai, and Ramanathapuram, the area along the coast that is below 10 m above current mean sea level is estimated to be at risk from a 1 metre SLR, because of the very high storm surges that already affect them (see **Figure 2.2 and Table 2.2**). For the remaining eight coastal districts, the coastal area that lies below 5 m elevation relative to current mean sea level is estimated to be at risk from a 1 metre SLR.

For purposes of simplicity, we have assumed that even those districts where future storm surges may slightly exceed 10 m are at risk only below 10 m. Similarly, Nagapattinam and Thiruvarur are expected to have future storm surges up to around 5.6 and 6.9 m, but we have assumed that the coastal zones up to 10 m are at risk in these districts. Given the likelihood of more frequent, if not more intense, storm surges and associated coastal erosion, the coastal area at risk from a given level of SLR will involve land that is well above the area below mean sea level. It should be noted that in other studies, e.g., McGranahan et al. (2007), the entire region below 10 m elevation near the coastline is delineated as the 'Low Elevation Coastal Zone' to designate the population affected from SLR.

The study estimates the total replacement value of infrastructure (ports, power plants and major roads) impacted by sea level rise to be between Rs. 47,418 and Rs. 53,554 crores (in 2010 terms). The present value of wetlands (estimated in terms of foregone ecosystem services through 2050) impacted by sea level rise is estimated to be between Rs. 3,583 and Rs. 14,608 crores. By far the largest impact will be on lost land itself, whose market value is estimated to be between Rs. 3,17,661 and Rs. 61,15,471 crores (**Table 2.3**). In comparison, Tamil Nadu's annual Gross Domestic Product is estimated to be around Rs.2,50,000 crores, indicating that very significant value is at risk along the coast due to climate change impacts on sea level rise alone.

Table 2.1 Land area inundated by a 1 metre rise in sea levels along the Tamil Nadu coast

Contour height (m)	Land area below contour (sq km)
1	1,091
3	2,289
5	3,835
10	7,796

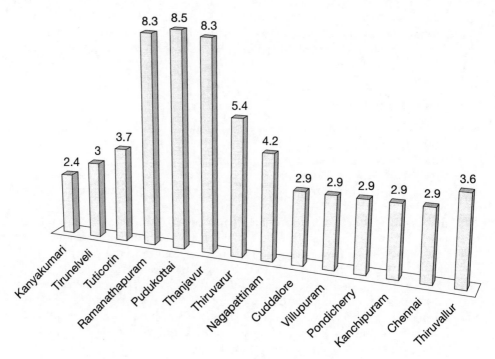

Figure 2.2 Probable maximum storm surge (PMSS) above tide level in Tamil Nadu
Source: Kalsi et al., 2007

Table 2.2 Future storm surge heights and corresponding areas at risk for different districts

District	S100 (m)	Future storm surge (m)	Area at risk
Thiruvallur	3.6	4.96	Below 5m
Chennai	2.9	4.19	Below 5m
Kanchipuram	2.9	4.19	Below 5m
Villupuram	2.9	4.19	Below 5m
Cuddalore	2.9	4.19	Below 5m
Nagapattinam	4.2	5.62	Below 10m
Thiruvarur	5.4	6.94	Below 10m
Thanjavur	8.3	10.13	Below 10m
Pudukottai	8.5	10.35	Below 10m
Ramanathapuram	8.3	10.13	Below 10m
Tuticorin	3.7	5.07	Below 5m
Tirunelveli	3	4.3	Below 5m
Kanyakumari	2.4	3.64	Below 5m

Table 2.3 Summary results with replacement value for infrastructure, present value of ecosystem services for wetlands, and market value for land in different coastal districts of Tamil Nadu with a 1 metre sea level rise

Coastal district	Ports		Power plants		Mangroves		Roads		Land	
In Rs. Crores	Min	Max	Min	Max	Min	Max	Min	Max	Min	Max
Thiruvallur	9,106	9,794	13,814	13,814	–	–	–	–	33,939	9,24,130
Chennai	7,639	9,786	–	–	–	–	6	16	2,29,976	4,59,951
Kanchipuram	500	500	–	–	–	–	63	173	7,882	14,30,749
Villupuram	400	830	–	–	–	–	24	65	5,277	63,871
Cuddalore	3,825	3,825	–	–	710	2,894	64	176	7,615	4,64,531
Nagapattinam	1,873	1,873	–	–	2,421	9,871	374	1,029	7,120	22,33,596
Thiruvarur	–	–	–	–	–	–	57	157	4,347	2,08,356
Thanjavur	–	–	–	–	–	–	122	336	1,860	94,547
Pudukottai	–	–	–	–	–	–	117	321	874	10,930
Ramanathapuram	–	–	–	–	452	1,842	301	827	17,344	1,30,021
Tuticorin	8,585	9,456	–	–	–	–	16	44	1,149	86,151
Thirunelveli	532	532	–	–	–	–	–	–	33	7,160
Kanyakumari	–	–	–	–	–	–	–	–	246	1,479
TOTAL	32,460	36,595	13,814	13,814	3,583	14,608	1,144	3,145	3,17,661	61,15,471

Recommendations

1 Comprehensive vulnerability assessment of the entire coast should be conducted

This report is a first approximation of the replacement value of coastal infrastructure, market value of land and present value of ecosystems at risk from SLR. Further analysis at higher levels of resolution and more detailed information for the entire coastal region of India needs to be conducted in order to estimate the total risk to land, infrastructure, ecosystems, human population and livelihoods. This must include analysis of the potential for erosion and shoreline retreat, expected flooding and storm surges at different levels of SLR, subsidence, and the impact of other human activities such as ports, commercial activity and groundwater withdrawal on the coastal zone.

2 Climate change considerations should be integrated into coastal infrastructure development

Existing structures in the area of high risk will need to be modified to withstand SLR and its impacts. Development in areas of high risk needs to be limited and proposed structures need to consider SLR and its associated impacts in the evaluation. Except for infrastructure that is essential along the coast, including indispensable ports, new development should be planned at considerable distance from the shoreline.

3 Wetlands need to be protected

The high protection value of wetlands along the Tamil Nadu coast as well as elsewhere in the peninsula needs to be taken into consideration whenever any development threatening their survival is proposed (Das and Vincent, 2009). To the extent existing threats to wetlands can be mitigated or removed, necessary actions should be carried out.

4 Coastal protection measures should be carefully assessed and carried out if necessary

These could include the following:

- providing assistance to at risk communities, building resilience;
- establishing early warning systems;
- improving our understanding of the role of coastal ecosystems acting as a guard-rail;
- anticipating migration, preparing inland facilities and preparing at-risk communities.

The Tamil Nadu government and other state governments with large tracts of coastal land may want to consider the implications of extensive infrastructure development in coastal areas in light of these findings. The analysis carried out here is based on commonly accepted methods and data that are publicly available (except for land estimates, which were based on interviews with real estate agents). Similar studies may well be conducted for states such as Andhra Pradesh, Orissa and West Bengal – all subject to even more severe cyclones from the Bay of Bengal than Tamil Nadu – as well as Maharashtra and Gujarat, which have much higher levels of investment along the coast.

Note

1 This chapter is based on a report that was published by Centre for Development Finance, IFMR in November 2010. The full report can be found at the Centre for Development Finance, IFMR, website: http://cdf.ifmr.ac.in/.

References

Bengtsson, L., Hodges, K.I. and Roeckner, E. (2006) 'Storm tracks and climate change', *Journal of Climate*, 19, pp. 3518–3543.

Blanchon, P. and Shaw, J. (1995) 'Reef drowning during the last deglaciation: evidence for catastrophic sea-level rise and ice-sheet collapse', *Geology*, 23(1), pp. 4–8.

Church, J.A., White, N.J., Aarup, T., Wilson, W.S., Woodworth, P.L., Domingues, C.M., Hunter, J.R., and Lambeck, K. (2008) 'Understanding global sea levels: past, present and future', *Sustainability Science*, 3(1), pp. 9–22.

Coch, N.K. (1995) *Geohazards: Natural and Human*, Englewood Cliffs, NJ: Prentice Hall.

Das, S. and Vincent, J.R. (2009) 'Mangroves protected villages and reduced death toll during Indian super cyclone', *Proceedings of the National Academy of Science, USA*, 106, pp. 7357–7360.

Dasgupta, S., Laplante, B., Murray, S. and Wheeler, D. (2009) 'Sea-Level Rise and Storm Surges: A Comparative Analysis of Impacts in Developing Countries', Policy Research Working Paper 4901 (Washington, DC: World Bank).

Emanuel, K.A. (2005) 'Increasing destructiveness of tropical cyclones over the past 30 years', *Nature*, 436, pp. 686–688.

ENVIS (2008) 'Database on Coastal Information of Tamil Nadu', Prepared by Prof. Dr. R. Ramesh, Dr. P. Nammalwar, Dr. (Mrs) V.S. Gowri; Report submitted to Environmental Information System (ENVIS) Centre; Department of Environment, Government of Tamil Nadu, January 2008, http://tnenvis.nic.in/PDF/coastal%20data.pdf, accessed 24 August 2010.

Gunawardena, M. and Rowan, J.S. (2005) 'Economic Valuation of a Mangrove Ecosystem Threatened by Shrimp Aquaculture in Sri Lanka', *Environmental Management*, 36(4), pp. 535–550.

Hansen, J.E. (2007) 'Scientific Reticence and Sea Level Rise', *Environmental Research Letters*, 2, pp. 1–6.

IPCC (2007) *Climate Change 2007: Impacts, Adaptation and Vulnerability*, Working Group II contribution to the *Fourth Assessment Report of the IPCC*, Cambridge University Press, Cambridge, United Kingdom.

Ivins, E.R. (2009) 'Ice Sheet Stability and Sea Level', *Science*, 324(5929), pp. 888–889.

Jarvis A., Reuter, H.I., Nelson, A. and Guevara, E. (2006) 'Hole-filled seamless SRTM data V3, International Centre for Tropical Agriculture (CIAT)', http://srtm.csi.cgiar.org, accessed 24 August 2010.

Kalsi, S.R. Jayanthi, N. Raj, Y.E.A. and Bhomik, S.K.R. (2007) 'Probable Maximum Storm Surge Heights for the Maritime Districts of India', Indian Meteorological Department, New Delhi.

Landsea, C.W., Harper, B.A., Hoarau, K. and Knaff, J.A. (2006) 'Climate change: Can we detect trends in extreme tropical cyclones?', *Science*, 313(5786), pp. 452–454.

McGranahan, G., Balk, D. and Anderson, B. (2007) 'The rising tide: assessing the risks of climate change and human settlements in low elevation coastal zones', *Environment and Urbanization*, 19(1), pp. 17–37.

50 Byravan, Rajan and Rangarajan

Nicholls, R. (2009) 'Adaptation costs for coasts and low-lying settlements', in Parry et al., *Assessing the Costs of Adaptation to Climate Change: A Review of the UNFCCC and Other Recent Estimates*, International Institute for Environment and Development and Grantham Institute for Climate Change, London.

Nicholls, R.J., Hanson, S., Herweijer, C., Patmore, C., Hallegatte, S., Corfee-Morlot, J., Château, J. and Muir-Wood, R. (2008) 'Ranking port cities with high exposure and vulnerability to climate extremes: Exposure estimates', *OECD Environment Working Papers*, No. 1, Paris, OECD Publishing.

Oppenheimer, M., O'Neill, B.C., Webster, M. and Agrawala, S. (2007) 'The limits of consensus', *Science* 317(5844), pp. 1505–1506.

Rignot, E. and Kanagaratnam, P. (2006) 'Changes in the velocity structure of the Greenland ice sheet', *Science*, 311, pp. 986–990.

Sathirathai, S. and Barbier, E.B. (2001) 'Valuing mangrove conservation in Southern Thailand', *Contemporary Economic Policy*, 19(2), pp. 109–122.

SCAR (2009) 'Antarctic climate change and the environment', Scientific Committee on Antarctic Research, Scott Polar Research Institute, Cambridge, UK.

Shanker, K., Namboothri, N., Rodriguez, S. and Sridhar, A. (eds), (2008) 'Beyond the tsunami: Social, ecological and policy analyses of coastal and marine systems on the mainland coast of India', Post Tsunami Environment Impact Report, UNDP/UNTRS, Chennai and Ashoka Trust for Research in Ecology and Environment, Bangalore.

Stern, N.H. (2007) *The Economics of Climate Change*, Cambridge, UK, Cambridge University Press.

Tol, R. (2002) 'Estimates of the Damage Costs of Climate Change. Part 1: Benchmark Estimates', *Environmental and Resource Economics*, 21(1), pp. 47–73.

UNEP/GPA (2003) 'The Economic Valuation of Alternative Uses of Mangrove Forests in Sri Lanka', Report prepared by Dr B.M.S. Batagoda, www.gpa.unep.org, accessed 24 August 2010.

WBGU (2006) *The Future Oceans: Warming Up, Rising High, Turning Sour* Berlin, WBGU (German Advisory Council on Global Change).

3 The impact of climate change on a shift of the apple belt in Himachal Pradesh[1]

*Ranbir Singh Rana, R.M. Bhagat,
Vaibhav Kalia and Harbans Lal*

The earth is warming up. Climate change is one of the biggest long-term challenges around the world. In Himachal Pradesh, evidence of global warming is suggested by changes like receding snowfall in the Himalayas, retreating glaciers and a shift in the temperate fruit belt upward, shifting and shortening of the *rabi* (winter) season, and disrupted rainfall pattern (Bhagat *et al.*, 2004). The impact of climate change has also been observed in production of apples and Satsuma mandarins in Japan. It has been predicted that regions favourable to the cultivation of apples and Satsuma mandarins will gradually move northward (Sugiura and Yokozawa, 2004).

Apples are a predominant fruit crop of Himachal Pradesh and in recent years they have emerged as the leading cash crop amongst fruit crops. In 2006, apples alone accounted for 46 per cent of total area under fruit crops and 76 per cent of total fruit production in the state. The area under apple cultivation has increased from 400 hectares in 1950–51 to 88,560 hectares in 2005–6 (Department of Economics and Statistics, 2006a). In 2005–06, the crop alone contributed more than Rs. 987 crore (\$220 million approx.)[2] towards the state gross domestic product, which was Rs. 20,919 crore (\$ 4.97 billion). The production level has gradually touched 540.3 metric tonnes with 5.6 tonne productivity in 2006 (Department of Economics and Statistics, 2006b). Impacts on apple cultivation are, therefore, of considerable importance to the economy of the state and the livelihoods of its farmers.

Over the past few years the production of apples has gradually increased but the productivity has fallen with a rate of 0.016 tons/ha annually between 1985 and 2009 (Vijayshri Sen, 2010). Of the various productivity-reducing factors, climate is the most difficult to manage. The changes in climate in the form of erratic precipitation, increase in temperature, fewer days serving as the chilling period have started affecting the mountain agricultural production systems and ultimately the food security of the people.

There is evidence in the literature that climatic changes can considerably affect apple cultivation. Apple and stone fruit trees remain dormant until they have accumulated sufficient 'chilling units' (CU) of cold weather. The chilling unit requirement for apple standard variety is 800–1100 (Byrne and Bacon, 1992). Daily temperatures of 70°F and higher for 4 or more hours received by the plant during a 24 to 36 hour period can actually negate chilling. As long as there have been enough CUs the flower and leaf buds develop normally. Byrne and Bacon (1992) have reported that if the buds do not receive sufficient chilling temperatures during winter to completely release dormancy, trees will develop one or more of the physiological symptoms associated with insufficient chilling: 1) delayed foliation; 2) reduced fruit set and increased buttoning;

52 Rana, Bhagat, Kalia and Lal

and 3) reduced fruit quality. These physiological symptoms consequently affect the yield and quality of the fruit.

The objective of this study is to examine change in climatic parameters, especially chilling units, in Himachal Pradesh over time, and the associated changes in apple productivity. These results are further complemented by recording and analysing farmer perceptions of a changing climate and its impact on apple cultivation.

Approach and methods

Study sites

Apples are grown in all the districts of the state except Una and Hamirpur.

For the study, three sites in three apple growing districts, viz. Kullu, Theog (Shimla) and Lahaul and Spiti, representing different elevations, were selected to examine the perceptions of farmers for climate change and to relate the chill units with apple cultivation in the face of climate change. Kullu represents the lowest altitude, Theog the next highest, and Lahaul and Spiti the highest altitude among the areas studied.

Kullu Valley: The study site is located in Kullu district at 1,200–2,500 metres above mean sea level (msl). This elevation zone represents 16 per cent of the total geographical area of Himachal Pradesh. The geography of the region represents mid hill to high hills. The region also receives snowfall in the high hills during the winter months and serves as a great source of fresh water in Beas Basin of Himachal Pradesh. The climate of the region is by and large sub-temperate in lower hills to temperate in high hills. The ambient temperature ranges between 7.9°C and 25.6°C around the year. Temperature during the *rabi* season hovers around 12.7°C whereas during the *kharif* (monsoon) season average mean temperatures remain below 23.0°C. The mean annual temperature remains 17.0°C in the region (Bhagat *et al.*, 2007). The met station is located at 31°50′ N latitude and 77°10′ E longitude. The average mean annual rainfall is 1,095 mm. Parts of this region are known for the production of off-season vegetables, while the apple crop dominates in the higher hills (Bhagat *et al.*, 2007).

Theog Region (Shimla District): This study site is located in the district of Shimla and represents elevations of 2,200–3,250 msl. The area comprises mid- to high hills. The region is dominated by horticultural crops, viz. apple, pear and other temperate fruits. This elevation zone represents 8.8 per cent of the total geographical area of the state. It is located at the south eastern part of the state. Agricultural crops, mostly off-season vegetables, provide the majority of farmers of the region with their livelihood.

The meteorological observatory in the region is located at 31°10′ N latitude and 77°25′ E longitude. The average annual rainfall of the region varies between 1,100 mm to 1,533 mm annually from South to North. The major part of the annual rainfall is received during the south-western monsoon season. However winter rains are important for successful cultivation of apples in the region. The average mean temperature of the region is at its lowest of 7.7°C during January whereas the maximum temperature goes up to 20.7°C during June. The mean annual temperature of the region is 15.4 °C. December to February is cooler and temperatures start rising during March (Bhagat *et al.*, 2007).

The apple belt in Himachal Pradesh 53

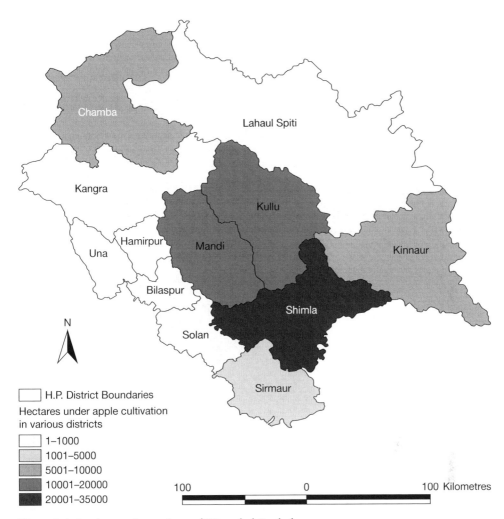

Figure 3.1 Apple growing regions of Himachal Pradesh

Lahaul and Spiti: The northern part of the state, which constitute Lahaul and Spiti, part of Chamba, part of Kullu, Shimla and Kinnuar district experience annual mean temperature below 14°C. The winter season starts from November and temperatures start decreasing until minima are obtained in January. The temperature again starts rising during the month of February, and May and June are the hottest months. Data has been gathered for farmer perceptions in Lahaul and Spiti but similar data is not available for weather trends and trends in chilling units.

Socioeconomic survey

Socioeconomic surveys were conducted in Kullu, Theog (Shimla), and Lahaul and Spiti regions of Himachal Pradesh in 2006–7 to examine how apple farmers in Himachal Pradesh perceive climatic change. Weather data from 1986 to 2009 was used to

54 Rana, Bhagat, Kalia and Lal

measure the accuracy of the farmers' perceptions. Perception of climate change is structured for the three valleys (Kullu, Theog in Shimla, and Lahaul and Spiti) with a multistage stratified sampling technique by knowledge of crop climate interaction and by differential apple performance outcomes associated with the changed conditions. To understand farmers' perceptions regarding climate change and its impact on apple cultivation, local perceptions of the climate variables to apple production were noted from forty farmers from each region (19 marginal, 16 small and 5 large farmers from Kullu, 4 marginal, 9 small and 27 large from Theog, and 9 small, 18 marginal and 13 large in Lahaul and Spiti). Perceptions were recorded on the basis of gathering data of two periods (1995 and 2006 years) of snowfall, temperature and rainfall.

Climatic elements trends

The climatic elements trends for Kullu valley and Theog region were worked out using the standard procedure from the past two to three decades weather database. Snowfall trends in the past two to three decades were also calculated for 22 sites representing different elevations ranging from 1,500 to 4,000 metres above sea level located in Sutlej basins of Himachal Pradesh.

Chill unit calculation models used

The cumulative chill units' requirements of apple for Kullu and Theog (Shimla) regions were calculated using the method developed by Ashcroft *et al.* (1977) and the Utah model (Byrne and Bacon, 1992). The Ashcroft model uses only average temperature of coldest months, whereas the Utah model uses daily maximum and minimum temperatures. The Utah model also introduces the concept of relative chilling effectiveness and negative chilling accumulation (or chilling negation) as follows:

1 hour below 34°F = 0.0 chill unit, 1 hour 35–36°F = 0.5 chill units

1 hour 37–48°F = 1.0 chill units, 1 hour 49–54°F = 0.5 chill units

1 hour 55–60°F = 0.0 chill units, 1 hour 61–65°F = –0.5 chill units

1 hour >65°F = –1.0 chill units

Recent apple productivity and area trends in Himachal Pradesh

Apple productivity trends for the past two decades of apple growing areas and total productivity of Himachal Pradesh were also analysed. The trends of area under apple were also worked out for different region to examine the expansion of areas under apple cultivation at different elevations.

Results and discussion

Farmers' perceptions

The socio-economic survey was conducted in Kullu, Theog (Shimla) and Lahaul and Spiti regions of Himachal Pradesh. Table 3.1 summarizes farmers' perceptions

The apple belt in Himachal Pradesh 55

Table 3.1 Farmers' perceptions regarding climate change and its impact

Particulars	Kullu Valley	Theog Region (Shimla)	Lahaul and Spiti
Increasing temperature during summer	85	80	–
Prolonged summer season	66	48	–
Short summer season	10	8	–
Delayed in the onset of rainy season	85	80	–
Uneven distribution of rainfall	88	96	–
Insufficient rainfall during rainy season	77	72	–
Delay in the outset of winter season	68	48	60
Very low temp. in winter season	–	12	80
Short winter period	94	88	80
Temp. above normal during winter	92	88	15
Reducing snowfall in winter	100	100	88
High humid weather	40	36	22
Increasing foggy days in winter	16	52	–
Increasing cloudy days in winter	16	18	28
Unpredictable rainfall	76	52	–
Threat of floods	88	50	88
High velocity winds	–	–	–
Mud slides	–	–	20
High intensity of rainfall	20	–	–

recorded. One hundred per cent of farmers of Kullu and Theog regions of Himachal Pradesh perceived a definite reduction in snowfall overtime during the winter season. Farmers perceived snowfall events in two general parameters related to the intensity and the change in the timings of snowfall. Farmers reported that the onset of early snow in December and January has occurred more infrequently over time and the period of snowfall now extends through the months of February and March.

There is a perception that the temperature distribution has undergone a significant shift in addition to an overall increase in temperature. Eighty-five per cent farmers of Kullu and 80 per cent farmers of Theog (Shimla) noticed an increase in temperatures. 88 per cent farmers of Kullu and 96 per cent of farmers of Theog (Shimla) reported uneven and insufficient distribution of rainfall during the rainy season.

The other signs of climate change which were reported by the farmers were: short summer season, humid weather, increasing foggy days in the winter and unpredictable rainfall. The perception of a reduced intensity of snowfall leads to the perception of a changed climatic pattern on the whole. According to farmers, late snowfall in February and March occurs mostly as a mixture of sleet and rain, resulting in lower temperatures and thereby a late onset of spring. Farmers also claimed that the winter period has shortened and there is a delay in the onset of the winter season, number of chilling hours and thereby the time of bud break. For normal pollination and fruit-bearing conditions for an apple crop a snow level of 2.5 to 3 ft is required in higher hills. Early snow is regarded as durable, long lasting and full of nitrogen. Late snow on the other hand, is described as watery, transitory and understood to adversely impact pollination and apple fruit bearing.

The socioeconomic survey concludes that between 1995 and 2005 land-use pattern in all farmer classes, small, marginal and large, has shifted toward orchard cultivation in Lahaul and Spiti, while the area under orchard per farmer decreased in Kullu and

56   Rana, Bhagat, Kalia and Lal

Theog (Table 3.2). In Kullu and Theog, there is a remarkable increase in the area under off-season vegetable cultivation. The survey also revealed that average areas per farmer under apple cultivation increased by 0.60 hectare in Lahaul and Spiti whereas Kullu and Theog showed a decrease in areas under apple cultivation. The data (Table 3.2) reflects that the income of farmers from fruits increased by more than 10 per cent in Lahaul and Spiti between 1995 and 2005. However, for the same period, the other two apple growing regions showed a sizeable decrease of 27 to 30 per cent. Off-season vegetables have shared more than 84 per cent of the area under field crops in Theog region.

Climatic elements trends in the apple growing region

Kullu Valley Climate change is apparent in this region due to a perceptible shift of apple cultivation to higher hills. Mean annual temperature in Kullu Valley showed an increase of 4.1°C over the last two decades from 1986 to 2005. During the *rabi* season the temperature showed an increase of nearly 5.5°C whereas the *kharif* season showed a decrease in temperature of 1.7°C. Moreover, the temperature from June to September showed a decreasing trend. Rainfall in the region showed an exceptional decrease of 270 mm. *Rabi* season showed a decreasing trend of rainfall of 18 mm per year whereas *kharif* season showed increasing trends. Evaporation showed decreasing trends of 14.5 mm annually during *rabi* and 8.6 mm during *kharif*. However, the decrease was more during *kharif* season.

Theog Region (Shimla) The Theog valley in the Shimla district showed more increase in rainfall in *rabi* season than *kharif* season. During the period 1990 to 2009, the mean temperature recorded at CPRI Shimla showed an increase of 1.54°C annually. An increase of the order of 2.4°C was observed during *rabi* season whereas it was 1.2°C during the *kharif* season. June alone showed a decrease in temperature. Rainfall showed a decreasing trend during *rabi* season and increasing trends by 5.1 mm during

Table 3.2 Change in land-use pattern, apple area and income from fruits per farmer in apple-growing regions of Himachal Pradesh

District	All farmers (small, marginal and large)	
	1995	2005
Land-use pattern (Orchard)		
Kullu	27.0	21.0
Theog	22.8	21.7
Lahaul & Spiti	1.93	4.34
Apple area (ha)		
Kullu	0.55	0.45
Theog	0.62	0.60
Lahaul & Spiti	0.48	1.09
Income from fruits (per cent)		
Kullu	69.9	39.6
Theog	59.3	32.8
Lahaul & Spiti	17.2	29.1

The apple belt in Himachal Pradesh 57

kharif season. Annual rainfall showed decreasing trends by 27 mm annually. Rainfall decrease during September to February was unprecedented.

Cumulative chilling units

As discussed earlier, changes in chilling units can have a substantial impact on apple cultivation. Vedwan and Robert (2001) report that the lack of early cold in December and January adversely affects the chilling requirements, which ranges from 700 to 1200 chill unit hours per year. Late cold during April can delay blossoming and reduce the pollination activity of bees. Jindal *et al.* (2001) report that winter temperatures and precipitation, especially in the form of snow, are very crucial for induction of dormancy, bud break and ensuring flowering in apples. They further report that the apple crop requires 1,200–1,500 hours of chill depending upon its variety. Fewer than 1,000 chilling hours results in a poor fruit set which consequently leads to poor yield of the crop. The period of November to February is important for chilling hours. However, November to January is more beneficial than February. Jindal and Mankotia (2004) report that at least 1,200 chilling hours are required for proper bud and flowering in Mashobra conditions of Himachal Pradesh. Apple size and quality are mainly dependent upon climatic conditions in summer as they influence fruit development during April to June.

The results for the areas under study here are reported in Figures 3.2–3.5 and in Table 3.3. The Utah model showed a decrease of more than 6.4 chill units' hours every year due to increase in surface air temperature at Bajaura in Kullu (Figure 3.2). Similar trends are reported for Shimla (Figure 3.3) Central Potato Research Institute (CPRI, Shimla) at –19.0 CU per year and Bhang in Kullu (Figure 3.4) at –3 per year. For the highest altitude site, Dhundi in Kullu, the data report an increasing trend of 26 over the period (Figure 3.5).

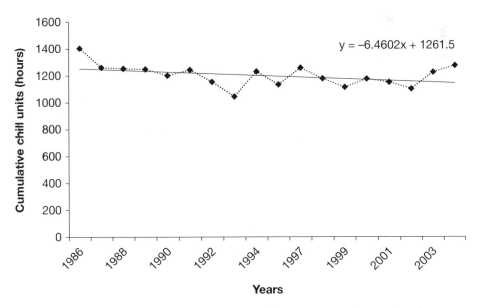

Figure 3.2 Cumulative chill unit trends (Utah model) at Bajaura in the Kullu Valley, 1986–2003

Turning to data for particular months (Table 3.3) the data for Bajaura in Kullu on cumulative chill units of coldest months (November–February) showed a decline of more than 9.1 units per year in the last 23 years of period (Table 3.3). The reduction was greatest during November and February months from 1986 to 2006.

In Shimla (CPRI, Shimla) the decrease of chill units during November to February ranged between −3.5 and −17.9 per year, with particularly steep declines from December to February due to the late onset of snow in the region (Table 3.3).

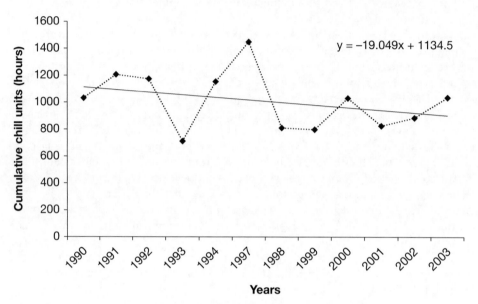

Figure 3.3 Cumulative chill units (Utah model) of Shimla, 1990–2003

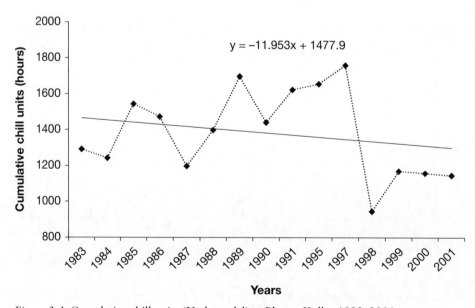

Figure 3.4 Cumulative chill units (Utah model) at Bhang, Kullu, 1983–2001

The apple belt in Himachal Pradesh 59

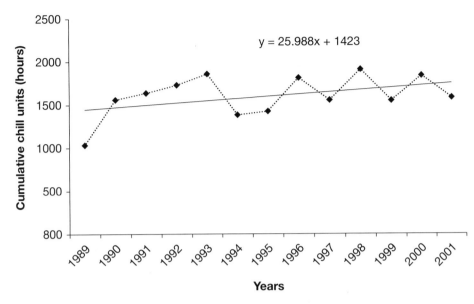

Figure 3.5 Cumulative chill units (Utah model) at Dhundi, Kullu (2700 msl), 1989–2001

Table 3.3 Cumulative chill unit trends (mean monthly model) equations for different winter months at Kullu (Bajaura) and Shimla (CPRI, Shimla)

Month	Kullu (Bajaura) Equations	Slope	Shimla (CPRI, Shimla) Equations	Slope
November	Y = −14.35+788.7	−14.35	Y = −3.55+585.0	−3.55
December	Y = −9.10+1034.1	−9.10	Y = −15.03+932.7	−15.03
January	Y = −10.85+1159.3	−10.85	Y = −17.94+1164.3	−17.94
February	Y = −13.28+1043.5	−13.85	Y = −14.96+1085.6	−14.96

The broad picture above is further reinforced by snowfall data. The snowfall trend in the two recent decades from 1984/85 to 2005/06 over different sites representing elevations ranging from 2,000 to 4,000 msl showed a decrease of 36.8 mm annually in the last 22 years averaged over 22 sites (Figure 3.6). The decrease was greater in recent decades. The decline in snowfall is one of the major regions in reduction of chill units in apple growing regions.

Monthly snowfall analysis indicated a sharp decrease of snowfall over the past 22 years from 22 observation sites during the period September to December, which is important for temperate crops. The snowfall showed increasing trends during January (27 mm per year) and February (23 mm) which revealed delay of snowfall.

The analysis clearly indicates that snowfall in the past two decades decreased due to an increase in temperature/change in climate as evident from the temperature analysis of apple growing regions. The delay of snowfall occurrence and early withdrawal of snowfall occurrence is reflected in a decrease in apple yield. Such trends in snowfall occurrence in high altitude areas increased the opportunity of growing more

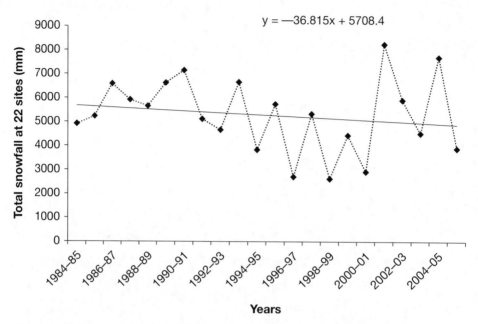

Figure 3.6 Annual average snowfall trends in Satluj catchment, 1984–2005

crops during March to October. The decrease in snow fall during early winter season and early withdrawal of seasonal snowfall contributes towards the decreased cumulative chill units for apple cultivation.

The trend reported here is further reinforced by data from other studies by other researchers. The chill unit trends calculated for different sites representing different elevations (Table 3.4) combining our work and other studies showed decreasing trends up to elevation of 2,400 msl in Sarbo (Kinnaur) whereas the chill units calculated for site Dhundi in Kullu (Figure 3.5) which is situated 2,700 metres msl revealed an increasing trend of chill unit at the rate of 25 CU per year in the recent decade. This reflected that areas above 2,500 msl are becoming suitable for apple cultivation in the most recent decade. These findings were also supported by the socio-economic survey conducted in Kullu and Lahaul and Spiti. The majority of farmers in Kullu and Lahaul and Spiti are of the opinion that the apple crop is shifting upward to higher elevation. The secondary data (Department of Economics and Statistics, 2006b) also reported an increase in area under apple crop in Lahaul and Spiti and Kinnaur in the most recent decade. The majority of croplands are above 2,500 msl in Lahaul and Spiti and Kinnaur. The upward shift in apples was also reported by Partap and Partap (2002) in a case study conducted on apple crops in Kullu districts.

The climate data and data on chill units in Table 3.4 shows that lower altitudes have become less suitable for apple cultivation, while higher altitudes have become more suitable. Cultivation data indicates corresponding changes on the ground.

The area under apple cultivation in recent years has fallen from 92,820 ha in 2001–2 to 88,560 ha in 2005–6 in the entire state. However, the area under apple cultivation in Lahaul and Spiti and Kinnaur district, which lies above 2,500 msl, showed an increase in cultivation under apple every year between 1995–96 and 2006–07. It went

The apple belt in Himachal Pradesh   61

Table 3.4 Cumulative chill unit trend equations for different sites and at different elevations (Utah model)

Sr No.	Stations	Elevation (msl)	Chill unit trend equations	Slope of trend equation	Remarks
1	Bajaura (Kullu)	1221	$Y = -6.4+1261.5$	−6.4	
2	Katrain (Kullu)	1420	$Y = -25.93+2299$	−25.93	Reported by Verma *et al.* (2007)
3	Bhang (Kullu)	2192	$Y = -11.953+1477.9$	−3.2	
4	CPRI Khalini (Shimla)	2159	$Y = -19.0+1134.5$	−19.0	
5	Mashobra (Shimla)	2250	$Y = -37.8+1930.5$	−37.9	Reported by Verma *et al.* (2007)
6	Sarbo (Kinnaur)	2400	$Y = -32.0+1399.3$	−32.0	Reported by Verma *et al.* (2007)
7	Dhundi (Kullu)	2700	$Y = 25.99+1423$	+25.99	

up to 621 hectares in 2006–7 from 334.0 ha in 1995–96 and 8151 ha in 2006–07 from 5,516 ha in 1995–96, respectively. Farmer perceptions reinforce the findings reported here. Surveys of farmers revealed that per farmer area under apple showed a decrease in Kullu and Shimla of 18.2 and 3.3 per cent respectively. The area at higher elevation (above 2,500 msl) namely Lahaul and Spiti valley showed substantial increase by more than 127 per cent over the recent decade.

Conclusion

The temperature in apple growing regions of the mountain state of Himachal Pradesh showed increasing trends whereas precipitation showed decreasing trends. The chill units requirements for apple cultivation showed decreasing trends up to 2,400 msl from Bajaura in Kullu at 1,221 msl to Sarbo in Kinnaur at 2,400 msl. The Dhundi observation station situated at 2,700 msl showed increase of chill units of the order of 25.0 CUs per year. The increasing trends of chill unit at 2,700 msl suggested that the area is becoming suitable for apple cultivation at a higher altitude. These findings have also been supported by farmers' perceptions which clearly reflect that apple cultivation is expanding to a higher altitude in Lahaul and Spiti. The average land use per farm in Lahaul and Spiti showed more than a 2 per cent shift towards apple cultivation but it showed a reverse trend in other apple growing regions situated at low elevations. The income of the farmers increased more than 10 per cent in Lahaul and Spiti whereas it showed a decrease of more than 27 per cent in Kullu and Shimla districts from fruits in recent decade compared to 1995. Climate change has demonstrated its impact with the decreasing productivity of apple crops in recent years at lower elevations, providing opportunity for more apple cultivation at higher elevation regions of Himachal Pradesh.

Notes

1 This chapter was first published in the ISPRS Archives XXXVIII–8/W3 *Workshop Proceedings: Impact of Climate Change on Agriculture*. The research could not have been completed without the assistance of Dr. P.K. Aggarwal, National Professor, and Project Coordinator, Division of Environment Sciences, IARI New Delhi and Dr G.G.S.N. Rao National coordinator, CRIDA Hyderabad for sanctioning the project and providing the financial sanctions. The data on snowfall from 22 sites provided by the Bhakra Beas Management Board Chandigarh is highly acknowledged. The authors are also thankful to CSK Himachal Pradesh Agriculture University for providing the necessary facilities to carry out the research.

2 The figure is a round approximation. For all such conversions in this chapter: $1 = INR 45.

References

Ashcroft, G.L., Richardson, E.A. and Seeley, S.D. (1977) 'A statistical method of determining chill unit and growing degree hour requirements for deciduous fruit trees', *Horticultural Science* 12(4), pp. 347–348.

Bhagat, R.M., Vaibhav Kalia, V., Chitra Sood, C., Pradeep Mool, P. and Bajracharya, S.R. (2004) 'Himachal Pradesh Himalaya – Inventory of glaciers and glacial lake outburst floods (GLOFs) affected by global warming in the mountains of Himalayan region'. Project report submitted to APN-START/UNEP, Japan.

Bhagat, R.M., Rana, R.S., Prasad, R., Lal, H., Kalia,V. and Sood C. (2007) 'Project Progress Report', (2004–07) of project entitled 'Impact Vulnerability and Adaptation to Climate Change' submitted to Network Project on Climate Change, ICAR, New Delhi.

Byrne, D.H., and Bacon, T.A. (1992) 'Chilling estimation: its importance and estimation', *The Texas Horticulturist* 18(8).

Department of Economics and Statistics (2006a) *Economic Survey of Himachal Pradesh*, Department of Economics and Statistics, Himachal Pradesh, pp. 30–39.

Department of Economics and Statistics (2006b) *Statistical Outline of Himachal Pradesh*, Department of Economics and Statistics, Himachal Pradesh, pp. 86–89.

Jindal, K.K. and Mankotia, M.S. (2004) 'Impact of changing climatic conditions on chilling units, physiological attributes and productivity of apple in western Himalayas', *Acta Horticulture* 662, pp. 111–117.

Jindal, K.K., Chauhan, P.S. and Mankotia, M.S. (2001) 'Apple productivity in relations to environmental components'. In: K.K. Jindal and D.R. Gautam (eds.) *Productivity of Temperate Fruits*, Y.S. Parmar University of Horticulture and Forestry, pp. 12–20.

Partap, U. and Partap, T. (2002) 'Warning signals from the apple valleys of the Hindu Kush-Himalayas'. In A.B.M. Shreshtha (Ed.) *Productivity Concerns and Pollination Problems*, Centre for Integrated Mountain Development (ICIMOD), PO Box 3226, Kathmandu, Nepal.

Sugiura, T. and Yokozawa, M. (2004) 'Impact of global warming on environments for apple and Satsuma mandarin production estimated from changes of the annual mean temperature', *Journal of the Japanese Society for Horticultural Science* 73(1), pp. 772–778.

Vedwan, N. and Robert, E.R. (2001) 'Climate change in the Western Himalayas of India: a study of local perception and response', *Climate Research* 19, pp. 109–117.

Verma, K.S., Mankotia, M.S., Bhardwaj, S.K., Thakur, C.C. and Thakur, M. (2007) 'Project Progress Report (2004–07)' of project entitled 'Impact Vulnerability and Adaptation to Climate Change', submitted to Network Project on Climate Change, ICAR, New Delhi.

Vijayshri, Sen (2010) M.Sc (Environmental Sciences) thesis submitted to CSK Himachal Pradesh Agriculture University, copy on file with author.

4 India in the Intergovernmental Panel on Climate Change

R. Ramachandran

The Intergovernmental Panel on Climate Change (IPCC) is a novel mechanism intended to synthesize and provide the authoritative compilation and interpretation of climate science, so as to inform policy. Understanding India's engagement with climate change, therefore, also requires understanding India's role at the IPCC. That is the purpose of this chapter.

Ideally, a full exploration of this question would also be informed by a detailed examination of Indian science, and social science, in the area of climate change. However, such a broad exploration, though necessary, is beyond the scope of this chapter. Instead, here I focus more directly on painting an impressionistic picture of Indian engagement in the IPCC, covering both numbers of participants, and some flavour of their contribution. I also discuss high profile issues such as the controversy about Himalayan glaciers.

The first section that follows provides a summary of the IPCC process and criticisms of this process intended to help readers understand both the rigor of the process and contextualize Indian involvement. I then turn to an exploration, quantitative and qualitative, of Indian involvement in the IPCC. The final section summarizes particularly noteworthy contributions from India to the IPCC process, followed by conclusions.

The IPCC process

The stated objective of the IPCC is to assess the available scientific, technical and socioeconomic information relevant for understanding the risk of climate change. This is reflected in its Assessment Reports (ARs) whose aim is to inform governments and serve as guideposts for international climate negotiations.

The preparation of the IPCC reports constitutes a unique global scientific enterprise. The reports represent the *collective* wisdom of a sizable fraction of the global scientific community and have the approval and acceptance of the IPCC member nation-states. The governments are as much responsible for what is contained in the reports as the authors of the reports are, because the governments and their experts have sufficient opportunity to review and comment on the contents. In India, the Ministry of Environment and Forests (MoEF) is the focal point for climate change research, participation in the IPCC process and international climate negotiations.

The IPCC itself *does not* carry out new research nor does it monitor climate-related data. The assessment in its reports is based chiefly on published and peer-reviewed scientific literature. It is a massive undertaking in which hundreds of volunteer scientists examine all available scientific literature relevant to climate change and put that through a rigorous process of assessment trying to arrive at a comprehensive sense of the climatic trends. Each AR is divided into three volumes, corresponding to three Working Groups (WGs), each covering one broad aspect (Figure 4.1).

The IPCC has so far released four ARs: the First (FAR/AR1) came out in 1990 with a Supplementary Assessment to it in 1992, Second (SAR/AR2) in 1995, Third (TAR/AR3) in 2001 and the most recent Fourth (AR4) in 2007. AR5 is scheduled for release in 2013–14. In addition, the IPCC also releases a 20-page Summary for Policy Makers (SPM), an optional Technical Summary (of 50–70 pages) and a Synthesis Report, a summary report that integrates the key findings of all the three WG Reports.

The IPCC has several co-chairs and a bureau comprising the IPCC Chair, the Vice-Chairs, the Co-Chairs and Vice-Chairs of the WGs and the Co-Chairs of the Task Force. The Bureau is elected by the Panel during the Plenary Session such that there is a balanced representation of all regions of the world. The IPCC principles state, 'There should be at least one, normally two or more from developing countries'.[1] The country-level representation is apparently often a contentious issue (Ravindranath, 2010). However, as is well known, the Chair of the IPCC since 2002 is an Indian, Rajendra Pachauri, the Director-General of The Energy and Resources Institute (TERI) but the IPCC is clear in stating that the Chair does not represent any country.

Currently, there is no Indian on the IPCC Bureau. There is also a practice[2] that a member of the IPCC Bureau can bring one person from his/her country to attend the Bureau meetings. Apparently after persistent demand from the MoEF, the Chair has been taking Subodh Sharma, Advisor to the MoEF, for the AR5 meetings of the Bureau in return for the government's financial contribution and support for running an independent office of the Chair. Though the IPCC has detailed process and procedures for the preparation of its reports (Figure 4.2) and the topics an AR will cover are decided

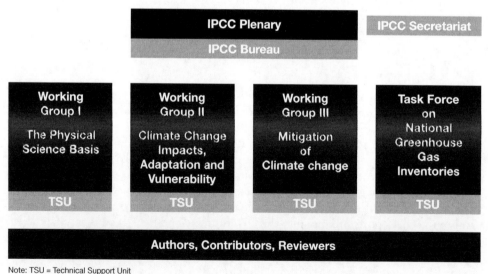

Figure 4.1 IPCC structure

Note: TSU = Technical Support Unit

by the governments at the 'scoping meeting' of the IPCC involving policy makers and experts, and not by just a few experts, the MoEF feels that this would ensure that India's perspectives on controversial issues in climate change science, such as Asian Brown Cloud (ABC), black carbon and Himalayan glaciers, are reflected better in the reports.[3]

For the selection of authors the IPCC invites the governments (and participating organizations) to nominate experts who can serve as authors – Coordinating Lead Authors (CLAs), Lead Authors (LAs) and Review Editors (REs) – and expert reviewers. The authors/reviewers are selected by the relevant WG bureau based on the nominees' publications and work. Sometimes experts besides the governments' nominations may also be chosen directly by the bureaus to meet any gap in the available expertise. In addition, CLAs and LAs may enlist (and generally they do) other experts as Contributing Authors (CAs) to assist with their work.

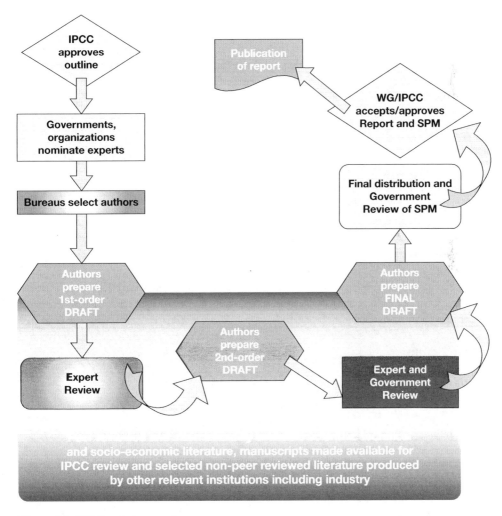

Figure 4.2 IPCC review procedure

Note: Data provided by MoEF

66 *Ramachandran*

The contribution and responsibility levels flow from CLA to LA and then to CA. The preparation of the reports is undertaken by the CLAs and the LAs, who will be responsible for the content of the authored chapters. LAs are responsible for assigned sections of a chapter 'on the basis of the best scientific, technical and socio-economic information available' and these designated parts *need not be* directly related to their research. LAs may assign specific parts of their sections (say, a para or a box or graphs or data) to a CA with knowledge in that specialized domain. CLAs are essentially LAs but with the added responsibility of ensuring that major sections are completed to a high uniform standard and they synthesize the contributions to conform to an overall high quality style. REs ensure that significant differences in opinion on scientific issues are kept track of.

The multi-layered review of the reports takes place in five stages (see Figure 4.2). REs, working in conjunction with the LAs, ensure that all substantive expert and governmental review comments are addressed adequately and advise the authors on how to handle contentious/controversial issues. While full reports are accepted as such during the plenary, the SPM actually goes through a line-by-line approval by the governments attending the session. Changes in the SPM can only be done in agreement with the LAs to ensure that the final text is consistent with the underlying report. The SPM therefore represents the point of agreement.

The following will give an idea of the numbers involved in the process. For the AR4 WG2 (Impacts, Adaptation and Vulnerability) report, for example, there were two scoping meetings to outline 20 chapters, 176 LAs and 46 REs from 72 countries, 232 CAs from 48 countries, over 8,000 peer-reviewed publications were cited, over 40,000 comments were received from 1,181 expert reviewers from 92 countries and 41 governments. [For the complete AR4, there were 489 CLAs/LAs from 130 countries and another 800 served as CAs. About 2,500 experts provided more than 90,000 review comments.][4]

Given this complicated process, with iterative revisions of the initial draft texts, by and large, the final form any individual's contribution takes becomes unrecognizably different from the original. So to talk of an individual's contribution to an IPCC report, save perhaps in very few cases, seems misplaced. But a country's participation in the IPCC process, as mentioned earlier, helps to ensure that the country's perspective and research findings on climate change issues get reflected in the reports.

Indeed, that is why the IPCC procedures require that there be proper regional representation in the WG teams. Authors from developing countries can, for instance, ensure that claims of developed countries' scientists are substantiated. The methane emission from rice fields is a case in point to which we will return shortly. When it comes to reports of WG2I and WG3 (Mitigation of Climate Change), they would be sensitive to statements such as those requiring greater mitigative actions or setting up exaggerated impact scenarios that are not backed by adequate science. The presence of developing country scientists can also provide, for example, appropriate inputs on GHG emission inventories by bringing in unorganized sectors, an important element in developing countries, into focus.

The IPCC process has received considerable recognition. AR4, which was released in February 2007, brought the issue of climate change to the centre stage of global discourse in science, economics, politics and social science. In tow came the Nobel Peace Prize awarded jointly to the IPCC, on whose behalf Pachauri had the honour of receiving the award, and Al Gore, the former US Vice-President. However, in the years since the release of AR4, the IPCC has also come in for serious criticism.

In the run-up to the Copenhagen Summit (COP-15) in December 2009 there was a spate of controversies, which began with criticisms of AR4's conclusions – in particular, the statement, 'the warming in the climate system is unequivocal' – by climate sceptics and the media. This was following an internal leak of thousands of emails and other documents from the University of East Anglia's Climate Research Unit, many of whose researchers had served the IPCC. But the IPCC stood by its robust findings – which were the result of measurements by various institutions – and the integrity of its authors. In his response, Pachauri stated that the IPCC would review the incident to identify lessons to be learnt and clarified that the IPCC itself would not carry out any investigation.

Then came the three major controversies, which were specific to the contents of WG2 report of AR4, the Himalayan glacier controversy that concerned India (to which we will return in some detail later) being the most significant one. All these were based on information in grey literature; that is, non-peer reviewed publications. While the IPCC has clearly laid down guidelines for accessing grey literature,[5] there were clearly lapses in adhering to them.

These controversies led the IPCC Chair and the UN Secretary-General to commission, on March 10, 2010, an independent review of the processes and procedures of the IPCC in the preparation of its reports by the Inter-Academy Council (IAC, 2010c). This review report was released on August 30, 2010 (IAC, 2010a, b). As the IPCC reports have, over the years, become the guiding documents for nations' responses to climate change, such a complete review by an external agency was timely and important to restore IPCC's credibility.

India's participation

Assuming that the selection process is apolitical and unbiased and is based solely on scientific credentials of individuals, one way to have a rough measure of India's contribution to the IPCC process is to look at the number of Indian scientists associated with each AR. Table 4.1 gives the number of CLAs and LAs associated with AR4. This number is a function of the amount, intensity and quality of research work done in the country and, of course, the process of nomination – in terms of numbers and institutional/regional distribution – by the Indian government and the basis of selection by the WG bureaus.

India and China account for a similar share in the numbers. Whether it is by design (of the IPCC bureau) or is a true reflection of their global presence in the field, cannot be stated with certainty. This similarity in the level of participation between the two countries seems to run through all the ARs (Table 4.2). China seems to have been slowly inching ahead of India since AR4. But, in general, why is the Indian share low? Is it a reflection of the level of expertise and the quality of research being done in the country? Or does the fault lie with the MoEF in not identifying the right kind of people?

How the MoEF actually goes about doing this is a moot question because the ministry itself, in all probability, does not have the technical capacity to assess Indian literature in climate science and make appropriate nominations. While the extent of Indian participation is partly a reflection of the differences that exist between the levels of expertise in developed and developing countries, according to one author,[6] the developed country co-chair tends to be more active because WG bureaus – the

68 *Ramachandran*

technical support arms of the WG teams – are located in developed countries. So far no developing country has hosted a WG though nothing prevents them (except perhaps for the high costs involved) from offering to do so.

If one looks at not just the numbers but also the names of individual scientists across the ARs, one would quickly discover that a few names keep cropping up as LAs. One

Table 4.1 Number of authors from selected regions contributing to the Fourth Assessment Report (AR4) of 2007

Countries	WG 1		WG 2		WG 3		
	CLA	LA	CLA	LA	CLA	LA	Total
India	0	5	3	4	3	5	20 (4.1%)
China	1	7	2	4	1	11	26 (5.3%)
Brazil	0	2	1	1	1	2	7 (1.4%)
Japan	0	6	2	3	1	12	24 (5.0%)
UK	3	13	4	10	2	6	38 (7.7%)
USA	7	28	6	18	6	25	90 (18.4%)
Africa	1	6	5	6	0	16	34 (7.0%)
Others	9	55	25	85	11	65	250 (51.1%)
Total	21	122	48	131	25	142	489 (100.0%)

Note: WG = Working Group, CLA= Coordinating Lead Author, LA = Lead Author

Source: Ravindranath (2010)

Table 4.2 Comparison of numbers of authors from India and China for the five IPCC Assessment Reports (ARs)

		WG1				WG2				WG3				Total
		CLAs	LAs	CAs	REs	CLAs	LAs	CAs	REs	CLAs	LAs	CAs	REs	
AR1 (FAR)	India			5 (+1)		1		2 (+1)		2				10 (+2)
	China			8 (+5)				5 (+1)		2				15 (+6)
AR2 (SAR)	India	2	3			10	11			7	2			33
	China	2	4			6	16			1	0			29
AR3 (TAR)	India	0	2	5	1	1	4	6	3	2	5	7	4	40
	China	0	10	4	1	1	4	8	3	0	8	1	0	40
AR4	India	0	5	2	1	3	4 (+3)	5	1	3	4 (+3)	2	1	31 (+6)
	China	1 (+1)	8 (+2)	12	1	3	3 (+2)	7	0	1	11 (+1)	3	1	51 (+6)
AR5	India	1	7		1	3	4		2	3	12		1	34
	China	0	13		4	3	6		1	3	11		1	42

Note: WG = Working Group, AR = Assessment Report; CLA = Coordinating Lead Author; LA = Lead Author; CA = Contributing Author

FAR: First Assessment Report of the IPCC; SAR: Second Assessment Report of the IPCC; TAR: Third Assessment Report of the IPCC

The figures in parenthesis refer to the numbers of authors associated with Special Reports.

India in the IPCC 69

also notices that certain institutions figure more frequently than others. This can be traced to the way in which India's engagement with the IPCC has evolved.

Evolution of climate change studies in India

At the time when AR1 was released in 1990, researchers in India were working on climate, and not climate change, and many climatologists have since switched to climate change. There is a subtle difference in the definitions of climate change of UNFCC and IPCC, with the latter definition including natural variability as well. This partitioning has never been easy. The Asian Development Bank (ADB) had commissioned an assessment of climate change in the region due to anthropogenic causes. This was a precursor to ADB's post-UNFCCC Asia Least-Cost Greenhouse Gas Abatement Strategy (ALGAS) Project, which was designed to assist countries of the region to meet their commitments under the Convention. The MoEF took the initiative to identify people who were sensitive to climate change issues more through a search of the available knowledge base.

Studies were initiated at IIT Bombay, Jawaharlal Nehru University (sea-level rise), Indian Agriculture Research Institute, Indian Institute of Science (forests, carbon flows), Indian Institute of Communicable Diseases, and the National Physical Laboratory (NPL) (GHG emissions). The outcomes of these studies were reflected in AR2, in particular with regard to national GHG inventory required under the UNFCCC, according to the MoEF. Under the guidance of Dr A.P. Mitra of NPL, his team, together with the Council of Scientific and Industrial Research (CSIR) and university network and research institutions, started the initial phase of GHG inventories in 1992 in 19 sectors (including energy, industry, land use, waste and forestry). Since then MoEF has apparently been inventorying people and institutions with domain expertise.

Even as this work progressed it was realized that the ALGAS programme was geared towards mitigation while the government was not mentally prepared for abatement at all. This required devising our own methodologies for inventories for which MoEF started intensifying the institutional work for performing in-depth calculations. Preparatory work for the first National Communication (NATCOM) began in 2001 by which time the number of institutions engaged GHG inventory had grown to 108 and number of experts to 153.[7] While organizing this work and during the NATCOM workshop more people got inducted and this, according to the MoEF, has been a continuing story. This evolving expert base has today become large enough for the MoEF, in October 2009 to launch the Indian Network for Climate Change Assessment (INCCA) comprising 127 institutions to make country-specific climate change analyses and assessments.

According to this evolving database of the ministry on climate science, for which long-term observations are required, even today many Indians are not actively working in this area. On other dimensions of the issue many more people have been associated with the IPCC. But, in general, the knowledge base and the ability to understand implications of climate change at the national level has remained inadequate and fragmentary. The overall numbers too have not grown significantly over the years and the low participation of Indians in the IPCC process is perhaps a reflection of this true shortage. Compounding this would, of course, be the bureaucratic process at the MoEF as least effort is involved in forwarding the same set of names during every IPCC call.

70 *Ramachandran*

For AR5, the Ministry has apparently been more proactive than before in identifying a new crop of people, particularly younger scientists, and having better geographical/institutional distribution. According to the ministry, 137 scientists were identified and invited to participate in AR5, 98 of whom responded. The positive 92 responses received were forwarded to the IPCC Bureau, and 34 were selected, which is about a 40 per cent success rate.[8] This is an improvement over the selection of 22 from 85 nominations for AR4. (These numbers includes only CLAs, LAs and REs.)

For AR5, in all 831 authors (CLAs/LAs) were selected based on over 3,000 nominations received, which is 50 per cent more than AR4. According to the IPCC, about 30 per cent are from developing countries or Economies in Transition (EITs) and women authors constitute 25 per cent of the selected. More than 60 per cent of the names are supposed to be new to the IPCC process. Indian scientists/experts selected thus constitute only about 4 per cent of the global total.

Indian domain expertise

Notwithstanding the limited perspective that the IPCC numbers reveal, can one say something about Indian climate science? In the process of selecting authors, assuming this is an unbiased process, someone at the IPCC has done the hard work of sifting through their research contributions and assessed their expertise and credibility. So, if we create another matrix of numbers against the subject areas for which they have been chosen, one may get an empirical idea, albeit a crude one, of the available expertise in the country in the respective areas of climate science.

Table 4.3 shows the distribution of Indian IPCC authors against broad subject areas. Indeed, as MoEF has perceived, physical science aspects seem to be our weakness, particularly climate modelling. Even atmospheric science does not seem to be very strong. Policy-related areas, both with regard to impact-adaptation-vulnerability and mitigation (WG2 and WG3), seem to be our strength. But even within areas related to WG2, specific impact studies seem to be lacking; expertise on health is noticeably weak. The area of regional impact studies on Asia demonstrate some limited experience but there is clearly a decline in numbers in this area in AR5, perhaps a consequence of the unfortunate errors in the IPCC on the Himalayan glaciers to which we will return later. In WG3-related areas too, besides policy-related subjects, there seem to be major areas of weakness.

Specific Indian contributions

Perhaps most illustrative of India's role in the process are a few key episodes and instances of detailed engagement with the IPCC.

Agricultural methane emission

Emission Factors (EFs) are the crux of the GHG inventory reporting (Total emission E = Activity × EF). The IPCC Guidelines offer a default methodology that includes default EFs and, in some cases, default activity data. MoEF's first comprehensive GHG inventory estimation in 1992, which formed the basis of India's first NATCOM, generally used the IPCC's default EFs. An important exception was, however, related

Table 4.3 The distribution of Indian IPCC authors by subject area

Area	AR1				AR2				AR3				AR4				AR5				Total
	CLA	LA	CA	RE	CLA	LA	CA	RE	CLA	LA	CA	RE	CLA	LA	CA	RE	CLA	LA	CA	RE	
Physical science basis Atmosphere constituents incl. aerosols & RF			2			3	1			1			1		1			3			12
Climate variability & cl. change		1					3					3	2	2	1						12
Surface atmosphere & oceanic cl change			2			2	1							2	1			1+r			9
Climate models (global & regional)										1				2		1	1	1			6
Palaeoclimatic studies														1			r				1
Impacts, adaptation & vulnerability Dev. issues, assessment & methods & tools			1			4	3					1+r[2]	1	1	1	1	1	r	1	1	16
Water resources management							1							1							2
Ecosystems including coastal						1	1							1							3
Food, agriculture and forest products	1[2]	1				2	1					r	1							r	6
Human health										1				r							1
Industry settlement & society							1			1				1			1	2			6

Table 4.3 Continued

Area	AR1				AR2				AR3				AR4				AR5				Total
	CLA	LA	CA	RE	CLA	LA	CA	RE	CLA	LA	CA	RE	CLA	LA	CA	RE	CLA	LA	CA	RE	
Regional impact studies: Asia									$1+1^2$	1	7				3			1			13
Small island states										1											1
Mitigation Development issues & policies, tech. choices, CB analysis	1					1^3			r	3	4	2	r	1	1+4		2	5		1	25
Emission scenarios, & stab. pathways										3	1			1	1			1			7
Industry						1			1				1				r				3
Transportation & infrastructure																1		3			4
Agriculture						1	1							1							3
Forestry including LULUCF							1		r	4+r		1		r				r			6
Policies, tech. tr., instruments, co-op.					4	7	l+r	4		1			1	r			r				18

Notes: CLAs= Coordinating Lead Authors, LAs = Lead Authors

Entry r means the repeat of the same name which has occurred under an earlier AR. Superscript numbers refer to the same person authoring different sections of the same AR. This has been done to avoid multiple counting in assessing the available expert base.

to EFs developed for methane emitted from rice cultivation, which had been the subject matter of WG1 (The Physical Science Basis) report of FAR/AR1 in 1990, for whose estimation an indigenous exercise was mounted. And this work constituted one of the first very significant contributions that came from developing country studies. The EF developed for methane was based on extensive measurements carried out in the country in a sustained manner, involving 10 national laboratories. The work established coefficients for various types of harvesting practices for different water regimes and external organic inputs. This was further refined during ALGAS, the Methane Asia Campaign in 1998 and more recently in 2002 (Mitra et al., 2004).

FAR/AR1 had given an estimate of globally averaged CH4 emission from rice paddies as 25–170 Tg of CH4/yr or MT/yr. AR1 had noted, 'One difficulty in obtaining correct estimates is that almost 90 per cent of the world's harvested area of the rice paddies is in Asia, and of this about 60 per cent are in China and India from which no detailed data are available'. But Dr Mitra's group at the NPL had pioneered novel measuring techniques for methane from paddy fields and had determined the average methane flux from Indian paddy to be ~ 4 Tg/yr, about tenth of what was being attributed to India in Western literature that had fed into AR1. In 1992, the IPCC issued Special WG1 and WG2 Reports and WG1 included Mitra as one of the authors. It said: 'The 1990 estimate of the CH4 flux from rice paddies was based on a very limited amount of data . . . While WMO (1992) decided to retain the same quantitative emission estimate of 100 Tg as IPCC (1990), a detailed analysis of the available data, particularly that from India, suggests a global annual emission nearer the lower end of the range.' Indeed, Indian data led to a change in IPCC methodology by adopting the concept of seasonal emissions.

There has not been any other very specific contribution arising from Indian research to the IPCC process, despite its key presence in some other areas. However, it is reasonable to assume that Indian scientists would have been instrumental in providing a balanced perspective to the statements made based on significant Indian work. These areas include:

Monsoon variability and modelling extreme events

Monsoon research is an area in which Indian scientists have done highly original and significant work for years and this has been reflected in the Indian presence at the IPCC since the 1990s. In AR4, for example, J. Srinivasan and Rupa Kumar Kolli were LAs in WG1 for chapters on 'Climate Models and Their Evaluation' and 'Regional Climate Projections' respectively.

In the former chapter, Indian research contributed to the point that the skill of existing Atmosphere-Ocean General Circulation Models (AOGCMs) is not very good in simulating monsoon variability. On the other hand, as the chapter noted, notwithstanding their coarse-grained nature, these models were able to predict extreme temperature events quite well but were not as good at predicting extreme precipitation events. In the latter chapter, Kolli contributed to a discussion on how the ENSO-Monsoon correlation that seems to exist today might get affected due to climate change, and what its implications would be for regional projections of climate, particularly monsoon trends, over Asia.

For AR5, which has a significant sub-continental monsoon component in the WG1 assessment, the MoEF has also proactively taken some unprecedented steps. Former

74 Ramachandran

MoEF Minister Jairam Ramesh wrote to the Chair on January 30, 2010, informing him of the specific higher grid resolution (25 km × 25 km) regional models for the Indian sub-continent to be run by a research group constituted by the ministry and requesting that the results of this research work be taken as inputs for AR5.[9]

Article 2 on Dangerous Anthropogenic Interference

Since AR4, a new, politically sensitive topic has been introduced into the IPCC discourse which is to address key vulnerabilities in the context of Article 2 of UNFCCC.[10] A significant issue here is how 'dangerous anthropogenic interference (DAI)' is to be defined. In this context, key vulnerabilities need to be assessed on the basis of what science has to say. A paper co-authored by an Indian scholar, Anand Patwardhan, along with S.H. Schneider and S. Semenov (2003) appears to have been a key input on this point. The three co-authors were also the LAs for Chapter 19 in WG2 Report of AR4 on 'Assessing Key Vulnerabilities'. Patwardhan, says:

> One of the perspectives that I was able to bring to the Chapter was that ultimately judgments regarding DAI result from a complex socio-political process, and while they can be informed by science, they are not purely scientific judgments. We, therefore, were careful not to suggest any particular target (like 2°C). At the same time, we tried to assess the literature pertaining to decision-making and the ways of evaluating options in a multi-criteria, multi-objective manner.

This cross-cutting issue is expected to be a part of AR5 as well.

The Himalayan glacier issue

Perhaps the most publicized component of India's presence at IPCC is the grossly wrong projection that the Himalayan glaciers would disappear within the next two and a half decades if the present rate of warming continued. This erroneous statement was contained in WG2 report of AR4 in its Chapter 10 on 'Asia'. Section 6.2 of the chapter addressed the issue of Himalayan glaciers. Citing a 2005 report of the World Wide Fund for Nature (WWF, 2005), a non-peer-reviewed (grey literature), paper reported that:

> Glaciers in the Himalayas are receding faster than in any other part of the world . . . and, if the present rate continues, the likelihood of them disappearing by the year 2035 and perhaps sooner is very high if the Earth keeps warming at the current rate. Its total area will likely shrink from the present 500,000 to 100,000 km^2 by the year 2035.

The section was authored by one of CLAs of the chapter, M. Lal, an atmospheric scientist formerly of IIT Delhi and who was the Chairman of Climate, Energy, Sustainable Development Analysis Centre (CESDAC) at the time the report was written. M. Lal had been a frequent contributor to the IPCC reports in different capacities since AR2. The WWF report had, in turn, cited a 1999 report of Working Group on Himalayan Glaciology (WGHG) of the International Commission for Snow

India in the IPCC 75

and Ice (ICSI). The ICSI Chairman at that time was the well known Indian glaciologist Syed Iqbal Hasnain, formerly of the Jawaharlal Nehru University (JNU) and now with The Energy and Resources Institute (TERI), New Delhi. The ICSI report had also resulted in a *New Scientist* article in June 1999 that quoted Professor Hasnain as saying that Himalayan glaciers would vanish within 40 years as a result of global warming (see Pearce, 1999).

However, the WG2 report section did not refer to the ICSI report, whose purported statement the WWF report had lifted from an April 1999 report of *Down to Earth* without checking. As it turns out the ICSI report never contained any such statement. Quoting IPCC prediction of 1996, the ICSI report had, in fact, said that quarter of the presently existing mountain glacier mass is likely to disappear by 2050. 'There is a possibility that shrinkage of Himalayan glaciers will be much more than that of other glaciers in the world, since the summer accumulation type glaciers are sensitive to air temperature,' it added. In recent times, Hasnain has stated that Himalayan glaciers are likely to shrink by over 40 per cent by 2070 and by 75 per cent by the end of 21st century if the present rate of warming continues.

The controversy actually broke out following the release of a discussion paper on 10 November, 2009, by the Minister of Environment and Forests that challenged the conclusion that Himalayan glaciers were all retreating and claimed that actual measurements had revealed that some Western Himalayan glaciers were actually expanding. The report stated: 'Himalayan glaciers, although shrinking in volume and constantly showing a retreating front, have not in any way exhibited, especially in recent years, an abnormal retreat, of the order that some glaciers in Alaska and Greenland reported' (Raina, 2009).

Pointing out that some have retreated, some have remained the same and some have advanced, the report said, 'Glaciers in the Himalayas, over a period of the last 100 years, have behaved in contrasting ways . . . It is premature to make a statement that glaciers in the Himalayas are retreating abnormally because of global warming.' This report, however, elicited derisive remarks from Pachauri and he asked why the minister was supporting such unsubstantiated science. Hasnain, on the other hand, remarked that the discussion paper was unscientific and biased. It had ignored scientific papers published in peer-reviewed journals after the 1980s when the impact of long-lived greenhouse gases became more visible, he claimed (Raj, 2009).

Investigating the error in the WG2 report, the Inter-Academy Council (IAC) (2010a, b, c) (which reviewed the workings of the IPCC in the wake of the controversies and whose report was released on August 30, 2010) examined the draft text of the chapter in question and the relevant reviewer comments. The Council's analysis showed that six experts reviewed this section in the first draft and, interestingly, none of their comments was critical. However, at the stage of the second draft, which is sent to both the governments and the expert reviewers, two comments were related to the erroneous statement on Himalayan glaciers, but they were not from the Indian government or any Indian expert.

One of them was from Hayley Fowler of Newcastle University, who questioned the conclusions of the section and referred to the work that arrived at different conclusions. Fowler pointed out that measurements by Hewitt suggested that Western Himalayan glaciers were expanding and added that the climatic changes in precipitation and temperature trends, which he along with D.R. Archer had observed, also supported this conclusion (Fowler and Archer, 2006).

76 *Ramachandran*

Fowler and Archer had said in their 2006 paper:

> The observed downward trend in summer temperature and runoff is consistent with the observed thickening and expansion of Karakoram glaciers, in contrast to widespread decay and retreat in the eastern Himalayas. This suggests that the Western Himalayas are showing a different response to global warming than other parts of the globe.
>
> (Fowler and Archer, 2006).

These observations seem to conform to the statements made by Raina in his discussion paper. The upshot of this debate is that given the vast expanse of the Himalayan region, comprising 9,375 glaciers covering a total area of 38,000 km^2, one cannot make generalized statements. Detailed mass balance studies on all glaciers across the Himalayan region need to be taken up and indeed such a Study Group has been set up under the Principal Scientific Advisor (PSA) to the Government of India.

Lacunae in the review process under MoEF

In contrast to the final version of the WG2 report, the final version of the SPM, however, did not have any statement on the Himalayan glaciers. This is because when the (second) draft version of the report was received by the Indian government (Stage (4) of the Review process) it elicited a response from the Indian government but, interestingly, none from any expert.

The remark included in the draft SPM from the section in question was: 'If the current warming rates are maintained, Himalayan glaciers could decay at very rapid rates, shrinking from the present 500,000 km^2 to 100,000 km^2 by 2030s'. The government had commented: 'This is a very drastic conclusion. Should have a supporting reference otherwise should be deleted'(IAC, 2010a). In response, the writing team removed the contentious statement from the SPM.

But what is interesting to note here is the shortcoming in the review process that the government has put in place. While it had succeeded in raising the flag on the remark included in the 20-page SPM, the experts that it had appointed to review failed to detect the more drastic statement in the main chapter. It is not clear whether the set of reviewers to whom the chapter was sent included people like Hasnain and Raina. This puts a big question mark on the general process of selection of reviewers by the MoEF.

Conclusion

There is a need to have a better Indian presence in the IPCC process at all its levels, in particular in the number of CLAs, LAs and reviewers. Increasing the nominations from MoEF alone may not be enough. The research of Indian scientists has to become more intense and of high quality. The number of scientists engaged in climate science research has to increase. Perhaps the setting up of a Climate Research Centre at Pune and MoEF's INCCA initiative will help in achieving that. Scientists too must strive to become visible by publishing in quality international journals so that they come to the notice of the IPCC bureau and are easily identified when the selection process for IPCC authors and reviewers begins.

Notes

1 http://www.ipcc.ch/pdf/ipcc-principles/ipcc-principles-appendix-a.pdf
2 Personal communication with R.K. Pachauri.
3 Personal communication with Jairam Ramesh, Former Minister MoEF.
4 http://www.ipcc.ch/activities/activities.shtml
5 Annex 2 of IPCC principles at http://www.ipcc.ch/pdf/ipcc-principles/ipcc-principles-appendix-a.pdf
6 Personal communication with P.K. Aggarwal, International Water Management Institute, New Delhi, August 2010.
7 Personal communication with Subodh Sharma, MoEF, December 2010.
8 Data provided by MoEF.
9 Letter from Jairam Ramesh to R.K. Pachauri dated 30 January, 2010. Copy on file with author.
10 Article 2: 'The ultimate objective of this Convention and any related legal instruments that the Conference of the Parties may adopt is to achieve, in accordance with the relevant provisions of the Convention, stabilization of greenhouse gas concentrations in the atmosphere at a level that would prevent dangerous anthropogenic interference with the climate system. Such a level should be achieved within a time-frame sufficient to allow ecosystems to adapt naturally to climate change, to ensure that food production is not threatened and to enable economic development to proceed in a sustainable manner.'

References

Fowler, H.J. and Archer, D.R. (2006) 'Conflicting signals of climatic change in the Upper Indus Basin', *Journal of Climate,* 19, pp. 4276–4293.

IAC (Inter-Academy Council) (2010a) 'Climate change assessments: Review of the processes and procedures of the IPCC', Committee to Review the Intergovernmental Panel on Climate Change,

—— (2010b) 'Inter-Academy Council Report Recommends Fundamental Reform of IPCC Management Structure', http://reviewipcc.interacademycouncil.net/ReportNewsRelease.html, accessed 12 May 2011.

—— (2010c) 'UN Letters to IAC Co-Chairs', http://reviewipcc.interacademycouncil.net/UN_Letters_to_IAC_Co-Chairs_10_March_2010_WITH_TOR.pdf, accessed 12 May 2011.

Mitra, A.P., Sharma, S., Bhattacharya, S., Garg, A., Devotta, S. and Sen, K. (eds.) (2004) *Climate Change and India: Uncertainty Reduction in GHG Inventory Estimates,* Universities Press (India) Pvt. Ltd., http://reviewipcc.interacademycouncil.net/report/Climate%20Change%20Assessments,%20Review%20of%20the%20Processes%20&%20Procedures%20of%20the%20IPCC.pdf, accessed 12 May 2011.

Pearce, F. (1999) 'Flooded Out', *New Scientist,* 5 June.

Raina, V.K. (2009) 'Himalayan Glaciers: A State-of-Art Review of Glacial Studies, Glacial retreat and Climate Change', Ministry of Environment and Forests, Discussion Paper.

Raj, N. Gopal (2009) 'Controversy over Himalayan glaciers hots up', *The Hindu,* 19 November.

Ravindranath, N.H. (2010) 'IPCC: Accomplishments, controversies and challenges', *Current Science,* vol. 99, July 10.

WWF (2005) *An Overview of Glaciers, Glacier Retreat, and Subsequent Impacts in Nepal, India and China,* assets.panda.org/downloads/himalayaglaciersreport2005.pdf, accessed on 27 June 2011.

Part II

Past as prologue

Early Indian perspectives
on climate change

5 Global warming in an unequal world

A case of environmental colonialism* (selected excerpts)

Anil Agarwal and Sunita Narain

The idea that developing countries like India and China must share the blame for heating up the earth and destabilizing its climate, as espoused in a recent study published in the United States by the World Resources Institute in collaboration with the United Nations, is an excellent example of environmental colonialism.

The report of the World Resources Institute (WRI), a Washington-based private research group, is based less on science and more on politically motivated and mathematical jugglery.[1] Its main intention seems to be to blame developing countries for global warming and perpetuate the current global inequality in the use of the earth's environment and its resources.

A detailed look at the data presented by WRI itself leads to the conclusion that India and China cannot be held responsible even for a single kg of carbon dioxide or methane that is accumulating in the earth's atmosphere. Carbon dioxide and methane are two of the most important gases contributing to global warming. The accumulation in the earth's atmosphere of these gases is mainly the result of the gargantuan consumption of the developed countries, particularly the United States.

. . .

WRI's calculations: faulty and prejudiced

The figures used by WRI to calculate the quantity of carbon dioxide and methane produced by each country are extremely questionable. Heavy emphasis has been placed on carbon dioxide production due to deforestation and methane production from rice fields and livestock as compared to carbon dioxide production from the use of fossil fuels like oil and coal. Since developing countries are more responsible for the former, the heavy emphasis on deforestation and methane generation tends to overplay their contribution while underplaying that of the developed countries.

Brazil, for instance, is a clear case where deforestation estimates have been overstated. Even though Brazil's deforestation did peak in 1987, several Brazilian sources point out that they have reduced substantially since then. Its carbon dioxide emissions since 1987, and on average during the 1980s, are much lower than those taken by WRI to calculate carbon dioxide emissions. Similarly, in India, deforestation rates do not seem to be the same as those of the 1970s, that is, 1.5 million hectares a year – the figure taken as the yearly average by WRI for the 1980s. . . . For other developing countries also, the accuracy of the forest-loss estimates used by WRI to calculate carbon dioxide levels is very shaky. . . .

82 *Agarwal and Narain*

The fact remains that forest-loss data in the world is still extremely poor and it is difficult to use it for any set of calculations of carbon emissions to the same level of precision as fossil fuel-use data.

The methane issue raises further questions of justice and morality. Can we really equate the carbon dioxide contributions of gas guzzling automobiles in Europe and North America or, for that matter, anywhere in the Third World with the methane emissions of draught cattle and rice fields of subsistence farmers in West Bengal or Thailand? Do these people not have a right to live? But no effort has been made in WRI's report to separate out the 'survival emissions' of the poor, from the 'luxury emissions' of the rich. Just what kind of politics or morality is this which masquerades in the name of 'one worldism' and 'high minded internationalism'? [emphasis in original].

Centre for Science and Environment (CSE) calculations

CSE's analysis presented in this report does not question the data that WRI has used to calculate each country's production of carbon dioxide and methane, even though, as argued above, they definitely can be questioned. Yet CSE's analysis shows India and China cannot be blamed for any of the methane or carbon dioxide that is appearing in the atmosphere.

As a senior UNEP official has put it, nature serves two major economic functions – one, as a source of raw materials and, two, as a sink for absorbing wastes.[2] Ideally, the approach should have been to prepare each nation's budget of greenhouse gas emissions by taking into account each nation's sources of emissions and its terrestrial sinks, i.e. its forests, other vegetation and soils. This exercise would have given an idea of the true emissions of each nation. These emissions would have to be further matched with each nation's just and fair share of the oceanic and tropospheric sinks – a common heritage of humankind. Only then could the net emissions of a nation that are accumulating in the atmosphere be calculated. But nothing of this sort has been attempted by WRI.

The earth's environment has a considerable ability to absorb wastes. The ocean is an important sink for absorbing carbon dioxide produced through human activity. According to the estimates of the Intergovernmental Panel on Climate Change, the ocean absorbed, during the 1980s, carbon dioxide to the tune of 1,200 to 2,800 million tonnes of carbon equivalent every year. There could also be terrestrial sinks for carbon dioxide but scientific knowledge about them is still uncertain. The various models prepared world-wide for estimating the accumulation of carbon dioxide in the atmosphere reveal a substantial 'missing sink' which scientists now believe could be a terrestrial sink. The predicted amount of carbon dioxide increase in the atmosphere ideally should be equal to the amount of carbon dioxide emitted by human made sources less the amount absorbed by the oceanic sinks. But models find that instead the predicted amount is more than what is actually accumulating in the atmosphere, indicating the presence of yet another cleansing mechanism in the world. There is a growing belief that various land processes like vegetation and soil could possible account for this surplus. Some preliminary models even suggest that these terrestrial sinks could be possibly even larger than the oceanic sinks. But much of this is still unknown.

The sink for methane is primarily removed by a reaction with hydroxyl radicals (OH) in the troposphere. This reaction represents a sink of about 400 to 600 million

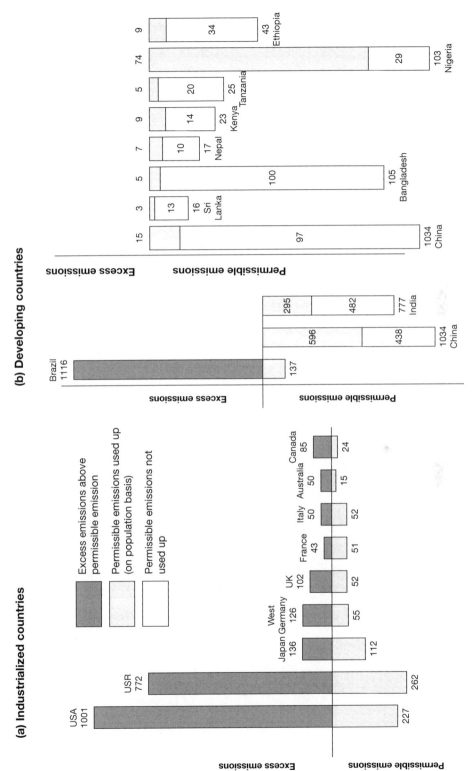

Figure 5.1 Permissible emissions vs total emissions of carbon dioxide of select countries on the basis of population (in million tonnes of carbon equivalent) as calculated by CSE

84 Agarwal and Narain

tonnes per year. Soils may also be contributing in removing methane to the tune of 15 to 54 million tonnes each year.

WRI's legerdemain actually lies in the manner that the earth's ability to clean up the two greenhouse gases of carbon dioxide and methane – a global common of extreme importance – has been unfairly allocated to different countries [emphasis in the original]. According to WRI figures, the world produces every year 31,100 million tonnes of carbon dioxide and 255 million tonnes of methane. But in reality, the increase in the atmosphere every year is only 13,600 million tonnes of carbon dioxide and 43 million tonnes of methane. In other words, the earth's ecological systems – its vegetation and its oceans – absorb 17,500 million tonnes of carbon dioxide and 212 million tones of methane every year. Global warming is caused by over-exceeding this cleansing capacity of the earth's ecological systems. The WRI report makes no distinction between those countries which have eaten up this ecological capital by exceeding the world's absorptive capacity and those countries which have emitted gases well within the world's cleansing capacity. India, for instance, has been ranked as the fifth largest contributor of greenhouse gases in the world.

Compared to its population – 16.2 per cent of the world's population in 1990 – India's total production of carbon dioxide and methane amounted to only six per cent and 14.4 per cent, respectively, of the amount that is absorbed by the earth's ecological systems. How can, therefore, India and other such countries be blamed even for single kg of the filth that is accumulating in the atmosphere on a global scale and threatening the world's people with a climatic cataclysm? In fact, India can double its total carbon dioxide emissions without threatening the world's climate. And if it controls its deforestation, then it can increase its carbon dioxide emissions from fossil fuels several times.

On the contrary, the United States, with only 4.73 per cent of the world's population, emits as much as 26 per cent of the carbon dioxide and 20 per cent of the methane that is absorbed, every year. It is the production of carbon dioxide and methane by countries like USA and Japan – totally out of proportion to their populations and that of the world's absorptive capacity – which is entirely responsible for the accumulation of unabsorbed carbon dioxide and methane in the atmosphere. In addition, these countries emit large quantities of CFCs – chemicals which do not get absorbed at all. Japan accounts for 7.4 per cent and USA for 25.8 per cent of the world's consumption of CFCs.

Not even one tonne of CFCs released into the atmosphere can get absorbed because there is no natural sink for it. As concerned environmentalists, we should propose that no country should be 'allowed' to produce such chemicals which the atmosphere has no ability to cleanse naturally and all production of such chemicals should be added to the net emissions of the individual countries.

But the WRI report does not take countries like USA or Japan to task. On the contrary, it adopts a mathematical technique which puts the blame on several poor countries. WRI has calculated the proportion of the world's greenhouse gases produced by a country like India and has then used this proportion to calculate India's share in the quantity of gases that are accumulating in the atmosphere.

· · ·

Global warming in an unequal world   85

Sharing a crucial global common

How can we calculate each country's share of responsibility for the accumulation of gases such as carbon dioxide and methane in the earth's atmosphere?

It is obvious that the concept of sustainable development demands that human beings collectively do not produce more carbon dioxide and methane than the earth's environment can absorb. The question is how should this global common – the global carbon dioxide and methane sinks – be shared amongst the people of the world?

Several studies on the global warming problem have argued, and we argue ourselves, that in a world that aspires to such lofty ideals like global justice, equity and sustainability, this vital global common should be shared equally on a per capita basis.

Using this principle, CSE has adopted the following methodology to ascertain the net emissions which are posing a threat to the world's climate:

1   The natural sinks for carbon dioxide and methane have been allocated to each nation on a population basis. These quantities then constitute the permissible emissions of each country. As no natural sinks exist for CFCs, no permissible shares for CFCs have been calculated.
2   The total emissions of each country of carbon dioxide and methane (as calculated by WRI) have then been compared with its permissible emissions (as calculated by CSE) to ascertain the quantity of emissions that are in excess of the permissible emissions.
3   The unused permissible emissions of countries like India and China have been traded with the excess emitters on a population basis.
4   The permissible emissions, traded from low emitting countries have been subtracted from the excess emissions of each country to obtain the quantity of each country's net emissions to the atmosphere of carbon dioxide and methane.
5   The total greenhouse gas emissions have been obtained by adding the net emissions of methane and carbon dioxide (as obtained by CSE) with the total emissions of CFCs (as given by WRI).

CSE's calculations clearly show that there is one set of nations in the world which is emitting greenhouse gases well within its share (or, in other words, its permissible limits) whereas there is another set of countries which is exceeding its permissible limits by leaps and bounds. . . .

Lack of Third World research

The entire episode also emphasizes the fact that Third World nations must undertake their own research in this crucial area. They cannot depend on Western institutions to present a true picture of the global situation and safeguard their interests. The manner in which the methane and carbon dioxide emissions of several developing countries have been calculated is itself open to questions. The database on contributions from deforestation, irrigated rice farming and livestock management is still poor. It is vital that a reliable system of measuring deforestation annually on a global and national basis is developed urgently. . . .

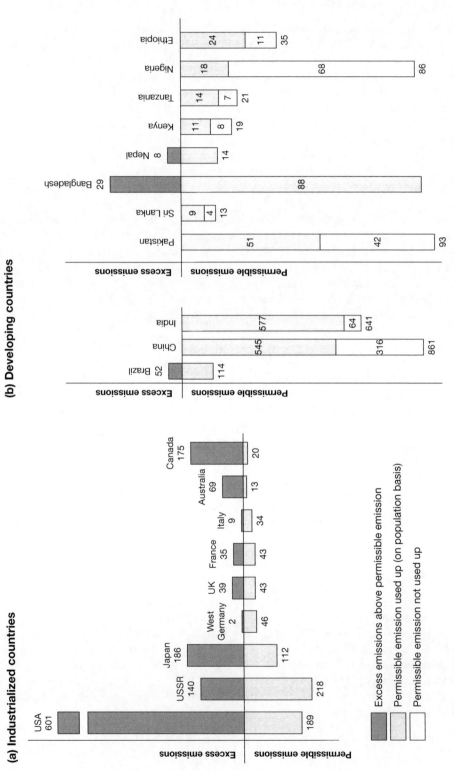

Figure 5.2 Permissible emissions vs total emissions of methane of select countries on the basis of population (in million tonnes of carbon equivalent) as calculated by CSE

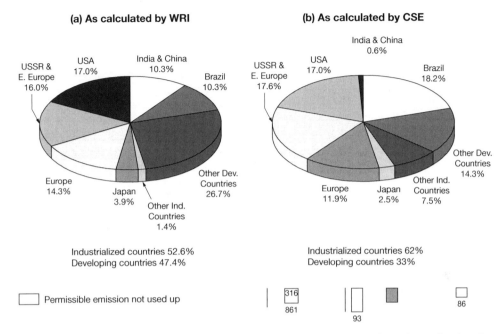

Figure 5.3 Percentage distribution of net emissions of greenhouse gases by industrialized and developing countries

Action in India

None of this means that India should not regenerate its environment or that it should not be efficient in its use of energy. This will also be our best defence against any possible impact of global warming. Only if the diverse ecosystems of India are functioning at optimum levels of productivity, will the effects of the expected changes in the global climate become somewhat manageable. But if, as today, our land and water resource base remains highly stressed and degraded (and even normal conditions constitute a near-crisis situation), climatic perturbations will throw society into a state of total emergency.

But to carry out this strategy to improve land productivity and meet people's survival needs development strategies will have to be ecosystem-specific and holistic. It will be necessary to plan for each component of the village ecosystem, and not just trees, from grasslands, forest lands and crop lands to water. To do this, the country will need much more than just glib words about people's participation or wasteland development. It will demand bold and imaginative steps to strengthen and deepen local democracy by creating and empowering democratic and open village institutions. Only then will the people get involved in managing their environment. It will mean dismantling the inefficient and oppressive government apparatus and changing laws so that people can act without waiting for a good bureaucrat to come along. As present laws stand, planting trees on government wastelands can land villagers in jail. The government is the biggest and the worst land and water owner in the country.

Those who talk about global warming should concentrate on what ought to be done at home. The challenge for India is thus to get on with the job at hand and leave the

88 *Agarwal and Narain*

business of dirty tricks and dirtying up the world to others. In this process, we will help ourselves, and maybe even the rest of the world.

Notes

* Excerpted from Anil Agarwal and Sunita Narain (1991), *Global Warming In an Unequal World: A Case of Environmental Colonialism*, Centre for Science and Environment, New Delhi. Reproduced with permission from the Centre for Science and Environment.

1 World Resources Institute (1990), *World Resources 1990–91: A Guide to the Global Environment*, Oxford University Press, New York.

2 Yusuf J. Ahmad (1990), 'Energy Issues in Environmental Economics', paper presented at a Seminar on the Economics of Sustainable Use of Forest Resources, April 1990, Centre for Science and Environment, New Delhi, *mimeo*.

6 Present at the creation

The making of the UN Framework Convention on Climate Change

Chandrashekhar Dasgupta

Few major global agreements have been negotiated as expeditiously as the UN Framework Convention on Climate Change.[1] The negotiations commenced in February 1991 and were completed by May 1992, in time for the Convention to be opened for signature in the following month at the UN Conference on Environment and Development (UNCED) in Rio de Janeiro. It took only 15 months for the Intergovernmental Negotiating Committee (INC) to conclude this path-breaking agreement. By contrast, the Law of the Sea negotiations covered a full decade.

Initial differences

This achievement is all the more remarkable since the initial positions of the parties were far apart. The negotiations reflected a deep North–South divide as well as major differences within both these groups.

In general, developing countries pressed for an agreement based on equity, reflecting the fact that anthropogenic climate change was the result of cumulative emissions of greenhouse gases (GHGs) originating mainly in the developed countries. The developed countries, on the other hand, sought to minimize the link between commitments under the agreement and responsibility for causing climate change. The United States refused to recognize the link altogether, maintaining that countries should contribute to an international effort 'in accordance with the means at their disposal and their capabilities' (United States of America, 1991), ignoring the question of responsibility for causing climate change.

India's position was based on the principle that every human being had an equal right to the global atmospheric resource. As head of the Indian delegation, I stated our position as follows at the outset of substantive negotiations:

> The problem of global warming is caused not by emissions of greenhouse gases as such but by *excessive levels* of per capita emissions of these gases. If per capita emissions of all countries had been on the same levels as those of the developing countries, the world would not today have faced the threat of global warming. It follows, therefore, that developed countries with high per capita emission levels of greenhouse gases are responsible for incremental global warming.
>
> In these negotiations, the principle of equity should be the touchstone for judging any proposal. Those responsible for environmental degradation should also be responsible for taking corrective measures. Since developed countries with high

90 *Dasgupta*

per capita emissions of greenhouse gases are responsible for incremental global warming, it follows that they have a corresponding obligation to take corrective action. Moreover, these are also the countries which have the greatest capacity to bear the burden. It is they who possess the financial resources and the technology needed for corrective action. This further reinforces their obligations regarding corrective action.[2]

This statement introduced an Indian 'non-paper' setting out the full text of a draft framework convention (India, 1991). The core provisions of the draft were incorporated in the article on 'commitments', which focused on the responsibilities of the developed countries. It set out the long-term objective of:

stabilizing the concentration of greenhouse gases in the atmosphere . . . on the basis of an equitable formula requiring, inter alia, that anthropogenic emissions of carbon dioxide from states should converge at a common per capita level, and which would take into account net carbon dioxide emissions during the century.

Towards this goal, the draft convention proposed that:

Developed country parties shall, as immediate measures: (a) declare, adopt and implement national strategies to stabilize and reduce their per capita emissions of greenhouse gases, particularly carbon dioxide; stabilization . . . should be achieved by developed country parties at the latest by the year 2000 and should be set at 1990 emission levels, with the goal of achieving at least a (20%) (30%) (40%) (50%) reduction on these stabilized levels by the year 2005; (b) provide new and additional financial resources for developing country parties for the objective described in paragraph 4 below . . . ; (c) provide assured access to appropriate, environmentally sound technology on preferential and non-commercial terms to developing countries; and (d) to support developing countries in their efforts to create and develop their endogenous capacities in scientific and technological research and development directed at combating climate change.

4. Developing countries may, in accordance with their national development plans, priorities and objectives, consider feasible measures with regard to climate change provided that the full incremental costs are met by provision of new and additional financial resources from the developed countries.

(India, 1991, p. 5)

Our proposals received wide support among developing countries. China, which had submitted a non-paper calling upon the developed countries to assume the 'main responsibility' in addressing climate change, stated that the Indian non-paper to a large extent reflected the common views of many developing countries.

As already noted, the developed countries sought to minimize or ignore the link between responsibility for causing climate change and the burden of addressing the problem. They called upon developing countries also to accept some form of a binding mitigation commitment. Within this overall approach, however, there were significant differences of detail. Thus, Germany recognized that the developed countries have a special responsibility 'since these countries have been the main sources of the increase in atmospheric concentrations of climate-relevant gases', while also calling upon the developing countries to accept commitments because 'it is only with their broad participation that the global challenge can be met effectively' (Germany, 1991). France, whose nuclear power plants met the bulk of its energy requirements, declared that it was prepared to limit its per capita emissions below 2 tonnes of carbon equivalent by 2000, provided other industrialized countries accepted the same commitment (France, 1991). There were no takers for this offer among other developed countries. (In 1991–92, European Community policies were coordinated much more loosely than they are today.) At the other end of the scale, the United States simply refused to recognize the question of historical responsibility.

The North and the South were divided not only on the nature of the commitments of the developing countries but also on the related question of financial and technological support. Developing countries, in general, refused to accept binding commitments, maintaining that their commitments would be conditional on receipt of finance and technology transfers from developed countries to cover the full incremental costs of response measures. The United States rejected outright the demand for developed countries to assume financial commitments to support mitigation and adaptation actions in developing countries. Other OECD countries were prepared to offer 'assistance' to developing countries to cover 'agreed' (as distinct from 'full') incremental costs but this fell far short of the expectations of the South. The industrialized countries also rejected calls for technology transfer on anything other than commercial terms.

While maintaining a common front in insisting that the developing countries should assume binding mitigation commitments, the industrialized countries were deeply divided on the question of their own commitments. The European Community (EC) proposed that industrialized countries should, in general, stabilize their emissions by the year 2000 at 1990 levels. Norway presented a similar proposal, calling for stabilization by OECD countries by the same date but at 1989 levels (Norway, 1991).

The United States opposed calls for such time-bound stabilization or reduction targets. It took the position that 'specific commitments for emissions reductions should not be included in the framework convention, because of the need for flexibility in nations' choices of their own measures' (United States of America, 1991). Britain sought to find common ground between the EC and US positions by calling for stabilization 'as soon as possible' (United Kingdom, 1991).

Japan advocated a 'pledge and review' agreement, in which every country 'makes public a pledge, consisting of its past [sic] performance strategies' to limit emissions and targets or estimates of emissions resulting from these strategies. These would be subject to periodic reviews (Japan, 1991).

Sweden urged all countries to limit greenhouse gas emissions on the basis of the best available technology and good practices. It prescribed a series of energy efficiency measures for groups of countries selected on the basis of presumed ability to implement the commitments (Sweden, 1991). This approach set aside questions of responsibility and equity.

As in the case of the North, there were significant differences also within the South. In particular, there was a major divergence between the positions of the countries whose economies were largely dependent on oil exports and the countries forming the Association of Small Island States (AOSIS). The oil exporters, led by Saudi Arabia, were concerned about the potential impact of carbon mitigation measures on petroleum

92   Dasgupta

markets. They were opposed to ambitious mitigation commitments, even for the developed countries. On the other hand, the low-lying island states were deeply concerned about the possible submergence of their territories as a consequence of sea-level rise resulting from climate change. They therefore pressed for the strongest possible convention. India, China and many other developing countries tried to steer a middle course in an effort to hold together the 'G-77 and China' group.

Coalition diplomacy

Both of the major groups – G-77 and China and the OECD countries – made strenuous efforts to bridge internal differences. The developing countries tried hard to arrive at a common negotiating text. These efforts were partially successful. Agreement was reached within the group on the section on 'principles' (initially proposed by China). Reflecting our position on the conditional character of developing country commitments, G-77 and China agreed that 'commitments that might be entered into by developing countries under this Convention are contractually dependent on the fulfillment of the financial and technology transfer obligations that must be entered into by developed countries who are in the main responsible for the urgency of the present situation'. Agreement was also reached on the need for 'adequate, new and additional resources' and technology transfer to developing countries on 'favourable, concessionary and preferential terms'. However, differences persisted on a number of issues, including the question of the admissibility of reviews in regard to developing countries. Most importantly, there was no agreement within the group on the crucial question of specific emission reduction commitments for developed countries because of the wide differences between AOSIS and the oil exporting countries.

By the end of 1991 it became clear that G-77 and China would not be in a position to reach a consensus text on commitments. Our proposals would have to be advanced through a more compact group. Accordingly, at the year end, India joined hands with 53 other developing countries (including China) to submit a common text on 'commitments' (General Assembly, 1991). The text called on the developed countries, on the basis of assessed contributions, to 'provide on a grant basis new, adequate and additional financial resources to meet the full incremental costs of developing country Parties' in connection with mitigation and adaptation measures. It incorporated the demand of the developing countries for technology transfer on 'concessional, preferential and most favourable terms'. Developing countries would be required 'in accordance with their national development plans, priorities, objectives and specific country conditions to consider taking feasible measures to address climate change, provided that the full incremental costs' are met by the developed countries. They might also, on a strictly voluntary basis, take additional nationally determined measures.

The OECD countries were initially less successful in forging a common position. The EC made an early attempt to reach such a consensus on the basis of the Japanese proposal for a 'pledge and review' agreement. In June 1991, the EC proposed that the Convention 'should include what has come to be called a pledge and review proposal', pointing to the need for 'flexibility' (a crucial concern for the US). Its own proposal for a time-bound emission stabilization commitment for developed countries was now described as being merely 'an example of a commitment that should preferably be embodied in a protocol'.[3]

The new EC approach came under fire not only from the developing countries but also, very importantly, the NGO community. Developing countries pointed out that the new statement diluted the specific commitments of the developed countries and unfairly imposed binding obligations on the developing countries. Moreover, in the absence of agreed criteria and guidelines, a review could only be an arbitrary exercise. The NGO news letter, ECO, launched a devastating attack on 'pledge and review', describing it as 'hedge and retreat' proposal.

Coming under strong attack, the EC beat a hasty retreat. In the next session, held in September 1991, it recognized that the 'concept of Pledge and Review had caused a great deal of confusion. We are quite ready to admit that this was also the case among Member States of the European Community. The Group of 77 was, therefore, completely right when it stated, through its Chairman, that the concept of pledge and review lacked precision and transparency.'[4]

The OECD countries then attempted to arrive at a common text on the basis of the EC stabilization proposal. There was some movement on the part of Japan, Canada, Australia and others but positions remained far apart. The United States rejected any stabilization target. The final outcome of the negotiations between the OECD countries was a heavily bracketed text on stabilization and no less than four alternative formulations! The EC expressed its 'regret that the positions reflected in the document are as far apart as is the case' (Portugal, 1992).

Impasse

Thus, as late as in December 1991, the INC deliberations had a trilateral character. Most OECD countries, led by the EC, sought an agreement with commitments for all parties, including time bound emission stabilization targets for all developed countries. The United States wanted a very general agreement focused on further scientific studies on climate change; it refused to accept time-bound emission reduction – or even stabilization – targets or any obligation to provide financial resources or to transfer technology to the developing countries on anything other than commercial terms. The developing countries – in particular, the 54 countries presenting a common negotiating text – called upon the developed countries to commit themselves not only to emission limitation targets but also to provide financial resources to developing countries and transfer technology to these countries on preferential terms. They emphasized that any obligations they assumed would be conditional on receipt of adequate financial and technological support from the developed countries.

The 'negotiations' took the form of a drafting exercise, with hardly any attempt at resolving substantive differences through bargaining. The net result by the end of the penultimate session in December 1991 was a 'consolidated working document' in which all the core provisions – covering the sections on 'Principles', 'General Commitments', 'Specific Commitments', and 'Special Situations' – were placed within square brackets, reflecting divergent views. In fact, only a single word in these sections was unqualified by a bracket – the word 'commitments' figuring as a title!

We drew a blank in our efforts to sound the EC and USA separately on the possibility of a deal. I came to the conclusion that neither of these parties was prepared to enter into substantive negotiations with the developing countries until they succeeded in forging a common position between themselves. (As noted earlier, the attempt to

94 Dasgupta

resolve differences within the OECD came to naught in the December 1991 session.) The result was a deadlock in the INC.

The fifth and final session of the negotiations opened in New York in February 1972, with only four months remaining for the Rio de Janeiro summit on Environment and Development. But little progress could be achieved even at the February meeting.[5]

The original plan was to complete negotiations on the framework convention by the fifth session of the INC in February 1992. However, in view of the impasse in the negotiations, the INC decided to resort to a typical UN device. It was decided to 'resume' the fifth session in May, in the hope of a breakthrough.

Breakthrough

In my report to New Delhi on the outcome of the February meeting, I ventured the following assessment:

> At the present moment the prospects of a successful conclusion of the negotiations in May are not promising. Nevertheless, it is possible that a last minute effort will be made to bridge the differences between the US and the EC by adoption of an ambiguous formulation concerning stabilisation and reduction of emissions of developed countries. This could be the basis of an attempt to shift the balance of responsibility from the North to the South. Our delegation would have to be prepared for this eventuality.

In May, an agreement of sorts was finally reached between the EC and the United States. This was the result of a last minute British initiative to bridge the divide. Anglo-US talks in Washington produced a formulation on the mitigation commitments of the developed countries. This was riddled with ambiguities concealing the substantive differences between the US and EC positions. The EC Environment Commissioner initially rejected the formulation as 'completely unacceptable' but member countries finally accepted it with minor amendments (Bodansky, 1993, p. 491). Thereupon, the US–EC draft was incorporated verbatim in a 'Chairman's text' presented at the beginning of the 'resumed' fifth session in May.

When the text was debated in plenary, Philippines, on behalf of G-77 and China, sought clarification on no fewer than fifteen obscure points in the formulation. Supporting the G-77 position, I pointed out the artful ambiguity of the formulation, describing it as legal 'striptease'. In response to my intervention, the Chairman acknowledged that the ambiguity reflected lack of agreement between the industrialized countries (ECO, 1992).

The Chairman's text was weighted in favour of the developed countries. In keeping with the EC position, all countries would be required to 'coordinate' their economic and administrative instruments in the context of a climate change response, in order to avoid so-called 'distortions' in international trade. Financial support to developed countries would cover only 'agreed', not 'full', incremental costs. In a partial concession to the South, the term 'review' was eschewed in relation to the developing countries but these countries were asked to link proposals for financial support with their 'national communications'. This opened the possibility for reviews of policies and measures reported by developing countries in their 'national communications'. Above all, the chair sought to treat as sacrosanct the US–EC text on commitments of the developed countries, insisting that re-opening the issue would inevitably lead to the collapse of the negotiations.

On the Chair's suggestion, negotiations were largely confined within an 'enlarged bureau', which included, in addition to members of the bureau, countries which he regarded as 'key' players. In response to the Chair's position on the non-negotiable nature of the US–EC text on the mitigation commitments of the developed countries, we insisted that the Chair's text as a whole was under negotiation, reserving our right to press for an amendment on the US–EC formulation.

Vigorous negotiations ensued in the 'enlarged bureau' (Dasgupta, forthcoming). One of our earlier successes in the session was an agreement on provision of financial resources to developing countries to cover the 'agreed full incremental costs'. Co-ordination of economic and administrative instruments was limited exclusively to developed countries. It took much longer to secure acceptance of our position on the inadmissibility of reviews of developing country actions. A 'review' implies a binding commitment and is, therefore, inapplicable in respect of actions that are purely voluntary. We were prepared to communicate information about our national policies and measures but only for the purpose of estimating global trends, not a review of these policies and measures. We were finally able to exclude all references to a review of the voluntary actions of developing countries.

Perhaps the most difficult negotiations concerned a paragraph drafted by us. This read as follows in its final form:

> The extent to which developing country parties will effectively implement their commitments under the Convention will depend upon the effective implementation by developed country parties of their commitments under the Convention related to financial resources and transfer of technology and will take fully into account that economic and social development and poverty eradication are the first and overriding priorities of the developing country Parties.

We were able to secure agreement on this crucial paragraph only after very hard and protracted negotiation. It stands as Article 4, paragraph 7 of the convention.

Thus the Framework Convention conforms to our basic position concerning the voluntary and non-negotiable nature of the actions taken by the developing countries without international support. Developing countries have no obligation to implement mitigation measures involving incremental costs, unless these costs are met in full by the developed countries. When thus supported, developing countries assume a con-tractual or conditional commitment but unlike the binding commitments of the developed countries.

However, there was an unfinished task at the conclusion of the negotiations. The US–EC formulation incorporated in the Convention as Article 4.2 (a) and (b) failed to specify time-bound emission reduction targets for the developed countries. The Kyoto Protocol, adopted in December 1997, filled this lacuna.

Prospect and retrospect

More than a decade later, North and South have once again locked horns in the current climate change negotiations. In a nutshell, the developing countries are seeking *enhanced implementation* of the Framework Convention and the Kyoto Protocol,

96 Dasgupta

while the developed countries are pressing for a *new agreement* that would have the effect of amending or overwriting the basic provisions of the existing agreements.

In pursuing this revisionist agenda, the developed countries are trying to resurrect proposals that were laid to rest in 1992. Thus, demands are being made once again that developing countries should take on new, legally binding commitments. The Annex II countries are seeking to renege on their commitment to provide financial resources to developing countries in order to cover 'agreed, full incremental costs', restricting these at best to Least Developed Countries and Small Island Developing States. A major attempt is being made, on the basis of the so-called Copenhagen Accord, to resurrect the 'pledge and review' approach, rejected as early as in 1991 not only on grounds of equity but also as being totally inadequate for achieving the required deep cuts in emissions. In negotiating the Convention, the international community rejected a proposal calling for universal 'coordination' of economic and administrative measures in order to avoid alleged trade distortions. Some developed countries are now holding out threats of border levies or similar charges on exports of countries declining such 'coordination'.

We stand at a cross-road in the negotiations. One road leads to enhanced implementation by all countries – developed and developing alike – of their respective obligations under the agreed climate change regime. The other road leads to the effective dismantling of this regime, reopening of every basic issue and returning the negotiations to the starting point in 1991.

Notes

1. For more detailed accounts by the author of the negotiating history of the Convention, see, Dasgupta (1994, pp. 129–148) and Dasgupta (forthcoming).
2. Statement by the leader of the Indian delegation, Second Session of the INCFCCC, Geneva, 19 June 1991. Copy on file with the author.
3. Intervention by the Netherlands delegation on behalf of the European Community and its Member States, Second Session of the INCFCCC, Geneva, 28 June 1991. Copy on file with the author.
4. Intervention by the Netherlands on behalf of the European Community and its Member States, Third Session of the INCFCCC, Nairobi, September 1991.
5. For details of the limited outcome of the February meeting, see Dasgupta (1994, pp. 141–142).

References

Bodansky, D. (1993) 'The United Nations Framework Convention on Climate Change: A Commentary', *Yale Journal of International Law*, vol. 18, pp. 451–558.

Dasgupta, C. (forthcoming) 'Negotiating the Framework Convention on Climate Change: A Memoir', in K. V. Rajan (ed.) *The Ambassadors' Club*, HarperCollins, New Delhi.

Dasgupta, C. (1994) 'The Climate Change Negotiations', in I. M. Mintzer and J. A. Leonard (eds) *Negotiating Climate Change: The Inside Story of the Rio Convention*, Cambridge University Press, Cambridge, UK.

ECO (1992) NGO News Letter, 5 May.

France (1991) *Suggestions concerning the limitation of greenhouse gases*, in INCFCCC (Intergovernmental Negotiation Committee for a Framework Convention on Climate Change) *Preparation of a Framework Convention on Climate Change*. A/AC.237/Misc. 1/Add.1. pp. 10–14.

General Assembly, United Nations (1991) *Draft report of the Intergovernmental Negotiating Committee for a Framework Convention on Climate Change on the work of its second session, held at Geneva from 19 to 28 June 1991*, A/AC.237/WG 1/L.7.

The making of the UNFCCC 97

Germany (1991) *Non-paper: Important elements for an international climate convention*, in INCFCCC *Preparation of a Framework Convention on Climate Change*. A/AC.237/Misc.1/Add.1. pp. 15–23.

India (1991) *Non-paper: Draft framework convention on climate change*, in INFCCC *Preparation of a Framework Convention on Climate Change*. A/AC.237/Misc.1/Add.3. pp. 3–17.

Japan (1991) *Informal paper: Pledge and review process as a possible mechanism to implement commitments defined on the basis of the convention*, in INCFCCC *Preparation of a Framework Convention on Climate Change*. A/AC.237/Misc.1/Add.7. pp. 3–5.

Norway (1991) *Non-paper*, in INCFCCC *Preparation of a Framework Convention on Climate Change*. A/AC.237/Misc.1/Add.2. pp. 10–31.

Portugal (1992) 'Statement by the Portugal on behalf of the European community and its member states, New York', *ECO*, 28 February.

Sweden (1991) *Non paper: Commitments in Chapter IV.1 (submitted on 19 June 1991)*, in INCFCCC *Preparation of a Framework Convention on Climate Change*. A/AC.237/Misc.1/Add.6. pp. 3–5.

United Kingdom (1991) *Draft paper: Possible elements for inclusion in a framework convention on climate change*, in INCFCCC *Preparation of a Framework Convention on Climate Change*. A/AC.237/Misc.1/Add.1. pp. 83–88.

United States of America (1991) *Submission of the United States to the Intergovernmental Negotiating Committee on Climate Change*, in INCFCCC *Preparation of a Framework Convention on Climate Change*. A/AC.237/Misc.1/Add.1. pp. 89–95.

Part III

The international climate negotiations

Stakes, debates and dilemmas

7 International climate negotiations and India's role[1]

Sandeep Sengupta

The issue of climate change has grabbed the attention of the world today as never before. This chapter aims to provide an introduction to how India has engaged in the international negotiations on climate change over the last two decades. It is organised in four parts. The first part provides a synopsis of the key events in international climate negotiations to date, tracing its rise from being an issue of relative scientific obscurity to becoming the 'defining challenge of our age' (UN, 2007). The second part focuses on India's behaviour in the climate negotiations, noting the key contributions that it made and the policies and strategies that it adopted. The third part attempts to explain the continuities and changes seen in India's foreign policy behaviour on this issue. The fourth concludes with a brief assessment of India's current evolving role.

Contrary to the common perception of developing countries being more 'rule-takers' rather than 'rule-makers' in the international system vis-à-vis the developed world (Hurrell and Woods, 1999), this chapter argues that on climate change, at least, India has been a major international force since the earliest days of the negotiations. It has played a vital role in constructing the international regime, norms, rules and institutions governing this issue, working to ensure that these are in line with its self-perceived national interests. However, while India's engagement on climate change over the last twenty years has been largely a story of continuity, the period leading up to the 2009 Copenhagen Summit saw a serious reconsideration of views, both within and outside government, on what India's interests and positions on this issue ought to be. While the debate in India continues to remain contested, the recent policy shifts and the divisions surrounding them reflect the hard choices and trade-offs that the country now faces on this issue.

The climate change story so far

It was scientists who first brought the problem of climate change to the attention of the world. Conferences such as the 1979 First World Climate Conference highlighted the long-term danger that excessive accumulation of greenhouse gases (GHG) in the Earth's atmosphere – caused by human activities such as industrialisation, burning of fossil fuels and deforestation – posed to its climate system and to human wellbeing (Paterson, 1996). However, the issue formally emerged on the international political agenda for the first time only in 1988, when the UN General Assembly passed a resolution recognising climate change to be a 'common concern of mankind', and urged governments to treat it as a 'priority issue' (UNGA, 1988). The resolution also endorsed the setting up of the Intergovernmental Panel on Climate Change (IPCC) to

102 *Sengupta*

study its scientific basis in greater detail. In 1989, the UN General Assembly passed another resolution that called on member states to urgently prepare a 'framework convention' to address this global issue through international collaboration (UNGA, 1989). The release of the IPCC's First Assessment Report in 1990 confirmed that anthropogenic GHG emissions were on the rise, and that stabilizing their concentrations in the atmosphere would require 'immediate reductions . . . of over 60%' (IPCC, 1990, p. xi). Following this, the UN General Assembly established a negotiating body called the Intergovernmental Negotiating Committee (INC), and directed it to launch formal negotiations to develop an 'effective framework convention on climate change, containing appropriate commitments' (UNGA, 1990). After 15 months of intense negotiations in the INC, countries adopted and signed the United Nations Framework Convention on Climate Change (UNFCCC) at the Rio Earth Summit in June 1992.

The UNFCCC laid out the basic international political, legal and normative architecture to address climate change. The core principle agreed under it noted that countries should protect the climate system on the 'basis of equity' and in accordance with their 'common but differentiated responsibilities and respective capabilities' (UNFCCC, 1992, Article 3.1). Noting that the 'largest share of historical and current global emissions' originated in developed countries, it called on them to 'take the lead' in addressing this challenge (Preamble and Article 3.1). Specifically, it asked developed countries to aim to return their GHG emissions to 1990 levels by the year 2000 (Article 4.2 a and b). However, given the level of reduction that the IPCC's First Assessment Report had demanded, and also the ambiguous language used in its framing (see Dasgupta, this volume), the UNFCCC noted that it would be necessary to 'review the adequacy' of this central commitment at its first Conference of Parties, once the agreement entered into force. The Convention exempt developing countries from any similar specific GHG mitigation commitments, noting that their 'per capita emissions' were still 'relatively low', and that their share of global emissions would need to grow in the future to meet their 'social and development needs' (Preamble).

The UNFCCC entered into force in March 1994. Its first Conference of Parties (CoP-1), which was held in Berlin in 1995, reviewed the 'adequacy' of the above commitment made by developed countries. Although nearly everybody agreed that stronger commitments were needed beyond 2000 to effectively address climate change, there were strong differences over how this should be done. While most developing countries, particularly the Alliance of Small Island States (AOSIS), demanded that industrialised countries take on more stringent emission reduction targets by adopting a legally binding 'protocol' to the UNFCCC (as the Montreal Protocol to the Vienna Convention had previously done to combat ozone layer depletion), this was resisted by a group of developed countries, particularly the United States (Oberthur and Ott, 1999). However, with the European Union (EU) also favouring the development of a protocol, a decision called the 'Berlin Mandate' was finally adopted at the end of CoP-1, which called for formal negotiations to begin to develop a protocol with legally-binding 'targets and timetables' to reduce industrialised country emissions (UNFCCC, 1995). The release of the IPCC's Second Assessment Report in 1995, which noted a 'discernible human influence' on the global climate (IPCC, 1995, p. 5), gave further impetus to this process. Following two years of intense intergovernmental negotiations, the Kyoto Protocol to the UNFCCC was formally adopted at CoP-3 in December 1997.

Under the Kyoto Protocol, developed countries agreed to take on individual, quantified, legally-binding emission reduction targets to reduce their collective emissions by

International climate negotiations 103

5% below 1990 levels over a commitment period of 2008–12 (UNFCCC, 1997, Article 3.1). The various CoPs that followed focused mostly on developing the modalities and rules for operationalising the Kyoto Protocol, including its three 'flexible' mechanisms of 'emissions trading', 'joint implementation' and the 'clean development mechanism' (CDM).[2] These were mechanisms that the US, in particular, had insisted upon in exchange for their acceptance of the Kyoto treaty. The rules for implementing the Kyoto Protocol were formally adopted at COP-7 of the UNFCCC in 2001 in the form of the 'Marrakesh Accords'.

The release of the IPCC's Third Assessment Report in 2001, which noted 'new and stronger evidence' of anthropogenic global warming, now also brought into sharp focus the fact that some degree of climate change was unavoidable (IPCC, 2001, pp. 9–11). This led to the issue of climate 'adaptation', which had been largely neglected in the negotiations until then, gaining greater prominence between CoP-8 and CoP-10. However, the decision of the US – the world's largest cumulative GHG emitter – not to ratify the Kyoto Protocol in 2001, following the election of George W. Bush, on claims that the agreement was unfair and harmful to its economy since it exempted major developing countries like China and India from similar emission restrictions, placed a question mark on the future of the treaty. The ability of the Kyoto Protocol to deliver actual change on the ground was also put in doubt by the continually growing emissions of OECD countries between 1990 and 2004, with most of them remaining far 'off track' their agreed Kyoto targets (UNDP, 2007, p. 54).

Nevertheless, with the EU still supporting the treaty, and with Russia's ratification, the Kyoto Protocol succeeded in entering into force just prior to CoP-11 in Montreal in 2005. This automatically triggered a process to initiate discussions on the emission reduction commitments that developed countries that had ratified the Protocol would need to adopt in their 'second' commitment period beyond 2012 (UNFCCC, 1997, Article 3.9) However, realising that this alone would not be enough, especially with the US remaining outside the treaty, and with emissions from the developing world, especially the major emerging economies, on the rise, CoP-11 also initiated a parallel 'dialogue' process to discuss other options that could 'enhance' the implementation of the UNFCCC and deliver 'long-term cooperative action' on climate change (UNFCCC, 2006).

Following two years of this 'dialogue', a decision on what to do next was finally taken at CoP-13 in December 2007. Called the 'Bali Action Plan' (BAP), this decision reiterated the urgency of addressing climate change, noting in particular the finding of the IPCC's Fourth Assessment Report that the threat of climate change was now 'unequivocal' (IPCC, 2007, p. 2). The BAP stressed that 'deep cuts in global emissions' were needed to achieve the ultimate objective of the Convention (to stabilise atmospheric GHG concentrations at safe levels), and called for the initiation of 'comprehensive' formal negotiations to enable the 'full, effective and sustained implementation' of the UNFCCC 'now, up to and beyond 2012' (UNFCCC, 2008). Specifically, it called for an 'agreed outcome' to be reached by CoP-15 on a 'shared vision' for 'long-term cooperative action' (LCA) that would include a 'long-term global goal for emission reductions' and agreements on the four key unresolved areas that had dogged climate negotiations until then: 'mitigation', 'adaptation', 'technology' and 'finance'.

The period between 2007 and 2009 witnessed extensive intergovernmental discussions on each of the above issues. The formal negotiations took place within two 'ad-hoc working groups' (AWGs) that were officially set up under the UNFCCC to

104 *Sengupta*

negotiate respectively: (1) the post-2012 'second' commitment period emission reduction targets of developed countries party to the Kyoto Protocol (AWG-KP) and (2) 'local-term cooperative action' as envisaged under the Bali Action Plan to cover what non-Kyoto developed countries like the US, and other developing countries, would do (AWG-LCA). In addition, climate change was also discussed at various other international fora, including the G-8+5 Summits, the Major Economies Forum (MEF), the G-20, and even the UN Security Council. The period also saw a slew of influential reports on how to tackle climate change, such as the Stern Review, as well as the build-up of unprecedented media, civil society and private sector attention on this issue across the world. These finally culminated at CoP-15 in Copenhagen in December 2009. However, amidst serious differences between the North and South, no agreement could be reached on either the AWG-KP or AWG-LCA tracks. Ultimately, the Copenhagen Summit concluded with countries agreeing to extend the negotiating mandates of both the AWGs till CoP-16, and by 'taking note of', but 'not adopting', the controversial 'Copenhagen Accord', a three-page political document hastily negotiated on the final day of the conference by a small group of states led by the United States, China, India, Brazil and South Africa.

The failure to realise an 'agreed outcome' at CoP-15 brought to fore the deep political fissures that existed between leading developing and developed countries over what sort of international regime could deliver effective action on climate change. While the former continued to insist on the implementation of a 'top-down', 'differentiated', 'legally-binding', 'targets and timetables'-based approach exemplified by the UNFCCC and its Kyoto Protocol; the latter, especially the US, advocated a radically-altered regime that would replace Kyoto with a less legalised, 'bottom-up', 'pledge and review'-type system that would also require significant mitigation commitments and accountability from key developing countries.

International negotiations in 2010 focused mostly on how the political understandings reached under the Copenhagen Accord (on restricting temperature rise to 2 degrees C; registering and monitoring the mitigation commitments and actions of developed and developing countries; provision of fast-track finance; technology mechanism; etc.) could be legally anchored and taken forward in the formal UNFCCC process, and how the basic conflict about the nature of the post-2012 climate regime could be resolved. Despite the reduced expectations, CoP-16 held in Mexico in December 2010 managed to keep the multilateral process alive by delivering the 'Cancun Agreements'. While for some, this represented progress, for others it set the stage for the eventual replacement of the original UNFCCC/Kyoto regime by a new international arrangement on climate change that would be less 'differentiated', require less of developed countries, and demand more of developing countries (Khor, 2010).

India's role and contribution

India has played a key role in international climate negotiations over the last two decades. It has been: (1) an influential voice and defender of the global South; (2) an important producer of ideas and international norms and rules on climate change; (3) an effective coalition-builder; and (4) an aggressive protector of its own interests. Each of these roles has typically fed off, and reinforced, one another.

That India intended to play an active role in the international debate on climate change was clear from very early on itself. Even before the formal negotiations

Table 7.1 Timeline of key events in climate change negotiations

Year	International events	Indian events
1979	• First World Climate Conference	
1988	• IPCC established • UNGA Res. 43/53 recognises climate change as 'common concern of mankind'	
1989	• UNGA Res. 44/207 calls for 'framework convention'	• Ministry of Environment and Forests (MoEF) constitutes 'Expert Advisory Committee' on global environmental issues
1990	• IPCC First Assessment Report • UNGA Res. 45/212 establishes Intergovernmental Negotiating Committee (INC)	• India hosts 'Conference of Select Developing Countries on Global Environmental Issues'
1991	• INC negotiations commence	• Economic crisis in India
1992	• UNFCCC signed at Rio	• India signs UNFCCC
1993		• India ratifies UNFCCC
1994	• UNFCCC enters into force	
1995	• CoP-1 adopts 'Berlin Mandate' • IPCC Second Assessment Report	
1997	• Kyoto Protocol adopted at CoP-3	
2001	• IPCC Third Assessment Report • Marrakesh Accords adopted at CoP-7	
2002	• CoP-8 prioritises 'climate adaptation'	• India ratifies Kyoto Protocol • India hosts CoP-8
2003		• India establishes National CDM Authority
2005	• Kyoto Protocol enters into force • AWG-KP established to discuss 'second commitment period' targets • 'Dialogue' launched on long-term cooperative action (LCA)	
2006	• Asia-Pacific Partnership on Clean Development and Climate (APP) launched	• India joins APP
2007	• G-8+5 Summit at Heiligendamm, Germany • IPCC Fourth Assessment Report • Bali Action Plan (BAP) adopted at CoP-13 • AWG-LCA established	• Prime Minister's Council on Climate Change (PMCCC) established • PM's pledge at Heiligendamm
2008	• AWG-KP and AWG-LCA sessions	• National Action Plan on Climate Change (NAPCC)

106 *Sengupta*

Table 7.1 Continued

Year	International events	Indian events
2009	• MEF Leaders Declaration at L'Aquila recognises '2 degree C' limit • CoP-15 'takes note of' Copenhagen Accord • AWG-KP and AWG-LCA mandates extended to CoP-16	• India signs MEF declaration • India announces voluntary 'emissions intensity' cut
2010	• 'Cancun Agreements' adopted at CoP-16 • AWG-KP and AWG-LCA negotiating extended to CoP-17	• Planning Commission establishes Expert Group on 'low carbon economy'

commenced, India took the lead in constructing a Southern coalition to develop a common developing country strategy on this issue. At a conference on 'global environmental issues' that it hosted in April 1990 – the first of its kind for developing countries – India succeeded in securing the general support of the South for its basic international positions on climate change. It was agreed at this meeting, for instance, that the primary responsibility for reducing GHG emissions belonged to the North; that no emission reduction obligations could be accepted by the South; and that the developed world would have to provide developing countries with both clean technology and finance to help them address this challenge.

Similarly, India also played a vital role in shaping the background conditions against which the INC negotiations were held. For example, the original draft of the IPCC's First Assessment Report had noted that both developed and developing countries had 'common responsibilities' on climate change. However, recognising that what got agreed to here could have significant implications for the future commitments that countries would have to accept, India worked closely with other developing nations to ensure that this was amended to become the 'common but differentiated responsibility' (CBDR) of industrialised and developing countries (Rajan, 1997, p. 108).[3] It also played a key role in determining what should be the 'appropriate' negotiating forum for conducting the convention negotiations. While many developed countries favoured using the IPCC itself, developing countries, led by India and Brazil, which had been unhappy with how the IPCC had gone about its work, insisted that the negotiations be conducted under the direct authority of the UN General Assembly via a separately-constituted INC that would ensure 'openness, transparency, universality and legitimacy' and the 'full participation' of all states (cited in Rajan, 1997).

Having helped to create a level-playing negotiating field, India went on to play a major role in shaping the substance of the Convention itself, which has been detailed elsewhere in this volume (see chapter by Dasgupta). Although it was not able to get everything that it wanted (such as agreement on 'per capita convergence'; concrete emission reduction commitments from the North; and technology transfer on 'preferential' terms), it was nevertheless successful in getting its preferred principles, norms and conditionalities (on 'equity'; 'CBDR'; 'new and additional' finance to cover 'agreed full incremental costs'; an 'equitable and balanced' financial mechanism; and especially Article 4.7) embedded within the UNFCCC to a significant extent. As the head of India's delegation to the INC later acknowledged, its main objective in the convention

International climate negotiations   107

negotiations was to ensure that the obligations imposed on developing countries like itself were 'minimal', and that 'differentiation' was maintained between developed and developing countries 'in all areas'. Overall, his assessment was that the outcome of the INC negotiations was 'entirely satisfactory' from India's point of view (Rajan, 1997, p. 151–2).

India's principal objective in the entire post-UNFCCC negotiations on climate change – from Rio right up to Copenhagen – has been to defend this 'differentiated' architecture of the climate regime that it had worked to inscribe within international law, and to ensure that no fresh legal obligations were placed on it. CoP-1 at Berlin in 1995 was the first major test of India's resolve in this regard. As noted by Dasgupta, some developed countries had called on developing countries to accept mitigation commitments during the INC negotiations itself. At CoP-1, a US-led coalition including Japan, Canada, Australia and New Zealand (JUSCANZ); and EU countries led by Germany, raised this issue again during the debate over 'adequacy' of commitments. Noting that climate change was a 'global problem' that needed 'broad international participation', they called on the 'more advanced' developing countries (code for China and India) to also accept mitigation commitments and for the establishment of 'new categories' in the UNFCCC beyond the 'developed/ developing' (Annex I/non-Annex I) divide (Oberthur and Ott, 1999). However, this was widely perceived by the South, which wanted the North to implement its own agreed commitments under the UNFCCC first, as a ploy to break their unity and shift the responsibility of tackling climate change to the developing world.

India used its coalition-building skills to considerable effect at this point to ward off this Northern demand. Observing that the EU and AOSIS countries were strongly in favour of a legally binding protocol with 'targets and timetables', while the JUSCANZ and OPEC countries were strongly opposed to the same, India convened a 'Green Group' of 72 like-minded developing states (including AOSIS but excluding OPEC), that jointly called for the development of a strong legal protocol but *without* any additional commitments for developing countries (Paterson, 1996). Leveraging the support of international climate NGOs, who also advocated a strong protocol, and were sympathetic to Southern concerns, India then impressed upon Germany and the EU that they would need to choose between having a strong protocol or additional commitments for the 'more advanced' developing countries. Ultimately, the India-led coalition succeeded in winning over the EU to its side and in persuading the JUSCANZ group to drop its insistence on additional developing country mitigation commitments. Consequently, the Berlin Mandate called for the development of a protocol with quantified emission reduction targets *only* for developed countries, and explicitly noted that the process should 'not introduce any new commitments' for developing countries (UNFCCC, 1995). This was a striking example of India's ability to engineer creative alliances and shape the climate negotiations to protect its own narrowly defined interests on this issue. Similarly, in the Kyoto Protocol negotiations between 1995 and 1997, India worked closely with other like-minded G-77 states, especially China, its long-standing ally on climate change, to exclude the concept of 'voluntary commitments' for developing countries, which several developed countries had now tried to introduce, and also in limiting the reach of the Kyoto 'flexible' mechanisms (Oberthur and Ott, 1999).

India was initially deeply sceptical of these flexible mechanisms and actively opposed their inclusion in the Kyoto Protocol. For instance, when discussions were first held

108 *Sengupta*

on the applicability of 'joint implementation' (JI) in developing countries after Rio, it viewed this primarily as another attempt by the North to avoid taking any serious domestic emission reductions of their own, and to 'lure' the South to do their mitigation for them on the cheap (Agarwal et al., 1999, p. 44). India feared that mechanisms like JI would not only shift the burden of tackling climate change to the developing world, but also that the South would be left disadvantaged in the future if they sold off their cheapest emission reduction options (or 'low hanging fruits') to the North (Parikh, 1995). To address these concerns, it was agreed at CoP-1 to set up a voluntary, non-crediting, 'pilot phase' for JI projects in developing countries (under the title of 'Activities Implemented Jointly'), whereby this mechanism could first be properly tested in the field. It was also agreed that a final decision on this would be taken only after a review of the pilot phase in 2000. However, in the Kyoto negotiations in 1997, the idea of JI in developing countries managed to resurface again under the guise of the 'clean development mechanism' (CDM), with the US cleverly managing to reformulate a separate Brazilian proposal on compliance to push it through. India, on its part, strongly opposed this subterfuge. However, with its ally, Brazil, now taking ownership of the CDM, it ultimately acquiesced to its inclusion in the Protocol.

However, it is important to note here that despite India's initial opposition to the concept, the CDM has been one of the few issue areas on which its thinking and policies have undergone a complete turn-around over time, from opposition to support. By the time of the Marrakesh Accords in 2001, India had begun to realise that it could significantly gain from this new mechanism. This was partly born out of a recognition that CDM projects were, after all, not very different from the sort of 'contractual commitments' that India was anyway willing to accept even during the INC negotiations (see Dasgupta, this volume). It was also facilitated by the entry of new policymakers in government who actively supported India's participation in the new mechanism, and the work of organisations like The Energy and Resources Institute (TERI), Development Alternatives and the Confederation of Indian Industry (CII), who argued that JI/CDM could be a useful conduit for Indian industry to gain external technology and finance (Jakobsen, 1998; Das, this volume). Consequently, India played an active role in designing the principles, rules and institutions governing the CDM, ensuring that it could benefit the most from them. The fact that India accounted for over 20 per cent of total CDM projects registered worldwide by the UNFCCC by the end of 2010, with its private sector actively engaged in this process, is both a testament to how much it has gained from this mechanism, and also why it continues to actively support its inclusion, and further expansion, in any future climate regime (UNFCCC, 2010a; MoEF, 2009). Apart from the CDM, another important area where India made a major contribution in the post-Kyoto negotiations was on 'climate adaptation', which it helped to prioritise, particularly at CoP-8 in New Delhi in 2002.

Following the entry into force of the Kyoto Protocol in 2005, when the debate increasingly began to turn to what would happen to the international climate regime post-2012, India remained an active, if cautious, participant in these discussions. Although it engaged in various bilateral and multilateral arenas on this issue, including in non-UN fora like the US-led Asia-Pacific Partnership (APP), it repeatedly emphasised that the UNFCCC was the only legitimate forum where formal negotiations on this topic could be conducted. This was also a time when concerted pressure began to be applied by the North on emerging developing countries, especially China and India, to do more on climate change. This was manifested most prominently by Northern

International climate negotiations 109

attempts to shift the focus of the climate debate from the question of who was responsible for the 'stock' of past global emissions to who would be responsible for their future 'flow' (see Jayaraman et al., this volume).

Drawing on the fact that India's total emissions had grown by 97 per cent between 1990 and 2004, which was noted to be 'one of the highest rates of increase in the world' (UNDP, 2007, p. 152); and that China had, in 2007, surpassed the US as the world's largest aggregate emitter of GHGs, a number of developed countries forcefully argued that no long-term solution to climate change could be found without the active participation of these fast-growing developing states. Moreover, with India projected to become the world's third largest GHG emitter by 2015, and the energy use of both China and India expected to more than double between 2005 and 2030 (IEA, 2007), they asserted that anything that developed countries did to reduce their own emissions would simply be neutralised by the actions of these emerging economic giants. These points were repeatedly articulated by Western leaders and amplified widely across the world by the global media.

In an effort to counter this growing drumbeat of views that countries like India were not acting responsibly on climate change, India's Prime Minister, Manmohan Singh, sought to restate and defend the legitimacy of the country's position at the G8+5 Summit held in Heiligendamm, Germany in June 2007. Noting that its GHG emissions were 'among the lowest in per-capita terms', and accounted for 'only around 4% of the world's emissions' even when considered in aggregate terms, Singh stressed that India 'recognise[d] wholeheartedly' its 'responsibilities as a developing country' and would 'add [its] weight to global efforts to preserve and protect the environment'. While he noted that the time was 'not ripe' for developing countries to take on 'quantitative targets', he made a unilateral and voluntary announcement that India's 'per-capita GHG emissions' would never 'exceed' that of the developed world (Singh, 2007). Although significant in some ways, this carefully worded pledge was, however, essentially consistent with India's longstanding position that 'per capita convergence' was the only equitable long-term solution to climate change, and hence did not reflect a major change in its international stance on this issue.

India also played a prominent role in the negotiation of the Bali Action Plan in December 2007. Since this was a crucial document that would guide future negotiations, it worked closely with other developing countries to ensure that its content remained consistent with the framework and principles of the UNFCCC and Kyoto Protocol as far as possible. In particular, it tried to ensure that a clear 'differentiation' was maintained between what developed and developing countries would each be required to do on climate mitigation in the future, and in the conditions under which any international measurement, reporting and verification (MRV) of developing country mitigation actions would be permitted. The two years between Bali and Copenhagen were essentially a period of North–South deadlock in climate negotiations. Although the Indian government took a number of significant steps domestically during this period, which signalled the growing importance that it accorded to tackling this issue – including the establishment of a Prime Minister's Council on Climate Change (PMCCC) in June 2007, the appointment of a Special Envoy of the Prime Minister, and the launch of a National Action Plan on Climate Change (NAPCC) in June 2008 – its international position remained largely unaltered.

The first signs of change in India's foreign policy on climate change were seen in July 2009, when Prime Minister Manmohan Singh signed the MEF Leaders Declaration on

110 *Sengupta*

Energy and Climate at a meeting held alongside the G-8 Summit in L'Aquila, Italy. The declaration specifically recognised, for the first time, that the rise in global temperature 'ought not to exceed 2 degrees C', and that MEF countries would work together to identify a 'global goal' to reduce 'global emissions by 2050' (MEF, 2009). While only a political declaration, and not legally binding, India's signing on to this '2 degree C' limit nevertheless signalled its willingness to concede, in theory at least, an implicit cap on its future emissions, even though this was left ambiguous and unstated (Ramachandran, 2009).

However, the fact that India's political leadership was now seriously reconsidering its international stand on climate change became further clear when Jairam Ramesh, the country's new Minister for Environment and Forests, actively attempted to reframe India's traditional position on this issue in the six months leading up to the Copenhagen Summit. Stressing repeatedly that India was highly vulnerable to climate change, and also that it needed to be seen internationally as 'a leader, as a proactive player, as somebody who is shaping the solution' on this issue, Ramesh argued that it was now in the country's own interest to go beyond its original 'per capita convergence' position, and adopt a more aggressive 'per-capita plus' approach, whereby specific 'performance targets' could be assigned through domestic legislation or executive action to key sectors of the country's economy – energy, transportation, industry, etc. – to help reduce their emissions (Ghosh, 2009). He also suggested taking a more flexible stand on the question of allowing external reviews of India's domestic mitigation actions, including through more frequent and detailed national communications to the UNFCCC, and even IMF/WTO-style reviews (Sethi, 2009).

These new ideas provoked a great deal of domestic debate in the country, including within government, which saw strong concerns about the seemingly unilateral nature of these concessions being expressed by senior members of India's official climate negotiating team itself (TNN, 2009). It also led to India's foreign policy on climate change being extensively debated in Parliament on at least three separate occasions (see Chapter 17 on Parliamentary debates, this volume). In the final parliamentary debate held just prior to CoP-15, the Environment Minister declared that India would go to Copenhagen with a 'positive frame of mind' and prepared to be 'flexible', but stressed there were three 'non-negotiables' that it would not compromise on: (1) it would not accept any 'legally binding emission reduction cut'; (2) it would not accept any 'peaking year'; and (3) it would not allow unsupported mitigation actions to be subject to the same type of scrutiny as those that were externally supported. He also announced – in a clear shift of position from the pre-Kyoto days, and even from the Prime Minister's 2007 statement at Heiligendamm – that India would voluntarily reduce the 'emissions intensity' of its GDP by 20–25 per cent by 2020 compared to its 2005 level through domestic mitigation actions, arguing that to do so would be in India's own best interests, and would help to strengthen its hand in future climate negotiations (Lok Sabha, 2009).

At CoP-15 in Copenhagen, India coordinated extremely closely with a core group of similarly placed large developing countries (China, Brazil and South Africa) through the newly-formed BASIC group to jointly resist the mounting pressure that they now each came under from a largely unified, US-led, North. The latter insisted that the BASIC states not only accept stronger mitigation commitments but also that the Kyoto Protocol, which they considered as deeply flawed, be replaced by a new, 'undifferentiated', international agreement on climate change, where all major GHG emitters, developed and developing alike, would have similar mitigation obligations subject to similar levels of scrutiny.

This Northern attempt to bypass the Kyoto Protocol, and dilute the foundational norm of 'differentiation' that had been built into the UNFCCC, was strongly opposed by the BASIC group and most other developing countries. It was in this intractable situation that the 'Copenhagen Accord' was uneasily born on the final night of CoP-15, as a last-minute compromise between the BASIC countries and the US at their heads-of-state level. In the Accord negotiations, India worked actively to ensure that none of the three 'non-negotiables' that it had promised to its Parliament were fundamentally violated, although its success in this regard was questioned post-Copenhagen (see Chapter 17 on Parliamentary debates, this volume). India also played a major role in brokering agreement on the sensitive question of MRV by suggesting the alternative language of 'international consultations and analysis' to review unsupported developing country mitigation actions (Chauhan, 2010). The BASIC group collectively also ensured that some of the fundamental principles and provisions of the UNFCCC (such as 'CBDR'; 'equity'; 'new and additional' finance; and recognition for the 'over-riding priorities' of poverty eradication and development) were suitably acknowledged and referenced in the Accord (UNFCCC, 2010b). A 'differentiated' framework for recording the 'quantified economy-wide emissions targets' of developed countries and the 'nationally appropriate mitigation actions' of developing countries that both agreed to submit under the Accord was also ensured. The BASIC group also succeeded in getting the negotiating mandates of both the KP- and LCA-AWGs extended to CoP-16.

Following Copenhagen, India has continued to reiterate its seriousness in tackling climate change. At the domestic level, its Planning Commission constituted an Expert Group in January 2010 to prepare a strategy for a 'low-carbon economy' for India that could be integrated into its Twelfth Five-Year Plan process over the 2012–17 period. Several state governments also launched or announced state-level action plans to combat climate change. India also officially communicated its willingness to be associated with the Copenhagen Accord, and for the voluntary emissions intensity reduction target that it had announced earlier to be internationally recorded. At CoP-16 in Mexico, during the negotiation of the Cancun Agreements, India played a particularly notable role in attempting to bridge the gap between developed and developing nations, especially on 'equity', 'international consultations and analysis', and the 'technology mechanism'. Furthermore, Environment Minister Ramesh also signalled India's willingness to consider altering the voluntary nature of its mitigation pledges in the future, suggesting in his address to the plenary that 'all countries must take on binding commitments in an appropriate legal form' (Ramesh, 2010).

As in the lead up to Copenhagen, some of these recent moves made by India at Cancun have been the subject of intense domestic scrutiny. Leading environmental activists and opposition parties have both questioned the logic of these seemingly unilateral concessions, as have some prominent former negotiators who have even characterised them as a capitulation of India's national interests (NDTV, 2010; Dasgupta, 2011). However, these shifts have also garnered considerable international and some domestic praise (PTI, 2010). Even as climate negotiations remain in play, what is clear is that India's foreign policy thinking on climate change is presently at a moment of change. In terms of understanding what is driving these shifts, a comprehensive analysis is not possible in the brief space available here. But the following

112 *Sengupta*

section notes some key historical and analytical factors that can help to understand and explain India's evolving foreign policy behaviour on climate change.

Explaining India's foreign policy behaviour on climate change

First of all, it is important to understand that India's international behaviour on climate change has deep historical roots, and has been intimately shaped by how it has conceptualised its overall national interest over time. India's primary national purpose, after independence in 1947, was to eradicate its deep-rooted poverty and achieve modernisation and development by following the well-trodden Western model of industrialisation and economic growth. At the international level, its foreign policy traditionally rested on a determination to safeguard its post-colonial sovereignty, maximise its space for autonomous action, and regain what it considered to be its 'rightful place' in the world (Saran, 2006). Through policies based on 'non-alignment' and Third World solidarity it also consistently sought to improve the post-1945 international economic and political order into which it had emerged, and which it viewed as being deeply flawed and skewed against developing country interests.

It was against this backdrop that when global environmental issues first emerged on the international agenda in the early 1970s, framed by the West as a need for 'limits to growth' (Meadows et al., 1972), that India, and other developing countries, took it as an unfair, even neo-colonial, Northern attempt to thwart the South's development aspirations, and to interfere in their domestic resource-use choices and policies. Taking up the cudgels on behalf of the global South, India helped to reframe the international discourse and norms on global environmental protection at the time, first as 'environment *and* development', and then as 'sustainable development' (Desai, 2007; Gandhi, 1972). When the more specific issues of ozone layer depletion, biodiversity conservation and climate change entered the intergovernmental agenda in the late 1980s, it was this same basic concern to safeguard the country's developmental interests and its sovereignty from external interference that drove India's foreign policies on these issues. On climate change, in particular, there was a realisation, very early on within government itself, that any international agreement to curb GHG emissions, which were intrinsically connected to national energy use, economic growth and development, would not just be an environmental treaty but rather a 'major multilateral economic agreement', where '[t]he sharing of costs and benefits implied . . . could significantly alter the *economic destinies* of individual countries' (Dasgupta, 1994, p. 131, emphasis added).

This particular interest-based conceptualisation, coupled with an equally strong normative sentiment that tackling climate change was not the responsibility of the South since it was a problem caused primarily by the North, played an important role in determining India's initial international responses to it. Another key factor that influenced India's behaviour during the INC negotiations was the extremely weak and vulnerable position that it found itself in following its economic crisis of 1991. This was a time when the Cold War had just ended, and the US-led Western world was at the peak of its 'unipolar' moment. Under these unfavourable circumstances, it was entirely rational for India's negotiators to use principled arguments based on equity and justice, and adopt Southern coalition strategies, to ensure a climate regime that had minimal obligations for India, and which did not constrain its future development prospects or foreign policy ambitions in any significant manner. Among other factors, a key reason why India was able to successfully secure much of what it wanted in the

International climate negotiations   113

UNFCCC was because the environment was one of the few issue areas at the time on which the South had any meaningful leverage vis-à-vis the more powerful North.

Reasons for continuity

Regarding the subsequent continuity seen in India's foreign policies on climate change from Rio right up to Copenhagen, there are at least four additional factors that helped to contribute to this. First, even though a clear North–South bargain had been struck at Rio in 1992 on how to tackle climate change, there was little movement from the North to actually deliver on its promises, either in terms of reducing its own GHG emissions, or in providing technology and finance to the South. On the contrary, the entire effort of the North, from CoP-1 onwards, seemed focused on undoing and revising the terms of the original Rio deal. In this situation, there was little reason for India to unilaterally change its foreign policy on this issue, especially now that it had international law on its side.

Second, for most of this 20-year period, there was a general domestic consensus within India (among government negotiators; political parties; environmental NGOs; business groups; scientists; and the media) that India's external position on climate change was legitimate and valid, and did not require any changing. One of the striking features that illustrates this pan-national feeling is that even environmental NGOs that actively criticised the government's domestic environmental policies at home, rallied to strongly defend its foreign policies on climate change abroad. For instance, the Centre for Science and Environment (CSE), a New Delhi-based environmental NGO, played a critical role in providing some of the most persuasive normative arguments used by the Indian government in the climate negotiations (Agarwal and Narain, 1991), and in marshalling support for its positions among international climate NGO networks at key junctures.

A third reason for the long continuity in India's climate foreign policy stems from the nature of the policymaking apparatus and process itself. Formulating India's external climate policy has traditionally been the preserve of a relatively small group of serving and retired government officials and diplomats, who have been engaged in climate negotiations since its earliest days, and who believe they are right, and have found little reason to change their worldviews and normative positions on this issue over time. Linked to this is also the generally limited role that science and scientists, barring some exceptions, have played in determining India's official policies on climate change over the years. Notwithstanding the successive IPCC reports, economic and developmental considerations, and not environmental concerns or science, have been the predominant forces that have driven India's external thinking and policies on this issue. Moreover, given limited governmental capacity, the natural tendency of the Indian state and its bureaucracy has been to stick to existing defensible positions rather than venture out into new uncertain territory.

Finally, an important structural reason for the continuity seen in India's foreign policy on climate change is the inherent nature of the international system itself, where the primary motivation of all states has been to safeguard their own economic competitiveness, and their relative positions in the hierarchy of nations, rather than to collectively and meaningfully address the problem of climate change. Given the underlying power/interest-driven logics and bargaining that have underpinned climate negotiations, India has often had little option but to defend its turf on this issue.

114 *Sengupta*

Reasons for change

However, as this chapter shows, India's foreign policy on climate change has now transitioned into a very significant period of change. While the most immediate and visible reason for this is the ascendancy of new policy makers in government, such as Ramesh, who have significantly differing worldviews, threat perceptions, and normative commitments on this issue than those who have traditionally been in charge of Indian climate policymaking, it is important to note that there are at least four deeper structural forces driving this shift as well.

First, domestic consensus on this issue within India is no longer as solid as it used to be, with dissenting voices questioning the sagacity of India's traditional stand emerging from not only academia, civil society and other interest groups, but also from within Parliament itself (Rajamani, 2007; see also Chapters 12, 14 and 17 this volume). This, in part, has been driven by growing scientific knowledge on climate change, and increased awareness of the risks that it poses particularly to a country such as India.

Second, India itself has changed considerably over the last two decades. From being in a position of severe economic vulnerability at the end of the Cold War in 1991, it has now emerged as a powerful economic and political actor on the global stage. While this has, on the one hand, led to increased calls by the North for countries like India and China to do more on climate change, especially as their emissions rise; it has, crucially, also led to India's own political leadership reappraising the necessity of pursuing an entirely defensive external strategy on this issue. Although climate foreign policy-making remains contested within government, there is a growing sentiment within powerful sections of India's political and policy-making establishment that a rising, more confident, India should be more willing to shed its hard-line image as a 'naysayer' in international negotiations as it assumes a position of greater power and responsibility in the world, not just on climate change but across other areas of global governance as well (Narlikar, 2006). This has also been enabled by a growing sense that taking proactive action on climate change can position India well to benefit from the emerging growth and business opportunities in clean technology, and to transition to a new more efficient and energy-secure form of development.

Third, the fact that its fellow emerging powers in the international system – China, Brazil and South Africa – all announced voluntary mitigation targets of their own prior to Copenhagen, generated considerable 'peer pressure' on India to do so as well. This was further driven by a fear that unless India was seen to be acting progressively on this issue, it could be isolated and blamed internationally in the event of failure, which would risk its reputation and desire to be seen as a globally responsible state.

Finally, it is clear that the changing configuration of global geopolitical alliances has also impacted India's thinking and policies on this issue. Some have critiqued and attributed the recent shifts in India's climate change policies to the growing bilateral ties between the United States and India in particular, evidenced most powerfully by the 2005 Indo–US nuclear deal (see Raghunandan, Chapter 12, this volume). However, a different way of looking at this would be to note that these increasing ties have opened up new avenues for practical collaboration and mutual gain, and thereby made it less logical for India today to simply pursue a line of uni-dimensional opposition to the US and the wider developed world on climate change.

However, rather than any single factor, it is ultimately the cumulative effect of all of these different drivers, catalysed by the intense global pressure and expectations brought about by the Copenhagen Summit, that helped to crystallise these changes in

India's international climate policy. Yet, it is important to note that these incipient policy changes are still quite fragile, and, given the continued domestic opposition, they are by no means irreversible, especially as the underlying logics for continuing with the traditional stance are simultaneously also at play. Whether or not the recent shifts will be sustained will depend on a number of factors, including the personalities involved, how the future negotiations go, and the reciprocity that is shown.

Conclusion

As the world's second most populous nation, an emerging economic powerhouse, and a significant future emitter of GHGs, India will undoubtedly continue to remain a major force in international climate negotiations in the future. As this chapter has shown, India played a key role in developing the architecture, norms and rules of the climate regime in the past in ways that suited its own interests, and that of its coalition partners. The future role that India plays will also be determined to a large extent by how it chooses to define its interests and partners on this issue.

Looking back over the last twenty years, arguably the single most notable achievement of Indian climate negotiators was that they succeeded in building an international climate regime that secured 'legal cover' and 'bought time' for India to proceed on unrestricted economic development, at a time when it needed it the most. The generally defensive role that India then played in successive years can also be justified, by some normative standards at least, by the North's consistent refusal to honour the commitments that it made under international law.

Nevertheless, given the continued deadlock on this issue, and the inability of the South (despite the growing clout of BASIC) to coerce the North to deliver on its promises, it now seems prudent for countries like India to take pause and reappraise their strategies on this issue. Although it still has a long way to go before it achieves its full developmental aspirations, there is no doubt that India is a richer and more powerful country today than it was 20 years ago. On the one hand, this has increased its ability to hold its ground and resist Northern revisionism if necessary, as was partially demonstrated at Copenhagen. Yet, on the other hand, India's emergence as one of the key powers of the 21st century has also generated greater global expectations of it playing its full part as a responsible member of international society – a role that it has always valued and held dear, and ostensibly attempted to fulfil at Cancun. Moreover, it may be argued that India has already substantially reaped the benefits of its past foreign policies on climate change, and that, now, as a more secure power, it needs to pragmatically weigh their continuity against a range of other foreign policy objectives and priorities that may also be of interest and value to it.

Apart from such *realpolitik* considerations, of course, is also the very real fact that India cannot afford to ignore the emergence of new scientific evidence on climate change, and the pressing question of its own vulnerability. Equally, it cannot afford to ignore domestic voices that may be at variance with its traditional stance on this issue, or even critical external views (see Huq and Metz, this volume, for instance), especially if these are driven by better and more legitimate arguments, and a genuine concern for India's long-term welfare and interests. As international climate negotiations enter a new and uncertain phase, India thus faces a complex array of choices and trade-offs on this issue. What is vital is that these choices and trade-offs are made in an intelligent, balanced and reasoned manner, based on widespread consultation and the best available evidence, rather than on either dogma or whim.

116 *Sengupta*

If India's national interest on climate change is to be best served, then it must combine aggressive domestic action to combat climate change with tough and clear-eyed bargaining in its international negotiations. Equally, as it attempts to play a new 'bridging role' between the North and South, India needs to manage its various alliances, old and new, in a sensible manner, based obviously on its own interests, but also keeping in mind its professed values of securing a fairer international order that will protect weaker nations against the strong. However, in the ultimate analysis, any decision that India takes on climate change will be judged primarily by how much and how quickly it enables the country to leapfrog to a smarter, sustainable and technologically superior developmental pathway that advances the future well-being and prosperity of all its citizens, and enhances the overall security and prestige of the country. It is these criteria that should guide it forward on this issue.

Notes

1 The author would like to thank the editor and other contributors to this volume for their valuable feedback.
2 Under 'emissions trading', developed countries are permitted to buy and sell excess emission allowances from each other to help meet their Kyoto targets. Under 'joint implementation' they are allowed to invest in emission reduction projects in other developed countries and gain credits in exchange to help meet their own targets. Under the 'clean development mechanism', they are allowed to gain credits by investing in emission reduction projects in developing countries. For more details, see: http://unfccc.int/.
3 This notion of 'differentiation', which was extremely important for India, was subsequently integrated into the UNFCCC in the form of the principle of 'common but differentiated responsibilities and respective capabilities', which became the core foundational norm of the treaty (see also Rajamani, this volume).

References

Agarwal, A. and Narain, S. (1991) *Global Warming in an Unequal World: A Case of Environmental Colonialism*, Centre for Science and Environment, New Delhi.

Agarwal, A., Narain, S. and Sharma, A. (eds) (1999) *Green Politics: Global Environmental Negotiations 1*, Centre for Science and Environment, New Delhi.

Chauhan, C. (2010) 'US, China close in on carbon accord', *Hindustan Times*, 3 December.

Dasgupta, C. (1994) 'The Climate Change Negotiations', in I. M. Mintzer and J. A. Leonard (eds) *Negotiating Climate Change: The Inside Story of the Rio Convention*, Cambridge University Press, Cambridge.

Dasgupta, C. (2011) 'Sweet Surrender: Jairam Ramesh has turned India's climate change policy on its head', *The Telegraph*, 17 January.

Desai, N. (2007) 'Sustainable Development', in K. Basu (ed.) *The Oxford Companion to Economics in India*, Oxford University Press, Delhi.

Gandhi, I. (1972) 'Man and Environment', Address to the Plenary Session of the United Nations Conference on the Human Environment, Stockholm, 14 June.

Ghosh, P. (2009) 'I want to position India as a proactive player: Jairam Ramesh', *Mint*, 29 September.

Hurrell, A. and Woods, N. (eds) (1999) *Inequality, Globalization, and World Politics*, Oxford University Press, Oxford.

IEA (2007) *World Energy Outlook: China and India Insights*, International Energy Agency, Paris.

IPCC (1990, 1995, 2001, 2007) *The IPCC Assessment Reports*, Intergovernmental Panel on Climate Change, Geneva, Switzerland.

Jakobsen, S. (1998) 'India's Position on Climate Change from Rio to Kyoto: A Policy Analysis', *CDR Working Paper 98.11*, Centre for Development Research, Copenhagen.

Khor, M. (2010) 'Complex Implications of the Cancun Climate Conference', *Economic & Political Weekly*, Vol. XLV, No. 52, pp. 10–15.

Lok Sabha (2009) *Transcript of the Minister's Response in the Lok Sabha*, Parliament of India, New Delhi, 3 December, pp. 228–47.

Meadows, D. H., Meadows, D. L., Randers, J. and Behrens, W. W. (1972) *The Limits to Growth*, Universe Books, New York.

MEF (2009) *Declaration of the Leaders of the Major Economies Forum on Energy and Climate*, L'Aquila, Italy, 9 July.

MoEF (2009) *Climate Change Negotiations: India's submissions to the United Nations Framework Convention on Climate Change*, Ministry of Environment and Forests, Government of India, New Delhi.

Narlikar, A. (2006) 'Peculiar Chauvinism or Strategic Calculation: Explaining the Negotiation Strategy of a Rising India', *International Affairs*, Vol. 82, No. 1, pp. 77–94.

NDTV (2010) 'BJP, Left slam Jairam Ramesh on shift in climate stand', 10 December.

Oberthur, S. and Ott, H. E. (1999) *The Kyoto Protocol: International Climate Policy for the 21st Century*, Springer, Berlin.

Parikh, J. (1995) 'North–South Cooperation in Climate Change through Joint Implementation', *International Environmental Affairs*, Vol. 7, No. 1, pp. 22–43.

Paterson, M. (1996) *Global Warming and Global Politics*, Routledge, London.

PTI (2010) 'Cancun talks: Germany praises Jairam Ramesh', *Business Standard*, 13 December.

Rajamani, L. (2007) 'India's Negotiating Position on Climate Change: Legitimate but Not Sagacious', *CPR Issue Brief*, No. 2, Centre for Policy Research, New Delhi.

Rajan, M. G. (1997) *Global Environmental Politics: India and the North–South Politics of Global Environmental Issues*, Oxford University Press, Delhi.

Ramachandran, R. (2009) 'Climate Change and the Indian stand', *The Hindu*, 28 July.

Ramesh, J. (2010) *Letter to Members of Parliament on the Cancun Agreements*, 17 December.

Saran, S. (2006) 'Present Dimensions of the Indian Foreign Policy', Address by Foreign Secretary, *Shanghai Institute of International Studies*, China, 11 January.

Sethi, N. (2009) 'India ready for global scrutiny on emissions', *Times of India*, 28 September.

Singh, M. (2007) 'PM's Intervention on Climate Change at the Heiligendamm Meeting of G8 plus 5', 8 June 2007.

TNN (2009) 'Jairam persuades negotiators to join climate talks', *Times of India*, 7 December.

UN (2007) 'Secretary-General Ban Ki-Moon's address to the Intergovernmental Panel on Climate Change in Valencia', United Nations, Department of Public Information, New York, 17 November.

UNDP (2007) 'Fighting Climate Change: Human Solidarity in a Divided World', *Human Development Report 2007/2008*, Palgrave Macmillan, Basingstoke.

UNFCCC (1992) *United Nations Framework Convention on Climate Change*.

UNFCCC (1995) 'Berlin Mandate', Decision 1/CP.1 in FCCC/1995/7/Add.1, 6 June.

UNFCCC (1997) *Kyoto Protocol to the United Nations Framework Convention on Climate Change*.

UNFCCC (2006) 'Dialogue on long-term cooperative action', Decision 1/CP.11 in FCCC/CP/2005/5/Add.1, 30 March.

UNFCCC (2008) 'Bali Action Plan', Decision 1/CP.13 in FCCC/CP/2007/6/Add.1, 14 March.

UNFCCC (2010a) 'Registered Projects by Host Party', *CDM Statistics*, http://cdm.unfccc.int/Statistics/index.html, accessed 28 December 2010.

UNFCCC (2010b) 'Copenhagen Accord', Decision 2/CP.15 in FCCC/CP/2009/11/Add.1, 30 March.

UNGA (1988) *United Nations General Assembly Resolution 43/53*, 6 December.

UNGA (1989) *United Nations General Assembly Resolution 44/207*, 22 December.

UNGA (1990) *United Nations General Assembly Resolution 45/212*, 21 December.

8 The reach and limits of the principle of common but differentiated responsibilities and respective capabilities in the climate change regime[1]

Lavanya Rajamani

Introduction

The principle of common but differentiated responsibilities and respective capabilities (CBDRRC)[2] has, from the inception of the climate dialogue, underpinned the efforts of the international community to address climate change. At the Second World Climate Conference, 1990, countries recognized that the 'principle of equity and common but differentiated responsibility of countries should be the basis of any global response to climate change' (Hague Declaration, 1989; Noordwijk Declaration, 1989; Second World Climate Conference, 1990, paragraph 5). This principle finds reflection in the Framework Convention on Climate Change (UNFCCC, 1992) and is the basis of the burden sharing arrangements crafted under the FCCC and its Kyoto Protocol (UNFCCC, 1997b). The CBDRRC principle is also highlighted in numerous FCCC Conference of Parties (COP) decisions (Berlin Mandate, 1995; Bali Action Plan, 2007; Cancun Agreements, 2010), as well as the controversial Copenhagen Accord, 2009. Yet, the core content of the CBDRRC principle, the nature of the obligation it entails, as well the applications it lends itself to, are deeply contested, which in turn raises questions about its legal status and operational significance. This chapter explores the debates surrounding the constituent elements of the CBDRRC principle which shed light on the legal status and operational significance of the CBDRRC principle, as well as the ability (or lack thereof) of this principle to offer substantive guidance to Parties in the design of the post-2012 climate regime.

Dissecting the CBDRRC principle

Beneath the surface of the seemingly authoritative and intuitively attractive CBDRRC principle that India, among other developing countries, relies on in the climate process, lie a host of contestations. These contestations are best explored by dissecting the CBDRRC principle into its constituent elements. Such a dissection will help flesh out the core content of the principle as well as determine the nature of the obligation it entails, both of which, as will be evident, are contested, and subject to differing interpretations.

Common but differentiated responsibilities 119

'Principle'

Although, the term 'principle' appears to signify a high level of legal authority, principles are of various kinds, from the merely aspirational to the legally binding. At its most basic 'when we say that a particular principle is a principle of law we mean that the principle is one which officials must take into account if it is relevant as a consideration' (Dworkin, 1977, pp. 24–27). While a principle may sway decision-makers in a particular direction it does not necessitate a predetermined action. In this sense it is open-ended (Bodansky, 1993, pp. 501–502). Depending on a series of factors a principle of law could be given more or less weight. The debate surrounding the negotiation of FCCC Article 3 and the US efforts to circumscribe its legal effect is illustrative of this point (Bodansky, 1993, p. 502, footnote 308). As a result of the United States-sponsored alterations to the text of FCCC Article 3 during its nego-tiation, the notion of CBDRRC within the FCCC cannot technically be termed a 'principle'; it is couched in discretionary and guiding rather than prescriptive language and applies only to Parties in relation to the FCCC (Bodansky, 1993, p. 502, footnote 308).

This is not to suggest that 'principles', even where circumscribed as in the CBDRRC case, have limited legal gravitas. As, the International Court of Justice (ICJ) in the *Gabcikovo-Nagymaros* case noted 'new norms and standards have been developed, set forth in a great number of instruments during the last two decades. Such new norms have to be taken into consideration and such standards given proper weight.'[3] What constitutes 'proper' weight, and how the principle must be 'taken into consideration' will depend on context and circumstance, which in turn leaves room for negotiation between Parties.

'Common'

The notion of 'common' responsibility derives from the notions of 'common concern' (Inter-American Tropical Tuna Convention, 1949, preamble), 'common heritage of mankind' (GA, 1970; UNCLOS, 1982, preamble) and 'province of mankind' (Outer Space Treaty, 1967, Article 1), notions as old as international environmental law itself. The Rio treaties, the Convention on Biological Diversity and the FCCC recognize biological diversity and climate change, respectively, as matters of 'common concern' to humankind (Convention on Biological Diversity, 1992, preamble; UNFCCC, 1992, preamble). The precise legal import of these different notions varies, but, in their use of language signifying a global interest, they form the backdrop to our discussion on 'common responsibility'.

The significance of a term such as 'common concern' or 'common responsibility' in a treaty is that it could arguably give all parties a collective and individual interest in the enforcement of the treaty (GA, 2002, Article 48). Article 48 of the Articles on State Responsibility recognizes that states, by virtue of their participation in a multilateral regime or as a consequence of their membership in the international community, have a legal interest in the performance of certain multilateral obligations.[4] As such it recognizes the right of states to protect and enforce obligations entered into in the collective interest. Terms akin to 'common concern' indicate the existence of collective interest and arguably create *erga omnes* (towards all) obligations. Some scholars suggest that the *erga omnes* character of 'common concern' treaties should be viewed

120 Rajamani

less as an issue of standing before the ICJ and more as a method for the international community to hold individual states accountable before the institutions created by the respective treaties (Birnie, Boyle and Redgwell, 2009, pp. 131–132). Indeed, treaties under which accountability or compliance mechanisms have been created recognize the right of every state to report a defaulting state to the compliance committee (UNEP, 1998, paragraph 1; UNFCCC, 2002, paragraph VI (1) (b)).

It could be argued, more generally, that 'common concern' treaties, with the attendant notion of *erga omnes* obligations, create greater accountability in the regime-building process as well as function as levers for moral suasion. 'Common concern' treaties create greater accountability for they legitimize an interest in, opinion on, and the right to question the polluting behaviour of states. It is not open to countries to shield their national actions from the international gaze, to claim that it is their sovereign right to pollute as they will, or to justify national measures on the ground that, in their sovereign wisdom, they consider it an adequate response to a global problem. While this obligation may yet be sourced to customary international law,[5] 'common concern' treaties demand this and more. They require states, *inter alia*, to take actions, driven by a sense of common destiny, rather than national interest; to take the global nature of the problem into account in national policy-making, state practice and negotiating positions; and, to arrive at outcomes which reflect progressive solidarity on a global environmental problem, rather than horse-trading between multiple vested interests. Where a state does not reach this standard of behaviour, 'common concern' treaties recognize the right of other states to at least remind the state of its obligations. This is in effect a 'diplomatic form of a solidarity measure' (Bodansky, Crook and Crawford, 2002, p. 881).

'But'

A few words about the significance of the chosen coordinating conjunction, 'but', in this principle: the use of the conjunction 'but' signals a distinction between the 'common' responsibility that states share and the 'differentiated' responsibility that particular states have. To appreciate the significance of the use of this conjunction, it might be worth considering an alternative such as 'and'. Should Parties have chosen to use the conjunction 'and', it would have signalled that the latter ('differentiated' responsibility) is chronologically sequential or a result of the former ('common' responsibility). Clearly this was considered not to be the case. This can be read to suggest that the basis for 'common' responsibility is different from the basis for 'differentiated' responsibility. And, indeed even the term 'responsibility', as will be evident from the discussion below, has different meanings in different contexts. Arguably the 'common' responsibility states share flows from 'common concern' – 'responsibility' in this context is akin to a moral duty. 'Differentiated' responsibility on the other hand flows from, as will be argued below, from causal agency in creating the problem and the fruits (i.e. 'capabilities') of those actions that caused the problem.

'Differentiated' – based on contribution to environmental harm and/or 'respective capabilities'

The term 'differentiated' signals the need for differentiation between Parties, but the principle explicitly indicates only one basis for such differentiation – 'respective

Common but differentiated responsibilities 121

capabilities'. There is, however, another basis for differentiation implicit in this principle.

In the eighties, in the process leading up to Rio,[6] and at Rio, in particular in the climate negotiations (Hague Declaration, 1989; Noordwijk Declaration, 1989; Second World Climate Conference, 1990, paragraph 5), there was a growing,[7] albeit not universal acknowledgement,[8] of industrial country contributions to the global environmental crisis. This acknowledgement was articulated as the CBDR principle in Rio Principle 7. Rio Principle 7 by its terms assigns a leadership role to industrial countries based on their enhanced contribution to environmental degradation. The terms of FCCC Article 3 are, however, less clear. FCCC Article 3, unlike Rio Principle 7, contains no reference to the enhanced contributions of industrial countries to global environmental degradation, and it places both common but differentiated responsibilities and respective capabilities on the same plane. While it could be argued that the FCCC's use of the phrase 'common but differentiated responsibilities' is enriched by Rio Principle 7, and therefore the FCCC incorporates some level of contribution-based responsibility, at least some industrial country negotiators believed that by excluding the specific language of contribution they had contrived to make such an interpretation of Article 3 implausible (Biniaz, 2002, p. 366). During the negotiations most industrial countries opposed the inclusion of Article 3 in the FCCC as it could potentially introduce a note of uncertainty into the context of FCCC obligations. When it became clear that an article on principles would be included, they opposed language pertaining to contribution to environmental degradation. Further, the United States introduced various amendments to circumscribe the legal potential of Article 3 and ensure that the principles, unofficially so titled, applied only to the parties and only in relation to the FCCC, not as general law (Bodansky, 1993).

The ambiguity created in the notion of CBDR due to the differing terms of FCCC Article 3 and Rio Principle 7 has resulted in two incompatible views on the basis on which responsibilities between Parties are 'differentiated'. One, that the CBDR principle 'is based on the differences that exist with regard to the level of economic development' alone (Kellersmann, 2000, p. 335). And, the other that CBDR principle is based on 'differing contributions to global environmental degradation and not in different levels of development' (International Law Association, 1995, p. 116).

Arguably, however, Rio Principle 7 and FCCC Article 3 reinforce each other. The terms of Principle 7 emphasize both the enhanced contribution of industrial countries to environmental degradation as well as the developmental challenges faced by developing countries. FCCC Article 3 refers to 'common but differentiated responsibilities and respective capabilities'. If CBDR, as some argue, refers to differentiation based on capability alone the use of the term 'respective capabilities' would be superfluous. It follows that the negotiated agreement intended to highlight differentiation based on two markers – one based on capability and the other, drawing from Rio Principle 7 which contains the authoritative definition of CBDR, based on contribution to environmental harm. It is also worth noting that although there are two distinct markers for differentiation in the CBDRRC principle, these are linked. Enhanced capabilities are a direct result of industrialization, which in turn resulted in the spike in GHG emissions that is causing climate change.

122 Rajamani

'Responsibilities'

The term 'responsibility' is a term of art in moral and legal philosophy. In common parlance the term is used to signify agency in having caused particular acts – in the sense that one is *responsible for* certain events/acts having occurred. This can translate into accountability – in the sense that one is *held responsible* for those acts/events (Morris, 1961, pp. 1–51). The fact that one has caused certain acts leads, often but not inevitably, to accountability for those acts. There is also a distinction between moral and legal responsibility. Even if one is morally responsible for certain acts it does not necessarily translate into legal responsibility. Much will depend on how and why those acts occurred, and the extent to which the acts were voluntary, intentional, and done with foresight of the consequences that would occur. It is here, for instance, that the roots of the 'historical responsibility' conundrum in the climate change debate lie.

Industrialized countries have drawn, and indeed continue to draw, from the Earth's assimilative capacity far in excess of what a per capita entitlement would permit them to. Their excessive use, whether by reference to ecological or equitable criteria, of environmental resources and atmospheric space, in conjunction with other factors, has worsened environmental conditions and reduced the ecological space for others. Yet, the impacts of climate change are unevenly distributed between states. Small island states and the African dry regions are likely to lose their territories and cultures to climate change, but they have done little to precipitate climate change. This presents a clear case of historical injustice from which, arguably, a valid claim for recognition, compensation and correction could arise.[9] Yet industrial countries degraded the environment in the absence of scientific knowledge establishing such degradation to be irreversible, and damaging to others across time (Grubb, 1995, p. 491; Schokkaert and Eyckmans, 1998, p. 206), and in the absence of international rules prohibiting states from degrading the environment. In the face of this 'ignorance challenge' (Gosseries, 2004) and the lack of applicable legal rules at the time, to what extent are industrial countries *responsible* for past contributions to environmental degradation? There are effective arguments against the 'ignorance challenge' – current generations in industrialized countries benefit from the fruits of industrialization, and therefore should bear the consequences as well.[10] It is also possible to mount a valid response to the legal case against historical responsibility. Although no specific international legal prohibitions existed when GHGs emissions first began to spike, this did not translate into absolute freedom for states to engage in polluting behaviour.[11]

In the context of the CBDRRC principle, the use of the term 'responsibilities' is subject to differing interpretations. States, the principle posits, have a 'common' responsibility – but given the vastly differing (in some cases non-existent) contributions of states to causing climate change, this must signal a *responsibility to* or a *duty towards* not a *responsibility for* creating the problem. The principle also posits that states have 'differentiated' responsibilities – but given the fact that this principle is drawn from Rio Principle 7, this must signal both a *responsibility for* (in the sense of having caused the problem) and a *responsibility to or duty towards* (deriving from the *responsibility for* causing it).

Needless to say, the purpose of this discussion is not to provide an authoritative account of the term 'responsibilities' as used in the CBDRRC principle, but merely to highlight the many interpretations it lends itself to, and the multiple layers at which it can be read.

The Legal Status of the CBDR & CBDRRC Principle

The disagreements over this principle's content and the nature of the obligation it entails have spawned debates over the legal status of this principle. Is it 'soft law—a nonbinding norm—or has it already emerged as a robust, acknowledged principle of international environmental law' (Joyner, 2002, pp. 358–359). Has it indeed reached the status of customary international law binding on all states? Scholars have differing views. Brown Weiss describes CBDRRC as an 'emerging principle of international environmental law' (Weiss, 2000, p. 350). Birnie, Boyle and Redgwell describe it as 'framework principle' that is 'legally significant' (Birnie, Boyle and Redgwell, 2009, p. 135) whilst Stone denies that 'a new normative "principle" is in play' (Stone, 2004, p. 300).

The CBDR principle does not fulfill the criterion necessary for it to constitute 'customary international law' that is binding on states. In addition to the differences with respect to its core content and the nature of the obligations it entails, it is doubtful whether in and of itself the principle is of a 'norm-creating' character.[12] This is not to suggest, however, that it does not have considerable legal gravitas. The CBDR principle is referred to in the Rio Declaration, the FCCC, and the Johannesburg Plan of Implementation, 2002.[13] In addition differential treatment, the application of CBDR, is evident in its varying forms in most international environmental agreements, including the Vienna Convention, 1985, Montreal Protocol, 1987, Convention on Biological Diversity, 1992, the FCCC and the Convention to Combat Desertification, 1994, five multilateral environmental agreements with near-universal participation. It could be argued that the CBDR principle, repeatedly endorsed in international fora and seen in practice in at least five treaties with near universal participation, is the bedrock of the burden sharing arrangements crafted in the new generation of multi-lateral environmental treaties.

In the climate change regime CBDRRC is the overarching principle guiding the future development of the regime. It is found in two operational, rather than pre-ambular paragraphs of the FCCC, a binding treaty with near universal participation and reiterated in the preamble of the Kyoto Protocol. It is also frequently referred to in FCCC COP decisions and Ministerial Declarations (e.g. The Berlin Mandate, 1995; Bali Action Plan, 2007). Even though this principle does not assume the character of a legal obligation in itself, it is a fundamental part of the conceptual apparatus of the climate change regime such that it forms the basis for the interpretation of existing obligations and the elaboration of future international legal obligations within the climate change regime (Rajamani, 2006).

The operational significance of the CBDRRC principle

The CBDRRC principle in the FCCC and Kyoto Protocol

Notwithstanding the rich legal and philosophical debate that this principle has spawned, at its core the CBDRRC principle permits differential treatment between countries in the fashioning of treaty obligations. Accordingly, the FCCC and its Kyoto Protocol requires developed countries to take the lead in assuming and meeting ambitious greenhouse gas (GHG) mitigation targets. The Kyoto Protocol puts in place an elaborate institutional architecture to oversee this division of responsibilities including a compliance system which references the CBDRRC principle, and applies

124 *Rajamani*

differently to developing and developed countries (UNFCCC, 2006). This has proven problematic for certain countries. The United States' rejection of the Kyoto Protocol in 2001 can be sourced, in part, to a resistance to this interpretation and application of the CBDRRC principle.[14]

The current impasse in the negotiations over the future and fate of the Kyoto Protocol can also be sourced to the particular vision of CBDRRC and differential treatment it contains: a vision that translates demonstrable leadership from developed countries into differentiation in favour of developing countries, in particular in the context of the central obligations (GHG mitigation targets and timetables) in the treaty. Many developed countries are in favour of replacing the Kyoto Protocol with a new instrument that would possess a Copenhagen Accord-style architecture. Such an instrument would substitute a regime of *differentiation in favour of developing countries* with a regime of *differentiation for all countries,* providing flexibility for all. This would, through architectural sleight of hand, recast the contours of the CBDRRC principle – rendering the issue of differentiation for developing countries irrelevant. The Cancun Agreements take a step in this direction (Rajamani, 2011).

The CBDRRC principle in the post-2012 climate negotiations

In the negotiations to design a post-2012 climate regime, launched by the Bali Action Plan in 2007, the CBDRRC principle has been raised by Parties in several contexts, including differentiation between states in: undertaking mitigation actions/commitments; providing and receiving finance and other support; measurement, reporting and verification obligations; and, compliance procedures and consequences.[15]

Not surprisingly, given the many interpretations the CBDRRC principle lends itself to, States often claim inspiration from this principle in support of incompatible positions, as for instance on the stringency of actions required from developing countries and on the need to differentiate between developing countries. The Bali Action Plan requires Parties to arrive at a 'shared vision' for long-term cooperative action. This vision is required to be in accordance with the provisions and the principles of the Convention, in particular the CBDRRC principle (Bali Action Plan, 2007, paragraph 1(a)). The Bali Action Plan also uses the terms 'developing country parties' and 'developed country parties', rather than the FCCC categories of 'Annex-I' and 'non-Annex I' Parties. This is intentional, in that certain Parties wished to permit the categories of developing and developed countries to be negotiated anew. The reference to the CBDRRC principle and the possible re-negotiation of the categories of Parties is linked. Many developed countries are in favour of a more flexible and evolving categorization of Parties which will permit differences within and between developed and developing countries to be taken into account in fashioning obligations under the future climate regime. And they point to the CBDRRC principle as permitting and indeed requiring this. The USA, for instance, refers to the CBDRRC principle in its submissions to the FCCC (USA, 2008a, pp. 85, 87). The USA notes, however, that 'the notions of "responsibilities" and "capabilities" evolve as the circumstances of countries evolve in the global economy'. The specific circumstance of countries to which it refers are those relating to 'evolving global emissions and economic development trends', which in its view are central to addressing the issue in an environmentally effective and economically sustainable manner. The USA therefore envisages a focus for all countries on 'nationally appropriate actions that are measurable, reportable,

Common but differentiated responsibilities 125

and verifiable' with an understanding that 'meaningful contributions from countries with a significant emissions profile will be critical' (USA, 2008a, pp. 85, 87). It expects 'major emitters' and 'emerging economies' to take on similar commitments (USA, 2008b, p. 71). In its April 2010 submission it records 'serious differences of view' regarding the application of the CBDRRC principle, and notes that in its view 'the principle of common but differentiated responsibilities and respective capabilities' 'inherently recognizes a spectrum or continuum of effort among all countries, not just between categories of countries' (USA , 2010, pp. 79–80). In a similar vein, Japan believes that some developing countries based, *inter alia*, on their economic development, response capabilities, shares of GHG emissions in the world, should be expected to undertake sectoral GHG intensity targets (Japan, 2008, p. 14). Both Japan and the USA also believe that there is insufficient attention paid to the 'common' responsibility that states share.

China, on the other hand, believes that the CBDRRC principle requires countries like the USA to undertake a 25–40 per cent emission reduction target from 1990 levels, and for developing countries to take 'nationally determined mitigation actions' (China, 2008, p. 18). It also considers that any further 'sub-categorization' of countries runs counter to the Convention (China, 2008, p. 18). India (2008, p. 156) and Brazil concur (Brazil, 2009). In other words these countries advocate a *de facto* continuation of differentiation in the central obligations of the treaty, such that industrialized countries have legally binding targets and developing countries do not. This is but one illustration of the divergent and incompatible applications to which the CBDRRC principle lends itself, or at least is perceived as lending itself to. There are many others.

Whilst the wide-spread referencing of the CBDRRC principle is a testament to its universal appeal, the array of incompatible positions it is interpreted as supporting is evidence of the limits of this principle, as currently understood, in performing a standard setting role, and providing guidance to Parties in the design of the future climate regime.

It is worth noting that although the recent Cancun Agreements refer to the principle of common but differentiated responsibilities and respective capabilities (Cancun Agreements, 2010, LCA decision, para 1), and even unusually, to 'historical responsibility', (UNFCCC, 2010, LCA decision, introductory para 2 to section III.A), there has been a gradual erosion of differentiation between developed and developing countries, and an increase in the incidence of symmetrical obligations (Rajamani, 2011, pp. 512–513)

Conclusion

The CBDRRC principle, frequently referred to in India's submissions and interventions in the climate negotiations, is a fundamental part of the conceptual apparatus of the climate change regime. This principle offers authoritative guidance in certain respects – it requires efforts from all states in service of the common environmental goal, and it requires differentiation between states based both on capacity to do so and GHG contributions. Current obligations must be interpreted and future obligations structured in accordance with these basic tenets of the CBDRRC principle. Beyond this, the precise contours of the principle await further examination and elaboration by Parties.

There are differences between Parties on the core content of this principle including on the source, nature, contours, extent and relative weight of the 'common'

126 Rajamani

responsibility shared by Parties; the source, nature, contours, criterion for, extent and relative weight of the differentiated responsibility individual or groups of Parties have; the significance and legal import of the term 'responsibilities'; and the significance, legal import, and relative weight of the term 'respective capabilities' as well as the relationship between 'responsibilities' and 'respective capabilities'. Flowing from these many contestations, there are differing views on the applications this principle lends itself to, the nature of the obligations it entails, as well as the legal status and operational significance of the principle. The contours of the CBDRRC principle are still in evolution. Submissions from Parties as well as the eventual interpretations that come to hold sway in the climate process can usefully be mined at some point in the future to offer a definitive account of the intuitively appealing CBDRRC principle, but for now this principle, as also the climate change regime, is work in progress.

Notes

1 This article draws from and builds on a body of previously published work including Rajamani (2006) and Rajamani (2007), and is part of a longer-term project on the evolution of the CBDRRC principle in international environmental law.

2 It is worth noting that while FCCC Article 3 includes the phrase 'and respective capabilities', Rio Principle 7, the other, albeit soft law, articulation of the principle of common but differentiated responsibility, negotiated in parallel with the FCCC, does not. Although there are inconsistencies in the articulation of this term in submissions from Parties, the text of FCCC Article 3, as well as numerous Decisions of the FCCC Conference of Parties, such as the Berlin Mandate and the Delhi Ministerial Declaration on Climate Change and Sustainable Development, as well as the non-binding Copenhagen Accord, use the phrase 'principle of common but differentiated responsibilities and respective capabilities'. Since this chapter deals with the articulation of this principle in the climate change regime the less popular yet more accurate term 'common but differentiated responsibilities and respective capabilities' will be used, except where the reference is to the Rio Principle 7 articulation of this principle.

3 Gabcikovo – Nagymaros (Hungary/Slovakia), 1997 ICJ Rep. 15, 24, at paragraph 140, discussing 'sustainable development'.

4 See, GA (2001, p. 322). See also, Barcelona Traction Light and Power Company Ltd., second phase, 1970 ICJ Rep. 3, 32 noting an essential distinction between obligations owed to particular states and to the international community as a whole; all states have a legal interest in the protection of the latter, which are obligations *erga omnes*.

5 See, Trail Smelter Arbitration, 3 Rep. Int'l Arb. Awards 1903–1982 (1949) noting that 'under the principles of international law ... no State has the right to use or permit the use of its territory in such a manner as to cause injury by fumes in or to the territory of another State or the properties or persons therein, when the case is of serious consequence and the injury is established by clear and convincing evidence'. This principle is widely regarded as having attained the status of customary international law.

6 The discussions at the Second Meeting of the Parties to the Montreal Protocol, London, 1990, formed part of the backdrop to Rio. At the London Conference, developing countries led *inter alia* by then Indian Minister, Maneka Gandhi, took the position, '[w]e did not destroy the ozone layer, you have done that already. Don't ask us to pay the price.' See, Gandhi (2002, p. 12).

7 See, for example, GA (1992a) and GA (1989) (noting that developed countries have the 'main responsibility' for pollution abatement).

8 See GA (1992b, paragraph 16) for the US reservation on principle 7. The US noted, 'the United States understands and accepts that principle 7 highlights the special leadership role of the developed countries, based on our industrial development, our experience with environmental protection policies and actions, and our wealth, technical expertise and capabilities'.

9 Historical responsibility has long been discussed in the negotiations. Brazil proposed quantifying the sharing of the cost of combating climate change according to the 'effective

responsibility' of each country in causing the climate change problem. See, UNFCCC (1997a). More recently the Bolivarian Alliance for the Americas has argued for a regime based on historical Responsibility (Bolivia, 2010).

10 See for a sophisticated analysis of this issue in the climate context, Shue (2009).
11 A full legal response is offered in Rajamani (2006, pp. 142–144).
12 See Rajamani (2006, pp. 158–162).
13 See, World Summit on Sustainable Development (2002). There are six references to CBDR.
14 Text of a Letter from the President to Senators Hagel, Helms, Craig, and Roberts, The White House, Office of the Press Secretary, 13 March 2001.
15 All submissions of Parties to the Ad Hoc Working Group on Long-Term Cooperative Action (AWG-LCA) are available at UNFCCC, 'Submissions by parties', http://unfccc.int/meetings/ad_hoc_working_groups/lca/items/4578.php, accessed 12 February 2011.

References

Biniaz, S. (2002) 'Common but differentiated responsibilities', *American Society of International Law Proceedings*, vol. 96, pp. 358–368.

Birnie, P., Boyle, A. and Redgwell, C. (2009) *International Law & the Environment*, 3rd edn, Oxford University Press, Oxford, UK.

Bodansky, D. (1993) 'The United Nations Framework Convention on Climate Change: A commentary', *Yale Journal of International Law*, vol. 18, pp. 451–558.

Bodansky, D., Crook, J. R. and Crawford, J. (2002) 'The ILC's articles on responsibility of States for internationally wrongful acts: A retrospect', *American Journal of International Law*, vol. 96, pp. 894–890.

Bolivia (2010) Submission by the Plurinational State of Bolivia to the Ad-Hoc Working Group on Long-term Cooperative Action, in UNFCCC Additional views on which the Chair may draw in preparing text to facilitate negotiations among Parties. FCCC/AWGLCA/2010/MISC.2. pp. 14–39.

Brazil (2009) Views and proposals on paragraph 1 of the Bali Action Plan, in UNFCCC Ideas and proposals on the elements contained in paragraph 1 of the Bali Action Plan. FCCC/AWGLCA/2009/MISC.1. pp. 17–18.

China (2008) China's comments on the implementation of the Bali Action Plan, in UNFCCC. Views regarding the work programme of the Ad-Hoc Working Group on Long-term Cooperative Action under the Convention. FCCC/AWGLCA/2008/MISC.1. pp. 18–19.

Convention on Biological Diversity (1992) *International Legal Materials*, vol. 31, p. 818.

Dworkin, R. (1977) *Taking Rights Seriously*, Harvard University Press, Cambridge, USA.

GA (General Assembly, United Nations) (1970) Declaration of principles governing the sea-bed and the ocean floor, and the subsoil thereof, beyond the limits of national jurisdiction, G.A. Res. 2749.

GA (1989) United Nations conference on environment and development, G.A. Res. 44/228.

GA (1992a) *Development and environment*, G.A. Res. 2849.

GA (1992b) Report of the United Nations conference on environment and development, A/CONF.151/26, Vol. IV.

GA (2001) Draft articles on responsibility of states for internationally wrongful acts, UN Doc. A/56/10.

GA (2002) Responsibility of States for internationally wrongful acts, Annex, G.A. Res. 56/83.

Gandhi, M. (2002) 'A lesson for humanity: The London meeting', in Anderson, S.O. and Sarma, K.M. *Protecting the Ozone Layer: The United Nations History*, Earthscan, London.

Gosseries, A. (2004) 'Historical Emissions and Free Riding', in L. Meyer (ed.) *Justice in Time: Responding to Historical Injustice*, Nomos Verlagsgesellschaft, Baden-Baden.

Grubb, M. (1995) 'Seeking fair weather: Ethics and the international debate on the climate', *International Affairs*, vol. 71, pp. 463–496.

128 *Rajamani*

Hague Declaration on the Environment (1989) *International Legal Materials*, vol. 28, pp. 1308–1310.

India (2008) Mitigation actions of developing countries under the Bali Action Plan (paragraph 1(b)(ii), in UNFCCC Ideas and proposals on the elements contained in paragraph 1 of the Bali Action Plan. FCCC/AWGLCA/2008/Misc.5/Add.2 (Part I). pp. 155–156.

Inter-American Tropical Tuna Convention (1949), 80 UNTS 3.

International Law Association (1995) International Committee on Legal Aspects of Sustainable Development, Report of the Sixty-Sixth Conference, Buenos Aires.

Japan (2008) Japan's submission on application of sectoral approaches, in UNFCCC Ideas and proposals on the elements contained in paragraph 1 of the Bali Action Plan. FCCC/AWGLCA/2008/MISC.5/Add.2 (Part II). pp. 14–22.

Joyner, C.C. (2002) 'Common but differentiated responsibilities', *American Society of International Law Proceedings*, vol. 96, pp. 358–368.

Kellersmann, B. (2000) *Die Gemeinsame, Aber Differenzierte Verantwortlichkeit Von Industriestaaten Und Entwicklungsländern Für Den Schutz Der Globalen Umwelt*, Springer, Heidelberg, Germany.

Morris, H. (ed.) (1961) 'Responsibility', in *Freedom and Responsibility: Readings in Philosophy and Law*, Stanford University Press, California.

Noordwijk Declaration on Atmospheric Pollution and Climatic Change (1989) *American University Journal of International Law and Policy*, vol. 5, p. 592.

Outer Space Treaty (Treaty on Principles Governing the Activities of States in the Exploration and Use of Outer Space, Including the Moon and Other Celestial Bodies) (1967), 610 UNTS 205.

Pogge, T.V. (2004) 'Historical injustice: The other two domains', in L. Meyer (ed.) *Justice in Time: Responding to Historical Injustice*, Nomos Verlagsgesellschaft, Baden-Baden.

Rajamani, L. (2006) *Differential Treatment in International Law*, Oxford University Press, Oxford, UK.

Rajamani, L. (2007) 'The nature, promise and limits of differential treatment in the climate change regime', *Yearbook of International Environmental Law*, vol. 16, pp. 81–118.

Rajamani L. (2011) 'The Cancun Climate Agreements: Reading the Text, Subtext and Tea leaves,' *International and Comparative Law Quarterly*, vol. 60, pp. 499–519.

Schokkaert, E. and Eyckmans, J. (1998) 'Greenhouse negotiations and the mirage of partial justice', in M. Dore and T. Mount (eds) *Global Environmental Economics: Equity and the Limits to Markets*, Wiley-Blackwell, New Jersey.

Second World Climate Conference: Ministerial Declaration, 1990.

Shue, H. (2009) 'SBSTA technical briefing, historical responsibilities', http://unfccc.int/files/meetings/ad_hoc_working_groups/lca/application/pdf/1_shue_rev.pdf, accessed 30 January 2011.

Stone, C. (2004) 'Common but differentiated responsibilities in international law', *American Journal of International Law*, vol. 98, pp. 276–301.

UNCLOS (United Nations Convention on the Law of the Sea) (1982), 1833 U.N.T.S. 397.

UNEP (United Nations Environment Program) (1998) *Report of the Tenth Meeting of the Parties to the Montreal Protocol on Substances that Deplete the Ozone.* UNEP/OzL. Pro.10/9.

UNFCCC (United Nations Framework Convention on Climate Change) (1992) UN Doc. A/AC.237/18 (Part II)/Add. 1.

UNFCCC (1995) The Berlin Mandate: Review of adequacy of Articles 4, paragraph 2, sub-paragraph (a) and (b), of the Convention, including proposals related to a Protocol and decisions on follow-up. Decision 1/CP.1, FCCC/CP/1995/7/Add.1.

UNFCCC (1997a) Implementation of the Berlin Mandate: Additional proposals from Parties. FCCC/AGBM/1997/Misc.1/Add.3.

UNFCCC (1997b) Kyoto Protocol to the United Nations Framework Convention on Climate Change. FCCC/CP/1997/L.7/Add.1.

Common but differentiated responsibilities 129

UNFCCC (2002) Report of the Conference of the Parties on its seventh session, held at Marrakesh from 29 October to 10 November 2001. FCCC/CP/2001/13/Add.3.

UNFCCC (2006) Procedures and mechanisms relating to compliance under the Kyoto Protocol. Decision 27/CMP.1, FCCC/KP/CMP/2005/8/Add.3.

UNFCCC (2008) Bali Action Plan. Decision 1/CP.13, FCCC/CP/2007/6/Add.1.

UNFCCC (2010) Copenhagen Accord. Decision 2/CP.15, FCCC/CP/2009/11/Add.1.

UNFCCC (2011) Cancun Agreements. Decision 1/CP.16, FCCC/CP/2010/7/Add.1 and Decision 1/CMP.6, FCCC/KP/CMP/2010/ 12/Add.1.

USA (United States of America) (2008a) Submission of the United States under the Bali Action Plan, Decision 1/CP.13, FCCC/AWGLCA/2008/MISC.1. pp. 85–88.

USA (2008b) Submission on the AWG-LCA Chair's assembly document, FCCC/AWGLCA/2008/MISC.5/Add.2 (Part II). pp. 71–75.

USA (2010) Submission of the United States to the AWG-LCA Chair, FCCC/AWGLCA/2010/MISC.2. pp. 79–85.

Weiss, E.B. (2000) 'The rise and fall of international law', *Fordham Law Review*, vol. 69, pp. 345–372.

World Summit on Sustainable Development (2002) 'Plan of implementation', www.un.org/jsummit/html/documents/summit_docs/2309_planfinal.htm, accessed 12 February 2011.

9 Equity and burden sharing in emission scenarios

A carbon budget approach

T. Jayaraman, Tejal Kanitkar and Mario D'Souza

Introduction

The reduction of greenhouse gas (GHG) emissions of anthropogenic origin across the globe, to prevent dangerous interference with the Earth's climate beyond the point of no return, and to minimize such human interference with climate is today the most pressing issue in global environmental governance. Article 2 of the United Nations Framework Convention on Climate Change (UNFCCC), emphasizes that the 'ultimate objective' of the Convention is the 'stabilization of greenhouse gas concentrations in the atmosphere at a level that would prevent dangerous anthropogenic interference with the climate system' (UNFCCC, 1992). Article 3.1 further enjoins: 'The Parties should protect the climate system for the benefit of present and future generations of humankind, on the basis of equity and in accordance with their common but differentiated responsibilities and respective capabilities' (UNFCCC, 1992).

The elaboration of Articles 2 and 3.1 to ensure their operationalization has been one of the most contested issues in international climate negotiations. At the heart of this debate is the question of the relative responsibilities of different Parties to the effort required to move away from all forms of economic activity that contribute to the emissions of GHGs. Burden-sharing in mitigation, as this relative sharing of the responsibility of reducing GHG emissions is referred to in climate speak, is one of the most divisive issues in the negotiations. In this chapter we will review the question of burden-sharing in mitigation and the variety of approaches that deal with this question, keeping in view especially the implications for India.

Among the general category of burden-sharing schemes, a first key difference in approach is between those that incorporate some aspect of Article 3.1 in their formulation, even if in a somewhat indirect way, and others that do not fall into this category. In the latter we may include in particular some classes of economic models of climate change impacts, especially of the kind that work with a rough disaggregation of the world into a finite number of regions (economic models that treat the globe as a single region have, of course, little to say about burden-sharing and may fix only a global agenda). However in this chapter we will focus only on proposals that bear some relationship to Article 3.1 as these appear the most relevant in the real world of climate negotiations.[1]

The significance of Article 3.1 for burden-sharing in mitigation is immediately clear. The principle of 'common but differentiated responsibilities and respective capabilities' immediately offers a broad principle for determining the respective share of various countries in fulfilling their duty to 'protect the climate system for the benefit of the

Equity and burden sharing in emission scenarios 131

present and future generations of humankind'. For the developing countries this principle is one of the cornerstones of the UNFCCC, while for some developed countries it is clearly not of such overriding importance (see Rajamani, this volume). The significance of this fault-line can be gauged from the fact that one of the most potent criticisms in the armoury of developing countries is the criticism that the principle of common but differentiated responsibilities (CBDR) is being violated. Moreover, although the second sentence of Art 3.1 reads: 'Accordingly the developed countries should take the lead in combating climate change and the effects thereof' (UNFCCC, 1992), several developed countries refuse to countenance undertaking any substantial mitigation action themselves until and unless large developing countries like China and India are also ready to undertake substantial emissions reduction commitments.[2]

For our purpose here, an important feature of the debate and contestations around Article 3.1 is the relative lack of emphasis in the literature (and in the negotiations until recently) on the reference to equity in Article 3.1. Much of the literature tends to focus on the principle of CBDR while the preceding phrase 'on the basis of equity' has received little attention. Indeed it appears that in many interpretations of Article 3.1 the question of equity is considered to be synonymous with the principle of CBDR. The distinction between the two appears to have been only sporadically registered in the literature. On this particular question however concrete proposals in the climate negotiations have led the considerations in the academic literature. Especially in the negotiations in the Ad-Hoc Working Group on Long-Term Co-operation a number of countries have been associated with such proposals.[3]

The debate over the term 'equity' in Article 3.1 is in reality to be seen as part of a larger debate relating to the need of developing countries for 'developmental space' that in practice means reduced access to fossil fuels for an extended period beyond the immediate present. Developing countries have consistently maintained that they need to be able to utilize fossil fuels by virtue of the fact that proven developmental pathways, as opposed to potential or conjectural pathways, continue to rely in more than significant measure on the use of fossil fuels.

However these broad considerations in conceptual terms such as equity and CBDR have to be translated into operational statements relating to the amount of Greenhouse Gases (GHG)s that every country will be allowed to emit. It is important to note that this translation is not an easy exercise at all. This conversion of the broad principles of the UNFCCC into concrete statements and allocation of emissions for a potential agreement involves a non-trivial understanding of some quantitative aspects of climate science.

In this chapter we will examine the nature of the operational translation of Article 2 and Article 3.1 in the light of recent developments in climate science. We will begin with a brief review of the broad classes of schemes and proposals that fall within the category of the burden-sharing approach and the reading of climate science that promotes this understanding.

In the next part, we discuss how, in relation to Article 2, following a gradual shift of emphasis in the scientific literature, the term 'stabilization' is better understood in a modified way compared to its use earlier in the Third and Fourth Assessment Reports of the Intergovernmental Panel on Climate Change (IPCC). In this modified view the key recognition is that cumulative emissions and maximum temperature increase are better and more robust indicators of 'stabilization' rather than a trajectory of rising atmospheric concentration that then levels off at a particular value.

132 *Jayaraman, Kanitkar and D'Souza*

Following on this shift of emphasis in the scientific understanding we will argue that the notion of burden-sharing in mitigation also needs to shift correspondingly. A new approach to burden-sharing in this view must be understood in the context of cumulative emissions and the entitlement to cumulative emissions space of different nations.

Burden-sharing in mitigation and emissions scenarios

The old approach to burden-sharing in mitigation approaches relies basically on a view of stabilization of GHGs in the atmosphere that depends on understanding the flow of emissions (on an annual basis or based on some similar short time period) and the rise and subsequent fall of the concentration of these gases in the atmosphere. Emissions scenarios for the stabilization of atmospheric carbon concentrations were described in terms of an emissions trajectory for the Earth as a whole, which typically (including the well-known WRE scenarios[4] and other related ones) had a slow reduction in emissions after reaching a peak. Burden-sharing in mitigation has similarly been based on the emissions scenario perspective, including particularly the notion of an explicit emissions trajectory for every country.

In this view, mitigation at the global level is considered to be the effort required to move the world from some reference or baseline scenario of projected emissions (without any action directed at reducing emissions to limit anthropogenic global warming) to an emissions trajectory that would lead to stabilization. Typically the reference or baseline scenarios have been constructed using various variants of Integrated Assessment Models that produce projections of economic growth, energy use and corresponding emissions using a large number of exogenous and endogenous variables. Several such models have been constructed and several scenarios have been investigated (see for instance, Nakicenovic and Swart, 2000). In most of these models the global scenario is built from bottom-up considerations based on the globe divided into several regions, with the regions being linked through trade and investments, etc.

Even though these scenarios have been typically presented with the caveat that they are meant to be illustrative and not predictive, they have however in discussions on burden-sharing inevitably become a predictive measure of business-as-usual with respect to which mitigation actions may be measured. The discussion of burden-sharing in mitigation in Working Group III of IPCC AR4 is clearly dominated by these perspectives.

Having defined the global goal that is required in terms of the flow of emissions, subsequently there are two approaches in determining burden-sharing that are somewhat different. In one approach, a sharing formula is used to determine the contribution of each country in shifting the emissions trajectory from the projected global business-as-usual scenario to the global emissions trajectory that is required to achieve stabilization. In the second approach, a sharing formula is independently determined whose parameters are then adjusted to values that would then ensure that the global mitigation goal is met. However some effort is required to ensure that in any of these approaches, with reference to Article 3.1, what the relevant equity principle is that is operationalized and how the formulation of CBDR is implemented.

A typical example of the first approach is the Greenhouse Development Rights (GDR) approach.[5] In this approach equity is ensured by the process of assigning for every country a certain amount of emission rights automatically, in proportion to the

Equity and burden sharing in emission scenarios   133

number of people below the poverty line. CBDR is implemented through the provision of sharing the remainder of the shift (after the poverty-based emissions rights for all countries is implemented) from the business-as-usual to the target trajectory by a formula that accounts for both the responsibility aspect (based on cumulative emissions from 1990) and the aspect of capability (that is based on per capita GDP).

A typical example of the second approach is the well-known contract and converge approach (C&C).[6] In this approach, the equity principle is the equality of per capita emission flows. To this end, the developed countries are required to cut their annual emissions down while the developing countries are allowed to increase their emissions, both at such rates so that the annual emission flows of both groups converge to a common value at some pre-determined year.

A number of variations are of course to be found in both the approaches. One particular form is that of contract and differentiated convergence (CDC). Another variation, a particular version of the C&C approach that is relevant to India, is the so-called Manmohan Singh Convergence Principle. This refers to the offer made by India's Prime Minister at Bonn in 2008 that India's per capita annual emissions would never exceed the per capital annual emissions of developed countries. In the figures below we present a comparison of the allowed emissions for India and some select countries based on three different approaches (the material is reproduced from work done by Höhne and Moltmann, 2009).

In climate negotiations themselves, the burden-sharing perspective has manifested itself in the focus on the specification of emissions trajectories as the possible basis for long-term agreement and cooperation in mitigation. Thus typically discussions have been focused not only on reductions of emissions by 2050 but also on specifications of the peaking year for emissions and the rate of reduction of emissions in different sub-periods in the overall time-period of 2000–2050.

From the preceding discussion it should also be evident that it is not easy to determine the precise nature of what aspect (or aspects) of equity are satisfied and to what extent they are satisfied and similarly for CBDR in these discussions. A variety of operational interpretations of equity are possible, as also for CBDR.

In the next section we will argue that, based on recent scientific evidence and results, cumulative emissions appear to be a better indicator for limiting temperature rise compared to stabilization pathways. However in burden-sharing in mitigation this problem is exacerbated by some other features. Perhaps the most significant of these is the counter-factual nature of baseline scenarios. As the wide variety of scenarios testifies, there is room for considerable divergence on what the world would look like without any action to mitigate climate change. Using this as a basis from which to measure effort is clearly deeply problematic.

A notable case in point is that of the GDR approach that we have mentioned above. Notwithstanding the close attention paid to questions of equity in formulating the burden-sharing principle, the point remains that any estimate of what a particular country can emit is severely dependent on the baseline that is chosen from which to measure the effort. Another common feature of many baseline scenarios is their potential to underestimate the growth trajectories of many developing nations, large and small.

The second problematic aspect of the emissions pathway approach has been that it provides little indication of how developing countries, especially the large developing countries with high absolute quantum of emissions, could be persuaded to contribute

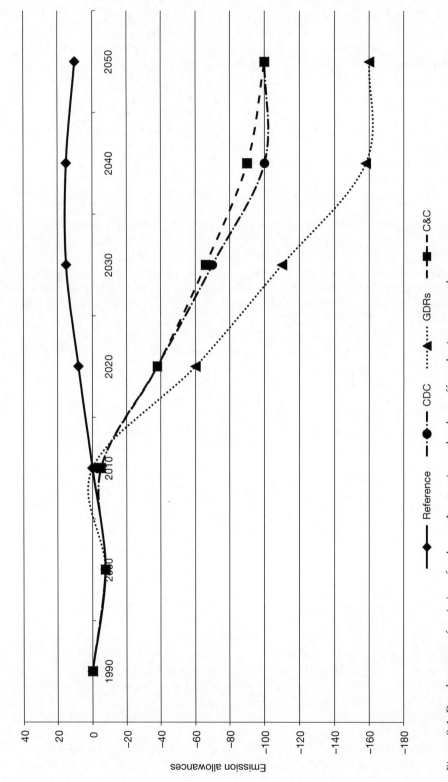

Figure 9.1 Development of emissions for Annex-I countries under three effort-sharing approaches

Source: Höhne and Moltmann, 2009

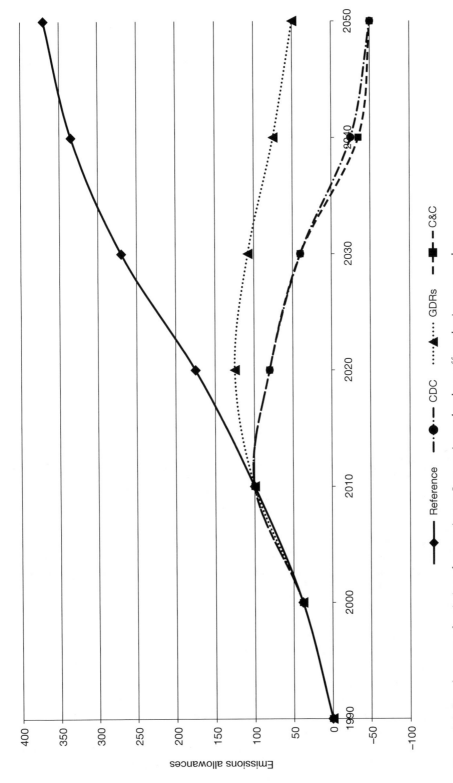

Figure 9.2 Development of emissions for non-Annex-I countries under three effort-sharing approaches

Source: Höhne and Moltmann, 2009

136 Jayaraman, Kanitkar and D'Souza

to mitigation. In view of the persistent demand of the developing countries that their requirements for development do not enable them to undertake any short- or medium-term emission reduction commitments, it is not clear what the basis would be for their eventual inclusion in a scheme to reduce emissions globally to the desired levels. We may add that while the developing countries have certainly a strong case for not entering a regime of mitigation with absolute emission targets right away, there is clearly no moral or ethical case, or indeed a scientific case, for not accepting such limits in a suitably equitable arrangement in the future.

For developed countries it is evident that, given their high levels of current emissions and their historical record of high emissions, a straightforward prescription of how much they should reduce from their emissions in 1990 or any appropriate base year is an unambiguous prescription.

With regard to other approaches such as C&C, the invidious consequence of such schemes is that the developing countries (the majority that is) reach the prescribed (equity-based) base level from below while the developed countries do so from above. This is not to deny the obvious fact that in the short term and maybe the medium term, developed-country emissions will still be above developing countries (not in absolute terms but with respective to the equity criteria used for equalizing access). But in effect such prescriptions sharply limit the flexibility and room for manoeuvre that developing countries have with respect to their development trajectory and consequently their emissions trajectory in the future. This last point has more often than not been ignored in the literature and will become clearer in the following sections of this chapter, only when we examine this issue from a different viewpoint.

Developments in climate science and cumulative emissions

We will now briefly summarize a line of recent results in climate science (over the last four to five years) that shift the emphasis from emissions trajectories to cumulative emissions. While no doubt the atmospheric concentration of GHGs would reduce as a result of emissions reduction (once the emissions fall below the absorption level of the carbon sinks), the earlier emissions in absolute terms would continue to drive temperatures higher. Hence, if the desired objective of the scenario is to specify the maximal temperature that will be reached, then clearly it is necessary that the emissions scenario specifies all the carbon that will be emitted, following which all emissions would cease. Thus the focus should be on the cumulative emissions in emissions scenarios. If it also turned out that the rate of increase and final reduction of emissions was not relevant, that would be even more helpful, as then the only variable in question would be cumulative emissions alone. Several scientific developments enable the conversion of this rough-and-ready argument into a coherent scientific statement.

First, in recognizing that the critical parameter of climate impact is the temperature increase that results from increased emissions the following steps are involved in relating the two quantities. The initial step is the effect of increased emissions on the carbon cycle, the second is the climate change response to increased concentrations of carbon, and the third is the feedback between climate change effects and the carbon cycle. In computer simulations Matthews et al. (2009) noted that (for cumulative emissions up to 2 GtC) the temperature increase due to a unit increase in carbon emissions was approximately independent of both atmospheric concentration as well as time.

Equity and burden sharing in emission scenarios   137

Matthews et al. defined an approximately linear climate-carbon response function that assigns a definite increase in temperature to every ton of carbon emission.[7]

In a related development, Allen et al. (2009) showed that while the overall warming response to increased atmospheric emissions under a stabilization scenario was subject to many uncertainties, the peak warming due to a given amount of cumulative emissions was much better constrained. Remarkably, the peak warming was insensitive to the emission pathway, including both the timing of emissions and the peak emission rate. The results also showed two other interesting facts. First was that the reduction in emissions in 2050 relative to 2010 was significant for peak warming only in so far as this was related to the cumulative emissions in this period, reiterating that it was cumulative emissions that mattered and not the shape of the emissions pathway. Second it also showed that the long-term warming response (for the period 2000–2500) was very similar to the peak warming response due to the cumulative emissions between 2010 and 2050. This suggested that cumulative emissions, even if emitted over a shorter period, commits us to a considerable degree of warming over a longer time scale (that may be even ten times larger than the time period when these emissions were committed).

In the work of Meinshausen et al. (2009) the scope of such studies was extended to include not only carbon dioxide but also the effects of other GHGs. In particular their paper focused on lower emission scenarios over a shorter time scale, and provided quantitative estimates for carbon budgets over the period 2000–2050 that would keep peak temperature rise below 2°C with a specified probability. In particular they found that for 1000 Gt of CO_2-eq, the mean probability for a temperature rise of 2°C was well below 50 per cent, while for 1440 Gt of CO_2-eq (from 2000 to 2050), the mean probability for a 2°C rise rose to 50 per cent. It is the latter budget that we have used for some further considerations below.

In sum, it is clear that there is a fit case for shifting the focus in emissions scenarios from specific trajectories and the 'stabilization pathway' paradigm to considerations of cumulative emissions over time-periods of a half-century and a century with the cumulative emissions over 500 years as an auxiliary estimate. As these results are very recent, all of them indeed are from 2009, it is clear that they have to go through the IPCC process for its Fifth Assessment Report. However this shift has already made itself evident in an authoritative evaluation by the US National Academy of Sciences. The report reviews 'stabilization' scenarios from the perspective of cumulative emissions, while also indicating how these are related to the earlier version based on the evolution of concentrations (National Research Council, 2011).

Mitigation in the cumulative emissions scenario: the carbon budget approach

From the perspective of cumulative emissions, the carbon budget approach suggests itself as the most intuitive means of burden-sharing in mitigation. In this view, human society as a whole is allowed a specified amount of carbon that it can emit from the beginning of the industrial era to a specified target date in the future to ensure that temperature rise stays within 2°C. Of course, it is presumed that the budget for future periods, after this target date, is so limited as to not disturb the decreasing temperature trend that has been set in motion.

One of the most significant outcomes of this recent scientific work on cumulative emissions is that, at least at the scientific level, it removes any ambiguity regarding

138 *Jayaraman, Kanitkar and D'Souza*

historical responsibility for emissions. In the earlier atmospheric concentrations-based view, there has been much ambiguity, including suggestions that to subtract the amount of GHGs absorbed in the oceans will absolve nations from responsibility, to provide carbon space in sinks for future emissions, including the role of ocean and other forms of sink absorption in computing responsibility with some doubt as to the relative weights of past and future responsibility for emissions, and so on. All these ambiguities are now removed, and in terms of their contribution to temperature increase, all carbon emitted during the industrial era carries equal weight. This is particularly significant in the context of the Brazilian proposal[8] that was the first to propose the idea of historical responsibility in its specific linkage to responsibility for temperature increase.

However the key conceptual advance that follows from consideration of cumulative emissions is the extent of access to atmospheric carbon space that can be allowed to each country. In most of the earlier proposals on burden-sharing, the implications of historical responsibility for future emissions allowances was not very explicit. On the other hand, for the developing countries, the problem, to reiterate, was the reconciliation of the global environmental constraint vis-à-vis the emissions that they could be allowed to meet their development needs.

In the cumulative emissions approach, both these problems are satisfyingly resolved. All we need clearly is an allocation rule or a set of rules whereby the share of the total carbon budget of the entire world could be distributed between nations. Obviously such a rule would be based on Article 3.1 of the UNFCCC that enjoins all Parties to protect the climate based on equity. Given such rules, historical responsibility is clearly related to the cumulative emissions from each country that have contributed (and are contributing) to temperature rise. Historical responsibility can be easily quantified as the difference between the actual contribution in terms of cumulative emissions and the share of the carbon space that is due to every country by whatever allocation rule has been specified. All countries will now have to live within their share of the carbon budget as specified by the allocation rules and this will determine the rate of reduction of emissions (modulo the overall flexibility available to them in determining the precise trajectory) so that they stay within their allocations. Those countries that have used less than their allocation of carbon space at the current time would have, of course, the freedom to increase emissions.

Equity-based allocations of carbon space

What is the rule by which carbon space may be equitably allocated? (See also Rao, this volume.) The most notable candidate for such an allocation rule has been the distribution of the total carbon space available (from the pre-industrial era to the future specified target date) on the basis of an equal per capita allocation. The standard procedure that advocates of this approach have followed is to consider the population with respect to a single base year, usually from the recent period, though varying population could also be used in the criteria.

Variants of this allocation rule can, however, choose not the pre-industrial era as the starting point (typically taken as 1850) but more recent dates such as 1970 or 1990 to mark different moments of heightened awareness of the problem of climate change. This clearly does not account for full historical responsibility in its original form, as the earlier contribution to temperature rise is simply neglected. However, 1970 provides the possibility of a formulation that accommodates both the Northern reluctance to

Equity and burden sharing in emission scenarios 139

accept full historical responsibility as a principle and the South's insistence that it is the North that is responsible for the bulk of emissions in the atmosphere. Even with 1970 as the base year, the numbers show that developed countries have contributed emissions far beyond their entitlement. The tables below show a comparison of the allocation of carbon space for different nations with different years as the base year.

It may be argued that a per capita cumulative emissions criterion does not adequately reflect the insistence of Article 3.1 on CBDR and respective capabilities). At the outset it is worth noting that it is common to conflate the term 'common but differentiated responsibilities and respective capabilities' to 'the basis in equity' that the Article refers to. However the necessity of interpreting 'the basis in equity' as prior to CBDR seems not to have been explored. Particularly in the case of the per capita allocation of cumulative emissions it is clear that reference to equity is not identical to CBDR. The per capita allocation refers only to the equity part. Common but differentiated responsibility actually arises in this view in the fact that the developed countries have over-occupied carbon space far above their fair share, to the extent that they have even overdrawn their budgets for the period 2010–2050. On the other hand, the developing countries, the majority at least, have not even exhausted half their total allocation for the 1850–2050 period.

Table 9.1 Entitlements to carbon space: 1850 basis

1850 Basis [All Values in GtC]	Total entitlements between 1850 and 2050 (GtC)	Actual current contribution (1850–2009)	Future entitlements (2010–2050)
USA	29.1	95.6	−66.5
EU	45.5	86.7	−41.1
Other Annex- I	43.0	63.1	−20.1
India	110.0	8.6	101.3
China	123.9	33.2	90.7
Brazil	17.7	3.0	14.7
South Africa	4.4	3.7	0.8
Other Emerging Economies	72.7	24.2	48.4
Rest of the World	185.8	13.9	171.9
	632.0	332.0	300.0

Table 9.2 Entitlements to carbon space: 1970 basis

1970 Basis [All Values in GtC]	Total entitlements between 1970 and 2050 (GtC)	Actual current contribution (1970–2009)	Future entitlements (2010–2050)
USA	24.2	54.9	−30.8
EU	37.8	44.8	−7.0
Other Annex-I	35.7	48.4	−12.7
India	91.4	7.4	83.9
China	102.9	30.4	72.5
Brazil	14.7	2.5	12.2
South Africa	3.7	2.9	0.8
Other Emerging Economies	60.4	21.6	38.8
Rest of the World	154.4	12.2	142.2
	525.0	225.0	300.0

We may also remark that in the emissions flow approach it does appear that, without some specific extraneous input (in the sense of being extraneous to the question of industrial activity and emissions), equity is identical to the principle of CBDR. The Kyoto Protocol may be regarded in some sense as the high watermark of this viewpoint. However with the Bali Action Plan and the introduction of the question of the shared vision for long-term co-operation action (UNFCCC, 2007), equity clearly needs to be distinguished from CBDR.

CBDR in the carbon budget view is actually strengthened by the observation that given the gross over-occupation of carbon space by the developed countries and the fact that carbon dioxide is a long-lasting GHG, the developing countries by and large will fall far short of attaining their fair share of carbon space. Only a few developing countries, including China and some other emerging economies, will come anywhere attaining their fair share. Thus differentiated responsibilities are already inherent in the facts of the matter, given the effort required of the developing countries to erase their full developmental deficit with a planet that is in effect far smaller than the one that the developed nations have enjoyed en route to prosperity. Respective capabilities would actually be quite adequately reflected in the fact that developing countries close to achieving their allocation of carbon space will need to mitigate their emissions earlier than the rest of the developing world.

It may still be argued that the allocation rule should perhaps be modified to take care not only of the per capita cumulative principle but also take into account HDI, and GDP per capita or other such indicators. In point of fact, this issue is of relevance only to a small subset of developing nations. Second, it is easy to show that there is a strong correlation between per capita cumulative emissions and per capita cumulative GDP (see Figure 9.3 below). In a rank correlation test, the correlation is of the order of 0.8. A regression analysis shows that the log of cumulative emissions is strongly correlated to log of cumulative GDP and that cumulative GDP accounts for roughly 54 per cent of cumulative emissions. However, with the removal of three outliers,[9] this figure goes up to 71 per cent, suggesting that in the vast majority of country cases, the link between cumulative GDP and cumulative emissions continues to be very strong.

Entitlements vis-à-vis the actual availability of carbon space

A further advantage of the advantage of the carbon budget perspective is that it clearly distinguishes between the allocations of emission allowances based on an equity principle vis-à-vis the actual carbon space that countries are likely to get under various scenarios of action by the developed nations. Keeping the entitlement to carbon space independent of the actual possibility of realization of that entitlement is another key aspect of the implementation of differentiated responsibilities in the carbon budget approach, and ensures that such an emissions right does not actually become a right to pollute. The key fact of the current actual use of global carbon space is the gross over-occupation by the developed countries that is best illustrated by the cumulative emissions of Annex-I countries compared to the cumulative emissions of the rest.

	Cumulative emissions (1850–2009) [GtC]	Cumulative emissions (1970–2009) [GtC]
Annex-I	245.68	149.175
Non-Annex-I	86.32	75.825

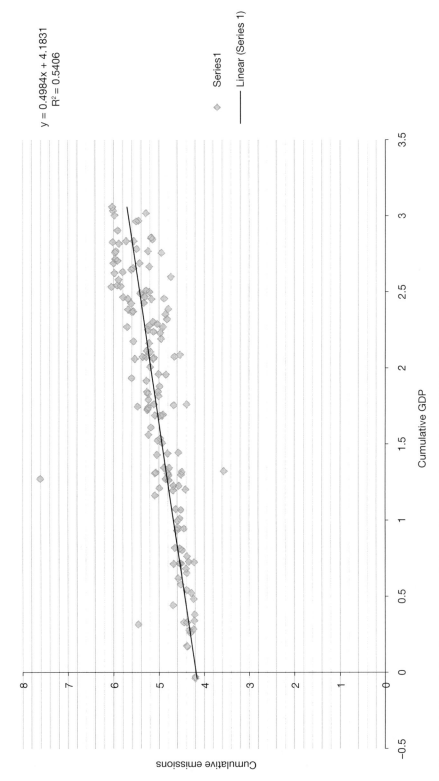

Figure 9.3 Correlation between cumulative emissions and cumulative GDP for all countries

142 Jayaraman, Kanitkar and D'Souza

We present in the following table the entitlements to carbon space for various nations compared to what they have actually accessed in the past. We also present, based on an optimization model (TISS-DSF model)[10] how much carbon space these countries are likely to access based on a set of rules that privilege the move towards an equitable access for developing countries while at the same time the constraint of the global carbon budget is kept firmly in place. This optimization model (based on the GAMS code) computes the carbon space that would physically accrue to countries and regions based on three rules.

The first rule allows countries that are currently below their fair share of carbon space to increase their emissions while those above their fair share of carbon space have to begin cutting. The second rule is that cumulative emissions from all countries/regions from the present (2010) to 2050 (the period over which the model is run) must adhere to the specified carbon budget. This budget works out to approximately 300 Gt C-eq. This gives the probability of a 2°C rise to be 50 per cent. The third rule is that among those countries who have less than their fair share of carbon space, those whose current emissions flow rate is above the world average have to start cutting earlier while those whose current emissions flow rate is below world average can start cutting emissions later. These three rules are applied universally to all countries/regions in the model. The model parameters of particular interest are the rates at which emissions reduction take place for specific situations; varying these parameters provides a number of scenarios that have been studied in detail.

The bottom line from the results of these optimization exercises is that, as a consequence of the gross over-occupation of carbon space by the Annex-I countries, the bulk of the Third World will obtain less than half its entitlement to carbon space. For India too, in particular, we see that eventually it would obtain a little less than half its entitlement of carbon space. For some other large developing countries, the situation is somewhat improved, and a country like China can attain much closer to its fair share of carbon space.

This aspect, where we try to estimate what will actually be available as carbon space to developing countries in physical terms, is a computation that is rarely considered in the carbon budget or cumulative emissions approaches. In much of the literature on the subject it is assumed that once the carbon space allocations, and hence entitlements, are fixed within a global constraint, the problem reduces to one of allowing trading (or direct compensation) in terms of the corresponding carbon space allowances. While this approach seems plausible, it is not clear whether such an approach is sufficient to ensure that the global constraint is not actually violated.

A more careful consideration of the actual physical carbon space available to the developing countries has also appeared to elude those who have focused on the cumulative emissions approach for another reason. Most of the analytical literature on climate policy from developing countries has focused on entitlements but has been slow to recognize that even developing countries would need to undertake substantial mitigation action in order to maintain global emissions within the global environmental constraint.

Especially in the emission flow perspective, such a question does not even present itself properly. A particularly negative feature of the flow approach is that it does not provide a proper analytical basis for developing countries to develop a considered approach to mitigation action, and thus leaves them somewhat querulously defending a position of climate inaction in the international arena On the contrary, from the

Equity and burden sharing in emission scenarios 143

Table 9.3 Entitlements and potentially realizable carbon space: 1850 basis

1850 basis [all values in GtC]	Total entitlements between 1850 and 2050 (GtC)	Actual current contribution (1850–2009)	Future entitlements (2010–2050)	TISS–DSF model (potentially realizable carbon space: 2010–2050) (Based on 48% cuts (of 1990 levels) by 2020 and 97% cuts by 2050 by Annex I)[*]	TISS–DSF Model (potentially realizable carbon space: 2010–2050) (Based on 63% cuts (of 1990 levels) by 2020 and 99% cuts by 2050 by Annex I)[#]
USA	29.1	95.6	−66.5	18.4	14.5
EU	45.5	86.7	−41.1	14.4	11.4
Other Annex-I	43.0	63.1	−20.1	17.4	13.7
India	110.0	8.6	101.3	45.1	56.3
China	123.9	33.2	90.7	90.0	88.3
Brazil	17.7	3.0	14.7	5.4	5.7
South Africa	4.4	3.7	0.8	1.5	1.2
Other Emerging Economies	72.7	24.2	48.4	31.8	30.5
Rest of the World	185.8	13.9	171.9	76.4	75.8
	632.0	332.0	300.0	300.4	297.4

[*]This scenario assumes that the maximum reductions possible for countries that have already occupied more than their fair share are 48% of 1990 levels by 2020 and 97% of 1990 levels by 2050

[#] This scenario assumes that the maximum reductions possible for countries that have already occupied more than their fair share are 63% of 1990 levels by 2020 and 99% of 1990 levels by 2050

emphasis on cumulative emissions in the carbon budget perspective, developing countries have a perspective from which to view their own contribution to keeping peak global warming to acceptable levels that can be formulated in terms that keep explicit track of equity concerns in a quantitative manner.

Thus the problem of burden-sharing in mitigation (or equivalently allocating carbon space within a global budget) would appear to have two parts. The first would be the question of redressing the over-occupation of carbon space by the developed countries. The second would be related to the actual distribution of physical carbon space. In the approaches we have so far, the second part has been done by an optimization program based on some normative rules. It would be interesting to see whether this can be replaced, most probably approximately, by a more analytical and simple formula.

Another way of getting a handle on India's requirements of physical carbon space is to actually develop models of India's requirement for energy and developmental imperatives in quantitative terms and derive a projection of India's likely emissions into the future. Such models however typically do not have a time horizon of more than 20 or 30 years. In some variants such models are connected with general equilibrium models in a combination of top-down and bottom-up approaches to this problem. We present in the table below, a comparison of the carbon budget for India for the period 2010–2050 based on a number of models[11] and compare them with the corresponding number from our optimization (TISS-DSF) model for the same period.

144 *Jayaraman, Kanitkar and D'Souza*

Table 9.4 Comparison of budgets allocated by various economic models

Model	Budget 2010–2030 [GtCe]	GHGs considered
NCAER-CGE (2030,31)	14.86	(CO_2 & N_2O)
TERI-MoEF (2031–32)	14.27	(CO_2)
IRADe AA (2030–31)	15.20	(?)
TERI Poznan (2030–31)	19.97	(CO_2)
McKinsey India (2030)	19.75	(all GHG)
TISS-DSF model – 1850 Scenario (2030)	18.11	(CO_2)
IEA-450 Scenario	10.61	(CO_2)

However it must be emphasized that all economic models have higher levels of uncertainty and it is unlikely that any developing country's requirement of carbon space can be reliably estimated from such economic models, and that too over an extended time-horizon of 40–50 years.

There is some policy pressure to generate rough ball-park figures of this kind and one may make a good case that the official publication of such numbers should be guided by political and climate negotiation considerations rather than by pure economic modelling considerations. Even by these admittedly raw considerations it is evident that India's accessible carbon space (under the best case scenarios of Annex I reductions, it must be emphasized) falls below the larger predictions and somewhat above the lower end of the projections. It is also significant that India by the IEA scenario gets much less. This is illustrative of the base-line determination problems that are characteristic of such studies.

Conclusions

It is the argument of this note that cumulative emissions and carbon budgets, both global and national together, provide a viable basis on which to seek a way forward in the operationalization of Article 2 and Article 3.1. Looking beyond the current narrowly defined discourse, it is evident that the carbon budget perspective provides a way to articulate the burden due to every country in checking GHG emissions, and it does so with a clear basis in equitable access to common property resources.[12] The crux of the problem is that equity cannot be really achieved in physical terms, not at least without the developed countries taking recourses to 'negative' emissions. However it is evident that the developed countries would obtain carbon space only by taking away the rightful share of the developing nations, in return for which the latter can legitimately lay claim to financial and technology transfer. Indeed the gap between rightful share and the physically attained share provides an unambiguous starting point for computing the value of such financial and technology transfers which had hitherto been always bogged down in more nebulous computations. This approach also makes evident India's unique position among the large developing countries.

It is clear that by any account India is not currently a major contributor to the flow or the stock of GHG emissions. While further growth and development may increase the flow of emissions, India would still remain below its population share of cumulative emissions for an extended period. Further it would never be able to access its fair share of cumulative emissions, especially if the global budget is around 300 Gt of

Equity and burden sharing in emission scenarios   145

carbon for the period 2010–2050. The critical question is the balance between what we are likely to get by way of physical carbon space eventually compared to the needs of India's developmental paradigm. To add to the difficulty of estimating this, which is difficult enough, one may add the difficulty of estimating India's needs for carbon space within a paradigm that ensures a decent level of material and spiritual well-being for the vast majority of the population. In the absence of a convincing response to this consideration, it would appear essential for India to conserve and claim as much as is possible physically of its carbon space in the short and the medium term.

Notes

1 For a useful survey that covers some major varieties of proposals see for instance Baumert et al. (ed.) (2002).
2 In his speech at the University of Michigan Law School on October 8, 2010, US Special Envoy for Climate Change, Todd Stern said, 'As noted, the United States, as well as a number of other countries, would not accept legally binding commitments unless China and other emerging markets did so as well, and they have made abundantly clear that they will not'. The entire speech is available here: http://www.state.gov/g/oes/rls/remarks/2010/149429.htm
3 Among the more prominent such proposals are the Bolivian proposal, and the negotiating text insertions by various parties including India, referring to 'equitable access to global atmospheric space'. This last phrase was present also in the negotiating text coming out of COP-15 at Copenhagen. For relevant references see, for instance, the Bolivian proposal at http://unfccc.int/resource/docs/2010/awglca10/eng/misc02.pdf
4 WRE is an acronym for the authors Wigley, T.M.L., Richels, R., and Edmonds, J.A. See Wigley et al. (1996).
5 Material related to the Greenhouse Development Rights framework can be accessed at http://www.gdrights.org
6 See http://www.gci.org.uk/index.html for a more detailed explanation of this approach.
7 In terms of specific numbers, Matthews et al. (2009) estimate that 1000 GtC would cause a temperature increase of 1–2.1°C (5%–95% confidence interval). Equivalently the cumulative emissions for a 2°C rise in temperature would lie in the range 1000–1900 GtC with a best estimate of 1400 GtC.
8 See 'Development of work on the Brazilian Proposal' at http://unfccc.int/methods_and_science/other_methodological_issues/items/1038.php
9 The three outliers are Eritrea, Vanuatu and Vietnam. It is somewhat surprising that these three outliers should have an impact, but it is a statistically correct fact for which we have no ready explanation at this time.
10 For an earlier version of the TISS-DSF model see Kanitkar et al. (2009). The model used in this chapter, based on a non-linear optimization, has been presented in Kanitkar et al. (2010).
11 Results of five model runs, namely, NCAER-CGE, TERI-MoEF, IRADe AA, TERI Poznan and McKinsey India appear in MoEF (2009).
12 We have not gone into this aspect of property rights on common property resources with respect to the global carbon sinks in detail here, which in many ways naturally leads to the notion of entitlements defined in terms of equal per capita cumulative emissions. For a broad defence of the per capita approach, see for instance, Sinden (2010).

References

Allen, M.R., Frame, D.J., Huntingford, C., Jones, C.D., Lowe, J.A., Meinshausen, M. and Meinshausen, N. (2009) 'Warming caused by cumulative carbon emissions towards the trillionth tonne', *Nature* 458, pp. 1163–1166.

Baumert, K.A, Blanchard, O., Llosa, S. and Perkaus, J. (ed.) (2002) *Building on the Kyoto Protocol, Options for Protecting the Climate*, World Resources Publication, Washington.

146 *Jayaraman, Kanitkar and D'Souza*

Höhne, N. and Moltmann, S. (2009) 'Sharing the effort under a global carbon budget', http://www.ecofys.com/com/publications/brochures_newsletters/sharing_the_effort_under_global_carbon_budget.htm, accessed on 15 March 2011.

Kanitkar, T., Jayaraman, T., D'Souza, M., Purkayastha, P., Raghunandan, D. and Talwar, R. (2009) 'How much "carbon space" do we have? Physical constraints on India's climate policy and its implications', *Economic and Political Weekly*, vol. XLIV, no. 41, pp. 35–46.

Kanitkar, T., Jayaraman, T., D'Souza, M., Purkayastha, P., Raghunandan, D. and Talwar, R. (2010) 'Conference on global carbon budgets and equity in climate change, Discussion Paper, Supplementary Notes and Discussion Report' Tata Institute of Social Sciences, available on the web at http://moef.nic.in/downloads/public-information/tiss-conference-cc-2010.pdf, accessed on 15 March 2011.

Matthews, H.D., Gillett, N.P., Stott, P.A. and Zickfeld, K. (2009) 'The proportionality of global warming to cumulative carbon emissions', *Nature* 459, pp. 829–833.

Meinshausen, M., Meinshausen, N., Hare, W., Raper, S.C.B., Frieler, K., Knutti, R., Frame, D.J. and Allen, M.R. (2009) 'Greenhouse-gas emission targets for limiting global warming to 2 deg C', *Nature* 458, pp. 1158–1163.

MoEF (Ministry of Environment and Forests), Government of India (2009) 'India's GHG Emissions Profile: Results of Five Climate Modelling Studies', http://moef.nic.in/downloads/home/GHG-report.pdf, accessed on 15 March 2011.

Nakicenovic, N. and Swart, R. (eds) (2000) 'Emissions Scenarios', Intergovernmental Panel on Climate Change, Cambridge University Press, Cambridge.

National Research Council (2011) 'Climate Stabilization Targets: Emissions, Concentrations, and Impacts over Decades to Millenia', http://dels.nas.edu/Materials/Report-In-Brief/4344-Stabilization-Targets, accessed on 15 March 2011.

Sinden, A. (2010) 'Allocating the Costs of the Climate Crisis: Efficiency Versus Justice', *Washington Law Review*, vol. 85, pp. 293–353.

UNFCCC (1992) Text of the Convention, http://unfccc.int/essential_background/convention/background/items/1349.php, accessed on 15 March 2011.

UNFCCC (2007) Bali Action Plan, http://unfccc.int/resource/docs/2007/cop13/eng/06a01.pdf#page=3, accessed on 15 March 2011.

Wigley, T.M.L., Richels, R. and Edmonds, J.A. (1996) 'Economic and environmental choices in the stabilization of atmospheric CO2 concentrations', *Nature* 379, pp. 240–243.

10 Equity in climate change
The range of metrics and views

Narasimha Rao

Eighteen years after the inception of the United Nations Framework Convention on Climate Change (UNFCCC) at the Earth Summit in Rio in 1992, 125 governments agreed to limit global temperature rise to 2°C in the Copenhagen Accord of 2009. Conspicuous by its absence in this Accord, however, was any agreement on how countries should share responsibility for reducing and adapting to climate change. For almost twenty years, developing countries (non-Annex I) have argued for equity, framed as a fair distribution of the earth's capacity to absorb human greenhouse gases (GHG). However, this position has remained largely a political stance, rather than a basis for dialogue in negotiations.

Despite, or perhaps due to, this impasse, the literature on climate equity has grown in two directions: philosophers and other scholars began writing about climate ethics; in parallel a number of new burden-sharing proposals have emerged, some as variations of their predecessors but in relative isolation from the philosophical literature. Are these various interpretations of equity substantially different, both in their ethical foundations and their practical implications? Does their similarity reflect their shared strength of principle, or do their differences undermine them? In this section, I explore very briefly the core ethical bases and differences between these proposals, with an emphasis on recent ones that quantify countries' obligations. Comprehensive surveys of equity proposals can be found elsewhere (den Elzen and Lucas, 2003; Klinsky and Dowlatabadi, 2009). I focus on distributive principles for climate change mitigation, rather than on corrective justice for damages already committed, because the former has been explored in greater depth. As this handbook has a focus on India, I also discuss the practical implications for India of implementing some of these burden-sharing proposals. I conclude with a brief reflection on the importance of resolving differences among equity views for moving international negotiations forward.

Equity principles

There are two broad families of proposals that differ fundamentally in how they frame the distribution problem. The dominant paradigm, which has spawned most of the literature on climate equity, frames justice as a claim to an environmental resource – the earth's carbon absorption capacity. A second approach treats the reduction of emissions as a cost to be shared. The problem is to define a fair distribution of these costs. Within each approach, several variations with distinct underlying distributive principles have been proposed. I look at these more closely.

148 Rao

Resource-sharing frame

Proponents of this view, pioneered by Agarwal and Narain (1991), view earth's capacity to absorb human GHGs as a global common on which all humans depend. Once use of this common has to be limited, its capacity has a scarcity value. Each country ought to have a claim to this common corresponding to their population share of the planet. States should have to mitigate only those emissions that are above their population's collective entitlement. This position has found support among several philosophers as well (Jamieson, 2001; Singer, 2002; Vanderheiden, 2009). This egalitarian distribution rule has been justified as a default, as the only just distribution of this scarce resource, in the absence of any other justifiable way to allocate it (Vanderheiden, 2009).

One of the first proposals on this basis was the Contraction and Convergence (C&C) proposal by the Global Commons Institute (GCI). All countries converge to a science-driven individual quota for emissions by a specified year, typically 2050. However, this proposal faced a number of objections, even among proponents of this broad view.

Some proponents of resource-sharing object that C&C is a 'time-slice' approach that ignores the cumulative effects of GHGs. C&C accounts only for the need for the planet to reach an equilibrium level of GHGs that matches earth's absorption capacity, or rather as a pipe where limited flow capacity must be shared. However, the atmosphere behaves more as a storage container where GHGs accumulate over time (that is, as a stock, rather than a flow).[1] Developed countries have already 'filled up' the atmosphere over the last 150 years during their industrialization with emissions far above this sustainable quota, which causes the need to limit future flows in the first place. Developing countries would not have that opportunity, given the urgency of reaching this steady state in the next 40 years.[2]

Scholars have responded to this concern with two types of modifications to the convergence approach: one type differentiates convergence targets for non-Annex I countries by their timing, sectoral emissions or other factors; and a second type provides for convergence to a per capita share of carbon 'stock', rather than flow. Among the first, a variation of C&C provides for a dynamic threshold for non-Annex I countries' participation. Non-Annex I countries would be obligated to undertake mitigation only once their average emissions reach a certain percentage of Annex I countries' average per capita emissions (Höhne et al., 2006).[3] Other proposals include similar staged, or differentiated, targets for non-Annex I countries for convergence, such as Triptych, which requires, among other things, that only certain sectors of the economy converge to a common threshold.[4]

A number of proposals define an individual entitlement to the stock of carbon 'space'. Other than sharing this principle, they differ in many respects among themselves. They differ with respect to the stringency of the scientific target that defines the allocable carbon space, whether they impose additional annual emissions constraints, and more critically, whether historical carbon space ought to count. Two proposals, from India (Kanitkar et al., 2009) and China (Pan et al., 2008), define the allocable space as the cumulative carbon space in the post-industrialization period, from 1850/1900 to 2050. An alternative proposal, from German scholars (WBGU, 2009), allocates only the remaining, cumulative budget between 2010 and 2050 to nations on a per capita basis.

The primary objection to including historical carbon use in estimates of the size of the allocable space is that of ignorance. Prior to knowing the risks of global warming, people in Annex I countries had emitted GHGs without knowing their future impacts.

Equity in climate change   149

However, it is not obvious how far back in time such claims of ignorance have merit. Some scholars have proposed 1970, based on when global warming was known to have been discussed in the US scientific community (Kanitkar et al., 2009). Certainly by 1990, after the release of the first Intergovernmental Panel on Climate Change (IPCC) report, it is widely accepted that ignorance can no longer be considered an excuse for inaction. Still, with regard to the Indian and Chinese proposals, the moral validity of including historical emissions *prior* to 1970 or 1990 turns on whether Annex I countries should be accountable for having 'used' their quota without having known they had one.[5] It has been argued that Annex I countries have, despite their ignorance in that period, reaped the benefits of these emissions (Caney, 2009). However, if the *benefits* derived from the use of carbon space influence whether their emissions count, then countries ought to distribute responsibility for mitigation directly based on these benefits, whose distribution may differ considerably from that of emissions.[6]

Another notable feature of these proposals is that they allocate carbon space to countries, albeit in proportion to their populations, even though the language of 'per capita' suggests an individual entitlement to carbon space. What is the ethical justification for population as a basis for allocation, if not to assure each individual an equal share of a putatively necessary, scarce resource? And if this entitlement is indeed for individuals – as many philosophers who support this view take for granted – then how should one deal with the practical reality that emissions are far from equitably shared within countries? This issue is discussed under the heading, Pushing boundaries in climate equity. What is noteworthy regarding the literature is the relative absence of discussion on this issue.

Burden-sharing frame

Under this view, scholars define various moral bases for allocating the burdens of mitigation. The Brazilian Proposal (1997) first raised the idea of allocating mitigation costs in proportion to countries' historical contribution to global warming potential (GWP). This proposal spawned a number of others that allocate mitigation costs to countries based either on responsibility for causing global warming (such as GWP or emissions) or the capacity to absorb the burdens of mitigation (e.g. average GDP or Human Development Index (HDI)), or a combination thereof. Consistent with the Aristotelian dictum, 'what is proportional is just' (Müller, 2001), Parties with the same levels of either responsibility or capacity should bear the same mitigation burden.

Most of these proposals combine responsibility and capacity in different ways to develop targets for emissions reductions below business as usual (BAU) trajectories for non-Annex I countries. Greenhouse Development Rights (GDR) allows for policy-makers to choose the relative weight of cumulative responsibility (since 1990) and capacity as the distributive principle for allocating mitigation costs to countries (Baer et al., 2008). Michaelowa (2007) suggests gradually deeper targets for countries based on an index of roughly comparable weight of per capita annual emissions and income, starting with an exemption from any targets for those below a threshold value of the index. Frankel (2007) suggests that non-Annex I countries start with modest targets related to current BAU emissions, which subsequently index to per capita income, and then in the long-run transition to population-based targets, equivalent to per capita emissions entitlements. However, these proposals seem to underestimate the difficulty

150 *Rao*

and ramifications for burden allocation in defining 'BAU' emissions trajectories. Past trends – the usual basis for their projection – may not adequately reflect changes in the economy, particularly in low income countries, that may lead to a substantial deviation from historical trends in carbon intensity.

Several burden-sharing proposals constrain countries' mitigation obligations to avoid impinging on populations' basic needs. These entitlements are often interpreted as 'subsistence emissions', particularly among those who frame mitigation obligations in terms of emissions (Pan et al., 2008; Müller et al., 2009).[7] GDR frames these rights as 'development rights', which are quantified as income. Both forms of exemption rest on the principle that all human activities – and consequently the emissions they generate – do not have the same moral priority in determining which ought to be sacrificed for mitigation. People below this specified income – or emissions – threshold should not be encumbered by mitigation costs. But who should be exempt from bearing mitigation burdens? On what basis should their eligibility be determined? An income measure, adjusted for price differences across countries, is a step closer than emissions for encapsulating people's eligibility for exemption, but does not universally correlate with aspects of human well-being, such as health or education, which are hard to measure.

The quest for a reasonable indicator of human well-being will always entail a tension between inclusiveness and measurability: this is a universal endeavour that is not unique to climate change. However, for any chosen metric, at what level should a threshold be set? The wide range of thresholds used reflects the subjectivity inherent in such an exercise. Müller et al. (2009) subtract 2 tCO_2eq for each person earning below \$1 and \$2/day (in different scenarios) from countries' cumulative emissions. Chakravarty et al. (2009) exempt all emissions below 1 tCO_2, which varies in income terms across countries and over time, but is in the range of \$5–10/day. At the other extreme, Baer et al. (2008) use a threshold of ~\$20/day, which is higher than even the US poverty line of ~\$13/day. As discussed under the heading, Implications for India, the financial ramifications of these choices are significant.

In summary, there is significant support in the climate equity literature for a distribution of future mitigation burdens in proportion to countries' historical emissions, and for the proposition that certain poor segments of society should not have to bear mitigation burdens. However, both principles have been applied with a wide range of thresholds, which indicate that the underlying moral premises are difficult to objectively operationalize. The definitions of these thresholds may not only be tied to deeper moral issues of entitlement that extend beyond climate change, but may also require country-specific definitions to reflect contextual differences.

Pushing boundaries in climate equity

In this section, I raise two moral questions about the scope of these equity proposals. The first concerns the importance of extending distributive concerns from the national to the individual level; and the second concerns the duties and obligations of non-Annex I countries.

We have seen that in seeking to exempt certain populations from mitigation burdens, some burden-sharing proposals incorporate *intra*-national income, or emissions, distribution into global burden-sharing arrangements. In doing so, they invoke an explicitly individualistic moral principle. Resource-sharing proposals, on the other hand,

Equity in climate change   151

strictly avoid intranational equity, but nevertheless base their national entitlements on population, derived from a 'per capita' entitlement to carbon space. This raises the obvious question: should an equity proposal that is founded on individual entitlements not be concerned that individuals receive the benefits of those entitlements? Some philosophers have recognized this disconnect (Singer, 2002), but many of the proposals are silent on this issue. This is particularly important in light of the widespread prevalence of income inequality and inequitable patterns of development. Would justice obtain if countries, hypothetically, receive mitigation exemptions consistent with these proposals, but deprive a section of their population of their share? Alternatively, if countries deserve emissions entitlements in *proportion to their* population, not necessarily for individuals to enjoy equally, but for general economic growth (for e.g., for 'collective emissions', such as from power plants), the fruits of which states may choose to distribute at their discretion, there needs to be some justification for such a distribution, particularly if it can entail some members being deprived of their basic needs as an indirect result of other members' mitigation commitments.

Another question that emerges from the literature is, should non-Annex I countries be *obliged* to identify and pursue 'no-lose' strategies for mitigation in exchange for an exemption from mitigation?[8] There is a rich literature on the importance of and opportunities for sustainable development paths and policies (Sathaye et al., 2007). Some equity proposals indeed suggest that non-Annex I countries voluntarily pursue such 'no-lose' mitigation strategies (Höhne et al., 2006; Baer et al. 2008) or adopt emissions intensity-based targets (den Elzen and Lucas, 2003; Birdsall and Subramanian, 2009). In principle, foregone opportunities of this kind would be tantamount to an avoidable use of carbon space that deprives other non-Annex I countries in much the same way that Annex I country emissions would. From this perspective, it seems reasonable to expect that *all* countries should keep carbon intensity to a minimum. But there are practical concerns that such options may be difficult to identify or involve hidden institutional costs. The challenge is to operationalize this principle in a manner that provides countries with the right incentives but without unreasonable expectations of institutional change.

Implications for India

How do the various proposals compare in their assessment of India's mitigation obligations? Tables 10.1a and 10.1b shows a number of metrics and features of the main equity-based proposals and their implications for India. A number of caveats are in order. Comparing proposals' mitigation allocation outcomes borders on comparing apples and oranges – proposals use numerous assumptions that can differ across them, including the scope of commitment (based on GHG concentration target and the timeframe for GHG stabilization), countries' growth, emissions and income characteristics, mitigation cost assumptions, and the output metrics, among others. Second, there are *numerous* proposals, with different degrees of quantification and detail. A comprehensive review is beyond the scope of this chapter.

In the following exercise, the focus was to compare how much of the global mitigation burden India would have to bear and *when*. Only certain scenarios have been picked from the various proposals, with the intent of capturing the range of obligations India would face. Finally, some of these estimates are approximate because they are drawn from numbers and graphs in executive summaries.

Table 10.1a Comparison of resource-sharing proposals – Indian perspective

Proposal[1]	Allocation time period	Exemption threshold (Global)	Average remaining carbon entitlement[2] $(tCO_2/per/yr)$	Peaking year (India)	Peak per capita emissions (India)	Stabilization target (Year)
Convergence approaches						
Common & differentiated convergence[4]	2050	90% of world avg per cap tCO_2	2.9	2030	4.8 tCO_2	~30% below 2005 (2050)
Princeton	2030	1 tCO_2 per cap (~$5.5/day in 2003)	9.6[6]	>2030	Unspecified	~20% below 2005 (2030)
Budget approaches						
WBGU– German	2010– 2050	–	2.7	~2030	4 tCO_2	See Note 7
TISS–India (Scenario IV)	1970– 2050	–	~4.5[3]	~2040	6–7 tCO_2	57% below 2005 (2050)
Chinese Acad. Community	1900– 2050	–	~4.5[5]	>2050	7.3 tCO_2	50% below 2005 (2050)

1 Shows particular scenarios, which are not necessarily the only ones calculated by the authors.
2 Based on achieving 450ppm, using constant population (Kanitkar et al., 2009; WBGU, 2009; Pan et al. (2008), except for differentiated C&C, which is based on 550ppm stabilization and uses variable population.
3 Kanitkar et al. (2009): Table 6 (Converted using 3.66 CO_2/C , and 1.18 b (2009 population))
4 Höhne et al. (2006), the only proposal on the table based on a 550ppm target stabilization
5 Pan et al. (2008): Table 4 (Converted using 1.1 b (2005 population)
6 Chakravarty et al. (2009). Represents an interim target for 2030, hence is not comparable to the others.
7 2050 target emissions unavailable, but likely lower than the TISS-India proposal, because the carbon budget is smaller (750 $GtCO_2$ vs. 1,100 $GtCO_2$ in the period 2010–2050).

Table 10.1b Comparison of burden-sharing proposals – Indian perspective

Proposal[1]	Allocation period	Exemption threshold	Mitigation cost (India)[2]
GDR (Capacity-based)	–	$20/day	~$114 b[1]
GDR (Responsibility-based)	1990–2030	$20/day	$143 b[1]

1 Other proposals referenced in the text do not have sufficient quantification to include here.
2 Based on an assumption that annual global mitigation costs are 1% of Gross World Product, starting in 2012 (*Greenhouse Development Rights*, Baer et al. (2008)).

Equity in climate change   153

The most notable aspect of this comparison is that under all the resource-sharing proposals, including the 'time-slice' variants, Indian emissions can grow unencumbered at least till 2030. Under the stock-based versions, Indian emissions can 'do nothing' until 2040, and even till 2050 in the Chinese case. Put another way, India may not have to mitigate until average per capita emissions exceed anywhere from 4 to 7 tons. In a report of the Climate Modelling Forum, only one of five climate model projections of India's emissions in 2030 puts India's average emissions in this range, at 5 tons per capita (Climate Modelling Forum, 2009). Furthermore, in the Indian and Chinese proposals, 'negative entitlements' of developed countries – historical emissions in excess of their fair share – should be treated as a debt to be repaid to developing countries, which would amount to up to $90 billion in the Chinese case.

In GDR, the $114–144 billion mitigation obligations for India are based on a fairly arbitrary assumption of global mitigation costs being 1 per cent of gross world product (GWP). Another interpretation of their result is that India's share of global mitigation burdens increases gradually from zero in 2010 to ~1 percent of GWP by 2030. Note that this may be an overestimate, since 'BAU' in GDR most likely does not incorporate current trends of fairly aggressive reduction in the carbon intensity of the Indian economy (Rao et al., 2009).

On the one hand these results seem to vindicate India's political position that its high total emissions belie its vast poverty, a condition that even when compared to other countries in the next two decades requires that it remain free from the burden of climate mitigation. On the other hand, barring GDR and the Princeton proposal, the resource-sharing proposals give India's growing upper classes a free ride. Further, they allow India to forego significant opportunities to improve efficiency and find more sustainable growth paths as India more than doubles its infrastructure in the next decade.

The other observation of note is that indeed these proposals vary widely, in their scope, principles, assumptions and outcomes. The difference between peaking in 2030 vs. 2050, spending $100 billion or not, exempting the poor below $5/day or below $20/day, or whether to differentiate populations at a subnational level at all, seem substantial. What should one make of these differences?

Getting the principles right – does it matter?

It is ironic that while governments of developed countries in negotiations have moved towards grandfathering their historical emissions, many recent equity proposals place even greater demands on developed countries than earlier proposals. This growing divergence between international climate politics and equity scholars gives cause to reflect on the relationship between them. Whether equity formulations are a strategic tool of non-Annex 1 countries' negotiators, or the moral standard against which public advocates battle to hold negotiators, they seem to have had little success in engaging countries in a constructive dialogue on equity. Further, their practical implications of absolving many developing economies of any obligation to pursue opportunities for reducing carbon intensity are politically controversial, and arguably morally unconvincing. In either case, however, there seems to be a need to rethink the role and strategy of equity proposals for international climate negotiations.

In this introspection, one question that stands out for equity scholars is, how important is it for achieving a fair distribution of responsibility in practice that these

154 Rao

various positions converge? As the synthesis above has shown, despite general agreement that Annex I countries should bear the bulk of mitigation costs, there are significant differences among different equity camps, both in principle and in their burden-sharing outcomes. One can subscribe to at least the following, fairly disparate, positions with regard to the importance of reconciling these differences:

> 1 A morally compelling formulation of justice is the only way to incorporate equity substantively into political dialogue. Defensible, widely supported equity principles are the most likely to have traction in negotiations. Equity scholars need to address some of their moral ambiguities, or demonstrate the unity of their practical implications and their immunity to subjective differences in their moral premises.

Alternatively:

> 2 A strong non-Annex I equity position, even if morally rough around the edges, is the only negotiating position that can stave off Annex I countries' efforts to disregard equity considerations. Equity positions are a posturing tool in a political environment that will not entertain moral arguments. Equity scholars would be wasting their time sorting out their internal disagreements.

The implications of these positions for equity scholars and their efforts to influence future negotiations can be quite different. Sorting out the motives of scholars in revising equity formulations may be a good place to start.

Notes

1 Carbon dioxide (CO_2) is the most potent GHG because it lasts for hundreds of years in the atmosphere. Methane, the next most important GHG, has 25 times the global warming potential of CO_2 (over a 100 year period), but a residence time of <12 years.
2 In principle, non-Annex 1 countries could exceed and revert to this steady state level by 2050. However, the demands such a pace of change would impose on institutions would be unprecedented and unrealistic.
3 This exemption rule also addresses a practical consideration that allocating excess allowances to poor countries would entitle them to financial transfers that would be politically controversial in Annex I countries.
4 See Höhne et al. (2006) for a review of these proposals.
5 Note that this question is different from whether non-Annex I countries are liable for the damages that have already occurred (or will occur) due to their historical emissions. That is, whether poor countries should be compensated for their adaptation to climate damages is a separate matter from whether the poor countries should be compensated for the lost opportunity to use the carbon space to which they have no access because of Annex I countries' prior use of that space. There may be legal and moral precedent for the former, but which does not necessarily apply to the latter.
6 Income, for example, though correlated with emissions up to a certain level, varies widely on an average basis across and within countries. See Chakravarty et al. (2009).
7 Note that the calculation of states' mitigation obligation resembles that of the resource-sharing view, where a certain amount of emissions is subtracted from states' total emissions, where the level of exemption is based on the extent of intranational poverty in the first case, and on ownership of carbon 'property rights' in the latter.
8 'No-lose', or 'no-regrets' mitigation strategies are those that have net positive developmental benefits. They should be implemented anyway, even in the absence of climate considerations.

References

Agarwal, A. and Narain, S. (1991) *Global Warming in an Unequal World: A Case of Environmental Colonialism*, Centre for Science and Environment, New Delhi.

Baer, P., Athanasiou, T., Kartha, S. and Kemp-Benedict, E. (2008) *The Greenhouse Development Rights Framework: The Right to Development in a Climate Constrained World*, Christian Aid, Heinrich Boll Foundation, EcoEquity and the Stockholm Environment Institute, Berlin.

Birdsall, N. and Subramanian, A. (2009) *Energy Needs and Efficiency, Not Emissions: Re-framing the Climate Change Narrative*, Center for Global Development, Washington DC.

Brazil (1997) *Proposed elements of a protocol to the United Nations Framework Convention on Climate Change, presented by Brazil in response to the Berlin Mandate*, in UNFCCC, *Implementation of the Berlin Mandate*. UNFCCC/AGBM/1997/ MISC.1/Add.3 GE.97.

Caney, S. (2009) 'Justice and the distribution of greenhouse gas emissions', *Journal of Global Ethics*, vol. 5, no. 2, pp. 125–146.

Chakravarty, S., Chikkatur, A., de Coninck, H., Pacala, S., Socolow, R. and Tavoni, M. (2009) 'Sharing global CO_2 emission reductions among one billion high emitters', *Proceedings of the National Academy of Sciences*, vol. 106, no. 29, pp. 11884–11888.

Climate Modelling Forum (2009) *India's GHG Emissions Profile: Results of Five Climate Modelling Studies*, Ministry of Environment and Forest, Government of India, New Delhi.

den Elzen, M.G.J. and Lucas, P. (2003) *FAIR 2.0 – A Decision-support Tool to Assess the Environmental and Economic Consequences of Future Climate Regimes*, RIVM Report No. 550015001, Bilthoven, Netherlands.

Frankel, J. (2007) 'Formulas for quantitative emissions targets', in J.E. Aldy, and R.N. Stavins (eds) *Architectures for Agreement: Addressing Global Climate Change in the Post-Kyoto World*, Cambridge University Press, Cambridge, UK.

Höhne, N., den Elzen, M.G.J. and Weiss, M. (2006) 'Common but differentiated convergence (CDC): A new conceptual approach to long-term climate policy', *Climate Policy*, vol. 6, pp. 181–199.

Jamieson, D. (2001) 'Climate change and global environmental justice', in P. Edwards and C. Miller (eds) *Changing the Atmosphere: Expert Knowledge and Global Environmental Governance*, MIT Press, Cambridge, MA.

Kanitkar, T., Jayaraman, T., D'Souza, M., Sanwal, M., Purkayastha, P. and Talwar, R. (2009) 'Meeting Equity in a Finite Carbon World: Global Carbon Budgets and Burden Sharing in Mitigation Actions', Background paper for the Conference on 'Global Carbon Budgets and Equity in Climate Change', 28–29 June, 2010, Tata Institute of Social Sciences, Mumbai.

Klinsky, S. and Dowlatabadi, H. (2009) 'Conceptualizations of justice in climate policy', *Climate Policy*, vol. 9, pp. 88–108.

Michaelowa, A. (2007) 'Graduation and deepening', in J.E. Aldy and R.N. Stavins (eds) *Architectures for Agreement: Addressing Global Climate Change in the Post-Kyoto World*, Cambridge University Press, Cambridge, UK.

Müller, B. (2001) 'Varieties of distributive justice in climate change', *Climatic Change*, vol. 48, no. 2, pp. 273–288.

Müller, B., Höhne, N. and Ellermann, C. (2009) 'Differentiating (historic) responsibilities for climate change', *Climate Policy*, vol. 9, pp. 593–611.

Pan, J. (2004) 'Common but differentiated commitments: A practical approach to engaging large developing emitters under L20', in *Post-Kyoto Architecture: Toward an L20?*, Council on Foreign Relations, New York.

Pan, J., Chen, Y., Wang, W. and Li, C. (2008) *Carbon Budget Proposal, Global Emissions under Carbon Budget Constraint on an Individual Basis for an Equitable and Sustainable post 2012 International Climate Regime*, Research Centre for Sustainable Development, Chinese Academy of Social Sciences, Beijing.

156   Rao

Rao, N.D., Sant, G. and Rajan, S.C. (2009) *An Overview of Indian Energy Trends: Low Carbon Growth and Development Challenges*, Prayas Energy Group, Pune, India.

Sathaye, J., Najam, A., Cocklin, C., Heller, T., Lecocq, F., Llanes-Regueiro, J., Pan, J., Petschel-Held, G., Rayner, S., Robinson, J., Schaeffer, R., Sokona, Y., Swart, R. and Winkler, H. (2007) 'Sustainable Development and Mitigation', in *Climate Change 2007: Mitigation*, Contribution of Working Group III to the Fourth Assessment Report of the Intergovernmental Panel on Climate Change [B. Metz, O.R. Davidson, P.R. Bosch, R. and Dave, L.A. Meyer (eds)], Cambridge University Press, Cambridge, United Kingdom and New York, NY, USA.

Singer, P. (2002) *One World: Ethics of Globalization*, Yale University Press, New Haven.

Vanderheiden, S. (2009) *Atmospheric Justice: A Political Theory of Climate Change*, Oxford University Press, New York.

WBGU (German Advisory Council on Global Change) (2009) *Solving the Climate Dilemma: The Budget Approach*, Special Report, Berlin, http://eeac.hscglab.nl/files/DWBGU_SolvingtheClimateDilemma_Dec09.pdf, accessed 25 February 2011.

11 Climate change debate
The rationale of India's position[1]

Prodipto Ghosh

Introduction

The debate on multilateral action on climate change between the developed and developing countries has been sharply polarized for a long-time. If one may mix a metaphor with a descriptive term, India has been in the eye of this storm since the beginning of multilateral concern on climate change in the 1980s, since it has invariably and forcefully brought in the 'development' and 'poverty eradication' sides of the argument, and seems not to buy into the response from many developed countries that the concern for the preservation of the planet's present climate supersedes the former, or that aggressive climate action is consistent with maintaining, or even enhancing growth rates and poverty eradication efforts.

The positions of both sides, developed and developing, seem to have become further entrenched over time, in particular since the rejection of the Kyoto Protocol by the US Congress on the stated plea that GHG mitigation action by the USAwould be negated rapidly, unless 'key developing countries', i.e. China and India, (but also Brazil; South Africa, Mexico, and South Korea), also undertook similar actions. The US rejection, and the stated grounds for it, subsequently spawned a massive political effort by many developed countries, in particular the EU, Japan, Canada, and Australia, to reach a 'comprehensive' global arrangement that would also include the USA and these 'key developing countries'. Other developing countries are not as serious a target of these efforts.

The key feature of these 'key developing countries' distinguishing them from other developing countries, is, of course, their *size*. Brazil is slightly smaller in size in terms of land area (8.514 million sq km) and about 60 per cent population (187 million) as the USA (9.632 million sq km and 299.8 million), the largest developed country. India is slightly under 4 times the US in population (1,134.4 million), but with only about 34 per cent of its land area (3.287 million sq km – the area under crop agriculture is, however, about the same). China is more than 4 times the USA in population (1,313 million), with about the same land area (9.598 million sq km).[2] Surely, the developed country argument goes, the rapid growth of the economies of these countries, involving increasing use of energy, would lead to such massive quantities of GHG emissions, that no matter how stringent the emissions curbs in developed countries, the planet's climate would, in short order, be at severe risk.

The broad response to this argument, as of course is immediately pointed out by these very countries, is that they are all still very poor,[3] no matter that they have experienced high GDP growth rates in recent times; that their per capita energy use (and consequently per capita GHG emissions are just a fraction of those of the developed countries; and in terms of the accumulations of GHGs in the atmosphere, which is what actually leads to climate change their responsibility is miniscule or negative[4] (depending upon the methodology employed). Moreover, endless media repetition has led to several myths in developed countries, about the alleged energy profligacy and environmental irresponsibility of these 'key developing countries'.

This chapter presents the gist of the arguments made by India, as one of the targeted 'key developing countries', and as also broadly reflecting the concerns not only of this group, but also of a much broader set of developing countries, since, apart from scale, India is in most respects pretty typical of the poorer half of the developing world.

India's development and environmental challenges

Despite several impressive technological attainments, for example in space exploration, nuclear energy, information technology, automobile engineering, and agriculture, and a thin sliver of prosperity and cosmopolitanism in its teeming metro cities, India remains one of the world's poorest countries. Of the 1 billion+ population,[5] more than 800 million people (79.9 per cent of the population), a population larger than that of North America and EU combined, still subsist on less than US$ 2 per day. Within this group, more than 450 million people, about the population of the US, live on less that US$ 1.25 per day.[6] More than 700 million people still cook on traditional cookstoves using crop waste and animal residue – a majority of this group, more than 400 million people, live without electricity. One of the enduring images of India's periodic national and state elections is that of the rural poor mobbing legislative candidates, demanding electricity, so that their children could do their school homework! Electricity enables literacy, as also health-care, immunization, safe water,

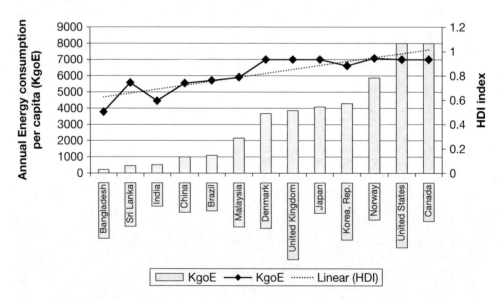

Figure 11.1 An international comparison between Human Development Index and per-capita energy consumption

Source: World Development Indicators Database

India's position in the climate change debate 159

and sanitation, which would enable India to improve its human development indicators[7] (global rank: 128, HDR value: 0.610, life expectancy at birth: 63.2 years, adult literacy rate: 61.0 per cent, GDP per capita: US$ in PPP 3,452), that are next only to Sub-Saharan Africa.

No country in history has improved its level of human development without a corresponding increase in per capita use of energy. To expect India to do so would be unrealistic. At present, India's per capita energy consumption is about 20 per cent of the global average, just 4 per cent of the US, and even in relation to China, just 28 per cent.

Nevertheless, India has proactively addressed its energy use and GHG emissions, as other chapters in this volume attest. Further, India has been highly vulnerable to climate variability (floods, droughts, cyclones, ocean surges) for millennia. Not just the present-day policy-makers, but the erstwhile British administrators, and before them, successive Indian dynasties over the centuries grappled with the impacts of the fickle climate. For many decades, India has had major, publicly funded programmes to address both the direct impacts, or prevention and control, of climate risks. In addition, other major public programmes focused on creation of infrastructure, or poverty eradication, have had, as a major objective, the reduction of vulnerability to climate risks. At present, India's Central (Federal) Government, spends no less that 12 per cent of its annual budget, or 2.63 per cent of the GDP on these programmes. *In point of fact, this is more than India's annual defence expenditure!* Figure 11.2 provides some recent data on the aggregate expenditures, while Figure 11.3 shows the programme areas where the money was spent. The programme areas were identified on the basis that each included programme would have among its stated objectives, reducing vulnerability to climate variability.

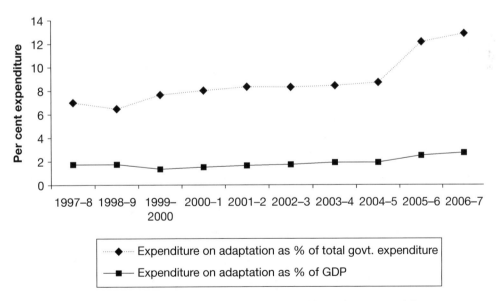

Figure 11.2 Annual central government expenditures to address climate variability, 1997–2000

Source: Data from Government of India Budget Documents, several years

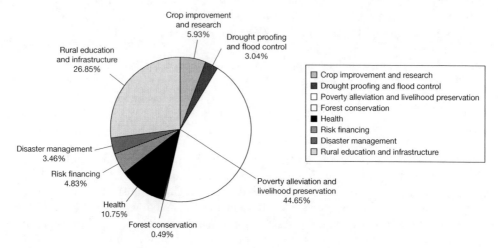

Figure 11.3 Components of adaptation expenditure, 2006–7
Source: Data from Government of India Budget Documents, 2007–8

The issue of lifestyles

A curious perception is that India's low level of current and historical responsibility for climate change simply reflects its large-scale poverty, and that as people become better off they would quickly assume the life-styles prevalent in developed countries, but without the attendant environmental safeguards. The view does not account for the strong environmental ethic, specifically, a 'waste not' mindset, and deep reverence for nature and all living forms, that is deeply embedded in the culture of the people, and which remains unchanged with increased prosperity. Nor does it reflect awareness of the comprehensive policy and regulatory structure, besides publicly funded programmes, that are in place to address environmental concerns. Some international comparisons are given below to illustrate, first, the fact that India has a strong environmental performance in terms of key sustainability parameters which are indexed to eliminate the effects of incomes; and second, the outcomes traceable to environmental interventions of the government.

In case of India and China, the CO_2 emissions from the food sector per kCal of food are an order of magnitude below that of the developed countries shown. A break-up of the emissions in each case into the respective contributions of the food production and food processing (including packaging) components shows that in the case of developed countries, the latter dominates the CO_2 emissions. Indians prefer fresh produce to processed food, and irrespective of economic status, buy fresh produce *each day*. Moreover, there is very little meat consumption (in terms of percentage of daily calories intake from meat), and this remains true even when people become richer.[8]

Figure 11.5 presents comparative data on recycling rates of municipal waste for India and three developed countries.[9] India is well-ahead of even Japan, the developed country with the most aggressive regulations to promote recycling. What accounts for the Indian performance? Very simply, India has a long, cultural tradition of recycling (as well as repair and re-use) – even wealthy households recycle everything possible – paper, metal, glass, plastic. A well-established network of non-formal sector recyclers

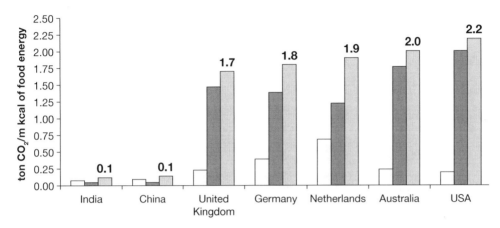

Figure 11.4 CO$_2$ emissions from the food sector – from field (production) to table (processed food) excluding cooking

Source: TERI Analysis, various data sources

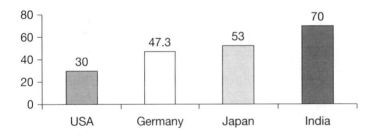

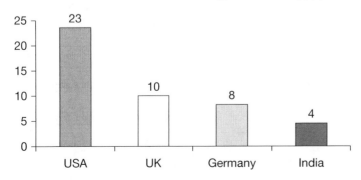

Figure 11.5
Recycling of solid waste and waste-related emissions

Source: TERI Analysis, based on national communications of different countries

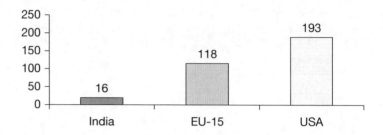

Figure 11.6
CO_2 emissions from passenger transport

Source: TERI Analysis, 2005, various data sources

visits every household at least once a month to buy the recyclables from the households. Stripped bare of recyclables, the actually disposed municipal garbage consists mainly of kitchen waste, which too is largely made into compost, rather than land-filled.

Another indicator of sustainability is CO_2 emissions from passenger transport.

A comparison is presented in Figure 11.6 of data from India, EU-15, and the USA, on CO_2 emissions per passenger-kilometre of transport use. Again, India's emissions are less than one-seventh those of EU-15, and just one-twelfth those of the USA. What accounts for this enormous difference? Notwithstanding the recent increase in ownership of private vehicles, public and mass-transport, i.e. rail and bus, account for the major share of transport demand, including the annual incremental increase. Even in respect of automobiles, there is a strong cultural preference for fuel-efficient vehicles,[10] i.e. cars and two-wheelers, and there is a rapid increase in vehicles powered by natural gas, and more recently, especially in case of two-wheelers, electric vehicles.

There are numerous other dimensions of India's culture that are conducive to sustainability. Most Indians are, in fact, not vegetarians, but almost all Indians are mostly vegetarian, signifying that only a small proportion of daily calorie intake is from foods of animal origin. Indians bathe twice a day, every day, but with a single bucket of water (25 litres). They switch off all appliances promptly when not required.[11] They do not waste food. These habits do not change when Indians become richer – they do not consume more meat, for instance. The National Geographic's Greendex, which evaluates a large set of developed and developing countries for environmental sustainability, has in May 2009, ranked India as the world's most environmentally sustainable society.[12]

A further demonstration of sustainability is provided by a comparison of the so-called 'Environmental Kuznets Curve (EKC)' of India and some other countries. The EKC reflects a near-universal phenomenon, that as countries grow, their environmental parameters at first worsen, and then improve, as higher incomes raise public environmental consciousness, and also enable public resources to be spent on environmental management. A typical turning point for developed countries in respect of several sustainability parameters is an income level of c.US$ (PPP) 6,000–7,000. The concept of the EKC is illustrated in Figure 11.7.

In the following tables, estimates of the turning points (in terms of per-capita incomes) of the statistically estimated EKC curves from India and several other countries by various authors are presented.

Table 11.1 presents the estimates of the EKC turning points for India and a set of 32 countries, which include both developed and other developing countries, for two key municipal wastewater parameters in the receiving waters. The estimated turning points for India by various authors are much lower than for the set of 32 countries.

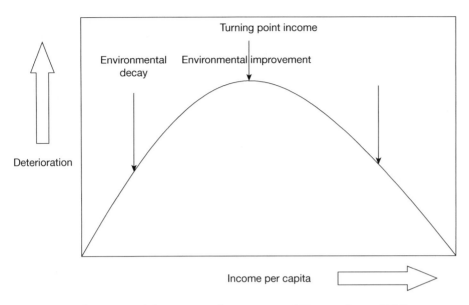

Figure 11.7 Illustration of the concept of Environmental Kuznets Curve (EKC)

Table 11.1 EKC estimates of turning points of India and a set of 32 countries (developed and developing) for wastewater treatment

	Countries	BOD	COD	Wastewater
MK ^	India		$523	
GK ^	Up to 32 countries	$7,623	$7,853	
CSB ^	India	$2,369		
NP ^^	India	$65 **		
Current study	India	$548 and $2,388**	$1,668**	$3,150 (CI cities) $1,694 (CII cities)

MK = Mukherjee and Kathuria (2006)
GK = Grossman and Krueger (1995)
CSB = Chandra Sahu and Bali (2006)
NP = Narayanan and Palanivel (2003)

* N shaped, ** U shaped
^ in 1985 US $
^^ in 1995 US $

For the study by MK, a composite index of pollution including 63 environmental indicators has been used as the dependent variable.

Note: 'Current study' refers to a TERI Study, 2008. 'BoD' is Biological Oxygen Demand, and 'CoD' is Chemical Oxygen Demand. 'CI' cities refers to Class I cities (5 metros), and 'CII' cities refers to Class II cities – in India cities are classified in terms of size.

164 *Ghosh*

Similarly, Table 11.2 gives the estimated EKC turning points for several key urban air quality parameters, i.e. sulphur dioxide (SO_2), suspended particulates (SPM), and nitrogen oxides (NOx). Once again, the estimated turning points in the case of India are much lower than for the other sets of countries.

Table 11.3 presents estimates of the EKC turning points for India and several other country groups in respect of energy intensity of the GDP. All three developing countries (Bangladesh, India, Sri Lanka) accomplished their turning points at much lower income levels than the three developed countries (Japan, Norway, Switzerland). Of all countries, the turning point in respect of India was at the lowest per capita income level.[13]

The way forward – India's perspectives

Given this background, I now look at what India's proposals are, so far, for moving forward on the key issues in the global climate change agenda.[14] For the sake of convenience, I look at India's approach in terms of the 'building blocks' and some other key elements of the Bali Action Plan (BAP).

GHG mitigation

In India's view, developed countries need to commit to deep, long-term, legally binding GHG reductions, consistent with the espoused level and time-frame of GHG

Table 11.2 Air quality: comparisons of EKC turning points for India and several other country groups

	Countries	*SO2*	*SPM*	*NO$_x$*
MK ^	India	$523		
CRB ^	11 OECD	$6,900	$7,300	$14,700
GK1 ^	Up to 32 countries	$4,107		
GK2 ^	Up to 32 countries	$4,053		
P1 ^		$3,000	$4,500	$5,500
P2 ^	30 developed and developing	$5,000		
SS ^	22 OECD and 8 developing	$10,700	$9,600	$21,800
S ^	31 countries	$3,670	$3,280	
Our estimates	India (industrial, transport and residential sectors)**	$1,695	$1,640*	$1,707
		$957	$1,440*	$1,413*
		$1,752	$1,840	$1,770

MK = Mukherjee and Kathuria (2006)
CRB = Cole et al. (1997)
GK1 = Grossman and Krueger (1993)
GK2 = Grossman and Krueger (1995)
P1 = Panayotou (1995)
P2 = Panayotou (1997)
SS = Selden and Song (1994)
S = Shafik and Bandhopadhya (1994)

^ in 1985 US $
* U shaped
** industrial, transport and residential sectors, respectively for the study by MK, a composite index of pollution including 63 environmental indicators has been used as the dependent variable.

Note: 'Our estimates' refers to a TERI study, 2008

Table 11.3 Energy intensity of GDP: EKC turning points for India and several other countries

	Specification	Shape	Turning point	Current income*
Bangladesh	Quadratic	EKC	$1,377	$1,827
India	Country	EKC	$501	$3,072
Japan	Quadratic	U	$22,675	$27,817
Netherlands	Linear	Monotonically decreasing	–	$29,078
Norway	Quadratic	EKC	$10,274	$36,849
Pakistan	Linear	Monotonically decreasing	–	$2,109
Sri Lanka	Quadratic	U	$4,092	$4,088
Sweden	Linear	Monotonically decreasing	–	$28,936
Switzerland	Quadratic	EKC	$26,122	$31,701
UK	Linear	Monotonically decreasing	–	$29,571

*GDP per capita at constant 2000 international $, PPP in 2005

Note: Where the EKC curve is stated to be 'monotonically decreasing' sufficient past data has not been available to estimate the turning points.

Source: TERI Study, 2008

stabilization. GHG mitigation actions by developing countries must be enabled and compensated by financial transfers and technology from developed countries. There can be no differentiation of 'key developing countries' from other developing countries.

Without a meaningful discharge of the historical responsibility of developed countries (see other chapters in this volume), based on an explicit recognition that all humans have equal rights to the atmospheric resource, besides termination of their current unsustainable emissions levels, no climate regime would be seen to be fair, or to solve the problem. On the other hand, significant mitigation actions by developing countries beyond the efforts that they are even now making, will lead to major diversion of their resources away from development and poverty eradication, unless these are adequately compensated, and the necessary technology is provided at low cost. The development challenges of the so-called 'key developing countries', are typical of other developing countries. They cannot be penalized by abridging their development on the argument of 'size', when they have, in fact, enabled the developed countries to industrialize, and their energy or CO_2 intensities are no different from those of developed countries in general.

The Copenhagen Accord endorsed a global temperature stabilization target at 2°C (the baseline, however remains unspecified. Several Small Island Developing States (SIDS) urge a still lower level of global temperature increase at 1.5°C above pre-industrial levels. Neither target is objectionable in itself, although the practical feasibility of accomplishing the latter target is open to question. However, the issue is of how the available atmospheric space, corresponding to whichever target is eventually accepted, is to be shared across countries. India's view is that this is to be done on the basis of cumulative historical responsibility with equal per-capita entitlements from the start of the industrial revolution till the agreed date of stabilization. If this means that several developed countries would have negative emissions entitlements from now on, till stabilization, this is neither a physical impossibility (think of afforestation, biomass based power generation with carbon capture and storage, etc.), nor is it the case that the difference between the entitlements (negative) and actual emissions (positive) cannot be purchased from the global carbon market.

166 *Ghosh*

Sectoral targets

In India's view, sectoral emissions targets by developing countries in line with externally imposed norms will only create a market opening for technologies closely held by a few developed country firms; these may be inappropriate to the situations in developing countries and will involve high, uncompensated technology costs due to cartelization by the suppliers. In any event, no 'sector' can be defined unambiguously, after taking into account vintages, technology pathways, differences in raw materials, finished products, transport linkages, etc., and as such, sectoral norms are in practical terms, a non-starter.

Externally imposed sectoral targets are an inefficient, and impractical means of GHG mitigation. They are primarily intended to gain market access, and in any event are not permissible under the Bali Action Plan (para 1(b) (iv)), which speaks only of enhancing implementation of para 4.1(c) of the UNFCCC, which, in turn, speaks only of promotion and cooperation in development, application and diffusion of technologies, practices and process for mitigation of GHG in relevant sectors.

'Nationally Appropriate Mitigation Actions'

The Bali Action Plan requires developing countries to formulate and implement 'Nationally Appropriate Mitigation Actions' (NAMAs), supported and enabled by finance, technology, and capacity building, that are 'monitorable, verifiable, and reportable' (MRV). In India's view 'Nationally Appropriate' signifies that the plans must be prepared by the countries themselves, without external dictat or 'adjustment of ambition'.[15]

Mitigation actions by developing countries should proceed on this basis, and the actions themselves, provided these are supported by finance, technology, and capacity building, as well as the support provided are accountable in the MRV sense. Actions carried out by developing countries on their own, without international support, cannot be not subject to MRV accountability.

The Copenhagen Accord, however, provides for 'international consultations and analysis' for unsupported mitigation actions, but acknowledges that these must be under 'guidelines that respect national sovereignty'. What exactly such guidelines would be is a focus of the post-Copenhagen negotiations. While responsible countries should respond positively to requirements of 'transparency' of their actions, it is important the such 'consultations' do not become a forum for international dictat of developing countries' growth and poverty eradication policies, or a means of review of the adequacy of implementation by them of their voluntary actions, or of the adequacy of their 'levels of ambition'.

Financing

In India's view, financial support for NAMAs, or adaptation action plans of developing countries is not 'aid', but a discharge of responsibility by developed countries, scaled both by their historical responsibilities for climate change, and the capabilities they have acquired thereby.

The 'aid' paradigm involves discretion by 'donors' as regards volume of resources, the purposes or actions for which they may be used, the sources of skills, equipment and technologies to which the aid may be applied, the countries and organizations

India's position in the climate change debate 167

within them that may receive the 'aid', and the institutions through which the 'aid' may be provided.

The responsibility-based approach, on the other hand, signifies that the resources must be 'new and additional' (i.e. not diverted from 'aid'), assessed and not discretionary, and must be administered by a financial mechanism answerable to the Conference of Parties serving as the Meeting of Parties to the Kyoto Protocol (CMP), with a unique governance structure. Financial resources amounting to 0.5–1 per cent of aggregate GDP of developed countries are necessary to address GHG mitigation in developing countries. The amount foreseen in the Copenhagen Accord, i.e. a total of $ 30 billion till 2012, and scaling up to an annual level of $ 100 billion a year by 2020 is a start, but, given the estimates of developing country GHG mitigation costs by responsible international agencies such as the World Bank and UNFCCC it is inadequate.[16]

Technology

In India's view, *technology is the key* to addressing climate change in both the aspects of mitigation as well as adaptation. It comprises three elements:

1   A global effort on R&D, including adaptive R&D to enable the deployment of available technologies in developing countries, as well as the development of new, cost-effective, clean technologies. This will involve significantly stepped-up public as well as corporate financing on R&D in developed countries. In addition, R&D efforts should involve partnerships between institutions in developed and developing countries, with sharing of intellectual property rights (IPRs), and these collaborative R&D efforts may be financed through the financial mechanism of the UNFCCC.
2   Available and new clean technologies must be available to developing countries for their climate change actions on non-commercial terms. This signifies that (a) the existing social contract on IPRs must be tempered to balance the rewards to the innovator with addressing the global imperative of saving the climate, involving negotiated or regulated,[17] rather than monopolistic licence fees, as indeed the international community has agreed in case of drugs needed for HIV/AIDS; and (b) that where particular clean technologies are of wide applicability in developing countries, the financial mechanism may purchase the technology rights for their use in the context of their climate change actions.
3   A network of regional technology innovation centres should be set up in developing countries to catalyse collaborative R&D, provide reliable information on available technologies, their costs and performance, and enable capacity building on deployment of clean technologies and their further innovation.

Adaptation

Adaptation has been the Cinderella of the climate change regime. It is clear from various studies, as well as country experience, for example India's experience discussed above, that the resource, and technology needs for adaptation are of the same order of magnitude as for mitigation. 'Mainstreaming' adaptation actions into development programmes must not involve a diversion of development resources to adaptation, whether the country's own, or externally provided. All vulnerable regions, and not

168   Ghosh

only the least-developed or small-islands must receive adaptation funding from the Financial Mechanism, as indeed the UNFCCC and Bali Action Plan contemplate, even though LDCs, Africa, and SIDS should have priority (as the Copenhagen Accord provides).

Sustainable production and consumption

High per-capita GHG emissions in developed countries are the inevitable outcome of unsustainable lifestyles, comprising unsustainable patterns of production and consumption. These need to be addressed in the future climate change arrangements, and it must be recognized, on the one hand, that human well-being is not conditional on unsustainable life-styles,[18] and on other that an argument that the present life-styles of certain countries are sacrosanct, is untenable.

Conclusion

I hope that the above narrative will persuade the reader of three things:

First, that India's (and all developing countries') concerns about economic growth and poverty eradication are legitimate, and must be fully respected in any global climate regime, as indeed stated unequivocally in the UNFCCC, the Bali Action Plan, and the Copenhagen Accord.

Second, that the cause of climate change, and one which is continuing, is the unsustainable emissions of developed countries. They have to take leadership to drastically reduce their emissions, and this will involve modification of their life-styles, but no one is suggesting that they become poor.

Third, that the proposals made by India (and other developing countries) in respect of the future climate regime are constructive, and must be given serious consideration in any future discussions on global climate action.

Notes

1 The views expressed in this chapter are the author's own.
2 Data sources: Population: Human Development Report 2007–08; area: World Development Report, 2009.
3 HDI ranks Brazil: 70; China: 81; India: 128; South Africa: 121. Source: HDR 2007–8.
4 Signifying that they have lived within a morally defensible allocation of environmental space, making the surplus available to others who have exceeded their environmental space.
5 Population in 2007: 1,123 million.
6 The latest official estimates of poverty following broadly the Expert Group (1993) method, based on calorie intake norms, and using the uniform reference period (URP) of 30 days, indicate that below poverty line (BPL for short) population was 28.3 per cent of the rural population (described as headcount ratio or poverty ratio) and 25.7 per cent of the urban population in 2004–5. These official estimates released by the Planning Commission are based on: (a) the 1973–4 rural and urban poverty line baskets originally at 1973–4 prices adjusted for price changes between 1973–4 and 2004–5; (b) a uniform reference period (URP for short) of 30-days for canvassing consumption of all items of current household consumption in NSS; and (c) rural and urban size distributions of per capita total consumer expenditure (PCTE for short) data collected during the 61st (quinquennial large sample) round (July 2004 to June 2005) on household consumer expenditure of the National Sample Surveys (NSS) (*Source: Planning Commission*). Other estimates are: (i) Arjun Sengupta (estimated on 2004–5 data) based on monetary value of per capita daily consumption: 'Below Poverty Line' (Rs 11.6 pcpd): 21.8 per cent of total population; 'Poor and vulnerable'

India's position in the climate change debate   169

(*c*.$2 per day), 77 per cent of total population (i.e. 836 million); (ii) Tendulkar Committee (estimated on 2004-5 data). Based on the urban poverty line basket for household goods and services consumed: 25.7 per cent urban and 41.8 per cent rural; (iii) World Bank. For 2005 based on international poverty line of consumption levels of $ 1.25 pcpd and $2 pcpd: 456 million and 828 million respectively. These have been criticized by, among others, Surjit Bhalla.

7 Source: *Human Development Report*, 2007–8.

8 Each calorie of food of animal origin requires *c*.10 times the energy required for producing the calorific equivalent of plant-based food.

9 Repair and re-use is not included in the data presented.

10 This may be seen in advertisements for cars and two-wheelers. Even luxury vehicle manufacturers are careful to point out the fuel mileage of the vehicles.

11 Visitors to India observe that at night there are virtually no lights left on in office and commercial buildings. This contrasts with what one observes in almost all developed countries.

12 The first edition of the Greendex, in 2008, jointly placed India and Brazil as the world's most environmentally sustainable societies.

13 Sufficient past data was not available to estimate the turning points in respect of the other countries studied (Netherlands, Pakistan, Sweden, UK).

14 In fact, India's approach to the global regime is entirely consistent with the UNFCCC, the Kyoto Protocol, and the Bali Action Plan. Most elements also have the endorsement of the group of G77 and China.

15 It is sometimes argued by developed country policymakers that without such external oversight, a developing country's supported NAMA actions may be negated by actions outside the supported NAMAs. This demand is unreasonable on three counts. First, a country's public policies, legislations, regulations and budgets are always public knowledge. Second, it would be irrational for a developing country to deviate from a baseline action to an economically suboptimal action *outside* the supported NAMAs. Third, would any developed country accept such external oversight in respect of its own policies, legislation, regulations and budget?

16 For example, the World Bank's 'Economics of Adaptation to Climate Change' (EACC) study, 2009, estimated the costs of Adaptation in developing countries as *c*. $80–100 billion a year. Costs of GHG mitigation, which would be additional, are variously estimated at $200–500 billion a year.

17 There is a widespread misconception that developing countries are asking for technology to be provided 'free'. A regulated licence would be no more free, nor provide insufficient incentive to the innovator (entrepreneur), than regulated tariffs for any natural monopoly, say, electricity.

18 For example, the assertion that commuting to work every day in an SUV with single occupancy, facing traffic congestion arising from everybody else doing the same, as opposed to commuting by safe and efficient mass transport, enhances well-being, is risible.

12 India's official position
A critical view based on science

D. Raghunandan

India's official position on climate change as reflected in international negotiations has often been seen as representing a consistent stance over the years, certainly till the Copenhagen Summit, based firmly on the principle that historical per capita emissions should form the basis for determining responsibility for the problem and for its amelioration. This strongly held position strengthened the foundation of the Kyoto architecture while also defending India's interests and those of other developing countries which lay in recognition of their right to economic growth and, implicitly, growth in emissions while developed countries reduced their clearly excessive emissions. According to this narrative, India abruptly committed to emissions mitigation in the run-up to and at Copenhagen, and changed its position in other ways too, even as developed nations also suddenly started diluting their commitments.

A closer critical examination, as attempted here, would reveal a rather more complex story and one with greater significance both for India and the unfolding global negotiations. It should be emphasized that this chapter deals with India only, even though many of the conclusions drawn may well apply to other so-called 'emerging economies' too. It seeks to show that India had not fully grasped the science, which in fact called for much greater emission reductions than either the developed nations had earlier committed to and were now reneging on, or large developing countries were themselves prepared for. It would also show that, over an extended period of time before the Copenhagen Summit, India had gone along with certain developed country positions that were to prove fateful not only in significantly lowering the bar as regards mitigation but also undermine the very basis of the Kyoto Protocol at Copenhagen. And finally, that the G5 and India in particular, rather than forging a strong alliance with the vast majority of developing countries, especially the Least Developed Countries (LDCs) and the Small Island Developing States (SIDS) so as to put effective pressure on the developed countries, increasingly distanced themselves from the former leaving them disgruntled and with little future option but to go along with the bullying and blandishments of the latter. Certainly as far as India goes, poor understanding of the science combined with poor geo-political understanding and tactics, has meant ceding the upper hand to the USA and its allies to the detriment of global climate control.

The science: more certainty, more gravity

To understand the unfolding dynamics, it is necessary to grasp the fundamentals of the science, especially as obtaining after the release of the Fourth Assessment Report of the Intergovernmental Panel on Climate Change (AR4) in May 2007. IPCC/AR4 brought a fresh intensity and urgency to the climate debate. Not that its findings brought totally new revelations, since scientists had for some time been warning, more vociferously and with greater agreement, that atmospheric concentrations of greenhouse gases (GHGs) especially carbon dioxide had been increasing to alarming levels, and that indications of rising global temperatures and significant changes in climate were becoming more unambiguous.

But IPCC/AR4 marked a sharp departure from its predecessor Third Assessment Report (TAR) of 2001 in three important ways. First, AR4 put an end to the needless debate with climate deniers over whether or not the accumulation of GHGs and consequent temperature rise was man-made. AR4 revised the assessment of the anthropogenic nature of climate change from 'likely' or having 68 per cent probability in TAR of 2001 to 'very likely' with over 90 per cent probability, and declared that 'warming of the climate system is [now] unequivocal' (IPCC, 2007a), this revised understanding being based on tens of thousands of peer reviewed papers and referee comments, a vast amount of fresh scientific evidence including atmospheric measurements by instruments on board satellites or balloons, as well as both physical and computer-based modelling studies. Despite all the controversies that later swirled around the IPCC Report, AR4 undoubtedly represents to date the broadest scientific consensus on climate change namely, that climate change is very real and is undoubtedly societally induced.[1]

Second, AR4 pronounced, again without any significant contestation within the scientific community, that atmospheric GHG concentrations then at around 425 ppmv (parts per million by volume) were extremely close to a 'tipping point' beyond which changes in climate could become irreversible (IPCC, 2007b). Yet AR4 held that even at this late stage, it was still possible to pull back to a stabilization level of around 450 ppmv provided concerted, global and decisive steps were taken very soon so as to allow for the time-lag between emissions and their effects on global temperature rise and climate change.

By concluding that the world was confronting not just climate change, but a climate *crisis* calling for drastic and virtually immediate action, AR4 decisively changed the tenor and urgency of global climate negotiations leading up to the Bali Summit of 2007 which set the deadline of Conference of the Parties (COP) 15 in Copenhagen in December 2007 for arriving at a global agreement. The public mood in many developed countries reflected this urgency and pushed political decision-making towards more forceful mitigation commitments. So much so that even the George W. Bush US administration, hitherto among the foremost deniers, was forced to concede 'the scientific knowledge as represented in the recent IPCC reports' in the statement of the G8 Summit at Heiligendamm, Germany, in 2007 (G8 Summit, 2007).

Finally, AR4 made specific recommendations as regards mitigation trajectories required to prevent runaway climate change. AR4 stated that global GHG emissions should peak and start declining by 2015, and reduce by 50 per cent by 2050 which, in turn, would require Annex-1 developed countries to reduce their emissions by around 40 per cent by 2020 and 90–95 per cent by 2050 (IPCC, 2007a). So the science clearly demanded, for the second commitment period of the Kyoto Protocol currently under negotiation, a steep upward revision of the emission reduction targets for the first commitment period, which were around 5.6 per cent reduction by developed countries from 1990 levels.

172 *Raghunandan*

The most significant elements of the story of global climate negotiations leading up to and beyond Copenhagen have been the adamant refusal of the developed countries to live up to these obligations as demanded by the science, and, as we shall see, the failure of India and other large developing countries to adopt tactics to pressure them to do so.

But AR4 also stressed a point that large developing countries had preferred to ignore or downplay even then. It suggested that, in order for emissions to achieve stabilization levels, besides the deep cuts required of developed countries, developing countries too needed to 'deviate below their projected baseline emissions within the next few decades' (IPCC, 2007a). This requirement was borne out by independent modelling exercises undertaken in India (Kanitkar, Jayaraman, D'Souza, 2009) and was to become central to the emergence of new thinking in India as discussed later. It must certainly have influenced the later re-think on mitigation actions by countries such as China, Brazil, Mexico, Indonesia and some other large developing countries. However, the fact that official India did not respond in a timely manner to this clear pointer from the IPCC showed once again its lack of attention to the science, and also prevented India from taking a reasoned position early and increasing its bargaining power, rather than be subjected to pressures at a later stage.

Indian position outlives its usefulness

The Indian position as it evolved needs to be examined against this backdrop, painted largely by AR4 and the changes in the tone and content of the international climate debate and the global negotiations that it wrought. Two major geo-political developments also need to be noted and will be discussed further below. First, the gradual evolution of a platform of 'major economies' which, although it went by different names at various times and served different purposes, brought the large developing countries into an enlarged grouping of 'major powers' straddling the divide between developed and developing countries. Needless to say, this G20 or G22 grouping was led by the G8 grouping of industrialized nations, itself an enlargement of the G7 group of advanced capitalist states bringing Russia into this geo-political elite. Second, and clearly linked to the first, the sudden spurt in economic growth and emissions first of China and then of India, and the growing gap this opened up between these large states and other smaller developing nations.

India's negotiating position in the early years of the UNFCCC and Kyoto Protocol negotiations owed much to its geo-political assessment of the stance taken by the developed countries in many different arenas of multilateral engagement. There was strong evidence that developed countries were approaching the climate issue through a prism of global domination and advancement of self-interests, and therefore required to be dealt with in like fashion. India's early and consistent advocacy of the yardstick of per capita emissions to determine responsibility of nations for atmospheric GHG accumulation, sharply underlined the difference between consumption patterns in developed and developing nations as regards accountability for the problem and for its amelioration through emissions abatement. On the other hand, the USA and other developed states repeatedly and explicitly sought to avoid responsibility for historically accumulated emissions, resisted emission reduction targets, stonewalled on transfer of funds and technologies to developing countries and continually tried to push the burden of mitigation onto developing countries. The principle of common

A critical view of India's official position   173

but differentiated responsibility (CBDR) was built into the UNFCCC and embedded in the Kyoto Protocol precisely to counter these efforts by the developed countries (see Dasgupta; Ghosh this volume).

While India's position remained correct in principle, considerable doubt arises as to the extent to which this position was informed by a deep scientific understanding of societally induced GHG emissions, global and national trends in emissions trajectories, and the mitigation actions required for amelioration. Official India seemed constantly to be warding off pressures to control emissions, and citing low per capita emissions in its defence, and was often over-concerned about fund flows from developed countries. Its position on occasion could even have been interpreted as tantamount to climate denial in that down-playing the dangers of climate change was also used to reduce pressure to do something about it. To be sure, all nations engage in global climate negotiations in such a manner as to defend and advance their national interests, and COP meetings often degenerated into naked defence of narrow self-interests by states, but India's official position remained mired in this traditional defensive mindset with several consequences.

India's position had not taken into account, or been calibrated with respect to, its recent rapid economic growth, the resulting rise in emissions and the discernible shifts in perceptions of India among both developed and developing countries. India's geopolitical ambitions and foreign policy stance were undergoing profound shifts, as were India's potential leverage in world affairs, which was however not reflected in her position in the climate change negotiations. The Indian position therefore appeared increasingly out of sync with what was demanded by the changed circumstances in respect of global emissions and its consequences, and also in terms of geo-political dynamics.

Some numbers in AR4 and in India's official submissions to the UNFCCC, as well as some back of the envelope projections, would convey why India needed to change its position (see Jayaraman et al. this volume).

Total global emissions in 2004–5 were around 49 Giga tonnes (Gt) of CO_2-equivalent and developed countries were emitting about 46 per cent of it or around 22.5 Gt. Developing countries were already more than half of global emissions at around 26.5 Gt and were expected to go up to about 75 per cent of global emissions by 2050. If total emissions in 2050 were to be brought down to half of current levels as AR4 required, or about 24.5 Gt, this clearly meant a reduction in developing country emissions even if developed country emissions were brought to zero! India and China were already registering emission growth rates of around 4 and 6 per cent per year (Government of India, 2004; China, 2007). Clearly, the emissions mitigation circle cannot be squared unless emissions of developing countries, of which China, India and another handful of countries contributed the overwhelming amount, also followed trajectories of declining emissions growth rates to some future point at which they too would have to start declining absolutely.

With China galloping at double-digit economic growth rates and India too growing rapidly albeit at a lower level and rate, neither country could any longer count on getting a free pass to unfettered emissions growth. Evidently a deceleration in emissions growth by large developing countries was required and must inevitably be part of any solution to the climate crisis. Yet there was no indication this was even being contemplated in official circles in India.

174 *Raghunandan*

Shifting geopolitics

To some observers of international developments in the climate negotiations and on climate issues in general, it was also becoming apparent that the Island States and many LDCs were getting impatient at the lack of progress in climate negotiations and were increasingly holding large developing countries at least partly responsible. The Island States were already feeling the impact of global warming with the rise of sea levels, and saw themselves as the 'canaries of climate change', the early signals that should warn the rest of the world. While they too, of course, saw the developed countries as historically responsible, and therefore the ones to take on most responsibility for mitigation as also to pay for adaptation necessities already looming large, they had begun to increasingly call upon 'all countries' or 'high-emission nations' to come together to tackle emissions and evolve a common position that would bring about the urgently required reduction in emissions that were called for (see AOSIS, 2009a; b). The LDCs too had begun to find common cause with AOSIS (Association of Small Island States) and, although this did not manifest in any open revolt by these countries and a unity of purpose among the developing nations continued to be maintained, the strains were getting more obvious and manifested themselves even more clearly in the run-up to Copenhagen and at the summit itself.

No one need have been surprised by this. Nations of the former groupings were already feeling substantial impacts of climate change, were reeling under poverty and economic hardship, and had few resources to cope with these problems especially in the absence of any fund flows from the developed countries either as part of the Kyoto treaty or any other agreement. In effect they were being left to fend for themselves, even while the large developing economies such as China and India were experiencing unprecedented economic growth and were increasingly seen at the high table of world powers.

Under US leadership and starting in 2007, the so-called G5 large developing countries namely China, India, Brazil, South Africa and Mexico had started becoming regular invitees at the G8 Summits. The G5 were first invited as 'outreach nations', then as part of an informal G8+5 with some other developing countries from different continents being roped in as invitees at each Summit. Whereas these Summits mainly focused on financial, economic and trade issues of the time, climate change also became a regular topic of discussion. The G8+5 and variations involving other large developing countries gradually morphed into the 'Major Economies Forum' or MEF, and statements from the annual MEF Summits on climate change came to be seen as major pace-setters for the global negotiations process. Not coincidentally, these MEF nations (and later the nations that came to constitute the G20 or G22) together represented over three-quarters of the global GDP, trade, population and emissions, so much so that some wags had even taken to calling the MEF the 'major emitters forum'.

Several consensus formulations on climate change emanated from the G8+5 or MEF Summits which were forerunners of formulations seen later at Copenhagen. At first glance they conveyed the idea that the big powers of the world were deeply concerned about the climate crisis and that they had indeed arrived at some modicum of consensus about tackling it. The MEF Statements agreed on limiting temperature rise to 2°C which, while appearing to be a firm target, disguised the fact that temperature rise was an outcome that could not be controlled whereas the quantum of emissions

A critical view of India's official position   175

could be monitored and regulated. Tellingly, the MEF statements did not specify emission reductions targets for developed countries nor did they address in any concrete manner the issue of fund or technology transfers from developed to developing countries. On the contrary, as might have been expected from a forum led by the USA and others subscribing to neo-liberal policies, they overemphasized the role of market forces in guiding economic and technology choices that would determine emissions trajectories, stressed the primacy of preserving intellectual property rights of new climate friendly technologies, and made quite clear that financial transfers would be hedged in by various conditions and mechanisms (See Raghunandan 2007a; 2008; 2009a).

That India agreed to go along with these formulations has been a great pity, and paved the way for disaster at Copenhagen. When these vague formulations were repeated in the Copenhagen Accord, India and other G5 nations could hardly protest. This stemmed in large part from the defensiveness of India's position from which standpoint staving off pressure to reduce emissions was seen as an achievement in itself. There is also little doubt that India's position in the G8+5/MEF gatherings was heavily influenced by the burgeoning 'strategic partnership' now developing during the Bush presidency between the USA and India.

The USA was drawing India into its geo-strategic and security calculus while India was cosying up to the USA in all areas. In the climate arena this was coming increasingly to the fore when India went along with several US initiatives which were widely regarded as undermining the UNFCCC platform, the Kyoto Protocol and its core principles of binding emission reduction targets for developed countries while exempting developing countries from such targets along with compensatory fund and technology transfer obligations from the former to the latter for mitigation and adaptation actions. The USA, especially during the first term of President Bush set up and pushed several parallel platforms and multilateral initiatives such as the Asia-Pacific Partnership, the new technologies initiative and shifting the main locus of discussions to the G8/MEF forums away from the UNFCCC and other global platforms under UN aegis which the Bush administration viewed with undisguised dislike and contempt.[2]

The pursuit of 'consensus' statements with the G8 countries, and the satisfaction of supposedly getting the USA on board, in fact undermined the effort at mounting greater pressure on the developed countries. It also crucially helped to bridge what had been a wide chasm between the EU and the USA but, instead of drawing the USA closer to the EU position, as fondly hoped by the latter, it dragged the EU towards the lowest common denominator approach of the USA. That the USA was able to use the MEF grouping at Copenhagen also created perhaps a fatal cleavage between the G5 on the one hand and the LDSs and AOSIS nations on the other.

The hollowness of the MEF 'consensus' became apparent as the deadline of December 2009 set at the Bali conference drew nearer and the stalemate continued. Neither of the two tracks of the negotiating process as pursued under the Ad Hoc Working Groups (AWG) on the Kyoto Protocol, which was to arrive at emission reduction targets for the developed countries, and that on the euphemistically named Long-term Cooperative Action (LCA), which was actually meant to delineate mitigation actions by developing countries supposedly with fund and technology transfers from developed nations, was making progress. With developed countries continually taking steps backwards, any breakthrough ideas had to come from developing states.

Towards a new Indian position

One such new position was suggested by the People's Science Movement in India (Raghunandan et al., 2007b). It recommended that India should *conditionally* offer to reduce its emissions growth rate *provided* the developed countries agreed to undertake the deep cuts to reduce their emissions as called for by AR4 as outlined above. Setting some mitigation targets for itself would bring about more accountability and also enable India to chart alternative policies to promote low-carbon development trajectories and reduce energy inequalities (Raghunandan et al., 2007b: 84–87). These ideas rapidly gathered momentum within civil society and were soon endorsed by many experts, think tanks, NGOs and social movements (Campaign for Progressive Climate Action & Policy, 2011).

The above position was refined and bolstered through exercises on a new computer model developed and subsequently further elaborated through a social movement–academic partnership. The model showed the results from different emissions reductions scenarios by different countries or groups of nations in terms of GHG concentrations vis-à-vis IPCC's stabilization target of 450 ppmv. The model brought out clearly, and far better than the back-of-envelope projections discussed above, that not only did developed countries have to undertake deep emissions cuts but that about 20 large developing countries, especially China, India and a few others too, would have to take on serious mitigation efforts reducing current emissions growth rates if the IPCC's stabilization target was to be met. Further modelling exercises showed the scenarios obtaining if accumulated GHG stocks were taken into account rather than only current or future emission flows.[3]

Such a position, it was argued, could galvanize the global negotiations, put the onus for forward movement back squarely on the developed countries, and would demonstrate to the world that India acknowledged the changed circumstances in terms of both the climate crisis and its own economic growth and capabilities. It would also allay the growing doubts among the LDCs and AOSIS nations towards the larger developing countries such as India and China as regards climate change, and restore India to a leadership role among developing nations and in the world of ideas on the global stage.

When India finally did announce a goal of reducing emissions intensity by 20–25 per cent by 2020, it did so as an also-ran, much after China had announced a similar target in its National Action Plan and after Mexico, South Africa and Indonesia had put forward similar or even more radical plans on mitigation.

Importantly, though, neither India nor any of the others had made these offers conditional upon the deep emission cuts required of the developed countries. This allowed the USA and others to simply ignore these major announcements by large developing countries. At Copenhagen where the USA and other developed nations announced watered-down targets, they even claimed the developing countries had not announced any *new* mitigation targets, brushing aside the earlier unilateral announcements. The unilateral nature of these new developing country targets has been criticized by some commentators for giving the game away and surrendering a crucial bargaining chip. India's Environment Minister, perhaps in an effort at public relations to convince what he thought would be a sceptical public about government's intentions, compounded the problem and confused public understanding of climate change when he posited in his statement to Parliament that India was taking unilateral steps on mitigation in order to address domestic climate impact, thus confounding the fact that climate change is caused by global emissions and atmospheric accumulation of GHGs (Raghunandan, 2009b).

A major opportunity was thus lost to reshape the global negotiations and to reposition India on the global stage with respect to a major international challenge such as climate change and also as a leader of developing countries. The denouement at Copenhagen and the 'Copenhagen Accord', virtually parachuted into the Summit through a non-transparent back-room process by-passing the two-year long arduous, messy but participatory and democratic twin-track process, saw India standing along with the USA and other developed countries. A large number of developing countries, even those who finally went along with it in the spirit of something is better than nothing, voiced deep reservations about both the content of the Accord and about the process which had delivered it. There are many shades of opinion about the Copenhagen Accord, but this author feels strongly that it has sharply cut the ground from under the Kyoto Protocol and paved the way for what the USA has long been pushing for and has now succeeded in dragging the whole world into, namely a completely new international architecture to control and monitor GHG emissions. Far from being a win-win compromise, the Copenhagen Accord is likely to be a loss-loss deal both for the climate and the developing world.

Conclusion and remarks for the future

This assessment appears to be borne out by subsequent developments, in particular the Cancun Agreements arrived at in COP 16 around the time of writing. The Cancun Agreements have in the main, in the opinion of this author and that of several other commentators, reiterated the basic elements of the Copenhagen Accord, this time within the UNFCCC ambit unlike at Copenhagen where the Summit merely 'noted' it (see Raghunandan, 2010; Khor, 2010). The core idea of bottom-up pledges by both developed and developing countries rather than the binding targets of the Kyoto Protocol, is a decisive move towards a single framework architecture for which the USA has been pushing as against the Kyoto Protocol's sharp differentiation between developed and developing countries, and a severe dilution of developed country commitments on finance and technology transfers that were to underpin actions by developing countries. All these elements contained in the Cancun Agreements are now firmly entrenched in the COP process. It is highly unlikely that this trajectory in international negotiations, now clearly well set from Copenhagen to Cancun, will be reversed leading up to and beyond the next Summit at Durban. It will probably form the cornerstone of a new post-Kyoto climate architecture. Once again, lip service was paid at Cancun to the science. Not only will the pledges made most likely lead to considerably more warming than the 2°C ritually promised but also the pledges of developed countries will thrust the bulk of the burden on to developing countries (UNEP, 2010). Regrettably, not only were the leading developing countries, India included, unable or unwilling to press for a shift back in favour of the Kyoto Protocol framework, the Cancun Summit saw the USA and its developed country allies succeed in persuading many Island States and LDCs to accept the new framework albeit through blandishments and barely veiled threats.

This was only to be expected. India had started from a defensive position concerned mostly about warding off threats to national interests, but the utility of this posture

178 Raghunandan

waned after the initial years and the coming into effect of the Kyoto Protocol. India did not, however, pay adequate attention to the growing severity and immediacy of the climate crisis or the bigger picture locating climate science in the geo-political scenario. It had remained in this posture despite the enormous changes in climate science and the understanding of the climate crisis, as well as the changes in India's economic and political standing on the global stage. To the extent that the latter was factored in to India's climate policy, especially at the highest levels of government, this was heavily influenced by the now blossoming Indo-US strategic partnership and the compulsion felt by the Indian political leadership to draw closer to the USA on all issues and, more importantly, to avoid disagreements, let alone articulating strongly conflicting positions. Thus positions taken by India at the G8+5/MEF meetings and the nature of the 'consensus' forged there often conflicted with positions in formal negotiations as also with the tone and tenor of other discussions in global fora.

Admittedly India is not alone in its complicity with this development. Yet India, which has invested a great deal in championing the principles underlying the Kyoto Protocol, needs to introspect deeply and re-fashion its position on the climate crisis so as to try and bring these principles back into play if not to centre-stage.

However, official India is still floundering. It needs to make up its mind on where it stands with regard to the Copenhagen Accord, the twin-track negotiation process and the fundamentals of the Kyoto Protocol. It has not yet built stable bridges with the majority of LDCs and the AOSIS nations, or come to terms with divergences among the large developing countries and areas of possible common ground with major developed countries such as the EU. India needs to evolve a coherent framework or perspective within which to locate its climate policy, rather than dealing with each situation or meeting or group of nations in an ad hoc manner. India perhaps also needs to recall that the Kyoto Protocol was agreed upon, signed up to and came into effect, all without the USA, the first major international agreement to do so. Is it time to consider whether the same path can be followed again?

Notes

1   The term 'societally induced' is far better than 'man-made', 'human induced' or 'anthropogenic'. These latter terms, although widely accepted and used throughout the IPCC reports, are in fact misleading as regards the underlying causative factors of GHG emissions and therefore of climate change. These latter terms owe their origins and popularity to the need to demarcate these emissions and their climate effects from those attributable to natural causes such as climate cycles or solar activity, etc. Unfortunately, they also attribute the emissions and their consequences to activities by *all* humans or by humankind in general. In actual fact, as is well known and specifically acknowledged in the IPCC reports and other literature, excessive GHG emissions are a result of certain types of activities such as fossil-fuel burning power generation or industries or automobiles engaged mostly in certain types of social formation with their specific forms of production and distribution. Subsistence-level tribal society obviously makes little contribution to GHG emissions whereas the globalized industrial-capitalist social formation is clearly responsible for the bulk of accumulated GHGs and current emissions.
2   See several articles by D. Raghunandan on the Delhi Science Forum website at www. delhiscienceforum.net for a closer analysis of these developments.
3   A collaboration between the Delhi Science Forum, a leading member-organization of the All India Peoples Science Network, and the Centre for Science, Technology & Society of the Tata Institute of Social Sciences, Mumbai has developed and is continually working to upgrade computer models to show results of different emission reduction scenarios by different countries or groups of nations. The model now also addresses accumulated stocks

A critical view of India's official position 179

of CO_2 and historical emissions, and not just current emission flows. Detailed papers discussing the model and its findings can be found in Kanitkar et al. (this volume).

References

AOSIS (Association of Small Island States) (2009a) Summit Declaration, www.sidsnet.org/aosis/.../AOSIS%20Summit%20Declaration%20Sept%2021%20FINAL.pdf, accessed 3 February 2011.
—— (2009b) Press Briefing, 10 July 2009, http://www.un.org/News/briefings/docs/2009/090710_AOSIS.doc.htm, accessed 3 February 2011.
Campaign for Progressive Climate Action & Policy (2011) 'Statement', http://progressiveclimatepolicycampaign-ind.blogspot.com/2009/10/campaign-for-progressive-climate-action.html accessed 9 March 2011.
China (2007) 'China National Climate Change Programme', http://en.ndrc.gov.cn/newsrelease/P020070604561191006823.pdf, accessed 3 February 2011.
—— (2007b) 'Contribution of Working Group III to IPCC/AR4: Summary for Policymakers', http://www.ipcc.ch/pdf/assessment-report/ar4/wg3/ar4-wg3-spm.pdf, accessed 3 February 2011.
G8 Summit (2007) 'Joint Statement by the German G8 Presidency and the Heads of State and/or Government of Brazil, China, India, Mexico and South Africa on the occasion of the G8 Summit in Heiligendamm', Germany, 8 June 2007, http://www.g-8.de/Content/EN/Artikel/__g8-summit/anlagen/o5-erklaerung-en,templateId=raw,property=publicationFile.pdf/o5-erklaerung-en.pdf, accessed 3 February 2011.
Government of India (2004) 'Initial National Communication to the UNFCCC', http://www.natcomindia.org/flashmain.htm, accessed 3 February 2011.
IPCC (2007a) 'Synthesis Report for Policymakers', http://www.ipcc.ch/publications_and_data/ar4/syr/en/spms1.html, accessed 3 February 2011.
—— (2007b) 'Contribution of Working Group III to IPCC/AR4: Summary for Policymakers', http://www.ipcc.ch/pdf/assessment-report/ar4/wg3/ar4-wg3-spm.pdf, accessed on 3 February 2011.
Kanitkar, T., Jayaraman, T. and D'Souza, M. (2009) 'How Much "Carbon Space" Do We Have? The Physical Constraints on India's Climate Policy and its Implications', http://delhiscienceforum.net/images/paper-final-dsfversion.pdf, accessed 3 February 2011.
Khor, M. (2010) 'Complex Implications of the Cancun Climate Conference', *Economic and Political Weekly*, Vol. xlv, No. 52, 25 December, New Delhi.
Raghunandan, D. (2010) 'Kyoto Is Dead, Long Live Durban?', *Economic and Political Weekly*, Vol. xlv, No. 52, 25 December, New Delhi.
—— (2009a) 'G8 Climate Declaration: cart before the horse', Delhi Science Forum, http://www.delhiscienceforum.net/environment/383-g8-climate-declaration-cart-before-the-horse.html, accessed 3 February 2011.
—— (2009b) 'India's offer: each nation for itself', *Economic Times*, 7 December 2009, Delhi.
—— (2008) 'Hokkaido G8 Summit & Climate Change:G8 + O5 + MEM16 = 0', http://www.delhiscienceforum.net/environment/275-hokkaido-g8-summit-a-climate-changeg8-o5-mem16-0-.html, accessed 3 February 2011.
—— (2007a) 'G8+5: Numbers Don't Add Up For Climate Change', Delhi Science Forum, http://www.delhiscienceforum.net/environment/269-g85-numbers-dont-add-up-for-climate-change-.html, accessed 3 February 2011.
—— (2007b) 'Climate crisis: challenges and options', All India People's Science Network, Delhi and Tata Institute of Social Sciences, Mumbai.
UNEP (2010) *The emissions gap report*, http://www.unep.org/publications/ebooks/emissionsgapreport/pdfs/The_EMISSIONS_GAP_REPORT.pdf, accessed on 3 February 2011.

13 Views from outside

International perspectives on India's climate positions

Bert Metz, Saleemul Huq, Vicente Paolo Yu III, Ying Chen and Michael Levi

A view from Europe

Bert Metz

India played a crucial role at the first Conference of Parties (COP) to the United Nations Framework Convention on Climate Change (UNFCCC) in Berlin, in the spring of 1995. At stake was a decision on a mandate to negotiate a Protocol to the UNFCCC, strengthening the provisions of the Convention that entered into force the year before. Negotiations were very contentious, with the group of oil exporting developing countries (OPEC) firmly resisting any decision that would lead to stronger action to limit CO_2 emissions. Indian Ambassador TP Sreenivasan personally took charge of the so called 'Green Group', a breakaway group of the G77 and China. By leaving out the group of OPEC countries it was possible to form a strong alliance with the European Union to support a decision on the (Berlin) mandate and to have this approved by the Conference (Mwandosya, 2000). The decision ultimately led to the birth of the Kyoto Protocol, agreed at the third COP in Kyoto in 1997. This was India at its best as an international power broker.

Although the G77 and China group quickly reunited after strong intervention by the G77 leadership in New York, India continued to play a strong role in the negotiations towards the Protocol. It particularly focused on equity as the key issue. The Berlin mandate clearly stated that the new Protocol should not entail new commitments for developing countries over and above what the Climate Convention says. The main discussion on equity was thus about the differentiation between developed country emission reduction commitments. Proposals for a systematic framework for differentiation, using income, emission and other criteria, were not supported by developing countries, fearing that such a framework would later be applied to developing countries themselves. Nevertheless it was clear that the climate change problem could only be addressed effectively if, over time, all countries would make a fair contribution, according to the principle of Common but Differentiated Responsibility enshrined in the Climate Change Convention. Proposals were made by developed countries during the negotiations to start a process after agreeing on the Kyoto Protocol to discuss how over time developing countries also would, in an equitable manner, limit the growth of their GHG emissions.

India played a very active role in mobilizing the G77 and China Group against this idea (Mwandosya, 2000). The main argument was that the Berlin Mandate did not provide for it. This is a legalistic approach, driven by strong convictions that the

International perspectives: European Union   181

historic responsibility of developed countries justified them to take on the problem of climate change alone for the time being. It is also a defensive approach, apparently based on the premise (false in my view) that economic growth will suffer from actions to mitigate climate change.

India's positions in the negotiations towards a follow-up of the Kyoto Protocol have been quite similar to those during the pre-Kyoto Protocol period. In the Bali Action Plan (a negotiation mandate), agreed in 2007, the principles for a new instrument were set. The contribution to be made by developing countries was very narrowly formulated,[1] speaking of actions, not commitments to act. India had a big role in that debate. In the actual negotiations over the past three years India, for instance, consistently argued that new actions of developing countries should not be enshrined in a second commitment period of the Kyoto Protocol, because developed countries had not yet done enough to justify developing countries to step up to their commitments. Rather, developing country voluntary actions should be contained in other decisions or another instrument, separate from the Kyoto Protocol. This is a remarkable interpretation of the principle of CBDR and the spirit of the Kyoto Protocol. The logical way to proceed would have been to formulate appropriate commitments – to take actions, not to reduce current emissions – for developing countries as part of a second commitment period of the Kyoto Protocol, appropriately differentiated from the commitments of developed countries. Not following that logic shows again a very defensive attitude, using legalistic approaches (the text of the Bali Action Plan) and clearly aiming at minimizing action to mitigate climate change in order to protect economic growth, while justifying this approach on equity grounds. Proposals by the European Union to have all countries adopt a low-carbon development strategy as a basis for specifying particular policies and measures, were met with hostile arguments about imposing new conditions on financial and technological support from developed countries and interfering in the sovereignty of developing countries.

The key equity principle promoted by India is equal per capita emissions, usually interpreted as an equal share of cumulative emissions, starting from a historic date so that historic emissions of developed countries are included. This principle has been elaborated in various ways, but has always remained the cornerstone of Indian climate negotiation positions (Parikh and Parikh, 2002). At first sight it appears to be a fair approach. However, there are serious problems with using this principle as the basis for differentiating climate action:

- *It ignores natural resource endowments*: countries with large hydropower resources or large natural gas resources ought to be treated differently from countries that do not have large low-carbon energy resources but large domestic coal reserves.
- *It masks the presence of a substantial number of people with high emissions*: in developing countries with more advanced economies there are millions of people with CO_2 emissions equal to or larger than those of people in developed countries. Using average per capita emissions hides these responsibilities for contributing to climate change (Chakravarty et al., 2009).
- *Countries can only be held partially responsible for their historic emissions*: knowledge about the climate change impacts of fossil fuel use only recently became obvious; industrialization in most countries happened way before that.
- *It stimulates countries with low emissions to further lock themselves into using fossil fuels, while good low-carbon alternatives exist*: countries that have not yet

182   Bert Metz

locked in their infrastructure based on high fossil fuel use can shift to cheaper and easier low-carbon energy, provided they get the necessary international support. Just focusing on emission levels takes the incentive away for making this transition.

In addition, it has been demonstrated that resolving equity issues on climate change on the basis of an agreed principle has a very low chance of success (IPCC, 2001). There are different principles that are often held strongly by different countries. Combining principles and translating them into a pragmatic 'equity formula' enhances the possibility of agreement amongst a wide range of countries.

The most important problem with India's equity approach is the fact that it locks the debate into a climate-centric framework and frames climate action as detrimental to economic growth. It focuses attention on equitably sharing the shrinking atmospheric carbon space, rather than on opportunities to help develop a green economy that requires a much smaller carbon space. This is also visible in the way India has historically organized its national and international climate change efforts: a central role for the Ministry of Environment and Forests and limited involvement of the National Planning Commission and key socio-economic ministries. It does not, of course, mean that climate-focused actions to limit emissions of CO_2, improving energy efficiency or adapting agriculture to a changing climate, are useless. On the contrary, without firmly integrating climate action in a process of transformation to a low-carbon, climate resilient development trajectory, India will not be able to thrive economically in a changing climate. And such a transformation goes to the heart of the socio-economic decision making.

Recently more encouraging signals can be heard. The introduction to the National Action Plan on Climate Change clearly envisions the need for charting an ecologically sustainable development path. It was developed by the Prime Minister's Council on Climate Change and gives an important implementation role to all relevant ministries. Subsequently the National Planning Commission has established an Expert Group for the Low Carbon Economy to prepare a roadmap by which India can reduce its carbon dioxide emissions without affecting the growth of the economy. The National Solar Mission has set ambitious goals for the deployment of solar energy and the development of the National Green Mission to maintain forests and biodiversity is moving ahead irrespective of serious criticism that it is an obstacle to development projects. Minister Jairam Ramesh made personal calls to grab the economic opportunities that moving to a low-carbon economy brings. He also made the point that India is not asking for international financial support to make this transition. However, these remarks and the fact that India agreed with the Copenhagen Accord provisions on international monitoring of its domestic action have been criticized heavily in India, showing strong divisions in the leadership of the country on these issues. The Minister also is making strong statements strengthening the climate centric equal per capita emissions framework (Kanitkar et al., 2010).

It is time for a breakthrough initiative to revitalize international climate negotiations that have almost come to a standstill. Although agreement was reached at Cancun on some issues, it is very unlikely that a binding treaty, delivering adequate emission reductions to fend off serious climate risks, can be achieved in the coming years. The best opportunities for such a breakthrough lie in the concept of low-carbon, climate resilient development. There is a growing number of initiatives in developed and developing countries applying this concept in national development strategies and

International perspectives: Bangladesh   183

policies. The European Union and several of its Member States are actively pursuing it domestically. Korea, Costa Rica, Norway and Mexico have integrated it in their high level policy decisions. China, Indonesia, Brazil, Ethiopia and Peru are developing sectoral or regional elements of it. If India, based on its economic self interest, would become a champion of this low-carbon, climate resilient development framework and seek cooperation with the European Union and others, it could broker a breakthrough that would change the debate from 'how to avoid reductions of greenhouse gases' to 'how to use international cooperation to maximize the benefits of a low-carbon, climate resilient development strategy'. Once more India at its best as a power broker?

Note

1   See UNFCCC document FCCC/CP/2007/6/Add.1, http://unfccc.int/documentation/decisions/items/3597.php?such=j&volltext=/CP.13#beg

References

Chakravarty, S., Chikkatur, A., de Coninck, H., Pacala, S., Socolow, R. and Tavoni, M. (2009) 'Sharing global CO_2 emission reductions among one billion high emitters', PNAS, July 21 2009, vol. 106 no. 29, pp. 11884–11888.

IPCC (2001) Working Group III: Contribution to the Third Assessment Report, Cambridge University Press/New York.

Kanitkar, T., Jayaraman, T., D'Souza, M., Sanwal, M., Purkayastha, P., Talwar, R. and Raghunandan, D. (2010) Conference on Global Carbon Budgets and Equity in Climate Change, 28–29 June 2010, Discussion Paper, Supplementary Notes and Summary Report, http://moef.nic.in/downloads/public-information/tiss-conference-cc-2010.pdf, accessed 10 May 2011.

Mwandosya, M. (2000) 'Survival emissions: a perspective from the South on global climate change negotiations', CEEST, Dar es Salaam.

Parikh, J. and Parikh, K. (2002) 'Integrating climate change and sustainable development issues, opportunities and strategies', in P.R. Shukla et al. (eds) Climate Change in India, Tata-McGraw Hill, New Delhi.

Bangladesh: Some friendly reflections on India's climate change strategy

Saleemul Huq

India has played a key role on behalf of the developing countries, within the Non-Annex 1 (NA1) countries through the 'Group of 77 and China' (G77) since the inception of the United Nations Framework Convention on Climate Change (UNFCCC). It has championed the cause of equity and specifically the need for taking per capita emissions into account in agreeing the roles of the Annex 1 (A1) and NA1 countries in taking actions to reduce emission of greenhouse gases. In particular it has championed the principle of 'common but differentiated responsibilities' (CBDR) clause within the UNFCCC. More recently, during the run-up to the fifteenth Conference of Parties (COP15) in Copenhagen, Denmark in December 2009, it has also played a much greater role within the smaller sub-set of G77 countries namely the BASIC (China, India, Brazil and South Africa) sub-group.

These reflections on India's prominent role on behalf of the developing countries and BASIC countries are purely personal, offered from the perspective of the friend

184 *Saleemul Huq*

from a neighbouring country that is also a member of the Least Developed Countries (LDC) sub-group within G77.

At the time of the signature of the UNFCCC in 1992 at the Earth Summit in Rio de Janeiro, Brazil in June 1992, the division of the world into the two main blocs of 'rich and powerful' (A1) and 'the Rest' (NA1) made sense and was a reasonable description of the dichotomous nature of the world. It was also right and proper that the A1 countries had a greater responsibility to take action first and strongest to reduce their emission of the greenhouse gases that were predicted by the Intergovernmental Panel on Climate Change (IPCC) to cause adverse climate change impacts.

However, I would argue that almost two decades after the Copenhagen meeting took place the world has moved on in several important respects. First, the dichotomous division of the world into the 'rich and powerful' on one side and the 'rest' on the other no longer describes reality, as we now have another 'powerful but not yet rich' countries and then the 'rest'. The fact that four of these 'powerful but not yet rich' countries chose to form a sub-group within G77, namely BASIC, was an implicit acceptance of that reality.

The second major shift in circumstances is the fact that previous efforts to reduce emissions of greenhouse gases (such as through the Kyoto Protocol) have not achieved any significant reductions of those emissions and that (according to the third assessment report of the IPCC in 2001) the world is already locked into a certain amount of warming, and hence would need to deal with the adverse impacts of that warming. It is also clear from the IPCC report that these impacts would fall first and hardest on the poorest countries and communities on the planet.

Thus, I would argue that, whereas in 1992 it made sense to emphasize (as India has always done) the 'differentiated responsibilities' part of the CBDR principle, by 2009 it is now time to shift the emphasis to the 'common' part of the CBDR principle. In other words countries like China and India (and BASIC plus others more generally) need to step up to take on significant responsibilities for changing their development paths from a high greenhouse emitting trajectory to a lower emissions one. This is not to absolve the A1 countries from their primary responsibility to take stronger actions, nor does it require India to take on emission reduction targets like the A1 countries. Nevertheless it does require India (and BASIC countries) to examine ways in which it can deliver the development aspirations of its billions of (mostly poor) citizens without generating the emissions of greenhouse gases that would be emitted under a business-as-usual (BAU) development path of dependence on fossil fuels.

I would also argue that it makes sense for India (and BASIC countries) to explore and embark on this new development path sooner rather than later for its own good (and not just as a negotiating tactic against the A1 countries in the UNFCCC). The first reason is that India (more than the other BASIC countries) has a very large number of people living in extreme poverty (indeed it could be argued that India alone has more poor than all the LDCs put together) and these people are also extremely vulnerable to the adverse impacts of climate change. Hence India has much more to lose (compared to many other countries) if global temperatures were to rise above 2°C (let alone the 3.5°C towards which we are headed now). So reducing emission is good for India's poor and vulnerable.

The second reason is that, if we agree that the solution to the climate change problem at the global level in the longer term is a massive global shift away from fossil fuel-dependent growth to a less or non-polluting growth pathway, then India (along with China) has the capability to lead the world in this transition. I believe that China has already grasped this proposition and is taking measures (such as investments in clean technologies) to make itself a leader of this post-fossil fuel world. India, although taking strides in the same direction, could make itself a leader as well.

Finally, let me deal with the argument that India needs to tap its vast coal reserves to provide electricity and modern energy to its billions of poor and that it should not face any restrictions in doing so. My response to my Indian friends is as follows: I fully support your right to develop and provide a better quality of life for all your citizens (particularly the poor). However, if you can find options to develop without emitting more greenhouse gases then I ask that you look for those options. If those options are more expensive (in the short run) than using your fossil fuel reserves, then I also fully support your demand that the additional costs be borne by the richer countries (through transfers of funding or technologies or both). Thus I am fully in support of India's 'right to develop' but I feel I can no longer support the position that India has a 'right to pollute'.

I would therefore appeal to my Indian friends to examine seriously all options for development in a non-polluting manner and try your best to lead the world in transitioning to a post-fossil fuel world. In today's world every tonne of greenhouse gas emitted that could have been avoided is almost a criminal offence.

The Philippines: India and the global South: partners in promoting a development-oriented approach to global climate change policy

Vicente Paolo Yu III

Ever since its independence from the British Raj in 1947, India has been a champion of developing country interests in multilateral policy fora. Its role in the formation of, as well as continued active engagement in, the Non-Aligned Movement (NAM) and in the Group of 77 (G-77), the two premier multilateral institutions of developing countries that serve as the vehicles through which developing countries' collective perspectives are articulated in the United Nations, highlights an essential enduring aspect of Indian foreign policy – the promotion of developing countries' solidarity in global policy institutions in asserting and stressing those countries' right to development. This is seen as an important element in the promotion of Indian national interests.

In the current UNFCCC climate change negotiations under the Bali Action Plan which started in December 2007, India and many other developing countries through the G77 have asserted that the full and effective implementation of the UNFCCC must reflect the fact that economic and social development and poverty eradication continue to be the primary policy objectives of developing countries. For developing countries, any new arrangements on long-term international cooperation to address climate change under the UNFCCC must support and promote these policy objectives.

While there are major differences in terms of size of economy, population size, and other economic and social indicators among developing countries, there continue to be key development commonalities that require the collective assertion of their development interests at international level. These commonalities include, for most developing countries including India, large portions of their population living in poverty; challenges in providing for the basic social needs of their populations such as

186 *Vicente Paolo Yu III*

food, education and health; economic conditions that offer limited or no opportunities for decent work and upward economic mobility; diversified economies that support higher value-added agro-industrial activities; and institutional and physical infrastructure challenges. These development commonalities as the basis for the collective assertion of common developing country interests take on even more urgency in the context of climate change.

The overall gap between developed and developing countries continues to remain and, by some measures, has further widened over the past three decades. This is of grave concern to developing countries. Considering that, as highlighted by the IPCC and other scientific studies, the adverse effects of climate change are going to be much more severe in developing than in developed countries, these adverse effects have the potential to severely undermine any progress that developing countries may have achieved. This is particularly crucial for India, as the impact of accelerating extreme weather events (such as unseasonal or strengthening cyclones), reduced water availability flowing through its rivers fed by the receding Himalayan glaciers, desertification, and other environmental challenges resulting from climate change, may significantly constrain Indian agricultural and industrial production and diversification with corresponding adverse downstream impacts on employment, income growth, and social and political stability. This means that, unless adequately prepared with appropriate human, financial, technological, and institutional resources, India's future ability to develop and improve the standards of living of its people, coupled with equitable income distribution at the impressive rates of overall economic growth that have been seen in the first decade of the 21st century, may become significantly constrained. This development problem arising from climate change haunts not just India but also the broad range of other developing countries all over the world.

India's perspectives on climate change in the context of global policymaking under the UNFCCC have been shaped by these development realities and challenges arising from climate change. These are perspectives that are, by and large, shared and also articulated by many other developing countries. India's contributions in this regard have been significant, ranging from its championing of the principles of equity and of common but differentiated responsibilities in the UNFCCC, the need to ensure that UNFCCC commitments on the provision of finance and technology to developing countries are fully implemented, to its proposal in the negotiations under the Bali Action Plan that the definition of global GHG emission reduction goals must be on the basis of a paradigm to be agreed upon for the equitable sharing of atmospheric space.

For India and other developing countries, therefore, the climate change negotiations are not about how GHG emissions are to be reduced globally – although this is of course a major part of the substantive content – but about how their long-term development prospects can be both protected and advanced in the context of climate change. It is primarily about improving the climate change-adaptive capacity of their economies by ensuring that development and economic growth take place as fast as possible without necessarily causing the equally rapid rise in GHG emissions that has historically accompanied economic growth.[1] At the same time, however, India and, in fact, other developing countries understand that there is a great need for them to contribute towards the reduction of global aggregate emissions to the maximum extent possible consistent with their development priorities, if further long-term damage arising from greater climate change impacts is to be averted for future generations of their peoples.

International perspectives: Philippines 187

For developing countries, reducing GHG emissions growth will require significant changes in the energy infrastructure and energy consumption patterns (including appropriate shifts in their agro-industrial economic base) – changes that are likely to be highly capital- and technology-intensive. The existing financial and technological capacity of most developing countries may not be sufficient to undertake such changes fully, given the wide range of equally pressing development concerns that need to be addressed (such as the provision of basic social services like education, shelter, health for their population). This will therefore require significant finance and technology transfers to developing countries. This is already recognized in the UNFCCC – i.e. Articles 4.3, 4.4, 4.5 and 4.7 – as a matter of treaty obligation on the part of developed countries.

The UNFCCC, in particular Articles 2, 3, and 4.7, stresses that developing countries' pursuit of their development and poverty eradication is their first and overriding priority. Pursuing development requires, *inter alia* and in the context of growing populations in developing countries, pursuing an economic expansionary policy that would result in increases in aggregate GDP. That is, aggregate GDP needs to keep on growing in developing countries in order to pursue economic and social development and poverty eradication.

The current strong link between GHG emissions and GDP growth, under current fossil-fuel-driven industrial technologies,[2] underlies India's concern that requiring developing countries to reduce either their GHG emissions growth rates or their overall GHG emissions may have economic implications that will forestall the achievement of their national economic development objectives. For India and other developing countries, this link between economic growth and development and any concomitant rise in emissions can be broken in developing countries only through the establishment of stronger international co-operation arrangements under the UNFCCC that would support national efforts and which would deploy in developing countries the necessary financial and technological resources needed to, for example, build and expand the energy, agricultural and industrial production infrastructures that emit fewer GHGs, reduce or eliminate reliance on fossil fuels, or increase the use of renewable energy.

Essentially, these international co-operation arrangements, coupled with national efforts, would be aimed at effecting structural changes in developing country economies in order to make these better suited, despite the adverse effects of climate change, to provide improved standards of living for their growing populations by ensuring that the underlying structural conditions – i.e. governance and policy institutions, physical and human infrastructure, policy environments, the basis of domestic economic activities – are better adapted to present and projected climate change impacts.

This focus on the development aspects of climate change, and the international co-operation arrangements required to address them that India has consistently promoted in the climate change negotiations has resonated with many other developing countries that are similarly concerned with the development implications of climate change for their own development prospects.

Given the scale of the present and potential impacts of climate change on developing countries' development prospects, and given the development commonalities that India shares with other developing countries, India's contributions to strengthen a development-oriented perspective in relation to climate change have therefore been substantial. The long-term viability and sustainability of global efforts to address climate change therefore depend on the creation of strengthened international

188 *Vicente Paolo Yu III*

cooperation under the UNFCCC which takes into account and responds effectively to the development needs of developing countries. India's leading role in this regard in the global climate change policy discourse will be crucial – not only for India's development prospects but also for the development prospects of other developing countries in the face of climate change.

Notes

1 As the 2006 Stern Report pointed out, between 1960 and 1999, the correlation between emissions per head and GDP per head was 'nearly 0.9' – i.e. 1 per cent GDP growth per capita leads to 0.9 per cent emissions growth per capita. See Stern, N. (2006) *Stern Review on the Economics of Climate Change*, p. 179.
2 Economic growth using current technologies implies increased consumption of electricity in households and industries and the direct and indirect use of fossil fuels (especially coal and oil and petroleum product derivatives) in industries, transportation, and agriculture. For most developing countries, the primary energy issue is the need to expand the access to usable forms of energy to at least the energy sufficiency threshold of 100 KWh/person/day for their populations and to fuel their agricultural and industrial production, as compared to the need in developed countries to reduce their over-consumption of energy beyond the energy sufficiency threshold of 100 KWh/person/day.

Indian climate policy: A Chinese perspective

Ying Chen

As a big developing country and the fourth largest aggregate emitter of greenhouse gases (GHGs) worldwide, India plays an important role in international climate negotiations under the United Nations Framework Convention on Climate Change (UNFCCC) and the many other multilateral mechanisms to address climate change.

At the international level, India, standing alongside G77 and China, has always presented a tough counterpart to the western world. Indian negotiators often cited Mahatma Gandhi's wise dictum 'the earth has enough to meet our needs, but will never have enough to satisfy our greed' to emphasize the importance of the equity principle in building the international climate regime. India firmly insists on the per capita standard, which implies ensuring relatively low emissions per capita compared with the average level of the developed countries or equitable access to emissions space.

At the domestic level, India has taken action and is prepared to be more ambitious to build a low-carbon economy. India released the first National Action Plan on Climate Change (NAPCC) and announced a target to reduce its emissions intensity by 20–25 per cent in 2020 as compared to 2005. India also set up a target to increase the share of renewable energy to 10 per cent of total electricity generated.

India's position and approach are quite similar to China's. Climate change has been recognized as a great challenge. On the one hand, both countries are relatively vulnerable to the adverse impacts of climate change, on the other hand, with a large population, in pursing accelerated growth, carbon emissions will inevitably increase in the short and medium term. The governments have to make difficult decisions to keep a balance between climate protection and meeting the needs of economic development and poverty alleviation. Although unshakably refraining from making legally binding commitments at international level, numerous initiatives related to climate change mitigation have been started domestically in recent years. The West has often criticized such a position and approach, arguing that it indicates a lack of flexibility and creates incoherence between international commitments and domestic actions.

China and India have tightened their cooperation in the field of climate change to promote international processes and improve domestic policies of energy conservation and efficiency, renewable energy and forest management. In October 2009, China and India signed a Climate Change Co-operation Accord before the Copenhagen conference. Besides these bilateral arrangements, China and India have increasingly had more communications and discussions within the BASIC group, consisting of China, India, Brazil and South Africa. Up to now, there have been six ministerial level meetings. Along with the meeting of ministers, BASIC experts' meetings starting in Rio, Brazil in 2009, have become a very useful platform for experts from BASIC countries to exchange views and work together on a series of key issues in negotiations such as the equitable access to sustainable development and carbon tariffs.[1] Indian and Chinese experts share a lot of similar viewpoints on these.

What explains enhanced co-operation between the two largest developing countries? From the Chinese perspective, it is the universal principles of justice and equity as well as common political and economic interests for both. Both countries need emissions space for development and meet common challenges in the process of industrialization and urbanization.

Different people have different understandings of justice and equity. There exists some universal principle beyond national interests. Germany clearly supports the per capita approach. German experts have also developed their own carbon budget approach based on the perception that every citizen of the globe has equal entitlement to the global atmospheric space (WBGU, 2009). Assuming that a 2° target can be achieved, the global carbon budget in the period between 1900 and 2050 is equally distributed among everyone on earth (Pan and Chen, 2010). Here, justice points to what is right. Some criticize this as being unrealistic in the real world. Developed countries have achieved industrialization by occupying global atmospheric space unfairly and cannot withdraw their historical emissions. For example, the USA has emitted over three times its total carbon budget. However, the carbon budget approach tells us how far current reality deviates from a scenario of equitable distribution. It thus encourages the international community to think about what can be done to correct this wide variation with an equitable and effective international climate regime.

Some industrialized countries have explored the notion of a carbon tariff. However, a carbon tariff is unfair to developing countries, although it is unlikely to be implemented for trade in carbon-intensive goods in the near future, and will only have minor implications for Indian industries even if it is implemented. Recently, carbon tariffs resurfaced after the EU made the decision to include the emissions of international civil aviation into the Emissions Trading Scheme (EU-ETS) in 2012. This reinforces the concerns of developing countries on expanding such a sectoral approach to other carbon-intensive sectors such as steel and cement based on the grandfathering principle.

The Cancun Agreements were a step forward in the direction of global action on climate change but Cancun failed to reach a balanced agreement not only between the two tracks but also between the four topics under AWG-LCA negotiations. Developed countries keep trying to kill the Kyoto Protocol and shift the focus from their commitments on emissions reduction and financial assistance to a long-term goal,

190   *Ying Chen*

peaking year, nationally appropriate mitigation actions (NAMAs) and MRV (measurement, reporting, and verification) of developing country actions. This strategy has ensured that negotiations move away from the Bali roadmap. Even though India might be able to easily manage to address some of these issues, particularly MRV, it continues to oppose this deviation on the principle of justice. The BASIC ministerial meeting held in New Delhi in February 2011 made a clear statement highlighting that, 'the Kyoto Protocol is critical to achieving the global goal of ambitious emissions reduction and global peaking of emissions. The effective operationalization of the mechanisms for providing financial and technological support to developing countries was equally critical in enabling them to contribute to global efforts for addressing climate change.' It further added that 'the guidelines for MRV for developing countries should be less onerous than the rules for enhanced MRV for developed country parties' (BASIC, 2011: 2).

More importantly, China and India have common interests to be allied with each other. Population growth, accelerated urbanization and modernization of lifestyles, and rapid economic growth are the main driving forces behind increasing energy consumption and emissions in both countries. All these factors will continue to exist and are not easily changeable in the near future. It is true that currently India has a unique advantage in emissions both in absolute and in per capita terms. According to the latest data from WRI-CAIT database,[2] in 2007, India's total national emissions were about 1410 $MtCO_2$, a small fraction (4.8 per cent) of the world's missions, compared to about 20 per cent for China and the USA. India emits only 1.3 tons of CO_2 per capita, ranking 122 in the world, much lower than the 19.3 tons emitted by the USA, 8.2 tons from the EU-27 and even the 5.1 tons of China. Keeping these figures in mind, India does not need to worry too much about threats from the western world. But from a dynamic view, with its rapidly growing emissions India will face similar, perhaps even greater, challenges as China does today.

To further develop this point, the population of India increased from 343 million in 1947 to 1,155 million in 2009 and is projected to exceed China's around 2030, and 28.6 per cent of the population still lives a life below the poverty line. About 600 million people have no electricity access for modern energy services (Zhang, 2009). Beside electricity generation, industry is also a key sector with great potential for emissions increase. According to the latest projections from the International Energy Agency (IEA), total industrial energy consumption in India between 2007 and 2050 is expected to grow 3.5 times under the baseline low-demand scenario and 4.2 times under the high-demand scenario (IEA, 2011). Furthermore, the infrastructure system is not well built in India. Large-scale infrastructure construction will be unavoidable with rapid urbanization leading to a huge demand for energy-intensive products. Heavy industries will be shifted to India from China or somewhere else in the world just as happened to China at the time of globalization. Energy security has become a real threat for economic stability and development. Like China, India lacks oil resources. Its share of coal in the energy mix has increased from 33 per cent in 1990 to 39 per cent in 2005 (IEA, 2011).

Up to now India has experienced less international pressure than China, but it is wrong to assume that India gets no benefit from its alliance with China. Standing with the G77 and China, speaking frankly and loudly at international fora is an appropriate strategy for safeguarding its national interests. The West emphasizes the differences between China and India in order to isolate China from the developing camp and impose more political pressures. Will India accept a so-called 'more flexible' and 'constructive' approach and co-operate with developed countries, particularly the USA, for example, on accepting carbon tariffs in the context of a cap-trade bill, soften its position on key issues such as MRV and legally binding commitments to exchange benefits on clean energy technology and capacity building? From the Chinese perspective, India will not easily change its position and approach to diverge from the developing camp. It is not in its interests in the long term. Furthermore, it is unlikely that the USA would provide India with more advanced clean energy technologies and more money for capacity building. The USA sees clean energy as a key technology area for future competitiveness and will not help any potential counterparts, including India, to build capacity to compete with it. Regarding financial assistance, with current barriers from the Congress, the US Administration is experiencing difficulties in transferring public money to developing countries as international climate assistance.

China will make every effort to enhance dialogue and co-operation with other Parties, both developed and developing countries, under bilateral and multilateral mechanisms. Actually, there are enormous possibilities for co-operation between China and India to identify similarities and learn from each other. For example, clean energy technology is a promising field for South–South co-operation. Some Chinese technologies have been adjudged world-class and exported to developed countries. Some, such as solar heaters, biomass utilization etc., may not be the most advanced in the world but are cheaper and more suitable for use in developing countries. Co-operation between China and India, the largest developing countries, would be of mutual benefit for both societies and contribute a lot to the whole world. In the meantime, China also needs to be more active and constructive in speaking out and putting forth its own proposals in international climate negotiations. It is not strange that every country, particularly large countries with specific circumstances such as China and India, needs to be ready to protect its own interests at all times.

Notes

1   Joint Statement Issued at the Conclusion of the Sixth Basic Ministerial Meeting on Climate Change, New Delhi India, 26–27 February 2011
2   WRI-CAIT 8.0. http://cait.wri.org/.

References

BASIC (2011) 'Joint Statement Issued at the Conclusion of the Sixth Basic Ministerial Meeting on Climate Change', 26–27 February 2011, New Delhi, http://moef.nic.in/downloads/public-information/BASIC-Stat-6.pdf, accessed on 15 March 2011.
IEA (2011) 'Energy Transition for Industry: India and the Global context', http://www.iea.org/papers/2011/india_industry_transition.pdf, accessed on 15 March 2011.
Pan, J. and Chen, Y. (2010) 'Carbon Budget Proposal: a framework for a equitable and sustainable international climate regime', *Social Sciences in China*, 31(1).
WBGU (German Advisory Council on Global Change) (2009) 'Solving the Climate Dilemma: Carbon Budget Approach'.
Zhang, H. (2009) 'India: A Dramatic Role in the International Negotiations on Climate Change', *World Environment*, No. 1, pp. 30–33 (in Chinese).

192 *Michael Levi*

Indian climate policy: A US perspective

Michael Levi

India is a mystery to most participants in the US climate policy debate. It is usually grouped with China (unless it is being ignored), and is rarely addressed on its own merits. This is largely the product of basic unfamiliarity with India. That is unfortunate, since on essentially every important emissions-related measure, India is in a different category from China. Moreover, US policy-makers normally have a much greater affinity for India than China, given India's status as the world's largest democracy. To the extent that India separates itself from China in climate policy discussions, it will be able to find a more constructive relationship with the United States.

The basic facts are well known to most Indians who are involved in climate policy discussions. Indian emissions (on both an absolute and per capita basis) are much lower than Chinese emissions. A large slice of India, meanwhile, lacks access to electricity. The average Indian has a substantially lower income than the average Chinese, limiting India's ability to pay for those emissions reductions that are costly. India is also much weaker than China in the trade-exposed carbon-intensive industries (like steel and cement manufacturing) that are the focus of so much US concern about the competitiveness and employment impacts of US climate policy.

Yet despite its differences, India appears to have tightened its co-operation with China in the context of the global climate negotiations, reinforcing the unfortunate US tendency to hyphenate the two countries rather than distinguish between them. There was enormous frustration in the US climate policy community (including among both experts and policy-makers) over the Indian decision to align itself closely with China during (and after) the Copenhagen climate negotiations in 2009. It is not clear to US observers how India benefited from that alliance. The United States was not pushing to cap Indian emissions, so the China-India alliance was not necessary to prevent that. (To be certain, some rhetoric from conservative US politicians emphasized a need for Indian emissions caps, but that was disingenuous: those lawmakers, for the most part, were intentionally making demands that could not be met.) The China-India alliance also aimed to preserve the Kyoto Protocol – but the odds of keeping Kyoto in a form resembling its current state after the 2008–2012 commitment period are very low regardless. US observers, in any case, generally believe that the Kyoto Protocol has no future, and hence have trouble understanding strategies aimed at shaping that future. And Indian defence of the Chinese position in the final fight of the Copenhagen negotiations – strong opposition to US (and European) insistence on provisions for 'measurement, reporting, and verification' (MRV) of emissions-cutting actions, along with 'transparency' and 'review' of all countries' efforts – struck US observers as particularly peculiar, given the open nature of Indian government and society, which should have made Indian compliance with such schemes relatively easy. (China, in contrast, faces fundamental political and social barriers to cooperation with such schemes, and hence benefits from having India defend its position.) While many in the United States (particularly in the expert community) are sympathetic to arguments rooted in Indian interests, such as Indian opposition to hard emissions limits, they are far less understanding of Indian actions that appear to be unnecessary for India but that hurt the United States.

US attitudes have shifted significantly since COP16 in Cancun. While most lawmakers and the general public paid little attention to the meetings, the expert and policy-making communities did. The forward-leaning Indian approach, which sought compromises on transparency and technology, was widely applauded, and has lent a new level of trust to US participants in the discussion. Yet US observers still struggle to understand Indian strategy. What, in their eyes, explains the Indian approach? There is widespread belief among experts that the Indian strategy in climate negotiations has been characterized by excessive worry that the West, and the United States in particular, aims to somehow limit its economic development. This leads to highly defensive (and largely unnecessary) postures, such as that which India took together with China in Copenhagen. Such fears, as argued above, are unfounded. Throughout 2009, for example, Indian policy-makers railed publicly against US attempts to get Delhi to commit to emissions caps – even though no such attempts existed. Perhaps those policy-makers were well aware that the United States was not pushing them to cap India's emissions, and they were just playing to domestic audiences. Even that, though, is dangerous, since it can limit India's ability to enter into sensible international arrangements to deal with climate change.

India would benefit from a more constructive approach. The United States invariably casts a long shadow over global climate discussions, for better or worse. By helping Washington differentiate India from China, Delhi would be able to more effectively pursue its own goals. One place to start might be around low-carbon technology. India is wrongly grouped with China in US discussions of clean energy technology. While Suzlon is frequently held out as an example of an Indian firm that is competing with leading US firms on the world stage, the reality is that the number of Indian firms in world-leading positions is very small. Moreover, unlike in the case of China, Indian firms have acquired their positions largely without significant help from the state. (Chinese firms, in contrast, are increasingly the targets of US concerns about unfair trade practices.) Indian policy-makers would benefit from better educating their US counterparts on these differences. That would, among other things, make the United States government more willing to support clean energy technology cooperation, including in commercially sensitive areas like large-scale demonstration projects, which could benefit both sides. Indeed US experts and policy-makers have been very pleased with the active Indian engagement in the new Clean Energy Ministerial process, launched in 2009, which aims to strengthen international cooperation on clean energy technologies.

India would also benefit from a related shift in the focus of international climate policy discussions from goals to capacity. Most in the United States still think about climate policy in terms of how much others are *willing* to do. Few show an appreciation for the fact that there are many climate-friendly things that India (and others) may want to do but is *unable* to. (Increasing adoption of energy-efficient technologies and decreasing non-technical losses in electricity transmission are but two examples.) There is, however, a growing appreciation, at least in the expert community, of the importance of this part of the equation. To the extent that international discussions focus on capacity, rather than just goals, and on enabling states, rather than constraining them, India will benefit. To make such discussions work, though, India will need to take a more constructive approach to the international talks than it has in the past, emphasizing shared opportunities rather than focusing on demands.

India would also do well to help remove one persistent thorn in the bilateral climate dialogue. Several pieces of draft US cap-and-trade legislation have threatened to impose tariffs on certain carbon-intensive imports. (Cap-and-trade is, of course, a

194 *Michael Levi*

political nonstarter in the United States in the next few years, but variations on the theme are likely to eventually reemerge.) India has been strongly and vocally opposed. Such tariffs would be imposed at a level commensurate with the fees that US companies producing similar products would pay under a domestic cap-and-trade system. (Passage of a cap-and-trade bill, of course, appears highly unlikely at the time of this writing.) Such tariffs, or at least the threat of them down the road, appear to be a necessary prerequisite to passing cap-and-trade legislation in the United States. (They would ensure that US manufacturers did not lose domestic market share to foreign competitors as a result of domestic carbon pricing.) Many in India, however, have resisted such tariffs as unfair. This is received poorly in the United States, and reinforces the negative tone of the bilateral climate change dialogue. India can reasonably object to measures that would hurt its economy relative to business as usual. But to the extent that carbon tariffs would simply maintain the previously existing competitive playing field (by imposing similar new costs on domestic and foreign producers of the same goods), many US observers see Indian opposition as unfair: India is not only asking the United States to take action on climate change, but is arguing that it should be allowed to use that US action to gain a new source of competitive commercial advantage.

Indian acceptance of reasonable US carbon tariffs in the context of a cap-and-trade bill – or, even better, pre-emptive Indian action to levy similar tariffs on its exports, which would forestall US action and allow India to keep the proceeds – would be a show of good faith that would have at most small implications for the competitiveness of Indian industry.[1] India, of course, may have a legal case against such tariffs under the WTO. But that does not mean that bringing such a case would be wise. A consultative group could be established to provide a channel for Indian input into what tariffs would be reasonable and to help reassure Indian policy-makers that the tariff scheme would not be abused.

Climate policy would also benefit more broadly from greater informal interaction with relevant experts and policy-makers in India. The most intensive climate-related US–India relationships currently appear to be in the technology community. In particular, a host of Silicon Valley based investors and entrepreneurs have established ties with the growing Indian clean technology sector. (There are also extensive relationships among scientists, including at the US national laboratories.) This is important in its own right, as a conduit for international flows of technology and capital, but it is not a substitute for stronger dialogue among policy-makers and experts. In particular, the Silicon Valley technology community is often poorly informed when it comes to US policy. To the extent that its members present an inaccurate view of US policy and its likely evolution, its Indian interlocutors may not be well served.

There are clearly important debates underway within India over its approach to climate change. By differentiating itself from China, and seeking common cause with the United States, Indian climate policy could become much more effective.

Note

1 It should be noted that carbon tariffs might not be wise from a purely US perspective. That does not, however, justify Indian opposition.

Part IV
Domestic politics of climate change

14 Climate politics in India

Three narratives[1]

Navroz K. Dubash

A domestic politics around climate change is gradually emerging in India, albeit with a distinctly dual nature. Much of Indian climate politics continues to be focused on climate change as a foreign policy concern, and centred on global climate negotiations. At the same time, there is an emergent discussion tentatively exploring Indian domestic policy in a changing climate context, but located within a larger emphasis on development. Finally, there is some discussion on whether and how the two should be linked.

This shift in Indian climate politics has been catalysed, although by no means determined, by global climate politics. With the creation at Bali in 2007 of a global negotiation track for 'long-term cooperative action' – a euphemism for action by developing, or non-Annex 1 countries – India was placed under ever greater international pressure to signal a proactive stance on climate change. The result has been increased media reportage of climate change (Jogesh, this volume), a few high profile parliamentary debates on climate change in the lead up to Copenhagen (Parliamentary debates, this volume), a profusion of reports and meetings from business and civil society (Das, this volume), and a slew of government committees, expert groups, and advisory councils focused on climate change. The outcome is a more diverse, if still predominantly elite, national politics around climate change.

This impressionistic overview of Indian climate politics starts by identifying three points of tension, where long-entrenched conventional wisdom is increasingly coming under question. I then build on this discussion to outline three archetypical political perspectives on climate change held within India, as a way of sharpening and making clear differences. I conclude with some forward-looking reflections on Indian climate politics in the global context.

Climate conventional wisdom: point and counterpoint

The long-held Indian negotiating position has argued that India cannot reasonably be construed as a 'major emitter' of greenhouse gases (GHG), that equity considerations should form the foundation of a global climate regime, and, consequently, that Indian domestic policy should be largely insulated from the requirements of climate mitigation.[2] These continue to be compelling views with wide backing. At the same time, there are emergent perspectives pointing to shades of grey on each of these points. While not challenging the underlying point, they are calling for a more nuanced view, and therefore a different domestic and international stance.

198 Dubash

India: disadvantaged latecomer or major emitter?

Within India, climate change has typically been viewed as a problem of allocating responsibility for the accumulation over time of GHGs – a problem of allotting finite 'development space'. By this measure, India has contributed only about 2.3% of global stocks of GHGs while the industrialized countries of Annex 1 collectively account for about 75% of current GHG stocks and the US alone for 29%.[3] By contrast, by some calculations India's 'fair share' of carbon space based on an equal per capita allocation of space is around 17% (Kanitkar et al., 2010; Jayaraman et. al., this volume). By this metric, India can hardly be called a major emitter, and is more appropriately a disadvantaged latecomer to the development game, seeking its fair share of atmospheric space.

The 1992 United Nations Framework Convention on Climate Change (UNFCCC) broadly supports this view by stipulating that industrialized countries should 'take the lead' in combating climate change and its impacts, as an implication of the principle of 'common but differentiated responsibilities and respective capabilities' (UNFCCC, 1992, Article 3.1). However, this remains a contested point, both on legal grounds (Rajamani, 2006; this volume), as well as on interpretation of how best to blend and operationalize concepts of responsibility *and* capability.

While acknowledging and reinforcing this point, some voices from civil society are increasingly vocal that India cannot long avoid the tag of a major emitter if it does not also reconsider its own development trajectory to account for climate threats (Raghunandan et al., 2008; Raghunandan, this volume; Bidwai, 2010). They argue that climate-vulnerable countries will increasingly regard India with 'sullen antipathy' (Raghunandan et al., 2008) as a growing part of the problem. While way behind the two largest emitters, China and the USA, by 2007 India was already the fourth largest emitter in terms of annual emissions.[4] A research consortium backed by the Government of India (GoI) projects India's emissions rising from about 1.8GT CO_2e in 2005[5] to somewhere between 4 and 7.3 GT CO_2e by 2030–31(Climate Modelling Forum, 2009). If global emissions shrink, as it is hoped they will, from about 42GT in 2005 to perhaps half that (21GT in 2030), the lower end of this range of Indian emissions will still amount to about 25% of global emissions by 2030–31. Well before this point, the tag of a major emitter is likely to become unavoidable.

The first perspective views allocation of responsibility solely on the basis of contributions to stocks of GHGs, while the latter gives some credence to how much an individual country contributes to flows. The political importance of India's growing share of annual global emissions depends on how effectively India makes the case that stocks of GHGs are all important. However, the case of China – which has faced growing pressure since overtaking the US to become the single largest annual emitter on the basis of flows – perhaps suggests that there are limits to this strategy. As a growing proportion of global flows of GHGs falls under India's jurisdiction, India will come under increasing international pressure to modify those flows and domestic constituencies for more action are likely to grow.

Equity: Who is hiding behind whom?

National contributions to either stocks or flows are, however, only part of the story. From an equity perspective, per capita emissions also matter. Thus, India's emissions per capita of 1.7 tons CO_2e per capita in 2005 were but a fraction of Annex 1 emissions of 14.1 tons CO_2e per capita or China's emissions of 5.5 tons CO_2e per capita, and only 7% of US emissions of 23.5 tons CO_2e per capita. [6] These numbers tell a story of extremely low emissions per person as compared to other countries, signalling not only a considerable development challenge ahead, but also weak capacity to address the climate problem.

The development data support this perception. It is well known that the bottom third or so of India's population are extremely poor – 27.5% are below the official poverty line of about $ 0.70 a day in rural areas and $1.05 a day in urban areas (PPP adjusted).[7] Moreover, the bottom half of India, 78 million households, do not have access to electricity. Even if they were provided access, in the short- to medium-run they would emit emissions equivalent to about 1–5% of US emissions (Dubash and Bradley, 2005). The Indian poor are unlikely to contribute greatly to global emissions.

While acknowledging this point, some internal critics suggest that in seeking to avoid emission reductions, India is 'hiding behind the poor' – the title of a Greenpeace India study (Greenpeace, 2007). However, the numbers are not easy to parse or interpret, and there is a range of contending interpretations and views also in public discourse (Chakravarty and Ramana, this volume). However, to briefly place this debate in numerical context, consumption data from McKinsey Global Institute suggested that in 2005, only 1% of India's population, or about 10 million people, lived on more than $16 a day (PPP).[8] Given that the US poverty line is $13 a day, this means that only a few tens of millions of Indians at most, rather than hundreds of millions, are living profligate lives while hiding behind the country's poor. The growing consumption of India's rich, while worth debating, can certainly not be a pretext for industrialized countries to shed their responsibility.

Rather than the numbers, however, it is the larger point at the core of the critique that is worth considering: internal equity within India should matter as much as equity across countries. For India to credibly place equity arguments at the core of its international position, it cannot continue to sustain gross internal inequalities in GHGs.[9] As social justice NGOs critically observe, while India argues that we need to increase our emissions in the name of the poorest and most vulnerable in India, they are often not the beneficiaries of development projects constructed in their name.[10] In addition, the effects of climate change are particularly harsh on the poorest (Bidwai, 2010). Finally, there are also discussions about whether, in fact, India should benchmark itself against Western consumption lifestyles, although correctly arguing that the choice about whether to do so or not should be a domestic one. The hiding behind the poor debate, while empirically problematic, has nuanced India's climate discussions by embedding them within development challenges, rather than only considering them a diplomatic problem.

Burden sharing versus opportunity seizing

The language of equity and unfinished development frames mitigation of climate change as a potential burden to be defended against in international negotiations. Indeed, to the extent that climate mitigation leads to the adoption of higher-priced but cleaner power options, higher prices on fossil fuels, and expensive carbon clean-up operations such as carbon capture and storage, it will indeed impose a cost. Moreover, it is near impossible to imagine India upgrading its infrastructure of roads, electricity

200 Dubash

capacity and urban spaces without considerable increases in GHGs. And clearly, the costs of adaptation to climate change are likely to pose a significant cost and compound development challenges. This perspective has historically informed India's climate negotiating position.

While India's negotiating position remains centred on this premise, within Indian domestic policy debates a more nuanced perspective has emerged. This view holds that not all climate mitigation need come at the cost of growth or even at the cost of poverty alleviation. Some sustainable development policies that particularly benefit the poor – such as promotion of public transport – clearly achieve both objectives (Sant and Gambhir, this volume). This approach, given the label of 'co-benefits' informs the Indian National Action Plan on Climate Change (NAPCC), which seeks to pursue opportunities, while not binding the country to necessarily realizing those opportunities (GoI, 2008). Put differently, India has chosen to hedge against the possibility that the trade-offs between low carbon development and poverty reduction may, in fact, be considerable.

Some have taken this argument further, suggesting that far from a cost, climate mitigation presents an opportunity (Das, this volume; Mehra, 2007). From this perspective, concerns over equity or an unfinished development agenda are not terribly salient to national positions because there is no real trade-off between poverty alleviation and climate mitigation; there may even be positive interaction between the two. For example, leadership positions in clean energy technology will support, not deter, India from addressing energy poverty.

In its absolute version, this position seems hard to sustain. There remain considerable uncertainties over the pace of technological innovation, and therefore over the extent to which aggressive climate mitigation will pay off, or whether it will delay or increase the cost of development outcomes such as providing infrastructure. At minimum, any opportunity seizing will only win support if it is strategic and prudent, keeping in mind other objectives such as economic inclusiveness and local environmental objectives.

Instead, domestic policy seems to have settled, and appropriately so, around the more nuanced co-benefits logic. Thus, accelerated investment in clean energy has been justified primarily on the basis of energy security. A mission on enhanced energy efficiency makes eminent sense from energy access and energy security perspectives, while also promising climate gains. Climate change, therefore, appears to present an intriguing political opportunity, as new institutional spaces such as dedicated missions under the NAPCC, have emerged to pursue diverse agendas with new vigour.

So far, however, there appears to be an accidental quality to the co-benefits approach: we will pursue our development interests, hoping they lead, almost serendipitously, to climate gains. A more proactive framing of the co-benefits approach would call for actively seeking co-benefits and exploring cases where marginal changes in domestic policy lead to significant climate co-benefits.

Three strategic narratives

The emergence of these more fine-grained substantive discussions on climate change have also led to a growing diversity of political perspectives on the subject. To provide a framework within which to explore the diversity of opinion in India on climate policy, I map out the range of positions along two axes: the relevance of environmental concerns to domestic policy; and perspectives on forms of engagement with the global climate regime (Table 14.1). These categorizations are of necessity crude, and simply provide a way of sharpening and identifying broad positions, rather than pigeon-holing particular groups or individuals.

On domestic policy, I distinguish between advocates of growth-first, who typically argue that environmental reforms will ineluctably follow when adequate levels of economic well-being have been achieved, against those who argue for internalizing environment under the rubric of sustainable development, for reasons of long-term viability of the natural resource base, as well as for reasons of equity (Lele, this volume).[11] On the international negotiations, I distinguish two extremes on a spectrum. At one end are those who adopt a staunchly realist position on global negotiations, the realists, and argue that because currently global politics are deadlocked, there is little to be gained by countenancing shifts in negotiating positions. The other end of the spectrum is those who call for more sustained and focused efforts by India to build a robust global regime, the internationalists.[12] The distinction between these positions on negotiations is somewhat blurred, as both categories tend to agree on long-sacrosanct positions such as differentiated responsibility. But the difference lies in emphasis given to ensuring that India's elbow room for domestic policy is preserved, versus strengthening the global climate regime as a negotiating objective.

As Table 14.1 indicates, this categorization results in four categories, of which three – growth first realist, sustainable development realist and sustainable development internationalist – are each associated with a narrative about how India should engage the climate debate, both domestically and internationally. The fourth option is effectively a null set, since those who give low priority to domestic concerns domestically, tend also to give them low priority internationally. These narratives are important, because each provides an internally consistent rationale for policy engagement. Shifts in climate politics are likely to be preceded or at least accompanied by a shift in narrative.

Below, I flesh out each of these narratives, using a range of common descriptive characteristics to provide some basis for comparison across narratives. The result is necessarily a somewhat caricatured picture of each narrative, but the intent is to sharpen distinctions so as to identify key points of transition from one narrative to another. This comparison is summarized in Table 14.2.

In constructing these ideal types, I do not suggest they fully encapsulate actual positions of different actors. Indeed, frequently actors combine elements of each position. However, in concluding the description of each narrative, I do point to different actors who, at different times, have come closest to exemplifying each narrative, in order to somewhat ground the discussion in empirical context.

Table 14.1 Diversity of opinion on domestic and international climate policy engagement with global climate regime

Importance of environmental concerns in domestic economic policy	*Realists – Preserve domestic policy space*	*Internationalists – Strengthen global regime*
Low – defer to later	Growth-First Realist	–
High – precondition for growth and equity	Sustainable Development Realist	Sustainable Development Internationalist

202   *Dubash*

Table 14.2 Three strategic Indian perspectives on climate change

	Growth-First Realist	Sustainable Development Realist	Sustainable Development Internationalist
Political reading of climate change	Geopolitical threat	India as excuse for inaction – fatalism	India as excuse for inaction – cooperation
Foundational demand	Equity – external	Equity – globally and nationally	Equity – globally and nationally + climate effectiveness
Domestic agenda	Growth first	Co-benefits	Co-benefits
International strategy	Stonewall commitments	Implement change at home, de-link globally	Implement change at home *and* link domestic and global
Motto	It's our turn!	It's an unfair world!	Seize the moment!

The growth-first realist: 'It's our turn!'

A growth-first realist narrative projects the climate debate itself as a threat to Indian interests. It downplays climate science, or at minimum, sees the threat of reduced growth as a result of global pressures to mitigate as more immediate and/or greater than the threat of climate impacts. From this perspective, climate change negotiations are a geopolitical stratagem by industrialized countries to contain new and emergent economic powers, particularly China, but also India, Brazil, and South Africa.

Equity across nations is the foundational demand, in part out of principle, but also because it is a strategic device to hold the industrialized world at bay. The priority is to continue India's recent high growth rate, and resist any efforts to modulate or change the growth strategy. China's recent two-decade long environmentally unconstrained growth spurt provides a model for India; India will be much better placed to bear the costs of both mitigation and adaptation after a similar growth spurt. There is little patience in this construction for sentiments about the need for internal equity within India, which are constructed as yet another effort by industrialized countries to deny responsibility and create an obstacle to growth. However, this opposition creates a perception that a growth first support for global equity is more strategic than principled.

The international strategy that emerges from this narrative is to stonewall commitments for India. Indeed, given that their concern over climate impacts is muted at best, adherents of a growth-first realist stance would prefer a weak climate regime that allowed India unconstrained growth over a strong climate regime even if it required industrialized countries to do more. A motto for this point of view might be: 'It's our turn!'

This position has, in the past, been influential in shaping the GoI's position (see Ghosh, this volume), although there have always been dissenting voices. In recent times there has been a discernable shift away from this perspective, as I discuss further below (see also Sengupta, this volume). The growth-first stance continues to command strong adherence from outside the government as well. Through 2007, Indian business has had a growth-first attitude and has been in lock-step with the government and there

Three narratives on climate politics in India   203

are elements within business who continue to support this view (Das, this volume).[13] In addition, economists who feel India has only recently managed to get onto a high growth trajectory worry that this achievement may be compromised (Panagariya, 2009a).[14] Those subscribing to this narrative include observers of WTO negotiations who are deeply sceptical of Western intentions and of India's ability to hold its own in a negotiations process.

Sustainable development realists: 'It's an unfair world!'

Sustainable development advocates start from the premise that climate change and its likely impacts pose a serious threat to India. However, the realists among them are deeply cynical about the international process, which they see as increasingly inconsistent with addressing historical responsibility or advancing equity. The prospect of a growing India (and China), they suggest, has become an excuse for inaction by industrialized countries. The fact that evidence of India's high level of continuing poverty, low carbon intensity, and a track record of measures to further reduce intensity have not served to remove this excuse suggests to realists that industrialized countries are hiding behind India, and there is little India can do to affect this situation – India is being used as an excuse.

Based on a long tradition of advocacy and scholarship, sustainable development realists have argued that a per capita based burden-sharing architecture is the only equitable way forward for the climate regime (see Agarwal and Narain, this volume; Rao, this volume). However a lack of success in getting this approach internalized within the climate negotiations, combined with a perception that the North is hiding behind India, have bred a fatalism about the global negotiations process.[15] As a result, the narrative leads to a re-focusing of energies on the national debate, to argue for a shift in India's growth strategy in favour of more environmental sustainability and internal equity by pursuing 'co-benefits' at home. Given their lack of faith in the international process, advocates of this view have increasingly argued for India to do its part, but not to link legally these efforts to the international process. The sense of cynicism regarding the international process informs my choice of motto for this narrative: It's an unfair world!

This view has long been the dominant perspective of Indian environment and development NGOs (see also Lele, this volume).[16] Most remain deeply sceptical of the good faith of the industrialized world in the negotiations process, even while remaining fierce critics of the government. This stance often leads to positions that may seem incongruous from an international perspective. For example a recent call by a network of civil society groups active on climate change calls for the Government to set a national cap on emissions, but not to embed this cap in the international legal process.[17] Thus, despite battling the government on several domestic fronts, many Indian NGOs close ranks with the government on international climate negotiations.

There is evidence that between 2007 and 2009, the centre of gravity of the GoI's position has shifted from a growth-first stance to a sustainable development view (see Sengupta, this volume). India's National Action Plan, for example, aims at a 'qualitative shift' in the development trajectory toward greater environmental sustainability as a way of realizing co-benefits (GoI, 2008). It is also consistent with the Indian government's stated position in 2009 that it will only subject actions that are externally supported to the measurement, reporting and verification process of the global climate

204 *Dubash*

regime, and that the rest of its policies and measures, which are designed to meet domestic objectives, will remain outside the scrutiny of the international process (GoI, 2009).

Finally, while Indian business has been relatively silent on climate change, they too, would appear to be moving from a growth-first position toward a sustainable development position, in the sense that they increasingly embrace the language of climate as a business opportunity (CII, 2008; Das, this volume). But they would rather pursue this opportunity free of the obligations and constraints of an international regime and corresponding domestic constraints.

Sustainable development internationalists: 'Seize the moment!'

The sustainable development internationalist narrative, as the label suggests, shares many of the attitudes of the sustainable development realist view. Both perspectives suggest that the rich world is using India as an excuse for inaction, stress the need for an equitable climate regime, and argue strenuously for the aggressive implementation of actions that bring development and climate co-benefits. However, where the realist view is informed by a somewhat fatalistic attitude to the global process, an internationalist perspective holds that India can and should make a difference to global negotiation dynamics by explicitly aligning Indian interests with a strong global climate regime. Since climate impacts will hurt the poor worst, according to this view, an ineffective climate agreement will, in effect, also perpetuate and exacerbate inequality. Hence, posing the climate issue as a trade-off between equity and effectiveness is misleading; there is no choice but to strive for both.[18] From within this narrative, sticking to a purist equity stand risks placing principle before the pragmatic considerations of the poorest. Consideration of climate impacts, particularly on the poor, is therefore a defining concern for internationalists.

Domestically, this perspective emphasizes the need for an aggressive national program of co-benefits measures. But, advocates of this view are more likely than either growth-first or sustainable development realists to anticipate potential economic gains if India is a first-mover in developing low-carbon technologies. The major line of difference with the realist narratives is the openness to exploring linkage of national measures to the international regime. Doing so will allow India to seize the moral high ground, challenge the industrialized world to take on commensurately more ambitious mitigation at home and throw India's weight behind a global collective action solution. Sustainable development internationalists' motto might be: 'Seize the moment!'

The sustainable development internationalist narrative is of relatively recent vintage, and is articulated by a small, but increasingly vocal group, many of whom have made a transition from a perspective of political realism, motivated by growing concern with the impact of climate change. Most are drawn from civil society and academia, although they certainly include a sprinkling of political figures, former government representatives, and business (Raghunandan et al., 2009; Bidwai, 2010; Desai, 2009; Shourie, 2009). So far, these voices have not coalesced into a larger coordinated position.

Nonetheless, this perspective continues to be a minority, particularly compared to the sustainable development realist stance. There are few takers for an argument that a shift in India's position can do much to change entrenched global positions. Instead, the mainstream perspective, in government and civil society, and perhaps even in business, is that rich countries are hiding behind India and other emerging economies, and have little independent will to act. Under these conditions, internationalists' calls for a proactive stance are met with charges of naiveté and a prediction that Indian offers will lead only to more constraints and no improvement in the global regime. Unlocking progressive climate politics in India is conditional on a more progressive climate politics globally.

Conclusion

A growth first perspective on climate change in India, once dominant, seems to be on the wane, although by no means politically marginal. The remaining two perspectives, while sharing a conviction in sustainable development, are fractured due to differing interpretations of the international process. While internationalists see a compelling case to exercise the limited leverage India has toward a more effective and equitable regime, realists view the negotiations process with a jaundiced eye. Uncertainty over the international negotiations process also leads sustainable development realists to curb their progressive instinct to aggressively promote a domestic co-benefits agenda. They fear a forward looking domestic policy will become a *de facto* baseline of action under a global regime, and the flexibility of the co-benefits approach will be replaced by a lock-in to an international regime of scrutiny and monitoring. These fears thrust them closer to growth-first realists, a group with which they share few convictions other than mistrust of the global negotiations process.

For their part sustainable development internationalists have to grapple with hard questions about the possible downsides of what realists would term a naive idealism about the global process. For example, what might be the costs to India's domestic autonomy of a robust global regime (see Parliamentary Debates, this volume)? Are internationalists willing to accept dilution of the bedrock principle of differentiated responsibility in order to win an environmentally strong global regime, and to what extent?

Thus, while sustainable development realists and internationalists are potential allies, they are held apart by widely differing interpretations of the global negotiations process. Consequently, a shift in the global negotiations context, one that provides credible evidence of industrialized country intent to take serious measures, and one that provides more substantial evidence of attention to equity, would help create the space for knitting a shared narrative among the two sets of sustainable development advocates.

In the wake of the Copenhagen and Cancun meetings of the Conference of Parties to the UNFCCC, visions of a hard global climate regime based on strict targets and backed by credible compliance mechanisms have diminished (Rajamani, 2011; Raghunandan, this volume). While this is a considerable problem from the viewpoint of global collective action, it may have the ironic side effect of diminishing concerns of an intrusive global regime, providing space for sustainable development realists and internationalists to make common cause on domestic change.

The challenge ahead for sustainable development advocates – whether of the realist or internationalist sort – is to deepen and operationalize the concept of climate co-benefits, and work it into a broader political vision of a sustainable and inclusive society. Only such a broad vision can effectively bring climate change closer to India's political mainstream.

206 *Dubash*

Notes

1 This chapter is a shorter and updated version of 'Toward a Progressive Indian and Global Climate Politics', Centre for Policy Research Climate Initiative Working Paper 2009/1, September. The author is grateful to Girish Sant, Sharad Lele, MV Ramana and Lavanya Rajamani for discussion and feedback on the ideas in this chapter, even while he retains responsibility for all opinions and errors.
2 This is not a comprehensive description of India's negotiating position, but includes key elements central to my argument here. Various other positions, such as on climate financing, follow from these foundational arguments.
3 Data from cait.wri.org.
4 Data from cait.wri.org.
5 Data from cait.wri.org.
6 Data from cait.wri.org. The GoI has presented studies to show that by 2030–31, estimates of India's per capita emissions range from 2.77 tons to 5.0 tons CO_2e per capita (Climate Modelling Forum, 2009).
7 Computed by the author from GoI, Press Information Bureau, 'Poverty Estimates for 2004–05,' New Delhi, 21 March 2007.
8 Mc Kinsey counts those households with more than Rs. 500,000 annual income. Assuming a PPP conversion rate of Rs 17 to the dollar, and 5 members to a household, this translates to about \$16 a day per person. Computed from McKinsey Global Institute (2007).
9 For a discussion of this point, see also Rao (this volume).
10 Letter from 17 civil society organizations to the Prime Minister of India, 'NAPCC and the National Water Mission' 27 July, 2009.
11 Sustainable development is, of course, a broad and quite contested formulation, that does not lend itself to easy implementation. I use the term here in recognition of the appeal of the concept as a way of providing a large tent for disparate positions, but also cognizant of its intellectual and operational weaknesses.
12 The use of the term 'internationalist' rather than idealist, which is more typically paired with the category of realist, is deliberate. I understand internationalists to identify India's *interests* with a strong global climate regime, in addition to a value-based predisposition to well functioning global mechanisms of governance. Internationalists are also more likely to see ways past the realist deadlock in climate negotiations, in particular by re-framing the debate. In other words, internationalists are distinguished from realists by their greater attention to constructivist perspectives on international relations, and include in their calculus a strong interest-based rationale for support of the global regime.
13 For example, the Federation of Indian Chambers of Commerce and Industry (FICCI) released a report in late 2007 highlighting the importance of CDM, emphasizing the low energy intensity of the Indian economy, and stressing the potential high costs of any mitigation (FICCI, 2007).
14 This view is spelled out in detail at Panagariya (2009b).
15 See for example, Sunita Narain's forceful view that 'international negotiations on climate change stink' due to a progressive erosion of differentiated responsibility (Narain, 2008).
16 This stance has a long history in India. Indeed, a wariness of the international process was apparent even during negotiation of the UNFCCC, as evidenced by the closing line of a highly influential report laying out an argument for an equity-based climate regime: 'Those who talk about global warming should concentrate on what ought to be done at home. The challenge for India is thus to get on with the job at hand and leave the business of dirty tricks and dirtying up the world to others' (Agarwal and Narain,1991, 20).
17 Letter from 17 civil society organizations to the Prime Minister of India, 'NAPCC and the National Water Mission' 27 July, 2009.
18 This argument is elaborated in Dubash (2009).

References

Agarwal, A. and Narain, S. (2009) *Global Warming in an Unequal World*, Centre for Science and Environment, New Delhi, 1991.

Three narratives on climate politics in India   207

Bidwai, P. (2010) *An India that can Say Yes*, Heinrich Boell Stiftung, New Delhi.

Centre for Science and Environment (2009) *Richest Indians Emit Less than Poorest Americans*, Centre for Science and Environment, October.

Climate Modelling Forum (2009) 'India's GHG Emissions Profile: Results of Five Modelling Studies', Ministry of Environment and Forests, GoI.

Confederation of Indian Industries (CII) (2008) *Building a Low Carbon Indian Economy*, CII Discussion Paper, January, New Delhi.

Desai, N. (2009) 'Lower the Temperature', *Times of India*, 22 July.

Dubash, N. (2009) 'Changing Climate Policies', *Livemint* 26 April 2009.

Dubash, N. and Bradley, R. (2005) 'Pathways to Rural Electrification in India: Are National Goals also an International Opportunity', in R. Bradley and K. A. Baumert (eds.) *Growing in the Greenhouse: Protecting the Climate by Putting Development First*, World Resources Institute Washington DC.

FICCI (2007) 'Climate Change Task Force Report', Federation of Indian Chamber and Commerce, New Delhi.

GoI (2009) 'Climate Change Negotiations: India's Submissions to the United Nations Framework Convention on Climate Change' Available at envfor.nic.in.

GoI (2008) *National Action Plan on Climate Change*, July 2008, pmindia.nic.in., accessed on 11 March 2011.

Greenpeace India (2007) 'Hiding Behind the Poor', Greenpeace India Society, Bangalore, India.

Kanitkar, T., Jayaraman, T., and D'Souza, M. (2010) 'Meeting Equity in a Finite Carbon World', CASS Forum on Climate Justice, Beijing, 15–16 April.

McKinsey Global Institute (2007) 'Tapping into the Indian Consumer Market'. Presented at the Indo-European Investment Forum, 28 June 2007. Available at http://www.scribd.com/doc/306245/Mckinsey-The-India-consumer-story. Accessed 11 September 2009.

Mehra, M. (2007) 'Climate Change: Why India Needs to take Leadership', Centre for Social Markets.

Narain, S. (2008) 'The Mean World of Climate Change', *Down to Earth*, 31 July.

Panagariya, A (2009a) 'Say No at Copenhagen', *Economic Times*, 23 July 2009.

—— (2009b) 'Climate Change and India: Implications and Policy Options', Paper presented at India Policy Forum, New Delhi, 14–15 July 2009, http://www.columbia.edu/~ap2231/, accessed on 11 March 2011.

Press Information Bureau, Government of India (2007) 'Poverty Estimates for 2004–5', New Delhi, March.

Raghunandan, D., Jayaraman,T., Purkayastha, P., Karunakaran, C.E. and Venkateswaran, T. V. (2008) *Climate Crisis: Challenges and Options*, All India Peoples Science Network and Centre for Science Technology and Society, Tata Institute of Social Science, New Delhi.

Raghunandan, D., Purkayastha, P. and Jayaraman, T. (2009) 'Breaking the Climate Deadlock', *The Hindu*, 23 June.

Rajamani L. (2011) 'The Cancun Climate Agreements: Reading the Text, Subtext and Tealeaves,' *International and Comparative Law Quarterly*, vol. 60, pp. 499–519.

Rajamani, L. (2006) *Differential Treatment in International Environmental* Law, Oxford, Oxford University Press, pp. 138–144.

Shourie, A. (2009) 'Changing Course on Climate', *Indian Express*, 2–3 July.

UNFCCC (1992) 'United Nations Framework Convention on Climate Change: Text of the Convention', Bonn, Germany.

15 Climate change and the Indian environmental movement

Sharachchandra Lele

Introduction

Climate change has emerged in the past few years as *the* environmental problem at the global level, swamping all other environmental issues. Western environmentalists who focus largely on wilderness and biodiversity conservation have adapted easily, by showing how climate change will aggravate the problem of conservation – e.g., loss of polar bears, seals, penguins, or whales (see, for instance, Lovejoy and Hannah, 2006). But this kind of 'climate centrism' in the environmental discourse has been problematic for many environmentalists in the global South, as it threatens to divert attention from other more pressing local or regional issues such as water scarcity and pollution, indoor and outdoor air pollution, mining impacts, or solid waste management. Not surprisingly, many Indian environmentalists have been tentative and ambiguous about engaging with climate change, to the extent that this tentativeness has been interpreted in the North as 'foot-dragging' or even 'hiding behind the poor' (Ananthapadmanabhan *et al.*, 2007). More recently, one sees an upsurge in interest and engagement and the emergence of some new groups and coalitions. Although some are focusing exclusively on climate change, most others are critical of blind engagement and are grappling with how best to integrate the issue into their overall approach to environmentally sound development.

The purpose of this chapter is to understand the manner in which Indian environmentalists have engaged with climate change so far, and how they might better engage with it in the future. I will argue that although the initial lukewarm response and the recent urgency have been shaped to an extent by the changing 'scientific' understanding of the impacts, fully understanding the nature of engagement requires exploring the various shades of Indian environmentalism and the complex linkage between climate and other environmental issues. I will present the different normative and analytical dimensions of Indian environmentalism(s) and suggest that a normatively more inclusive and analytically more sophisticated environmentalism might provide a means of better engaging with and integrating climate change concerns into domestic environmental agendas.

No need to engage

In the mid-1980s, climate change seemed like a remote issue, another of those 'Northern' environmental concerns, similar to the ozone hole, that had little overlap with burning issues in the South. In comparison, local and regional issues of big dams

The Indian environmental movement 209

(Narmada), industrial disasters (Bhopal), water pollution (Ganga and Palar rivers), air pollution ('slow murder' in Delhi), forest degradation (Himalayas and Western Ghats), and water scarcity (Gujarat) were clearly more pressing and significant. For instance, the first two citizens' reports on the State of India's Environment (CSE, 1982; 1985) did not have chapters on climate change, but focused on land, water, energy, dams, air, wildlife, and habitat. Subsequent reports focused on floods in the Gangetic plain (CSE, 1992) and air pollution in Delhi (Sharma and Roychowdhury, 1996). Even today, solid waste disposal, river water sharing and conflict, mining and tribal lives in central India, dam impacts in the northeast, soft drinks and water resource exploitation in Kerala, and threats of environmentally triggered diseases such as chikungunya are pressing problems, whereas there is still enormous uncertainty over how and to what extent the climate is changing and especially about how exactly it is affecting the quality of human life and activities.

Moreover, some of the early models of climate change were ambivalent about the overall direction of impacts in the Indian subcontinent, and mentioned the possibility that higher rainfall may actually benefit agriculture in spite of temperature increases (e.g., Parry, 1989; Matthews, 1995). Not surprisingly, 'most developing countries view[ed] the challenge of development to be far more important than the threat of climate change' (Reddy, 1993).

Equity-based engagement

For a long time, the major environmental group engaging with climate change was the Centre for Science and Environment (CSE) in New Delhi. True to its political economy perspective, a perspective clearly visible in the second Citizen's Report (CSE, 1985), CSE played a crucial role in analysing the question of how the responsibility for global warming should be allocated. In a path-breaking study (Agarwal and Narain, 1991), they pointed out that by focusing on current flows rather than the historic build-up of CO_2 stock in the atmosphere, by using shorter time frames (thereby emphasizing the role of methane from paddy cultivation rather than CO_2), by focusing on gross emissions per nation rather than normalizing them to per capita, by using questionable figures of Amazonian deforestation, and by equating luxury consumption of the rich with the survival emissions of the poor, developed country analysts were assigning a much higher share of the responsibility to developing countries than was accurate or fair. What is required then is a 'per capita emission entitlement approach [in which] the emissions absorbed annually by the global atmospheric sinks [are distributed] equally among all the people of the world, providing each person with an equal entitlement' (Agarwal, 2002). Those who want to consume more than their 'fair share' would then have to purchase emission rights from those who do not use their full share, creating massive wealth transfer from the rich to the poor countries.

The Indian government was quick to adopt this position, although it did not otherwise accept the environmentalist critique of the conventional development model crafted by CSE and others. By pointing to the low-level of per capita emissions of developing nations and the need for these nations to not sacrifice their 'developmental rights' by accepting restrictions on emissions, the government was able to push the principle of 'common but differentiated responsibility' (CBDR) in international climate negotiations for quite some time. By doing so, the government was in fact protecting its approach of 'economic growth = development', an approach that blindly replicates

210 *Lele*

the Western developmental model – the model that has led to climate change in the first place. Nevertheless, in light of the complete refusal of the North to engage with the question of climate justice, Indian environmentalists of all hues felt justified in not challenging its government's position. Thus, what was supposed to be an 'ecologically effective, economically efficient, and equitable' approach (Agarwal, 2002) became branded internationally as stonewalling while hiding behind equity (Dubash, this volume), while Indian environmentalists became increasingly cynical of the international process and refocused on domestic environmental issues (Dubash, 2009).

Dilemmas of engagement

Even when some engagement without compromising the equity principle seems possible, issues are more complicated than they appear. The Kyoto Protocol was broadly consistent with the concept of CBDR, but it also came up with the idea of the Clean Development Mechanism (CDM) – a precursor to the more general carbon-trading approach being strongly advocated in the last few years. While Indian environmentalists supported the government on CBDR, they were and are divided on CDM and carbon offsetting in general. While some welcomed the mechanism as a way of earning much-needed revenues for no-regrets measures taken at home (Gupta, 2003; TERI, 2001), others have questioned the CDM approach for its conceptual flaws (absence of an initially defined set of emission rights) as well as its fundamental unacceptability because it allows the North to buy its way out of its responsibility to reduce emissions at home (Agarwal, 2002) – exposing deep divisions on the question of market-based approaches to environmental problems.

CDM and carbon-trading in general poses a particularly severe dilemma in the context of forests. Some analysts, including ecologists (Ravindranath and Somashekhar, 1995; Binkley *et al.*, 2002; Poffenberger *et al.*, 2001) and foresters (Kant, 2005) have supported taking money for carbon-sequestration through afforestation programmes, arguing that this is a win-win between income generation, climate change mitigation and the greening of wastelands, many other groups (typically grassroots activists and advocacy groups, but also several academics) have rejected this as yet another form of climate imperialism, harmful to local communities, especially to the poor, and only strengthening the hands of already dominant state forest agencies (Caruso and Modi, 2004; Gundimeda, 2004; 2005; CSD and NFFPFW, 2009).

Since about 2005, with the impacts of climate change becoming clearer, potentially more disruptive and imminent, there has been greater engagement by Indian environmentalists with the question of mitigation. This engagement has taken different forms. Some, such as the Centre for Social Markets, Indian Youth Climate Network or the Indian Network for Ethics and Climate Change have focused primarily on awareness building. Others have pushed for taking the equity-based position to its logical conclusion, insisting on internal equity in access to energy and limiting the 'excessive' emissions of the rich. The latter point was made sharply by Greenpeace India in its 'hiding behind the poor' report (Ananthapadmanabhan *et al.*, 2007), although their figures have been questioned and it has been argued that even the richest Indians emit less than the poorest Americans (CSE, 2009). Others have pointed out that the overall energy efficiency of the Indian economy is higher than the USA or China (Rao *et al.*, 2009). Lost somewhere in this debate is the question of whether even this 'low' level of fossil energy consumption of the rich Indians is locally sustainable or whether this

The Indian environmental movement 211

level of energy access can realistically be provided to the rest of the population. The reference point in this debate still seems to be the international negotiations, which is perhaps inevitable in the current juncture but limiting in the long run.

In the larger debate on energy pathways, several dilemmas have emerged that further exemplify the challenges in engaging with climate change. One dilemma relates to the role of nuclear energy (INECC, 2000) and the other to the role of big dams. Both options are certainly low-carbon alternatives to fossil-fuel based electricity generation, but both have other environmental impacts and have been strongly resisted by local environmental groups and human rights activists in the past. The climate-friendliness of these options strengthens the hands of state agencies that had already begun pushing for 'energy by any means feasible' to fuel the economic growth juggernaut (e.g., Anonymous, 2005). In addition to having to fight the battle on local environmental grounds, activists now have to counter the efforts to portray the dams as carbon-neutral and cash in on CDM funds to finance dam construction (e.g., SANDRP, 2010).

The issue of big dams has also spilt over into the adaptation debate. To the extent that climate change will make rainfall more erratic, conventional water resource planning suggests that one should build more and bigger dams to allow for greater within-year and carryover storage to accommodate the greater variation in inflows. But this will only increase the social and environmental costs imposed by such structures – a reason why the number of new large irrigation projects has decreased significantly and the grandiose 'interlinking of rivers' project was shelved. For many grassroots activists, focusing on climate change means risking the revival of such foolhardy ideas. Thus, whether it is energy, water, or forests, bringing climate change into the equation appears often to undermine painstakingly built positions and coalitions on local environmental issues.

Understanding Indian environmentalisms

Much of the earlier response, or lack of it, may be explained in terms of perceptions about the importance of climate change vis-à-vis other local and regional environmental issues and environment-development conflicts. It has also been argued (Dubash, 2009) that the subsequent 'closing of ranks' around the equity-based engagement with international negotiations reflects the fact that a large fraction of Indian environmentalists subscribe to the 'environmentalism of the poor' (Guha, 1997a). In this ideology of environmentalism, the normative concern is with equitable sharing of or access to natural resources (land, water, forests), with an additional social justice dimension – that the livelihood needs of the poor must be given higher priority than the profit aspirations of the rich or the corporate sector. Such an approach is evident in the Chipko movement, which was not about the preservation versus destruction of nature, but rather about who should have the right to extract forest resources: rural communities or timber contractors? Analytically, this environmentalism posits that communities living in close proximity with natural resources, especially the poor, are generally predisposed towards sustainable use of resources, and the problem of degradation originates in their powerlessness in face of takeover/handover of these resources by/to industry in the name of development. Similarly, this environmentalism posits that the impacts of pollution are borne disproportionately by the poor, as in the case of the victims of the Bhopal disaster. It also suggests that these problems are the likely outcome of technology that is immense in scale, complex and hence expert-

212   *Lele*

controlled, and designed to meet the wants of industrial economies, not the needs of the poor – as in the case of large dams and nuclear power.

It is no doubt true that a concern for equity and social justice, a rootedness in livelihood questions, and an awareness of the political economy of the environment and the destructive nature of modern development has been a feature of many Indian environmental movements, starting with Chipko, Jharkhand, Narmada and other anti-dam struggles, and recent struggles over mining in Niyamgiri. It is also true that climate change has been cast by some as a problem akin to Bhopal – where the polluters are distinct from (and vastly richer than) the pollutees (e.g., Narain, 2009). And certainly the stonewalling by the North (especially the USA) of any meaningful action towards emission reduction is patently unfair and by far the biggest issue in climate change mitigation policy today. Nevertheless, to characterize Indian environmentalism as simply an environmentalism of the poor and casting it as a polar opposite of the 'post-materialist' environmentalism of the North, is problematic both because it glosses over the diversity of environmental movements in India and also because it does injustice to the ethical and analytical breadth of environmentalism as a concept.

Environmental 'problems' are of different kinds: some which impose a negative externality in space (such as pollution), some impose it over time (such as carbon emissions), and some in more subtle combinations (such as biodiversity loss) (Lélé, 1994; Lee, 1993; Lélé, 1998). To be an environmentalist means to care about the impacts of one's action on others, on the future, and on the quality of life. Thus, normatively, environmentalism appeals to multiple moral impulses: fairness to other human beings (intra-general justice), sustainability (intergenerational equity) and also material and spiritual quality of life (the latter overlapping with the idea of fairness to other living organisms). Social justice, when combined with environmental concerns, asks us to treat the environmental actions of the poor with more consideration than those of the rich. Guha himself, in a later chapter in the same book, suggested a new environmental ethics that synthesizes these multiple dimensions (Guha, 1997b).

Explaining the occurrence of these different kinds of problems requires also multiple analytical frameworks. The first kind of problem – the existence of situations where one actor imposes pollution costs upon someone else here and now – may be explained through a political economy framework, i.e., the power of the polluter vis-à-vis the pollutee, such as the case of Harihar Polyfibres versus downstream farmers on the Tungabhadra river (CSE, 1982, p. 91). But other aspects complicate matters. Polluters and pollutees may not be fully aware of the health impacts (e.g., the early use of DDT). Having many dispersed polluters creates a commons problem (e.g., air pollution by vehicles). Interests may be interlinked – e.g., factory workers may receive both pollution and jobs from a factory. Political economy also explains why natural resource access is often unfairly distributed, as in the case of colonial appropriation of forests in India. Even here, ecology and technology play a role – upper reaches of rivers tend 'naturally' to get settled much after river mouths have been settled, setting up the kinds of conflicts one sees between Karnataka and Tamil Nadu on the Cauvery river.

Other environmental problems are better explained by other kinds of frameworks: open-access forests may degrade due to collective action problems – commonly known as 'the tragedy of the commons'. Forests may be converted to agriculture simply because short-term livelihood needs trump long-term forest benefits – a problem often related to poverty but not entirely explained by it, as even rich farmers may opt to do this. Adoption of green revolution technology may lead to outcomes that were not really anticipated, such as salinization of soils – the result of reductionist science more than anything else. Women's lack of voice within the household may explain why rural households that can afford gobar-gas or improved chulhas do not install them, causing health hazards and hardship to the women. Mahatma Gandhi would probably also have highlighted materialistic values that are not purely a product of social structures. These factors may interact, but they are still semi-independent explanations of the complex phenomenon we call environmental degradation (see Figure 3 in Lélé, 1991). One also needs to remember that the issue is not just about the environment, but about environment and development – what trajectory will be environment-friendly and yet achieve the developmental goals of poor nations.

Climate change is an enormously complex issue because it has elements of all three kinds of environmental problems. The atmosphere is a global scale common-pool resource and individual emission actions result in impacts that are dispersed and long-term. But climate change hurts some (such as small island nations) more than others, and some people emit enormously more emissions than others, so issues of environmental equity and social justice are relevant. At the same time, climate change is not a problem in itself – it is a problem because it threatens to undermine the material and non-material quality of life for many of us. Yet, we have not figured out a way to ensure what is today considered an adequate quality of life without the use of fossil fuels. Or alternatively, we have not managed to publicly define a 'good life' that is less emission-intensive than that of the European middle class or the Indian middle class.

Indian environmentalists have embraced all types of environmentalisms outlined above. The wildlife conservationists, who preceded many others in post-independence India, have focused on saving pristine wilderness to the exclusion of all other concerns, including the justice issues in evicting tribal groups from conservation areas and also the environmental impacts of their own lifestyles. Their analytical perspective has tended to blame population growth (e.g., WWF-India, 2010). Another set of activists emerged around various resource and livelihood movements, starting with Chipko. They highlighted state control as the cause, valorising communities as natural conservationists (Shiva et al., 1991). A third grouping is visible around urban environmental issues such as air pollution in Delhi. This grouping has been somewhat insensitive to issues of social justice (as pointed out by Baviskar, 2011). Sustainability arguments typically seem to come from groups that are more techno-economic, e.g., those arguing for regulation of groundwater use to prevent long-term depletion, or for long-term energy planning (e.g., Shukla, 1997).

Corresponding to these strands, the positions of Indian environmentalists on climate change have also varied. Given the single-minded focus of conservationists, they see climate change as aggravating the pressure on already threatened flora and fauna. They therefore call for larger and more protected areas, better interconnectedness between them (to allow species to move with climate shifts), and stricter protection (Karanth and Chellam, 2009), even if it involves greater cost to local communities. Those concerned about forest rights of local communities are, as mentioned earlier, ambivalent about the role of CDM and REDD – will these programmes increase the income of forest communities or become another form of 'imperial' forestry? (See Gopalakrishnan in this volume.) Those oblivious in the past to issues of displacement and social justice in general have advocated more dams (Mathur et al., 2003), and more nuclear power to reduce carbon emissions (Anonymous, 2008). Some who champion markets for development also adopt that strategy for climate change (e.g.,

214 *Lele*

Centre for Social Markets). To the extent that the domestic engagement with climate change is only beginning, these differences have not yet emerged sharply, but are likely to sharpen in the coming years.

A broad-based environmentalism and a plural engagement

Not all environmentalist positions are, however, mutually exclusive. In the 1980s and 1990s, many inclusive positions were also crafted. Some anti-dam activists crafted a broad-based critique of these technologies based simultaneously on loss of bio-diversity, loss of livelihoods, undemocratic processes, and limited developmental gains (Bhartari *et al.*, 1985; Patkar, 1999). Many scholars and activists working on forests see possibilities of simultaneously enhancing tribal livelihoods, long-term sustainability and biodiversity conservation (Kothari *et al.*, 1998; Lele *et al.*, 2010). Energy analysts like Amulya Reddy, initially focused on energy scarcity and its constraints on development, actively embraced questions of equitable access, priority for poverty alleviation, and environmental impact (Reddy *et al.*, 1995). Indeed, I would argue that the biggest contribution of Indian environmentalism to global environmental thought was its forging of a multi-dimensional notion of environmental concern. The first citizens' report on the State of India's Environment (CSE, 1982) epitomized this convergence. It argued that environmentalism was not just about saving birds or tigers, but related to all aspects of traditional and modern life – air, water, land, energy, forests, habitation, and so on, and was therefore inseparable from developmental considerations also. To a reader of this report, Indian environmentalism represented a broad environmental ethic embracing sustainability, environmental justice and conservation (even if the first two terms were not in vogue then). And analytically, it allowed for multiple explanations – colonialism, bureaucratic control, technological failures, gender, class, and so on.

Maintaining this common front has not been easy though. Indeed, the first fissures appeared as early as 1985, when the second citizens' report arrived (CSE, 1985) where the tone was more strident and excessively focused on political economy explanations. Perhaps the convergence of 1982 was superficial or premature. Perhaps the pressure of the post-liberalization era on both environment and poverty was too much, so that activists retreated from broad consensus-building to narrow issue-based agitation. Perhaps the external funding that poured into the NGO sector starting the mid-1980s led to the co-option of some groups and the splintering of the environmental movement. Perhaps the emergence of a new consumerist and westernized middle class has led to the strengthening of western-style asocial conservation thinking. Whatever the reasons, this common front has not lasted, and polarizations around 'tribals versus tigers', 'commercial wind farms versus local rights', 'integrated water resource management versus small-scale water harvesting', or 'biotechnology versus bio-safety' have emerged. The divergent stances on climate change have already been described above.

Nevertheless, it seems clear that neither non-engagement nor blind engagement will carry the day. Climate change is now too serious and too imminent, especially in a monsoon-dependent and poverty-ridden country like India, to be ignored. On the other hand, India's average per capita emissions are still below the per capita level that is considered sustainable if adopted globally (around 3 $tCO_2e/cap/yr$ (Byrne *et al.*, 1998), which means Indian emissions can only increase, and in any case unilateral

The Indian environmental movement 215

emission reductions will achieve nothing, given that India's share is only ~5%. But climate change offers one important lever to prise open the conventional growth paradigm within the country – viz., the carbon footprint. This provides a relatively simple criterion for assessing the sustainability of one's lifestyle: 3 tCO_2/capita/year. Other indicators have been much more difficult to estimate and are indeterminate. For instance, water availability per capita may be easily estimated in a particular region, but only if it is assumed that no water can be imported across the region's boundary, which is necessarily arbitrary, and no water can be reused, which is simply incorrect. Pollution levels vary from one pollutant to another, and one always thinks one can eventually do away with that pollutant. But atmospheric CO_2 has only one boundary – the globe – and the burning of fossil fuels is fundamental to the modern developmental paradigm.

Indian environmentalists may therefore be able to use climate change to strengthen an already emerging multi-dimensional critique of the industrialization and growth paradigm that is holding sway in India at present. There are of course no magic bullets. Emphasizing climate change may seem to undermine the case against nuclear energy and big dams. But to the extent that the case for absolute emission reductions by India as a whole is weak, to the extent that coal mining and coal-based plants are already being opposed by local communities, and questions of equitable access to energy are already being asked, pointing to climate equity at home might strengthen the case for more bottom-up, democratic, need-based energy planning rather than simple equations about development = growth = energy consumption (see chapter by Sant and Gambhir this volume). To the extent that other issues such as forests are also multi-dimensional and multi-scalar, involving local resource rights, downstream hydrological beneficiaries and national wildlife heritage, the introduction of a fourth, global, dimension in the shape of carbon sequestration only strengthens the argument for multi-layered democratic governance of forests without compromising the primacy of local claims. And integrating climate change considerations into urban planning might tilt the balance in favour of mass transport and other modes of low or zero-pollution transport and in favour of eco-friendly buildings, thus firmly turning the scanner on the question of consumption in urban areas when much of environmentalism had hitherto focused on the question of production in the hinterland.

References

Agarwal, A. (2002) 'A Southern Perspective on Curbing Global Climate Change', in S. Schneider, A. Rosencranz and J. O. Niles (eds), *Climate Change Policy: A Survey*, Island Press, Washington, DC, pp. 375–391.

Agarwal, A. and Narain, S. (1991) 'Global warming in an unequal world: a case of environmental colonialism', Centre for Science and Environment, New Delhi.

Ananthapadmanabhan, G., Srinivas, K. and Gopal, V. (2007) *Hiding Behind The Poor: A report by Greenpeace on climate injustice*, Greenpeace India Society, Bangalore.

Anonymous (2005) 'Draft Report of the Expert Committee on Integrated Energy Policy', Planning Commission, Government of India, New Delhi.

Anonymous (2008) 'Pachauri supports India's nuclear power quest', *The Economic Times*, 7 January, http://m.economictimes.com/PDAET/articleshow/2679735.cms.

Baviskar, A. (2011) 'Cows, Cars and Rickshaws: Bourgeois Environmentalists and the Battle for Delhi's Streets', in A. Baviskar and R. Ray (eds), *Elite and Everyman: The Cultural Politics of the Indian Middle Classes*, Routledge, New Delhi.

216 Lele

Bhartari, R., Kothari, A. and Bagla, P. (1985) 'The Narmada valley project: Development or destruction?', *The Ecologist*, 15(5/6): 269–284.

Binkley, C. S., Brand, D., Harkin, Z., Bull, Z., Ravindranath, N. H., Obersteiner, M., Nilsson, S., Yamagata, Y. and Krott, M. (2002) 'Carbon sink by the forest sector—options and needs for implementation', *Forest Policy and Economics*, 4(1): 65–77.

Byrne, J., Wong, Y.-D., Lee, H. and Kim, J.-d. (1998) 'An equity- and sustainability-based policy response to global climate change', *Energy Policy*, 26(4): 335–343.

Caruso, E. and Modi, A. (2004) 'Village Forest Protection Committees in Madhya Pradesh: an update and critical evaluation', Forest Peoples, available at http://www.forestpeoples.org/documents/asia_pacific/madhya_pradesh_oct04_eng.shtml, last modified on October 2004, accessed on 6 September, 2006.

CSD and NFFPFW (2009) 'Joint Statement on REDD Climate Scheme', Campaign for Survival and Dignity and National Forum for Forest Peoples and Forest Workers.

CSE (1982) 'The State of India's Environment: The First Citizens' Report', Centre for Science and Environment, New Delhi.

CSE (1985) 'The State of India's Environment, 1984–85: The Second Citizens' Report', Centre for Science and Environment, New Delhi.

CSE (1992) 'Floods, Flood Plains and Environmental Myths. State of India's Environment: Third Citizen's Report', Centre for Science and Environment, New Delhi.

CSE (2009) 'Richest Indians emit less than poorest Americans', Factsheet, Centre for Science & Environment, New Delhi.

Dubash, N. K. (2009) 'Environmentalism in the age of climate change', *Seminar*, 601: 63–66.

Guha, R. (1997a) 'The environmentalism of the poor', in R. Guha and J. Martinez-Alier (eds), *Varieties of Environmentalism: Essays North and South*, pp. 3–21.

Guha, R., (1997b) 'Towards a cross-cultural environmental ethic', in R. Guha and J. Martinez-Alier (eds), *Varieties of Environmentalism: Essays North and South*, pp. 77–91.

Gundimeda, H. (2004) 'How "sustainable" is the "sustainable development objective" of CDM in developing countries like India?', *Forest Policy and Economics*, 6: 329–343.

Gundimeda, H. (2005) 'Can CPRs Generate Carbon Credits without Hurting the Poor?', *Economic and Political Weekly*, 40(10): 973–980.

Gupta, S. (2003) 'India, CDM and Kyoto Protocol', *Economic and Political Weekly*, 38(41): 4292–4298.

INECC (2000) 'Position paper 2000', Indian Network on Ethics and Climate Change, Vishakhapatnam.

Kant, P. (2005) 'Raising 'Kyoto Forests' in the different bio-geographic zones of India: A profitability analysis', *Indian Forester*, 131(9): 1105–1120.

Karanth, K. U. and Chellam, R. (2009) 'Carnivore conservation at the crossroads', *Oryx*, 43(01): 1–2.

Kothari, A., Pathak, N., Anuradha, R. V. and Taneja, B. (eds) (1998) *Communities and Conservation: Natural Resource Management in South and Central Asia*, Sage Publications, New Delhi.

Lee, K. N. (1993) 'Greed, scale mismatch, and learning', *Ecological Applications*, 3(4): 560–564.

Lélé, S. (1994) 'Sustainability, Environmentalism, and Science', *Pacific Institute Newsletter*, 3(1): 1–2, 5.

Lélé, S. (1998) 'Resilience, sustainability and environmentalism', *Environment and Development Economics*, 3(2): 251–255.

Lele, S., Wilshusen, P. R., Brockington, D., Seidler, R. and Bawa, K. S. (2010) 'Beyond exclusion: alternative approaches to biodiversity conservation in the developing tropics', *Current Opinions in Environmental Sustainability*, 2(1-2): 94–100.

Lélé S. M. (1991) 'Sustainable Development: a critical review', *World Development*, 19(6): 607–621.

The Indian environmental movement   217

Lovejoy, T. and Hannah, L. J. (eds) (2006) *Climate Change and Biodiversity*, Yale Univeristy Press, New Haven, CT.

Mathur, J., Bansal, N. K. and Wagner, H. J. (2003) 'Investigation of greenhouse gas reduction potential and change in technological selection in Indian power sector', *Energy Policy*, 31(12): 1235–1244.

Matthews, R. (1995) *Modeling the impact of climate change on rice production in Asia*, CABI.

Narain, S. (2009) 'Let's not forget, we are climate victims', *Times of India*, 9 December, http://epaper.timesofindia.com/Default/Scripting/ArticleWin.asp?From=Archive&Source=Page&Skin=TOINEW&BaseHref=CAP/2009/12/09&PageLabel=17&EntityId=Ar01700&ViewMode=HTML&GZ=T.

Parry, M. (1989) 'The Impact of Climatic Variations on Agriculture', *Bulletin of the American Academy of Arts and Sciences*, 42(8): 30–36.

Patkar, M. (1999) 'Letter From Medha Patkar to the Prime Minister of India, Mr. A.B. Vajpayee', Narmada Bachao Andolan, Baroda.

Poffenberger, M., Ravindranath, N. H., Pandey, D. N., Murthy, I. K., Bist, R. and Jain, D. (2001) 'Communities & Climate Change: The Clean Development Mechanism and village-based forest restoration in central India – A Case Study from Harda Forest Division, Madhya Pradesh, India', Research Report, Community Forestry International, Inc., Santa Barbara.

Rao, N., Sant, G. and Chellarajan, S. (2009) 'An overview of Indian Energy Trends: Low Carbon Growth and Development Challenges', Prayas, Pune.

Ravindranath, N. H. and Somashekhar, B. S. (1995) 'Potential and economics of forestry options for carbon sequestration in India', *Biomass and Bioenergy*, 8(5): 323–336.

Reddy, A., DSa, A., Sumithra, G. and Balachandra, P. (1995) 'Integrated energy planning: Part I. The DEFENDUS methodology', *Energy for Sustainable Development*, 2(3): 15–26.

Reddy, A. K. N. (1993) 'Poverty-oriented energy strategies for sustainable development', paper presented at International Workshop on Environment and Poverty, organized by, at Dhaka, on July 22–24.

SANDRP (2010) 'Why Teesta 6 should not get CDM status', South Asia Network on Dams, Rivers and People, New Delhi.

Sharma, A. and Roychowdhury, A. (1996) *Slow Murder: The Deadly Story of Vehicular Pollution in India*, Centre for Science and Environment, New Delhi.

Shiva, V., Bandyopadhyay, J., Hegde, P., Krishnamurthy, B.V., Kurien, J., Narendranath, G. and Ramprasad, V. (1991) *Ecology and the Politics of Survival: Conflicts Over Natural Resources in India*, United Nations University Press and Sage Publications, New Delhi and London.

Shukla, P. R. (1997) *Energy Strategies and Greenhouse Gas Mitigation: Models and Policy Analysis for India*, Allied Publishers, New Delhi.

TERI (2001) 'Clean Development Mechanism Project Opportunities in India', Project Report (in collaboration with Pembina Institute for Appropriate Development), Tata Energy Research Institute, New Delhi.

WWF-India (2010) 'Conservation Challenges', World Wide Fund for Nature-India, available at http://www.wwfindia.org/about_wwf/priority_species/royal_bengal_tiger/conservation_chall enges/, accessed on 5 February, 2010.

16 The Hiding Behind the Poor debate

A synthetic overview

Shoibal Chakravarty and M.V. Ramana

Introduction

In October 2007, the Indian branch of the international environmental organization, Greenpeace, came out with a report entitled *Hiding Behind the Poor* (Ananthapadmanabhan et al., 2007) Based on a survey of 819 individuals divided into seven income classes, the report tried to assess CO_2 emission levels amongst different income classes in India. The report was produced just prior to the Bali Conference of Parties to the United Nations Framework Convention on Climate Change (UNFCCC), which was expected to be crucial in setting the stage for an agreement to follow the Kyoto Protocol.

Though not without its problems (that we discuss below) the Greenpeace report was an important intervention in the Indian climate debate, representing one of the few attempts at examining how emissions are distributed among different income classes. The oldest of such studies that we have been able to identify is from 1997 by J. Parikh and her collaborators (Parikh et al., 1997; Murthy et al., 1997). Parikh and her collaborators have produced a more recent attempt in 2009 at quantifying the 'differential emission effects of consumption pattern of different income classes in India' (Parikh et al., 2009). An indirect handle on the same question is provided by S. Pachauri, who has produced a series of papers and a book that examine the energy consumption patterns of various income classes in India (Pachauri 2004; Pachauri and Spreng, 2002; Pachauri, 2007; Pachauri and Jiang, 2008). However, since these works do not explicitly calculate emissions, we will discuss them in brief, only in the context of access to modern energy sources. And, finally, in 2009, the Centre for Science and Environment produced an analysis that attempted to calculate how emissions vary with income based on assumed income-elasticity of emissions (CSE, 2009).

These studies raise a number of questions about domestic and international justice in the climate and other arenas. These questions are likely to become harder to address in the future, as global emissions rise and leave less ecological space to be shared by a larger number of people. We first describe the contexts in which these studies were produced and circulated, before turning to the methodologies they used and their results. Finally, we do a simple projection into the future to show how the continuation of current trends will be unsustainable.

Contexts

In motivating the report, Greenpeace argued: 'While [the Bali] international meeting sets the debate for "climate justice" at a global level this study aims at raising the same

Hiding Behind the Poor debate   219

debate within the country. It asks the question – Is there climate injustice happening in India?' and claimed to present 'a case for the Indian government to implement the principle of "common but differentiated responsibilities" amongst the various socio-economic groups in the country.' Others in India also endorse this call for uniformity in applying climate justice internally and externally. The activist journalist Praful Bidwai, for example, has argued that the 'per capita norm is a shield that enables India's elite to hide behind the poor while indulging in profligate consumption and evading its responsibility towards the underprivileged in its own society – an overwhelmingly important imperative, to which it only pays rhetorical obeisance' (Bidwai, 2009).

Though Greenpeace's motivation might have been to move the domestic debate, the impact of the study, at least of the issues it raised, was more pronounced at the global level. Around the period when Greenpeace embarked on the survey, the Indian government's position, in essence, was that until there was an international agreement on an equity based sharing of emission rights, it would not take on any commitments.[1] This was widely seen as obstructing the progress of climate negotiations, a sentiment captured by *The Economist* magazine: 'India has acquired an ugly reputation on the global front against climate change. Among big countries, perhaps only America and Russia are considered more obdurate' (*The Economist*, 2008).

At the same time, industrialized countries, especially the United States under President George Bush, were using rapid economic growth and the consequent increase in emissions in India and China as a way of not fulfilling their commitments under climate agreements.[2] One argument that was commonly deployed was that even though India as a whole may have low per capita emissions, the middle classes and rich did not fit in that category (Myers and Kent, 2003; Prins and Rayner, 2007), what with their cars, household appliances, and aeroplane flights, and hence India would have to commit to emission reductions.[3] This argument was amplified after the release of the Tata Nano car and one might be justified in calling this concern about growing Indian emissions the *Nano effect*. For example, a spokesperson from Friends of the Earth UK was reported as saying, 'The Tata Nano makes motoring cheaper and growing car sales in India will lead to big rises in carbon dioxide emissions. This is another blow to efforts to tackle global climate change' (Buncombe, 2008).[4] Inflated estimates of the Indian middle class have contributed to this impression.[5]

Therefore, all these studies on emission distribution in India also considered the question: how did the emission profile of the rich in India compare to emissions in Western countries, especially the United States. Thus, even though Parikh et al., 2009 deals entirely with emissions of different income classes in India, the last line in its conclusion is 'The CO_2 emissions embodied in the consumption basket of the top 10% of the population in urban India is one-fifth the per capita emission generated in the US'. The CSE analysis focused entirely on this latter question.[6] At no point does it discuss the intra-country disparities in emissions even though these differences were implicit in their results. Even Greenpeace noted that the CO_2 emissions of the richest income class in their survey 'are a shade lower than the average global emissions of about 5 tonnes per person. This is less than half of the EU-25 states, given as 10.5 tonnes, and 4.6 times smaller than the average emissions of the USA.'

Greenpeace, however, dismissed, in effect, the comparison with the United States by arguing 'that the global distribution of CO_2 emissions needs not only to be equitable, but also sustainable. Today's CO_2 emissions already lead to a steady increase of global

220 *Chakravarty and Ramana*

temperature, and with a global population still rising, an average CO_2 emission of 5 tonnes would drive the planet into a state of climate crisis.' At the same time, Greenpeace did not argue that India should agree to fixed emission targets or that the United States and others did not have to act till India agreed to such targets. Rather, it argued that 'the industrialized world [owed] a debt to the developing world for its historical emissions' (Kennedy, 2009).

Methodological aspects of measuring emissions

The Greenpeace report, as mentioned earlier, was based on a survey. Some 819 households, spread across representative income classes covering metros, other cities, towns and rural areas, were interviewed to estimate CO_2 emissions from household electricity and fuel consumption, and emissions from transportation (also called direct energy use emissions). The emissions estimates were validated by independently estimating household consumption from appliances and cooking. For international comparisons, the survey results were scaled up by a factor of 3.3 to equate the survey average emissions to the national per capita emissions ($1.67\ tCO_2e$) to account for emissions 'generated from food and non food consumption and additional overheads due to public consumption' (Ananthapadmanabhan, et al., 2007)

Though this method provides an indicative emission profile it overestimates the emissions of low-income households. A major source of error is because emissions embodied in manufactured goods and services do not scale with income the same way as emissions from direct energy use (Parikh et al., 2009). In most countries, direct emissions from transportation, especially flying, and indirect emissions from the consumption of manufactured goods keep rising while emissions from food, heating, and other direct energy use categories tend to saturate with rising income. The situation in India is more complicated as a significant part of the direct energy needs of the poor are met by biomass which is not counted in energy use statistics, Finally, the figure of $1.67\ tCO_2e$ also involve about $0.5\ tCO_2e$ from agriculture, wastes, and other greenhouse gases which are difficult to attribute to private consumption. In a rapidly growing economy like India's, only 60% of the emissions come from households; the rest are due to capital investments, infrastructure development, and public or government consumption. There is no well-agreed mechanism to allocate these emissions to households. Indeed, this allocation problem is difficult and the two methodologies described below also suffer from it. As far as possible, we report both the distribution of household emissions and emissions scaled up to the national average if the study provides these numbers or if we can calculate them. These scaled up numbers can, at best, be used for rough comparison with per capita emissions of other nations.

A proper accounting for direct and indirect emissions in consumption should essentially account for the flow of emissions in the entire economy. One standard method for doing so is through the Input-Output (I-O) tables. The idea was developed by the economist Wassily Leontief to account for (the monetary value of) the flow or distribution of goods and services between various components of the economy – households, government, industries, and so on. In its most basic form each row in the table is a linear equation accounting for the flow of a good to various parts of the economy. This monetary flow can be converted to an equivalent energy or emissions flow and the average energy or emissions intensity of various goods and services in the economy can be calculated (Bullard and Herendeen, 1975). Combining this

Hiding Behind the Poor debate 221

information with detailed consumption data from national or regional household surveys provides a consistent account of the emissions, both direct and indirect, produced by household income and size, a technique first developed by (Herendeen and Tanaka, 1976). This approach is used in (Pachauri, 2007) for estimating energy consumption and in (Parikh et al., 1997) for estimating emissions. In (Parikh et al., 2009), a social accounting matrix (SAM) is used. The SAM is an extension of the I-O table that tracks taxes, capital, labour, government savings and consumption, and savings of representative households categorized into urban and rural expenditure classes (Saluja and Yadav, 2006).

The I-O table and household survey based method for estimating emissions from private consumption comes with its own set of problems regarding data quality, methodology and the time required in these data intensive studies. The I-O table involves collection and analysis of vast amounts of data and are usually produced every 5 years by the Central Statistical Organization (CSO). The most important source of household expenditure surveys is the National Sample Survey Organization (NSSO).[7] NSSO conducts annual surveys but it is the detailed survey conducted every five years that is used in these studies. Consequently, papers based on these data report emission numbers that are a few years out of date.[8] NSSO surveys and I-O tables from CSO have data consistency problems: estimates of total consumption in all households from the NSSO surveys often differ significantly from estimates derived from National Account Statistics of the CSO. Finally, it is likely that the surveys are unable to fully capture the consumption patterns of the very rich. Studies have found that NSSO surveys underestimate non-food goods and services that are consumed by the upper income classes when compared to National Accounts Statistics (Sundaram and Tendulkar, 2001; NSSO-CSO, 2005).

Finally, CSE's analysis is based on a simple model in which per capita emissions (E) vary with income (Y) through a power law relationship ($E \approx (Y)^e$), where e is called the income elasticity of emissions) (CSE, 2009). The parameter e is assumed to range between 0.7 and 1, corresponding to a range of emission elasticities from empirical studies, as tabulated in Chakravarty et al. (2009). This is a simple and popular model but it may not hold for very high incomes.[9]

Survey of results

The key results of the Greenpeace report, the Parikh studies, and the CSE study are shown in the tables and figure below. These span the period 1989–90 to 2009. We tabulate separate rural (R) and urban (U) columns if the study reports these. Finally, we also report annual emissions, direct energy use emissions, total household emissions, and total emissions scaled up to the national average CO_2 and CO_2e (CO_2 equivalent numbers that also account for other greenhouse gases) for different income categories. Emissions numbers for other countries which are quoted for comparison are from the Climate Analysis Indicators Tool maintained by the World Resources Institute (http://cait.wri.org).

We consider the two Parikh et al. studies first as they provide a useful comparison over the first decade of the liberalization era. They show evidence of:

- Significant disparity in rural–urban emissions. Average urban emissions per capita are about 2.5 times rural emissions.

Table 16.1 Distribution of emissions in 1989–90 by household expenditure

Expenditure class	Population (millions)		Total emissions from household consumption (tCO$_2$)		Total emissions scaled to national average (tCO$_2$)	
	R	U	R	U	R	U
Bottom 50%	303.6	102.0	0.22	0.38	0.36	0.63
40%	242.5	81.8	0.37	0.90	0.62	1.51
Top 10%	**60.5**	**20.5**	**0.78**	**3.20**	**1.30**	**5.36**
Total	606.6	204.4	0.33	0.87	0.56	1.46
National		811		0.47		0.78

Source: (Murthy et al., 1997), based on 1998–9, Input-Output (I-0) tables and consumption data from NSSO 1987–8 survey and NCAER Market Information Survey of Households (various years)

Table 16.2 Distribution of emissions in 2003–4 by household expenditure

Expenditure class	Population (millions)		Emissions from direct energy use (tCO$_2$)		Total emissions from household consumption (tCO$_2$)		Total emissions scaled to national average (tCO$_2$)	
	R	U	R	U	R	U	R	U
Bottom 10%	77.2	30.0	0.01	0.06	0.15	0.27	0.26	0.47
20%	154.4	60.0	0.01	0.10	0.22	0.43	0.37	0.74
40%	308.7	120.1	0.02	0.14	0.34	0.81	0.58	1.39
20%	154.4	60.0	0.04	0.22	0.68	1.57	1.17	2.70
Top 10%	**77.2**	**30.0**	**0.13**	**0.68**	**1.37**	**4.10**	**2.35**	**7.06**
Total	771.9	300.1			0.46	1.16	0.80	2.00
National		1072				0.66		1.14

Source: (Parikh et al., 2009) based on 2003–4 SAM, and expenditure classes from NSSO 1999–2000 surveys.

Table 16.3 Distribution of emissions in 2007 by income

Income class	Population (millions)	Emissions from direct energy use (tCO$_2$)	Total emissions scaled to national average (tCO$_2$)	Total emissions scaled to national average (tCO$_2$e)
Bottom 38%	432	0.34	0.80	1.11
35%	391	0.47	1.11	1.55
14%	156	0.69	1.64	2.28
6%	69	0.82	1.96	2.73
5%	53	0.83	1.98	2.75
2%	19	0.94	2.24	3.12
Top 1%	**10**	**1.49**	**3.58**	**4.97**
Total	1130	0.50	1.20	1.67

Source: (Ananthapadmanabhan et al., 2007), based on survey conducted in 2007

Table 16.4 Distribution of emissions in 2009 by income

Country	Per capita emissions (tCO$_2$e)	
	India	USA
Poorest 10%	0.4–0.8	4.3–8.0
Richest 10%	3.4–5.1	52–69
Richest 2%	4.6–6.8	73–111
National average	1.6	22.1

Source: (CSE, 2009), based on an income elasticity of emissions model

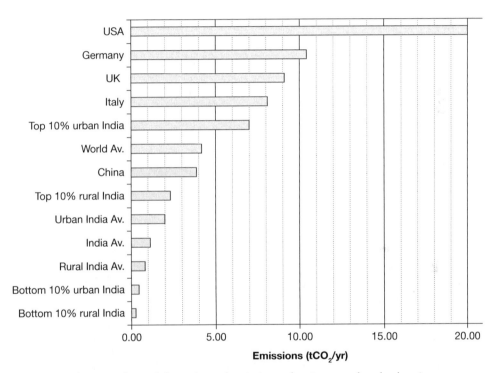

Figure 16.1 A comparison of the estimated emissions of various rural and urban income classes in 2004 with the average emissions of select countries of the world (Parikh et al., 2009)

Note: The household emissions calculated in (Parikh et al., 2009) are scaled up to national average emissions for the purpose of this comparison (see the section 'Methodological aspects of measuring emissions' for a discussion on this issue).

- Extremely low emissions of the poorest expenditure classes, especially the poorest 50%–60% of rural India and the poorest 30% of urban India.
- A higher inequality in emission in urban India as compared to rural India.[10]
- Significant disparity in emissions between the top 10% expenditure class in urban India and the rest of the population, especially the bottom 10% of urban and rural India.

224   *Chakravarty and Ramana*

One caveat is that rural India, especially the poorer half, depends on biomass for its energy needs, whereas the surveys that the Parikh et al. studies only account for commercial energy sources.[11] Thus, emissions from these sources are not included. The low emission numbers for rural India reflect the lack of access to modern sources of energy like electricity and LPG (Pachauri, 2007; Pachauri and Jiang, 2008).[12]

Coming to the top 10% of urban India (roughly 30 million people), in 2003–4 their emissions were about 15 times the bottom 10% of urban India, and about 27 times the emissions of the bottom 10% of rural India. The household emissions alone put the top 10% of urban India close to the world average (4.2 tCO_2), and between France (6.5 tCO_2) and Italy (8.1 tCO_2) when scaled up to the national average. Because of the problems with survey data of the rich mentioned earlier, it is likely that these figures might underestimate the emissions of the rich, thereby making these groups closer to the Italian average.

A comparison between the two studies does show some interesting temporal trends. Rural India's household emissions have grown slightly faster than urban India's (40% vs. 33%), with the emission of the top 10% of rural India (76%), an indication that the rural rich are moving toward modern energy sources and changing consumption patterns.

The Greenpeace study provides a detailed picture of direct energy use in households but shows significantly less inequality in direct emissions when compared to the (Parikh et al., 2009) study. The emissions of the lowest income group seem high when compared to similar expenditure classes in the (Parikh et al., 2009) study, perhaps an issue related to small sample size and insufficient coverage of rural India. It is likely that the Greenpeace study has better coverage of high income groups and reports finer detail there. Finally, we emphasize that scaling up direct energy use emissions to national average values might end up underestimating the emissions of the rich.

The CSE study likely overestimates the emissions of India's poor, especially the rural poor. The problem is that the simple income elasticity of the emissions model is unable to account for the reality of the India's energy economy: the rural poor obtain most of their direct energy needs from non-commercial energy sources like biomass which are not part of the emissions statistics.

The future

The studies on emission profiles show that there are significant inequalities amongst different income groups and that the emissions of the richest sections of society are reaching levels corresponding to averages in some industrialized countries. Given the current state of climate debate in India, the implications of these results for the questions of whether India should undertake unilateral climate actions and whether it should accept emission targets and so on, is contentious. However, the basis for action to reduce these inequalities and stronger climate mitigation will likely increase in the future if present trends continue. To see why, consider some simple projections of emission-income profiles.

As the basis for our projections, we used a 2009 report commissioned and published by the Ministry of Environment and Forests that projected India's per capita emissions in 2030 to be between 2.77 tCO_2e and 5.00 tCO_2e (India GHG Report, 2009).[13] We combined the results of this projection with the emissions distribution[14] of (Parikh et al., 2009) along with some simplifying assumptions:

- We consider two cases a. same emissions inequality for India as a whole (Gini coefficient of 0.46) as in 2003–4 and b. emissions inequality of rural India (which is lower at 0.38).[15]
- We project the emissions with the assumption that the average emission level is equal to the per capita numbers from the report. We also assume that these are CO_2 emissions not CO_2 equivalent (i.e., all greenhouse gases).
- We use household emissions per capita scaled up to the national average in 2004–5 for comparison with the projections.

Table 16.5 Projection of 2003–4 emission distribution to 2030

Scenario »	2003–4	2030		2030		2030	
	1.14 tCO_2	2.77tCO_2		3.9 tCO_2		5tCO_2	
Emission level (tCO_2)	I	R	I	R	I	R	I
<1	65.7	8.9	19.3	1.8	6.8	0.3	2.2
1–2	22.4	38.9	36.9	23.9	30.8	12.5	22.0
2–5	9.9	42.0	32.5	53.7	42.4	54.9	46.9
5–10	1.5	8.3	8.4	16.2	14.1	24.2	19.4
>10	0.4	1.9	3.0	4.5	5.9	8.1	9.5

Note: Authors' calculations. Columns labelled I and R refer to scenarios with the emissions inequality of India (higher) and rural India (lower) in 2003–4. The columns show the percentage of people within the specified emission slab.

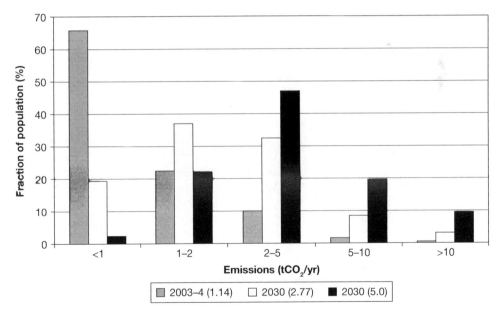

Figure 16.2 Projected evolution of the emission distribution of India, assuming that inequality in emissions stays the same as in 2003–4 (Parikh et al., 2009)

Note: The two 2030 per capita annual emissions used in this scenario (2.77 tCO_2 and 5.0 tCO_2) are the highest and the lowest emission projections given (India GHG Report, 2009).

226 *Chakravarty and Ramana*

This exercise is not meant to be a realistic estimate of future emissions, but a projection that provides some insight into the scale of emissions that one might expect under the specified circumstances. Nevertheless, it shows that assuming the same level of inequality as today we can expect most Indians to emit more than 1 tCO_2 per capita in 2030, and that about 30–130 million Indians will have emissions above 10 tCO_2 (assuming a 2030 population of 1.4 billion).

This conclusion, however, might underestimate the fraction of Indians with high emission levels in the future. This is because a significant trend since the 1990s has been an increase in inequality in general (Sen and Himanshu, 2005; ADB Key Indicators, 2007; Debroy and Bhandari, 2007). Though the All-India Gini coefficient is still low compared to most developing countries, it has increased from 0.32 in 1993–4 to 0.36 in 2004–5. The rise in urban–rural disparity, rapid rise in income inequality in many states, especially in urban areas, divergence in growth rates between states, and disparity in education levels have contributed to this. There is evidence that an increasing share of the benefits of India's growth is going to the top 10% of the population, especially the top 1% of India's population (Banerjee and Piketty, 2005; ADB Key Indicators, 2007).

Further, income inequality is likely to be less than, say, inequalities in electricity consumption and emission levels (Bhattacharyya, 2006). This is true in other countries that are going through a transition from biomass to modern energy services. Therefore, income inequality, if it continues to exacerbate, might indeed produce a significant number of high emitting rich (high by global standards) in a couple of decades.

Conclusion

Political choices underlie just about everything in this debate. Greenpeace's choice of comparing the emissions of the Indian rich to what they term a sustainable 2 tonne per capita level hides implicit assumptions and choices, for example, about the time at which the average value might or might not be achieved, the pathway between now and then, and how to deal with past emissions. In the same vein, the choice about whether one is comparing to the US average or the average of developed countries is also a political choice. So are choices about whether to compare emission intensities between different countries: those that use a market exchange rate will typically result in the developed countries appearing more efficient, whereas those that use a rate based on purchasing power parities will typically result in India looking as good as Germany or Japan. Greenpeace's report has an entire section on policy prescriptions at the end that seem fairly independent of the results of their survey.

Given this political nature of the debate, it is not surprising that the interpretation of the Greenpeace survey has been contentious. Though motivated by domestic considerations, the implications of this survey have been explored both in the domestic and international arenas. In the international arena, Greenpeace's results fed into a growing focus including in climate diplomacy circles, on growing consumption in developing countries, in part as a way to avoid discussing the absence of significant climate mitigation in the developed world. CSE, being an active participant in these international debates, was perhaps reacting to this current when it produced its analysis. This might explain its complete focus on international inequity and total avoidance of the question of domestic inequity or its implications. In this problematic international context, one natural view has been that the issue of internal inequalities should *not* be allowed to lead to an international explicit scrutiny nor implicit counter-

Hiding Behind the Poor debate 227

reaction that might weaken the ability of Indian diplomats to invoke equity. Others argue that our moral authority is weakened if we fail to take internal inequity seriously. Similar difference of opinion can also be found in other areas such as child labour and untouchability.

Domestically, there are two implications of the studies by Greenpeace and Parikh et al. worth highlighting. First, a large fraction of the population of the country has very low emissions because they are deprived of access to modern energy services in absolute terms. The imperative of remedying this situation as rapidly as possible has been widely stressed. The second implication is what we have been discussing all along, the growing emissions of the richest 10% of the population. The inequality inherent in the difference between the two ends of the spectrum has not been the subject of much domestic debate.

An important reason for this silence was laid out in the article on the report in *Frontline* magazine: 'It is a truism and so does not require detailed surveys to drive home its point: in India the disparities in living standards and consumption patterns, in particular of energy, between the rich and the poor are vast' (Ramachandran, 2007). In other words, the inequalities in emissions was only the latest manifestation of longstanding debates over India's development path.

This is, of course, not the place to recount the debates over development. But we might demarcate three broad categories. There are those who seem broadly comfortable with India's current path, and endorse continuing along a business-as-usual development path. For them, the presence of domestic inequality is only a sign that development as practised in India is an unfinished story and will eventually be addressed. The second category includes people who do not agree with the first on the development path, but agree that this subject should not be allowed to distract from the lack of action on the part of the United States and other industrialized countries, as well as the current trends in climate diplomacy, which are seen as moving away from the 'differentiated responsibilities' enshrined in the UNFCCC. Finally, there are those who feel that the current development path is wrong for other reasons, and for them the intra country inequalities suggest that the country should move away from current trends to a more equitable and environmentally sustainable path. The debate between these positions is likely to intensify in the future – and it should. Our simple projection of emission trends suggests, if present patterns of inequalities continue, then 'Hiding Behind the Poor' might become a reality.

Notes

1 At the Bali Conference of Parties, for example, Indian diplomats played an important role in making sure that any mitigation actions taken by India, or other developing countries, that are 'measurable, reportable, and verifiable' should be supported by international funding.

2 In his March 2001 letter to the U.S. Senate, for example, President George W. Bush wrote: 'I oppose the Kyoto Protocol because it exempts 80 percent of the world, including major population centres such as China and India, from compliance, and would cause serious harm to the US Economy'.

3 This argument is more often heard during coffee breaks at conferences and on the corridors of climate related meetings than in formal statements and papers.

4 But he went on to balance that statement with '[the] per-person emissions will still be much higher in the West. Our priority must be to increase efforts to cut our own emissions and to show the rest of the world how to develop a low-carbon economy'.

5 Estimates of the number of the Indian middle class are in the range of 200–300 million. While large in magnitude these numbers refer to the people whose incomes would mostly

228 *Chakravarty and Ramana*

fall under the poverty line of most developed countries. A recent study, (ADB Key Indicators 2010), defined the 'Asian middle class' as those making $2–$20 (2005, PPP dollars) per day. $20 per day is roughly the poverty line in Italy, (about Rs. 300/day using a PPP exchange rate of about 15 in 2005). The study estimates that 380 million are in the $2–$10 category (Rs. 30–150), 39 million in $10–$20 (Rs 150–300) and only 26 million earn more than $20/day (see Table 2.5 of ADB Key Indicators 2010). On the other hand, 90% of the developed world earns above $20/day.

6   Indeed, the CSE report's first line was definitive: the 'richest 10 per cent of Indians emit no more greenhouse gases per person than the poorest 10 per cent of Americans'.

7   Both the CSO and NSSO are part of the Ministry of Statistics and Program Implementation, Government of India.

8   For example, the Parikh et al. (2009) paper is based on the 2003–4 SAM where the 'I-O table for 1998–99 has been, first, updated to 2003–4 and then extended into various directions. The distribution of income is based on the data obtained from the MIMAP-India Household survey conducted by the NCAER for the year 1994–95' and the 'distribution of expenditure is based on the NSS survey on consumption expenditure for 1999–2000' (Saluja and Yadav, 2006, p. 23).

9   It is difficult to have good estimates of the number of people at high incomes without additional sources like tax data, for example. The income distribution used in this study is based on surveys that usually undercount the rich. The assumption of constant income elasticity of emissions might also not hold (for example, for the richest 1%–2% of a country).

10 India as a whole has the highest inequality because it also includes the rural–urban disparity.

11 These studies do not account for CO_2 emissions from biomass as they implicitly assume that it is sustainably used.

12 The use of these energy sources is also associated with indoor pollution and respiratory diseases. Approximately 400 million Indians, especially in rural India, also lack any access to electricity and a large number of Indians in rural India and small town India have unreliable sources of electricity even if they have power connections. The low emission numbers, especially low direct energy use emissions, reflect the prevalence of energy poverty, and lack of access to modern sources of energy. This lack of access is a combination of both extreme poverty and limited availability of these energy sources (esp. electricity and LPG) in rural India.

13 This would still place India's per capita emissions below today's global average.

14 We fit Beta-2 distributions to the rural and urban emissions tabulated in Parikh et al. (2009) as described in Chotikapanich et al. (2007).

15 The Gini coefficient is a standard measure of inequality and ranges from 0 to 1. The Gini is equal to 0 with perfect equality, and 1 with perfect inequality.

References

India's GHG Emissions Profile: Results of Five Climate Modelling Studies, New Delhi: Ministry of Environments and Forests. Available at: http://moef.nic.in/downloads/home/GHG-report.pdf. [Accessed 28 August, 2010].

Key Indicators 2010: The Rise of Asia's Middle Class, ADB.org. Available at: http://www.adb.org/Documents/Books/Key_Indicators/2010/default.asp [Accessed 28 August, 2010].

Key Indicators 2007: Inequality in Asia, ADB.org. Available at: http://www.adb.org/Documents/ Books/Key_Indicators/2007/default.asp. [Accessed August 28, 2010].

'China, India and climate change: Melting Asia', *The Economist*, 5 June 2008.

Ananthapadmanabhan, G., Srinivas, K. and Gopal, V., 2007. *Hiding Behind the Poor: A Report on Climate Injustice*, Bangalore: Greenpeace India Society.

Banerjee, A. and Piketty, T., 2005. *Top Indian Incomes, 1922–2000*. The World Bank Economic Review, 19 (1), 1–20.

Bhattacharyya, S.C., 2006. Energy access problem of the poor in India: Is rural electrification a remedy? *Energy Policy* 34, no. 18 (12): 3387–3397.

Bidwai, P., 2009. *An India That Can Say Yes: A Climate-Responsible Development Agenda for Copenhagen and Beyond*, Heinrich Boll Stiftung, New Delhi.

Hiding Behind the Poor debate   229

Bullard, C. and Herendeen, R.A., 1975. The energy cost of goods and services. *Energy Policy*, 3(4), 268–278.

Buncombe, A., 2008. 'Can the world afford the Tata Nano?' *The Independent* (11 Jan., 2008).

Chakravarty, S., Chikkatur, A., de Coninck, H., Pacala, S., Socolow, R. and Tavoni, M., 2009. Sharing global CO2 emission reductions among one billion high emitters. *Proceedings of the National Academy of Sciences*, 106(29), 11884–11888.

Chotikapanich, D., Griffiths, W.E. and Rao, D.S.P., 2007. Estimating and Combining National Income Distributions Using Limited Data. *Journal of Business and Economic Statistics*, 25(1), 97–109.

CSE, 2009. *Richest Indians Emit Less than Poorest Americans*, Centre for Science and Environment. Available at: http://www.indiaenvironmentportal.org.in/node/290547 [Accessed September 3, 2010].

Debroy, B., and Bhandari, L., 2007. Exclusive Growth – Inclusive Inequality. *Economic Developments in India*, vol. 116, Ed., Kapila, A. and Kapila, U., New Delhi, Academic Foundation.

Herendeen, R. and Tanaka, J., 1976. Energy cost of living. *Energy*, 1(2), 165–178.

Kennedy, M., 2009. 'In Delhi, doing as we do, not as we say', *Washington Post*, 22 Nov., 2009

Murthy, N., Panda, M. and Parikh, J., 1997. Economic growth, energy demand and carbon dioxide emissions in India: 1990–2020. *Environment and Development Economics*, 2(2), 173–193.

Myers, N. and Kent, J., 2003. New consumers: The influence of affluence on the environment. *Proceedings of the National Academy of Sciences*, 100(8), 4963–4968.

NSSO-CSO, 2005. Report on Cross-Validation Study of Estimates of Private Consumption Expenditure Available from Household Survey and National Accounts. *Sarvekshana*, xxv, no. 4 and xxvi no. 1(88). Available at: http://www.mospi.nic.in/servakshana_report.htm [Accessed 5 September, 2010].

Pachauri, S., 2004. An analysis of cross-sectional variations in total household energy requirements in India using micro survey data. *Energy Policy*, 32(15), 1723–1735.

Pachauri, S., 2007. *An Energy Analysis of Household Consumption: Changing Patterns of Direct and Indirect Use in India*, Dordrecht: Springer.

Pachauri, S. and Jiang, L., 2008. The household energy transition in India and China. *Energy Policy*, 36(11), 4022–4035.

Pachauri, S. and Spreng, D., 2002. Direct and indirect energy requirements of households in India. *Energy Policy*, 30(6), 511–523.

Parikh, J., Panda, M. and Murthy, N.S., 1997. Consumption patterns by income classes and carbon-dioxide implications for India: 1990–2010. *International Journal of Global Energy Issues*, 9(4–5).

Parikh, J., Panda, M, Ganesh-Kumar, A. and Singh, V., 2009. CO_2 emissions structure of Indian economy. *Energy*, 34(8), 1024–1031.

Prins, G. and Rayner, S., 2007. The Wrong Trousers: Radically Rethinking Climate Policy. Discussion Paper, Institute for Science, Innovation and Society. Available at: http://eureka.sbs.ox.ac.uk/66/ [Accessed 31 October, 2010].

Ramachandran, R., 2007. Class Injustice, *Frontline*, 24(24), December, 8–21.

Saluja, M.R. and Yadav, B., 2006. *Social Accounting Matrix for India 2003–04*, India Development Foundation. Available at: planningcommission.nic.in/reports/sereport/ser/sr_sam.pdf. [Accessed Aug. 28, 2010].

Sen, A. and Himanshu. 2005. Poverty and inequality in India: Getting closer to the truth. In *The Great Indian Poverty Debate*, Ed. Deaton, A., and Kozel, V., Delhi: Macmillan. Also available at: http://www.networkideas.org/featart/may2004/Poverty_WC.pdf.

Sundaram, K. and Tendulkar, S.D., 2001. NAS-NSS estimates of private consumption for poverty estimation a disaggregated comparison for 1993–94. *Economic and Political Weekly*, 36(2), 119–129.

17 Climate change and parliament

Excerpts from the Lok Sabha and Rajya Sabha debates

Commentary by Suresh Prabhu

The three sections in this chapter provide a collective snapshot of how India's parliament has engaged with climate change. An opening perspective by Hon. Suresh Prabhu, MP and former Minister, Environment and Forests, discusses both the potential for and limitations of India's Parliament as a primary point of interface with climate politics. Following this perspective are two sets of excerpts from debates held in the Indian Parliament: one before the Copenhagen climate negotiations in the Lok Sabha, and one after Copenhagen in the Rajya Sabha. Selections from these debates were chosen in order to provide a flavour of the breadth of the debate, and also to provide both critique and defence of government actions. These debates have been reproduced here with permission from the Hon. Speaker of Lok Sabha and the Hon. Chairman of Rajya Sabha. (*Editor's Note*)

Reflections on the role of parliament in climate change debates[1]

Debate on climate change in Parliament is a new and interesting phenomenon. But it needs to be seen within the larger context of legislative debates in India. The interest of the political class in climate change cannot always be determined by what happens in Parliament. This is because what gets debated in Parliament is not always the priority of the country. Often, what one says in Parliament can be at odds with the current priorities of the outside world. There is very limited time available for debate in Parliament. As a number of issues need to be raised in such a limited time not all issues that warrant action get debated. But this in no way is an indication of the priorities of MPs. It would be inadvisable to conclude that MPs do not attach any importance to climate change issues based simply on evidence from the floor of the house. MPs have to raise issues relevant to their own constituencies; there is pre-determined legislative business. So we cannot really judge the importance our MPs give to climate change by mere time devoted to its debate in Parliament. There are various other ways through which MPs engage with climate change issues including Standing Committees, letters to ministers, their own party fora, and public platforms on which they offer their comments.

The nature of the legislative process in India also has a bearing upon the debates. The Indian legislative process is very different from many other democracies of the world. For example, in the US, all the laws are made on the floor of the House, either in the Congress, or the House of Representatives or the Senate. This requires that all the bills originate from the members themselves. The situation in India, however, has been very different. Here all bills which become law are introduced by ministers as

Climate change debates in the Indian parliament 231

government business. Parties in power, then ensure passage of these into law by enforcing their majorities. In the past fifty-sixty years, I have not seen a single bill moved by an individual MP become law. In India, as private members, MPs have the right to move bills. But even if the proposed bill is good it is a very rare instance where the relevant minister acknowledges the bill's value and says, 'This is a good bill. I request you to please withdraw it so that the government can now move a bill on the same subject'. In effect, unlike in many other parts of the world, MPs are not the lawmakers in our country. Unlike in the US, MPs here make government bills into laws, but do not actually make the law themselves. This is a fundamental difference in the operation of the legislature.

The second difference is that no international treaty needs to be ratified by the Indian Parliament. In many other parliaments of the world, an international treaty that is binding upon future generations cannot be signed by the present government unless it is approved by the parliament. For example, why could the US not ratify the Kyoto Protocol? Though the US became a signatory to the Kyoto Protocol, it could not ratify the Protocol because the Senate refused to ratify it. It was not that the executive branch of the government was reluctant to put it before the Senate. The legislative branch of the government refused to ratify the Protocol because they thought it was not in the interests of the United States. Such a situation does not exist in India.

The Indian Executive, in my opinion, is one of the most powerful executives in the world. It can sign any document anywhere. It can commit to anything anywhere. It can do so without any mandate or even without any subsequent ratification from anybody. This is a unique characteristic of the system. It is within this broad context of the nature of Indian legislature that we should understand the significance of the debates on climate change in Parliament.

Often, debates in Parliament are undertaken by MPs to be noticed by the House or as a token ritual. Rarely do these debates concern themselves with how MPs might influence policy-making or regulate government action on a certain issue. Unfortunately, I don't see any policy-making taking place in Parliament. The Indian government has three branches: the Executive, the Legislature and the Judiciary, each with its own set of responsibilities. Over a period of time, the task of policy-making, which should solely have been the domain of Parliament, has been usurped by the Executive and the Judiciary. This is a fundamental problem in the Indian parliamentary system.

This system should work differently. In my opinion, all policies should be made by Parliament through open debates, in a transparent and participatory manner. The Executive should execute policies made by Parliament. Currently, the legislature is simply a bystander – watching what is happening and sometimes commenting on what goes on. This is unfortunately the situation not just on climate change but most other issues of significance. Parliament should be the forum where all issues are seriously debated, and where MPs work in a proactive manner to make, monitor and implement policies.

Shri Shivraj Patil made a remarkable and significant change in this parliamentary system to allow for more debating space. He introduced the concept of Standing Committees. Today, Standing Committees play a very important and proactive role in the functioning of Parliament. These Committees support the functioning of individual ministries. Standing Committee members are drawn from all political parties and work in a bipartisan manner. Ministers are not allowed to appear before the Standing

232 *Prabhu*

Committee. They are represented through a permanent secretary of the ministry. The other available space for debating important issues is the Consultative Committee. While the Standing Committee is chaired by an MP who is not a minister, the Consultative Committee is chaired by a minister. Before these changes were introduced issues were debated in Parliament plenary. It was only in the 14th Lok Sabha (17 May 2004–18 May 2009) where, for the first time, a parliamentary forum for climate change was created under Shri Somnath Chatterjee.

When we talk about MPs and climate change, we should remember that there are two Houses in Parliament with differing priorities. In the Lok Sabha MPs are directly elected by the people. For the Rajya Sabha states and territorial legislatures elect members. Both the Houses have some nominated members who are not elected by the people. Members of Rajya Sabha and Lok Sabha approach issues differently. This is because the former are not directly elected by the people. Therefore, the nature and range of debate in both Houses is also very different. The one common ground that both Rajya Sabha and Lok Sabha MPs share is over defined party positions. MPs are obligated to frame and present their responses on different issues according to party positions. For this reason Rajya Sabha and Lok Sabha debates are often similar in ideologies because MPs are directed to adhere to party lines. But on climate change there are no party positions. Thus, people end up presenting their individual positions when climate change is debated. What one also sees in debates on climate change is that there is a mixing of views across party positions.

Important as climate change might be for international relations and negotiations, it is yet to become a political catalyst in India. Climate change as an issue is not a constituency mover. On the floor of the House discussions on foreign policy are rare. There are two important points to be made with regard to climate change debates in Parliament. First, the time available to MPs for debate is very little. So what often gets priorititzed for discussion is what appears to be urgent government business. Second, because climate change in itself is not an electoral issue, members raise climate issues in different forms, as river erosion, floods, droughts, environmental degradation. It is not necessarily captured as a global environmental problem. The discussion in the Indian Parliament with regard to climate change is very different from other countries.

Further, the profile of the MPs and the constituencies they have been elected from affect how they think and argue in Parliament. There is a wide range of MPs in Parliament: Coastal MPs, MPs from hilly areas, rural MPs, metropolitan MPs, SC/ST MPs. MPs are most likely to argue on climate change in a way that resonates with their constituency.

This is not to say that individual members are not interested in climate change, quite the contrary. But for a parliamentarian public notice of issues is very important. Unless an issue appeals to their constituency they are unlikely to engage with it on the floor of the House.

The role of the media is very important here. The media can convey a very negative image of the MPs. The best speeches are never recorded while the worst misdemeanors are widely telecast. If an MP creates a controversy it immediately gets reported by the media. This encourages many MPs to only speak on issues which are likely to capture the media's attention and which would bring them publicity.

MPs are definitely interested in the issue of climate change. There is an all party agreement that this is an important issue. If one looks at the manifestos of the parties one will see that all manifestos list climate change as an issue. This shows that the

Climate change debates in the Indian parliament 233

Indian political class is serious about climate change and wants to act on it. There is a consensus that we should not change our position from what it has been so far. That consensus should not be broken.

With respect to the international dimension of climate change debates, there is complete unanimity across party lines on the issue of equity. There is also complete agreement with regard to the Kyoto Protocol and on India's stand not to take on binding commitments. Indian MPs swear by the UNFCCC process.

Given this background what should be the way forward on climate change? I feel that all international agreements and commitments should be subject to compulsory parliamentary ratification in India. We can even use the Standing Committee route to create more space for debate on climate change. On the issue of international obligations, we should have an all party mechanism and not just a brief from the MP's own party. Other parties should also have a say as the issue of climate change transcends party lines. Debate on climate change in Parliament is important because it can embarrass the Government, and thus, force accountability of actions.

Parliamentary Debates on Climate Change Pre-Copenhagen: Excerpts

Lok Sabha
Session: XV–III (19th November–18th December)
Title: Discussion Regarding Impact of Climate Change
Short Duration Discussions (Under Rule 193)
Thursday, 3 December 2009

(Reproduced from Lok Sabha Debates with the permission of the Hon'ble Speaker)

Shri M. B. Rajesh

Mr. Chairman, Sir, this discussion on climate change is being held in the context of the forthcoming global Summit on climate change in Copenhagen . . . Sir, this climate change will be the single largest threat to the existence of humanity . . . Sea levels have already started rising. Scientists have pointed out that sea levels of Maldives have risen by eight inches in the last 100 years. . . . The rivers may dry up; the rivers may even disappear in the long run . . . Sir, there is an apprehension that there will be a sharp decline in our food production and millions of people may go starving. When this global warming and climate change is affecting the entire humanity, it will be the poor who are going to bear the burden of this climate change . . .

Who is responsible for this kind of a situation? Is it the developing nations? The developed countries have been responsible for 72 per cent of Greenhouse gas emissions between 1952 and 2000. Our *per capita* emission is only 1.1 tonne as against 20.1 tonne of the United States. So, it is clear that the developed nations are responsible for this kind of a situation. This kind of a situation has been created because of the illegal appropriation and mindless exploitation of natural resources and global commons. Global commons include the global carbon space. Seventy-five per cent of this global carbon space has been occupied by the developed countries though their share in the world population is only 20 per cent.

234 *Prabhu*

Now, I would like to deal with some of the policy issues. There is much talk about flexibility, which our Hon. Minister of Environment and Forests, Shri Jairam Rameshji is appearing to be targeting widely. I would like to know what is the basic minimum, non-negotiable minimum of India in the forthcoming Copenhagen negotiations. What will this flexibility lead to? To what extent will this change our positions? Our minimum should be clear. First of all, the developed countries must begin to cut drastically their Greenhouse gas emissions. I feel that there is no flexibility on this question. I hope that the Hon. Minister will clarify whether there will be flexibility on the question of demanding more drastic cuts from the developed countries. . . ..

Sir, the developed countries want to erase the distinction between the developing and the developed countries. The distinction between the developing and developed countries, as far as this climate change negotiations are concerned, is fundamental. The Kyoto Protocol United Nations Framework has underlined the common but differentiated responsibilities. So, the developed countries should make drastic reduction in their emissions. According to this principle, the developing countries need only voluntary actions. The developing countries are not responsible for the global warming and they cannot be treated identically with the developed countries in this regard.

So, it is in this background that I would like to ask the Hon. Minister as to why he has promised that our NAMA and NAMOS will be available for international consultations.

Another aspect that I would like to highlight is regarding the unilateral action on the part of the Government of India. Our Minister is more enthusiastic in announcing unilateral action. Global warming and climate change is a global phenomenon. So, our unilateral actions will not help us from escaping the impact of global warming and climate change. It is tantamount to gifting away our carbon space.

. . .

Shri Prem Das Rai (Sikkim)

Most developing countries perceive the Bali Action Plan as distinguishing between developed country mitigation commitments and developing country nationally appropriate mitigation actions. This distinction is viewed as a 'firewall' by the developing countries, while some of the developed nations, notably the US, prefer to see it as a 'bridge'. The US and Australian proposals seek to create a new set of Parties and also attempt to extend mitigation 'commitments' to developing countries, contrary to the Bali Action Plan that prescribes only mitigation 'actions' for developing countries. Commitments signify acts that bind, while actions do not.

The developing countries on the other hand, have been arguing that they should be compensated for the damage caused by carbon emitted as developed countries have grown rich. Instead of imposing restrictions on developing countries, it would be more prudent to first determine the available carbon space that developing countries have in physical terms and then proceed to determine the optimal developmental roadmap to attain the goals set.

Glacial retreat in Sikkim

. . . Global warming has resulted in faster rate at which snow melts in the Sikkim glaciers, leading to huge quantities of water into glacier lakes. Once the water level in these lakes rises beyond the normal ranges, breaches of the dam formed of ice, boulders and sand give way. The surge of water and debris caused by outbursts of glacier lakes can change the entire course of rivers, also leading to a rise in the river level and causing floods in severe magnitudes in the Himalayan region.

...What needs to be noted by the House is that a study (Source: Sikkim Human Development Report, 2001) conducted by scientists in 1995 found that the Onglokthang and Rathong Chu glaciers are receding at a rapid rate, threatening the fragile economy of Sikkim. Studies have further revealed that since the Ice Age the Onglokthang glacier has retreated by about 500 metres, while the Rathong Chu glacier has rereated by about 600 metres. As per a study carried out in collaboration with JNU, the Zemu glacier has retreated by 963 metres from the year 1909 to 1999. Between 1998 and 2008, there has been a vertical thinning in the ice cover without any significant change in the snout position. ... This data indicates that there has been a continuous retreat at the rate of 13.6 metres per year between 1909 and 1965. Post 1965, the rate of retreat has been slower with an average of 5.8 metres per year between 1965 and 1999, without a significant change in the snout position from 1999–2008. These figures are in line with global trends. Although, we should strongly oppose taking legally binding emissions cuts, India must be willing to take greater and more serious steps to combat the threats of global warming. There remains an urgent need for us to make all possible efforts to tackle this menace at the domestic level as it will ultimately benefit us and our future generations. We have already embarked on an enhanced energy efficiency mission which will reduce carbon emissions.We should take this opportunity at the Copenhagen summit to showcase our efforts in the direction of environment protection and conservation to convince the larger global fraternity about our seriousness on this fragile issue without compromising our national interests.

. . .

Shri B. Mahtab (Cuttack)

...There is incontrovertible scientific evidence that global warming, a result of carbon dioxide emission, is making a far-reaching impact on our lives and will jeopardize the future of the planet. . . .

The Government has drafted a National Action Plan on Climate Change in June 2008. It looks great on paper. The basic foundation of the plan is faulty. It is complacent of the fact that the average per capita emission of India is only 1.5 tonnes, much lower than the world average of 4.5 tonnes. This hides the fact that about 150 million Indians have adopted the lifestyles of developed countries and are already on high carbon pathway.

Let us look at the energy and transport sectors. The share of coal in power generation is 67 per cent and the plan is to increase this with building more ultra-mega thermal power plants with capacities of 4000 MW each. Any industry that comes up, puts up a captive power plant and tries to get a coal block. . . . Efficiency of these captive power plants is very low. . . . Why are we allowing it? Are we going to put a check on it? Instead of addressing the issue of increasing the efficiency of the existing thermal plants, the Government, especially the Power Ministry, is eager to establish more coal-based power plants, and Orissa is becoming a victim of it.

In the transport sector, the Government is creating conditions to propagate private vehicles that add to carbon footprint and cause health problems. In our country, buses

236 *Prabhu*

are subsidized to the extent of Rs.33 lakh per day; cars are subsidized at Rs.72 lakh per day; and two wheelers are subsidized at Rs.151 lakh per day. This is stated in a study. Instead of minimizing these anomalies which actually favour the automobile industry, no attempt is being made to evolve policies to support public transport.

The biomass based economy of the rural households in the countryside is less prone to emission of greenhouse gases in comparison to the fossil fuel based economy of the urban rich in our country. The plan fails to recognize the positive contributions of the rural community and support them through policy initiatives. We know that energy is unlike any other commodity. The entire economy depends on access to dependable, affordable energy. Without this, nothing else can be successful. Today we have a genuine opportunity to build clean energy prosperity, if we act decisively. So, what can we do to capture this opportunity and how should our self interest be reflected in international negotiations?

There is a need to take advantage of efficiency and renewable energy technologies that are available today. Simple policies can help bring change. Adopt standards for efficient lights, compact fluorescents and LEDs.

Dr Jayant Sathaye of Lawrence Berkley National Laboratory has calculated that energy efficiency would save this nation over Rs.2.4 million crore by 2017 by eliminating blackouts that cripple the economy.

Secondly, let us accelerate the implementation of programmes to adopt clean technologies such as solar. Germany and Spain have special prices called 'feed-in tariffs' that have made solar and wind mainstream options. In our country it is still being contemplated. Why cannot we act? Long-term Government-backed power purchase agreement will create the appropriate environment for financing so that the private sector can develop innovative solutions.

India should lead in the negotiations during the Copenhagen Summit. Government has spelt out that India cannot accept a cap and that the ultimate carbon abatement, per capita, must converge for the rich and poor nations. But we need to do more. We need to become leaders in progressing the conversation and the best way to do this is to take our self-interest seriously, then commit to it internationally . . .

. . .

Shri Jayant Chaudhary (Mathura)

. . . I would like to start by quoting Einstein who said, 'Imagination is better than knowledge'. I think the peculiar situation that the Hon. Minister is now faced with, will require him to take a flexible approach to the whole problem. I know, sitting in the Opposition Benches and hearing the way the debate has gone . . . typically the stance has been that we must ensure equity. . . .

Talking about climate change, when we propagate the argument that we are not the ones who caused it, I think, it is a moronic argument and it does not matter because we are all a part of this world. We can no longer view environment as an individual property. We have not got a document with stamp duty saying that this is our river, this is our jungle etc., we own it. . . . So, we must change that mindset. I think, we are still in denial mode. We are not facing the facts. Climate change is not something that may happen after 2020. It is not about going to Copenhagen and getting a good deal or gaining anything. We are already losing. It is about how much we have lost already, it is about how much we stand to lose if we do not take action today.

Climate change debates in the Indian parliament 237

So, really, when we are not looking at gaining anything, our stance should be determined by how much we have to lose. Countries like India and China, with vast populations and agrarian economies, we have the most to lose. Therefore, we should perhaps not be afraid to give up the most.

In the papers we have recently read that there have been villages in Orissa who have had to move. Islands in Sunderbans are perhaps no more. So, it is a clear and present danger. It is no longer a choice. It is an imperative. It is not about national pride. I for one, talking on behalf of my party, will extend support to the initiatives that the Minister takes in this regard. While paying attention to the equity issues, we need innovative approaches. . . . We should create an environment within our domestic structures through laws enacting important legislations and empowering these so-called Missions, to bring these issues to the highlight. What I would like to find out is, say, the Solar Mission has already stated that by 2022 they are going to create 20,000 MW of capacity. Our approach up till now has been that we will provide incentives; we will provide some subsidies and private sector will come up. I think, unfortunately, though that has not happened in the renewable energy sector. A lot of the environmental standards that we already have are not being conformed to by industry because when they look at it from a cost-benefit analysis, it does not make sense. When they look at their income statements, balance sheet, cash flow, it does not make sense to invest in these technologies. Solar electricity has not taken off because people say it is expensive. When they are saying it is expensive, they are perhaps not taking into account the need for diversifying our energy sources; they are not taking into account the cost involved when there are regular floods, droughts, salinity of soil, loss of crop production and the threat that climate change poses. It is because these cannot be quantified in sheer numbers. . . . Perhaps the Central Government can look at becoming world's first green Government. Why do we not look at our Central Government buildings? Look at the footprint that they have in terms of emission, in terms of energy needs, and they can then be demonstrative. The good thing about solar technology is that it is democratic. The large distribution network, the large production facility, that model has failed in this country. Villages in our country, in any State you can talk about, they do not get more than four to six hours of electricity. There is wastage; there are people who are stealing electricity. It is not working. So, we should look at mini-grid setups. The Government should look at investing in it. Stepping up public investment through a public entity created for that purpose may not be such a bad idea.

. . .

Dr Tarun Mandal (Jaynagar)

It seems to me that this House of Politics has been turned into a House of Science, holding conferences on climate change with our honourable members are expressing concerns as scientists, researchers, discoverers and climate experts. I salute the concern of our members for our motherland due to climate change. But over-concern is bad, as bad as under-concern is . . . I have certain observations which will go in contradiction to many views on global warming. Anthropogenic carbon production is only 3 per cent in the world: 97 per cent comes from nature, by putrefaction of leaves, vegetables, algae of seas, etc. and volcanoes. So, the human contribution is minimal. Global temperature graphs from the history of climate change, as published by NASA, VOSTOK and

238 *Prabhu*

EPICA-type organizations, have shown maximum temperature rise. Our Globe had seen much before industrial revolution, when there were no questions of human carbon emission . . . Greenhouse gases are blessings to mankind. Without water vapour (H_2O), the major component of green house gases, responsible for contributing maximum heat and CO_2, life cannot survive. H_2O, (water) vapour gives a stable temperature as in the sea shores. It is the sea which gives maximum CO_2 exchange to the atmosphere. When temperature rises, the sea emits CO_2 and when temperature goes down, the ocean absorbs CO_2. It is also expressed as per the VOSTOK/EPICA graph that CO_2 is following temperature rise; but not that temperature is following CO_2. The great Al Gore has also used this graph in his Oscar winning production 'An Inconvenient Truth' but did not mention this bare truth. Even NASA has changed a graph what they published in the year 1999 and again in 2007, which seems to be a crime to manipulate scientific data to hoodwink the world's concern . . . Therefore, I find, may be this global warming theory is more political than scientific . . .

. . .

The Minister of State of the Ministry of Environment and Forests (Shri Jairam Ramesh)

. . . I want to spend this evening discussing some of the larger issues of policy that have been raised. I want to begin by saying that today I found remarkable degree of agreement that climate change is a serious issue. This is very important. . . .

Ever since I became the Minister on 29th of May, I have been trying to spread this single message that the most vulnerable country in the world to climate change is India, not Maldives, not Bangladesh and not America, but India. There is no country that is as much impacted by climate change as India.

. . . [L]et me talk a little bit about the Copenhagen process because that is the real issue that everybody wants to hear . . . On the international arena, when I took over as Minister for Environment and Forests on the 29th of May, the Prime Minister's instructions to me were: 'India has not caused the problem of global warming. But try and make sure that India is part of the solution. Be constructive; be proactive.' That was all he told me. Then I asked myself, What is India's position when it comes to international negotiations? The only position India had: 'Our per capita is very low; your per capita is very high; therefore we would not do anything.' Sir, per capita is an accident of history. It so happened that we could not control our population. That is why, we get the benefit of per capita. . . . It is an important point because per capita is the only instrument of ensuring equitable distribution. But it cannot be the only point. That is the point. So, when I first started looking at this international canvas, I was struck by the fact that India's position was: 'Our per capita is low and, therefore, we are entitled to pollute more till we reach your per capita levels. Since you have caused the problem, you must fix the problem'. That was, broadly speaking, our position. . . .

So, I ask myself this question: Can we go beyond per capita? Per capita is the basic position. Our per capita is low. Our Prime Minister has said that our per capita emissions will never exceed per capita emissions of the developed world. I said that our per capita emissions will remain below that of the developed world. My friends from the Left Parties accused me of compromising the Prime Minister's statement. Sir, this is English language. This is semantics . . . To my simple mind, I do not see any difference between 'will not exceed' and 'will remain below'. It is the same thing.

Climate change debates in the Indian parliament 239

Sir, there are some non-negotiables for us at Copenhagen. Let me categorically state what these non-negotiables are . . . The first non-negotiable is that India will not accept a legally binding emission reduction cut . . . I want to say this absolutely, clearly and categorically. There is no question of India accepting a legally binding emission reduction target . . . Second, there are some attempts by some countries to say that developing countries should announce when their emissions will peak. Let me say that this is the second non-negotiable for us. We will not accept under any circumstances an agreement which stipulates a peaking year for India . . . There is a third non-negotiable. Today, it is non-negotiable, but depends on the concessions that we can get from the western countries. Perhaps, we could modulate our position in consultation with China, Brazil and South Africa. We are prepared to subject all our mitigation actions, whatever we do, which is supported by international finance and technology to international review. There is nothing wrong with it as we are getting money from outside and we are getting technology from outside. The technology-giver and the money-giver is asking '*hisaab do toh usmein haemin koi appati nahi honi chahiye*'. The problem arises on the mitigation actions, which are unsupported, that is, that which we are doing on our own. We certainly would not like the unsupported actions to be subject to the same type of scrutiny that the supported actions are subject to. . . .

I separate domestic responsibility from international obligation. I want to be aggressive on domestic obligation and I want to be pro-active on international obligation because in international obligation there is only one thing that counts. Ultimately, when I go to Copenhagen, it is not G-77 or China or America or Brazil or South Africa, it is India's interest that counts.

Parliamentary Debates on Climate Change Post-Copenhagen: Excerpts

Rajya Sabha
Session 218
Tuesday, 22 December 2009

(Reproduced from Rajya Sabha Debates with the permission of the Hon'ble Chairman)

Shri Jairam Ramesh

. . . Before I get into the statement, Sir, let me say that this is the fourth time in the last four weeks that I am speaking in some detail on the issue of climate change reflecting our Government's transparency and keenness to keep the parliament fully informed at every step. It also reflects, of course, the great interest Hon. MPs themselves have taken in this important subject. There was a Calling Attention Motion in the Rajya Sabha on November 24th and a Zero Hour discussion on December 7th. The Lok Sabha had a five-hour discussion on December 3rd. Let me reiterate that I am more than prepared to discuss this issue in parliament at any time, in any form that the House desires and the Chairman directs . . .

240 *Prabhu*

The Leader of the Opposition (Shri Arun Jaitley)

Mr Deputy Chairman, Sir, I have heard and gone through the elaborate statement made by the Hon. Minister. I cannot, Sir, hide my disappointment under the present circumstances. Even when it became clear that at Copenhagen a multilateral accord or a statement was not going to be possible, what instead has happened is a plurilateral accord with a reasonable prospect of this plurilateral accord eventually slowly but surely being accepted by others and becoming the fresh basis for the furtherance of the negotiations . . .

In this detailed statement, Sir, the Minister has elaborately patted himself and the Government on the back for, what he calls, protecting the national interest. I do not know, Sir, whether the Government and the negotiators consciously agreed to the language, as has been framed, or they have been completely outwitted in the drafting of this language. Reports coming from across the world refer to this Accord as a global disappointment. It appears to be a complete betrayal of the poor and the weaker nations, the developing nations, and the more powerful nations have almost been left off the hook. And, after the Accord, what we find is a continuous campaign and spin-doctoring as a substitute for truth . . .

Sir, there are several questions which arise on the very language of the Accord. The first: If this plurilateral accord becomes a multilateral accord, which it is likely to, can it ever be reasonably argued that the Kyoto Protocol continues to subsist? . . .

Now, what do we find in the present document? It says that the reduction which is promised in the Kyoto Protocol and the subsequent declarations is now substituted. Now the Annexure-I Parties which are left off the hook by 31st of January, 2010, would file a fresh declaration with the Secretariat and the fresh declaration would be that they would now indicate as to what their rate of emission standards is going to be . . .

Yes, this Document does not say that Kyoto stand is abrogated. But the moment a route alternative to Kyoto Protocol is discovered and then obliged, there is an implied abrogation as far as the Kyoto Protocol is concerned. . . .

Shri Jairam Ramesh

Sir, if the Hon. Member can yield for half-a-minute, I just want to clarify . . . I just draw his attention to the fourth line at the very top of the Copenhagen Accord which recognises that there is a continuing mandate for negotiations under the existing tack of Kyoto Protocol. . . .

Shri Arun Jaitley

Sir, I am placing a very simple question today. If fresh set of obligations, less onerous obligations are to be cast under the Copenhagen Accord, you will continue giving lip-sympathy to the Kyoto Protocol which are the obligations which will be applicable in future . . . If there is a repugnancy between the two Documents, which of the two is going to be made applicable – the less onerous one or the more onerous one? After all, you can't have two sets of conflicting obligations occupying the same space. . . .

Now the Minister said that he has been very transparent and upfront. He told the parliament that there will be no peaking here and he is not agreed to a peaking here

Climate change debates in the Indian parliament 241

and the Document, in effect, says so. Let us read the fourth line of paragraph 2 of the document. It says, 'We should cooperate in achieving the peaking of global and national emissions as soon as possible, recognising that the timeframe for peaking will be longer for developing countries.' Now what happens in the next round of negotiations? . . . So, when the peaking of national emissions takes place, that peaking will be fixed. The only concession given is, the peaking will be more stringent for the developed countries, will be a little more liberal as far as the developing counties are concerned. . . .

The principle of peaking has been accepted; all that remains is the fixation of the specific year, as far as peaking is concerned . . . My third difficulty with this document is again an assurance given to this parliament and to the country that unsupported domestic action will never agree for any international verification. . . . The first thing that this document does, Sir, it completely obliterates the distinction between supported and unsupported actions. There is no distinction between the two . . . But, then, there is a next sentence, 'Non-Annexure parties will communicate information on implementation of their actions through national communications with a provision for international consultation and analysis under defined guidelines that will ensure that national sovereignty is respected.' Now, it does not stop with reporting. Your responsibility does not get over with that. After you report, there will be an international consultation. That is the first thing that will happen. Then, there will be an international analysis of whether you have achieved that or not. Both these things will be done by a process – and that is the whole art of outwitting in the process of negotiations – under guidelines which are yet to be framed. So, the Secretariat will frame the guidelines . . . Today, there is a statement made by the US Administration saying, 'We have now got India on hold and we will bind them by what is written therein, and we will make sure it is complied with.' And, this is the process by which they will make sure that it is complied with. There will be guidelines framed, whatever we tell the world, there will be analysis, there will be consultations, and once they find that there is something lacking, then, the consequences will follow and you will enter into an era of conflict, an era where even trade sanctions can be imposed upon you . . .

Sir, we are now being told that this Accord was not adopted in the entire multilateral conference, but it is a clear plurilateral agreement between us, look at the language, and, therefore, no legally-binding agreement arises. Sir, it is an argument which cuts both ways. If no legally-binding agreement arises, then, what will be the consequence if the developed countries by 31st of January don't make their submissions in the Schedule in which they are supposed to submit and say we are not bound by this outcome? Was what happened in Copenhagen, the meeting between the developed countries and the basic group, an exercise in futility? Admittedly, it was not. Admittedly, this document now promises to become the centre stage document as far as the climate negotiations are concerned. And, then the national parliament to be told, 'Well, this is not a binding document'. Paragraph 5, which is our obligation, starts with non-Annexure 1 parties to the Convention 'will' implement mitigation actions. Not 'may' implement, not 'could' implement, we 'will' implement, and what is it that we 'will' implement?

We 'will' implement what we make a declaration by 31st of January to the Secretariat that these are going to be what my emission cuts or energy intensity cuts are going to be. It hardly lies with the Government after entering into an Accord which uses the word 'will' implement, then to come back and say, 'Well, what I have signed is not binding; is not worth the paper it is written on'. . .

242 *Prabhu*

The Minister said, Sir, that the most important part of this agreement is the one relating to the funding . . . Please read paragraph 8 which deals with global funding. It clearly says, 'Funding for adaptation will be prioritised for the most vulnerable developing countries such as the least developing countries, small island developing States and Africa.' So the 'others' get priority; 'we' are not on the 'priority list.' In the context of meaningful mitigation actions and transparency on implementation, the developed world commit to a goal – now comes the most important world – of 'mobilising' – they are not going to take it out of their treasury and put it on the table – jointly US 100 billion dollars a year by 2020 to address the needs of developing countries. This funding will come from a wide variety of sources, public and private, bilateral and multilateral, including alternative sources of finance . . . Is the whole gambit of carbon trade going to be covered under this funding? And a very large part of that trade itself, which you would have got even without the Copenhagen Accord, is going to be a part of this amount of 100 billion dollars. So, this figure of 100 billion dollars is dressed up to say that you are making this concession; you are letting them off the hook of the Kyoto obligations; and they are going to pay for it. . . .

Sir, it is true that we should not be seen as the fall guys. But, at the same time, we should not allow our own interest to fall. And I am afraid in our entire attempt to please some and avoid being seen as the fall guys we have decided to let our own interests to fall as far as this Copenhagen Accord is concerned. Thank you, Sir.

Shri Sitaram Yechury

Sir, there are three points. Three windows have been opened up. One is to jettison the Kyoto Protocol and the entire framework of the UNFCCC and the Bali Declaration. The second window that has been opened up is on the question of MRV. The third window that has been opened up is on the question of what we talk of '4.7' of the Framework where our emission reductions will be contingent upon transfer of funding and technology by the developed countries. The '4.7' that you are talking of has been given a go-by whereby here the commitment is woolly commitment for financing, whereby they are not committing from their State exchequer. This is important. Please understand this. This is important because the entire climate change framework began by talking of a historical responsibility of the developed world which pillaged global climate and brought us to the situation. By not committing State finances, they are escaping from their historical responsibility. They are now talking of market forces and at a time of global recession market forces raising a 100 billion dollars annually is something that absolutely we can't accept. Therefore, this window that has also been opened up, they can violate. . . .

The fourth window is the window of technology transfers without the IPR regimen. Technology transfers without the IPR regimen was the demand that we have been putting, that has also been effectively negated in this Accord. Therefore, Sir, my only point is that we must be careful in the coming years. The effort by the West is to convert common but differentiated responsibility into common and undifferentiated responsibility. . . .

The Minister of State (Independent Charge) of the Ministry of Environment and Forests (Shri Jairam Ramesh)

. . . [T]here are some common concerns that have been expressed. . . . Sir, the first issue that has been raised is, have we agreed to the abandonment of the Kyoto Protocol. . . . [T]he Copenhagen Accord in no way spells the demise of the Kyoto Protocol. It accepts that the negotiations on the Kyoto Protocol will continue in 2010; but, I cannot disagree with him, that it provides an alternative alignment as well. But, we are committed. I want to reassure the House, to taking the negotiations forward in 2012 and which will culminate in Mexico.

But, the fact is, Sir, there are attempts to thwart the Kyoto Protocol. . . . The US has not ratified the Kyoto Protocol. The entire problem on the Kyoto Protocol has been caused by the fact that there is a common and differentiated responsibility within the developed countries. The Europeans do not want to say, 'we want to take obligations different than the Americans.' So, we have to bring the US into the mainstream of international environmental negotiations because they are the world's number two emitter, accounting for almost 22 per cent of the Greenhouse gases and emissions. Many countries want to leave the Kyoto Protocol. It is no secret that the country in which Kyoto is situated itself wants to leave the Kyoto Protocol, namely Japan. But, we are committed; the developing world is committed, the basic countries are committed. India is committed to completing these negotiations on this track and we are going to do our utmost to ensure that the emission reduction targets for the second commitment period, which is post-2012 period, will be negotiated with as much force as we can muster individually as well as collectively.

Sir, the second issue which is perhaps the most contentious issue today relates to the world international consultations and analyses. . . . Sir, before we went to Copenhagen, I did say that we will accept international information reporting as far as our unsupported actions are concerned. But, Sir, the fact of the matter is that when the negotiations on the Copenhagen Accord started, the issue was that it was not anything to do with India. . . .

This issue was really directed on China because today China has 23 per cent of the world greenhouse gas emissions and the world wants to bring China into the mainstream and they want to have confidence that the Chinese numbers, Chinese systems have some credibility. I can reassure this House, Sir, at no point of time, has any Government raised any doubt on our data, no Government; no head of State negotiator has raised doubts on our transparency. . . .

Sir may I say that the word 'consultations' is not new in international diplomacy. We have under the article four of the International Monetary Fund consultations that are held between the IMF and the Indian Government every year. It has been going on for decades. No sovereignty has been eroded as a result of those consultations. We should ensure that these guidelines do not lead to a proliferation of inspectors coming and seeing what we are doing and what we are not doing. But, the fact of the matter is, 'consultations' and 'analysis' does not mean review, scrutiny, verification or assessment. Let me give you one more example, because this is a very important issue that the Hon. Leader of the Opposition has raised and I want to address this directly. Sir, eighteen years ago, in 1990, the USA . . . put out a Report which said that Methane emissions from wet paddy cultivation in India is 38 million tonnes per year and it said that wet paddy cultivation in India is a major contributor to global Methane emissions.

244 *Prabhu*

There were some Indian scientists who challenged this data . . . They actually measured the Methane emission from wet paddy cultivation. And, their conclusion was that the annual level of Methane emissions from wet paddy cultivation in India was between 2 to 6 million tonnes per year, with a median value of 4 million tonnes per year. Sir, do you know that, today, the accepted international figure, including the USA, is not 38 million tonnes per year for Methane emission from wet paddy cultivation, but it is 4 million tonnes from wet paddy cultivation. So, I don't see why we should be defensive . . .

So, Sir, I agree that there is a difference between 'information' which I had committed to in this House and 'consultations' and 'analysis.' So, I plead guilty. Yes, I have moved from the word 'information' to 'consultations' and 'analysis.' I am not going to argue on that . . . this was a decision taken collectively by China, Brazil, South Africa and India. We decided that we will not be held responsible for the failure of Copenhagen. We decided that we will not be made the blame boys as far as the failure is concerned. A number of comments have been made on the USA. Let me also say that there was a statement made by the USA delegation during the negotiations. It said, 'we will not give money to countries like Bangladesh and Maldives if the issue of transparency is not settled.' The Bangladeshi delegates asked, 'why are you not settling the issue of transparency?' The Maldives delegation asked me, 'why are you not settling the issue of transparency?' So, the issue of transparency had become a big stumbling block and, Sir, frankly, of all the countries in the world, India should not feel defensive about transparency.

Sir, the Hon. Leader of the Opposition and many Hon. Members have referred to a statement made by Mr. Axelrod who is President Obama's close adviser. If I may be permitted, Sir, a small light-hearted comment, Mr. Axelrod is the Arun Jaitley of the Obama Administration. He is their top spin doctor. He has tried to give a spin to this Agreement . . . Mr Axelrod's statement was meant for domestic consumption. He has to convince the Congress that China and India have been brought in. He has to convince the trade unions that China and India have been controlled. I don't want to get into the statement of Mr Axelrod that has been made for purely domestic consumption. I go by what President Obama has himself said. And, nowhere has President Obama said that this record is meant to control or strangulate China and India. . . .

I was criticized for violating a commitment that I made on the floor of the House that we will not accept peaking year. On 16th November, the prospect was for an international agreement that would mention 2020–2025 as the peaking year for Developing Countries, like, India. This Accord does not mention a single year for peaking. That is a major accomplishment for us. It talks of global peaking, agreed. But it also talks of longer timeframe for Developing Countries, as the Leader of the Opposition read out. It also talks about the peaking in the context of the first and overriding priority being given to poverty eradication and livelihood security. This is not a new language. This was there in the L'Aquila Declaration. . . . What I want to convey to the Hon. Members is that the concept of peaking, when the Hon. Prime Minister made his commitment two years ago that all of you had applauded, which all of Indian media had applauded, which all of Indian NGOs had applauded, is that India's per capita emission will never exceed the per capita emission of the Developed World. We are implicitly accepting peaking. . . . What we have not done in this document is to mention a specific year for peaking. So, I do not plead guilty to this

Climate change debates in the Indian parliament 245

charge . . . But, I am sure, and Hon. Members will agree with me, that we should peak in the 21st century. Now, in which year in the 21st century, time alone will tell. But it should not be anybody's case that we should peak only in the 22nd century. We should peak sometime in the 21st century. If we don't peak in the 21st century, I think, then, we are having a very serious problem for us . . .

Sir, I also want to say one point on funding. Sir, a country like India, I believe, this is my belief, this is the belief of many people, does not need any international aid. We do not want international aid. We can stand on our own feet. Green technology is an area where India can emerge as a world leader. Ten years from now, Sir, India should be selling Green Technology to the world. Let us not always keep talking of technology transfer, technology transfer, technology transfer. Nobody is going to transfer technology to you. Technology has to be negotiated, technology has to be bought, technology has to be bought on commercial terms. I want to say that many Indian companies have already seen business opportunities in this. China has moved ahead. Today, of the top 10 solar companies in the world, four are Chinese. Let us see this as a business opportunity. This is an opportunity for Indian technology to move ahead and I am sure that in the next couple of years, we will, actually, be selling technology rather than keep repeating the stale mantra of technology transfer all the time. Yes, we require international financial assistance. I am not one who is suggesting we do not require international financial assistance. But, Sir, we are not in the same category as Bangladesh or Maldives or Ethiopia or Saint Lucia or Granada. There are countries in Africa, countries in small island States, countries in Asia which require more urgently than us for adaptation and mitigation. A country like India should be able to stand on its own feet and say we will do what we have to do on our own.

Note

1   This chapter is based on comments at a workshop of contributors to this volume, held at the Centre for Policy Research, New Delhi, 29th September, 2010.

18 Climate change and the private sector

Tarun Das

Background

In order to understand the present role of industry in India's climate debate, it is necessary to understand the changing relationship between business and government in India in the recent past. In general terms, 1947–1991 was a period of micromanagement of the economy and industry by the government. Production, manufacturing, export, import, prices, and distribution were controlled for many products. Essentially, it was a period of mistrust by government of industry; government held the view that industry had to be regulated and controlled.

Sectors of industry too preferred this policy approach in the short-term because of their ability to pre-empt capacities, markets and profits. Gradually, it dawned on both government and industry that this regime was not fulfilling the real national purpose of growth and development. In consultation with industry, government began the process of minor deregulation in the early '80s, and carried this forward in the mid- and late-'80s.

The by-product of this system of controls was inefficiency, complacency, the production of sub-standard goods, inadequate attention to the consumer and an uncompetitive industry incapable of generating exports. In fact, there was a general perception within and outside India that the nation suffered from weak entrepreneurship, and was unable to compete and survive. In this context, the question of addressing environmental issues did not seem relevant or important.

The economic crisis of the late 1980s and early 1990s led to a new paradigm of industrial development in India. June 1991 was the beginning of the deregulation of trade and investment controls, bringing with it a taste (which was initially sour for many) of competition, freedom of investment and a new challenge for entrepreneurs.

The period from 1991 to 2010 is a second phase of the development of industry in India. Competition has increased, growth rates are higher, profitability has been enhanced and entrepreneurs have started coming into their own, enjoying the space and freer environment for business. Some still complain that survival would be impossible, but this group is in the minority. The situation has steadily evolved with corporates now defending their borders and establishing footholds abroad through overseas investments and acquisition of companies. Globalisation has come full circle.

This changed context for industry has coincided with greater Indian and global business engagement with the environment. In 1991, the Business Council for Sustainable Development was established with a Swiss CEO as the chair, and with one representative from India, Ratan Tata, Chairperson of the Tata Group of companies. He

Climate change and the private sector 247

was supported in this work by the Confederation of Indian Industries (CII), through a new Environment Committee, led by the late Avininder Singh.

The 1992 Rio Conference was attended not only by the Indian government but also by Ratan Tata, Avininder Singh and a team from CII. On their return, they strongly encouraged CII to follow through on this start. With the funding support of the Tata Group, CII set up an Environment Management Division to promote the adoption of environment-friendly technologies and practices by Indian industry. The Division recruited technical experts and CII began a journey that would change industry practices and policies to build a cleaner environment.

The business response to climate change

Indian industry's initial reaction to climate change was dismissive. They perceived it as a product of the imagination of scientists or at best a scientific phenomenon that would not affect India any time in the near future. It was also thought to be another excuse for the West to impose non-tariff restrictions on Indian exports as a way of restricting India's growth. Much as the Indian economy was closed to the rest of the world, so was Indian industry closed to the idea of climate change.

But this reaction to climate change started to change once the Indian economy had opened and more businesses interacted with global markets. Nonetheless, progress was slow. Over time, measures that would reduce carbon emission intensity became popular with most businesses, not for environmental reasons, but because these measures made economic sense. For example, promoting energy efficiency was an obvious solution; one that would result in cost competitiveness for Indian industry.

Indian industry's lack of attention to climate change can also be attributed to the Government's defensive negotiation strategy, and the consequent signal to Indian industry that they would be insulated from climate measures. Until COP-13 at Bali, the Government of India (GoI) held the view that India was not required to take aggressive carbon emissions reduction actions but that the burden should rest exclusively on developed countries. Global emissions reduction was an obligation of the industrialised nations and India had its domestic development agenda as a priority. Low-carbon growth was decoupled from national development. That meant little action on domestic mitigation efforts and consequently no incentives for business to adopt low-carbon measures.

But there were 'green' mavericks all along, probably because India was among the first countries to create a ministry for non-conventional energy (early '90s). For example, Tata BP Solar's efforts at developing solar power generation (1989), Suzlon's leadership in wind energy (1995), and Reva's early leadership of electric cars (1994) were all examples. But none of these companies grew within India as much as in the industrialised world (Shah, 2010). There was not sufficient policy architecture to induce demand of an attractive size as India was still not seen as a market for climate or green technologies.

Other than these notable examples, only a handful of additional companies explored the problem of climate change in a manner that had business implications. By the mid-2000s companies such as ITC, some Tata Group companies, and public sector enterprises such as ONGC and NTPC, went public with their ideas, strategies or plans with respect to climate change (see, for instance, ONGC, 2010a; Jog, 2009).

Since then, many companies have matured with their comprehension and action to adapt to and mitigate climate change. To illustrate, ITC has been a carbon positive

248   *Das*

company since 2005–06, by sequestering more CO_2 than its operations emit (see ITC, 2006). It has been able to do so by leveraging business interests in agriculture and farm forestry.

ONGC is undertaking a carbon capture and storage project in Gujarat. Under this project, CO_2 from its Hazira gas processing plant is 'captured and transported to the nearby Ankleshwar oil fields and injected at the depleted reservoir as a part of [the] enhancing oil recovery (EOR) scheme'. With this project ONGC aims to reduce CO_2 emissions by 0.6 million cubic metres (ONGC, 2010b, 51). Several other projects for carbon capture and reuse are also on the anvil.

Similarly, the Tatas have also taken a lead in establishing a comprehensive climate change programme. Eventually, all the companies under the group are going to work under the stewardship of a climate change Steering Committee that will facilitate innovation and action on mitigation. With the help of Ernst & Young and McKinsey & Company the group is establishing baselines and benchmarks, cost-abatement curves, and training executives for undertaking enhanced action on low-carbon initiatives for five of its major companies (Dasgupta, 2008).

Indian industry's attention to climate change was heightened by two drivers – one external and one internal. First, from 2005 onward there was a global rise in geopolitical attention to climate change which also had echoes in India. The then British Premier Tony Blair put climate change on the global political agenda at the Gleneagles G8 Summit in 2005. The Stern report on the Economics of Climate Change in 2006 provided a high profile basis for climate economics. The IPCC Fourth Assessment Report followed in 2007. All these reports contributed to articulating climate change as a socio-political-economic issue and induced all governments, civil society and particularly business to act.

In this debate India was simultaneously positioned as a country that would be at the receiving end of the climate damage induced by the industrialised world, but also as a rapidly growing economy that is increasingly contributing to greenhouse gas emissions – a 'major emitter'. In the global public debate, the focus had moved from compensation for historic emissions to curtailing future emissions. India suddenly had to rethink its climate policy to exhibit global power responsibility.

Second, there was a string of natural disasters that killed hundreds and affected millions. Among the most notable ones were a cyclone in Orissa (1999), floods in Mumbai (2005), floods in Bihar (2008), and a cloud burst in Ladakh (2010). Though each of these events may not be attributed to climate change, they reinforced the message that climate-induced disasters will increase and undo much of the development the country has achieved, push people back into poverty, and damage property and infrastructure. The Mumbai floods hit business the most, because businessmen were victims. With many of their number trapped on the flooded streets of Mumbai on 26 July 2005, Indian business began collectively identifying climate change as a risk.

Transparency and ambition

The Carbon Disclosure Project (CDP), an independent not-for-profit initiative to compile corporate climate change information across the world, including India, provides some insights into how Indian business is approaching climate change (CDP, 2010).

Since CDP is based on voluntary reporting, one indicator of interest and awareness is simply the extent of participation in CDP. Indian companies' participation in this

Climate change and the private sector   249

transparency initiative has been steadily rising since the first CDP Report (2008). As compared to 33 per cent in CDP 2008, an overwhelming 85 per cent of responding companies shared their GHG emissions data for CDP 2010. This may have been a result of a combination of factors such as increased understanding of carbon disclosure and capacity building of companies done by CII-ITC, CESD and WWF India, and better data available with companies to disclose.

The CDP 2010 data shows that Indian companies compare favourably not just with their developing country counterparts on many indicators conveying their burgeoning ambition on mitigation, but also with developed countries. Seventy-one per cent of Indian companies are proactively seeking and implementing low-carbon solutions, compared to 87 per cent for both Europe, and the USA. Eighty-five per cent of India 200 have involved senior management in carving out a low-carbon business pathway indicating their seriousness on this issue. As the report states, these companies are 'helping to shape the future of Indian business' (CDP, 2010: 11).

Indian business responses also indicate a clear shift in perception, from seeing climate change as imposing barriers on business, to a potential opportunity for growth and diversification. Ninety per cent of India 200 foresee regulatory opportunities arising for business. Indian businesses are also taking steps to ensure they communicate with policymakers and work collaboratively to develop climate-friendly technologies for both mitigation and adaptation. Sixty-nine per cent of responding Indian businesses are undertaking this exercise, as compared to 66 per cent in Brazil and 57 per cent in China. Table 18.1 provides a quick snapshot of India 200's responses to basic indicators of transparency and low-carbon engagement, and how they compare with countries from the BASIC group, EU and US.

However, there remains substantial scope for improvement. Sixty-three per cent of India 200 have yet to identify and take on energy efficiency and emissions reduction targets (though 24 per cent are in the process of doing so). While 44 per cent continue to perceive regulatory risks from environmental regulation, which can only be allayed through greater interaction between business and policy makers at the national and global level.

Policy framework

India's climate policy too has moved up the evolutionary curve. From little domestic action under the shadows of its naysayer position in international negotiations, domestic climate policy has progressed to give some direction toward a low-carbon India. The country can achieve low-carbon growth with business participation within an appropriately enabling policy framework. However, arriving at this policy framework is a challenge since there are widely divergent views within government and business on the extent of and appropriate means for low-carbonisation in India.

Just as in the case of economic liberalisation in the early 1990s, CII held the view that Indian companies had to look for low-carbon strategies, that climate change could potentially risk business competitiveness, but also offered opportunities ranging from low-hanging fruits to long-term and strategic opportunities. CII sought government leadership on climate change, as it had on economic liberalisation.

One important area of industry policy advocacy was the design and implementation of the Clean Development Mechanism (CDM) in India. CII developed a detailed response on CDM and asked the government to create a policy that allowed industry

Table 18.1 Responses for Carbon Disclosure Project (CDP), 2010

Sample: geography/number of countries	% of sample answering CDP 2010	% of responders with Board or other executive level responsibility for climate	% of responders with management incentive	% of responders with emissions reduction targets	% of responders taking actions to reduce emissions	% of responders indicating that their products and services help third parties to avoid GHG emissions	% of responders seeing regulatory risks	% of responders seeing regulatory opportunities	% of responders engaging policymakers on climate issues to encourage mitigation or adaptation	% of responders reporting the company's response to climate change in mainstream annual filings/CSR reports	% of responders independently verifying any portion of Scope 1	% of responders independently verifying any portion of Scope 2
India 200	25	85	42	37	71	47	44	90	69	86	27	20
China 100	11	57	57	57	57	43	71	71	57	86	43	29
Brazil 80	72	68	29	23	57	55	61	78	66	74	28	28
South Africa 100	74	95	50	42	82	42	77	85	80	92	39	41
Europe 300	84	94	62	79	87	71	74	87	77	97	68	60
US Bond 180	82	78	62	70	87	55	60	71	88	91	54	46

Source: CDP, 2010

to participate in CDM and trade in carbon emissions. In order to attract investment to India, CII argued that the CDM should be developed as an efficient mechanism that uses market principles. Otherwise, Indian industry will not be able to compete with reductions from developed and transitional countries where market-based approaches are already being pursued to enable buyers and sellers of emission reductions to work together. Industry views CDM investments as a competitive endeavour, where industry in different developing and developed countries will compete to attract resources aimed to reduce global GHG emissions. With India's heavy reliance on coal, and significant potential for the use of renewable sources of energy, it is clear that CDM presents a huge opportunity to attract 'additional' investment to India.

CII further recommended that Indian industry should be eligible to certify emission reductions from CDM projects. The Ministry of Industry should be kept apprised as to how Indian industries can be 'designated' by the Conference of Parties or Meeting of Parties to engage in this new field of business.

Indian industry view has been that there is no need to define 'supplementarity'. Any ceiling on the use of CDM or other Kyoto mechanisms by developed countries will reduce potential flows of resources to India for emissions reductions. CDM investments will improve the efficiency and competitiveness of Indian industry.

CII further argued it would be important for the GoI to define and publicise India's priorities for sustainable development that are to be met through the CDM. These priorities should be transparent (obvious) and form part of India's domestic criteria for CDM projects, so that industry would be aware of any priorities and preferences before they begin to develop potential CDM projects. The result of this policy advocacy was that, at least for a period, India became the largest beneficiary of CDM projects in the world (see Pulver, this volume).

Following the election of the first United Progressive Alliance (UPA) government to power, CII also played an active role in fleshing out the national missions under the NAPCC. For example, CII's Godrej Green Business Centre (GBC) has been a pioneer of green buildings in India. Since its beginning in 2001, GBC has helped develop over 606 million square feet of green buildings in India. Its energy efficiency improvement projects with industry have accrued annual recurring savings of Rs 2100 million (CII, 2011). This leadership of CII was instrumental in providing a direction for the Sustainable Habitat and Energy Efficiency Missions in the Indian NAPCC.

The global connection

While these developments were taking place at the domestic front, India's climate negotiation policy was about to be given a makeover. In recognition of its emerging role in the global climate regime, India could not afford to be viewed as a naysayer in climate negotiations. India was already blamed by the US and the EU for stalling WTO's Doha round (Blakley, 2008) and it was at risk of receiving a similar reputation in climate negotiations. The brief given to Jairam Ramesh, India's Environment Minister, by the Prime Minister, was that India should become a proactive player in climate negotiations.

India began to engage with various countries, mainly the key emitters, on a renewed global climate regime. China had closed in on the US to emerge as a serious emitter. International pressure was building on India and China. Other countries such as South Africa and Mexico appeared to be more proactive on emissions reductions. Smaller

252 Das

countries, mainly those at risk of losing out to the consequences of climate change, increasingly asked India and China to take up legally binding cuts (PTI, 2009).

Appreciative of its global image and emerging role, and realising the benefits but also risks to domestic growth and development, India has decided to take on certain responsibilities. China had announced its voluntary targets just before COP-15 at Copenhagen. Jairam Ramesh was quick to announce in the Indian Parliament, India's voluntary emission intensity reduction target of 20–25 per cent by 2020 (see excerpts from Parliamentary Debates, this volume).

This announcement, unsurprisingly, shook many, including the industry. CII got down to number crunching to estimate the impact of such a target on industry and overall growth. In the meanwhile, another national-level industry association criticised the Minister for giving into global pressure and putting Indian industry's competitive advantage at risk (Das and Das, 2009).

However, CII displayed maturity. After making its calculations and conducting meetings with members and other experts, it issued support for India's intensity reduction target. According to CII, 20–25 per cent emission intensity reduction was easily achievable (CII, 2009). It also met with the Industry Ministry to explain the benefit. Clearly, the benefit was in having a long-term vision of sustainable growth.

Conclusion

Indian industry, as a collective union, has travelled some distance on its response to climate change. Of course, some sectors have travelled further than others, but, on average, there has been considerable movement. Having said this, low-carbon growth is a mammoth task. Indian industry still has a long way to go, just as industry in any other part of the world. Barring a handful of companies already mentioned, most companies are engaged in risk-mitigation. They need now to shift focus on embracing low-carbon growth as a business opportunity, without really waiting for anyone else (the government or China) to show them the way.

Indian industry is most likely to continue its support for a climate change-induced upgrade of regulation. Much of this support will be demonstrated in areas where a business angle is evident. In other areas, CII will continue to educate its membership and also work with governments to develop attractive incentives for industry participation. CII has been leading the way within the context of other industry-led organisations in India.

Now the countries have agreed to keep the rise in global average surface temperature below 2°C versus the long-term pre-industrial average (UNFCCC, 2011). This point alone will have massive repercussions for business and society at large. In order to achieve this, the global energy system will be zero carbon by 2050.

It probably means no fossil fuel combustion without carbon capture and storage. This can only be achieved with no fossil fuel use in mobile applications, since our world is unlikely to be able to economically capture and store tailpipe CO_2 emissions any time soon. This will require a total transformation of the ways in which energy is produced and consumed. Consider the impact when six out of seven top corporations in the world currently generate shareholder value by extracting, processing, distributing, and retailing liquid transport fuels.

CEOs cannot afford to hit a blind spot. They have to lead the transformative shift to low-carbonisation in business and economies.

References

Blakley, R. (2008) 'India blamed for Doha collapse by trying to protect poor farmers', *The Times*, 30 July, London.

Carbon Disclosure Project (2010) *India 200 Report*, CII, Centre of Excellence for Sustainable Development, WWF, http://assets.wwfindia.org/downloads/carbon_disclosure_project_2010_india_200_report.pdf, accessed on 10 March 2011.

CII (2009) Press Release: CII believes that Indian Industry is well-positioned to deliver on the 20–25 per cent emission intensity reduction, 8 December, http://www.cii.in/Pressreleases Detail.aspx?enc=ux3SiiK9SJm3sNXnC5Er4/GjrsYs0UKwp3DdkNGoLkvrmf6lmzyR2kxfIp MzIrtD7fk7WOiYFcmohKAC/aRNbg==, accessed on 10 March 2011.

CII (2011) 'Sohrabji Godrej Green Business Centre', www.greenbusinesscentre.com, accessed on 11 March 2011.

Das, S. and Das, S. (2009) 'Industry chambers split over emission target', *Financial Express*, 10 December 2009, http://www.financialexpress.com/news/industry-chambers-split-over-emission-target/552104/0, accessed on 10 March 2011.

Dasgupta, A. (2008) 'The Climate of Change', http://www.tata.com/aboutus/articles/inside.aspx?artid=f5KCaVEfP8s=, accessed on 11 March 2011.

ITC (2006) 'Sustainability Report', http://www.itcportal.com/sustainability/sustainability-report-2006/html/default.aspx, accessed on 10 March 2011.

Jog, S. (2009) 'NTPC plans Policy on Climate Change', *Financial Express*, http://www.financial express.com/news/ntpc-plans-policy-to-take-on-climate-change/495206/

ONGC (2010a) 'Policy on Climate Change and Sustainability', http://tenders.ongc.co.in/Notices/policy%20on%20sustain.pdf, accessed on 11 March 2011.

ONGC (2010b) 'Corporate Sustainability Report 2009–10', http://www.ongcindia.com//download/Corp%20Sust%20Report/ONGC_Sustainability_Report_2009-10.pdf, accessed on 11 March 2011.

PTI (2009) 'Jairam Ramesh to leave for Copenhagen on Friday', *IBN Live*, 10 December, http://ibnlive.in.com/news/jairam-ramesh-to-leave-for-copenhagen-on-friday/106868-3.html, accessed on 11 March 2011.

Shah, A. (2010) 'Green Investing in India – Is it worth your money?', 8 June, http://green worldinvestor.com/2010/06/08/green-investing-in-india-is-it-worth-your-money/, accessed on 11 March 2011.

UNFCCC (2011) Cancun Agreements, Decision 1/CP.16, FCCC/CP/2010/ and Decision 1/CMP.6, FCCC/KP/CMP/ 2010/.

19 Corporate responses to climate change in India

Simone Pulver

As an environmental issue, climate change is characterized both by irreversibilities and time lags. Greenhouse gases (GHGs) currently entering the atmosphere will remain there for centuries. The global warming experienced today thus traces back in part to emissions released decades ago. Moreover, those GHG emissions may themselves be the result of infrastructure and investment decisions made even longer ago. It is for this reason that decarbonizing the global economy is likened to piloting a supertanker. For a supertanker to avoid an obstacle in its path, turning procedures must be initiated far in advance.

From this perspective, the private sector in emerging economies stands as a crucial player in efforts to shift the future trajectory of global GHG emissions. Investments currently being made in China, India, Brazil and other emerging economies will shape the infrastructures of these economies for the next 30 years and these in turn will shape GHG emissions trajectories of the second half of the century. Yet, international climate policy and academic research communities have been slow to recognize the central role of the private sector in emerging economies in addressing the climate challenge. Large corporations based in the United States, Europe and Japan have been active in domestic and international climate politics – both as targets of regulation and as participants in negotiations – since the emergence of concern about climate change in the early 1990s. Likewise, academic research on corporate responses to climate change in advanced industrialized economies dates back to the same period (Tucker, 1997; Leggett, 1999). In contrast, corporations headquartered in developing countries have yet to establish a unique voice in the United Nations climate policy process. Moreover, academic studies of corporate responses to climate change in emerging economies are sparse.

Shifting attention to the climate-related activities of private sector actors in emerging economies reveals a variegated picture. In this contribution, I analyse patterns of corporate responses to climate change in India, in comparative context with other emerging economies. The first section summarizes data on corporate climate activities in the operational, political, and governance arenas. The second section focuses on the drivers of corporate responses to climate change, outlining both general patterns and sector-specific data from a study of climate action in the Indian sugar and cement sectors.

Corporate climate activities

Corporate responses to climate change can be evaluated based on activities in three areas: 1) operational practices, 2) political activities, and 3) corporate governance.

Operational practices are of greatest interest to policy makers and publics because of their direct impact on climate outcomes. Are private sector actors innovating new carbon-neutral technologies and markets? Are corporations reducing the GHG emissions from their own facilities and operations? Equal attention is garnered by corporate political activities. Do individual corporations support the regulation of carbon dioxide and other GHGs in various policy arenas? Are corporate lobbying and media efforts focused on undermining or bolstering the emerging scientific consensus on climate change? Finally, particular corporate business practices and political activities generally depend on a corporation's internal governance framework. Climate-friendlly shifts in business practices and political activities are possible only if senior management prioritizes climate change as a core issue of corporate strategy.

Operational practices

Climate-related operational practices can be evaluated based on both top-down and bottom-up data sources. Top-down, aggregate economic data place India in an intermediate position when evaluating the 'greenness' of its economy. Figure 19.1 compares the carbon intensity of the Indian economy, measured as carbon emissions per unit of economic output, with that of other emerging economies. Carbon intensity metrics reflect both the sectoral composition of an economy and the carbon content of dominant fuel sources. The Indian economy's reliance on fossil fuels, particularly coal, for economic production raises its carbon intensity. However, the relatively high contribution of agriculture to economic output has a mitigating effect. A more nuanced metric of aggregate corporate climate performance can be extrapolated from models of projected GHG abatement costs for the Indian economy. Such models indicate that India's power sector is the largest emitter of GHGs, followed by industrial production, specifically the steel and cement industries (GOI, 2004). Abatement cost curves developed by McKinsey & Company suggest significant room for improvement in the Indian power, cement and steel sectors. For example, they project negative abatement costs for various clinker substitution projects in cement and for energy efficiency in the steel industry (McKinsey & Company, 2009).

In contrast to aggregate top-down models, bottom-up approaches to studying corporate climate practices track the behavior of individual firms. At the firm-level,

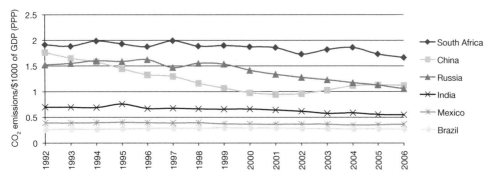

Figure 19.1 Carbon dioxide emissions from the consumption and flaring of fossil fuels per thousand dollars of gross domestic product (using PPP), 1992–2006

Source: EIA, 2006

256 *Pulver*

climate-friendly operational practices can take the form of investment in both new 'green' products and markets and energy efficiency and operational GHG reductions. A bottom-up view of corporate responses to climate change among Indian firms can be pieced together from single firm and sector case studies, industry surveys, international reporting initiatives (e.g. the Global Reporting Initiative (GRI), the Carbon Disclosure Project (CDP) and the UNFCCC National Communications), and from GHG emission reduction registries (e.g. the Clean Development Mechanism (CDM) project database).

The picture generated by synthesizing bottom-up, firm-level data is that Indian firms are aware of climate change and somewhat engaged in GHG reducing initiatives. For example, a 2008 survey of India's five hundred leading corporations – based on a multi-criteria index compiled by the *Financial Express* – documented that 96% of the 213 respondents to the survey self-assessed as having a fair (38%) or deep (58%) understanding of climate change (EVI and FE, 2008). Respondents to the survey included private Indian companies (69%), Indian subsidiaries of multinational corporations (17%) and public sector undertakings (14%) and were evenly distributed across a range of manufacturing and service sectors.

However, high levels of corporate awareness about climate change do not automatically imply action related to inventorying and reducing GHG emissions. Only 16% of the 213 survey respondents completed a full GHG emissions inventory, with another 38% completing a partial inventory. The 2010 Carbon Disclosure Project-India elicited similar results. Approximately 25% of the 200 companies approached for the project responded by providing information on their carbon disclosure practices (CDP, 2010). It is worth noting that these response rates, though low, are higher than for other emerging economies (CDP, 2010: 11). For companies that do take the first step of inventorying GHGs, additional action is likely. Of the 50 respondents in the 2010 CDP India survey, 97% identified business opportunities arising from climate change. The CDP survey also identified 17 companies that had voluntarily set corporate energy efficiency or GHG emissions reduction targets and an additional 15 companies that were in the process of doing so.[1]

The CDM registry, the most comprehensive database of GHG reducing projects initiated by firms in developing countries, reinforces the above picture.[2] To date, over 5000 CDM projects have been submitted for review from the group of emerging economies (UNEP/Risoe, 2011). Although some projects are initiated by NGOs or public authorities, the bulk of CDM projects represent firm-level investments in GHG reducing projects.[3] Firm investments generating CDM credits vary from sector to sector and reflect both investment in new green technology, such as solar power plants, and efficiency improvements in existing industrial processes, such as waste heat recovery. Internationally, the first CDM projects were approved in 2004. The market was initially dominated by projects initiated in Brazil. By late 2005, India overtook Brazil as carbon market leader, claiming 53% of projects. India remained the leader until 2007, when it was surpassed by China, which is currently host to the majority of CDM projects, measured both in numbers of projects and total emissions projected to be reduced through the CDM (Figure 19.2).

To date, over 1500 CDM projects have been initiated in India. Of these, 613 projects, have been approved and registered by the UN CDM Executive Board, the international approval authority that regulates the CDM. Projects in wind and biomass energy dominate India's CDM portfolio, both in terms of number of projects submitted and

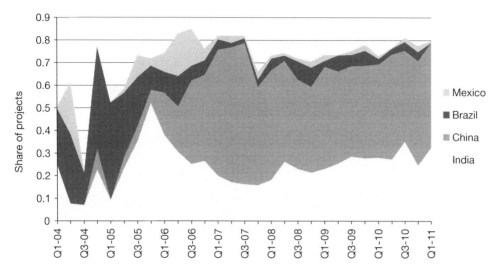

Figure 19.2 Share of total global Clean Development Mechanism projects by region, 2004–2011

Source: UNEP/Risoe, 2011

number of projects registered (Figure 19.3). The wind and biomass energy projects represent significant corporate investments in clean power sources. For example, Hultman et al. (in press) find that 14% of Indian sugar mills have invested in biomass-based electricity production and have sought CDM credits for their investment. Others further document the growth of renewable energy industries in India, including wind (Lewis, 2007), biomass (Dadhich, 1997; Purohit and Michaelowa, 2007), and solar (TERI, 2005). It must be noted that this growth in renewable energy industries comes at the same time as significant expansion in India's fossil fuel-based power system. Renewable energy will always supply a small fraction of India's power demand. Nevertheless, this is one area in which corporate action has climate consequences. Other examples of growing green product/markets in India include environmental consulting services, such as energy auditing and GHG emissions accounting (Knox-Hayes, 2010) and green building technology (McKinsey & Company, 2009).

A second category of Indian CDM project capitalizes on firm investments in process efficiency improvements. Such upgrades reduce energy consumption and may directly mitigate GHG emissions. They have been initiated in a range of sectors. For example, pulp and paper mills in India have invested in improving waste heat recovery, enhancing electrical energy efficiency, and optimizing steam consumption (Schneider et al., 2009). Perkins (2007) has shown a general pattern of environmental improvement in the steel industry. GHG specific projects in the steel sector include electricity generation based on waste gases and energy efficiency projects. Pulver and Hultman's study of the Indian cement industry documents GHG reduction activities among 40% of Indian cement factories. The most common cement project type reduces the fraction of clinker blended with other materials to create cement. Clinker production is both energy-intensive and a direct emitter of CO_2 (Hultman et al., in press).

In addition to showcasing patterns of green technology and efficiency investments by Indian firms, the CDM registry highlights several additional aspects of the overall

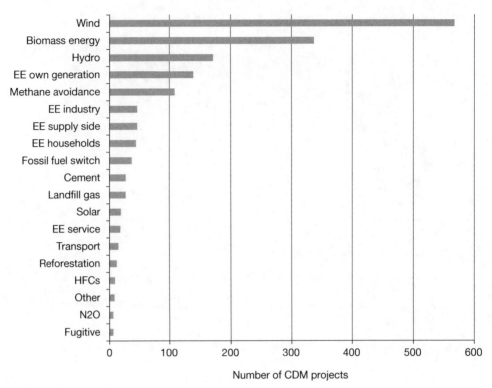

Figure 19.3 Number of Clean Development Mechanism projects in India by type
Source: UNEP/Risoe, 2011

corporate response to climate change in India. First, awareness of climate change, or at least of opportunities related to CDM, is widespread across a range of both large and small firms. Although large firms are generally more likely to seek CDM opportunities, CDM participation in India has also spread to smaller operations. In terms of GHG emissions reductions effected per CDM project, Indian projects are smaller than Chinese and Brazilian projects, reflecting in part the participation of small and medium enterprises in the Indian CDM market. To date, Indian CDM projects submitted for review are projected to generate over 441 million certified emissions reductions (CERs) by 2012, yielding an average project size of 0.23 million 2012 CERs in India, compared to 0.63 million 2012 CERs in China and 0.48 million 2012 CERs in Brazil (UNEP/Risoe, 2011).[4] A second unique characteristic of Indian CDM projects is that they are mostly unilateral, meaning that project financing is sourced from firm equity or Indian banks, rather than from foreign buyers of CDM credits (Krey, 2005; Lutken and Michaelowa, 2008). This suggests that Indian firms have sufficient access to capital to invest in clean technology and implement efficiency improvements. Finally, Indian CDM projects tend to rely on indigenous technology. In a study of technology transfer through the CDM, Dechezlepretre et al. (2008) show that only 12% of Indian projects had an international technology transfer component, compared to 59% in China, 40% in Brazil, and 68% in Mexico. This once again suggests sufficient technology development and expertise is available among Indian firms to move along the path of decarbonization (Dechezlepretre et al., 2009).

Political activities

While operational practices are the most direct way by which firms impact climate outcomes, companies also exert influence by shaping the organizational, informational, legal, and political contexts in which they operate and in which climate policies are debated. Such debates occur both at the international level and in domestic policy arenas. In international climate policy debates, Indian companies have not yet established a unique voice. The business lobby in the international climate negotiations tends to be dominated by general business associations, such as the International Chamber of Commerce, the International Emissions Trading Association, and the World Business Council for Sustainable Development. While such organizations have international memberships, they mostly draw their leadership from corporations headquartered in OECD countries (Pulver, 2002). There are regional and national business groups active at the international level, such as the US-based Global Climate Coalition, the E5 European Business Council for Sustainable Energy and the Latin American Business Council for Sustainable Development. According to participant data assembled by the UN Climate Change Secretariat, the Federation of Indian Chambers of Commerce and Industry (FICCI) and the Confederation of Indian Industry (CII) are the two Indian business associations formally registered to participate in the international climate negotiations. However, neither has been prominent in representing the South Asian business community, nor have individual Indian corporations established a high profile in the international negotiations. The one exception to this trend was the 2002 round of the climate negotiations (COP 8), which was held in New Delhi. Based on UN Climate Secretariat records, COP 8 featured two side events coordinated by Indian business groups. The first focused on corporate environmental performance, co-organized by CII and the Indian delegation. The second highlighted science and technology capacity building for climate change, co-organized by FICCI, the Indian delegation and the Indian Ministry of Science and Technology (UN Climate Change Secretariat, 2011). Officially, FICCI sent its first delegation to the 2004 round of the UN climate negotiations. CII became a registered participant observer after 2005.

Despite limited international activity, Indian business associations have incorporated climate change into their domestic agendas. However, even at the national level, business associations such as FICCI and CII have not acted as policy advocates. Rather, their focus has been on information provision, particularly around carbon market opportunities. For example, CII's climate programme produced a CDM handbook for its members, organized a series of national and state government workshops to build awareness of CDM and related investment possibilities, and worked with individual companies and sectors to encourage GHG inventorying and reporting. CII has also provided information about corporate responses to climate change to the Indian government. It has been contracted by the Indian government to catalogue GHG mitigation activities in 23 industrial sectors for India's Second National Communication on Climate Change. Finally, CII has provided some policy input into the national CDM policy process, offering a business perspective on the structure of the host country approval process and on the organizational location of the Indian CDM Designated National Authority, the agency that reviews the sustainable development contributions of CDM projects.

A second type of business association active in domestic politics are sector associations, such as the Cement Manufacturers Association (CMA) or the Indian Sugar

260 *Pulver*

Mills Association (ISMA). Like CII and FICCI, such groups have played a key role in disseminating information about climate change and carbon markets to their memberships through seminars and sector publications. The groups also serve as sites for more direct lobbying of national government agencies. For example, Indian cement companies worked through the CMA to influence the particular provisions of the new national government policy focused on setting sector and firm-specific environmental performance benchmarks. Looking ahead, increased climate policy engagement by Indian firms and business associations is likely as climate change becomes a more prominent issue on the domestic political agenda. The CDP survey of Indian industry indicated that 68% of respondents favored active engagement with policy makers and regulators (CDP, 2010).

Corporate governance

A third framework for assessing corporate responses to climate change focuses on corporate climate governance and investigates the extent to which climate concerns are integrated into firm management and decision-making structures. According to Ceres, a US-based environmental investor network, best practices related to corporate climate governance include: constituting a board of directors' committee with oversight of corporate climate change programs; periodic board of directors' review of those programs; a clear articulation by the chief executive of a company's views on climate change; executive compensation linked to meeting corporate climate policy goals; the pursuit of opportunities to reduce emissions, minimize exposure to climate-related physical and regulatory risks, and maximize low-carbon initiatives; public disclosure of corporate climate liabilities and corporate climate response strategies; externally verified carbon emissions data; and setting emissions reduction targets (Cogan 2006: 3).

Industry surveys provide the most systematic data on corporate climate governance activities in India. In 2007, McKinsey & Company conducted a global survey of over 2,000 corporate executives, including 150 executives from Indian firms (Enkvist and Vanthournout, 2007). Of these, 63% ranked climate change as somewhat or very important to corporate strategy. The percentage of Indian executives slightly exceeded the global average of 60%. Separately, 40% of Indian executives responded that climate change is taken into consideration in overall corporate strategy. This is a higher percentage than for any other world region including Europe (37%), China (34%), the rest of Asia-Pacific (34%), Latin America (25%), and North America (21%) (Enkvist and Vanthournout, 2007). Other surveys corroborate these findings. The FE-EVI report also documented commitment to corporate climate governance among Indian firms. In over 50% of firms surveyed, climate change risks were handled at the CEO or head of business unit level (EVI and FE, 2008). In the CDP report, over 84% of respondents assigned senior-level committees to develop corporate climate strategies (CDP, 2010).

Drivers of corporate responses

The previous analysis of operational practices, corporate political activities, and governance structures reveals the range of corporate response to climate change by Indian firms. What have been the primary drivers of this response? The McKinsey & Company survey identified nine potential motivations for corporate action on climate

Corporate responses to climate change in India   261

change: Corporate reputation, customer request, media attention, senior executive initiative, regulation, investment opportunity, competitive pressure, employee value proposition, and physical threats to assets. For the entire group of respondents, corporate reputation, customer requests and media attention ranked as the top three factors motivating behaviour (Enkvist and Vanthournout, 2007). The FE-EVI report, which surveyed only Indian companies, generated similar results. Over 70% of respondents identified better reputation among customers as a benefit of climate change management. Other commonly identified benefits included new business opportunities (53%) and greater operational efficiency (49%) (EVI and FE, 2008). The CDP India report highlighted the monetary savings harnessed by those companies actively increasing energy efficiency and reducing GHG emissions (CDP, 2010).

Hultman et al.'s (in press) in-depth study of CDM investment in the Indian and Brazilian sugar and cement industries adds nuance to the survey data presented above. The study, based on interviews with over 150 firms, sought to understand the drivers of firm investments in low-carbon technologies. The study replicates the CDP survey finding that revenue matters. In addition, Pulver and Hultman's research also documents the importance of reputational drivers. Most importantly, however, their research reveals that for many Indian firms, GHG emissions reductions are an afterthought. They are the co-benefits of investments aimed at minimizing the burden of high energy costs and or at enhancing firm revenues through electricity sales.

The Indian sugar and cement industries offer an instructive example. Both industries have made significant contributions to GHG emissions reductions over the past five years. Sugar mills have contributed to GHG mitigation by investing in technology that allows them to generate renewable electricity for sale to the grid, off-setting fossil fuel sources of grid electricity. Likewise, cement mills have reduced CO_2 emissions directly by altering the process of cement manufacturing and indirectly by reducing the fossil fuel energy used in the production process. The above investments have been made by a significant number of plants in both the sugar and cement sectors, 15% and 40%, respectively. Interviewees report that the GHG emissions reductions related to such investments are a welcome added benefit, but that the drivers for such investment originate elsewhere. For sugar mills, the revenue stream from electricity sales justifies the investment in new boilers and turbines that are needed to increase the electricity that can be generated at a sugar mill. For cement plants, high energy costs drive energy efficiency investments and the use of non-fossil alternative fuels in the production process.

While investments that resulted in GHG emissions reductions were primarily motivated by other concerns, the climate change mitigation aspects of such investments did play a role in firm decision-making. Cement companies and sugar mills identified both financial and reputational benefits coming from the CDM (Figure 19.4). On the financial side, the added revenues from CDM credits, while insufficient to justify the underlying investment, did offset risks related to investing in more advanced technologies, fluctuations in alternative fuel supplies, and marketing costs. Expected reputational benefits took the form of enhanced access to export and domestic markets, fewer delays in government approval of new initiatives, and increased brand value.

Looking at individual country-sector pairs gives a more detailed view. While all sectors rated the importance of the CER revenue stream as 3.5 or greater on a scale of 1–5 (with 1 = not important and 5 = very important), India-sugar had a very high rating of 4.4, while Brazil-sugar only rated as 3.5. The cement sector in both countries

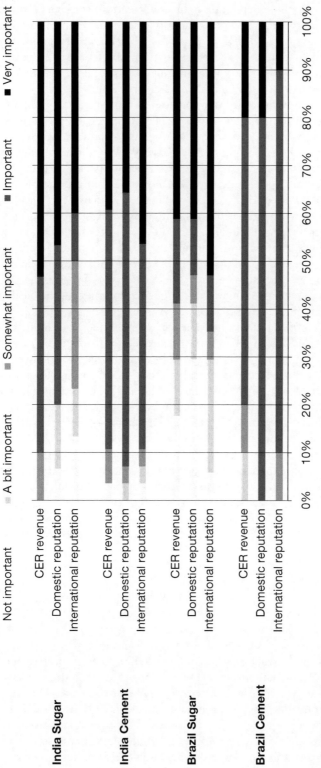

Figure 19.4 Financial and reputational drivers of corporate Clean Development Mechanism investment in the Indian and Brazilian sugar and cement industries

Corporate responses to climate change in India   263

was closer to 4, with a slightly greater weighting in India. These results may reflect the relative profitability of India-sugar relative to Brazil-sugar. Differences in the carbon intensity of grid electricity in Brazil and India mean that equivalent projects will earn significantly more CERs in India than in Brazil. Another interesting difference arose in the expected non-financial benefits to a firm's reputation: both domestically and internationally, cement firms provided evaluations of potential reputational benefits that were equal or higher to expected revenue benefits. These responses could reflect the more concentrated nature of the cement industry as compared to sugar, or possibly greater concern within the industry that its image was in need of burnishing. Alternatively, the brand image of cement may be much more important for cement sales, which tend to be directly to customers, than for sugar, where the product is usually sold to intermediaries (especially in India).

Conclusion

Most evaluations of the potential of developing-country firms as agents of environmental sustainability are pessimistic. Firms in emerging economies are often assumed to be environmental laggards, particularly in comparison with their industrialized country counterparts. It is argued that they are trapped in structures that dictate polluting practices as the only viable business model. This overview of corporate responses to climate change by Indian companies offers a different picture. Indian firms are largely aware of the climate challenge, and some have prioritized inventorying and reducing their GHG emissions, even in the absence of government regulation. However, rhetoric regarding climate-related business opportunities outpaces action in emerging economies, as it does in industrialized country settings. The firms mitigating their climate impacts constitute a small fraction of firms within the larger group that have not altered their business practices to minimize climate impacts. Moreover, among the corporations that have embraced action on climate change, climate-related activities remain a small component of the overall scope of business activities.

The primary drivers for corporate climate action in India are to be found outside the climate realm. GHG reductions often result as a co-benefit to investments in energy efficiency or renewable energy generation. The financial rewards of the latter motivate the investment, and GHG reductions are a welcome secondary benefit. While this pattern is problematic from the perspective of the current CDM architecture, it is promising from the broader perspective of addressing the climate challenge. A political economy that financially rewards GHG emissions reductions, even by indirect means, will be the most effective driver of change in corporate climate practices. That said, Indian firms also identified both direct financial and reputational benefits coming from proactive climate management.

Looking ahead, continued expansion of corporate action on climate change in India is likely. Several national government initiatives, such as trading in renewable energy certificates and trading based on performance benchmarks, will provide further financial incentives for corporations to tap into renewable energy sources and to improve operational efficiency. Such domestic, regulatory drivers of corporate action will dramatically expand the numbers of corporations reducing their GHGs. It is also likely that Indian corporations will become more active in both domestic and international policy arenas. As domestic regulation looms, corporations see the benefits of organizing a business voice and trying to shape the direction of domestic

264 Pulver

policy. Moreover, domestic regulation often motivates concerns about international competitiveness, which then spur international policy engagement.

Notes

1   The companies with voluntary GHG performance targets include ACC, Tata Steel, Mahindra & Mahindra, Ambuja Cements, ABB, Sterilite, Compton Greaves, Tata Consultancy Services and Wipro (CDP, 2010: 37).
2   The Clean Development Mechanism (CDM) is a policy framework created by the 1997 Kyoto Protocol. The CDM creates a structure by which GHG emissions reductions initiated in developing countries can be used by industrialized countries to meet the targets they agreed to under the Kyoto Protocol. The CDM is a project-based mechanism and UNEP/Risoe maintains an inventory of CDM projects initiated.
3   It is worth noting that the number of CDM projects initiated is not directly equivalent to the number of firms investing in GHG emissions reductions. For example, India is host to 61 projects in the cement sector. The projects involve activities at 51 individual cement production units, owned by 20 cement firms. The discrepancies arise because some firms initiate multiple projects at a single plant. Firms may also invest in carbon-friendly process innovations but not seek CDM credits and so would not be tracked in the CDM project database.
4   Many CDM projects produce emissions reductions over a multi-year period. CERs are projected to the year 2012 since this marks the end of the Kyoto Protocol's first commitment period.

References

CDP (2010) *Carbon Disclosure Project 2010 – India 200 Report,* British High Commission New Delhi, Confederation of Indian Industry-Centre for Excellence in Sustainable Development, and World Wide Fund for Nature, India, New Delhi, India.

Cogan, Douglas G. (2006) Corporate Governance and Climate Change: Making the Connection, Ceres, Boston, MA.

Dadhich, P. K. (1997) 'Cogeneration overview and potential', in *Cogeneration: Policies, Potential, and Technologies,* TERI, New Delhi.

Dechezlepretre, A., Glachant, M. and Meniere, Y. (2008) 'The Clean Development Mechanism and the International Diffusion of Technologies: An empiriical study', *Energy Policy,* vol. 36, no. 4, pp. 1273–1283.

Dechezlepretre, A., Glachant, M. and Meniere, Y. (2009) 'Technology Transfer by CDM Projects: A comparison of Brazil, China, India, and Mexico', *Energy Policy,* vol. 37, no. pp. 703–711.

EIA (2006) *World Carbon Intensity—World Carbon Dioxide Emissions from the Consumption and Flaring of Fossil Fuels per Thousand Dollars of Gross Domestic Product Using Purchasing Power Parities, 1980–2006,* Energy Information Administration, Washington DC.

Enkvist, P.-A. and Vanthournout, H. (2007) *How Companies Think About Climate Change,* McKinsey & Company.

EVI and FE (2008) *How Green is Your Business – FE-EVI Green Business Survey,* Emergent Ventures India and The Financial Express, New Delhi.

GOI (2004) *India's Initial National Communication to the United Nations Framework Convention on Climate Change,* Government of India, Ministry of Environment and Forests, New Delhi.

Hultman, N. E., Pulver, S., Guimaraes, L., Deshmukh, R. and Kane, J. (in press) 'Carbon Market Risks and Rewards: Firm perceptions of CDM investment decision in Brazil and India', *Energy Policy.*

Knox-Hayes, J. (2010) 'The Developing Carbon Financial Service Industry: Expertise, adaptation and complementarity in London and New York', *Journal of Economic Geography*, vol. 9, no 6, pp. 749–777.

Krey, M. (2005) 'Transaction costs of unilateral CDM projects in India – results from an empirical survey', *Energy Policy*, vol. 33, no. 18, pp. 2385–2397.

Leggett, J. (1999) *The Carbon War: Global Warming and the End of the Oil Era*, Penguin Books, London.

Lewis, J. (2007) 'Technology Acquisition and Innovation in the Developing World: Wind turbine development in China and India', *Studies in Comparative International Development*, vol. 42, no. 3/4, pp. 233–255.

Lutken, S. E. and Michaelowa, A. (2008) *Corporate Strategies and the Clean Development Mechanism*, Edward Elgar Publishing Ltd, Cheltenham, UK.

McKinsey & Company (2009) *Environmental and Energy Sustainability: An approach for India*, McKinsey & Company.

Perkins, R. (2007) 'Globalizing Corporate Environmentalism? Convergence and heterogeneity in Indian industry', *Studies in Comparative International Development*, vol. 42, no. 3/4, pp. 279–309.

Pulver, S. (2002) 'Organizing Business: Industry NGOs in the Climate Debates', *Greener Management International*, vol. 39, Autumn, pp. 55–67.

Purohit, P. and Michaelowa, A. (2007) 'CDM potential of bagasse cogeneration in India', *Energy Policy*, vol. 35, no. 10, pp. 4779–4798.

Schneider, M., Hoffmann, V. H. and Gurjar, B. R. (2009) 'Corporate Responses to the CDM: The Indian pulp and paper industry', *Climate Policy*, vol. 9, no. 3, pp. 255–272.

TERI (2005) *CDM Implementation in India: The National Strategy Study*, TERI (The Energy and Resources Institute), New Delhi.

Tucker, M. (1997) 'Climate change and the insurance industry: The cost of increased risk and the impetus for action', *Ecological Economics*, vol. 22, no. pp. 85–96.

UN Climate Change Secretariat (2011) '*Meetings Archive*', http://unfccc.int/meetings/archive/items/2749.php, accessed 5 February 2011.

UNEP/Risoe (2011) '*UNEP Risoe CDM/JI Pipeline Analysis and Database*', http://cdmpipeline.org/, accessed 5 February 2011.

20 A change in climate?

Trends in climate change reportage in the Indian print media

Anu Jogesh

Introduction

> Climate change is a notoriously difficult subject for journalists to report on, for editors to maintain interest in, and for audiences to grasp. (Painter, 2010: 3)

One morning in 2007, in a conference room packed with producers, reporters and department heads of a 24-hour news channel, I recall an exasperated senior editor challenging anyone to bring him 'three people' outside that room who knew anything more about climate change than the fact that it produced some sort of warming. The big news story in question, jostling with politics, sports and business developments, was the release of the final working group report by the Intergovernmental Panel on Climate Change (IPCC). The editor implied that most Indians, save a small minority, were neither interested in nor informed about the nuances of climate science and its governing politics. Its coverage therefore, could be 'cut down to size'.

Fast forward to 2009: Even a cursory glance at the extent of reportage on climate change both in the Indian print and television media reveals that a lot has changed since. If one were to follow the reasoning that the media coverage of the environment is heavily reliant on events and policy developments, then 2009 and early 2010 were significant for the climate cause (Olausson, 2009; Boykoff and Boykoff, 2007). The conference at Copenhagen was the big geo-political event that buoyed international climate coverage to new heights, but there were several other important developments (Boykoff, 2010; Painter, 2010) (see Figure 20.1). In November 2009 the very basis of climate science was questioned by the leak of e-mails belonging to scientists at the University of East Anglia (UEA). This was followed by the discovery of errors in the IPCC's Fourth Assessment Report in early 2010 pertaining to the extent of disappearance of the Himalayan glaciers. 2009 also saw the rise of emerging economies in the climate debate (Roberts, 2011; Aiyar, 2009b). Brazil, South Africa, China and India (BASIC), along with the US played a central part in devising the Copenhagen Accord in what is now regarded by many as a significant dilution of the UN-led multilateral process (Raghunandan, 2010). Providing further fodder for news, Jairam Ramesh as the new Minister of State for Environment and Forests seemingly disrupted the established order among Indian negotiators leading to reams of Indian newsprint being spent on domestic climate politics (Chauhan, 2009; Joy, 2009). With so many events unfolding in the scientific and geo-political arena, it is worth investigating how they were picked up and reflected in the Indian press. One needs to also examine if

Trends in reportage in Indian print media   267

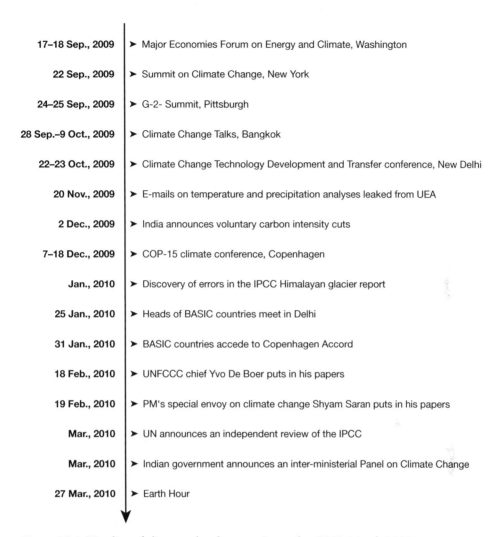

Figure 20.1 Timeline of climate-related events, September 2009–March 2010

narrative frames identified in previous studies on climate change and the Indian media still apply (Boykoff, 2010).

Climate change and the Indian print media

Much has been written about media representations of climate change in the western press, especially pertaining to countries like Sweden, the US and the UK (Antilla, 2005; Olausson, 2009; Carvahalo, 2007; Boykoff, 2007), however the study of the Indian media's coverage of climate change is still nascent. While there have been papers examining science and technology as well as general environmental reportage in the Indian newspapers (Dutt et al., 2008; Sekar, 1981), only three studies known to the author look at climate change in the Indian news context (Dutt et al., 2008; Billet,

268   *Jogesh*

2009; Boykoff, 2010). The paper by Billet (2009) examines climate news coverage in four Indian national dailies between 2002 and 2007 and states that the narrative of climate change in the Indian print media falls along a 'risk-responsibility divide'. He argues that the stand taken on climate change is strongly nationalistic and 'divides the issue along both developmental and postcolonial lines' (2009: 1). Billet states that while climatic risks are perceived as an Indian problem, the onus for action is almost unanimously placed on advanced countries. Boykoff's research, titled 'Indian media representations of climate change in a threatened journalistic ecosystem' (2010: 17), delineates the sharp rise in climate news coverage globally as well as in India during the Copenhagen summit despite media houses globally facing economic pressures and cutting down on specialized news resources (see Figure 20.2). The article acknowledges that the global political landscape had changed since the Billet chapter was published and that it would be interesting to study how narratives of climate action and responsibility are now being reflected in the Indian press.

Methodology

This study is therefore a temporal analysis of media coverage of climate change across nine national circulation[1] and business dailies between September 2009 and March 2010, namely: *The Times of India, Hindustan Times, The Indian Express, The Hindu, The Economic Times, Mint, Financial Express, The Hindu Business Line* and *Business Standard*. These newspapers have an Average Issue Readership between 7.1 million readers for *The Times of India* to 1.2 million readers for *The Hindu Business Line* according to the 2010 Indian Readership Survey (Angel Broking, 2010).

All of the papers used for this study are English language newspapers, which cater to the English speaking elite and middle classes. As such they are regarded as prime shapers of policy (Viswanath and Karan, 2000 cited in Sonwalkar, 2002). However, it is worth noting that Indian language newspapers still surpass the Indian English dailies in terms of absolute readership (Bunsha, 2002) and there are further local language newspapers with wide circulation, all of which are influential in shaping broad public perceptions. Consequently, it is important to keep in mind that this study focuses on a limited, if influential, slice of the media.

The period chosen for the analysis falls three months prior to the climate summit in Copenhagen in December and three months subsequent to it. Business dailies are included in the study because the frequency of their climate coverage during this period matched that of the mainstream print media thereby offering a more comprehensive picture of climate reportage by the Indian press. The study involved an online archival search and the newspapers were scanned for articles using the keywords 'climate change', 'global warming', 'greenhouse gas emissions', 'IPCC' and 'Copenhagen'. The study encompassed news reports, editorials as well as guest columns but did not include advertorials or letters to the editor. Following the approach of a media discourse analysis, the resultant sample was quantitatively and qualitatively analysed for narratives along pre-selected themes by devising a series of codes (Wodak and Meyer, 2009).

One of the overarching themes of the study is the frequency and distribution of the nature of the news content in the Indian press. Reports were coded and categorized into five areas: 'Climate science' and its impacts, 'Global politics and policies', 'Indian politics and policies', 'Business news', and climate-related 'Trends'. Under the umbrella

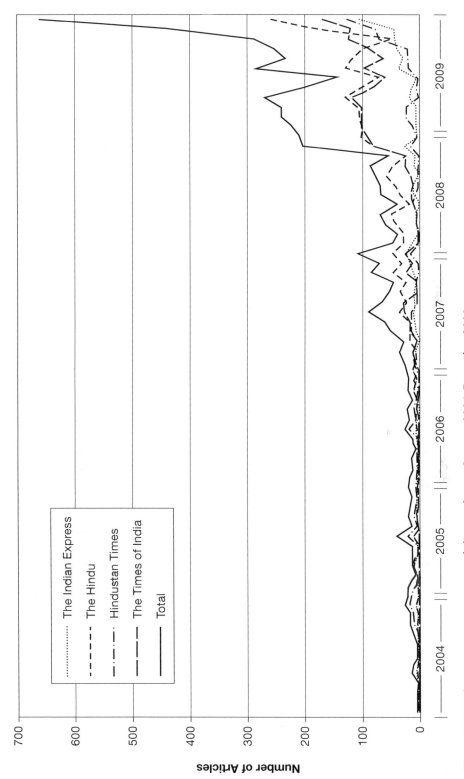

Figure 20.2 Indian newspaper coverage of climate change, January 2004–December 2009

Source: Boykoff, 2010

270 Jogesh

theme of science and impacts, articles were coded based on their narratives on the existence or denial of man-made climate change. The theme acquires added pertinence during this period in the face of climate controversies involving UEA's leaked e-mails and the IPCC report on Himalayan glaciers. The study therefore examined the treatment of these two incidents and also considered perceptions built in the media about IPCC and its chief R.K. Pachauri as an outcome. Additionally, the frequency and geographical distribution of climate risks and impacts was also analysed.

In global climate politics, one of the fundamental points of contention remains the allocation of responsibility of greenhouse gas emissions and the division of action among nations. The study therefore evaluates articles for narratives on climate responsibility and action. In the run-up to the conference and after, much noise was created in India over Jairam Ramesh's apparent break in protocol during the negotiations and what finally was negotiated (Parsai, 2009). A quantitative evaluation of the number of articles that dealt with domestic climate politics versus domestic policies was also carried out.

Olausson argues in her paper that 'Globalization notwithstanding, national media are still dominated by a national logic in the presentation of news' (2009: 421). With India effecting a shift in its negotiating position however, rifts were created internally among civil society, polity and the media about what was best for the country (Dasgupta, 2009). The study evaluates if there is a perceivable dichotomy in newspapers' reactions to India's altered stance. Codes were finally devised to gain a quantitative representation of the type of talking heads that were quoted in the news articles. The stories were also categorized either as in-house reports, agency wires, opinion pieces or internationally sourced articles.

Frequency of climate news coverage

The online archival search of nine Indian newspapers between September 2009 and March 2010 registered a total of 1,938 articles. The temporal distribution of the sample collected closely corresponds to the events and incidents that unfolded during the chosen period (Olausson, 2009; Boykoff and Boykoff, 2007). They are perhaps also reflective of the importance accorded to them by the Indian media. For instance in the month of December alone when the Copenhagen summit took place, the selected dailies carried 40 per cent of the reports, higher than the combined total present across the three months leading up to the conference. The graph reveals a steady rise in the frequency of reportage leading up to Copenhagen, followed by a sharp jump in December (see Figure 20.3). This was followed by a steady decline in January and February 2010, with a minor jump in articles in March. After the conference ended in December, a *Hindu Business Line* editorial stated: 'Climate change will retreat to where it belongs, namely, somewhere near the bottom of the national agenda' (*The Hindu Business Line*, 2009).

The frequency graph reveals that this has not been the case. The 'climate news fatigue' that one expected after the build-up and hype of a mega conference like Copenhagen was relatively short-lived. While the absolute number of articles declined between January and March 2010, events like the BASIC countries' meet in Delhi and the impending pressure on India to accede to the Copenhagen accord continued to ensure adequate column space to climate news. A major bulk of the news stories in March also pertain to the controversy generated over errors in the IPCC's Fourth Assessment Report and its impact on Pachauri's position as the IPCC chief.

Trends in reportage in Indian print media 271

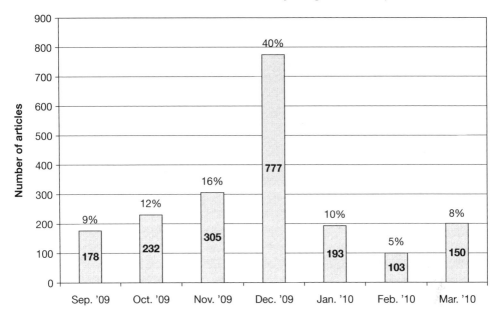

Figure 20.3 Frequency of climate news coverage across nine newspapers, September 2009–March 2010

Nature of news content

In terms of frequency and distribution of the overarching nature of the content pertaining to climate change, global politics and policies seemed to dominate the news space over the chosen period with 1,111 articles or 57 per cent of the news sample falling under this category. This included India's role in international global politics (see Figure 20.4). Apart from the much-anticipated conference at Copenhagen, a look at the timeline of events reveals a proliferation of other politically driven developments during this seven-month period (see Figure 20.1). In fact several articles pertaining to the leaked e-mails at UEA as well as the glacier errors were categorized under global politics and not science, as they dealt less with the science of climate change and more with the politics of recrimination and retaliation over the mistakes made (Sinha, 2010; Adam, 2010; *The Indian Express*, 2010).

Indian politics and policies formed the next highest category comprising 21 per cent of all news stories. This included articles about domestic policies such as research tie-ups and financial outlays under the National Action Plan on Climate Change as well as the launch of the National Solar mission. It also comprised news reports that detailed domestic climate politics. For instance negotiators in December threatened to pull out of the Copenhagen conference claiming that they had not been adequately briefed. Members of the Prime Minister's council on Climate Change as well as opposition parties also criticized policy moves by Jairam Ramesh terming India's announcement of carbon intensity cuts and annual reporting of its domestic actions to UNFCCC a 'sell-out' to the US (*The Hindu*, 2009; TNN, 2009).

Science-based news came third including 10 per cent of the total reportage in the sample ahead of business reportage, which registered just 5 per cent of the news content. This despite the fact that the study included news coverage across five financial

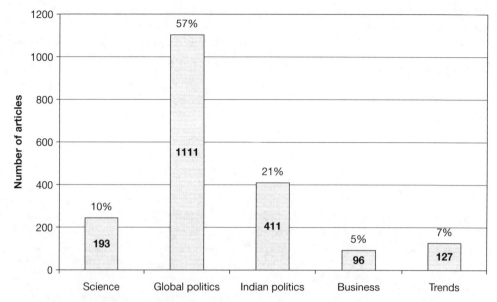

Figure 20.4 Distribution of content across nine newspapers, September 2009–March 2010

dailies. The frequency of business news was relatively lower perhaps because business papers too chose to direct their focus on the political side of the climate debate in the run-up to Copenhagen. This may also explain why climate-related business stories – essentially corporate dealings in carbon markets and company investments in green energy technology – doubled in number between January and March 2010 compared to September and November 2009.

Science of climate change

An international print media evaluation on the frequency of science reportage during the Copenhagen summit reveals that politics trumped science coverage globally (Painter, 2010). News content in the Indian press – as stated earlier – was no different, with just 10 per cent of the articles predominantly dealing with the science and impacts of climate change (see Figure 20.4). But if one were to focus specifically on climate-related impacts, then several articles tabled under international and Indian politics also drew upon this theme, sometimes just in passing, and often to highlight the urgency of achieving a meaningful outcome at Copenhagen. For instance an opinion piece in *The Financial Express* while making a case for India to adopt stringent energy efficiency measures states, 'Over 400 million people living in the Indo-Gangetic Plain will be affected (by climate change). It will affect the country's food production and self-reliance in the area, as a result of no water availability for irrigation, as well as shortage of drinking water' (Meattle, 2009).

The study finds that 310 articles reflected the risks and impacts of climate change.[2] An evaluation of the geographical distribution[3] of climate-related impacts in the Indian newspapers however reveals that reports were not just about climate change as a setback for India but for other developing as well as advanced nations (see Figure 20.5). This is an important deviation from the Billet paper (2009), which concludes that climate impacts were predominantly regarded as an indigenous problem by the Indian print media between 2002 and 2007. Studies for instance predicting the re-occurrence of dust bowl-like conditions in the US, or droughts in Australia, not to mention disappearing ice-shelves in the Arctic and Antarctic seem to reinforce the point that this is a phenomenon with global consequences. Many of these were sourced from international wire reports. For instance an Associated Press report in *The Times of India* quotes weather experts in the US: 'West Coast storms could get more frequent and severe with climate change' (*The Times of India*, AP 2010). However only 48 reports in the sample are based on local anecdotal instances or experiences, and a few of them are not Indian.

The period selected for this study between September 2009 and March 2010 also saw the science of climate change being questioned because of errors in the time-line predicted for the disappearance of Himalayan glaciers as well as the leaked UEA e-mails. Some sections of the media also highlighted other errors in the IPCC report such as the rate of decline of Amazonian forests. In November the Ministry of Environment and Forests (MOEF) released a paper by Indian glaciologist VK Raina stating that the rate of decline of some Himalayan glaciers was not as dramatic as predicted in the IPCC.

These events together resulted in a deluge of reports that the media projected as climate controversies. As many as 85 articles covered the IPCC's misreporting of the Himalayan glacier disappearance (80 of which were critical in their tone), compared to 42 that were critical of 'climate gate' as the UEA e-mail debacle came to be called (see Figure 20.6). The former incident clearly garnered higher interest in India because of the geographical proximity of its perceived impacts.

It is worth noting that as a fallout of these incidents, 69 articles were critical of the IPCC though as many as 42 pieces defended the institution (11 were neutral in their

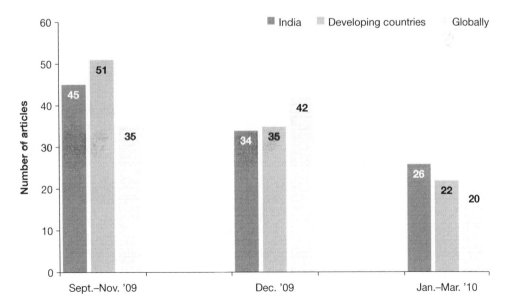

Figure 20.5 Frequency and geographical distribution of the coverage of climate impacts. Distribution of impacts across nine newspapers, September 2009–March 2010

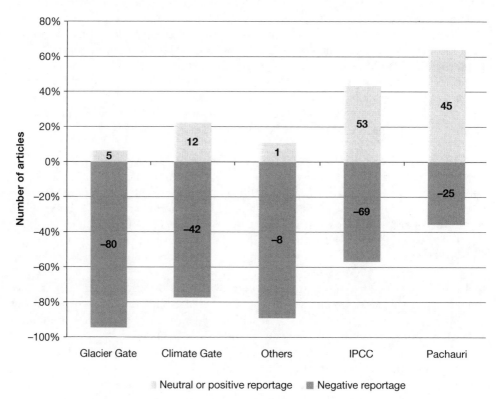

Figure 20.6 Media coverage of climate controversies. Distribution of coverage across nine newspapers, September 2009–March 2010

stance). RK Pachauri took some flak as well, with 25 articles criticizing his stewardship of the IPCC and demanding his resignation. Forty-five articles however, gave Pachauri and others, space to defend the former's position and counter those allegations. An opinion piece in *The Hindustan Times* for instance, comes to the defence of Pachauri and the IPCC stating: 'it does appear that vested interests – using British media – are seeking to discredit the IPCC' (D'Monte, 2010).

As a result of the climate 'controversies', the science of climate change came sharply into question in the western media (Bondre, 2010). However, it has been pointed out that unlike the international media the extent of climate scepticism in the Indian media has been virtually non-existent (Billet, 2009; Painter, 2010). And the study reveals the period between 2009 and 2010 was no different. The press seems to have largely accepted the veracity of anthropogenic climate change and progressed directly to the politics surrounding this scientific phenomenon. As many as 65 Indian and 10 international articles[4] attested to the existence and veracity of man-made climate change and only 10 articles questioned climate science; five of these were internationally sourced. However this does not mean that sceptics or their ideas were not given column space in the Indian press. As many as 32 articles either directly quoted or talked about climate sceptics and their ideas, but the overall tilt of these pieces lay firmly in favour of attributing climate change as a man-made phenomenon.

Politics of climate change

Domestic policies versus politics

As the above title suggests there were several articles in the study that touched upon the twin themes of domestic policies and politics.[5] Domestic policies essentially pertained to India's plans and actions involving mitigation, adaptation, research, and funding. For instance a *Business Standard* piece quotes Jairam Ramesh stating that, 'The Planning Commission will soon announce the constitution of an expert group to look at low-carbon growth strategies, called the National Network for Climate Assessment (INCCA)' (Suneja and Jain, 2010).

Domestic politics on the other hand revolved around the political machinations of politicians, bureaucrats, and other individuals linked to India's climate politics. The latter provided much fodder for news with opposition parties openly criticizing India's policies, and the growing discontent among climate negotiators and the environment minister. For instance a *Times of India* article in December alludes to two Indian negotiators threatening to pull out of Copenhagen talks because, 'they feared that the baseline of India's stand was being changed in the name of flexibility'. The article also states that they 'drew dark red lines by publicly confirming that they had differences (with Jairam Ramesh)' (TNN, 2009).

Also in January 2009, a *Hindustan Times* article talks about Shyam Saran resigning from his position as the Prime Minister's Special Envoy on Climate Change and quotes Jairam Ramesh stating that, 'There was a difference in style and perception (between Saran and Ramesh) . . . I am not a rubber stamp to the bureaucracy' (HT, 2009).

It is worth noting that the extent of column space devoted to such domestic political wrangling is significant, with the number of articles presenting domestic politics (281) being marginally lower in number to those that detailed domestic climate action (308) (see Figure 20.7).

India's new role in global climate politics

'It is a fact that in per capita terms, population growth in the US and EU contributes more towards addition of greenhouse gases than in countries in Africa and South Asia. Yet, with every passing day, the pressure on India to agree to binding cuts only increases.'

(*Mint* editorial, 2009)

'rice growers have been putting methane into the atmosphere for thousands of years, whereas the western countries have been putting carbon dioxide into the air for barely 250 years.'

(Aiyar, 2009)

Research and perspectives pinning responsibility for climate change, and thereby advocating equity and burden-sharing in terms of mitigating measures invite strong rhetoric among policy makers and the public. This study sought to make a distinction between narratives[6] in the Indian media that highlight which nations or blocs are primarily responsible for greenhouse gas emissions and those who should take measures to curb it, since the two are not necessarily interrelated. For instance there are many articles in which industrialized nations admit to being historically responsible but feel the burden of action needs to been divided among developing nations according to their

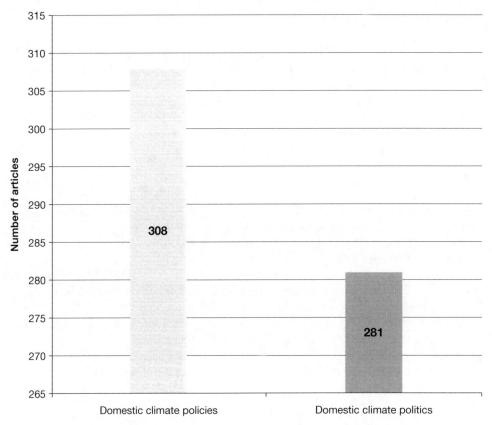

Figure 20.7 Domestic climate policies versus domestic climate politics. Distribution of coverage across nine newspapers, September 2009–March 2010

respective capabilities, or those who state that emerging economies are catching up in their emissions but should not be coerced into committing binding targets.

In terms of newspapers tackling the issue of allocating responsibility for climate change, five broad arguments were identified for which codes[7] were devised; 'industrialized nations are historically responsible', 'emerging nations are catching up in emissions', 'US is the number one emitter', 'China is the number one emitter', 'US and China are the top two emitters'. This sample was also divided between Indian and internationally sourced articles.

The study reveals that the highest count of articles (83) speak of industrialized countries as being historically responsible. Of these 10 are internationally sourced reports and 37 are opinion pieces (see Figure 20.8). It is not just Indian climate commentators who make this argument but blocs like the European Union as well as individuals in the US have been quoted in the Indian media stating the same. For instance a Hindu article refers to US Secretary of Energy Steven Chu and says, 'While conceding that it was the developed world which had put most of the carbon into the atmosphere, he stressed the need for all countries to realise that 'we are all in this together' (Joshua, 2009).

The next big category (with 69 reports) is that of articles that present the view that emerging economies are catching up in their emissions. Of these only 7 are inter-

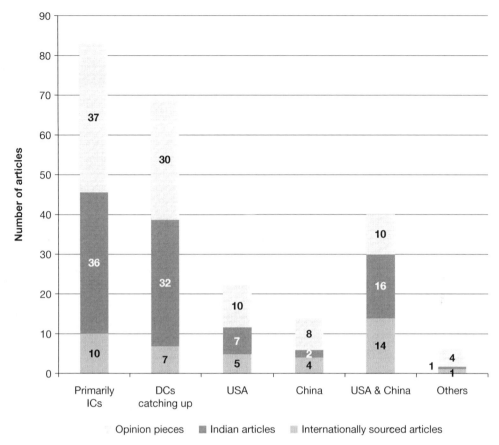

Figure 20.8 Narratives pertaining to responsibility for climate change impacts

ICs = Industrialized countries; DCs = Developing countries

nationally sourced, and 30 reports are opinion pieces (see Figure 20.8). Several Indian commentators – climate experts, guests and in-house columnists – in the sample argue that emerging economy emissions can no longer be ignored. For instance a guest columnist in *The Hindu Business Line* states that greenhouse gas emissions 'flows are contributed by both the developed and developing countries, particularly the fast industrialising ones . . . Hence, all countries should share the burden of compulsory mitigation' (Krishnan, 2009).

In fact Indian environment minister Jairam Ramesh also went on record to differentiate between the stock and flow of emissions into the atmosphere, and how India was unequivocally adding to the latter (Jebraj, 2010). Moreover the third largest count of articles (40) belong to narratives pinning the blame on the US and China together causing the lion's share of the climate problem. A Reuters report in *Business Standard* for instance calls the US and China: 'the world's top two emitters of greenhouse gases' (*Business Standard*, Reuters, 2009).

Only 14 of these articles are internationally sourced, the rest are driven by Indian reporters, columnists and agency wires. Many of these reports base their assumptions on studies over the last five years that argue that China has overtaken the US in terms

278   *Jogesh*

of absolute emissions (Zhang, 2010). What this indicates is that at least in terms of placing responsibility for climate change, the North–South divide that Billet (2009) promulgates has been somewhat diluted. There are also 22 articles that just blame the US as the single largest emitter and 14 that hold China responsible. Some of these articles also belong to climate commentators who were wary of India backing China during the Copenhagen summit since they believe that China is the bigger climate culprit. For instance a *Business Standard* piece calls the government's move to throw 'India's lot with China' at Copenhagen a 'dubious' strategy as: 'the two countries have a large gulf when it comes to both their per capita as well as aggregate levels of carbon emissions. China emits four and half times more CO_2 than India on a per capita basis and their development needs are also vastly different' (Aiyar, 2009).

As stated earlier, these changes have been driven by a broadening of the debate as well as shifts in the Indian political landscape. For instance in the sample of articles evaluated, Jairam Ramesh was quoted on a few occasions saying that the per capita approach was no longer tenable in India's negotiating debate especially if India wanted to be a 'deal-maker' during the climate conference (Jebraj, 2010). This meant that India made significant shifts in its negotiating position in the run-up to Copenhagen, most notably, taking on voluntary carbon intensity cuts and agreeing to international consultation and analysis of its unsupported mitigation actions. As a result the study devised four broad codes based on narratives in the Indian media pertaining to climate action; 'Industrialized nations need to take action', 'industrialized countries make deep emissions cuts and developing countries take on supported actions', 'emerging countries should do more', and 'emerging countries take on carbon intensity reductions'.

The results reveal that the highest number of articles (188) mention that industrialized nations need to take on most of the climate-related action with developing countries only agreeing to commitments that are supported by finance and technology from the developed world. This essentially follows the principle of common but differentiated responsibilities (CBDR) as laid out under the United Nations Framework Convention on Climate Change (UNFCCC) and the commentary in some of these pieces often just referred to CBDR without elaborating. What is noteworthy however is that as many as 94 pieces stated that emerging economies, including India, need to do more. Of these, 33 reports were in fact opinion pieces and only 8 were internationally sourced (see Figure 20.9). Moreover, 70 reports talked about emerging countries taking on carbon intensity cuts. Several newspapers during this period printed views and quotes of Indian climate commentators who argued as to why it was crucial for India to move away from its stated position and take on unsupported commitments to varying degrees (Krishnan 2009). Only 44 articles stated that industrialized nations need to make deep emission cuts. This low figure could be attributed to the fact that the largest category already calls for industrialized countries to take on binding emission reductions with developing countries agreeing to supported actions.

What is evident from the analysis of articles that touch upon climate change impacts as well as those that refer to action on climate change is that the 'risk responsibility divide' that Billet (2009: 1) talks about isn't always evident. Indian newspapers seem to be discussing climate risks that not just threaten India but the rest of the global landscape (see Figure 20.5). They also seem to present the view that India take on some form of responsibility for climate action, while still insisting that industrialized economies undertake more stringent commitments. As stated earlier this is because the scope of the debate seems to have widened as well as the ambit of speakers. It is no

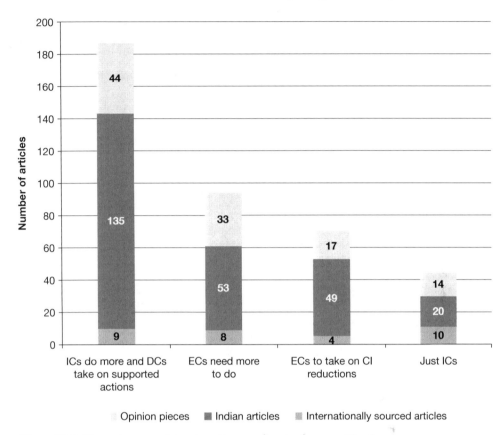

Figure 20.9 Narratives pertaining to action on climate change mitigation

ICs = Industrialized countries; **DCs** = Developing countries; **CI** = Carbon Intensity; **ECs** = Emerging countries

longer just NGOs or research organizations like The Energy Research Institute and Centre for Science and Environment driving the debate (Billet 2009), but a host of economists, academics, scientists, former diplomats and dedicated in-house reporters opining on the economics and ethics of the climate issue. It is perhaps worth noting that many of these individuals have not been long-standing commentators in the Indian climate debate. For instance an opinion piece in the *Economic Times* by Chandanathil P. Geevan, a scientist, argues that, 'Willingness to adopt binding commitments will help countries like India to bargain for economic opportunities that can ameliorate poverty and sustain the current high growth rates with significantly lower emission intensity' (Geevan, 2009). In addition, a *Hindustan Times* article quotes economist Kirit Parikh stating that there is 'no point in sticking to the idea that there should be no emission cuts for developing nations' (Chauhan and Halarnkar, 2009).

One of the aspects of this study has been to code and categorize the source of news reports in the sample. While an overwhelming 54 per cent of 1,938 articles carried a byline of an in-house reporter, columns and opinion pieces at 21 per cent formed the second largest category. They were larger in number than wire reports. One such guest editorial in *Mint* by the head of Morgan Stanley in India in December states:

280 Jogesh

All the arcane talk about greenhouse gases (GHG), melting glaciers, percentage cuts and relative fairness is lost on the average Indian. I would be willing to wager a tidy sum that most people have paid little attention to the issues, alternatives and magnitudes (indeed even the unit of measurement) related to environmental sustainability—leave alone have an informed view on the trade-offs.

(*Mint*, 2009)

Whether that is a precise observation is open to question. But running contrary to that belief, many of the guest writers and columnists offered content that was more often than not, heavily nuanced and sometimes numerically heavy or technical in nature in both the national and business dailies (Ganesan, 2009). In fact some of their views were also at odds with the stand adopted by some of the in-house reporters of those newspapers. For instance an *Economic Times* (*ET*) opinion piece by one of its editors, TK Arun, suggests that India 'accept a binding target for emission intensity' (Arun, 2009). This is at odds with an *ET* article by reporter Urmi Goswami which states that if India took on added commitments, it could undermine its position in subsequent negotiations (Goswami, 2009).

This brings us to the question of whether the Indian media, as stated in the Billet paper, is overtly nationalistic in its standpoint. Fernandes (2000) has spoken of how global issues in the Indian media are increasingly being tackled through 'nationalistic narratives' and more recently Olausson speaks of 'national logic' in the presentation of news despite the transnational character of environmental risks (2009). As the above examples however illustrate, the print media during the selected period provided room for varied opinions in the climate debate. The nationalistic narrative, though present in sizable numbers is by no means the only position being taken by reporters and climate commentators. There are equally vocal counter-arguments being reflected in the Indian press. In fact an analysis of all in-house reports and columnists that explicitly supported the various shifts in the government's negotiating stance – announcing carbon intensity reductions as well as agreeing to an annual reportage of its unsupported climate actions – versus those that were critical of it, reveals that while 27 articles openly advocated the government's position, as many as 55 opposed it (see Figure 20.10). And these were the personal viewpoints of reporters and columnists indicating that the nationalistic standpoint, or idea of what is right for India seems divided at this point.

Conclusion

This study finds that there has been a moderate shift in the climate of the overall debate pertaining to climate change in the Indian press. Narratives on the politics of climate change specifically with regard to responsibility and action are not always polarized along North–South lines. While the largest number of articles in the sample blamed industrialized nations as the historical polluters, a sizable number stated that emerging countries were catching up in emissions, followed by those who blamed the USA and China together. On the subject of climate action, while most of the articles called for deep cuts from industrialized countries and supported actions for developing nations, a notable number also stated that emerging economies needed to do more.

In terms of climate-related risks and impacts, the Indian print media presented a rather varied geographical division of the risks, indicating that the discourse does not always veer towards presenting India as the singular victim at the receiving end of runaway climate change. An examination of the division of articles based on their

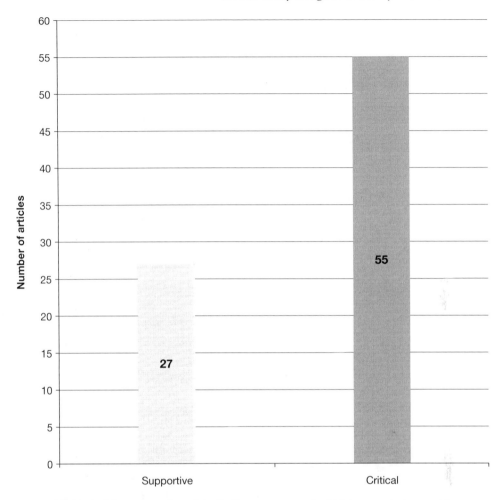

Figure 20.10 Articles supportive of the Indian government's shift in negotiating position on climate action versus articles critical of the government's negotiating stance

source indicates that while in-house reports are the largest in number, columnists represent the second most frequent source of news content. This is perhaps indicative of the fact that there is a greater mix of climate commentators – not all of whom have been associated with the topic in the past – appearing in the Indian print media today, presenting both varied and nuanced narratives on the climate debate.

Notes

1 The English dailies selected publish several editions, and have a pan-India presence to varying degrees. But none of them has a circulation that extends to all parts of the country. (Registrar of Newspapers for India, 2008.)
2 Articles that merely suggested catastrophic outcomes or temperature increases without mentioning any specific impacts were not counted.
3 Some articles were coded in more than one category. For instance if a report detailed regional climatic impacts as well as impacts specific to India, it was coded under India and Developing countries.

282 Jogesh

4   International articles pertain to both international agency wires (for e.g. Associated Press or Xinhua), as well as pieces sourced from the international press such as a *Guardian* report in *The Hindu*.
5   While 411 articles were coded as predominantly dealing with domestic policies and politics, a larger number of reports touched upon or made a mention of these themes.
6   The narratives essentially pertain to the overarching tilt of the article either as a result of what was predominantly quoted in the piece or the direct views of the reporter or columnist.
7   Some articles were coded across more than one category. For instance if a report quoted some individuals stating that industrialized nations were historically responsible and others in the same story argued that developing countries were catching up in their emissions, but the newspaper did not take a stand, then it was coded under both the categories.

References

Adam, D., 2010. Himalayan glacier report 'rigorous', says Martin Parry. *The Hindu* (Sourced from the *Guardian* report) [online] 18 February. Available at: http://www.hindu.com/seta/2010/02/18/stories/2010021850011500.htm [Accessed 15 March 2011].

Aiyar, P., 2009a. Hindi-Chini camaraderie at Copenhagen. *Business Standard*, [online] 18 December. Available at: http://www.business-standard.com/india/news/hindi-chini-camaraderie-at-copenhagen/379947/ [Accessed 10 May 2011].

Aiyar, P., 2009b. UN Climate meet showed the old North-South divide outdated. *Business Standard*, [online] 21 December. Available at: http://www.business-standard.com/india/news/un-climate-meet-showedold-north-south-divide-outdated/380211/ [Accessed 5 May 2011].

Aiyar, S. S. A., 2009. Carbon cuts: Penalty or insurance? *The Economic Times*, [online] 9 December. Available at: http://articles.economictimes.indiatimes.com/2009-12-09/news/28455859_1_global-warming-carbon-dioxide-climate-catastrophe/3 [Accessed 10 May 2011].

Anderson, A., 2009. Media, Politics and Climate Change: Towards a New Research Agenda. *Sociology Compass*. 3(2), pp. 166–182.

Angel Broking, 2010. Print sector update, IRS 2Q2010 analysis, [online], 13 September. Available at: http://www.scribd.com/doc/43954672/IRS-2Q2010-Analysis-Print-Media [Accessed 15 March 2011].

Antilla, L., 2005. Climate of scepticism: US newspaper coverage of the science of climate change. *Global Environmental Change*. 15(4), pp. 338–352.

Arun, T. K., 2009. For a binding climate target. *The Economic Times*, [online] 4 December. Available at: http://economictimes.indiatimes.com/articleshow/5298331.cms [Accessed 10 May 2011].

Bharvi, A. and Garg, K. C., 2000. An overview of science and technology coverage in Indian English-language dailies. *Public Understanding of Science*. 9(2), pp. 123–140.

Billet, S., 2009. Dividing climate change: global warming in the Indian mass media. *Climatic Change*. 99(1–2), pp.1–16.

Bondre, N., 2010. Whence climate scepticism?. *The Global Change NewsLetter*, [online]. Available at: http://www.igbp.net/documents/NL75_scepticism.pdf [Accessed 10 May, 2011].

Boykoff, M. T., 2007. Flogging a Dead Norm? Newspaper Coverage of Anthropogenic Climate Change in the USA and UK from 2003–2006. *Area*. (39), pp. 470–481.

Boykoff, M., 2010. Indian media representations of climate change in a threatened journalistic ecosystem. *Climatic Change*. 99, pp. 17–25.

Boykoff, M. T. and Boykoff, J. M., 2007. Climate Change and Journalistic Norms: A Case Study of US Mass-Media Coverage. *Geoforum*. (38), pp. 1190–1204.

Bunsha, D., 2002. The rise of print. *Front Line*, [online] 6 July. Available at: http://www.hinduonnet.com/fline/fl1914/19140810.htm [Accessed 29 May 2011].

Carvalho, A., 2007. Ideological Cultures and Media Discourses on Scientific Knowledge: Re-reading News on Climate Change. *Public Understanding of Science*. (16), pp. 223–243.

Chauhan, C., 2009. Manmohan agrees to attend climate summit. *Hindustan Times*, [online] 6

Trends in reportage in Indian print media 283

December. Available at: http://epaper.hindustantimes.com/ArticleText.aspx?article=06_12_2009_003_009&kword=&mode=1 [Accessed 1 May 2011].

Chauhan, C., 2009. Manmohan agrees to attend climate summit. *Hindustan Times*, [online] 6 December. Available at: http://epaper.hindustantimes.com/ArticleText.aspx?article=06_12_2009_003_009&kword=&mode=1 [Accessed 1 May 2011].

Chauhan, C. and Halarnkar, S., 2009. India cuts differences, won't cut emissions. *Hindustan Times*, [online] 13 December. Available at: http://www.hindustantimes.com/special-news-report/rssfeed/India-cuts-differences-won-t-cut-emissions/Article1-486146.aspx [Accessed 8 May 2011].

Chauhan, C., 2009. Jairam admits climate shift. *Hindustan Times*, [online] 23 December. Available at: http://epaper.hindustantimes.com/ArticleText.aspx?article=23_12_2009_001_012&kword=&mode=1 [Accessed 18 May 2011].

Dasgupta, S., 2009. Climate talk: India needs to be fearless. *The Hindu*, [online] 20 December. Available at: http://blogs.timesofindia.indiatimes.com/right-and-wrong/entry/climate-talk-india-needs-to [Accessed 6 May 2011].

D'Monte, D., 2010. Tragedy of errors. *Hindustan Times*, [online] 27 January. Available at: http://www.hindustantimes.com/Tragedy-of-errors/Article1-502386.aspx [Accessed 1 March 2011].

Dutt, B. C., Garg, K. C. and Kumari, P., 2008. Media Coverage of Climate Change: A Case Study of Indian English Language Dailies. In: *Biodiversity, Environment & Sustainability*. New Delhi: MD Publications, pp. 339.

The Economic Times, 2010. 'Global warming & natural disasters not wrongly linked'. *The Economic Times*, [online]. 27 January. Available at: http://articles.economictimes.indiatimes.com/2010-01-27/news/28447893_1_ipcc-climate-panel-fourth-assessment-report [Accessed 7 April 2011].

Fernandes, L., 2000. Nationalizing 'the global': media images, cultural politics and the middle class in India. *Media Culture Society*. 22(5), pp. 611–628.

Ganesan, M. R., 2009. Greening coal-fired power plants. *The Hindu Business Line*, [online] 11 November. Available at: http://www.thehindubusinessline.com/2009/11/11/stories/2009111150300700.htm [Accessed 26 April 2011].

Geevan, P. G., 2009. Copenhagen: Accountability is vital. *The Times of India*, [online] 1 December. Available at: http://lite.epaper.timesofindia.com/getpage.aspx?pageid=10&pagesize=&edid=&edlabel=ETD&mydateHid=01-12-2009&pubname=&edname=&publabel=ET [Accessed 2 May 2011].

Goswami, A. G., 2009. Quo vadis India from Copenhagen?. *The Economic Times*, [online] 17 November. Available at: http://articles.economictimes.indiatimes.com/2009-11-17/news/28408718_1_climate-change-political-statement-domestic-actions [Accessed 26 April 2011].

The Hindu, 2009. A damp squib: CPI. *The Hindu*, [online] 22 December. Available at: http://www.hindu.com/2009/12/22/stories/2009122260831000.htm [Accessed 14 May 2011].

Hindustan Times, 2009. There were differences with Saran. *Hindustan Times*, [online] 25 February. Available at: http://www.hindustantimes.com/There-were-differences-with-Saran/H1-Article1-512597.aspx [Accessed 3 March 2011].

The Indian Express, 2010. Pachauri's IPCC report faces fresh questions. *The Indian Express* (Sourced from The Press Trust of India), [online] 8 February. Available at: http://www.indianexpress.com/news/Pachauri-s-IPCC-report-faces-fresh-questions/576964 [Accessed 7 March 2011].

Jebraj, P., 2010. India may drop per capita stand. *The Hindu*, [online] 8 February. Available at: http://www.thehindu.com/news/national/article102623.ece [Accessed 12 March 2011].

Joshua, A., 2009. U.S. may not commit itself to emission cuts. *The Hindu*, [online] 14 November. Available at: http://www.hindu.com/2009/11/14/stories/2009111450040100.htm [Accessed 15 March 2011].

Joy, S. K., 2009. Opposition criticizes government over change in climate commitment. *Mint*, [online] 5 December. Available at: http://www.livemint.com/2009/12/04220346/Opposition-criticizes-govt-ove.html [Accessed 1 May 2011].

284 *Jogesh*

Krishnan, N. R., 2009. Copenhagen: An unequal dialogue. *The Hindu Business Line,* [online] 7 December. Available at: http://www.thehindubusinessline.com/todays-paper/tp-opinion/article1071046.ece [Accessed 2 May 2011].

Meattle, K., 2009. Heed the Global Warming. *Financial Express,* [online] 9 October. Available at: http://www.financialexpress.com/news/heed-the-global-warming/524642/ [Accessed 14 May 2011].

Mint, 2009. The return of Malthusian logic. *Mint,* [online] 30 November. Available at: http://www.livemint.com/2009/11/30211644/The-return-of-Malthusian-logic.html?h=B [Accessed 26 April 2011].

Olausson, U. 2009. Global warming!! Media frames of collective action and scientific certainty global responsibility? *Public Understanding of Science.* 18, pp. 421–436.

Painter, J., 2010. *Summoned by Science: Reporting Climate Change at Copenhagen and Beyond.* Oxford: Reuters Institute for the Study of Journalism, p. 137.

Parsai, G., 2009. Opposition slams government on Copenhagen. *The Hindu,* [online] 23 December. Available at: http://www.hindu.com/2009/12/23/stories/2009122360781300.htm [Accessed 7 May 2011].

Raghunandan, D., 2010. Kyoto is Dead, Long Live Durban? *Economic & Political Weekly.* 46(22), pp. 16–20.

Ramachandran, N., 2009. Smart growth, sans Copenhagen. *Mint,* [online] 16 December 2009. Available at: http://www.indianexpress.com/news/a-new-high-table/553749/0 [Accessed 4 May 2011].

Registrar of Newspapers for India, 2008. *Press in India Highlights for the Year 2008–2009,* [online]. Available at: https://rni.nic.in/ [Accessed 15 March 2011].

Roberts, T. J., 2011. Multipolarity and the new world dis(order): US hegemonic decline and the fragmentation of the global climate regime. *Global Environmental Change.* 21(3), pp. 776–784.

Sekar, T.,1981. The response strongly suggests a limited role of the Indian press in creating mass concern with environmental issues. *International Journal of Environmental Studies.* 17(2), pp. 115–120.

Sinha, N., 2010. Behind the clouds: decoding climate panel. *The Indian Express,* [online] 5 February. Available at: http://www.expressindia.com/latest-news/Behind-the-clouds-Decoding-Climate-Panel/575837/ [Accessed 12 March 2011].

Sonwalkar, P., 2002. Murdochization' of the Indian press: from by-line to bottom-line. *Media Culture Society.* 24(6), pp. 821–834.

Suneja, K. and Jain, K., 2010. India's action plan under Copenhagen Accord is ready: Jairam Ramesh. Business Standard, [online] 7 January. Available at: http://www.business-standard.com/india/news/india%5Cs-action-plan-under-copenhagen-accord-is-ready-jairam-ramesh/381914/ [Accessed 15 March 2011].

The Times of India, 2010. Frankenstorm: Mother of all squalls brewing in lab. *The Times of India* (Sourced from Associated Press), [online] 25 January. Available at: http://webcache.googleusercontent.com/search?q=cache:izQ_rngVMV4J:timesofindia.indiatimes.com/home/science/Frankenstorm-Mother-of-all-squalls-brewing-in-lab/articleshow/5500473.cms+Frankenstorm:+Mother+of+all+squalls+brewing+in+lab&cd=1&hl=en&ct=clnk&gl=in&source=www.google.co.in [Accessed 7 April 2011].

TNN, 2009a. Jairam persuades negotiators to join climate talks. *The Times of India,* [online] 7 December. Available at: http://articles.timesofindia.indiatimes.com/2009-12-07/india/28069926_1_climate-talks-carbon-intensity-cuts-chandrasekhar-dasgupta [Accessed 1 May 2011].

TNN, 2009b. Alternative track to Kyoto open. *The Times of India,* [online] 23 December. Available at: http://lite.epaper.timesofindia.com/getpage.aspx?pageid=11&pagesize=&edid=&edlabel=CAP&mydateHid=23-12-2009&pubname=&edname=&publabel=TOI [Accessed 14 May 2011].

TNN, 2010. Govt must explain why Saran quit: BJP. *The Times of India,* [online] 21 February. Available at: http://articles.timesofindia.indiatimes.com/2010-02-21/india/28146621_1_

shyam-saran-highly-detrimental-initiatives-terror-and-meek-submission [Accessed 15 March 2011].

Wodak, R. and Meyer, M (eds.), 2009. *Methods of Critical Discourse Analysis.* 2nd edn. London: Sage Publications Ltd., p. 216.

Zhang, Z., 2010. Is it fair to treat China as a Christmas tree to hang everybody's complaints? Putting its own energy saving into perspective. *Energy Economics.* 32(1), pp. S47–S58.

Appendix

Table 20.1 Frequency and distribution of news coverage across nine newspapers

Sept. '09	Oct. '09	Nov. '09	Dec. '09	Jan. '10	Feb. '10	Mar. '10
178	232	305	777	193	103	150

Table 20.2 Frequency and distribution of the nature of news content

S	GP	IP	BZ	TD
193	1111	411	96	127

Table 20.3 Source of news content

	Wires	*In-house*	*Opinion*	*International publications*
Sep.–Nov. '09	110	397	124	64
Dec. '09	152	404	165	45
Jan.–Mar. '09	120	246	58	23
Total	**382**	**1047**	**347**	**132***

*58 of 132 internationally sourced articles are opinion pieces

Table 20.4 Frequency and geographical distribution of climate-related impacts

	India	*DCs*	*All*	*Total*
Sep.–Nov.	45	51	35	131
Dec. '09	34	35	42	111
Jan.–March	26	22	20	68
Total	**105**	**108**	**97**	**310**

DCs = Developing countries

Table 20.5 Frequency of climate scepticism

	Yes	*No*	*Uncertain*	*Number of times scepticism quoted/spoken about*
Sep.–Nov. '09	11	1	3	5
Dec. '09	23	1	1	11
Jan.–March '09	31	8	4	16
Total	**65**	**10**	**8**	**32**

Table 20.6 Impact of climate controversies

Controversy	Negative coverage	Neutral or positive coverage
Glacier Gate	−80	5
Climate Gate	−69	12
Others	−8	1
IPCC	−69	53
Pachauri	−25	45

Table 20.7 Coverage during the Copenhagen Summit (7–18 Dec. 2009)

Publications	TOI	HT	IE	Hindu	ET	Mint	FE	BL	BS
Frequency of articles	83	47	51	36	38	38	58	21	40
Internationally sourced	25	4	10	14	12	7	6	3	3

Note: Articles generated: 412.

Table 20.8 Narratives on responsibility for climate change impacts

Narrative frames	Indian articles	Internationally sourced	Total
Common but differentiated	71	3	74
Industrialized countries	72	11	83
Specific nations	57	29	86
Some developing countries	57	7	64
Developing countries, but experts/newspaper disagrees	12	4	16

Table 20.9 Narratives on responsibility for climate change mitigation

Narrative frames	Indian articles	Internationally sourced	Total
Common but differentiated	177	11	188
Industrialized countries	34	10	44
Specific nations	3	4	7
Some developing countries need to take on commitments	89	9	98
Some developing countries take on carbon intensity cuts	66	4	70
Developing industrialized countries say some developing countries need to take on commitments, but experts/ newspaper disagrees	69	3	72

Table 20.10 Domestic politics versus domestic policies

	Domestic politics	Domestic policies
Oct.–Nov. '09	150	164
Dec. '09	86	63
Jan.–March 2010	45	81
Total	**281**	**308**

Part V

Integrating climate change and development

A sectoral view

21 Energy, development and climate change

Girish Sant and Ashwin Gambhir

Introduction

The energy sector is central to the debate on climate change. While the sector is vital for development, its emissions are large and growing (WRI-CAIT, 2010). On the one hand, low cost mitigation options like efficiency improvement are insufficient to contain the growth of emissions. On the other hand, options with abundant potential like solar energy are expensive and can defeat the fundamental objective of adequate supply at an affordable price, and hence hamper development. The complexity of the situation is further exacerbated by an excessive dependence on low cost fossil fuels in India, with its limited domestic resources adding to the climate problem. For a rapidly developing country like India, energy policy is therefore a multi-criteria optimization process: it must balance the urgent priority of expanding access to low cost energy, with minimal local social and environmental impacts, while keeping in mind future constraints of energy security and the climate.

Energy development linkage

Energy linked emissions form 64% of Indian GHG emissions, which are less than the global average of 75%, due to a large share of methane emissions in India (MoEF, 2010a; WRI-CAIT, 2010). With economic growth, however, the share of energy emissions is increasing. The scenario for the contribution of fossil fuels to the energy mix is similar. While the global average is over 81%, it is only 70% in India, due to a sizable share of biomass use (World Bank Indicators, 2010). With the growing use of commercial energy, and the increasing penetration of LPG, the share of fossil fuels in India is increasing as well (World Bank Indicators, 2010).

The country has a massive development imperative. Nearly half of its children are malnourished (World Bank, 2010a), 404 million people are without access to electricity, 75% of the population still relies on biomass as a cooking fuel (IAE, 2010), and 52% and 19% of rural houses are built partly (semi-pucca) or completely (kaccha) from mud, thatch and other low quality materials respectively (NHFS, 2005–06). The average GNI per capita in India, at $3,280 per year in 2009 $ PPP, is about a third of the world average, and a tenth of the OECD average (World Bank Indicators, 2010). This is also reflected in low fossil fuel use which stands at a quarter of the world average, and low energy emissions of only 1.1 T CO_2 per capita per year, against the world average of 4.4 in 2005 (WRI-CAIT, 2010).

Fossil fuel use, and hence energy emissions, are strongly linked with development. This is best understood by the following correlation.

Development ↔ Income (GDP) ↔ Energy use ↔ GHG emissions[1]

These linkages are strong but also somewhat flexible. Let us examine the linkages on the left hand side of the above correlation. It is correctly argued that GDP growth in itself is an insufficient measure of development (Daly, 1996). Special policies are required for eliminating hunger and poverty from the lives of large sections of the population. This issue is at times incorrectly portrayed to argue that poverty reduction will not require a significant increase in GDP and hence energy use. However, an increase in GDP is an important part of poverty reduction (Sen, 2011). Productive employment is associated with increased incomes and increased consumption of goods and services, both of which require increased energy use.

Internationally, development and overall energy use are seen to be strongly related (Reddy, 2000). Figure 21.1 plots Human Development Index (HDI), a frequently used indicator of development, as well as electricity use, which is a major part of energy use. This data for 114 countries displays a strong correlation between the two. A similar relationship is also seen between other development indicators, like child mortality, female life expectancy, or proportion of undernourished people, and energy use (Smil, 2010). Therefore, India must plan for its energy requirements based on the likelihood of a continuation of this relationship, without presuming that new technology or an alternative development paradigm will make it possible to completely break free from this relationship.

At the same time, Figure 21.1 offers another lesson. It shows that some countries have a higher HDI for the same level of electricity use as that of India. This lends support to critiques of the current development path, and underscores an urgent need for a more inclusive development process. It is of relevance here that providing basic services such as energy for lighting and cooking, though essential, are insufficient for wholesome development and poverty reduction. One should expect a 3- to 4-fold increase in electricity use in India, so as to achieve an HDI of 0.8. In short, addressing poverty no doubt requires change in policies, but it also needs a sizable increase in energy use.

In order to understand the linkages on the right hand side of the correlation above, a popular index called the emissions intensity of the economy is useful. The emissions intensity of the economy is obtained by dividing the energy emissions by the GDP measured in $ PPP. Figure 21.2 plots the emissions intensity of the economy for five major countries. It shows that due to low emissions intensity, for the same GDP, the Indian economy emits only 51% and 48% GHG emissions of those of China and South Africa respectively. Thus, India is using GHG emissions efficiently, despite its heavy reliance on coal, a high-carbon energy source.

The carbon efficient economy of India has several drivers. These are partly structural – compact cities with small homes, shorter travel distances, and a low share of manufacturing and heavy industries in the economy. Other drivers relate to unintended climate friendly policies which limit the energy use of the rich, such as high energy prices for the rich and industries, and electricity rationing due to shortages. The gasoline or industrial electricity prices in India, for example, are 50% higher than in the USA or China.[2] On the other hand, kerosene and agricultural electricity used by the poor, although subsidized, is highly rationed, which limits use.

Under the Copenhagen Accord, India has voluntarily committed to reduce the emissions intensity of its GDP by 20–25% by 2020 from 2005 levels (MoEF, 2010b) While this may appear to be an easy target due to the declining intensity of the Indian

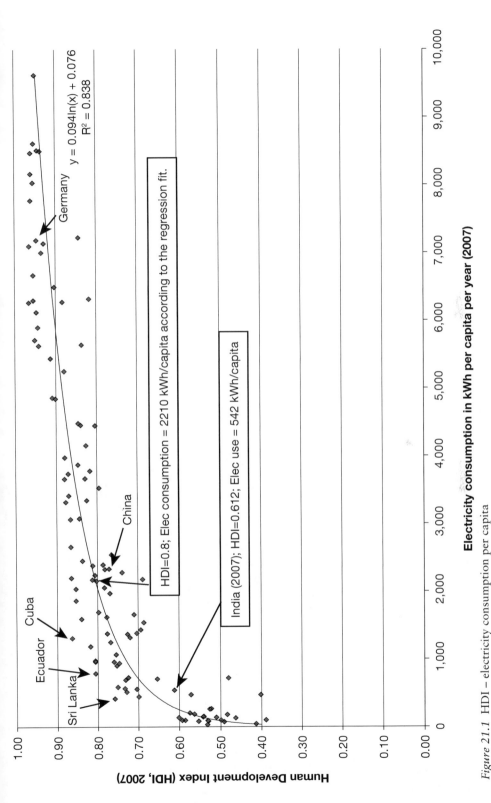

Figure 21.1 HDI – electricity consumption per capita

Source: Calculations by Prayas based on the electricity consumption data from the World Bank and HDI data from UN statistics.

Note: It can be observed that (a) HDI and per-capita electricity use are highly correlated, and that (b) India is below the best-fit curve, corroborating an urgent need for a pro-poor policy.

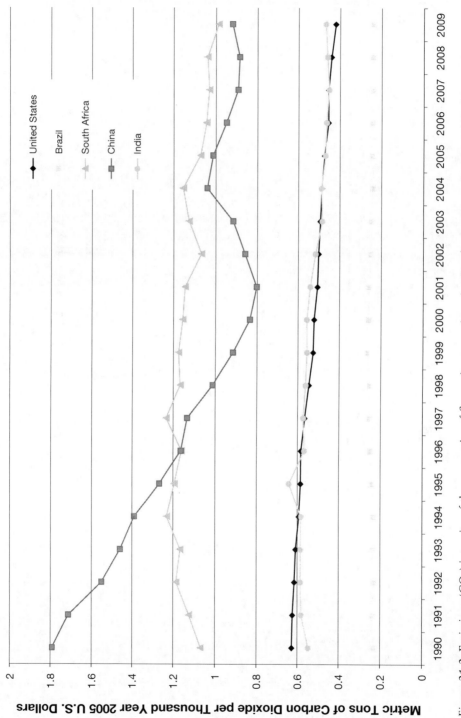

Figure 21.2 Emissions (CO_2) intensity of the economies of five major countries using Purchasing Power Parities, 1990–2009

Source: EIA International energy statistics, 2010

Energy, development and climate change

economy in the past, reducing intensity is not a certainty going ahead (Sant, 2011). As has been discussed in the following section, recent data indicate that India may see an upward pressure on intensity, like that of China, as India builds more infrastructure, removes power shortages, and shifts away from a service led economy to one with an increasing share of industry. The emissions intensity can then be reduced only by active interventions to promote energy efficiency and introducing more green energy in the energy mix. Therefore, the emissions intensity will predominantly be dictated by policies in the major energy consuming sectors.

In summary, options of inclusive development are urgent, but a substantial increase in total energy use should be planned for. The following two sections discuss trends, choices, and dilemmas in the major energy sectors of electricity and transport, which together account for over 78% of energy related emissions in India.

Electricity sector

About 150 GW (1GW = 1000 MW) of power plants in India emitted 0.72 Billion T CO_2 in 2007, accounting for 65% of the country's energy emissions. Over the 13 years from 1994 to 2007, electricity generation and its emissions have increased at a much faster rate, at 5.9% and 5.6% respectively, than the total emissions, which grew at 3.3% (MoEF, 2010a).

Growth in electricity use is expected to accelerate in the near future, due to rapid GDP growth, and the increasing electricity intensive nature of the economy (Figure 21.3). For two decades since 1985, the ratio of electricity growth rate to GDP growth rate (also

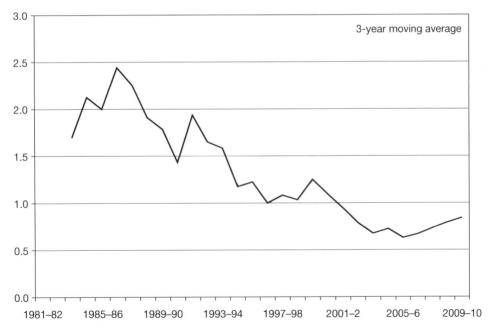

Figure 21.3 India's elasticity of electricity production to GDP, 1981–2010

Source: Calculations by Prayas based on data from the Central Electricity Authority, the Ministry of New and Renewable Energy, and the Ministry of Statistics and Programme Implementation, GoI

294 Sant and Gambhir

called elasticity of electricity to GDP) decreased steadily. Figure 21.3 plots elasticity since 1981. For the past decade, elasticity was below 1, which means that the electricity growth rate was lower than the GDP growth rate. However, elasticity has started increasing recently. Though several studies which estimate electricity demand in the future have widely varying estimates,[3] it is likely that an 8–9% growth in GDP will result in an increase of 7 to 8% p.a. in the electricity demand, resulting in a doubling of the power capacity in about 10 years.[4]

In addition to meeting the rapidly rising demand and alleviating persistent shortages, the power sector faces other daunting challenges as well. First, the burgeoning financial losses of power utilities need to be contained. Second, access to reliable and affordable electricity in rural areas must be quickly expanded. While meeting these objectives, India has to worry about its limited indigenous resources of fossil fuels including coal, and increasing pressure on land, water and the local environment exerted by power projects. Limiting CO_2 emissions is seen as yet another challenge that complicates policy choices further. But as discussed later, right choices for solving other challenges can also help the objective of GHG mitigation.

Table 21.1 shows the contribution of different sources to the electricity supply in 2010, and the expected rate of emissions of new plants from each source while using prevailing technology. The conflict between cost minimization and the objective of

Table 21.1 Share of Indian electricity generation by source (2010)

Source	% share capacity	% share generation	Specific CO_2 emissions (kg CO_2/kWh)	Typical cost (Rs/kWh)
Coal	54%		0.83–0.93	2.5–3.5
Gas turbines	10%	79.6%	0.42	3–4
Diesel generator-sets	1%		0.6–0.7	12
Large hydro	22%	13.3%	–	2–6
Indian nuclear	3%	2.3%	–	3 charged to consumers
Imported nuclear	0%		–	Uncertain, high
Wind power	7%		–	3.5–5.3
Small hydro	2%	4.8%	–	3.2–4.4
Biomass + Bagasse Cogen	1%		–	3.6–5.2
Solar (PV, thermal)	0%		–	11–12.5
Total	100%	100%		

Source: Central Electricity Authority, Ministry of New and Renewable Energy, Central Electricity Regulatory Commission, and Prayas estimates

Notes:
1 The total installed capacity of 170 GW excludes captive generation.
2 Energy generation of 804 Bn Units in 2009–10 excludes captive plants. Generation from renewable energy sources is estimated by the authors.
3 The emissions exclude those associated with the construction of plants, and methane emissions from hydro reservoirs. For further reading on methane emissions from large dams please see World Bank (2008) and Ivan B.T. Lima et al. (2007). The data for coal and diesel shows a range for available technology.
4 The wind, biomass and small hydro tariffs are as approved by Central Electricity Regulatory Commission; others are based on recently approved projects.
5 The Solar PV and CSP tariffs are representative of the tariffs discovered though the recent competitive bidding process under phase 1 of the JNNSM.
6 0.83–0.93 kg CO_2/kWh is for supercritical and sub-critical coal technologies respectively.

Energy, development and climate change   295

mitigation is clear in this table. The low cost but high emission coal,[5] and high cost but clean solar, represent the two extreme options for the sector.

With a third of the Indian population not having access to electricity, and an additional third not having reliable access, the growth of the electricity sector has bypassed the poor in the past (Rao et al., 2009). It is argued that a decentralized deployment of solar and other renewable sources should be used to bridge the access gap quickly (World Bank, 2010a). Though such measures are urgently needed, we must understand two factors. First, simple policy measures can ensure that grid electricity helps in rapid expansion of electricity access to the poor (Sreekumar et al., 2010). Second, expensive decentralized renewable solutions cannot meet the complete gamut of energy needs of society to generate jobs and bring about economic development. Hence, these sources cannot yet replace the low cost supply from fossil fuels.

The Rajiv Gandhi Grameen Vidyutikaran Yojana, which aims to expand the electricity grid in order to enhance access, is already facing a shortage of electricity. A rapid expansion of the low cost electricity generation is not only critical to ease this shortage, but is also essential to limit the burgeoning financial losses of power utilities. The accumulated losses of power utilities have already crossed 1% of GDP (or Rs. 70,000 crore in 2010–11) and are likely to increase further, as the high-tariff paying industrial consumers opt out, in favour of private generation.[6] While an increase in tariff for existing customers has its limitations, new rural customers with limited paying capacities are unlikely to afford even the existing tariff. Hence, to prevent utility losses from exploding, low cost supply is essential.[7]

Conventional supply options

Given the rapid economic growth and need for expanding low cost power supply, India is about to double its coal based capacity in less than a decade. In this context, concerns have been raised about the limitations of domestic coal reserves. These concerns were highlighted during the debate on banning coal mining in forest areas, which would have reduced accessible coal reserves. Estimates of indigenous extractable reserves of coal vary widely. Assuming a lower range of estimate of 40 BT corresponds to a peak coal capacity of 290 GW.[8] Hence, if coal is imported for about 75 GW,[9] and the bottlenecks in developing new coal mining and transportation are handled, India would be able to meet its electricity needs till 2030 with its domestic coal resources. However, these are not easy conditions, and also imply that based on existing proven extractable reserves no new plants can come up after 2030. This implies a sizable increase in GHG emissions, which are discussed later in this chapter. It also points to the need to shift to a low energy use trajectory much before 2030.

The potential of other options is limited in India. Hydro resources are not only limited, but are also located in difficult terrains of the north-east and the Himalayan ranges. These projects have large financial costs, significant socio-environmental impacts, and face a high hydrological risk due to receding glaciers and climate variability as a result of global warming. Hydro-power is expected to add less than 10 GW by 2020, which is less than 5% of the incremental electricity needs by 2020 – a marginal contribution.

The prominent and the most controversial option is that of nuclear power. India, with its limited uranium reserves, is investing in 'fast breeder' technology, which is yet to be proven and involves highly challenging reactor cooling systems. India is

296 Sant and Gambhir

also seeking foreign collaborations for light-water reactors and uranium supply (Bharadwaj, 2008). The price of electricity for imported reactors, as well as nuclear safety issues, have been hotly debated but post the Fukushima accident, the intensity of debate has peaked (CNDP, 2011, Maurin, 2011, Gopalakrishnan, 2011). The public opposition, likely high cost of electricity and slow pace of construction indicate that nuclear energy will remain a marginal contributor for the next decade.[10] It is doubtful that this situation will change even in the decade 2020–30.

The potential of natural gas to facilitate a transition to a low-carbon future for India is uncertain. Conventional gas reserves in India are limited and it has competing uses other than power generation. These include fertilizer production and as oil replacement in industry and transport, which have higher benefits in terms of improving energy security and reducing oil imports. Considering this, the power capacity addition based on domestic conventional natural gas is unlikely to be more than 15 GW (or 10% of the incremental requirement) by 2020.[11] The uncertainty about gas comes from two factors: India can import sizable quantities of LNG or piped gas, and reserves of shale-gas can be unexpectedly large (Prasad, 2011). These factors may allow India to add much more than the capacity stated above. Barring this uncertainty, the traditional alternatives to coal will play only a marginal role in the coming decade, and possibly even in the next decade until 2030.

Renewables and energy efficiency

This leaves three major options: (I) energy efficiency, (II) wind and (III) solar energy. Efficiency improvement is cost effective compared to adding new generation, and has more potential by 2020, than the combined potential of hydro, nuclear, and conventional gas. If properly exploited, it can reduce the need for new capacity by about 50 GW, a third or fourth of the required addition by 2020. The GHG saved would be about 200 MT per year by 2020 (Planning Commission, 2011), about a quarter of the present emissions of the electricity sector. Exploiting this win-win resource to its full potential involves radically different policy interventions that are consistent with Indian conditions and enable rapid scale-up of implementation. High penetration of super-efficient models of just four electric appliances can reduce the need of 15–20 GW of peak capacity or 40–60 TWh by 2020 (Chunekar et al., 2011). One promising approach to quickly achieve such market transformation at low transaction costs is national programs (NPs) through upstream incentives to manufacturers in combination of racheting up of minimum efficiency standards (Singh et al., 2011). Similarly ensuring that new buildings and industries, which would constitute over two-thirds of the 2030 stock, are built using the most efficient designs would help reduce pressure of electricity shortages.

India was the first country to set up a separate ministry for renewable energy, and also promote wind energy early on. The Indian power generation mix already has over 10% of renewable energy by capacity, which is comparable to that of the EU and China, and more than twice that of the USA. The second substantial source is wind power, the largest of the non-solar renewable sources.[12] Large wind generation in India has been achieved despite low wind resources. Official sources indicate a limited wind potential of roughly 50 GW, however, recent studies indicate a much higher potential of ~ 1000 GW.[13] Even considering this revised estimate, the Indian wind resource is much lower in quality and quantity in comparison to USA, China and EU. Hence, a substantial improvement in wind contribution in percentage terms is possible, but might carry a slight additional cost on account of grid integration and stability and transmission infrastructure.

Solar power is a sunrise technology with massive potential. Although an addition of 22 GW of solar capacity is planned by 2022 under the National Solar Mission (MNRE, 2010), it would generate energy equivalent to what is generated by 7 GW of coal plants. The estimated subsidy for the first phase of 1 GW of large solar projects is 15,000 Cr.[14] Even with the reduction in cost achieved by technology improvement and competitive bidding the present cost of solar energy is four times that of coal-based power. However, presently solar PV is highly economical for niche applications in remote, off-grid locations. About 10 GW of solar PV if used strategically can achieve massive and direct benefits to the poor through provisions of lighting, rural services for drinking water, primary health centres, and other key decentralized applications. Beyond such niche applications, subsidizing installations of several GW of grid-connected solar plants as a replacement for coal is difficult to justify at present costs. The focus of solar energy in India should be strategic and should be presently targeted towards decentralized applications, technology development and promotion of Indian industry and manufacturing.

With a reduction in the cost of solar energy, it will progressively become more economical for all off-grid, decentralized installations, followed by MW scale plants. Once this happens, the practically unlimited potential of solar will alleviate concerns of energy resources and emissions. Such a breakthrough will be required for Annex-I countries to reduce their emissions sizably by 2030, and can then be utilized by the rest of the world without having to bear the cost penalty.

The National Action Plan for Climate Change (NAPCC) suggests increasing the renewable energy contribution to 15% of electricity generation by 2020 (GoI, 2008). Given the intermittent operation and low capacity factors of RE plants, the RE capacity required will be about 30% of the total installed capacity in order to achieve this goal. This is an ambitious target, even from the perspective of resource availability, and is unlikely to be feasible.

Framework for choosing the mitigation options

The present debate on RE is centered on who should bear the high cost of promoting green technologies. The RE subsidy in India can be justified for the domestic considerations of (a) limitations of Indian coal reserves and risk in maintaining supply of imported coal, (b) local pollution due to coal plants, and (c) promotion of Indian RE industry. Justifying the RE subsidy for climate mitigation is difficult in India due to low emissions by India both historically and as expected in the future till 2030, and low affordability. The subsidy arising from the domestic considerations should be quantified, but is likely to be less than the subsidy required for large scale deployment of RE – which could be in the range of an incremental 10 billion US $ per year in years to come (Sant 2011).

Development being the first and overriding objective of India, it should adopt all low cost mitigation options. Options with large development benefits (low costs or social benefits) and climate mitigation as a co-benefit are an obvious priority. Options with large development benefits (electricity for the poor through coal) along with a minor climate penalty should be implemented. Similarly options with large climate

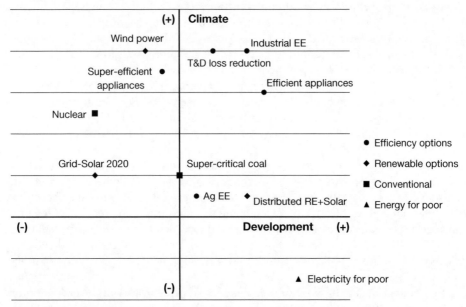

Figure 21.4 Balancing between climate and development objectives

Note: Development (social and economic benefits) considered for this exercise is subjective to technology and implementation. Climate benefit is generally proportional to the 2030 mitigation potential, except in the case of solar where it represents the 2020 capacity addition planned under the National Solar Mission. The location of points should be seen for the purpose of elaborating the concept.

benefits (wind power) and minor additional financial costs should also be promoted. However, investment in pro-climate options having large financial or social costs (nuclear and grid-connected solar) should be limited to strategic investments. Figure 21.4 shows this screening method, where x axis is the development benefit and y axis is the climate benefit. Hence, India should aggressively promote NAMAs (Nationally Appropriate Mitigation Actions)[15] and restrict investments in high cost mitigation options to strategic investments such as R&D in solar, rather than mass deployment of MW scale plants or investing in carbon capture and sequestration.

Implications for policy

The immediate developmental imperative for the power sector is at odds with the climate mitigation objective. In the next decade, about two-thirds of incremental energy is likely to come from coal, unless large reserves of unconventional gas are found or cost of solar falls rapidly. Considering Indian commitment to reduce emissions intensity by 20–25%, Indian GHG emissions are likely to be 2.9 and 4.2 T per capita, in 2020 and 2030 respectively. Total Indian emissions would be 4 and 6.2 BT in these years, just 9% and 17.7% of the global emissions if one considers the global budget to be 44 BT and 35 BT in 2020 and 2030 respectively (Elzen, 2010; UNEP, 2010). Considering the rightful need of the Indian population (which is projected to be 17.8% of the global population in 2030) and its low emissions historically, India should focus on domestic priorities of energy security, access and not pay a heavy price for costly climate mitigation.

Energy, development and climate change 299

However, for social and local environmental reasons, and energy security concerns, it is in India's interest to radically change its energy trajectory. Energy efficiency and renewable energy should be adopted for reaping developmental benefits of rapid reduction in shortages and social inclusion respectively. Low cost grid power should be preferentially used for rapidly ensuring reliable access for the poor, while high energy use by the rich should be used to pay for the high cost of RE development. The RE ambition can also be increased through financial support from the Annex-I countries under the climate agreement. Hence, increase in energy emissions are on the cards, but radical changes to meet domestic objectives of energy access, energy security, and limiting social and local environment can achieve a co-benefit of climate mitigation in the medium term.

Transport sector[16]

The transport sector accounts for about 13% of energy emissions and over 40% of oil use in India. Road freight and passenger transport each account for about 40% of the transport energy needs. The country's net oil import bill is 4% of GDP, compared to less than 2% for the USA, EU, Japan and China (IEA, 2010). With the possibility of 'peak oil' in sight and oil price volatility, this sector is of key national importance.

The developmental priorities of this sector – to facilitate mobility while enabling access for the poor, improve energy security, and reduce cost and pollution – are well aligned with the global objective of climate mitigation. The freight transport by railway is several folds more efficient than road freight, and also reduces oil use and pollution (Prayas internal calculations). Increasing the share of railway freight from say 40 to 47% can reduce GHG emissions by 21 million ton per year, and reduce annual oil imports worth Rs 14,000 Cr per year by 2020. Improved public transport and infrastructure for non-motorized transport can help improve mobility of the poor, and reduce the excessively high rate of road accidents in India. This will reduce the use of personal vehicles and resulting oil use as well as associated GHG emissions. Air travel, requires only 7% of transport energy in India, but energy consumed in the aviation sector has had an alarming annual growth of about 10.5% over the last 5 years (MoPNG, 2010 and MoEF, 2010a). China is rapidly building high-speed trains between major cities, a low energy, low cost alternative that can reduce oil dependence.

Conceptually, the transport sector reforms can be seen as a paradigm change towards an 'Avoid-Shift-Improve' paradigm. Maximum benefits are accrued when travel is 'avoided' through better city planning and optimal location of industries. Denser cities interspersed with housing for population of different income groups reduce the need for travel. Location of industries and power plants is also important to minimize the freight of raw material and finished products.

The second level of intervention is to help people 'shift' to better modes of transport. Shifting passengers from personal transport to public transport has a much higher benefit than simply improving say car technology. A large section of the urban population can benefit if they have safe cycle tracks, and travel distances are limited to 5–10 km. Allowing them this choice requires mixed land-use cities, and road infrastructure that is not monopolized by cars, but instead allows the safe movement of pedestrians and cyclists. A higher investment in public transport is now being seen as an essential prerequisite for habitable cities. These options promote inclusive growth, a cleaner local environment, and reduced oil use and GHG emissions.

300 Sant and Gambhir

The third level of intervention is to 'improve' the technology of vehicles being used. Making cars more efficient, or using electric vehicles, are some examples. Though the social and climate benefits of this intervention are far lesser than the first two interventions, being trendy it usually gets disproportionately more policy attention. This approach needs to be reversed.

In summary, in the transport sector, the climate and developmental objectives are largely aligned. However, implementation is a problem of governance and institutions. Actions are needed by multiple institutions at different levels – from central government to municipal authorities. The issues of motivation, incentives, and capabilities of these institutions need to be addressed quickly before we invest in inefficient infrastructure and city layouts.

Conclusion

India is already on a low carbon growth path but is going to require a sizable increase in energy to address its massive developmental imperative. India should adhere to rational sectoral policies with the objectives of inclusiveness and low cost, but should not commit to high-cost mitigation options. In other words, India should follow NAMAs.

For the power sector, going beyond the existing push for expanding low cost coal/gas based power, we urgently need a change in energy trajectory through an aggressive push for energy efficiency, strategic deployment of renewable energy, using grid power to ensure reliable access to the poor, and promotion of R&D in renewable and efficiency technologies. At the same time, considerations of social and local environmental issues, as well as long term resource availability, should be integral to the core of decision-making.

In the transport sector, there is a high convergence of climate and development objectives. India should aggressively pursue the 'Avoid-Shift-Improve' paradigm. It is in India's interest to follow a low carbon path, due to acute limitations of domestic oil/gas resources, and an already serious situation of urban congestion and pollution.

As India follows a pro-development path, it should see climate as a co-benefit. On this path, the country's per capita GHG emissions can remain much below the global average till 2020 and perhaps even until 2030. Hence, it is not appropriate for India to buckle under pressures to declare a 'peaking year' of emissions, or accept an emissions limit until 2030. At the same time, India should aim to follow a low carbon and inclusive development pathway, which in itself, calls for a sizable shift in energy policies.

Notes

1 We have explored only a few linkages within the above correlation, since exploring each link thoroughly would require a paper in itself.
2 The misleading discourse on oil subsidies arises due to an odd definition of subsidy by many agencies including IEA, which only points to the fact that Indian companies selling diesel or kerosene cannot recover the full price of diesel, inclusive of taxes. However, taxes even on diesel are pretty high, and the consumer price of diesel actually reflects a small net tax. Hence, diesel prices in India are slightly higher than those in the USA.
3 The McKinsey study estimates the needed power generation capacity of 760 GW by 2030, whereas the World Bank and CEA-17th EPS estimate the same at 730 and 778 GW respectively.
4 This assumes an elasticity (ratio of electricity growth rate to GDP growth rate) of 90%, and that it will not increase much as in the case of say China.
5 Cost of coal based generation is low even after accounting for externalities of local pollution.
6 The Electricity Act 2003 allowed large industries 'open access', i.e. to opt out of the local

Energy, development and climate change 301

utility supply and opt for captive generation or access to private power plants. But the practical feasibility has increased only recently, with the opening of the coal sector, and construction of a large number of private power plants.

7 The T&D loss reduction and improvement in operational efficiency can contribute to improved utility finances, but an increase in tariffs cannot be avoided, which are already at a high level.

8 This considers phased retirement of the existing 92 GW, and an addition of 250 GW of new capacity on Indian coal, and 25 year of plant life.

9 75 GW would need peak import of 0.25 Bn Ton of coal, against a global trade of steam coal of 0.7 BT in 2008 (World Coal Institute, 2009).

10 The Interim Report of the Expert Group on Low Carbon strategies for inclusive growth (Planning Commission, 2011) assumes additional nuclear capacity addition of 8–12 GW till 2020. The implicit capacity addition of about 1 GW/yr seems to be an overestimate.

11 This is important considering that India imports 80% of its oil requirement.

12 Biomass resources have limited potential in India due to competing biomass uses and high pressures on land, and hence have not been considered here.

13 A forthcoming report from LBNL, "Reassessing Wind Potential Estimates for India: Economic and Policy Implications" indicates a significantly higher potential of ~ 1000 GW at a hub-height of 80m and above. Draft report is likely to available in August 2011.

14 Calculations revised from Deshmukh et al. (2010).

15 The National Action Plan on Climate Change (GoI, 2008), 'identifies measures that promote our development objectives while also yielding co-benefits for addressing climate change effectively'.

16 This section draws on the report of the Working Group on Transport of the Expert Group on 'Low Carbon Strategy for Inclusive Growth' by the Planning Commission, 2010, which was convened by one of the authors.

References

Bharadwaj A. (2008) *Nuclear Power in India: The Road Ahead.*, CSTEP, Bangalore: CSTEP, http://www.cstep.in/docs/CSTEP%20Nuclear%20Report.pdf, accessed 8 March 2011.

Chunekar A., Kadav K., Singh D. and Sant, G. (2011) *Potential Savings from Selected Super-Efficient Electric Appliances in India*, Prayas publication, http://www.prayaspune.org/peg/publications/item/155.html

CNDP (2011) 'Courting Nuclear Disaster in Maharashtra: Why the Jaitapur Project Must Be Scrapped', http://www.sacw.net/article1914.html, accessed 8 March 2011.

Daly, H. (1996) *Beyond Growth: The Economics of Sustainable Development*, Beacon Press, Boston.

Deshmukh, R., Gambhir, A. and Sant, G. (2010) 'Need to Re-align India's National Solar Mission', *Economic and Political Weekly*, 20 March, 2010, vol. xlv, no. 12.

Energy Information Administration (EIA), USA (2010) *International Energy Statistics*, Government of USA, tonto.eia.doe.gov/cfapps/ipdbproject/IEDIndex3.cfm?tid=91&pid=46 &aid=31, accessed 23 December 2010.

Elzen, M. (2010) 'The Emissions Gap Report: Are the Copenhagen Accord pledges sufficient to limit global warming to 2°C or 1.5°C? A preliminary assessment', advance copy.

Gopalakrishnan, A. (2011) 'Nuclear power: The missing safety audits'. *Daily News and Analysis*, http://www.dnaindia.com/mumbai/report_nuclear-power-the-missing-safety-audits_1536223, accessed 2 May 2011.

Government of India (2008) 'National Action Plan on Climate Change', Prime Minister's Council on Climate Change, Government of India, New Delhi, http://pmindia.nic.in/climate_change.htm, accessed 13 May 2011.

International Energy Agency (IEA) (2010), *World Energy Outlook 2010*, IEA Paris.

International Institute for Population Sciences (IIPS) and Macro International (2007) *National Family Health Survey (NFHS) – 3*, India, www.nfhsindia.org/nfhs3.html, accessed 23 December 2010.

Lima, I., Ramos, F., Bambace, L. and Rosa, R. (2007) 'Methane Emissions from Large Dams as

302 Sant and Gambhir

Renewable Energy Resources: A Developing Nation Perspective', *Mitigation and Adaptation Strategies for Global Change*, 13(2), pp. 193–206.

Maurin, F. (2011) 'Fukushima: Consequences of Systemic Problems in Nuclear Plant Design', *Economic and Political Weekly*, March 26, vol. Xlvi, no. 13. pp.10–12.

Ministry of Environment and Forests (MoEF), India (2010a) *India: Greenhouse Gas Emissions 2007*, moef.nic.in/downloads/public-information/Report_INCCA.pdf, accessed on 8 March 2011.

MoEF (2010b) 'Press Release', 30th January 2010, http://moef.nic.in/downloads/public-information/UNFCCC%20Submission_press_note.pdf, accessed on 8 March 2011.

MNRE (2010) *Jawaharlal Nehru National Solar Mission: Towards Building Solar India; available online at* http://mnre.gov.in/pdf/mission-document-JNNSM.pdf, accessed on 10 February 2011.

MoPNG (2010) *Basic Statistics on Indian Petroleum & Natural Gas*, http://petroleum.nic.in/petstat.pdf, accessed 8 March 2011.

Planning Commission, GoI (2011) *Interim Report of Expert Group on Low Carbon Strategies for Inclusive Growth*, http://planningcommission.gov.in/reports/genrep/Inter_Exp.pdf, accessed in July 2011.

Prasad, G. (2011) 'Shale Gas in India is 300 times KG D-6', *The Financial Express*, 6 January.

Rao, N., Sant, G. and Rajan, S.C. (2009) 'An Overview of Indian Energy Trends: Low Carbon Growth and Development Challenges', Prayas Energy Group, Pune, http://www.prayaspune.org/peg/media/k2/attachments/overview__indian_energy_trends_101A01.pdf, accessed 8 March 2011.

Reddy A.K.N. (2000) 'Energy and Social Issues', in Goldemberg, J. et al., (ed.) (2000) *World Energy Assessment: Energy and the Challenge of Sustainability*, UNDP, Washington DC.

Sant, G. (2011) *India's Development needs and mitigation actions*. Indian presentation at the NA1 Mitigation Actions UNFCCC workshop; 4 April Bangkok, http://unfccc2.meta-fusion.com/kongresse/110403_AWG_Bangkok/templ/play.php?id_kongresssession=3466&theme=unfccc, accessed 13 May 2011.

Sen, A. (2011) 'Growth and Other Concerns', *The Hindu*, 14 February.

Singh, D., Bharvirkar, R., Kumar, S., Sant, G. and Phadke, A. (2011) *Using National Energy Efficiency Programs with Upstream Incentives to Accelerate Market Transformation for Super-Efficient Appliances in India*. Paper presented at the ECEEE Summer Study June 2011, http://www.prayaspune.org/peg/publications/item/158.html.

Smil, V. (2010) 'Science, energy, ethics, and civilization', in Chiao, R., Cohen, M., Leggett, A., Phillips, W. and Harper, C. (eds), *Visions of Discovery: New Light on Physics, Cosmology, and Consciousness*, Cambridge University Press, Cambridge, pp. 709–729.

Sreekumar, N. and Dixit, S. (2010) *Electricity for All: Ten Ideas Towards Turning Rhetoric into Reality*, Prayas Energy Publication, http://www.prayaspune.org/peg/publications/item/84.html, accessed 2 May 2011.

UNEP (2010) Copenhagen Accord Pledges Take World a Long Way Towards 2°C Path, But Should Go Further, 25 March 2010, http://hqweb.unep.org/Documents.Multilingual/Default.asp?DocumentID=617&ArticleID=6513&l=en&t=long, accessed on 20 February 2011.

World Bank (2008) Review of Greenhouse Gas Emissions from the creation of Hydropower Reservoirs in India, http://moef.nic.in/downloads/public-information/LCGEmisssionsHydro June2008.pdf, accessed 13 May 2011.

World Bank (2010) Indicators, data.worldbank.org/indicator/NY.GDP.PCAP.PP.CD, accessed on 21 December 2010.

—— (2010a) Empowering Rural India: Expanding Electricity Access by Mobilizing Local Resources,siteresources.worldbank.org/INDIAEXTN/.../empowering-rural-india-expanding-electricity-access-by-mobilizing-local-resources.pdf, accessed 9 March 2011.

World Coal Institute (2009) *Coal Facts*, http://www.worldcoal.org/bin/pdf/original_pdf_file/coal_factsnewversion09(15_09_2010).pdf, accessed 8 March 2011.

World Resources Institute (WRI), Climate Analysis Indicators Tool, cait.wri.org, accessed 2 October 2010.

22 Climate change and urbanization in India[1]

Partha Mukhopadhyay and Aromar Revi

Introduction

In the multiple transformations that South Asia will undergo over this century, urbanization occupies a vexed and poorly understood position, though if India's citizens are to realize their potential, it is both a necessary and an inevitable outcome. Concomitantly, it is intimately linked to climate change. On the one hand, migration induced by climate change-induced drought and environmental risk may lead to an involuntary spurt in urbanization. On the other, it could be a contributor to climate change via growth, consumption and emission. This chapter explores a limited set of emergent issues that will have to be considered as India develops its domestic approach to urbanization in the context of climate change. It is structured into two broad sections:(a) the feedback loops from urbanization to climate change and vice versa and (b) actions needed at multiple levels to influence these processes.

The core challenge

The processes which lead to an increase in greenhouse gases (GHG) are complex, non-linear and subject to multi-decade-long lags. This implies that a decline in emissions may take decades to affect critical climate variables. Urban capital stock is typically locked in, exacerbating these lags and making it difficult to effect changes even over decades. On an urbanizing planet, the struggle against climate change will therefore be largely lost or won in the cities of Asia and a few of the UNFCCC Annex 1 countries. China and India will play a central role in this because they lie at the centre of gravity of this planetary urban transformation.

These long lags also imply that mitigation actions alone may be insufficient to help the most vulnerable Indians. They will be forced to adapt to changes in their physical, resource and built environments. Many weather and geo-hydrological systems, e.g., the Ganga-Yamuna and Brahmaputra river systems, may never return to their former state. An unalterable change in such systems would be a watershed in the cultural and civilization identity of the subcontinent.

A series of coordinated actions are necessary, from the household, to state and national level and even internationally, if we want to preserve a strong continuity with our past. This will require not only a transformation of the material and energy metabolism of most national, firm and city economies; but changes in patterns of consumption, savings and investment and social behaviour in relation to resources in particular, and the global commons, in general.

304 *Mukhopadhyay and Revi*

India's role

Over the next 40 years, India could experience one of the most dramatic settlement transitions in history, with its urban population growing from about 300 million to more than 700 million. Three mega-urban regions: Mumbai-Pune-Nasik (50 million), the national capital region of Delhi (more than 30 million) and Greater Kolkata (20 million) may be among the largest urban concentrations in the world (Dyson, Cassen and Visaria, 2005, de Vries, et al. 2007).[2] A potential renaissance in the smaller Class I towns (i.e., those above 100,000) and the construction of many new cities ranging from industrial townships to Special Economic Zones (SEZs) may also take place. This urban transformation has two important relationships to global climate vulnerability:

(a) First, large numbers of India's urban poor and vulnerable households by the late 2030s could well be part of the first generation of climate change induced environmental refugees fleeing from the drought and flood-affected regions of rural India. Many will not find much comfort in these cities as our current pattern of development does not offer them effective participation options. But they will come to the city nevertheless.

(b) Second, if the Indian middle class aspires to Middle Eastern, East Asian and even OECD standards of consumption using existing technologies, the scale of rise in GHG emissions and potential resource conflicts will be clearly unsustainable for both India and the world unless there are dramatic countervailing drops in GHG emissions in developed countries.

The focus of attention of the international climate community is on the second, i.e., the mitigation challenge, while much of India's attention and resources may be consumed by the first. We now look at these challenges separately.

Effect of climate change on urbanization

Climate change risk in most Indian cities is typically associated more with vulnerability than hazard exposure (Revi, 2008). It is primarily expected to increase the frequency and intensity of current hazards and the probability of extreme events, and to spur the emergence of new hazards, e.g. sea-level rise. It will deepen as other environmental transitions, e.g., brown (water, sanitation and environmental health) and grey (air and water pollution), simultaneously play out. When taken in tandem with changes in freshwater systems, i.e., water availability and consequent drought, it could become a serious risk in time. These new climate-induced vulnerabilities are likely to accentuate and further degrade the resilience of poor and vulnerable communities through channels listed below that will typically be asymmetric in impact, based on gender, age and ability.

*   Loss of livelihood opportunities and hence income, directly via an interruption of economic activity, short and long-term displacement or loss of health and ability to work; and indirectly due to structural changes in livelihood opportunities, including housing, household and financial assets, tenure rights, means of identification and usufruct rights.
*   Loss of community and informal social safety nets due to dislocation, displacement or forced migration.

Climate change and urbanization in India   305

- Reduced resilience to future shocks and coping capacity due to frequent risk exposure, negative net incomes, livelihood and asset loss.
- Higher coping costs and consequent compression of discretionary expenditure and spending on basic needs.
- Greater vulnerability to unsustainable debt exposure and predation by commercial organised criminal and political patronage structures that could expand in times of crisis.

Taken together, this forms a body of mechanisms through which vulnerable households fall in or out of poverty due to income or asset shocks (Fuente, Lopes Calva and Revi, 2008).

A second-order impact of climate change on Indian cities can occur via migration. Migration in India has been constrained by a number of factors such as high urban poverty levels with dismal living and working conditions due to insufficiently viable urban livelihoods; neglect of rural education; and slow processes of social transformation (Dyson and Visaria, 2004).

Climate change may force the current gentle pace of rural–urban migration. It could turn the ongoing agrarian crisis in rural India into a migratory rout, driven by increases in extreme events, greater monsoon variability, endemic drought, flooding and resource conflict. On the other hand, severe stresses induced in urban areas due to a mix of resource scarcity and disease can lead to the persistence of a low level of rural–urban migration. This indicates the potential for climate change to induce bifurcation behaviour in migration, and to that extent urbanization trends.

Effect of urbanization on climate change

As societies urbanize, their energy consumption rises. We focus here on four major channels of increased energy consumption (a) appliances, (b) built form, (c) transportation, and (d) water supply and treatment.

Increased use of appliances

Energy consumption in urban households is higher than rural households at similar incomes (Pachauri, 2007). Though the share of consumption expenditure on fuel and light declines as income rises; the share of expenditure in rural households remains consistently below that of their urban counterparts. This declining share of expenditure on fuel and light indicates a possibly reduced price elasticity and hence weaker responsiveness to price signals in changing behaviour. On a regional basis, an analysis of the National Sample Survey data shows that while the ratio of urban to rural consumption varies widely across states, this ratio is declining over time across states, especially where there was a large initial discrepancy between urban and rural areas, thus indicating a growing convergence in energy consumption across regions.

Some of this difference in electricity use is attributable to the possession of consumer durables. Chandigarh and Delhi stand out as having high consumption as also high air conditioner ownership. Figure 22.1, which compares ownership of consumer durables for the top expenditure quintile across rural and urban areas, shows that as incomes increase in rural areas, one can expect to see more use of appliances and vehicles. Once some adjustment is made for income differences,[3] differences in the ownership of key

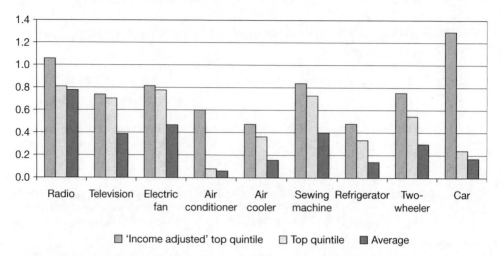

Figure 22.1 Ratio of rural to urban share of households with specific consumer durables

Note: The 'income adjusted' ratio refers to the ratio of share of households in the top rural quintile (80th to 100th percentile by expenditure) to the share of households in the fourth urban quintile (60th to 80th percentile by expenditure).

Source: Authors' calculations from NSS data

durables, like air conditioners and cars, reduce considerably. Further, urban consumption may also increase the aspirations of the rural rich.

Energy consumption by buildings

The ubiquitously emerging glass and steel constructions in India are designed for full time, full space air conditioning, rather than part time, part space air conditioning that is the more familiar pattern of use in India and often possibly, more efficient from an overall energy use perspective (as compared to efficiency of individual equipment). Widespread use of curtain wall design needs insulated glazing, air conditioning and insulation technologies to offset imposed heating and cooling loads. In addition, the embodied energy of these building systems, through their extensive use of energy intensive materials, like cement, steel, glass and aluminium, increases the carbon footprint of these aspirational spaces, while ignoring the large body of indigenous energy efficient design.

The use of green building standards, such as LEED (Leadership in Energy and Environmental Design), may not be an effective antidote to this affectation. Indeed, despite its apparently rising popularity, it could be inappropriate to the Indian context. Domestically developed ratings like GRIHA (Green Rating for Integrated Habitat Assessment) also exist for sustainable buildings but, according to one estimate, the number of green building area registered under LEED is 200 times more than that under GRIHA (TERI, 2009). Newsham, et al. (2009) find that, while, as a group, LEED buildings in the USA consumed less energy per unit area, up to a third of them used more energy and higher levels of certification did not imply better energy efficiency. Besides, benchmarks that appear aggressive in the USA could well be

Climate change and urbanization in India 307

irrelevant in India, given the nearly forty-fold difference in average electricity consumption levels.

While scrutiny of building standards is especially important given the lock-in effects that flow from the long-lived nature of building stock in urban areas, there is also a role for behaviour in determining actual energy consumption. Hwang, et al. (2009) present evidence from a field survey in Taiwan, documenting sharp differences in thermal adaptation behaviour at home and work. While the fact that cooling is costless at work presumably plays a role in this finding, the researchers noted that '*only a quarter of workplaces . . . visited [were] equipped with electrical fan or [had] sufficient operable windows to facilitate natural ventilation*', indicating a strong role for building design.

Finally, even if one were to understand and appreciate the kinds of buildings that needed to be built, it is not entirely clear that India has the capacity to build them given the poor quality of training available to construction workers in the country and their low levels of education (SEWA Bharat 2006).

Energy consumption by transport

In transport, there appears to be little difference between shares of consumption in rural and urban areas, for a given level of income. As of 2004–5, nearly 50% and 16% of the uppermost urban quintile in India own two-wheelers and cars respectively, as compared to 36% and 3% respectively for the next richest urban quintile. As incomes rise, if current trends continue, the use of private transport is likely to increase. This is made even more likely by the widespread absence of dependable public transport in India.

City form and public transport are thought to be closely related (Newman and Kenworthy, 1999; Mees, 2010). An examination of data for Indian cities from the Ministry of Urban Development (MoUD) (2008) shows that the status of a city as a state capital has a significant effect on the availability of public transport (see Table 22.1). Dense compact cities that encourage greater use of public transport (see World Bank, 2009) are seen as better for GHG mitigation. In India, while linear cities, like Kolkata and Mumbai can benefit greatly from rapid transit corridors, most of the larger cities in India are circular. They, especially if they are multi-focal, are public transport challenges. Most of these cities, like Bangalore and Delhi have a sequence of ring roads and a set of radial spokes. For a transport system to possess the ability to take a person from any point to any other point within the circle, it would need to have multiple modes (e.g. small vehicles, possibly non-motorized, that connect from interior to the ring roads and spokes),[4] predictable and frequent schedules on the rings and spokes and free or low-cost interchanges, so that routes can be customized by the passenger. Since it is relatively rare that such kind of public transport system is available, the default in such cities is the growing use of private transport, constrained in India by the affordability of such options. The extent to which the city fabric accommodates informal settlements also matters. In Mumbai, for instance, Baker et al. (2005) find that a high proportion of the poor walk to work, presumably because they can live, albeit squalidly, close to their workplaces. In addition, much of the decision as to whether one chooses public or private transport is as much social as economic and depends on how preferences are socially constructed. For example, the use of public transport among higher income groups is more in Mumbai and Kolkata than it is in Delhi.

308   *Mukhopadhyay and Revi*

Table 22.1 Capital cities and public transport availability

Public transport in capital cities	No	Yes	Total
No	17	36	53
Yes	1	20	21
Total	18	56	74

Source: Authors' calculations from data in MoUD (2008)

Energy consumption in water supply

In addition to the negative effect of climate change on freshwater availability, increasingly, as water begins to be transported over long distances, as in Bangalore, Indore and Delhi, a significant energy component is also embedded in water supply. In many Indian cities, even before they begin to treat their wastewater, electricity is among their main expenditures, so much so that in many states, fiscal transfers to them are made after deducting their dues to the state-owned electricity distribution company. When wastewater treatment becomes widespread; it would add to the energy bill. California, for example, uses 19% of its electricity to deliver, treat, and dispose of water (Government of California, 2008). This implies that the existing lower energy use for water in India is at the cost of increased pollution of water sources and the future would see a trade-off between mitigation pressures to reduce energy use and adaptation imperatives to treat wastewater.

Action space in adaptation

Since the response of the global climate system to mitigation actions will have a multi-decade lag adaptation measures are likely to be inevitable. Despite uncertainty over precise impacts due to the lack of downscaled climate data there is some agreement that enhanced risks in the foreseeable future will include (a) increased mean and peak temperatures, (b) changes in the mean, peak and the distribution of precipitation, (c) extreme weather events with associated storm surges and (d) sea-level rise (MEA, 2005; IPCC, 2007a, b).

These factors independently (or combined) lead to a large set of urban climate-related hazard risks for which some level of assessment and intervention already exists. The 'units of exposure' in an archetypical Indian city are people, enterprises, lifeline infrastructure elements, buildings, livelihood clusters and ecosystem services. Among these, populations, enterprises and livelihood groups can be vulnerable for many reasons: (a) location (b) multiple episodes of displacement (c) inability to ride out extreme events (d) disempowerment from entitlements (e) lack of capacity for preparedness and community and social safety nets.

City climate adaptation plan

This form of analysis is central to the development of detailed City Climate Adaptation Plans for operationalizing adaptation. Some concrete policy instruments and programmes that could help the blending of development, poverty and climate change agendas include:

Climate change and urbanization in India 309

(a) Hazard modification by repairing and strengthening strategic flood, storm surge and coastal defences. Detailed analysis will be needed to assess whether these investments are appropriate vis-à-vis other adaptation options.
(b) Enabling new construction to meet climate vulnerability norms. Considerable enterprise and institutional development inputs will be required to make this a reality. India's efforts towards formulating an Energy Conservation Building Code is a step in this direction.
(c) Technical measures to strengthen and retrofit buildings to have both adaptation and mitigation benefits. This would take considerable institutional and financial innovation.[5]
(d) Improving water use efficiency and conservation in conjunction with appropriate water management practices as a strategic defence against drought.

Relocation and rehabilitation as an adaptation measure should emerge as a policy option only after all other options have failed. Planning, market and financial instruments will be needed to adequately address local needs, with the recognition of the rights of residents to compensation. However, today even the most progressive rehabilitation policies rarely address climate change-related concerns.

Need for multi-level institutional co-ordination

A city climate adaptation plan would ideally need to link national, state and city policy, political and institutional arrangements, and interventions at local levels. It would also need to serve as a platform for dialogue between government functionaries, political leaders, CBOs and NGOs, and private entrepreneurs who could provide the motive power for adaptation implementation. Current governance structures and the institutional culture at city levels are inadequate for this task. A sketch for a possible framework at multiple levels is presented below.

(a) At the national level it is important to perform the following functions:
  (i) Articulate a clear definition of responsibilities that enables the integration of a cross-cutting climate change agenda into the national policy planning and investment process.
  (ii) Allocate the finances necessary for the effort and adopt the necessary fiscal measures.
  (iii) Assimilate and aggregate knowledge at a high level of granularity. The development of a national Risk and Vulnerability Atlas that includes climate change-related risks and estimates of potential effects could be an important first step.
  (iv) Assist in the creation of appropriate state and city institutional capacity to execute the adaptation agenda.

Among institutions, the National Disaster Management Agency (NDMA) could serve as a bridge between short and medium-term risk mitigation and long-term climate adaptation.

(b) As at the Centre, in the State, the finance and planning ministries will need to:
  (i) Integrate adaptation into medium-term planning and expenditure frameworks and try to synergize adaptation and mitigation investments across sectors.

310 *Mukhopadhyay and Revi*

(ii) Articulate the role of State Finance Commissions in enabling transfers and capacity building within ULBs.[6]

(iii) Make changes to appropriate housing and urban development, town planning and infrastructure legislations, to integrate disaster and climate change concerns into urban planning and development.

(iv) Build capacity of state public functionaries and bureaucrats in climate change risk assessment and adaptation planning.

But none of this is going to happen automatically. These governance developments remain a formidable challenge in a world where city growth remains tied to surplus extraction from real estate and where the dominant paradigm does not recognize the inter-relationships between the poorer and more vulnerable residents of the city with their better endowed neighbours. Climate change risks will only manifest themselves over a multi-decade period. While this provides an opportunity for pre-emptive actions to reduce the disruption to economic and social development processes, it also carries with it the danger of inaction, since its effects and benefits lie beyond the political and perception horizon.

Action space in mitigation

Many OECD countries, especially in Europe, are now engaged in decarbonizing their cities. This has led to improvements in energy and resource efficiency in appliances, vehicles and buildings. However, most such initiatives result in incremental changes, given an existing and locked-in urban infrastructure. The slow rate of urbanization in India means that lock-in is not yet an issue. Can this be taken advantage of to chart a lower-carbon path to urbanization?

India's National Action Plan on Climate Change (NAPCC) proposed a Sustainable Habitat Mission that sought to promote energy efficiency as an integral component of urban planning and renewal, through three initiatives: (a) application of the Energy Conservation Building Code; (b) urban waste management and recycling, including power production from waste and waste water recycling and (c) better urban planning and modal shift to public transport. Since then, the MoUD has released a document on a National Mission on Sustainable Habitat (NMSH), which is briefly described in Box 22.1.

The NMSH does not offer a radically new vision or set of instruments, preferring to stick to relatively traditional planning oriented approaches, even in the pilots it envisages. It is not clear how an approach presaged on better urban planning will help since India has not been very successful in applying building codes in urban planning and other approaches may be needed, e.g., incentive-based regulation imposing additional fees on buildings whose energy use exceeds a threshold.[7] Further, the priority for investments still focus on increasing supply, e.g. in water. While urban areas in India account for a fraction of total water consumption, they also consume water resources by discharging untreated wastewater. Indian cities need to demonstrate to the rest of her polity a concern for common use resources by reducing use of water. Much of the water consumption is by industry and higher income households and the use of pricing to reduce their use, albeit a minefield in India, needs to be discussed openly. Demand for fresh water could then be further reduced by recycling and reuse.[8] Such initiatives could, inter alia, form the basis of a much expanded pilot programme,

Climate change and urbanization in India 311

especially since it appears that the experience of these pilots will inform policy only after 2017. In the interim, the degree of lock-in can only be expected to rise.

The process of urban transformation in India is a collection of wicked problems to which one must now add climate change. As defined by Rittel and Webber (1973), wicked problems are often the symptom of deeper problems and their particular characteristics may override commonalities with similar problems elsewhere. They are affected by a multiplicity of poorly understood factors which do not offer themselves to manipulation. Every attempt to address the problem is consequential and creates new wicked problems, for which the solvers bear responsibility. Such problems are exacerbated in intensely pluralistic and transitional societies, such as in India.

BOX 22.1 NATIONAL MISSION ON SUSTAINABLE HABITAT

Consequent to the release of India's National Action Plan on Climate Change (NAPCC) in 2008, the Ministry of Urban Development released a document on a National Mission on Sustainable Habitat (NMSH) in 2010, with three main action areas, viz.: (a) legal and regulatory initiatives, (b) investments in physical infrastructure, and (c) pilot projects.

The legal and regulatory measures relate to increasing energy efficiency in the residential and commercial sectors, by developing standards and by-laws and mandating of certification of energy performance for buildings; development of transport planning norms, water harvesting and recharge, mandating water audit of utilities, and guidelines for managing solid waste, storm water and urban planning.

Under the NMSH, about three-fourths of the investment of over USD 11 billion planned over 2010–17 is shared equally between new water supply and sewerage connections and water saving through replacement of pipes. About a seventh is for recycling and reuse of wastewater and the rest is for solid waste treatment including bio-methanation, etc. Focus on reuse of water, though present in the NMSH, is thus, still nascent.

The NMSH is also proposing a number of pilot projects, over 2010–17, for increasing energy efficiency in buildings, improving urban transport, conservative wastewater management and solid waste management as well was a small allocation for a pilot climate adaptation plan. It also proposes the establishment of a National Commission on Sustainable Urbanization.

The NMSH document is available at http://www.urbanindia.nic.in/programme/uwss/NMSH.pdf.

Increasing use of public transport

The public transport debate seems to be around bus vis-à-vis rail mass transit. Urban metro rail systems are high investment and have a high lock-in character from a climate perspective with uncertain benefits in energy intensity. Despite this, many cities in India are attempting private sector rail based mass transit. In part, this is driven by governance failures that make road usage painfully slow. It also helps that high investment

312   *Mukhopadhyay and Revi*

modes offer more chances for rent seeking. If so, it is quite likely that in some cases at least, the lack of more and better trained traffic police may drive urban choices in an unsustainable direction. Yet, hiring and training traffic police is not thought of as a climate mitigating investment.[9]

Elsewhere, it appears unlikely that public transportation of indifferent quality or high cost with per trip fares can compete with the ease and economy of the two-wheeler, especially when the decision to provide public transport is not that of the city (see Table 22.1). However, low-cost modern ticketing systems, coupled with better predictability of service (using GPS and SMS technology) could indeed increase use of public transport. However, except for a few cities there appears to be little movement in this direction. Furthermore, intermediate modes like autorickshaws with per seat fares provide an option with low capital cost and low per vehicle capacity. Kolkata, for instance, runs an innovative short route-based system for auto-rickshaws that operates like a switched network. This allows frequent operation and increases the attractiveness of public transport, especially for the poor, but such modes are often neglected.

Not just within cities, transport can affect urban form across cities too. Here again, rail is a double edged sword. High speed rail has the potential to increase sprawl by reducing commute time, but it could also spawn a series of compact cities. This is a challenge not only because of lock-in effects, but because of a wide range of wicked problems that do not relate to standard building by-laws and master plans but refer to much broader economic policies that nevertheless seem to have an effect on the urban form.

Decentralization and service delivery

Another wicked problem is the relevance of local government. The 74th Amendment to the Indian Constitution places the tools traditionally used for moulding the city form – town planning – with the local government. But, not only have States not transferred this function to the city effectively, city form is also affected by broader economic policies, outside local control (Nivola, 1999).[10] However, GHG mitigation is a global public good and perhaps local governance should not be entrusted with producing it. The right allocation of responsibilities across levels of government remains a vexed question.

The responsibility of different levels of government is tied to intergovernmental financing. Much of the urban reform agenda in India is structured around improving property tax collection. However, it now appears that not only will climate change require much more investment in cities than property taxes can generate, the tax itself may be responsible for urban sprawl (Slack, 2006). The levels of income/property values in India may not permit the provision of services that induce sprawl based on such taxes alone just yet, but it is important to consider what the nature of the federal financial system should be. It can be argued that if the quality of local public goods remains high and equitable, there will be less interest in establishing separate communities. This requires addressing questions on the quality of service delivery and the appropriate mix of financing vis-à-vis local taxes and statutory transfers.[11] In India, this effect may be mitigated by private coping options. Today, over two-thirds of the urban school children go to private schools, obviating one of the needs to establish separate communities. It may appear odd to consider education delivery and fiscal transfers as climate change instruments, but they may be more relevant in determining urban form in terms of city shapes and location of cities over the long run, than traditional measures like better fuel efficiency.

Home ownership and transport demand

In addition to property taxes, the propagation of home ownership may also cause urban sprawl. The supply of such homes in the core city would involve densification, which, even if it was permitted by building by-laws, is difficult to provide, since it involves replacing existing structures. This is usually hard to do, except in countries like China. New homebuyers therefore move outside the core city resulting in urban sprawl. Added to this, the new labour market implies multiple job changes. Once a home is purchased, the costs of relocating closer to a new job are high, bringing distance between home and work. Over time, this leads to a rise in transport demand. In this context, increasing the supply of rental housing may prove to be climate-friendly.

One silver lining in this situation is that the search for a more climate-sensitive urbanization path is likely to result in a number of co-benefits in city efficiency, which can only add power to our economic engine, given that our economic activity is becoming significantly concentrated in our cities. Such efficiency innovations in urban systems are more likely to be replicated across Indian cities than other countries, with higher degrees of lock-in, thus increasing the competitiveness of our urban system even further.

Conclusion

Urbanization in India is both a necessary input and an inevitable consequence of growth. We have argued that climate change impacts are likely to affect urban residents adversely, especially the more vulnerable among them. They can lead to increased migration, especially of eco-refugees or discourage migration, by turning cities in even more hostile environments than they already are. Our urban lifestyle, building design, transportation behaviour, the way our cities now raid water from long distances, our current institutions and some of social values all contribute to a high carbon growth path.

Under these conditions, the immediate concern for India is to ensure that our cities adapt to adverse climate conditions and as such adaptation efforts will be privileged over mitigation actions without co-benefits. In this, we are constrained by the poor development of our local institutions and our inability to integrate the various different agencies that would need to respond, if climate change risks crystallized.

Over the medium term however, we must accept that existing urbanization models are unsustainable at Indian scale and there is no off-the-shelf alternative trajectory.[12] Unfortunately, India's approach in the NMSH suggests that we have not yet decided to look for alternatives. It is however true that charting a new urbanization path, that is dense, public transport-rich and compatible with the surrounding biome, is fraught with wicked problems for which we do not yet have the answers. What we do know is that the answers do not lie in the urban domain alone and that much of the conventional wisdom about issues like decentralization, fiscal federalism and homeownership may need to be re-examined. We need to discover policy levers that will drive our organic urban growth process in a more sustainable direction.

314 *Mukhopadhyay and Revi*

At a broader level, climate change-induced disruptions will force Indian cities to alter their extractive relationship with the countryside. *RUrbanism* or 'keeping the balance between rural and urban areas' could become increasingly important, as resource and socioeconomic conflicts becomes sharper (Revi et al., 2006). Maintaining two-way flows of food, biomass, water, energy, livelihoods, products and services across this *RUrban* continuum will be crucial to the development transition.

A critical part is the establishment of mutual trust across urban and non-urban spaces. We must recognize that despite their exclusion from the formal economy of the city, the poor survive and subsidize the better off through their poor living and working conditions. A significant decline in the productivity of the poor could seriously affect a city's development and competitiveness. Relief for the primary constraints of the poor lie not in the climate sphere but in the space provided by better and more accountable city governance, democratic decentralization and improving the functioning of public institutions, the re-creation of the commons through multiple political and institutional struggles. Mitigation and adaptation can thus come with significant co-benefits for the political harmony of the country.

But, how will these changes happen? Enabling the wide range of changes that have been articulated will require the development of a deep and systemic innovation system that functions within and across particular cities and regions. While the autonomy of technical progress has been compromised, it may still be our best hope. Technology can interface with society as digital communication helps a large number of dispersed but commonly aligned social movements coalesce into a critical mass. Greater equity, access to entitlements and markets, efficient and sustainable public services and access to commons such as knowledge, space, ecosystem services and biodiversity are values that will need to be nurtured and rediscovered in many parts of the world but equally so, within our borders. Only then can we expect our cities to enable the fullest realization of people's potential in a sustainable manner.

Notes

1 This is an updated and abridged version of a chapter previously published in *The Economic and Political Weekly*, vol. 44, issue 31 pp. 59–70 (August 2009). Reproduced here with permission from *The Economic and Political Weekly*.
2 Urban population projections at the city level are notoriously fickle. See, for example, Table 7.1 in World Bank (2009).
3 This is done in a relatively crude manner by comparing the top rural quintile to the penultimate urban quintile. The expenditure ratios for the 40th, 60th and 80th rural percentiles, as a proportion of 20th, 40th and 60th urban percentiles are 1.02, 0.92 and 0.87 respectively. The more careful approach would be to use a spatial price index to make urban and rural incomes comparable, but this is beyond the scope of this chapter.
4 Para-transit, especially that offered by low-capacity vehicles can often play a critical role in reducing the cost of access to public transport by linking mainline corridors to residential areas more frequently. Similar frequency using high-capacity public transport such as buses, would nullify their carbon advantage, due to low capacity utilization.
5 Retrofits have rarely been implemented outside OECD cities, but China has recently begun to move aggressively. During the Eleventh Five-Year Plan, it plans to retrofit 150,000,000 m^2 of existing residential buildings in three areas, viz.: building envelope, heat metering and heat source and systems. The intent is to realize an energy saving of 16 million tons of standard coal (33 $mtCO_2$) by the end of the plan period (Zhao and Wu, 2009).
6 An open question is the mix between own resources of cities, state level funding and national funding. The JNNURM provides one example of how the financial envelope of cities can change, though it remains mired in the existing three-layer hierarchy of governments.

Climate change and urbanization in India 315

7 The tax cannot be increasing in total consumption because it would discourage density. Furthermore, this assumes, reasonably in our opinion, that the effect of per capita intensity in the use of space on energy demand is negligible.

8 This may increase the energy intensity of water, depending on the distance of water transfers. However, California, which uses 19% of its electricity and 30% of its natural gas (non-power plant) to deliver, treat, and dispose of water, has determined that the balance would favour re-use (House, 2006). Within treatment too, a number of options are possible, with biological treatment, e.g., using artificial wetlands that may prove more energy efficient than chemical and mechanical methods.

9 A related issue is that of parking. A body of literature now discourages in-building parking as a disincentive for car ownership. However, in India, where illegal on-street parking is rampant, does such a policy achieve its purpose or does it simply increase emissions by increasing congestion? Here too, the traffic police seem to be part of the story.

10 Despite pious pronouncements to use it as an opportunity to build self-governing cities, JNNURM has been largely used as a means to build traditional infrastructure (with a strong focus on water supply and drainage systems, much like the NMSH), often executed by state government agencies.

11 Discretionary transfers, à la JNNURM can prove to be useful for specific actions and perhaps to advance the time when such actions are adopted, but are unlikely to affect long term structure, owing to their intrinsically temporary nature.

12 For a possible alternative, see Shukla (2008).

References

Baker, J., Basu, R., Cropper, M., Lall, S. and Takeuchi, A. (2005) 'Urban poverty and transport: the case of Mumbai', *Policy Research Working Paper* Series 3693, The World Bank.

de Vries, H.J.M., Revi, A., Bhat, G.K., Hilderink, H. and Lucas, P. (2007) 'India 2050: scenarios for an uncertain future', MNP Report 550,033002/2007 Netherlands Environmental Assessment Agency (MNP), Bilthoven.

Dyson, T., Cassen, R. and Visaria, L. (eds.) (2004) *Twenty-First Century India: Population, Economy, Human Development and the Environment*, Oxford New Delhi.

Dyson, T. and Visaria, P. (2004) 'Migration and urbanisation: retrospect and prospects', in T. Dyson, R. Cassen, and L. Visaria, (eds.) *Twenty-First Century India: Population, Economy, Human Development and the Environment*, Oxford, New Delhi, pp. 108–129.

Fuente, A. de la, Felipe, López-Calva, L.P. and Revi, A. (2008) 'Assessing the relationship between natural hazards and poverty: A conceptual and methodological proposal', ISDR Geneva.

Government of California (2008) 'Proposed Wetcat strategies and measures', http://www.climatechange.ca.gov/wetcat/documents/wetcat-strategy_summaries_3-24-08.pdf, accessed 3 May 2011.

House, L. (2006) 'Water Supply Related Electricity Demand in California', http://www.fypower.org/pdf/CA_WaterSupply_Electricity.pdf, accessed 6 May 2011.

Hwang Ruey-Lung, Ming-Jen Cheng, Tzu-Ping Lin and Ming-Chin Ho (2009) 'Thermal perceptions, general adaptation methods and occupant's idea about the trade-off between thermal comfort and energy saving in hot–humid regions', *Building and Environment*, volume 44, issue 6, pp. 1128–1134.

IPCC (2007a) *Climate Change 2007: Impacts, Adaptation and Vulnerability*, Contribution of Working Group II to the *Fourth Assessment Report of the Intergovernmental Panel on Climate Change*, M.L. Parry, O.F. Canziani, J.P. Palutikof, P.J. van der Linden and C.E. Hanson (eds), Cambridge University Press, Cambridge, UK.

IPCC (2007b) *Climate Change 2007: Mitigation*, Contribution of Working Group III to the *Fourth Assessment Report of the Intergovernmental Panel on Climate Change*, B. Metz, O.R. Davidson, P.R. Bosch, R. Dave, L.A. Meyer (eds), Cambridge University Press, Cambridge, United Kingdom and New York, USA.

316 *Mukhopadhyay and Revi*

Millennium Ecosystem Assessment (MEA) (2005) 'Ecosystems and human well-being: Synthesis', Island Press, Washington, DC.

Ministry of Urban Development (MoUD) (2008) 'Traffic and transportation policies and strategies in urban areas in India', Government of India.

Mees, P. (2010) 'Density and sustainable transport in US, Canadian and Australian cities: Another look at the data', 12th World Conference on Transport Research, Lisbon, July.

Newman, P. and Kenworthy, J. (1999) *Sustainability and Cities: Overcoming Automobile Dependence*, Island Press, Washington, DC.

Newsham, Guy R., Mancini, S. and Birt, B. (2009) 'Do LEED-certified buildings save energy? Yes, but . . .', *Energy and Buildings,* volume 41, issue 8, August, pp. 897–905.

Nivola, S. (1999) *Laws of the Landscape: How Policies Shape Cities in Europe and America*, Brookings Institution Press.

Pachauri, S. (2007) *An Energy Analysis of Household Consumption: Changing Patterns of Direct and Indirect Use in India, Berlin, Heidelberg*, Springer, New York.

Revi, A. (2008) 'Climate Change: an adaptation and mitigation agenda for Indian Cities', *Environment and Urbanization*, vol. 20, issue 1, Sage, London.

Revi, A., Prakash, S., Mehrotra, R., Bhat, G.K., Gupta, K. and Gore, R. (2006) 'Goa 2100: The transition to a sustainable RUrban design', *Environment and Urbanization*, vol. 18, issue 1; pp. 51–65, Sage, London.

Rittel, H. and Webber, M. (1973) 'Dilemmas in a General Theory of Planning', *Policy Sciences*, volume 4, pp. 155–169.

SEWA Bharat (2006) Socio-Economic Status of Construction Workers in Delhi: A Study http://www.wiego.org/news/E-Newsletters/2006/survey_report_socioecon_status_ construction_workers.pdf

Shukla, P.R. (2008) 'Alignment with Sustainable Development Goals', presentation at Symposium on Achieving a Sustainable Low-Carbon Society, 13 June, London.

Slack, E. (2006) 'The Impact of Municipal Finance and Governance on Urban Sprawl'. A paper sponsored by the Science Advisory Board of the International Joint Commission http://www.utoronto.ca/mcis/imfg/pdf/international joint commission paper Sep 6.pdf

TERI (2009) 'Sustainable Buildings and Construction for India-Policies, Practices and Performance: Influence of Indian buildings on Climate change, Background Paper', http:// www.teriin.org/events/DSDS/Sus_bldg_paper.pdf, accessed 2 May 2011.

World Bank (2009) *World Development Report Reshaping Economic Geography,* World Bank Washington, DC.

Zhao, Jing and Yong, Wu. (2009) 'Introduction: Theory and Practice on building energy efficiency in China', *Energy Policy*, Volume 37, Issue 6, p. 2053.

23 Agriculture in the environment

Are sustainable climate friendly systems possible in India?

Rajeswari Raina

Climate change is a bag of nettles in India's contentious, iniquitous and unsustainable agriculture sector. Climate change is expected to adversely impact agriculture through increased temperatures, inter-and intra-seasonal changes in precipitation and temperature regimes, and sea level rise. The expected result is an overall decline in food grain production in the country.

These anticipated changes carry potentially serious consequences, making adaptation a central issue for Indian agriculture. Nearly 60 per cent of the nation's workforce is in agriculture; most cultivator households are also food buyers, and many are poor and food insecure. In addition, many agricultural systems and their supporting ecosystems are stressed or in crisis. Already degraded, these systems must somehow be transformed to produce even more food.

Adaptation to climate change demands a shift from the current worldview of agriculture *versus* the environment, to one of agriculture *in* the environment, marked by increasing understanding and co-evolution of ecological and social systems. Climate smart agriculture would sustainably increase productivity, resilience and adaptation, and enhance achievement of national food security and development goals (FAO, 2010). Interestingly, however, this shift can also have the additional effect of mitigating emissions from the agriculture sector, as discussed further below. This is a significant additional gain, since agriculture contributed 17 per cent of GHG emissions of India in 2007, and even more if we take into account emissions associated with inputs like fertilizers and distribution – or 'food miles'.

This chapter begins with a brief overview of India's climate change agenda in agriculture, as proposed by the National Mission for Sustainable Agriculture (NMSA), part of the National Action Plan on Climate Change. The NMSA pursues the Indian predilection to re-invest in energy and input intensive agricultural production. This is part of a globally accepted worldview that equates increased production to food security and pushes agriculture against the environment – in the process pushing the livelihoods and ecosystems that sustain millions of rural poor into further distress. This approach is unlikely to help adaptation and resilience building.

The next section discusses how the highly acclaimed successes of the input intensive green revolution strategies have not helped achieve food security. Alternative approaches that seek food and environmental security, enabled by civil society initiatives and limited state support, conceptualize agriculture *in* the environment. They focus attention on the economic and ecological outcomes in each location. Contrary to the energy-guzzling capital intensive production systems being promoted, these alternative approaches ensure adaptation and mitigation.

318 *Raina*

But pursuing mitigation and adaptation through resilient and sustainable agro-ecological systems and regional food security is a significant political and social challenge. Fostering policies and practices that nurture diversity, local investments and employment, and reduce massive transportation, processing and trade requirements goes against the grain of how the business of agriculture is currently done.

BOX 23.1 GHG EMISSIONS FROM AGRICULTURE

Agriculture contributes anywhere between 10–12 per cent of global anthropogenic GHG emissions (IPCC, 2007). If the emissions from input production (especially fertilizers and other agro-chemicals) and the food miles till the consumer's table are added, then agriculture accounts for 25–30 per cent of all GHG emissions. Globally, the livestock sub-sector contributes 18 per cent of global GHG emissions (FAO, 2006).

Indian estimates show agriculture accounting for 17 per cent of GHG emissions in 2007, coming third following energy and industry accounting for 58 and 22 per cent respectively (INCCA, 2010). The inventory of emissions includes livestock – enteric fermentation (accounting for 63 per cent), rice cultivation (21 per cent), crop soils (13 per cent) and livestock manure and crop residue burning (2.7 per cent); it uses India specific emission factors that are lower than the IPCC default values (say 30 per cent lower for N_2O emissions from Indian cropping systems). Agriculture is the largest contributor to methane (77 per cent of total CH_4) emissions and nitrous oxide (60 per cent of the total N_2O) emissions from India (INCCA, 2010).

Globally, India accounts for only 5 per cent of GHG emissions. With a recorded increase of 65 per cent between 1990 and 2005, the projected emissions per capita by 2031 will still be lower than the global average of 4.22 tonnes of CO_2e in 2005 (CMF, 2009). Given that per capita emissions are 70 per cent below the global average and 93 per cent below that of the USA, and that agriculture accounts for only 23 per cent of the total emissions the focus in India is to enable adaptation to climate change and bargain for greater ecological space and more international support – especially finance and technology from the affluent North.

The current agenda: The National Mission for Sustainable Agriculture (NMSA)

The NMSA plans to 'support development of climate-resilient crops, expansion of weather insurance mechanisms and location specific agricultural practices' (PM-CCC, 2008). Given that 'progressive adaptation' is a key requirement, the agricultural research system will have to be 'oriented to monitor and evaluate climate change and recommend changes in agricultural practices accordingly' (PM-CCC, 2008). The NMSA has devised its agenda, seeking increasing convergence between traditional knowledge and practices, information technology, geo-spatial technologies and bio-technologies.

Sustainable climate friendly agriculture? 319

The NMSA has decided to focus on four areas that are crucial for the adaptation of Indian agriculture to climate change: (1) dryland agriculture, (2) risk management, (3) access to information, and (4) use of biotechnology.

India's drylands and Sub-Saharan Africa are slated to face the worst impacts due to multiple stresses, including the exclusive dependence on rainfed agriculture, already high incidence of poverty, inadequate attention from agricultural research and extension systems, weak institutional infrastructures and low adaptive capacity often worsened by contradicting policies (IAASTD, 2009; Lobell et al., 2008; Raina 2006; V&A Programme, 2009). Thereby, the NMSA's first focus is on dryland agriculture, accounting for over 60 per cent of the arable land in the country.

Both climate variability (the statistical distribution of weather over certain periods of time – say a few months or a season) and climate change (the long-term change) will affect crop production, reducing yields by 30 to 40 per cent of current yields and up to 63 to 82 per cent by the end of the 21st century (Brown and Funk, 2008; Smith et al., 2007). Given the estimated reduction in yields of staple crops – especially wheat (Nelson et al., 2009a), the NMSA's second focus is on crop insurance and other management support. Insurance to cover the risk due to increased adoption of standard capital intensive inputs that can enhance productivity, will be critical for the future. The third component, strengthening availability and access to information is also crucial, given that very little decentralized (meso-level variables) environmental and socio-economic information exists to support farming, and whatever little is present exists in a prescriptive mode for annual crop cycles with no interactive information support other than a few experiments with information technology (cell phones, computers or television). The fourth agenda on biotechnology is also important, given that many of the staple foods known today may not yield enough given increasing CO_2 levels and high variability in intra-seasonal temperature and precipitation (IPCC, 2007).

While the four areas of focus of the NMSA are important, there are concerns about the content and specific activities proposed and the assumption that inadequate research-extension linkages, and weak institutional capacities will correct themselves. How will these four focal areas help adaptation? Will NMSA's drought and pest resistant varieties help India's dryland agriculture? The future is one where rainfall intensity will increase in large parts of the *Deccan* plateau (Kumar et al., 2006), with high variability, changing the current relationships between precipitation, run-off, humidity and soil moisture which critically determine crop growth and output. Also, varieties cannot be bred or designed for progressive adaptation to climate change – because it is unlikely that there will be a steady pace or incremental change – most changes will be sudden or will arrive with significant variability inter- and intra-seasonal. How far will crop insurance help the farmers, when formal sources cover only 30 per cent of the agricultural credit used by Indian farmers? How will insurance schemes cover millions of women cultivators with no property deed or collateral to access formal credit, whose only option is recourse to low risk crops or crop-livestock combinations?

The NMSA agenda is dictated by the demand for agricultural production enhancement for national food security. In this framework, agricultural production technology and practices push agriculture *against* the environment.

320 *Raina*

An agenda in vain

Today, India is home to the largest number of undernourished people and malnourished children anywhere in the world (UNICEF, 2008). Almost 60 per cent of India's active workforce is employed in agriculture (compared to 2 to 4 per cent in developed countries). Cultivators and workers account for over 410 million in a total of over 740 million (2004–05), classified as rural work force (NCEUS, 2007). With the share of agriculture in national GDP declining from 50 per cent (1950–51) to less than 16 per cent in 2009–10, this increasing population dependent on a thinning share of the national income, is cause for concern because the magnitude of production and relative economic value of the sector will be affected by climate change.

Production policies and technologies contribute significantly to the economic and ecological distress in rural, agrarian India. Farming is largely unviable due to increasing costs of modern inputs – of fertilizers, chemicals, water, seeds, agro-machinery and implements, and declining factor productivity (Acharya and Jogi, 2007; Swaminathan, 2005). The doubling of the incremental capital output ratio from about 2 to 4 in less than two decades (Golait and Lokare, 2008), punishes farmers, since every rupee of output demands 4 times the investment. With increasing capital intensity comes declining growth of income per worker (Sen and Bhatia, 2004), and low and declining employment elasticity in agriculture (Palanivel, 2006). Moreover, there are increasing soil and water problems – both quantity (declining arable land and water tables) and quality (soil and water systems degradation) (ICAR, 1998; Government of India, 2005; 2008; Kulkarni and Vijayashankar, 2010), which further reduces the returns to inputs. Rural India offers limited opportunities for non-farm employment (NCEUS, 2007), though an average cultivator household relies heavily on non-farm income (30–80 per cent in different states).

Farmers' capacities to respond to climate variability and change are weakened further because of the technologies and interventions for food security, which ignore the location and interactions of farming with specific environmental and social contexts. Subsidies and pricing mechanisms push agriculture against these environments; subsidies for tube wells and fertilizers that lead to depletion of groundwater and soil degradation are prime examples. The input intensive production paradigm is part of a globally accepted framework of knowledge and policies, dictated by development theory. Whether practised in communist or capitalist regimes, this paradigm addresses the distribution of food, after food has been produced through ways that engender unemployment, environmental disruption and food crisis for the rural poor (Friedman, 1992; IAASTD, 2009; Lang, 2010). A targeted public distribution system, cheap food grains scheme, or guaranteed employment are not lasting solutions, because the environmental crisis in agriculture threatens future capacities for increased production (Nellemann et al., 2009), thereby leaving little to supply. Predictions of an unpredictable, inclement climate make matters worse.

The Indian picture mirrors the global food security paradigm. Globally, food security policy interventions ignore and interfere with the close relationships between many of the constituents of well-being and the provisioning, regulating and enriching components of ecosystems (UNEP-IISD, 2004; Nellemann, 2009). The rural poor (especially small farmers, women, herders, pastoralists and landless labour who constitute over 80 per cent of the poor anywhere in the developing world) have been (i) subject to the 'exclusionary practices – intentional or unintentional – by the 'non-poor' and thereby prevented from accessing the various services offered by ecosystems, and (ii) 'bear a disproportionately heavy burden of the impacts of ecosystem degradation . . . caused by the non-poor'; they are excluded from participating in an equitable manner in the commercial activities introduced into ecosystems converted to massive cereal production tracts to ensure food security (UNEP-IISD, 2004, pp. 21–22; Jodha, 1986).

India today accounts for 72 per cent of the undernourished population in South Asia, and 43 per cent of all undernourished people in the Asia-Pacific region (WFP and FAO, 2010). This staggering 300 million hungry and undernourished people, mainly in rural areas, must be seen in the context of the green revolution paradigm of blanket application of capital intensive technologies across diverse social and ecological contexts. Should the same paradigm be espoused in the current NMSA? The content of each of the four areas identified by the NMSA, buttressed with enhanced water supply and chemicals, risks adding to the distress already evident among millions of marginal and small farmers, dryland, coastal and mountain ecosystems. Coastal livelihoods that are threatened, given the estimates of sea level rise, do not even figure in the NAPCC – an omission that does not sit well with over 200 million people depending on coastal livelihoods. The silence on livestock – especially fodder (which is already a major constraint to the livestock sub-sector), diseases, and zoonoses, is alarming, given the pro-poor livelihood options that these sub-sectors offer. Current food security policy framework and technology choices have little to offer to these sub-sectors. They are ill-equipped to comprehend the complexity and constant evolution of knowledge and practices for survival in these sub-sectors.

Towards climate friendly, sustainable production systems

The climate debates within the country have discussed agriculture mainly in terms of adaptation capacities, with little or no attention given to the industrial appropriation of agriculture that has already happened. In the developed countries agriculture is today a net energy consumer, having lost its status as a net energy producer. Increasing industrial appropriation and substitution of agriculture with increasing fossil-fuel use has made agriculture – the fundamental source of energy for human beings – one of the worst polluters of the atmosphere (CO_2, CH_4, and NO_x emissions), soil, and water systems (nitrates, phosphorus, and several toxic chemicals). Value addition – by processing, storing, marketing, and transporting food across the globe – is sustainable only because energy and labor that feed into agribusiness and other industries are cheap to maintain (Pimentel and Pimentel 2008; IATP 2008).[1] Should India emulate these energy-guzzling, capital-intensive agri-food systems? Will climate change enable a re-consideration of current economic growth patterns, including the industrial appropriation of agriculture?

Many of the present estimates of decline in food production (Brown and Funk, 2008), priorities for climate change adaptation and food security (Lobell et al., 2008) and the amount of investment needed country-wise and crop-wise (Nelson et al., 2009b) are based on the assumptions and parameters of mainstream mono-crop cereal-based input intensive production systems. Food insecure tropical regions are regions where farming is 'manually conducted using a hoe and planting stick with few inputs', (Brown and Funk, 2008, p. 580). Contrary to such academic caricature, they are not tropical farms with 'far fewer options in their agricultural system' (*ibid*); they have multiple options, are highly risk aware and adept at adaptation.

322 *Raina*

The National Rainfed Areas Authority (NRAA, 2009) in India enumerates '34 predominant crops' in rainfed tropical areas compared to 2 or 3 in irrigated areas. Farmer's practices for soil moisture conservation are plenty in rainfed regions – while irrigated rice–wheat tracts, especially in North and West Indian states have few practices to fall back upon to conserve soil moisture when their precipitation and irrigation patterns will change. For instance, the formal policy and research actors are yet to acknowledge that India's drylands, accounting for over 60 per cent of the arable land, more than 50 per cent of foodgrain production, almost all the coarse grains, millets, and over 80 per cent of cotton and pulse production, have always faced low and erratic rainfall and frequent inter-and intra-seasonal changes in temperature (Shah, 2006). Many crop production techniques and associated social formations and capacities (such as traditional water harvesting and irrigation systems, modern integrated pest management (IPM) and systems of rice intensification (SRI)), in these regions, are under-researched and receive limited or no policy support. With annual rainfall ranging from 100–400 mm in arid areas and 400–800 mm in semi-arid areas, there is a history of adaptation to low and erratic rainfall (with the co-efficient of variation ranging from 40–70 per cent) (V&A Programme, 2009). Despite the food security rhetoric of Indian agricultural policy, the drylands receive less than 6 per cent of the agricultural subsidies in the country (Acharya and Jogi, 2007), even as they contribute significantly to food security of the poor!

Small farms make a massive contribution to food and environmental security (Altieri, 2009). India's small farmers (handling 86 per cent of operational holdings covering over 68 per cent of area cultivated), herders and pastoralists who produce a mixture of local food and animal (mainly small ruminants and poultry) products are the backbone of regional food security. They are flexible, adaptable and use diverse crops, cultivars and combinations thereof. With climate variability and change adding to challenges in agriculture, the world of science is now paying attention to the knowledge base of small farms (especially gendered know-how) that reduces crop loss – choice of drought tolerant or pest tolerant varieties, opportunistic weeding, agro-biodiversity management, furrow-bund planting, traditional chemical-free storage techniques, etc. Currently these features of small farms (scorned as 'laggards, non-adopters, resource poor, or unskilled') and village level or local networks and institutional support systems are not captured by any of the climate change models. These are knowledge systems and technologies that underscore the critical relationship between agricultural production and the environment. Agriculture is conceptualized and practiced as an activity within the environment.

Sustainable production systems allow us to consider the prospects for carbon mitigation without sacrificing farmer livelihoods. C sequestration or removal of atmospheric CO_2 by terrestrial ecosystems and converting the sequestered C into organic C is a great opportunity for mitigation, that co-exists with many adaptation practices that small farmers follow (IPCC, 2007 (Ch. 8); Lal, 2010; Wang et al., 2010). Pro-poor livestock development efforts that are consistent with mitigation (livestock accounting for 63 per cent of emissions from Indian agriculture) and adaptation (livestock being the main economic resource for the poorest rural households) practices and systems have been documented and analysed (INCCA, 2010; Ramdas and Ghotke, 2006), but are far from the national policy arena (V&A Programme, 2009). Optimization of the energy efficiency and productivity of Carbon (C) sequestration in agriculture, through cropping system changes, crop rotation, inter cropping, cover

Sustainable climate friendly agriculture? 323

cropping, low C crop-livestock combinations, etc., requires a different research strategy and support systems in agriculture. Former defensive breeding strategies and agronomic knowledge that built horizontal resistance to a range of stress factors (water, temperature, pests, etc.) will have to be recalled to replace the current offensive breeding and engineering of crops to withstand a single stress variable.

There is no universally applicable list of mitigation mechanisms; most of them, like agriculture itself, have to be evaluated at the meso-level, within specific agro-ecological systems with internally consistent edaphic and historical processes. What is important to note is that many mitigation mechanisms are consistent with adaptation capacities; they do not threaten food security, ensure environmental integrity and do need effective stakeholder participation and stewardship – in particular where small farms and traditional or local knowledge systems are critical (FAO, 2010; V&A Programme, 2009).

That adaptation measures can also help mitigation has been proven by several experiments like the ones initiated by CSOs. Experiments on rainfed crops, indigenous technologies, local agri-food systems, non-pesticide crop management practices, small-ruminant production systems, watershed development, soil and moisture conservation, local markets, organic production, village forestry and management, non-farm livelihoods, herders and pastoralists, and storage and exchange mechanisms, offer major lessons for co-jointed mitigation and adaptation. But these lessons come in the wake of some earlier and more poignant debates about land reform, land grab, pesticide contamination, food retail, or others like rainfed vs. irrigated agriculture, organic vs. chemical-based production, liberalization vs. protected markets, subsidies vs. investment, etc. These have already positioned the state against a range of local organizations, in particular those located in the drylands, mountain or coastal eco-systems. It must be acknowledged that state interventions in sustainable, eco-friendly alternatives such as the integrated pest management or local watershed development schemes, have succeeded only in cases where CSOs, relevant experts and local markets have played a major role in the design and implementation of schemes (Raina, 2009).

Given the current approach of measuring individual variables, it may be difficult to measure, report and validate the resilience of the climate friendly small farms, rainfed crop production, and crop-livestock systems. Inter-disciplinary knowledge, to explain and enable intervention in these systems relationships, especially in highly intractable and diverse terrains, has long been on the anvil of sustainable development research. (Lele, 2008). Social sciences inputs necessary to consolidate our natural science understanding of these relationships are underdeveloped and need substantial research support (Ehrlich, 2010). If market mechanisms are to be enabled to include the poor, say, small farmers or herders paid for their C-sequestration efforts, the knowledge gap in our understanding of sub-national or local impacts of climate change and limited capacities for decision-making must also be acknowledged (V&A Programme, 2009). There is concern about increasing rates of glacial melting and consequent floods in the Himalayan rivers fed by glaciers, though there is little agreement on the extent to which these rivers, crucial to India's irrigated plains, depend on glaciers (see USAID, 2010). However, the little technical or financial support for local adaptation and crop management is available will work only if there are substantial local capacities.

Many local capacities, and action to ensure the fundamental 'right to food' are being facilitated by civil society organizations; all in the midst of increasing concerns that climate change negotiations do not adequately address questions of human rights,

324   *Raina*

especially the right to food (see HBF, 2009). It might seem appropriate that the NMSA should strategically link its agenda to that of these rights and capacities at the community or local level; the nature of engagement necessary will then be more than technology development or dissemination. What are the ways in which the state can enable organic C build-up in the soil, to enrich agricultural production and productivity, soil moisture retention, and soil quality, to ensure that agricultural livelihoods and incomes become sustainable? Certainly, the expected returns to corporate investments in agriculture (say dams, or power stations or retail chains) may not work out if small changes in the structure of these dynamic systems trigger massive and cascading system changes. Markets can help only to a certain extent – flexibility and information will be central to conform with the new rules of variability and change laid out by nature. The state and CSOs as well as the corporate sector, as environmentally and socially responsible actors, will become central to climate adaptation and mitigation in agriculture.

Is there a way out?

Agriculture, which is a net energy producer and ideal C-capture medium, is expected to play its extractive role, proffering both, surplus output as well as labour for secondary and tertiary sector growth. In a system that will increasingly turn unpredictable and absolutely unmanageable by current centralized decision making, this worldview will change.

In India, policy making and implementation mechanisms find it impossible to engage with the prospect that mitigation is entirely consistent with agricultural and rural development goals, and can foster the long term sustainability of ecological and social systems. The need for 'new rules or institutions and policy processes that enable cross-sectoral policy integration, iterative methods for decision-making under conditions of uncertainty, vertical policy co-ordination across different scales of the economy and ecosystems, processes of devolution of knowledge and capacity for action, and ways of policy evaluation and continuous policy learning and change' has been stated time and again (Dovers and Hezri, 2010). But such academic pleas are not enough to elicit the changes in the norms of technocracy, selective perception, and target and control that govern policy formulation, choice of instruments and implementation mechanisms, and evaluation, within individual sectors like agriculture. The political vision and policy capacity to see agriculture *in* the environment, necessary to address production and system performance, biodiversity, soil and water quality, and overall sustainability, are missing in India today. The very fact that these goals are constitutive of the well-being and productivity of small farms, regional capacities to promote less impacted crops, and low carbon agri-food production and distribution systems (Li Chin et al., 2010; FAO, 2010), is yet to be acknowledged in policy circles.

The pointers signal a climate change agenda in agriculture that simultaneously addresses pro-poor development and sustainability; capacities for adaptation and mitigation. This agenda can gradually re-build the wealth of human and ecological systems in rural India.

Note

1 Fewer than 2 billion people in the developed countries use 70 per cent of global fossil energy annually, while over 4 billion in the developing countries live on less than 30 per cent (Pimentel 2009).

References

Acharya, S.S. and Jogi, R.L. (2007) Input subsidies and agriculture: Future perspectives, in Ballabh, V. (ed.) *Institutional Alternatives and Governance of Agriculture*, Academic Foundation and IRMA: New Delhi and Anand, Gujarat.

Altieiri, Miguel A. (2009) Agroecology, Small Farms, and Food Sovereignty, *Monthly Review*, July–August 2009, Monthly Review Foundation: New York. www.monthlyreview.org/090 810altieri.php

Brown, M.E. and Funk, C.C. (2008) Food Security Under Climate Change, *Science*, vol. 319 (5863): 580–581.

CMF (2009) *India's GHG Emissions Profile: results of five climate modeling studies*, Climate Modelling Forum, Ministry of Environment and Forests, Government of India, New Delhi.

Dovers, S.R. and Hezri, A.A. (2010) Institutions and policy processes: the means to the ends of adaptation, Interdisciplinary Reviews, *Climate Change*, vol. 1 (2): 212–231.

Ehrlich, P.R. (2010) The MAHB, the Culture Gap, and Some Really Inconvenient Truths, *PLoS Biol*, vol. 8 (4): e1000330.doi:10.1371/journal.pbio.1000330.

Fan, S. (2010) *Halving Hunger: Meeting the First Millennium Development Goal through 'Business as Unusual'*, IFPRI, Food Policy Report, IFPRI: Washington, DC.

FAO (2006) *Livestock's Long Shadow: Environmental Issues and Options*, FAO: Rome.

FAO (2008) *Climate Change, Water and Food Security*, FAO: Rome.

FAO (2010) *'Climate-Smart' Agriculture – Policies, Practices and Financing for Food Security, Adaptation and Mitigation*, The Hague Conference on Agriculture, Food Security and Climate Change, 31 Oct.–5 Nov, FAO: Rome.

Fischer, G., Shah, M. and van Velthuizen, H. (2002) Climate Change and Agricultural Vulnerability, in IAASA, *Contribution to the World Summit on Sustainable Development*, Johannesburg, International Institute for Applied Systems Analysis (IAASA): Luxembourg.

Friedmann, Harriet (1992) Distance and Durability: Shaky Foundations of the World Food Economy, *Third World Quarterly*, vol. 13(2), pp. 371–383.

Golait, Ramesh and Lokare, S.M. (2008) *Capital Adequacy in Indian Agriculture: A Riposte*, Reserve Bank of India, Occasional Papers, vol. 29(1), Summer 2008.

Goodland, R. and Anhang, J. (2009) *Livestock and Climate Change*, World Watch Institute: Washington, DC.

Government of India (2005) *Report of the Task Group on Revamping and Refocusing of National Agricultural Research*, Planning Commission, Government of India: New Delhi.

Government of India (2008) *Eleventh Five-Year Plan (2007–2012), Agriculture, Rural Development, Industry, Services and Physical Infrastructure*, Vol. III. Planning Commission, Government of India: Oxford University Press: New Delhi.

HBF (2009) *Climate Change and the Right to Food – A Comprehensive Study*, vol. 8, Heinrich Boll Foundation: Berlin.

IATP (2008) *Commodities market speculation: The risk to food security and agriculture*, Institute for Agriculture and Trade Policy: Minnesota http://www.tradeobservatory.org/library.cfm?RefID=104414).

IAASTD (2009) *Agriculture at a Crossroads, Synthesis Report, International Assessment of Agricultural Knowledge, Science and Technology for Development*, Island Press: Washington, DC.

ICAR (1998) *National Agricultural Technology Project – Main Document* ICAR: New Delhi.

326 Raina

INCCA (2010) *India: Greenhouse Gas Emissions*, 2007, Indian Network for Climate Change Assessments, Ministry of Environment and Forests, Government of India: New Delhi.

IPCC (2007) *Climate Change 2007: Synthesis Report*, Contribution of Working Groups I, II and III to the *Fourth Assessment Report of the Intergovernmental Panel on Climate Change*, (eds) Pachauri, R.K. and Reisinger, A., IPCC: Geneva.

Jodha, N.S. (1986) Common Property Resources and Rural Poor in Dry Regions of India, *EPW*, vol. 21(27): 1169–1181.

Kulkarni, H. and Vijaya Shankar, P.S. (2010) *Groundwater Knowledge Systems in India: Need for a Fresh Look*, SIID Working Paper No. 8, *Systems of Innovation for Inclusive Development* (SIID) Project, CPR: New Delhi.

Kumar, R.K., Sahai, A.K., Kumar, K.K., Patwardhan, S.K., Mishra, P.K., Revadekar, J.V., Kamala, K., and Pant, G.B. (2006) High resolution climate change scenarios for India in the 21st century, *Current Science*, vol. 30 (3): 334–345.

Lal, R. (2010) Enhancing Eco-efficiency in Agro-ecosystems through Soil C sequestration, *Crop Science*, vol. 50, S-120-S-130, March–April 2010.

Lang, Tim (2010) Crisis? What Crisis? The Normality of the Current Food Crisis, *Journal of Agrarian Change*, vol. 10 (1): 87–97.

Lele, S. (2008) Interdisciplinarity as a Three-way Conversation: Barriers and Possibilities, in Bardhan, P. and Ray, I. (eds.) *The Contested Commons: Conversations between Economists and Anthropologists*, Blackwell: London, pp. 187–207.

Li Chin, L., Dano, E., and Jhamtani, H. (2010) *Rethinking Agriculture, Third World Resurgence*, no. 223.

Lobell , D.B., Marshall, B.B., Tebaldi, C., Mastrandrea, M. D., Falcon, W.P., and Naylor, R.L. (2008) Prioritizing Climate Change Adaptation Needs for Food Security 2030, *Science*, vol. 319 (5863): 607–610.

NCEUS (2007) *Report on Conditions of Work and Promotion of Livelihoods in the Unorganized Sector*, NCEUS: New Delhi.

Nellemann, C., MacDevette, M., Manders, T., Eickhour, B., Svihus, B., Prins, A.G., and Kaltenborn, B.P. eds. (2009), *The Environmental Food Crisis: The Environment's Role in Averting Future Food Crises*, Oslo: Birkeland Trykkeri AS for the United Nations Environmental Programme.

Nelson, G.C., Robertson, R., Msangi, S., Zhu, T., Liao, X., and Jawajar, P. (2009a) Greenhouse Gas Mitigation: Issues for Indian agriculture, IFPRI Discussion Paper 00900, IFPRI: Washington, DC.

Nelson G.C., Rosegrant M.W., Koo, J., Robertson, R., Sulser, T, Zhu, T, Ringler, C., Msangi, S., Palazzo, A., Batka, M., Magalhaes, M., Valmonte-Santos, R., Ewing, M., and Lee, D. (2009b) *Climate Change Impact on Agriculture and Costs of Adaptation*, International Food Policy Research Institute: Washington, DC (www.ifpri.org/sites/default/files/ publications/pr21.pdf).

NRAA (2009) *Harnessing Opportunities in Rainfed Areas – A pathway to prosperity, Vision, 2025* National Rainfed Area Authority, Ministry of Agriculture, Government of India: New Delhi.

PM-CCC (2008) *National Action Plan on Climate Change*, Government of India: New Delhi.

Palanivel, S. (2006) Technical report on linkages between international trade and employment growth in Asia and the Pacific, UNDP: Colombo.

Pew Centre (2008) *Climate Change Mitigation Measures in India*, International Brief, 2, Pew Centre Global Climate Change.

Pimentel, David (2009) Energy Inputs in Food Crop Production in Developing and Developed Nations, *Energies*, 2(1), pp. 1–24.

Pimentel, D. and Pimentel, M. (1979, revised 2008) *Food, Energy, and Society*, Edward Arnold: London, and CRC Press: London.

Raina, R.S. (2006) Researching the Drylands, Seminar, 564: pp. 25–29.

Raina, R.S. (2009) Innovation for eco-friendly development – towards institutional reform in scientific research and policy-making, in Guimaraes-Perreira and Funtowicz (eds) *Science for Policy*, Oxford University Press: London and New Delhi, pp. 312–327

Ramdas, S. and Ghotke, N. (2006) India's Livestock Economy, Seminar, 564, pp. 20–24.

Sen, Abhijit and Bhatia, M.L. (2004) *Cost of Cultivation and Farm Incomes*, vol. 14, *State of Indian Farmers: A Millennium Study*, Academic Foundation, New Delhi.

Shah M. (2006) *The problem. Seminar: The Forsaken Drylands*, vol. 564, pp. 12–14.

Smith, P., Martino, D., Cai, Z., Gwary, D., Janzen, H., Kumar, P., McCarl, B., Ogle, S., O'Mara, F., Rice, C., Scholes, B. and Sirotenko, O. (2007) 'Agriculture', in *Climate Change 2007: Mitigation*. Contribution of Working Group III to the Fourth Assessment Report of the Intergovernmental Panel on Climate Change, (eds) Metz, B., Davidson, O.R., Bosch, P.R., Dave, R. and Meyer, L.A., pp 497–540. Cambridge, UK: Cambridge University Press.

Swaminathan, M.S. (2005) *India's Greatest Living Industry: Hundred Years Later*, IARI: New Delhi.

UNEP-IISD (2004*) Exploring the Links – Human Well-being, Poverty, Ecosystem services*, UNEP: Nairobi, IISD: Manitoba.

UNICEF (2008) *The State of the World's Children: Child Survival*, UNICEF: Paris.

USAID (2010) *Changing Glaciers and Hydrology in Asia – Addressing Vulnerabilities to Glacier Melt Impacts*, USAID: Washington, DC.

V&A Programme (2009) *Vulnerability and Adaptation Experiences from Rajasthan and Andhra Pradesh, SDC*, V&A Programme, India: Hyderabad.

Wang, Q., Li, Y., and Alva, A. (2010) Cropping Systems to Improve Carbon Sequestration for mitigation of climate change, *Journal of Environmental Protection*, vol. 1 (2): 207–215.

WFP and FAO (2010) *The State of Food Insecurity in the World*, FAO: Rome.

24 Framework for India's strategic water resource management under a changing climate

Himanshu Kulkarni and Himanshu Thakkar

Introduction

The reflection of a changing climate, particularly in the form of extreme events such as droughts, floods, heat-waves, will have far-reaching consequences on the lives and livelihoods of human population in a country like India. The Water Mission constituted under India's National Action Plan on Climate Change (NAPCC) summarizes the overall impacts of Climate Change in India as, 'the projected climate change resulting in warming, sea level rise and melting of glaciers will adversely affect the water balance in different parts of India and quality of ground water along the coastal plains'. Preliminary reports indicate that the impact of climate change will result in intensification of spatial and temporal variations in water resources resulting in severity in floods and drought-like situations (MoWR, 2009). In other words, scenarios stemming from increased frequencies and intensities of droughts and floods will become a common feature. Risks to future water availability and reliability are among the most damaging expected impacts of climate change to India. Yet, attention to this aspect of climate impacts cannot be independent of the history of water policy and management in India, as the past has set the physical and institutional conditions for future responses.

This chapter seeks to introduce thinking through the links between climate change and water in India. We approach this subject in four parts. First, we examine the scientific basis for understanding impacts of climate change on water in India. Next, we turn to a brief description of existing water conditions and management approaches, making the point in particular that there has been a historical lack of attention to groundwater. Third, we juxtapose this discussion against the likely implications of climate change, which leads to a fourth section presenting stylized models of thinking through water management under risk and uncertainty. We then turn to a discussion of India's climate policy with respect to climate change, before concluding that climate change may yet offer an intriguing opportunity to re-think water policy and management in India in a more fruitful manner.

Impacts of climate change on water in India

Climate change is likely to affect water resources due to changes in precipitation and evapo-transpiration. Rising sea levels may lead to increased salinity intrusion into coastal and island aquifers, while increased frequency and severity of floods may affect groundwater quality in alluvial aquifers. Increased rainfall intensity may lead to higher runoff and possibly reduced recharge (MoWR, 2009).

Water resource management in a changing climate 329

Studies on impacts of climate change on river runoff in various river basins of India indicate that the quantity of surface runoff due to climate change would reduce across river basins as well as sub-basins by the 2050s. An increase in precipitation in the Mahanadi, Brahmani, Ganga, Godavari and Cauvery basins is projected under some of the climate change scenarios. However, the corresponding total runoff for all these basins does not increase. This may be due to increase in evapo-transpiration on account of increased temperatures or variations in the distribution of rainfall. In the remaining basins, a decrease in precipitation is projected. For example, the Sabarmati and Luni basins show a drastic decrease in precipitation and consequent decrease of total runoff to the tune of two-thirds of the prevailing runoff. This may lead to severe drought conditions in the future. Flooding conditions may deteriorate in the Mahanadi and Brahmani river systems. Further, climate change may increase the severity of droughts and intensity of floods in various parts of the country (Ministry for Environment and Forests, 2010). Preliminary reports indicate that the impact of climate change will result in intensification of spatial and temporal variations in water resources resulting in severe floods and acute droughts (MoWR, 2009). In other words, increased frequencies and intensities of droughts and floods will become a common feature in India. A combination of increase in heaviest rainfall and reduction in the number of rainy days suggest the possibility of frequent and severe floods (MoWR, 2009).

The projections of precipitation indicate a 3% to 7% overall increase in all-India summer monsoon rainfall in the 2030s with respect to the 1970s. However, on a seasonal scale, except for the Himalayan region, all other regions are likely to have lower rainfalls in the winter period as well as pre-summer period. Spatial patterns of monsoon rainfall indicate a significant decrease in monsoon rainfall in future except in some parts of the southern peninsula (MoEF, 2010: 36).

Climate change impacts on water will have significant repercussions for the agriculture sector as well. Agriculture consumes between 78 and 83% of total water diverted in India. The impact of agriculture on climate change will be two pronged: crops will be affected due to changing temperatures, precipitations, humidity levels and they would also need more water as evapo-transpiration increases. For some crops better water management could help adapting to the changes. For others, the changes in cropping methods, varieties, and patterns may have to be changed. According to a recent paper published in *Science*, high temperatures will cut yields of the primary food crops like rice and maize by up to 20–40% (Battisti et al., 2009). This does not include the impact this will have on water supplies and soil moisture stressed by the higher temperatures (Thakkar 2009). Even if there is some exaggeration in these projections, the largest number of chronically hungry people in a single country in the world happens to be in India (FAO, 2008).

In discussing impacts it is important to sound one note of caution. While there appears broad agreement on the aggregate regional picture of potential climate change impacts on water resources in India, the diversity of India's water resource conditions and the highly disaggregated nature of water usage makes predictions of impacts at the local scale somewhat difficult.

Water resources in India

While the climate change story has unfolded at a global level, India's water story has also been unfolding over the past few decades. A close look at this history is a necessary starting point for discussions on climate change and water. Right from the 1950s onwards, irrigation programmes have focused on major and medium irrigation projects. There were 346 large dams in 1950; there are over 5,100 now (CWC 2009), with over 95% of them servicing irrigation projects. A large proportion of the water sector budget (65 to 80%) goes towards *large* irrigation projects, reflected also in the 11th Five-Year plan (2007–12). This budgetary provision has not included rain-fed agriculture, local water systems, groundwater resources development, repair and maintenance of created infrastructure (Thakkar, 2011). In fact, the share of surface water irrigation to the net irrigated area in the country has decreased while the share of groundwater irrigation has increased (Figure 24.1).

India spent more than Rs 150,000 crores on major and medium irrigation projects during the period 1990–2008. The total net and gross irrigated area in India in this period showed continued increase, as illustrated in Figure 24.2. This increase in net and gross irrigated area at national level, in spite of the decline of canal irrigation during the same period was possibly due to the increasing irrigation by groundwater during the period, as illustrated in Figure 24.2 (Thakkar, 2011).

The emphasis on large irrigation projects in India continues despite the growth of groundwater irrigation in the small land-holding region of India's hinterland. In fact, by the mid-80s, India had become the largest groundwater user in the world; by the turn of the century, South Asia alone had more area under 'groundwater irrigation' than all the rest of the world combined (Shah, 2009). In many ways, groundwater overuse has led to a reduced potential of groundwater resources acting as 'drought buffers' in areas where groundwater extraction far exceeds the potential annual

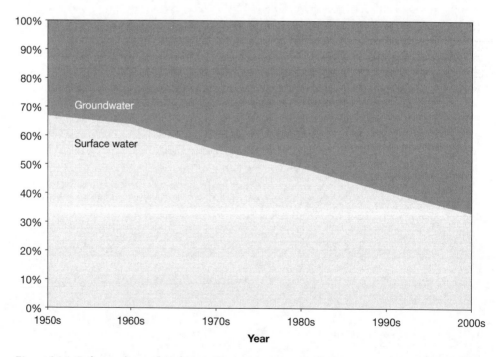

Figure 24.1 Relative share of surface and groundwater to India's net irrigated area, 1950 to 2000 (developed from Indian Agricultural Statistics, various issues; Shah, 2009)

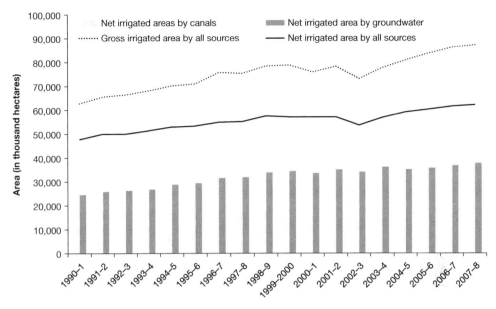

Figure 24.2 Trends in gross irrigated area, net irrigated area, irrigation by canals and irrigation by groundwater, 1990–2008

Source: Modified, after Thakkar, 2011

recharge to aquifers. This fact highlights the need for a groundwater management strategy in India, a strategy that ought to be inclusive of factors stemming from climate change, especially in the context of extreme events like floods and droughts, and given the fact that surface water irrigation has stagnated in large regions of India (Thakkar, 2010).

So far, two national groundwater assessments have formally taken place, in 1995 and 2004 (Central Ground Water Board, 2006). Administrative units, mostly 'blocks', are classified into safe, semi-critical, critical and overexploited categories based on the ratio between extraction and annual replenishment. Between 1995 and 2004, the proportion of districts in the semi-critical, critical and over-exploited categories has grown from 9% to 31%, area from 5% to 33% and population affected from 5% to 35% (Table 24.1). However, such data are limited in not only the extent to which they present the problem, but also being too gross to really provide strategic solutions to the problems of scarcity and quality, say at the scale of a village or a micro-watershed (Kulkarni et al., 2010). Moreover, India's current groundwater assessment does not represent the extent of the groundwater quality problem, clearly a requirement for developing rural drinking water security plans in India (Kulkarni et al., 2009; Shankar et al., 2011). As these data show, any discussion of water policy in India must pay considerable attention to groundwater.

India's water debate in the context of climate change

Let us consider the climate change phenomenon in the light of the preceding historical discussion of India's water context. The overarching change, about which there is

332 Kulkarni and Thakkar

Table 24.1 Comparative status of level of groundwater development, 1996 and 2004

Level of groundwater development	% of total districts		% of total area		% of total population	
	1995	2004	1995	2004	1995	2004
0–50% ('safe')	82	55	89	52	80	45
50–70% ('safe')	10	15	7	16	13	20
70–90% ('semi-critical')	4	13	2	14	3	17
90–100% ('critical')	1	4	1	5	1	3
>100% ('over-exploited')	4	14	2	14	3	15
TOTAL	100	100	100	100	100	100

Source: Central Groundwater Water Board, 2006

discussion at all levels – international, national even down to the districts and sub-districts in India – is bound to have major, even if unpredictable, implications for weather and climate at more local levels. Recharge to groundwater and flows to surface storages are influenced by climatic changes (at least in the medium and long terms) as a direct consequence of changing flow patterns, increasing temperatures, increasing losses, increasing extractions, water available for recharge and that available in the catchment of surface storages. There are also likely to be indirect or secondary impacts as discussed later in the chapter (Table 24.2). Both sets of impacts will influence the immediate state of water resources at a location – whether surface water or groundwater – and should play a major role in influencing responses under these variable scenarios.

There is also a 'time-dimension' involved in the development of water resources in the region, a dimension that has serious implications given climate change impacts. As Shah (2009), illustrates, a changing socio-economic milieu, including cropping shifts, the energy–irrigation nexus and so on, can lead to changing groundwater resources. The spatial variability in conditions governing water resources – catchment areas, ecology, water use, shifts in land-use and land-cover – and the constitution of the substrate and super-strate also makes for consideration of complex changes to groundwater resources over time. In sum, even prior to considering climate impacts, understanding water and in particular groundwater resources over time and space is extremely challenging, suggesting the need for a disaggregated approach to understanding the water resource. When adding on climate considerations, most hydrologic modeling, analysis and planning assumes that key climatic parameters are stationary (Moench and Stapleton, 2007). Such 'stationarity' practically forecloses the space for including uncertainty and risk that come with climate change compounded by a rapidly moving socio-economy such as India.

Increased uncertainty and risk associated with the changing climate will need to be dealt with while developing solutions in the water resources sector. Assured water supply is the principal input required for stable agricultural livelihoods in large parts of India. When water resources get depleted and degraded, normal climate variability, extended droughts and climate change can significantly affect agricultural economies and even compel shifts in livelihoods. Where agriculture is the only available livelihood option, true even today in many parts of India, migration, social unrest, economic instability and even famines can result. At the same time, India is transitioning in many ways, with urbanization and industrialization requiring an altogether different dimension of water demand, supply and treatment.

A conceptual framework

Given these challenges, we attempt to develop a conceptual basis for thinking through water resource policy in a context of greater uncertainty and risk in water, driven in part by climate change. In essence, we argue that a purely supply driven approach is unlikely to be adequate to future water challenges. Instead, we suggest more attention to demand orientation, combined with some supply augmentation.

We initially focus on the groundwater management challenge, an argument that can be extended to water resources in general, essentially with regard to demand, supply and changing availability (after Kakade et al., 2001; Kulkarni et al., 2011; Shankar et al., 2011). The concept, as explained here, is limited to the problem of groundwater scarcity and does not necessarily include water quality. Figures 24.3 and 24.4 provide a schematic view of the relationship between availability, demand and supply of groundwater at any given location. The availability (within a hydrologic/hydro-geologic unit) defines the upper limit for demand and supply, an aquifer in the case of groundwater resources (Figure 24.2). Availability is viewed here as the environmentally sustainable withdrawal of groundwater that the aquifer can support. In many rural areas of India, a single village usually has different episodes of supply

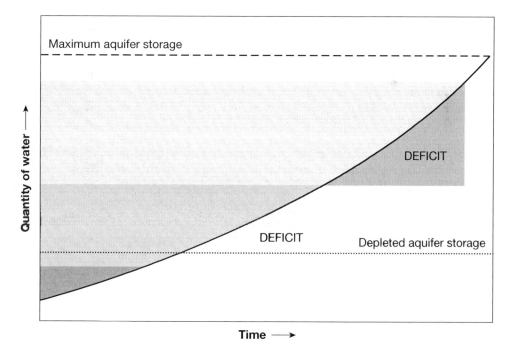

Figure 24.3 Groundwater resources: availability, demand and supply – business-as-usual approach

Source: Modified, after Kakade, Kulkarni et al. (2001); Kulkarni et al. (2011); Shankar, Kulkarni et al. (2011)

augmentation – in other words, 'water supply schemes' or 'well excavations' that simply try to fix ever-increasing demand with 'sources' of water supply. Such an approach has meant engineering access-structures that cater to a certain 'demand range'. Hence, they work for a certain period in time, after which demand outstrips the supply range and a deficit is created (shown as deficit in the figure), for which another scheme (supply-step) is created. Each increment in supply, as Figure 24.2 illustrates, meets demand only for a fixed period, after which deficits develop once again between a demand that outstrips the 'designed' supply from time to time. Moreover, in drought-like situations, or over-exploitation of the aquifer, the useful life of any given supply enhancement further diminishes, leading to calls for exogenous water imports through tankers or piped water schemes. This 'supply-driven approach' characterizes many parts of rural India.

Figure 24.4 illustrates the concept of sustainability through augmentation by appropriate artificial recharge (or resource augmentation) programmes, so that depleted water availability is restored. In addition, conserving such storages on a sustainable basis would be possible only through some degree of demand regulation. Even a slight reduction in the demand-line (Figure 24.4) demonstrates that supply becomes sustainable. The regulated demand makes a slight difference to the availability–supply situation in early stages of the time-line, but as demand increases, the regulated demand ensures a more effective supply. Simply put, a water supply scheme in a village or a town tends to run over a longer period of time, through a combination of appropriate augmenta-

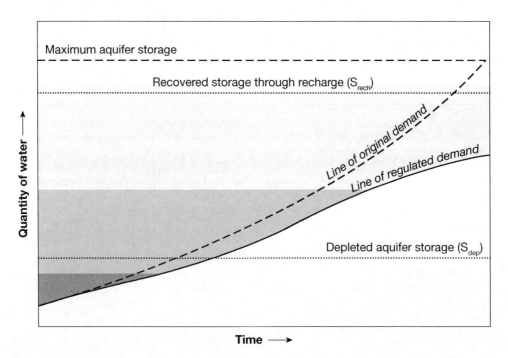

Figure 24.4 Groundwater resources: availability, demand and supply – managed resource approach

Source: Modified, after Kakade, Kulkarni et al. (2001); Kulkarni et al. (2011); Shankar, Kulkarni et al. (2011)

tion (recharge) and regulated demand. Regulated demand also includes the notion of effective utilization, including water-use efficiency measures. Managing demand would also include preparedness in water management for overarching climate change impacts, especially during prolonged dry spells as also in dealing with smaller storages that operate on the basis of an annual water availability criterion.

A similar concept holds true for water resources in the mountain ranges, such as in the case of Himalayan springs. A rising demand is likely to hasten the water crisis in Himalayan and other mountain systems as spring discharges get reduced by a variety of factors such as land-use change in catchment areas, changing precipitation patterns, glacial retreat etc. (Figure 24.5). The response to such a crisis is possible through a two-fold approach that combines augmenting systems that feed springs – catchment area treatment, protection of existing local storages, augmenting where necessary and groundwater recharge – and demand regulation including reducing demands, reusing, and recycling appropriately. Only a three-fold approach will ensure sustainable restoration and/or protection of many mountain hydrologic systems (Figure 24.6).

India's policy response to water resources and climate change

India's policy response to the challenge of water and climate change focuses on two missions, the Green India Mission and the National Water Mission, both formulated as part of the National Action Plan on Climate Change. Other missions such as the Mission for Sustainable Agriculture, Himalayan Ecosystem Mission and the Urban Habitat Mission also have a significant bearing on the water sector in India. The Green India Mission (MoEF) specified key innovations in tackling the climate change challenge in India.[1] It focuses on quality of forests, ecosystem services, democratic decentralization, on creating a new cadre of community youth as foresters and on

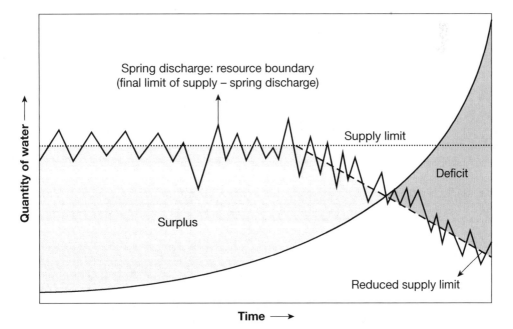

Figure 24.5 Springs – increasing demand, climate change and decreased discharges

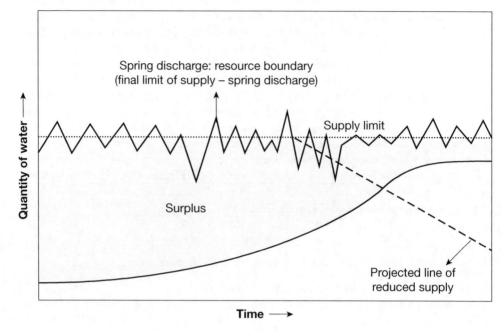

Figure 24.6 Springs – spring recharge, managed demand and sustainable discharges

adoption of a landscape-based approach in tackling the water resource challenge. The National Water Mission has identified several measures as part of the action plan on climate change (MoWR, 2009):

- comprehensive water database in the public domain and assessment of the impact of climate change on water resource
- promotion of citizen and state action for water conservation, augmentation and preservation
- conservation of wetlands
- increasing storage
- focused attention on areas where groundwater resources are over-exploited
- increasing water-use efficiency by 20%
- promotion of basin level integrated water resources management.

While these lists of measures appear useful, there are indications of limited thinking in the approach of these missions. First, the Green India Mission focuses on forests, whilst the MoWR focuses on water, risking a problem of institutional silos in what is a systemic problem dealing with various facets of the environment. Second, in the absence of a concrete implementation strategy, and given the biophysical and socio-economic diversity across India, the effectiveness of the so-called innovations would remain questionable, unless institutional, programmatic and geographical silos break down. The Green India Mission approach focuses on forests as major domains of interventions, although there is a reference to non-forest areas as well. The National Water Mission promises to look into a water-related database, but major questions

Water resource management in a changing climate   337

would remain in connection with appropriateness of scale, especially while planning, decision-making, implementing and operating projects. Third, sufficiency and appropriateness of knowledge systems, data and information could be major hurdles in efficient implementation of the key innovations laid down on paper. Protection of key forest areas from a 'water security' perspective is an example where such mission documents draw a big blank because data, information and knowledge about the precise linkages between forest areas on the one hand and surface and groundwater systems on the other hand are simply not available or addressed as a basis for action.

The above is just an illustrative list of possible complexities arising out of climate change. Based on this discussion, it may be useful to go through the exercise of not only identifying impacts, but also looking at the resultant second order effects or 'impact of impacts' under a climate change scenario. Table 24.2 represents an initial effort at such an exercise, pointing to the strategic responses that are required, and which, so far, find little space in India's policy making.

Neither the impact of impacts nor the responses presented in Table 24.2, are an exhaustive list. However, these impacts lead to three large-scale effects that must form an integral part of a national level strategic thinking on water management and climate change. First, clearly there are impending dangers for water and food security because of these impacts, with the resultant impact being passed on to the poor and under-privileged sections of society. Second, the co-terminal changes (changes from drivers other than the changing climate) in socio-economic conditions might impose huge shifts in livelihood patterns and stimulate large-scale migration from highly vulnerable regions. Third, the cumulative effect of the summarized impacts suggests broader environmental threats including loss of vegetative cover, salinization and changes in fragile ecosystems that are crucial in protecting certain aspects of the water resource and livelihood systems.

Looking ahead: using climate change as an opportunity for improved water management

India's water situation is complex to say the least. The complex nature and diverse contextual regime of water problems in India compel the development of a strategic approach to managing water. Policies, planning, projects and implementation strategies remain driven by supply-side mega solutions. Although increasing efficiency in supply (Planning Commission, 2007) is stated as one of the major objectives in the planning process, equitability and sustainability remain only slogans. In this light, the development of strategies to respond to groundwater over-use and deteriorating groundwater quality requires a process-based approach that incorporates the potential impacts of a changing climate on one side and the impacts stemming from a growing demand on a depleting-deteriorating water resource regime on the other.

Adaptation occurs in response to changes in the water resource conditions as well as to those happening in the purely social and economic contexts; such adaptations are beginning to emerge into a formal regime, both within the larger risk arena of extreme events and climate change but also within a rapidly globalizing context (Moench and Dixit, 2004). In India, such changes are especially occurring around changes in water resources at regional and local levels. Water resource systems are more stable when compared to climate and weather systems, but patterns of water use are sensitive to climate, and especially to the weather. Trends in long-term annual

Table 24.2 Impact of impacts – water resources and climate change

Climate change impacts	Some of the compounded impacts (very broad) of CC impacts – to be used as parameters for water resource planning and management	Strategic responses as part of various policies and programmes
1 Increase in temperature – both in terms of rise in dailies as well as in the number of 'hot' days	Increased evaporation and evapo-transpiration losses; increased water demands; changed precipitation trends; relative humidity in dry season drops; crop stress and increase of uncertainty in agriculture	Soil moisture management, including: increase organic content in soils; secure protective irrigation for rainfed crops; increase efficiency of irrigation; increase investments in dryland farming
2 Untimely and changed patterns of rains, especially on monsoonal pattern, including onset of monsoon, gap between rainy days	Crop failure due to monsoonal excesses on one hand and delayed onset and even long dry spells affecting regions without access to alternative sources of protective irrigation; reduced recharge to aquifers further compounding availability during dry seasons and impacting productivities as well as access to drinking water; increased competition/conflicts for water resources	More robust forms of weather insurance, especially for rainfed farmers; innovative groundwater recharge programmes with links to demand-management; conjunctive use of surface and groundwater at sub-basin scales; protection of resources that provide safe drinking water, protection of existing groundwater recharge systems
3 Glacial retreat	Extreme wet and dry conditions as river flow hydrology downstream changes; impact on irrigation systems in Himalayan region, on hydropower generation	Flood-control measures; large-scale promotion of local water systems, efficient irrigation practices; soil-moisture management and protective irrigation for dry-season crops, ensuring that glacier melting is not accelerated through local actions (e.g. hydropower, roads, township projects in fragile regions close to the glaciers)
4 Drying up of rivers	Reducing groundwater recharge; destruction of riverine biodiversity including fisheries and related livelihoods; reduced flows into storages, compounded by stress on alternative sources such as groundwater	Strategies of river basin (and sub-basin) management based on improved hydrologic data, ensuring that rivers have freshwater flow all round the year; improved decision support systems to manage small, medium and large storages; increased base-flow contribution through groundwater management in basin; groundwater recharge
5 Decline in spring discharges, especially for springwater in mountain systems	Drying up of some springs, perennial springs becoming seasonal; severe impact on drinking water and irrigation systems in hill and mountain regions; impact of livelihoods, changes in water quality of springs; reduced dry season flows in streams and rivers because of reduced spring flows	Major programme on spring water conservation and management across the Himalayan region; improved understanding of spring–forest relationships leading to integration of forest-conservation and water management, promotion of local water systems and forests in spring catchments
6 Flash floods, cloud bursts in mountains	Disasters	Disaster preparedness

rainfall, for example, are important in understanding climate change; however, water resources planning under such change would require inputs such as rainfall intensities (and changes therein), changed number of rainy days and so on. Data disaggregation holds the key in such planning, as understanding and managing the availability, demand and supply of water resources at various scales ranging from micro to meso to mega, becomes all the more significant.

Climate change offers a unique opportunity to revisit our water resources in terms of understanding, planning and management. It also provides an opportunity to learn lessons from past approaches to water resources development and management in a credible way. The purpose for a revamped water policy could be that of equitable, sustainable, participatory and transparent approach to water management; an approach based on sound knowledge and data to make decisions. Further, this approach would need to include a protection strategy for forests, wetlands, water bodies and groundwater reserves, as well as demand side management measures, along with a definition of the clear linkages between these domains.

The process of water resources planning and management would need to include resource understanding, supply management (including getting optimum benefits from existing infrastructure, best options for augmentation) and instruments to manage the growing demand. These three aspects of water management would therefore require special reference to units and scale – river basins, aquifers, watersheds etc., for which an enhanced understanding of surface and groundwater resources is required. Management of supply would require special focus on managing groundwater recharge, engineering (and re-engineering) schemes of water supply to an optimum limit to minimize losses. Managing demand would be possible through various measures, the selection of measures being a function of situations, and including instruments such as participatory regulation (social fencing), formal legislation and indirect mechanisms including efficiency of *applying* water as well as that of regulating power supply intelligently.

Finally, the process outlined above is not simple and requires integration between not only communities, governments, institutions and departments, but across disciplines of expertise, for example, between science, technology, engineering, sociology, economics and ecology. The process is a challenging task, but seems a way forward, especially if India needs to take on the triple challenge of mitigating climate change, bridging existing gaps in water governance and management, and dealing with a rapidly developing economy and society.

Note

1 http://moef.nic.in/downloads/public-information/2011-02-23%20Press%20Brief% 20%20Green%20India%20Mission%20approval.pdf, accessed on March 4, 2011

References

Battisti, D.S. and Naylor, R.L. (2009) 'Historical warnings of future food insecurity with unprecedented seasonal heat', *Science*, vol. 323 (5911), pp. 240–244.
Central Ground Water Board (2006) 'Dynamic ground water resources of India (as on March, 2004)', Central Ground Water Board.
Central Water Commission (2009) 'National Register of Large Dams', Central Water Commission, New Delhi.

340 *Kulkarni and Thakkar*

Food and Agriculture Organization (2008) 'The state of food insecurity in the World: high food prices and food security – threats and opportunities', FAO, Rome.

Indian Agricultural Statistics, Ministry of Agriculture, various issues, http://dacnet.nic.in/eands/latest_2006.htm.

Kakade, B., Kulkarni, H., Marathe, A, Petare, K., Neelam, G. and Nagargoje, P. (2001) 'Integration of drinking water supply-sanitation and watershed development' (a research study covering seven micro-watersheds from five states of India), DFID-WHIRL Project Working Paper 5, as part of the UK DFID's project R7804 on 'Integrating drinking water needs in watershed projects'.

Kulkarni, H. and Vijay Shankar, P.S. (2010) 'Sustainable Groundwater Management: Challenges for the 21st Century', International Conference on Dynamics of Rural Transformation in Emerging Economies, New Delhi, April 2010.

Kulkarni, H., Vijay Shankar, P. S. and Krishnan, S. (2009) Synopsis of groundwater resources in India: status, challenges and a new framework for responses. *Report submitted to the Planning Commission, Government of India. ACWA Report ACWA/PC/Rep – 1.*

Kulkarni, H., Vijay Shankar, P.S. and Krishnan, S. (2011) 'Groundwater governance: backing CPR principles with a process-based approach', IASC-2011, Hyderabad, India.

Ministry for Environment and Forests (2010) 'Climate change and India: A 4 x 4 Assessment: A Sectoral and Regional Analysis for 2030s', Government of India.

Ministry of Water Resources (2009) 'Comprehensive Mission Document of National Water Mission under National Action Plan on Climate Change', vols. 1 and 2, Government of India.

Moench, M. and Dixit, A. (eds.) (2004) *Adaptive Capacity and Livelihood Resilience: Adaptive Strategies for Responding to Floods and Droughts in South Asia*, Kathmandu, and Boulder, USA, ISET, 214pp.

Moench, M. and Stapleton, S. (2007) 'Water, climate, risk and adaptation', *Working Paper 2007–8.* Co-operative Programme on Water and Climate, 80pp.

Planning Commission, Government of India (2007) 'Report of the Expert Group on Groundwater Management and Ownership', Planning Commission, New Delhi, 61pp.

Planning Commission, Government of India (2010) 'Mid-Term Appraisal for Eleventh Five-Year Plan: 2007–2012', Government of India. (http://planningcommission.gov.in/plans/mta/11th_mta/MTA.html)

Shah, T. (2009) 'Taming the Anarchy: Groundwater Governance in South Asia, Resources for the Future', Washington DC and International Water Management Institute, Colombo, 310pp.

Shankar Vijay, P.S., Kulkarni, H. and Krishnan, S. (2011) 'India's groundwater challenge and the way forward', Special Article, *Economic & Political Weekly*, vol. xlvi (2).

Thakkar, H. (2009) 'There is little hope here: India's National Action Plan on Climate change', South Asia Network on Dams, Rivers & People, New Delhi, 56pp.

Thakkar, H. (2010) 'India's Tryst with the Big Irrigation Projects', http://www.sandrp.in/irrigation/Failure_of_Big_Irrigation_Projects_and_Rainfed_Agriculture_0510.pdf.

Thakkar, H. (2011) 'India's Water Sector: Performance and Challenges'. South Asia Network on Dams, Rivers & People, New Delhi. http://www.sandrp.in/wtrsect/India_Water_Sector_Performance_and_Challenges_March_2011.PDF accessed on March 4, 2011

World Meteorological Organization's Co-operative Programme on Water and Climate, et al. (2006), in Moench, M. and Stapleton, S., *Water, Climate, Risk and Adaptation*. Working Paper 2007–1. Co-operative Programme on Water and Climate, 80pp.

25 Mitigation or exploitation?

The climate talks, REDD and forest areas

Shankar Gopalakrishnan

While most articles in this handbook are on climate change itself and its likely impacts, this article focuses on a different angle: the impact of the climate change talks. A major area of such talks today is the agreement on Reducing Emissions from Deforestation and forest Degradation, (REDD), which was one of the few outcomes of the Cancun talks. REDD has been described as a 'low hanging fruit', a win-win solution for all.

But there is an old adage that when enemies suddenly agree, others should be suspicious. In that context, this chapter is concerned with looking at this agreement, and asking why all seem to support it. We will briefly explore the issue and the dynamics of forest policy to look at what the current forest-related negotiations are actually about, in the broad sense. Eventually, this chapter argues, the old proverb is right – there is indeed a great deal to be suspicious about.

Background: forests and climate change

Forests clearly are a significant factor in both driving and mitigating climate change. The Food and Agricultural Organisation estimates that forests currently cover 31% of the world's land area and store approximately 289 gigatonnes of carbon, more than the total amount of carbon in the atmosphere (FAO, 2010). But the world's forest area is shrinking, with a net loss of 5.2 million hectares per year over the last decade (FAO, 2010). Such deforestation, in turn, is a significant cause of climate change emissions: the Intergovernmental Panel on Climate Change's Fourth Assessment Report estimated deforestation's share of global emissions in the 1990s at approximately 20% (UNFCCC, 2009).

The reason for such mammoth statistics is the fact that forests, and trees in particular, absorb considerable amounts of carbon dioxide as they grow, with the carbon extracted being used to build their biomass (branches, leaves, etc.). Equally, therefore, cutting down or burning forests results in the release of large amounts of carbon dioxide into the atmosphere. Indeed, as per the IPCC's estimate, deforestation contributed more carbon dioxide to the atmosphere in the 1990s than pollution from air and land transport.

From this stark logic, it is indisputable that protecting forests has to be a significant part of any effort at combating climate change. But, as we shall see, drawing out a strategy for doing so is far more complex than it might appear – and in the process, interests motivated by entirely different dynamics can hide themselves behind what looks like a neutral, technical approach to mitigating climate change. To understand these dynamics, a good starting point is the basis of the current negotiations – what might be called the 'incentives' approach.

342 *Gopalakrishnan*

Forests and 'incentives'

The Nature Conservancy, one of the major international NGOs supporting the proposed agreement, describes the problem in these terms on their website:

> Forests are home to more than half of the world's terrestrial species and they provide food, water, shelter and income to millions of people around the world. Yet the world's forests are disappearing at an alarming rate ... Currently, countries have few economic incentives for preserving their forests. With no price put on the value of the carbon stored in trees, forests are considered more valuable for timber, cropland, or pasture than they are as standing, healthy systems. . . . [Through] activities that place a value on healthy forests—and through the creation of carbon trading markets that allow developing nations to sell credits attained through forest protection—developing countries can generate income from protecting forests rather than destroying them.
>
> (Nature Conservancy, 2010)

The logic is straightforward. In this view, the reason forests are destroyed is that they have less value than the resources they hold. The route forward for forest protection is to increase their value, i.e. to provide incentives to protect them.

In the international negotiations, after various efforts in other directions, this logic is now sought to be operationalized through the REDD agreement referred to above. This agreement is concerned with methods of providing incentives to developing countries, communities and companies to protect forests. Such incentives will be paid by the developed countries (and potentially their companies). By creating a sustainable system of incentives, it is said, REDD will ensure that the world's forests become more valuable alive than dead. This, in turn, will reduce emissions from deforestation and potentially increase absorption of carbon dioxide by forests, thereby addressing climate change.

Or, to use the language of the UN Collaborative Initiative on Reducing Emissions from Deforestation and forest Degradation (UN-REDD for short):

> REDD is a mechanism to create an incentive for developing countries to protect, better manage and wisely use their forest resources, contributing to the global fight against climate change. REDD strategies aim to make forests more valuable standing than they would be cut down, by creating a financial value for the carbon stored in trees. Once this carbon is assessed and quantified, the final phase of REDD involves *developed* countries paying *developing* countries carbon offsets for their standing forests. REDD is a cutting-edge forestry initiative that aims at tipping the economic balance in favour of sustainable management of forests so that their formidable economic, environmental and social goods and services benefit countries, communities, biodiversity and forest users while also contributing to important reductions in greenhouse gas emissions.

Thus, in addition to mitigating climate change, proponents of REDD also claim many other potential benefits, such as increased protection of biodiversity, benefits to forest dependent communities from both forest protection incentives and from the preservation of forests themselves, and a relatively cheap route to mitigation. The last

The climate talks, REDD and forest areas   343

point is particularly important in the context of the current intense resistance by the industrial nations to financial obligations; REDD is often advertised as an 'easy' way to achieve mitigation gains, a 'low hanging fruit' that should be seized at the earliest opportunity.

Some governments, including and especially India, have gone beyond REDD in this form and argued that afforestation (tree planting) should also be rewarded with incentives. As the Ministry of Environment and Forests recently argued at the Oslo conference on REDD, 'Reduction of deforestation and conservation and enhancement of forest carbon stocks should be treated at par; fairness requires that a unit of carbon saved should be treated the same as a unit of carbon added' (MoEF, 2010). This principle has largely now been accepted in the international talks, and is described as 'REDD-plus'.

At the moment, all the major industrial countries, including the US, support REDD-plus, and the major developing nations such as Brazil, India, Indonesia, China and so on also support the agreement, or at least do not object to it. In short, REDD currently enjoys a greater degree of support than hardly any other international climate initiative.

On the surface, this appears natural. Through this approach, industrial countries can cheaply contribute to addressing climate change; developing countries can get access to increased funds; what are often described as 'some of the world's poorest people' will receive collateral benefits; and there are other environmental gains. REDD seems like a 'win-win' solution. The only outstanding questions are whether REDD finances will come from a 'carbon trading' model, and whether industrial countries will get to claim that they have reduced emissions by financing REDD.

This rosy picture, however, rests on an extremely shaky foundation. In fact, practically none of the arguments made for this incentives approach to forest protection, and for REDD in particular, hold up under deeper scrutiny. There is far more to forests and forest policy than they address. Let's start with a basic question: what exactly is a forest?

The nature of forests and forest land

The online version of the Oxford dictionary defines a forest as a 'a large area covered chiefly with trees and undergrowth'. This definition immediately runs into problems. Is a pine plantation a forest? Perhaps. Is a stand of bamboo a forest? Maybe. What about a scrub jungle, a form of vegetation so common in India? Or a grassland, which is 'covered chiefly by undergrowth' but not necessarily by trees?

Meanwhile, it turns out that Indian law contains no definition of the term 'forest', excepting that of a Supreme Court order in 1996 which defined the term to mean any area recorded as a forest in any government record, or any area satisfying the 'dictionary definition' of a forest. As we have seen, the dictionary is not of much help. As far as government records are concerned, even a brief glance reveals a situation of bewildering complexity. According to the Forest Survey of India, 23.41% of the country's land area is recorded as forest (FSI, 2009); this is primarily based on data from State Forest Departments. But the actual area under tree cover is around 21%, and this includes areas under crops such as sugar cane, coconut, etc. that appear similar to forests in satellite mapping. Further, in 2005, the FSI undertook a sample survey to see to what extent the recorded forest areas matched the actual forests of the country. They found that, in the four States they studied, 'of the total forest cover

344 *Gopalakrishnan*

of 77,152.2 sq km in these States/UTs, only 48,983 sq km or 63.5% lie inside the recorded forests and quite a substantial proportion of forest cover (36.5%) exists outside the recorded forests' (FSI, 2005). Meanwhile, in several States, the recorded forest area is far larger than the actual forest cover. In short, more than a third of forest cover is outside areas recorded as forest, and much of the recorded area has no forest on it.

To add a further twist to this tale, the Ministry of Agriculture's Land Use Statistics for 2004–2005 (which are largely drawn from State Revenue Departments) show an area under 'forest use' that differs from the 2005 Forest Survey by more than 66,000 square kilometers (for the 22 States that have comparable statistics; the total for the whole country would be larger). In the Northeastern States, the differences are particularly striking; in Manipur, for instance, the Forest Survey reports a recorded forest area of 17,418 square kilometers, while the Ministry of Agriculture reports a recorded forest area of zero. There are particular historical and legal reasons for this that are outside the scope of this chapter, but the difference in itself is very significant.

Indeed, the closer one looks, the more chaotic things become. Thus, under the Indian Forest Act, all forest areas under the categories of reserved and protected forests (the two major categories of government forest) have to undergo a 'survey and settlement' to record land rights and other rights of people who live in them and in surrounding areas. In the case of reserved forests, a specific procedure is required in the Act, while protected forests are meant to be settled under the revenue laws. Yet in 2004 the Madhya Pradesh government informed the Supreme Court that 82% of its forest blocks had never been surveyed or settled and that it would take one and a half centuries to complete the job.[1] Similar requirements apply to national parks and sanctuaries under the Wild Life (Protection) Act; in 2005, as per affidavits filed in another Supreme Court case, this had not been done in 60% of national parks and 62% of sanctuaries, in some cases for more than 25 years.[2]

Superficially, it would appear that this chaos of records is merely caused by bureaucratic inefficiency. But in reality it results from a specific policy followed in the forest lands of India for the past 150 years. If we understand REDD and the incentives model in the light of that policy, the problems become apparent.

Understanding the chaos of Indian forests[3]

Contrary to the current environmental discourse that is often used to justify it, India's system of forest management did not originate in concerns for ecological or environmental preservation, as we now understand those terms. Rather, it had its roots in the British drive for timber extraction in the nineteenth century. For British industrial capitalism at the time, timber was a key raw material, both within India (for the railway networks that strengthened imperial control and allowed more efficient extraction of resources) and in the UK itself (particularly for ship building). Having exhausted their own timber resources, the British naturally looked to India's vast forests as a major source of supply. But the systems of forest control that existed in India at the time, where village communities, religious institutions, local rulers and tribal societies operated multiple and complex systems of management, did not permit easy extraction. They also did not serve British interests, since timber trees were not necessarily given high priority in such management systems. The British therefore described these systems as 'wasteful' and 'profligate', requiring replacement with 'scientific forestry'

The climate talks, REDD and forest areas   345

to increase timber yields; but to do this, they needed to override these systems and force both Indians and their own agents to accept one centralized framework. As a result, the British created the Forest Department and passed a series of three Forest Acts – in 1865, 1878 and 1927 – to essentially bring India's timber resources under their control and provide a legal–institutional form for their management. The 1927 Act, as mentioned above, remains India's main forest law.

The British Forest Acts were based on the principle of expropriation: any area could be declared to be a government forest, whereupon rights in this area would have to be respected/settled (the process varied over the course of the three acts and over the type of forest). As the scope for this expropriation expanded through the law, the form of people's rights was whittled down to essentially individual land rights by the time of the 1927 law, and, in the case of reserved forests, even these were subject to the decision of a forest settlement officer. The resulting failure to record even the individual rights of *Adivasis*, *Dalits* and most other forest dwelling communities is well documented. This process continued and was consolidated after independence, excepting in the Northeast.

This process resulted in two key consequences for these areas. The first was that, as with enclosures anywhere, it sought to reduce what were essentially territories and landscapes to commodities (timber, in this case). The variations in pre-colonial management systems notwithstanding, none of them was based on principles of commodity management; though often far from democratic or egalitarian, they were concerned with regulation of use and (at most) extraction of revenue. Their purpose did not revolve around the extraction of a single commodity; this was an innovation of the British.

But, unlike the classical enclosures of England, the enclosure attempt in India's forests failed – bringing about the second consequence. The attempt to seize most of central India's forests met with fierce resistance, being one of the triggers for a series of *Adivasi* uprisings across central India (the tribals of the Northeast having largely fought off British control from the beginning). The British lacked the force to clear these areas of people and suppress their management systems. The post-colonial Indian state, which retained the British forest law system and expanded it to the former princely States and partially excluded areas, has also repeatedly attempted this with as little success. The result has been to create a landscape of unclear property rights, governed by an autocratic system of centralized control. The result is uneasy peace at best and violent conflict at worst.

Over the years, even as the justification for this system has changed from 'scientific forestry' to industrial needs, and then to environmental conservation, the system itself has remained almost entirely unchanged (until the significant dent made in it by the 2006 Forest Rights Act). Forest dwellers continue to exist in a kind of legal twilight zone, and forests continue to be treated as if they are a commodity – to be safeguarded (in the conservationist view), sacrificed (in the developmentalist view), or traded (in the neoclassical view), but never to be democratically *governed*.

It is for this reason, fundamentally, that the state of records in forest areas is in such chaos. It was always far easier to issue notifications of forest land on paper than it was to survey and actually settle these lands, for the latter involved confronting the reality of people's rights and various degrees of popular resistance. A paper notification further offered the advantage of bringing the full draconian machinery of forest law into operation, for use in favour of all those the state favours (such as industry, mines

346 *Gopalakrishnan*

and, locally, contractors) and for use against those who the state wishes to repress. Once the legal regime is activated, decisions on forest management become controlled by various ways of estimating the 'value' of a forest – whether on the basis of silviculture, which remains the main focus of the training of forest officials, or on the basis of other considerations such as the value of the minerals or the land that the forest is occupying. The fate of forests and the ecosystems, territories and social systems they house becomes hostage to forces that seek, in one way or another, to *extract* their resources.

It should be clear that a large number of interests, from the local forest guard to multinational mining corporations, benefit from this system. As such, any attempt to change it meets with intense resistance. For instance, the earlier-mentioned Forest Rights Act of 2006 was the first law since 1865 to provide for at least a partially democratic process of deciding on forest rights. Its passage and notification was delayed by almost three years by a media campaign about it triggering forest destruction, and it has since faced systematic sabotage in implementation, with forest officials illegally insisting on additional evidence and blocking recognition of rights.[4]

The incentives model and Indian forests

In light of this situation, there are serious problems with accepting the incentives model as an accurate way of understanding Indian forests. We already have earlier experiences to this effect. Joint Forest Management (JFM), a huge scheme introduced across India in 1990, was supposed to provide a 'participatory' system by which communities and the Forest Department would 'jointly manage' forests. The scheme was a classic incentive model, in that communities were to produce micro-plans for forest management and participate in protection, in exchange for community development facilities and sharing of revenue from timber or forest produce sales. Very large sums of money have been put into this scheme in the name of enhancing 'conservation and livelihoods'; indeed, at last count, there are more than 2,500 crores worth of externally funded forestry projects in India, most of which involve a JFM component.[5]

But incentives and democratic participation are not in fact compatible; those providing incentives wish to intensify their control, not reduce it. The result has been that JFM has achieved the opposite of its stated goal of participation. Every JFM Committee has the local forest guard as its secretary and joint account holder, and JFM committees are federated into 'Forest Development Agencies' whose office bearers are also all forest officials. The entire institution is thus controlled by the Forest Department, and in most forest areas JFM committees are now seen as Department proxies which are run by the Department and local elites (such as contractors, MFP traders, etc.). Community planning is unheard of and revenue sharing frequently does not take place (Sarin, 2009). A 2001 public hearing report in Harda, Madhya Pradesh – cited at the time as a 'model' of JFM – provides a graphic illustration of what JFM has become. It found that 'the villagers want the JFM committees to be disbanded as these have become a means of increasing the exploitation of adivasis, rather than benefiting them... Their formation has created conflict within villages... [and] between villages... Work for which villagers used to receive wages prior to JFM has now been converted into begari (unpaid labour)... The villagers have no idea how much money has come into their account from any scheme and how it is being spent' (Diwan et al., 2001). The same story is repeated across the country. As a survey across three States

The climate talks, REDD and forest areas   347

put it, 'Existing institutional arrangements that are more locally legitimate, more democratically accountable, and more sensitive to local livelihood needs –although not always equitable and gender sensitive – are being replaced by institutions amenable for extending state control' (Sarin et al., 2003).

Meanwhile, the Forest Department and the Environment Ministry are today playing a very active role in denying recognition of the community rights recognized in the Forest Rights Act, most actively in the case of the right to protect, manage and conserve community forest resources under the Act.[6] As a statutory right, the latter in law is superior to and overrides JFM, which is a mere administrative scheme; but in practice, all Ministry funds, resources and implementation are channeled to the latter, while the former is systematically blocked. Thus the institutional and political-economic interests of the Forest Department and the state override even the law itself.

REDD in the context of the political economy of forests

At a conceptual level, the REDD model repeats exactly the same mistake that underlies the problems of the earlier system: whereas forests were once valued for their timber, and today are valued for their land, REDD proponents would have us value them for their carbon content. But to reduce a socio-ecological system to a single value leads, inevitably, to resource grabbing.

Let us play this out in the context of the history of Indian forests. If incentives are provided based on the carbon absorption capacity of existing forests, there will be an immediate rush by powerful interests – Forest Departments and, if they are permitted, corporates – to 'lock down' these 'assets' and prevent any 'damage' to them. This will only intensify the autocratic regime in these areas and further deprive people of their rights (whatever legal protections might say). For instance, in a 'carbon forestry' project in Brazil by an American NGO working on a REDD style model, the local indigenous and poor communities found that they were prevented from fishing, hunting rodents and eventually from even entering the forest; a special police force was set up, which used extreme brutality to prevent people from using what had once been their forest (Shapiro, 2009).

Nor will REDD-style incentives result in better protection for forests, whether one understands them as carbon storehouses or as ecosystems. A trading and incentives model offers ample scope for manipulation and cheating. Firstly, while it is relatively easy to measure carbon emissions from a forest, it is very difficult to reliably predict how much carbon that forest will absorb, since this depends on a variety of natural factors. For instance, in one existing carbon forestry project in Bolivia, the estimates of carbon emissions saved by the project declined by ten times over the life of the program (Greenpeace, 2009). Secondly, in a situation where records are chaotic and mutually inconsistent, there is ample scope for forgery. Deforestation can simply be shifted from one area to another, and the old area then claimed as a 'forest protection project.' In short, the net result of REDD could be large amounts of money pouring into agencies and companies that are not in fact protecting forests at all. When they do do so, they will do it in a manner that is both unjust and unecological (since protecting 'carbon' may not always be compatible with the environmental needs of a system, such as the frequent forest fires or grazing that characterize many scrub jungles).

The model proposed by the Indian government – REDD plus – is even more dangerous. Though plantation and afforestation policies in India are often described as a

348 Gopalakrishnan

success, their negative aspects are rarely noted. Afforestation programs often take place on cultivated lands (including shifting cultivation fallows), village commons, community pasture lands, etc. that actually belong to and are being used by people. Such programs are already leading to evictions of people and/or displacement from their livelihoods in several areas.[7] They are a standard method by which the Forest Department asserts its power over lands. Indeed, in October 2008, the Parliamentary Standing Committee on Environment and Forests[8] stated that 'afforestation ... deprives forest dwellers and adivasis of some or all of their lands and impacts their livelihoods and basic needs – for which they are neither informed, nor consulted, nor compensated.'

In such a context, to provide financial incentives for afforestation may easily lead to a wave of land grabbing for plantation programmes. Such plantations are, once again, not necessarily environmentally friendly. Plantations often replace grasslands, scrub jungles and other habitats with monocultures planted with one or a few species of trees. This has a negative effect on wildlife, biodiversity and, depending on the species planted, potentially on the water table as well. Once again, we already have direct experiences of the link between climate change agreements and such impacts. There are two existing forestry projects in India under the Clean Development Mechanism; in one, by ITC in Andhra Pradesh, all the trees being planted are eucalyptus, with predictable implications for the local water table (Ghosh, 2006). The people in the area were not even told that carbon credits have been earned for the project.

Finally, REDD will most likely involve provision of financial incentives through a 'carbon trading' model. This in turn will create even larger financial incentives for wholesale takeovers of forests. A recent survey found that the world's largest investment companies are tracking REDD very closely (WWF, 2009). With such funds, there will be a rush by private companies seeking access to public forest land for plantations as well as control over official forest protection programs. Reliance, ITC and other companies have been demanding access to 'degraded' forests for commercial afforestation for many years, and this scheme could legitimize their demand (for the most recent example, see Sethi, 2006).

Possible safeguards

In light of these circumstances, it is not surprising that REDD is so popular with so many governments. For industrial nations, it offers a route whereby relatively small payments can be made for nominally large emissions reduction gains, thereby saving them from actually reducing their own emissions. For developing countries, it offers an opportunity for state agencies and private companies to expand and intensify their control over lands and forests while earning money through 'incentives.'

In the process, though, the result is unlikely to be any major mitigation of climate change; rather there is likely to be greater land grabbing, intensifying conflict and greater impoverishment in forest areas. Thus the 'win win' solution is in fact more of a lose-lose one, excepting for those who financially or otherwise benefit from the process.

Some have sought to argue that these and other issues can be addressed through safeguards in the REDD agreement. The most recent and far-reaching proposal of this type was made by the Government of Bolivia, following on the 'Cochabamba People's Agreement' of April 2010. Some of the key changes suggested in this proposal were:[9]

The climate talks, REDD and forest areas   349

- a guarantee of indigenous rights as protected by international law;
- a bar on the use of REDD by industrial countries to offset their domestic emissions;
- a bar on conversion of natural forests to plantations;
- a requirement for 'transparent and participatory' mechanisms to resolve disputes over rights and access; and
- mandating the free, prior and informed consent of indigenous peoples to any action under REDD.

It would appear that these safeguards should be sufficient to address the major concerns about REDD raised here. Without getting into the details of each safeguard, however, there is a fundamental problem with the safeguards approach itself. The lesson of Indian forest law is that policy and legal safeguards are implemented in the manner, and to the extent, that is permitted by the larger power dynamics at play. In India's forests, these dynamics are driven by a coalition of powerful forces (the state machinery, corporate capital, and organized criminal elements) that profit from expropriation of forests. The same is probably true around the world.

Thus, safeguards are only of value where they provide space and institutional frameworks for countervailing forces that can resist these pressures. In most countries, and particularly in India, international agreements simply do not provide such spaces. Affected communities will have no access to forums where such provisions could ever be enforced, except in very rare cases. The interpretation and use of such safeguards will therefore remain with the same forces that they are intended to guard against. As an international joint statement of climate justice organisations recently put it,[10] 'Despite efforts to create safeguards to prevent the violation of the human rights of Indigenous Peoples and forest-dwelling communities, there is no guarantee to their effectiveness. In the worst case, REDD could inaugurate a massive land grab . . . the idea that REDD could help secure the territories or consolidate the rights and livelihoods of forest-dependent peoples is ludicrous.'

In any case, the fate of such safeguards is already quite clear, both domestically and internationally. In India, the Ministry of Environment and Forests has consistently projected JFM as its answer to international pressure for 'participatory' approaches to REDD implementation (see for instance ICFRE, 2009 and MoEF, 2010). The discussion above, however, indicates what the impact of JFM actually has. Meanwhile, the references to indigenous rights have no legal value in India, since the government refuses to recognize that there are any indigenous communities in the country at all. Meanwhile, at the international level, the subterfuges are even more glaring. The Bolivian text simply disappeared from the negotiating text presented by the chair to the AWG-LCA at Cancun; at the time of writing, the parties have 'agreed' to use the chair's text, effectively removing the Bolivian proposal from the table (Lang, 2010).

Conclusion

The problem with the incentives approach behind the logic of REDD is that it is based on a fundamentally flawed understanding of the reasons for forest destruction. Increasing the 'value' of forests is not the issue; the issue is one of power to decide what is valuable and what is not. What is needed is not a new way of valuing forests but a new way of governing them. Breaking the autocratic stranglehold of 150 years of

350 Gopalakrishnan

extractive processes on India's forests, forest lands and forest peoples is the only way forward for forest protection. Moving towards genuinely democratic institutions, which regulate forest use on the basis of the local community's rights, will be far more effective in the long run, as it permits collective control over these spaces and resources rather than the private control of profit-seekers. Unfortunately a full discussion of the possibilities of such a transformation is out of the scope of this chapter, but it is clear that, whatever it may be, such a transformation looks nothing like REDD.

Notes

1 From affidavits filed by the Madhya Pradesh government during hearings in WP 202/95, *T.N. Godavarman Thirumalpad and Ors. vs. Union of India and Ors.*
2 Compiled from affidavits filed by State governments in *CEL, WWF-India vs. Union of India and Ors.*
3 For a more detailed exploration of this argument, see Gopalakrishnan (forthcoming) and Gopalakrishnan 2010. Also see the considerable literature on the history of Indian forest management.
4 For more details please see www.forestrightsact.com.
5 Annexure to answer to Unstarred Question No. 2529, dated 22.07.2009, by Minister of State for Environment and Forests to Shri Vikrambhai Arjanbhai Maadam in the Lok Sabha.
6 For more information on this see Council for Social Development (2010).
7 An illustrative list is available here: http://www.forestrightsact.com/climate-change/item/download/29.
8 194th report of the Standing Committee on Science and Technology, Environment and Forests, on the Compensatory Afforestation Fund Bill 2008.
9 See Option 1, Chapter VI of draft negotiating text, AWG-LCA, document number FCCC/AWGLCA/2010/14, dated 13.08.2010.
10 'No REDD! No REDD Plus! Global Sign On Campaign Against Schemes for Reducing Emissions from Deforestation and Forest Degradation', December 2010.

References

Council for Social Development (2010) 'Summary Report on the Implementation of the Forest Rights Act', April 27, Copies available from the Council for Social Development, New Delhi, or from the author.
Diwan, R., Sarin, M., and Sundar, N. (2001) 'Summary Report of Jan Sunwai on Forest Rights at Village Indpura, Harda District, 26 May 2001', Obtained by personal communication with authors.
Food and Agricultural Organisation (FAO) (2010) *Global Forest Resources Assessment 2010*, March, FAO, Geneva.
Forest Survey of India (FSI) (2005) *State of Forests Report 2005*, Forest Survey of India, Dehradun.
—— (2009) *State of Forests Report 2009*, Forest Survey of India, Dehradun.
Ghosh, S. (2006) 'Myths and Reality: ITC and its Social Forestry/Carbon Forestry plantations in Khammam District, Andhra Pradesh', Unpublished manuscript, received by personal communication from author.
Gopalakrishnan, S. (2010) 'Forest Areas, Political Economy and the 'Left-Progressive Line' on Operation Green Hunt', *Radical Notes*, May 30, http://radicalnotes.com/content/view/137/39/, accessed on September 13, 2010.
—— (forthcoming) 'Forests and Forest Rights', *Social Development Report*, Council for Social Development, New Delhi.
Greenpeace (2009) *Carbon Scam: Noel Kempff Climate Action Project and the Push for Sub-national Forest Offsets*, October 15 http://www.greenpeace.org/carbon-scam, accessed on September 6, 2010.

The climate talks, REDD and forest areas 351

Institute for Council on Forestry Research and Education (ICFRE) (2009) 'Forest and Tree Cover: Contribution as a Carbon Sink', Technical Paper, August http://moef.nic.in/downloads/home/contri-carbon-sink.pdf, accessed on September 17, 2010.

Lang, C. (2010) 'REDD in Cancun, part 1: What happened to Bolivia's text in the AWG-LCA?', posted at www.redd-monitor.org, accessed on December 7, 2010.

Ministry of Environment and Forests (2010) 'India's Presentation on its Forestry and Climate Change Initiatives', http://moef.nic.in/downloads/publicinformation/OsloREDDConference.pdf. May 30, accessed on September 8, 2010.

Nature Conservancy (2010) 'Climate Change: Why Reducing Deforestation is Crucial', http://www.nature.org/initiatives/climatechange/strategies/art13747.html, accessed on September 8, 2010.

Sarin, M. (2009) 'Undoing Historical Injustice: Reclaiming Citizenship Rights and Democratic Forest Governance through the FRA', paper presented at 'Beyond JFM' conference in Delhi, September 2009, on file with author.

Sarin, M., Singh, N.M., Sundar, N., and Bhogal, R.K. (2003) 'Devolution as a Threat to Democratic Decision-making in Forestry? Findings from Three States in India', Working Paper 197, Overseas Development Institute, London.

Sethi, N. (2006) 'Private Affairs', *Down to Earth*, April, Centre for Science and Environment, New Delhi.

Shapiro, M. (2009) 'GM's Money Trees', *Mother Jones Magazine*, November/December.

UNFCCC (2009) 'Fact sheet: Reducing emissions from deforestation in developing countries: approaches to stimulate action', June, http://unfccc.int/files/press/backgrounders/application/pdf/fact_sheet_reducing_emissions_from_deforestation.pdf, accessed on 11 March 2011.

World Wildlife Fund (2009) 'Investors ready for forest carbon market if Copenhagen and countries supply certainty', WWF Forest Carbon Initiative Press Release, September 28.

26 The technology agenda

Anand Patwardhan and Neha Umarji

Introduction and rationale

Climate change resulting from the anthropogenic emissions of greenhouse gases is now recognized as perhaps the most serious environmental problem facing humanity today, requiring an urgent global and national response. Since greenhouse gas emissions are inextricably linked to energy use and economic activity, effective response will likely require transformative changes in the energy system. Technology could play a key role in this transformation, by helping decouple emissions and other negative impacts from energy use. Such a decoupling could be achieved by increasing the efficiency of energy use and by switching to primary energy sources that have a reduced environmental footprint. The next section examines in greater detail the extent of technology change required to meet climate mitigation objectives.

While considering the role of technology in the response to climate change, an immediate question is the extent to which the technology agenda is basically a financing agenda. An oft-heard view is that if the policy environment provides the right incentives, investments will be attractive, and technologies will follow. This is true, but only partly. For one, given the magnitude and rate of the change required it is unlikely that it could be achieved only through existing technologies. Much of it can, but quite a bit is still dependent on technologies that are in the lab stage or in early stages of research and development. Second, 'technology push' is often as important as 'market/demand pull' for bringing new technologies to market, although this is less visible in the energy sector than, for example, in the information and communication technology (ICT) sector. And third, the conventional view of technology transfer, that it consists of mature technologies first developed and deployed in the North (developed countries) that are then transferred to the South (developing countries), is being challenged by rapid changes in the global economic environment. Emerging markets may well be the first points of market entry for clean technologies, and developing country firms are increasingly engaging in merger and acquistion (M&A) activity that is driven by technology, in addition to considerations of operational efficiency and market access.

These reasons suggest that when considering the role of technology in responding to climate change, a broad view of the innovation process is required, and policy interventions need to address all of the elements of the innovation system, including applied research, early-stage technology development, new venture creation, incubation and venture capital. The process of technology change is described further in a subsequent section.

The technology agenda also needs to be placed within the broader context of national policy response to climate change. In this regard it is instructive to note that the National Action Plan on Climate Change (GoI, 2008) emphasizes the generation of climate mitigation and adaptation co-benefits, while pursuing a policy of inclusive and rapid economic growth. Technology choices have an important role to play in 'greening' this growth (i.e. generating mitigation co-benefits), and making it more climate-resilient (i.e. generating adaptation co-benefits).

Consequently, it is important to consider the technology dimensions of the Missions through which the NAPCC is being operationalized. These dimensions are particularly important for missions such as the National Solar Mission that have identified ambitious targets for deployment of solar energy generation technologies or the Mission on Sustainable Agriculture, where an important element is the development and dissemination of crop varieties that are better able to handle water and thermal stress. The section on 'Science and technology in India' further elaborates the national circumstances and priorities with regard to science and technology.

Climate change is a global problem, requiring a global response. Indeed, national responses to climate change need to be developed and implemented in the context of the broader multilateral response, and there is an expectation that these responses will be supported and enabled by the multilateral process. Therefore, the final section of this chapter examines the multilateral response, focusing on the technology-related elements of the response, and the state of play at the end of the recent Conference of Parties (COP) in Cancun.

Overall, the chapter aims at giving the reader a perspective of the potential of technology in addressing climate change, and the requirements for realizing that potential in practice.

The significance of technology in climate change

Article 2 of the United Nations Framework Convention on Climate Change (UNFCCC) specifies that the ultimate objective of the Convention is 'to achieve the stabilization of the GHG concentrations in the atmosphere at a level that would prevent dangerous anthropogenic interference with the climate system. Such a level should be achieved within a timeframe sufficient to allow ecosystems to adapt naturally to climate change, to ensure that food production is not threatened and enable economic development to proceed in a sustainable manner' (UNFCCC, 1992). While the Convention does not specify what would constitute 'dangerous anthropogenic interference', there has been a convergence in recent years around the goal of limiting global warming to 2°C relative to pre-industrial levels.

The Fourth Assessment Report (AR4) of the Intergovernmental Panel on Climate Change (IPCC) concluded that for this goal to be achieved with reasonable certainty, global carbon dioxide (CO_2) emissions would need to be reduced from 2000 levels by 50%–85% by 2050 (IPCC, 2007). The AR4 highlights the changes required in various economic sectors for this reduction. See, for example, Figure 3.33 from Chapter 3 of the report of Working Group 3 of the AR4 (Fisher et al. 2007). Three main categories of changes are prominent: reduction in demand (for example through increased end-use efficiency), switching to low GHG emitting energy sources (such as renewable energy and nuclear) and CO_2 capture and storage technologies (to reduce the carbon footprint of existing fossil-fuel based energy sources).

There is an ongoing debate in the literature regarding the role of technology for these transformative changes. While some authors suggest that existing technologies will not be adequate to deliver the extent of mitigation required (for example, Hoffert et al., 2002), others argue that at least for the near to mid-term, accelerated deployment of existing technologies might suffice, although there will be a need for research and technology development in the latter half of this century (for example, Pacala and Socolow, 2004).

More recently, the International Energy Association (IEA) Energy Technology Perspectives report (IEA, 2010) describes a scenario (BLUE scenario) that leads to a 50% reduction in CO_2 emissions by 2050 and a stabilization of CO_2 concentration at 450 ppmv (IEA, 2010).

In terms of meeting the 2°C climate target with reasonable certainty, the BLUE scenario is clearly desirable. However, realizing the BLUE scenario will require radical and immediate steps for decoupling growth from GHG emissions. Technologies, both new and existing, will play a key role in achieving this target.

Figure 26.1 depicts the transformation required in different sectors. While a reduction in emissions is required in all sectors, the most important sectors are power generation and transport on the supply side and demand side respectively. With regard to power generation, Figure 26.2 indicates that a substantial increase in solar, wind and carbon capture and storage (CCS) is required.

In the transportation sector, the technology change primarily involves the transition to electricity and/or hydrogen as fuels in the medium to long term as seen in Figure 26.3.

While some of the technologies identified in Figures 26.2 and 26.3 are commercially available, many are currently at different stages of research and development. For example, active R&D efforts are on-going with regard to fuel cells, energy storage and new solar cell technologies to increase efficiency and reduce cost. Further, the BLUE scenario assumes the need for a rapid expansion in nuclear power. If this were not to happen, an even more rapid increase in renewable energy technologies would be required in order to meet the mitigation targets. Uncertainties in the pace of technological change, and unanticipated technology risks pose further challenges for a technology agenda, and require a dynamic and adaptive approach towards technology policies.

An understanding of the process of technology change and innovation is therefore essential for designing policies for technology where we have to look at all stages of

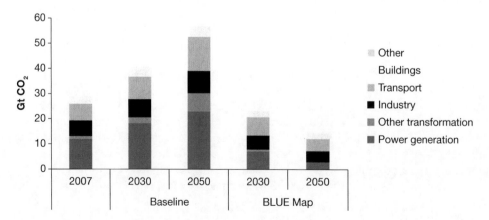

Figure 26.1 Transformation from Baseline to Blue Map scenario

Source: IEA, 2010

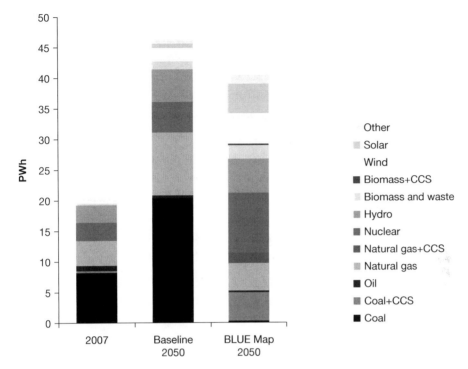

Figure 26.2 Power generation mix
Source: IEA, 2010

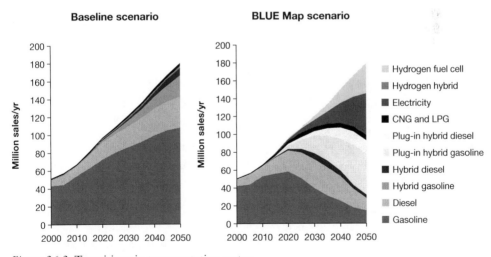

Figure 26.3 Transitions in transportation sector
Source: IEA, 2010

356 Patwardhan and Umarji

the technology cycle, and not only the adoption or transfer of mature technologies, noting that 'transfer' goes beyond just the process of capital supply of high-tech equipment, and includes the transfer of enhanced knowledge, integrated human and management skills and technical and maintenance capabilities to the recipient party.

The process of technological change

Technological change is often seen to follow a number of well-defined and distinct stages (Grübler, 1998):

1   Invention (the creation of a novel concept or idea, often, but not always, resulting from a formal research and development process).
2   Innovation (conversion of the idea into a product or service that can be introduced into the market).
3   Niche markets (early adoption, initial, small-scale applications that are economically feasible under specific conditions).
4   Diffusion (wide-spread adoption and evolution into mature markets, eventually ending in saturation followed by decline through substitution or replacement).

The technology life-cycle (TLC) and the product life-cycle (PLC) are analytical constructs that are often used to characterize the evolution of technology through these stages. The process of technology development is dynamic and context-specific; i.e technology choices and technology development patterns vary from country to country and even sector by sector depending upon the extent of infrastructure, technical capacity, the readiness of the markets to provide commercial opportunities and supporting policy frameworks.

Collectively, factors such as institutions, legal and regulatory environments, and the factor and product markets relevant to new technologies influence the rate, scope and nature of innovation, and are often referred to as a 'national innovation system'. The view of innovation as a systemic process emphasizes its dynamic nature and the interplay of technology and market factors. Innovation policy then needs to address not only technology issues such as research and development, but institutional and market issues including new venture creation, barriers for market adoption, learning-by-doing and financing of early-stage technology.

In broad terms, technology policies may be grouped into those that drive a technology push, and those that create a market pull. Technology push emphasizes the role of policies that stimulate research and development, especially those aimed at lowering the costs of meeting long-term objectives with technology that today is very far from being economical in existing markets. This might include measures such as public funded R&D or R&D tax credits, as well as measures that support learning and spill-overs. Such measures typically include education and capacity-building.

Demand-pull policies emphasize the use of instruments to enhance the demand for lower-emission technologies, thereby increasing private incentives to improve these technologies and inducing any learning-by-doing effects. Demand–pull instruments might include emissions taxes or more direct approaches, such as renewable portfolio standards, adoption subsidies, or direct government purchases. Figure 26.4 illustrates some of these policies and their interactions.

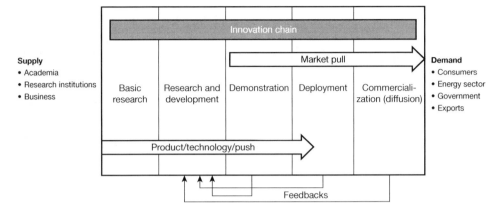

Figure 26.4 Technology development cycle and its main driving forces

Source: Adapted from Halsnaes et al., 2007

The significance and relevance of different policies is dependent on the stage of technology development. For example, as technologies mature, market mechanisms and commercial incentives play an increasingly important role to further progress of technologies. Many of the new, efficient technologies pose a problem in being too expensive for commercial deployment.

Learning by doing that results from the accumulation of experience is an important source of cost reduction. Therefore it is important to characterize and assess learning in low carbon technologies as an input for assessing economic feasibility and guiding policy decisions (Jamasb and Köhler, 2007). For example (Nemet, 2006) uses the learning curve idea to estimate the time required to reach grid parity for solar photo-voltaics. Assuming that the historical rate continues in the future, grid parity would be achieved by 2027. A similar illustration is provided in Figure 26.5 (IEA, 2000) that describes the implications of future progress ratios on the quantum of learning investments required.

Given that subsidies may be required until 'grid parity' is reached, there is a direct implication for the duration for which subsidies may need to be provided and the total burden on public funds for the subsidy. Assumptions about learning curves and the associated cost reductions thus have significant implications for the viability of different technology support schemes such as the Jawaharlal Nehru National Solar Mission (JNNSM), which aims at establishing 20,000 MW of grid-connected solar power along with an additional 2,000 MW of off-grid generation by 2022.

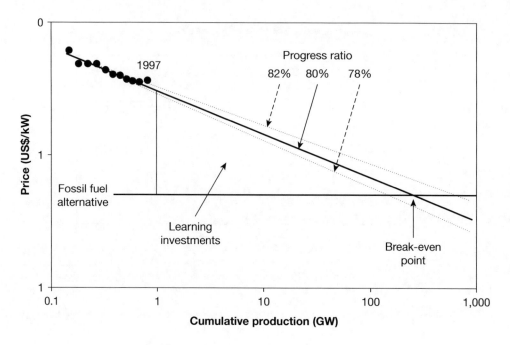

Figure 26.5 Effect of progress ratios on break-even point and learning investments
Source: IEA, 2000

Science and technology in India

Over the years, India has demonstrated impressive capabilities relating to science and technology development in strategic sectors such as defence, atomic energy and space. Development of indigenous technology capabilities was of particular importance during the 80s and 90s as India faced a technology denial regime. Private sector investment and involvement in R&D was quite limited, and even though this is now changing gradually post-liberalization, the public sector still accounts for more than two-thirds of the R&D expenditure. While the gross expenditure on R&D has not increased beyond 0.8–0.85% of GDP over the years, the S&T Policy of 2003 (Ministry of Science and Technology, 2003), for the first time set a target of 2% of GDP – at par with the level of R&D expenditure in the developed world. Increasing private sector investment in R&D is one of the main challenges for achieving this target.

The S&T policy of 2003 also recognized the significance of innovation, technology development and diffusion and that the transformation of new ideas into commercial successes is of vital importance to the nation's ability to achieve high economic growth and global competitiveness. Accordingly, government policies are now emphasizing not only R&D and the technological factors of innovation, but also the other equally important social, institutional and market factors needed for adoption, diffusion and transfer of innovation to the productive sectors.

The science and technology system has also undergone significant institutional change in recent years. For example, leading academic institutions such as the Indian Institutes of Technology are now placing an increased emphasis on research, innovation and technology commercialization. In many cases, academic and research institutions are creating interface structures and organizations to support the innovation and commercialization activities (such as the Foundation for Innovation & Technology Transfer, or FiTT at IIT-Delhi, the Society for Innovation & Entrepreneurship or SINE at IIT-Bombay and the Society for Innovation and Development, or SID at IISc, Bangalore). There is substantial growth in externally funded research, including contract research, and research funded by the private sector. That said, the role of academic institutions in India in the innovation and technology development process is still limited, and the base of activity rather narrow. For example only about a fifth of the academic institutions in the country are involved in patent filing (Nezu et al., 2007).

Publicly funded R&D institutions form a distinctive and key element of the Indian S&T system. These include, in the civilian sector, the R&D laboratories of the Council for Scientific and Industrial Research (CSIR), the Indian Council for Agricultural Research (ICAR) and the Indian Council for Medical Research (ICMR). In addition, several socio-economic ministries have dedicated R&D organizations or R&D units associated with public sector enterprises. These institutions play a key role in applied research and technology development, and have seen significant change and growth in the past decades. For example, the CSIR laboratories have emerged as significant generators of IPR along with substantial private sector funded contract research and collaborative R&D. This institutional base needs to be further mobilized and leveraged for supporting innovation and the development and commercialization of new technologies.

At the policy level, there is increasing interest and efforts for exploring new forms of public-private partnership or creating facilitating structures such as technology business incubators (TBIs) or science, technology entrepreneurship parks (STEPs). New financing approaches and support mechanisms for early-stage technology development are also being attempted, such as the Small Business Innovation Research Initiative (SBIRI) programme of the Department of Biotechnology and schemes of the Department of Science and Technology and the Department of Scientific & Industrial Research. India has also adopted policies and a legal framework for intellectual property rights (IPR) that is compliant with the requirements of the WTO and TRIPS. Patenting activity has increased rapidly, both with regard to patenting in India and patenting by Indian organizations in developed countries (Ministry of Science and Technology, 2009).

One of the most important inputs to R&D is manpower. In order to match the rise in R&D expenditure to a level of 2% of the GNP, a corresponding increase in the number of R&D personnel is required. One way to increase this strength is by encouraging industries to contribute by inducting R&D personnel on a larger scale (Ramarao, 1998). As of 1 April 2005, 3.91 lakh personnel have been employed in R&D establishments of which only 39.6% are primarily engaged in R&D activities (Ministry of Science and Technology, 2009). India had 140 researchers per million people as compared to 7,681 in Finland, 6,139 in Sweden, 5,713 in Singapore, 5,546 in Japan and 5,277 in Denmark. The total number of researchers in India is 1,54,840 as compared to 13,90,649 in USA, 12,14,912 in China and 7,09,888 in Japan (Ministry of Science and Technology, 2009). Figure 26.6 provides a comparison of the Global Expense on R&D (GERD) as a

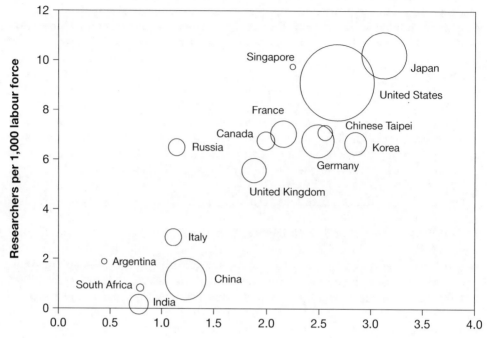

Figure 26.6 Global expense on R&D (GERD) as a % of the GDP for various countries
Source: IEA 2008

percentage of the GDP of various countries, along with the number of researchers per 1,000 persons in the labour force.

Indian technology agenda for climate change and energy

Over the years, India has been investing significantly in technologies of significance for mitigation and adaptation responses to climate change. Energy R&D was identified as a priority area in the 11th Plan (2007–2012), with a separate Working Group on Energy R&D. The report of the Working Group (GoI, 2006) provides some useful insights into the priority technology areas identified for the energy sector and the overall R&D directions. Some of the technology areas identified in this report of high relevance for climate mitigation include:

- developing methods for exploiting energy sources, currently considered unviable such as development of in-situ gasification for recovery of coal buried deep in the earth,
- breakthrough technologies for exploiting renewable sources, particularly solar which has a very high potential in the country,
- developing clean-coal technologies (ultra-super critical technology, integrated gasification combined cycle, atmospheric fluidized bed combustion, pressurized fluidized bed combustion) suitable for Indian coal, which is characterized by high ash content,

The technology agenda   361

- bringing in efficiency in the use of non-commercial energy sources (such as animal residue, bio-mass, urban and rural waste including agricultural waste),
- continuing measures to improve energy efficiency of industry and transport,
- hydrogen (production, storage and end use) technologies as alternate energy carrier.

Technology priorities and needs have also been identified during the course of the development of the NAPCC, and particularly the Missions under the NAPCC. Many of the NAPCC missions have significant technology implications and include components for research and technology development. The technology-related aspects of some of these missions are described in Table 26.1 below.

Table 26.1 Science and technology-related aspects of some NAPCC missions

Mission	Targets	Technology implications
Solar mission	To increase grid-connected solar power generation to 1000 MW within three years (by 2013), an additional 3000 MN by 2017 through the mandatory use of the renewable purchase obligation by utilities backed with a preferential tariff. An overall target of 20 GW of solar power by 2030.	There is a wide variety of technology approaches, including solar photovoltaic, solar thermal and the use of solar energy for power and thermal applications. Underlying technologies span the range from lab-stage to mature. The key challenge is of reducing the cost of power quickly to ensure economic viability.
Sustainable habit	Mission includes a focus on material and urban waste management, an increase in energy efficiency in buildings and the use of solar technologies for building energy demand.	Development and deployment of waste to energy and related technologies, including biochemical conversion, wastewater use, sewage utilization and recycling options.
		The solar evacuated tabular panel technology is available internationally for solar water heating systems but needs to be transferred for diffusion in the Indian market.
		A national networked initiative for the next generation of LEDs, particularly white LEDs.
Sustainable agriculture	Increasing the resilience of agriculture to climate stress.	Development of drought- and pest-resistant crop varieties.
Strategic knowledge for climate change	Generating the information base for technology choices, and developing technology strategy that effectively utilizes domestic strengths and leverages the various international collaborative mechanisms.	Research in key substantive domains of climate science to improve understanding of key phenomena and processes.
		Global and regional climate modelling to improve the quality and accuracy of climate change projections for India.

362 *Patwardhan and Umarji*

Formulating and implementing a national science and technology agenda in the context of climate change is an urgent priority and a challenge as well. Given the economic growth targets, the need for inclusion, and the need for simultaneously achieving environmental and climate related goals, a careful evaluation of technology choices is warranted. This will need to reflect resource endowments, domestic capabilities and technical and economic feasibility. Implementing a technology agenda will require effective institutional structures to deliver and manage resources, to connect public institutions and private firms, and blend technology-push and market-pull policies.

Technology in the multilateral process

National responses to climate change need to be placed in the context of the multi-lateral and global response and the principles underlying that response. The UNFCCC and its Kyoto protocol serve as the foundation for the global response to climate change that is based on the principle of '*common but differentiated responsibilities (CBDR) and respective capabilities*' of Parties. Under Article 4.5 of the UNFCCC, Annex II Parties are specifically committed to 'promote, facilitate and finance the transfer of, or access to, environmentally-sound technologies and know-how' to developing countries to enable them to 'implement the provisions of the Convention'. This commitment includes supporting the development and enhancement of endoge-nous capacities of developing countries. The extent to which the multilateral process has concretely supported and enabled the transfer of low-carbon technologies is debatable. Three issues have often been identified as posing barriers:

1 *Provision of finance*
   Although there are many mitigation options that are low-cost, options that have large mitigation potential (such as renewable energy technologies or CO_2 capture and storage) also have high additional costs. The mobilization of, and access to, adequate, predictable and sustainable financial resources remains a challenge.
2 *Intellectual Property Rights*
   IPRs identified as a barrier to technology transfer need further consideration. The following possible solutions, among others, have been suggested: regulating the patent regime to balance rewarding technological innovation with access to a common public good; removing barriers to accessing technologies in the public domain; and increasing access to clean technologies by granting compulsory licences for these technologies.
3 *Lack of capacity*
   A key obstacle is often the lack of capacity to utilize climate friendly technologies, as well as limited awareness of available climate-friendly options among decision-makers in developing countries and financial and development institutions. Enhancing technology absorption capabilities, taking into account national circum-stances, is therefore a priority. Mechanisms for technology transfer should include measures that will enable the enhancement of absorptive capacities, keeping in mind the targets of such technology interventions.

The technology agenda   363

Agenda for the multilateral process

In order to realize the full potential of technology it will be important to realize that the challenge is to accelerate the entire technology cycle – from idea to concept to early adoption and finally widespread diffusion. While the focus so far has been on the transfer of mature, commercialized technology, it will have to be broadened to address all the three key initial stages of the technology cycle – research, development and early adoption, and the financing instruments and mechanisms that are put in place will need to match the varied requirements of each of these stages.

Research: There is need to drastically increase the scale and scope of public-funded research in relevant sectors, particularly energy. While this will typically take place through domestic actions, the UNFCCC process could help by internationalizing these efforts. For example, multilateral funds could support the participation of developing country entities in R&D projects, with suitable IPR sharing. They could also support placing certain research outputs in the public domain (by 'buying out' the IPR, for example), and also support open platforms and open source approaches for development.

Development: Technology risk is still quite high, and there is a sound rationale for public support of technologies. Just as in the case of research, multilateral funds could support the internationalization of this stage; for example by supporting developing country entities to participate in consortia projects; or by supporting joint, collaborative technology development between public and private partners in developed and developing countries.

Market entry and early adoption: In the case of the energy sector, where affordability and access are key requirements and the final consumer only sees the energy service, rather than the technologies themselves, it is usually the state that has to serve as the 'early adopter'. For this reason, there is an important role for public funds to help move technologies quicker along the learning curve for cost reduction and for demonstrating and validating technologies to address concerns of technology risk and viability. Public–private partnerships, demonstration projects and the provision of risk capital are all mechanisms that have been used in this stage.

Unfortunately, none of the existing financing mechanisms and arrangements address these early stages of the technology cycle. The CDM, as an offset mechanism, works only for technologies for which cost and performance baselines are known at scales being proposed, and there is little or no technology risk. The Global Environment Facility, which is also a source of financing, has, unfortunately, moved steadily away from the early-stage technology space.

The most recent COP to the UNFCCC (COP 16 at Cancun) has led to some progress with regard to technology transfer through the adoption of the Cancun Agreements. Through these decisions, a Technology Mechanism has been created, comprising of Technology Executive Committee (TEC) and Climate Technology Centre and Network (CTCN). Together the TEC and CTCN propose to provide guidance in choosing appropriate technologies and assistance in actual implementation and deployment of the same. However, 'one significant flaw in the Cancun text is the lack of any mention of IPR-related issues, even though it has been cited as a priority issue in technology

364 *Patwardhan and Umarji*

transfer negotiations by the developing countries' (Khor, 2011). Much more progress is also required on other elements of the agenda mentioned earlier, particularly early-stage technology development and market adoption supported by appropriate financing mechanisms and institutions.

Conclusions

India is faced with the dual challenge of maintaining economic growth for socio-economic development while addressing the climate change issue. The transition to a low-carbon, climate-resilient future will require transformative change in many sectors, including energy, transport and urban habitat. This will require an enabling environment, for which focused attention needs to be given on three main points: building a knowledge and technology base; devising innovative mechanisms to finance the transition; and strengthening the institutional and policy framework.

The NAPCC and the eight missions that form the core of the NAPCC give concrete expression to the national response for climate change. Technology has a key role to play for the succcess of these missions. As discussed earlier, the importance of learning and technological change cannot be overlooked if the ambitious targets set in these missions are to be realized. The timing and the prioritization of the investments in R&D will bear a great effect on the realization of the goals. Streamlining and accelerating the technological change cycle, most importantly the early stages of research, development and market entry will be required.

India has been a front-runner in the Information and Communication Technology sector. The challenge is to replicate the successes of this sector in sectors such as energy and transport to achieve sustainable development goals. The private sector contribution towards R&D needs to be increased. In order to enable the collaboration between industry and academia, effective mechanisms supported by a policy and regulatory regime that addresses questions of IPR, commercialization and new venture creation are needed. Technology foresight will play an important role in this process.

The national response needs to be effectively supported and enabled by the multilateral process. This may require appropriate institutional structures and financing. Given the magnitude and urgency of responding to climate change, rapid progress is required at the multilateral level to realize the potential of technology.

References

Connor, J. (2011) 'Reignition: the positive side of Cancun', http://ecosmagazine.com/paper/EC10077.htm, accessed 21 April 2011.

Fisher, B.S., Nakicenovic, N., Alfsen, K., Corfee Morlot, J., Chesnaye, F. de la, Hourcade, J.-Ch., Jiang, K., Kainuma, M., Rovere, E. La, Matysek, A., Rana, A., Riahi, K., Richels, R., Rose, S., van Vuuren, D., Warren, R. (2007) 'Issues related to mitigation in the long term context', in *Climate Change 2007: Mitigation*, Contribution of Working Group III to the Fourth Assessment Report of the Inter-governmental Panel on Climate Change [B. Metz, O.R. Davidson, P.R. Bosch, R. Dave, L.A. Meyer (eds)], Cambridge University Press, Cambridge, United Kingdom and New York, NY, USA.

Foxon, T. and Pearson, P. (2008) 'Overcoming barriers to innovation and diffusion of cleaner technologies: some features of a sustainable innovation policy regime', *The Journal of Cleaner Production*, 16S1, pp. S148–S161

The technology agenda 365

Government of India, (2006) 'Report of the Working Group on R&D for the Energy Sector for the formulation of the Eleventh Five Year Plan (2007–2012). Submitted to the Planning Commission by the Office of the Principal Scientific Adviser to the Government of India.

Government of India (2008) 'National Action Plan on Climate Change'.

Grübler, A. (1998) 'Technology and Global Change', Cambridge University Press, UK.

Halsnæs, K., Shukla, P., Ahuja, D., Akumu, G., Beale, R., Edmonds, J., Gollier, C., Grübler, A., Ha Duong, M., Markandya, A., McFarland, M., Nikitina, E., Sugiyama, T., Villavicencio, A., Zou, J. (2007) 'Framing issues', in *Climate Change 2007: Mitigation*, Contribution of Working Group III to the Fourth Assessment Report of the Intergovernmental Panel on Climate Change [B. Metz, O.R. Davidson, P.R. Bosch, R. Dave, L.A. Meyer (eds)], Cambridge University Press, Cambridge, United Kingdom and New York, NY, USA.

Hoffert, M.I., Caldeira, K., Benford, G., Criswell, D.R., Green, C., Herzog, H., Jain, A.K., Kheshgi, H.S., Lackner, K.S., Lewis, J.S., Lightfoot, H.D., Manheimer, W., Mankins, J.C., Mauel, M.E., Perkins, L.J., Schlesinger, M.E., Volk, T. and Wigley, T.M.L. (2002) 'Advanced technology paths to global climate stability: Energy for a greenhouse planet', *Science*, 298, pp. 981–987.

International Energy Association (2000) 'Experience Curves for Energy Technology Policy', International Energy Association and Organization for Economic Co-operation and Development.

International Energy Association (2008) 'Energy Technology Perspectives 2008 – Scenarios and Strategies to 2050', International Energy Association.

International Energy Association (2010) 'Energy Technology Perspectives 2010', International Energy Association.

IPCC (2000) *Special Report 'Methodological and technological issues in technology transfer'*, [S. O. Andersen, W. Chandler, R. Christ, O. Davidson, S. Devotta, M. Grubb], http://www.ipcc.ch/pdf/special-reports

IPCC (2007) *Climate Change 2007: Mitigation*, Contribution of Working Group III to the *Fourth Assessment Report of the Intergovernmental Panel on Climate Change*, [B. Metz, O.R. Davidson, P.R. Bosch, R. Dave, L.A. Meyer (eds)], Cambridge University Press, Cambridge, United Kingdom and New York, NY, USA.

Jamasb, T., and Köhler, J. (2007) 'Learning curves for energy technology and policy analysis: a critical assessment', *Delivering a Low Carbon Electricity System: Technologies, Economy and Policy*', Cambridge University Press.

Khor, M. (2011) 'Complex implications of the Cancun Climate Conference', Climate Policy Brief no. 5, South Centre, Geneva.

Levin, K. and Bradley, R. (2010) 'Comparability of Annex I Emission Reduction Pledges', WRI Working Paper, World Resources Institute, Washington, DC.

Ministry of Science and Technology (2003) 'Science and Technology Policy, 2003', Department of Science and Technology, Government of India.

Ministry of Science and Technology (2009) 'Research and Development Statistics', Ministry of Science and Technology, Department of Science and Technology, Government of India.

Nemet, G.F. (2006) 'Beyond the learning curve: factors influencing cost reductions in photovoltaics', *Energy Policy*, Vol. 34, pp. 3218–3232.

Nezu, R., Kiang, C., Ganguli, P., Nithad, K., Nishio, K., Tansinsin, L., Yi, H., Yujian, J. (2007) 'Technology transfer, intellectual property and effective university–industry partnerships: The experience of China, India, Japan, Philippines, the Republic of Korea', World Intellectual Property Organization (WIPO), Singapore and Thailand.

Pacala, S. and Socolow, R. (2004) 'Stabilization wedges: Solving the climate problem for the next 50 years with current technologies', *Science*, 305, pp. 968–972.

Raghavan, S.V., Bharadwaj, A., Thatte, A., Harish, S., Iychettira, K., Perumal, R., Nayak, G. (2010) 'Harnessing Solar Energy: Options for India', Centre for Science, Technology and Policy (CSTEP), Bangalore.

366 *Patwardhan and Umarji*

Ramarao, P. (1998) 'The Shaping of Indian Science: 1982–2003', Presidential Address, *Proceedings of the 85th Indian Science Congress Association*, Vol. 8, Part III.

UNFCCC (1992) *United Nations Framework Convention on Climate Change*, Bonn.

UNFCCC (2007) Annual Report of the Expert Group on Technology Transfer for 2007.

Part VI
Looking to the future

27 Mainstreaming climate change

Shyam Saran

The international momentum which was built up for global action on climate change in the run up to the Copenhagen Climate Summit of December 2009, has now largely dissipated. The Conference of Parties to the UN Framework Convention on Climate Change at Cancun, Mexico, in December 2010, reached a consensus on a set of Cancun Agreements, but only after a significant dilution of the original mandate adopted at Bali in 2007. This is regrettable because the challenge posed by climate change has only become more urgent and compelling. The window of opportunity still open to avoid irreversible and possibly catastrophic consequences to our planet's fragile ecology has probably narrowed even further.

Energy and its use lie at the heart of the climate dilemma. Since the industrial revolution began in the eighteenth century, modern production and consumption patterns have advanced through the adoption of progressively more energy-intensive processes. While great progress has been achieved, modern industrial production and the consumption patterns based on it have continued to rely upon the burning of carbon, in the form of coal, oil and now gas. And while this remains the prevailing and dominant pattern of economic activity, the phenomenon of global warming, linked to greenhouse gas emissions from such energy use cannot be tackled with any realistic prospect of success. The logical corollary to this is the need for a worldwide strategic shift from the current reliance on fossil fuels to a pattern of development based on renewable sources of energy, such as solar, and clean sources of energy, such as nuclear power.

This strategic shift cannot be accomplished through the perpetuation of the current pattern of production and consumption in one part of the world, while advocating a costly switch to renewable energy in another part of the world. It cannot be accomplished if energy-intensive and often wasteful consumption, that is the hallmark of affluent lifestyles in developed economies, is considered sacrosanct while frugality and modest expectations are preached to the aspiring populations of emerging economies. Standard setting is invariably led by the more successful and wealthy economies. It is inevitable that late-comers will aspire to the same standards, particularly in today's interconnected and globalized world. Therefore, a different approach is required, and the essence of that approach is the principle of equity. It will be impossible to construct an effective global response to climate change on the basis of a Nuclear Non-Proliferation Treaty (NPT)-type approach i.e. the developed, industrialized countries get to keep their living standards unchanged because they got there first, while others stay where they are or at a more modest level of affluence, because they are late-comers. This cannot be justified in the name of tackling climate change as a global

370 *Saran*

cross-cutting issue. In this day and age, in an increasingly shrinking world, this two-track approach will simply not sell. Therefore, we will need to advance together towards a shared vision of sustainability with benchmarks for success that are common to all. We may reach this goal at variable speeds and through different pathways; some may be more successful than others. The important point here is that our standards for success in pursuing ecologically sustainable development should be convergent. We will not be able to proceed if there is a perception that there are double standards being applied while promoting sustainability.

There is another aspect to meeting the challenge of climate change. If climate change is an urgent and compelling challenge, if it is a threat to the very survival of humankind and to our planetary home, then our collective response must match this ringing rhetoric. An extraordinary challenge deserves an extraordinary response. Such a response must by its very nature be collaborative. It cannot be delivered by relying mainly on market forces. For example, already there are climate friendly technologies whose widespread adoption would make a significant contribution to mitigating GHG emissions. Does it not make sense to disseminate, as rapidly as possible and as widely as feasible, such technologies as global public goods? Is it not worthwhile to pool the scientific talents and technological capabilities from across the world to generate the innovative technologies that we would require to enable us to move away from carbon-based growth? A truly global and collaborative response cannot be delivered through competitive style inter-governmental negotiations, which by their very nature will deliver a least common denominator result. Rather than aiming to preserve one's turf or press one's advantage, countries would come together in the realization that they need to pool all the talent and ingenuity available across the world to deal with a challenge which recognizes neither national nor regional boundaries. Such a global, collaborative effort can be mobilized quickly and effectively, if it incorporates the equity principle. Equitable burden-sharing will ensure that each participating country pools all of its energies to contribute to a common cause.

I stated earlier that energy and its use lies at the heart of the climate dilemma. There is no future for an energy-intensive carbon-based production and consumption pattern, but energy intensity is only one aspect of the larger phenomenon of resource-intensive growth. The truth is that we are extracting from Mother Nature well beyond her inherent regenerative capacity. We are living on a resource overdraft. When there was only a small cluster of industrialized economies with access to resources around the world, the assumption of unlimited resources was a viable one. Constant technological innovation could further stretch resource availability through more efficient processes. Competition for resources was confined largely to this small cluster of countries with the rest of the world serving as its resource hinterland. The production pattern which resulted from this was mostly a once-through process, transforming raw materials into finished goods, which require constant replacement after use. The quantitative increase in the total output of a country in each cycle of the production process thus represented growth and rising wealth. This pattern of production and the consumption patterns, or lifestyle based on it, are not sustainable in a world which has several more countries that are too engaged in resource-intensive growth. Since at least two of these countries, India and China, are populous, continental-sized economies, the world is already confronting a growing resource crunch. What is the answer to this challenge? It cannot be the halting of growth in developing countries, nor a competitive rush for cornering resources in different parts of the world. The answer lies in extending the scope of the global collaborative response referred to earlier to promote sustainable development in all its aspects. Once-through production processes must give way to those which generate zero or minimal waste and integrate the recycling of goods into the production chain. We must generate technologies which are water-neutral or even water-positive and thus contribute to global water security. There should be a shift to sustainable agriculture where water-intensive fertilizer and pesticide intensive methods give way to those which are economical in the use of water and rely on maintaining and augmenting the natural fertility of the soil to ensure high yields.

A joint study between the Resource Optimization Institute, Bangalore and Yale University mapped the industrial ecosystem in Nanjangud Industrial Area, Karnataka (NIA) (Bain et al., 2010). NIA is a unique industrial area, with a high density of diversified industries. The study found that of all wastes among all NIA facilities (which includes paper, textile and sugar mills, plywood manufacturers and distilleries among others), only 0.5 per cent was actually discarded! The rest of the waste was either reused or recycled in the plants themselves, or by other industrial units within a 20 km radius. Carbon dioxide produced from a distillery is re-used in a bottling facility. Alkaline effluents from a textile mill and spent acid from a chemical manufacturer are mixed to neutralize each other, and the product is used to irrigate a small nearby sugar cane plantation. With a little foresight and spatial planning, many material and waste flows in industrial parks can be synergized to minimize waste.

And a shift in production patterns is only half the story. Modern lifestyle values disposability over durability; it prefers 'use and discard' to 'reuse and recycle'. Advertising reinforces these attitudes. Such a value system which is constantly in search of novelty generates a wasteful lifestyle which an unsustainable production pattern feeds into. This must change in societies in both rich and poor countries. But the rich must take the lead and set the standard so that aspirations among the developing countries also get influenced in a positive direction.

Taken collectively, even individual consumer decisions can make a difference. In 2005, the Maharashtra State Energy Distribution Corporation implemented a pilot program in Nashik to test the effects of demand-side management (subsidizing the cost) while distributing compact fluorescent lamps (CFLs). These were meant to replace less efficient light sources. Prayas Energy Group's analysis of this program shows that there were significant benefits for both consumers and utilities (Singh et al., 2007). Urban consumers saved Rs.11/month and rural consumers saved Rs.15/month through this program. The payback period for buying CFLs was less than a year. And perhaps most importantly, there was an estimated 12–16 MWs of saving and an estimated peak demand reduction of 7–9 MW. Imagine the potential effects if such projects could be scaled up to a national level.

In this context, I believe India has a unique role to play. On the one hand, it must continue to champion the principle of equity in international negotiations. We must take the lead in rejecting a two-track world in which permanent inferiority *remains* the lot of a vast swathe of humanity. On the other hand, irrespective of what transpires in the international negotiations on a global climate change regime, there is every reason for India to chart out its own path for sustainable growth. We are still at a relatively early stage of our own development and much of our infrastructure and manufacturing capability remains to be built. We are not irretrievably locked into a highly energy-intensive and resource-intensive pattern of growth. It is possible for us to traverse a different more sustainable road. This will need to be accompanied by a

372 *Saran*

mindset change which looks upon development and wealth from a broader perspective than GDP alone. We are fortunate in being heirs to a civilizational legacy that placed a high value on sustainability, never extracting from Nature what could not be renewed and regenerated. As a people we need to recapture the spirit of oneness with all living and non-living beings and the sense of interconnectedness of our universe that pervades Indian spirituality. This India will lead the world in the redefinition of the concept of development, rather than hasten along a well-trodden path which now leads to a dead end.

References

Bain, A., Shenoy, M., Weslynne, A. and Chertow, M. (2010) 'Industrial Symbiosis and Waste Recovery in an Indian Industrial Area', *Resources, Conservation and Recycling*, Vol. 54 (12), pp. 1278–1287.

Singh, D., Sant, G. and Kadam, R. (2007) 'Review of Nashik Pilot CFL Program of Maharashtra State Electricity Distribution Co. Ltd', Prayas (Energy Group), http://www.prayaspune.org/peg/publications/item/download/95.html, as on 21 April 2011.

28 The geopolitics of climate change

Nitin Desai

The essential problem with the current threat of climate change is that it is man-made and that the pace of change will challenge the adaptive capacities of all societies. [1] Humans can mitigate the threat by containing their contribution to the accumulation of greenhouse gases. But this requires a global framework as emissions in one part of the globe affect every other part. The geopolitics of climate change is about how these efforts to mitigate the threat and adapt to it impinge on the relationships of power between political jurisdictions, which, in today's world, are basically the states that constitute the international system.

The links between climate and international relations are an important part of the classical discipline of geopolitics. But the tendency there was to treat the climate as a constant that determined each country's resource basis, particularly its capacity for feeding its population, and in, the more racist versions, the mentality of the inhabitants. This is hardly the issue today. The geopolitics of climate change is not about the static impact of climate on national vigour, as determined by armchair theorists, but about the dynamic impact of climate change on the balance of power relations and each country's perception of the threat posed and the most appropriate response.

Governments will look at the threat of climate change in terms of its impact on their primary charge, the provision of 'national security' for their territory and their citizens. The implications of climate change for security can be looked at from a very broad or very narrow definition of the term 'national security'. If security is defined in terms of a wide concept of human security then the total impact of climate change will fall within the remit of this geopolitical analysis. It is doubtful if such a wide conception will truly help to clarify options. Hence in this chapter the focus is on implications more-or-less directly connected with geographical factors. Of course even this geographical approach has to look beyond the impact on military activities conventionally defined to areas such as energy security, food security, water security and similar areas where there is a clear international dimension.

A word of caution is necessary at this point. Climate change is not a security threat in any conventional sense. It is not some sudden trigger event that can precipitate violent conflict. It will take place gradually over a long period of time with the impacts building up slowly. For instance the intrusion of a rising sea level in the Ganges delta will not take place as some sudden tsunami-like inundation but as a gradual loss of land to the sea inch by inch. In that sense the impacts of climate change are unlikely to provide the triggers for specific security threats. They will operate more as factors that condition the probability of trigger events and act as a threat multiplier that amplifies the impact of other threats to security. Moreover there is a great deal of

374 *Desai*

uncertainty about the scale of impact and timing so that one cannot say with confidence that this particular change will take place at this time.

The impact of climate change on power relations in the international system will come from:

- the way in which the international system negotiates its response (i.e. climate diplomacy),
- the mitigation actions that the members of the international system will take unilaterally or as part of an agreed multilateral programme, and
- the impact of the changes in climate that climate actions cannot avert.

The time profile of these three sets of impacts is very different. Climate diplomacy is already under way and its impact on power relations can be observed here and now. Mitigation actions have begun but the greater part of what can be expected as countries institute programmes and policies for mitigation and adaptation is still to come. The impact of these actions on power relations will play out over the next few decades.

Leaving aside the entirely unlikely possibility of an agreement that averts all risks, some degree of climate change is unavoidable. But this change is not going to happen tomorrow, though some early harbingers of what is in store are already evident. These projected changes will take place well into this century and the impact on power relations, say from potential changes in water availability, will be some decades in the future.

This staggered time profile of impacts is why this chapter deals first with the geopolitics of climate diplomacy, then the geopolitical consequences of the mitigation actions it engenders and then with the longer-term consequences of the changes in climate that seem likely at present.

The geopolitics of climate diplomacy

Climate diplomacy has to rest on climate science as governments are being asked to take action before the full impact of climate change is evident.[2] However given the uncertainty about the causes, the magnitudes and the impacts of climate change a consensus-building process that brings together scientists was necessary. This led to the establishment of the Intergovernmental Panel on Climate Change in 1988. It was a product of three factors – the emergence of ecosystem research as an influential academic discipline, the global scientific cooperation promoted by organisations like UNESCO, WMO and UNEP, and the influence of world-wide NGO networks on national and international environmental policy.

The case for immediate policy action was not as readily accepted, with resistance coming from major emitters like the USA and the energy-supplying countries, particularly the OPEC, though the very influential Brundtland report (1987) had sought action on energy in a broader context that included local pollution management and resource depletion concerns.

The pressures for action came to a head at the Second World Climate Conference held in Geneva in November 1990, when the Rio Earth Summit was in the early stages of preparation. They led to the constitution of the UN negotiating process on climate change which culminated in the UN Framework Convention on Climate Change

Geopolitics of climate change 375

(UNFCCC) opening for signature at the UN Conference on Environment and Development (the Rio Summit) in 1992.[3] From a geopolitical perspective what matters is the interplay of power reflected in the outcome of the negotiating process.

The Rio Earth Summit and the Climate Convention were both launched in a narrow window of opportunity when the Cold War was at an end, multilateralism was in the ascendant with the successful UN-sanctioned action in 1991 to undo Iraq's invasion of Kuwait. South Africa was being liberated from apartheid and an Oslo process was under way leading to an agreement in 1993 between the PLO and Israel. But unfortunately this window of opportunity for multilateralism came at a time when the government of the largest emitter, USA, was dominated by oil and coal interests.[4] This power of organized industry lobbies is also a part of the geopolitics of climate diplomacy. The Framework Convention that emerged was a compromise between European demands for immediate and strong action and US reluctance (with many others like Japan, Canada and Australia sheltering under the US umbrella).

Though India played a major role in the negotiations,[5] most developing countries (including China) were peripheral to the main line of discussion in the negotiations which remained a battle between Europe and the USA. Within the G-77 interests were widely divided with small islands arguing for immediate and strong action,[6] the oil producers becoming spokesmen for the climate sceptics in order to protect their economic prospects and the large emerging economies not wanting any constraint on their development ambitions from any sort of carbon emission obligation. Despite this the G-77 remained united and insisted that the primary, almost the sole responsibility for action rested with the developed countries and that development, which would inevitably increase GHG emissions, remained the primary objective of policy for them. But already, at that stage the desire of the developed countries to bring the large developing countries within the ambit of the commitments was evident. The principle of 'common but differentiated responsibility', which was a delicate compromise, that allowed all to see what they wanted in it, was the product and has now become absolutely central to the negotiating stance of China, India and the other developing countries (see Rajamani, this volume).

The Convention that was opened for signature at Rio was merely a framework that did not impose any binding obligations on emission reductions on the parties. When it was clear that the indicative goal of holding emissions at 1990 levels by 2000 was not going to be reached the clamour for legally binding targets grew. The main demand for strong action came quite understandably from the small island countries with some support from Western Europe where a combination of North Sea Gas and nuclear power facilitated low carbon growth.

A difficult negotiation process led finally to the Kyoto Protocol in which the industrial countries accepted binding obligations on emission reductions by 2008–2012 and that also brought the developing countries indirectly into the mitigation effort through the Clean Development Mechanism (CDM). This mechanism was the product of a strange marriage between a Brazilian proposal for a fund to help developing countries experiment with carbon saving programmes and the US demand for a flexibility mechanism that would reduce costs of compliance by allowing the purchase of carbon credits from lower cost mitigation activities in developing countries.

The Kyoto Protocol was not a mitigation plan worked out on the basis of goals for allowable temperature increase and related emission targets. The distribution of mitigation effort between the industrial countries was not based on worked-out criteria.

376 *Desai*

The more-or-less arbitrary targets were more a product of the European eagerness for any sort of agreement, the Japanese desire to ensure success for a conference held on home turf and hard ball bargaining by the USA and Russia. To cap it all with the election of a new administration, the USA backtracked on its commitment. [7]

The Kyoto Protocol came into force on 16 February 2005, more than seven years after it was adopted. The actual performance by most of those who did ratify it is significantly short of what they had promised (UNDP, 2008). In fact only the collapse of the old economy in Russia and Eastern Europe and the dramatic fall in their energy consumption creates the illusion of achievement and that too because they were given very generous Kyoto targets.

Towards the end of the Kyoto period a fresh round of negotiations was needed for the second commitment period beyond 2012. But by this time the geopolitics of climate diplomacy had changed substantially. The focus now is on China where the combination of rapid growth and coal dependence has led to a rapid increase in emissions. The pressure on the other emerging economies is really a consequence of this concern about Chinese emissions growth. The basic argument is that any reasonable goal for allowable temperature increase is unattainable unless the large emerging economies join in the mitigation effort. As a consequence, the G-77 is more central to the process but its unity is under serious pressure.

Another reason for this change of stance by the industrial countries is their concern that both China and India (and some of the other emerging economies) are emerging as major competitors in the global marketplace. In the nineties, Europe, with its access to low carbon gas supplies, saw no threat to its economy from any carbon restriction commitment while the USA did. The OECD countries have now made common cause in demanding action by the large developing countries on the argument that if they are free from carbon abatement obligations the consequences for industrial competitiveness would be substantial. There is even talk of compensatory trade measures. The countries have responded to this pressure with measures for carbon abatement in different forms (see, WRI, 2010).

All of these changes in the matrix within which negotiations take place were responsible for what happened at the Copenhagen meeting of the Conference of Parties to the UNFCCC in December 2009. This meeting saw the emergence of what could be called a 40:40:20 power structure in climate diplomacy. These proportions reflect the share in emissions of the countries concerned. They are a rough rather than an exact measure of influence.

The first 40 per cent includes the two largest emitters – the USA and China. Emissions in the USA, are growing faster than in most other Annex I countries. China is now the world's largest emitter and their emissions are also growing at a rate higher than the average for non-Annex I countries. These two countries have a de facto veto power because their staying out of any mitigation agreement makes it a trifle pointless as a big chunk of emissions remains beyond global purview.

The second 40 per cent consists of the EU, a 10 per cent power, Russia, Japan and India, each of them a 5 per cent power, and a string of 2 per cent powers like Brazil, South Africa, Mexico, Indonesia, South Korea, Saudi Arabia, etc. The individual members of this second group, with the exception of the EU, do not matter in the way that USA and China do as their absence from an agreement does not greatly undermine the global effort. The EU is now so publicly committed to a strong global agreement that they have lost their potential power of opting out. A more positive spin would be

Geopolitics of climate change   377

that they are setting the bar which others have to try and reach. India is a middle level power in this structured global oligarchy and must act without any illusions about its relative status. The last 20 per cent covers the smaller states whose influence comes from their membership of some larger group like the Association of Small Island States or the African Group.

The end-game at Copenhagen reflected this balance of influence where an agreement between the USA and China was a necessity but not sufficient to secure a consensus outcome. Obama's wooing was directed at China and the understanding was that an agreement between them would seal the deal and the others would either have to accept that or do without a deal. This is not just a consequence of the changing power equations in climate diplomacy. It is also a product of domestic political compulsions in the USA. India, Brazil and South Africa were there at the end game because China engineered events so that it was not alone in striking a deal with the USA.

The smaller players can acquire influence only occasionally when a full global consensus is needed. At Copenhagen the big and medium players decided that what mattered was what they committed to each other and the consent of the smaller players was not crucial. But they could not ride rough-shod over everybody. In the end game the worm turned and the smaller states used the consensus procedures of the UN to deny this oligarchic agreement the imprimatur of legitimacy. Yet they could not prevent it from becoming the de facto basis for cooperative global action as 142 countries communicated their acceptance of the Copenhagen Accord.

The geopolitics of mitigation actions

The Copenhagen Accord includes an agreement that the goal should be to contain the likely temperature increase to 2°C. The commitments on emissions that have been put on the table for the 2020 target date by the Annex I countries and, as unilateral national targets by some non-Annex I countries like India and China, fall well short of the time profile of emissions reduction required. However inadequate these may be, it is reasonably clear that significant steps will be taken to reduce the carbon content of energy use and the intensity of energy use per unit of GDP. One can also expect some accelerated action on forestry in this medium term time frame. The geopolitical implications of these mitigation actions will be modulated through their impact on the global energy economy, the role of major forested countries in providing carbon sinks and the edge that it could give to leaders in low carbon technologies.

Energy security has always been a major geopolitical concern of all major economies, including the emerging economies of China, India and Brazil. This has generally taken the form of securing supply sources, mainly for oil, with exploration and production-sharing contracts, military presence where possible and other diplomatic moves. What climate diplomacy has done is to modify the classical approach of looking at energy security largely in terms of oil demand and supply by factoring in the growing global concern about climate change.

The shift to non-carbon energy is unlikely to amount to much in the 2020 or even 2030 frame and the global dependence on the very unevenly distributed oil reserves will not be greatly affected. Most projections of world petroleum demand and supply show a growing dependence on Gulf oil as about two-thirds of the world's oil reserves lie in West Asia. The production of oil in the Gulf region will have to double by 2030 and much of this increase will be on account of rising demand from China and India (Energy Information Administration, 2006).

The mitigation actions arising from any global climate agreement are unlikely to alter the geopolitics of global energy markets. The basic features of the power play in the oil economy will remain as they are, viz.:

- the capacity of Saudi Arabia and other Gulf States to adjust production up and down for strategic rather than commercial reasons,
- the clout that the US enjoys because of the dependence of the Gulf States on its security umbrella,
- the potential of Iran and Iraq for tactical disruption of Saudi strategies,
- the continued stranglehold of the Western oil majors on the logistics of the global oil economy,
- the growing clout of Russia as the key supplier to Europe and to China from Siberian reserves,
- an aggressive pursuit of concessions in fringe production areas by China and, less effectively, by India.

Change may come from the attraction of gas as a transitional fuel for coal dependent India and China. They are the only viable clients for the large gas reserves in the Gulf and cultivating this market may well serve the geopolitical interests of the Gulf States. A new factor is the supply potential of the Central Asian 'stans' and the power play between China, Russia and the USA in this region reflects at least partially the impact of climate geopolitics.

The world coal trade will be more significantly affected by the actions engendered by climate diplomacy. As big importers like China come under pressure to contain their carbon emissions and shift to more carbon-friendly fuels like natural gas, the impact will be felt by major coal exporters like Australia.

In the medium term to 2020 the main source of carbon mitigation will be policies to stimulate energy efficiency and deforestation avoided. The latter is already an important part of the REDD plus negotiations under the UNFCCC. Deforestation avoided is one of the most attractive options for carbon mitigation and is attracting substantial support from potential sources of concessional fund. The scope for big gains from this are concentrated in the countries with large areas under forest cover like Brazil and Indonesia. In the geopolitics of climate change this not only increases the leverage of these countries but also introduces a wedge between them and other large emerging economies like China and India.

Energy efficiency gains depend largely on known technologies, and no particular impact on power balances is likely to arise from the central role that these technologies will play in the climate mitigation effort. In the longer run, and even in a 2030 time frame, carbon mitigation and, by implication, energy security will increasingly depend on access to renewable energy and other carbon saving technologies. This will stimulate collaboration in technology development for high cost items like carbon sequestration and nuclear energy. But it will also increase the leverage of the technology super-powers like the USA in the global game of energy security. New players like China and India can become significant global players in lower cost options like energy efficiency and solar, wind and geothermal energy. China is already a leading player in solar and wind power. But this is unlikely to give it much more than commercial leverage in energy markets.

Basically the scale of mitigation efforts in the medium term will be most likely modest in their aims. They will not alter the geopolitics of the global energy economy very substantially. The larger impacts will come over the longer term as the pace of carbon mitigation builds up to the point where fundamental shifts in energy production and consumption will be required. This is some decades into the future. But at that time what will matter are the competencies that have been built up in these new energy technologies over this transitional period. Hence the main geopolitical impact of climate mitigation actions will be the edge it will give to those countries and corporations that invest now to establish their presence in this technology space of the future.

Geopolitics of climate change impact

The mitigation actions that are likely to be undertaken as part of a multilateral agreement or unilaterally will not be able to stop the momentum of climate change that has already been built up because of past emissions. Nor is there any realistic prospect of containing future increases in greenhouse gases to the point at which the climate is fully stabilized. Even the stated goal of policy now involves a 2°C temperature rise. Hence some measure of climate change and, with it, a change in the geography of international relations is unavoidable. That is why the intersection of climate science and security analysis has become a growth industry (see for instance, Campbell et al., 2007; European Commission, 2008; IDSA, 2009; Halden, 2007; Maas and Tänzler, 2009).

The paradigms that underlie climate change and security analysis differ in several ways and combining the two is not easy. First the unit of analysis for climate scientists is the ecosystem, which, in the case of carbon is the earth system as a whole. International relations and security analysis tends to work with states as the unit of analysis. Second, the time horizon of analysis varies: very long term in the case of climate change and short to medium term in security studies. Third, climate analysis focuses on slowly changing processes while security analysis is specially interested in trigger events that can precipitate conflict.

Security analysis tends to look for factors that can lead to insecurity and conflict. But the links between resource shortages, environmental stress and conflict are often overstated. In fact the causation may even run the other way with violent conflict leading to a worsening of environmental stresses. Thus famines do not cause wars; wars lead to famines. Climate change is a slow process that will affect resource availability and environmental conditions over periods measured in decades. Its geopolitical impact will be felt more through its slow impact on human security rather than through any sudden impact on physical geography.[8]

Two areas of potential tension caused by the predictable climate change impacts are frequently mentioned – the worsening of disputes over shared waters, and the movement of people displaced by worsening agricultural conditions and sea level rise.

The principal areas of concern in the case of shared waters are the Jordan River in West Asia, already the scene of some violence, the Nile Valley and some other rivers in Africa. Central Asia is served by rivers that are snow fed, and glacier melt may alter the timing of flows in a manner that challenges existing agreements. This may also

380 *Desai*

happen in the snow melt-dependent Indus system. But much of this will be more an irritant than a *causus belli*. In fact the frequent references to water disputes as a potential cause of war between states is not borne out by the historical record, and shared resources are as likely to lead to cooperation as to conflict.[9] An outstanding example of this is the Indus Waters Treaty between India and Pakistan that has withstood several decades of confrontation between the two states.

The links between displacement and environmental stress have been recognized by many.[10] The movement of people displaced by the impact of temperature and sea level rise on agriculture and human settlements has led to many guesstimates of the number of 'environmental refugees', a misleading term that appropriates a legal concept applicable to persons who cross national boundaries to seek asylum from persecution. Seasonal migration and longer-term emigration of some family members to seek urban employment are part of the coping strategy of people who live in vulnerable environments.[11] Whether climate change will lead to an increase in such migration is still an open question. In South Asia the most widely touted possibility is the pressure of illegal migration from Bangladesh to India as the Ganges Brahmaputra delta feels the impact of sea-level changes. The other flow that is much talked about is from Africa to Europe as agricultural conditions in the Sahel deteriorate.

Climate change matters more when strategy planning takes account of transnational threats, vulnerabilities and instabilities that can affect national options. Nowadays this includes consideration of the implications of deepening economic interdependence and the competition for natural resources. Climate change can be viewed as a multiplier that enhances the impact of all of these factors. Some of the areas where such threat/vulnerability multiplier effects may be seen are listed below:

- Food security will be affected by the fall in agricultural productivity in most of Africa and Asia because of the impact of climate change on precipitation and river water flows.
- Water security will be affected by the large changes in the volume and timing of river flows because of glacier melt and precipitation changes.
- Energy security will be affected by the impact of climate change in crucial supply areas like the Gulf and Central Asia and by its impact on Israel–Arab conflict.[12]
- Maritime security will be affected by the impact of sea level changes on coastal installations and coastal populations.
- Border security will be affected if changing sea levels and river flows open up new disputes on land and maritime border demarcation and if sea-level rise leads to illegal migration across national boundaries.
- Health security will be affected by the changes in breeding conditions for disease vectors.

From an Indian perspective the geographical changes that are more or less committed and that have a direct security implication are:

- The warming of the Himalayan-Hindu Kush-Tibetan highlands and its impact on water flows in the Indus, Ganges and Brahmaputra river systems.
- The rise in sea levels and its impact in the Ganges-Brahmaputra delta.
- The impact of both these on the conditions for military operations in the Himalayas and in coastal seas.

Geopolitics of climate change 381

Other large-scale geographic changes are possible but not considered probable at present. However, a failure to contain temperature rise would increase the risk of these occurring. Some of these potentially huge geographical changes have been studied (see Lenten et al., 2008). One of these, Arctic sea ice melt has moved from the realm of the possible to the probable already. This is opening up new waterways and international trade routes between North America, Europe and Asia through passages running north of Canada and Russia. It will reduce the distance between the USA and China, allow submarines to come through the Bering Straits and thus alter the strategic equation between USA and China. Russia also will acquire all-weather ports on its Northern shore and that too will have significant strategic impact. In addition, the increased accessibility of the enormous hydrocarbon resources in the Arctic region is changing the geo-strategic dynamics of the region with potential consequences for international stability and European security interests. The resulting new strategic interests are illustrated by the recent planting of the Russian flag under the North Pole and other manoeuvres to stake territorial claims (Crawford et al., 2008).

The other potential tipping points are not predictions but projections of what the new equilibrium of the earth system could look like when it adjusts fully to a higher temperature regime. The extent of temperature increase required for each of these tipping points and the time frame are still speculative. However the consequences of some of the tipping points, for instance the collapse of the monsoon or the Antarctic ice sheet would be hugely catastrophic. These speculative tipping points are reminders that the downside surprises that greatly worsen the impact of climate change are far more likely than any upside surprises that reduce the threat. The tipping points identified by climate scientists are a further reason to take out insurance and act now to avert the worst of the consequences.

Conclusion

Climate diplomacy, climate actions and climate impacts are unlikely to change the basic features of the global power balance. The changes that can be expected in the next couple of decades are as much a product of other forces, such as the shift in the balance of the global economy towards Asia, the growing presence of emerging market players in the global investment and technology flows and the increase in the military capacities of countries like China and India.

The geopolitical impact of climate change in the medium term will be felt more in the form of marginal shifts in international relations. An interesting dimension to this is the argument that climate diplomacy can become a vehicle for strengthening co-operation in other areas.[13] Some of the impacts that may be seen are:

- pressures on the transatlantic relationship because of the differences of approach between Europe and the USA,[14]
- the intrusion of a new element in the delicate balance of superpower relations between NATO and Russia, between US and China and between China and Russia,
- regional powers like India, Brazil, South Africa and Mexico using their centrality to a climate agreement to leverage a role in superpower politics,
- a lowered salience for the 'oil weapon' as the basis for the power plays of the Gulf oil states,
- the growing importance of technological competence as the key to global power.

382 Desai

In the longer run, looking beyond the next two decades, climate change can lead to new sources of tension and potential conflict in the Arctic region and perhaps in West Asia because of its impact on water resources. Other sources of tension induced by climatic changes may be too slow and diffused to trigger conflict. In these areas climate change is not a cause but a condition that could shape the direction taken by other potential sources of conflict. It could be a threat multiplier that pushes some disputes into the realm of active conflict. However there is so much uncertainty about the timing and scale of such long-term impacts that they are hardly likely to alter the strategic stances of today.

The real case for action on the threat of climate change has to rest on its impact on human security rather than on state security. In fact a geopolitical perspective hides the inequities that underlie the climate change problem.[15] Moreover for effective action, states will have to step outside a framework where the protection of national interests is the sole basis for security and for foreign policy.[16]

The assessment of geopolitical implications presented here implicitly assumes that sooner rather than later the governments of the world will secure an agreement that specifies:

- The acceptable limit for the temperature increase.
- The implied time profile of global carbon dioxide and other GHG emissions.
- The distribution of allowable global emissions between countries.
- The treatment of forestry and land use changes.
- The mechanisms that would allow flexibility in fulfilling commitments.
- The mechanisms that would support adaptation actions.
- The financial and technology transfer commitments.

If an effective climate agreement is not secured in the present round of negotiations then all bets are off. Some of the tipping points may become a reality, and climate geopolitics will change drastically as the survival of hundreds of millions is threatened. This chapter stops short of spelling out such a doomsday scenario in the hope that the political masters who rule our fate know and understand the consequences of inaction. What we need in order to manage the geopolitics of climate change is not just a consensus-building process for the underlying science and a negotiating process between states for reciprocal obligations, but also the evolution of a climate ethic that the common but differentiated responsibility we have accepted involves not just responsibility as culpability, but also responsibility as a duty to future generations.

Notes

1 At a climate conference held in cold Ottawa it was agreed that it would be more politic to refer to the threat as climate change rather than as global warming, which, in that frigid environment seemed a good idea. The term that people at a village level seem to respond to best is actually 'climate instability'. They seem to have a better fix on the problem than the scientists.

2 The scientific consensus took time to evolve, the most contentious issue being the extent to which observed changes could be attributed to anthropogenic influences of natural forcing factors. A definitive statement that observed and likely changes were due to human actions and therefore controllable by modifying these actions did not come till the IPCC's third assessment report issued in 2001 and was asserted forcefully only in its fourth assessment report issued in 2007.

3 For the cut and thrust of these negotiations see Dasgupta (this volume).

Geopolitics of climate change   383

4 The US, which hosted the first negotiating meeting for the Climate Convention, was, at this time, under a Bush administration, heavily influenced by sceptics like John Sununu, the then White House Chief of Staff, and by powerful oil industry interests.

5 It is a moot question whether this reflected any serious discussion of alternatives in Delhi, which, at that time was preoccupied with the resolution of the big economic crisis at home. Fortunately for Delhi, the USA, whose support was crucial for the management of the domestic economic crisis, was sceptical about the need for any action beyond data gathering and research when it came to climate change.

6 They emerged as an organized lobby after a Commonwealth-supported meeting: Small States Conference on Sea Level Rise, 14–18 November 1989, Male, the Maldives.

7 'In terms of the classical narrative of the tragedy of the commons what happened in the [Kyoto] climate negotiations was that there was a general agreement that there are too many cows in the field. Then, instead of working out how many there should be, the agreement was that those of us who have the largest herds will withdraw some cows. Of course the biggest cattle owner has simply refused to go along saying that he will teach his cows to behave better' Desai (2005, 10).

8 '[C]limate change in itself will not be a cause of conflict. Instead, climate change will likely produce knock-on effects, which may catalyse processes leading to tensions and eroding institutions' (Maas and Tänzler, 2009, 3).

9 '[T]he record of acute conflict over international water resources is historically overwhelmed by the record of cooperation' (Wolf, 2006). 'There is a very limited number of situations in which it would make strategic sense for a country today to wage war in order to increase its water supply' (Podesta and Ogden, 2007, 121).

10 '[T]he Darfur conflict began as an ecological crisis, arising at least in part from climate change' (Ban Ki Moon, 2007).

11 '[A]lthough environmental degradation and catastrophe may be important factors in the decision to migrate, and issues of concern in their own right, their conceptualization as a primary cause of forced displacement is unhelpful and unsound intellectually, and unnecessary in practical terms' (Black, 2001, 1). See also Brown (2007).

12 'Roughly two-thirds of the Arab world depends on sources outside their borders for water. The Jordan and Yarmuk rivers are expected to see considerable reduction in their flows affecting Israel, the Palestinian territories and Jordan. Existing tensions over access to water are almost certain to intensify in this region leading to further political instability with detrimental implications for Europe's energy security and other interests. Water supply in Israel might fall by 60 per cent over this century. Consequently, a significant drop in crop yields is projected for an area that is already largely arid or semi-arid. Significant decreases are expected to hit Turkey, Iraq, Syria and Saudi Arabia . . . Central Asia is another region severely affected by climate change. An increasing shortage of water, which is both a key resource for agriculture and a strategic resource for electricity generation, is already noticeable. The glaciers in Tajikistan lost a third of their area in the second half of the 20th century alone, while Kyrgyzstan has lost over a 1,000 glaciers in the last four decades' (European Commission, 2008, 7).

13 'A climate policy that induces China to join the rules-based global regime for dealing with global warming – independent of the fine details of that policy – would contribute to the broader project of cementing China's commitment to the world order, which in turn could create payoffs in building a positive security relationship' (Busby, 2007).

14 '[T]he EU will likely cement its position as the most responsible and united regional organization on the issue of climate change' (Podesta and Ogden, 2007, 131).

15 'It is the most wealthy people in the most wealthy countries that have the most power to change the political and economic systems that sustain the problem of climate change. This more subaltern and class-based view of climate geopolitics is hidden by the popular geopolitical imaginary of climate change as a "global" and environmental problem to be addressed by the community of states' (Barnett, 2007, 1372).

16 'It is the job of governments to articulate the national interest. But if they do that in a narrowly conceived short-term form, finding common ground for an agreement is particularly difficult. Interest based arguments must be accompanied by a willingness to accept a science based discourse as the basis for negotiation. In addition there must some framework of values to limit the play of national interest. In essence, environmental management is about justice between polluters and victims of pollution, between early users

384 *Desai*

of common property resources and new comers, between current and future generations. Justice cannot be secured with economics alone. There has to be a global ethic that cooperation is better than confrontation, that unrequited harm to another country is not justified, that sovereignty involves not just rights but responsibilities' (Desai, 2005, 12).

References

Barnett, J. (2007) 'The Geopolitics of Climate Change', *Geography Compass* 1(6), pp. 1361–1375.

Black, R. (2001) 'Environmental Refugees: Myth or Reality', Working Paper No. 34, United Nations High Commission for Refugees, Geneva.

Brown, O. (2007) 'Climate Change and Forced Migration: Observations, Projections and Implications', *Human Development Report Office Occasional Paper*, United Nations Development Programme, New York.

Brundtland Commission (1987) 'Our Common Future', Report of the World Commission on Environment and Development, Oxford University Press.

Busby, J. (2007) 'Climate Change and National Security: An Agenda for Action', *CSR* No. 32, Council on Foreign Relations.

Campbell, K., Gulledge, J., McNeill, J.R., Podesta, J., Ogden, P., Fuerth, L., Woolsey, R.J., Lennon, A., Smith, J., Weitz, R. and Mix, D. (2007) 'The Age of Consequences: The Foreign Policy and National Security Implications of Global Climate Change', Center for Strategic and International Studies (CSIS) and the Center for a New American Security (CNAS), November 2007.

Crawford, A., Hanson, A. and Runnalls, D. (2008) 'Arctic Sovereignty and Security in a Climate-changing World', International Institute for Sustainable Development, Canada.

Desai, N. (2005) 'Global Environmental Security' in *Emerging Global Order and Developing Countries*, University Press Limited (UPL), Dhaka.

Energy Information Administration (2006) 'International Energy Outlook', US Dept. of Energy, Washington.

European Commission (2008) 'Climate Change and International Security', Paper from the High Representative and the European Commission to the European Council, 14 March 2008, S 113/08, Brussels.

Halden, P. (2007) 'The Geopolitics of Climate Change: Challenges to the International System', FOI, Swedish Defence Research Agency, Stockholm, Sweden.

Institute for Defence Studies and Strategic Analysis (2009) *Security Implications of Climate Change*, Report of the IDSA Working Group, Academic Foundation, New Delhi.

Lenton, T.M., Held, H., Kriegler, E., Hall, J., Lucht, W., Ramhstorf, S. and Schellenhuber, H. (2008) 'Tipping elements in the Earth's climate system', Proceedings of the National Academy of Sciences of the United States (PNAS), pp. 1786–1793, http://www.pnas.org/content/105/6/1786.full.pdf+html.

Maas, A. and Tänzler, D. (2009) 'Regional Security Implications of Climate Change: A Synopsis', A Study Conducted for DG External Relations of the European Commission, Adelphi Consult GmbH, Berlin.

Moon, B.K. (2007) 'A Climate Culprit in Darfur', *Washington Post*, June 16.

Podesta, J. and Ogden, P. (2007) 'The Security Implications of Climate Change', *The Washington Quarterly*, Winter 2007–8.

UNDP (2008) 'Human Development Report 2007/8: Fighting Climate Change: Human Solidarity in a Divided World', UNDP.

Wolf, A. (2006) 'A Long Term View on Water and Security: International Waters, National Issues, and Regional Tensions', A Report to the German Advisory Council on Global Change (WBGU), available at http://www.wbgu.de/wbgu_jg2007_ex08.pdf.

WRI (2010) 'Summary of GHG Reduction Pledges Put Forward by Developing Countries', World Resources Institute available at http://pdf.wri.org/summary_of_non_annex1_pledges_2010-06.pdf.

Index

Note: Page numbers ending in 'f' refer to figures, ending in 'n' refer to notes and ending in 't' refer to tables.

Abbot, K. 21
Acharya, S.S. 320, 322
Adam, D. 271
adult literacy rate in India 159
aerosols 34–5
Agarwal, A. 108, 113, 148, 206n, 209, 210
Aggarwal, P.K. 23n, 37
agriculture 19, 317–27; adaptation to low rainfall 322; carbon mitigation in sustainable production systems 322–3, 324; climate change impacts on water and repercussions for 329, 332; crop insurance 319; drought resistant crops 319, 322; drylands 319, 322; GHG emissions from 317, 318; National Mission for Sustainable Agriculture (NMSA) 317, 318–19, 321, 324, 353, 361t; NMSA 318–19, 321, 353, 361; numbers working in 317, 320; production technologies for food security 319–21; rice fields methane emissions 66, 70, 73, 243–4; share in GDP 320; small farmers 321–2, 323, 324; temperature increases and problems for 35, 37–8, 329; towards sustainable production systems 321–4, 371; in tropical regions 321–2; *see also* apple cultivation in Himachal Pradesh
air travel 299
Aiyar, P. 266, 275, 278
Ali, S.I. 34
Allen, M.R. 137
Alliance of Small Island States (AOSIS) 91, 92, 102, 107, 174, 175, 176, 178
Altieri, M.A. 322
Ananthapadmanabhan, G. 208, 210, 218, 220, 222t
Antarctic ice sheet 41, 42, 381
Antilla, L. 267
apple cultivation in Himachal Pradesh 6, 51–62; approach and methods 52–4; area

under cultivation 51, 60–1; changing land-use patterns by site 51, 55–6, 56t, 60–1, 61; chill unit calculation models 54; climatic elements trends 54, 56–7, 59–60, 60f; cumulative chill unit trends 51–2, 57–61, 58f, 59f, 59t, 60, 61, 61t; farmers' perceptions of climate change and impact 54–6, 55t; findings 54–61; productivity and area trends 51, 54; socioeconomic survey 53–4, 54–6, 56t, 61; study sites 52–3
Archer, D.R. 75, 76
Arctic 30, 381, 382
Arun, T.K. 280
Ashcroft, G.L. 54
Asia Least-Cost Greenhouse Gas Abatement Strategy (ALGAS) Project 69, 73
Asia-Pacific Partnership (APP) 105, 108
Asian Development Bank (ADB) 69, 226, 228n
Atmosphere-Ocean General Circulation Models (AOGCMs) 73
autorickshaws 312
'Avoid-Shift-Improve' paradigm 299–300
Axelrod, D. 244

Bacon, T.A. 51, 54
Baer, P. 9, 149, 150, 151, 152t
Bain, A. 371
Baker, J. 307
Bali Action Plan (BAP): CBDRRC principles in 118, 124–5; comments in parliamentary debate on 234; development policy objectives of developing countries 185–6; formulation of NAMAs 166; India's role in negotiations 109, 181; seeking agreement on GHG emissions 103–4
Banerjee, A. 226
Bangladesh 34, 86f, 380; delegates to

386 Index

Copenhagen Summit 244; EKC turning point 165t; perspective on climate change strategy of India 183–5
Barbier, E.B. 44
BASIC bloc 2, 189, 202; Copenhagen Accord and 210, 244; on Kyoto Protocol 190; and need to embark on lower emissions strategy 184–5
Battisti, D.S. 35, 329
Baviskar, A. 213
Bazilian, M. 22
Benedick, R.E. 8
Bengtsson, L. 43
Berlin Mandate 102, 107, 108, 118, 180
Betsill, M. 4
Bhagat, R.M. 51, 52
Bharadwaj, A. 296
Bhatia, M.L. 320
Bhattacharya, S.C. 38, 226
Bhopal disaster 209, 211, 212
Bidwai, P. 17, 198, 199, 204, 219
Billet, S. 267, 268, 272, 274, 277–8, 279, 280
Biniaz, S. 121
Binkley, C.S. 210
biomass energy 191, 224, 236, 256–7, 258f, 289, 294t, 355f
Birdsall, M. 151
Birnie, P. 120, 123
Blair, T. 248
Blakley, R. 251
Blanchon, P. 41
Bodansky, D. 20, 22n, 94, 119, 120, 121
Bolivia 145n, 347, 348–9
Bollasina, M. 37
Bondre, N. 274
Boykoff, J. 266, 270
Boykoff, M. 266, 267, 268, 269f, 270
Boyle, A. 120, 123
Brandt Commission 8
Brazil: Brazilian Proposal 108, 138, 149, 375; 'carbon forestry' project in 347; CDM projects 256, 258; deforestation 81; developing climate-friendly technologies 183, 249; drivers of corporate CDM investment study 261–3, 262f; as a key developing country in climate change debate 157–8; references to CBDRRC principle 125; size of 157; technology transfers through CDM 258
Brown, M. 319, 321
Brown, O. 383n
Brundtland Commission 8, 374
buildings: and city warming 29, 32; energy 306–7; green 251, 296, 306–7, 310; Indian regulations 310; NMSH projects on energy efficiency in 311; retrofit of 309, 314n

Bulkeley, H. 4
Bullard, C. 220
Buncombe, A. 219
Bunsha, D. 268
burden-sharing in emission reductions 132–6, 134f, 135f, 149–50; burden sharing versus opportunity seizing scenarios 199–200; carbon budget approach to cumulative emissions scenario 137–8, 140, 143, 144, 152t, 153; CBDRRC principle in 130–3; contract and converge approach (C&C) 133, 136, 148; contract and differentiated convergence (CDC) 133, 152t; emissions flow perspective 133, 142–3; entitlements on an equity basis vis-à-vis availability of carbon space 140–4; equity-based allocations of carbon space 138–40, 147–50, 151, 182, 198; Greenhouse Development Rights (GDR) approach 132–3, 149–50, 152t, 153; implications for India 151–3; Indian perspective on 164–5; and issues of historical responsibility 138–9, 148–9, 153, 165, 170, 172, 233–4, 276–7; Manmohan Singh Convergence Principle 133; media coverage of equity issues and 275–7, 278, 279–80, 286t; resource-sharing frame 148–9, 150–1, 152t, 153; susbsistence emissions 150
Bush, G.W. 103, 171, 175, 219
business associations 15, 259–60
Business Council for Sustainable Development 246–7, 259
business sector and climate change: *see* corporate responses to climate change; private sector and climate change
Business Standard 268, 269f, 275, 278
Byrne, J. 51, 54, 214

Campaign for Progressive Climate Action & Policy 176
Campbell, K. 379
Canada 86f, 93, 107, 157, 360f
Cancun Agreements 4, 104, 125, 177, 189–90; bottom-up pledges in developed and developing countries 125, 177; CBDRRC principle 124, 125; India's role in xxi, 111; technology transfers 363–4; US shift in attitude since 192–3
Caney, S. 148
cap-and-trade legislation 193–4
carbon budgets: calculations in TISS-DSF model 142; CBDR in 140; comparisons for India based on different models 143, 143t; cumulative emissions and carbon budget approach 137–8, 140, 143, 144,

152t, 153; estimates for 2000–50 137; German approach 189
carbon capture and storage 165, 199, 252, 298, 354, 354f; project 248; in sustainable agriculture 322–3, 324
carbon credits 348, 375
carbon dioxide: calculation of cumulative emissions and impact on temperature 136–7; CSE report calculating production by country 82–4, 83f, 87f; emissions per $1000 of GDP 255f; food sector emissions 160, 161f; impact on regional climate change 30; increase in atmosphere 31; IPCC Fourth Assessment Report on 29–30, 35, 353; lack of third world research on emissions 85–6; passenger transport emissions 162, 162f; sinks for 82, 85, 138; WRI report calculating by country 81–2, 84, 87f
Carbon Disclosure Project (CDP) 248–9, 250t, 256, 260, 261, 264n
carbon space: 1850 as basis for entitlement to 138, 139t, 143t; 1970 as basis for entitlement to 138–9, 139t, 149; calculating India's share of 142, 143–4, 143t, 144–5, 144t; entitlements on an equity basis vis-à-vis availability of 140–4; equity-based allocations of 138–40, 148–9, 151, 182, 198; optimization (TISS-DSF model) 142, 143, 143t, 144t
carbon tariff 189, 191, 193–4
carbon trading 210, 242, 342, 343, 348
Caruso, E. 210
Carvahlo, A. 267
Cassen, R. 259, 304
CBDR: see common but differentiated responsibility (CBDR)
CBDRRC: see common but differentiated responsibilities and respective capabilities (CBDRRC)
cement industry 260, 261–3, 262f
Central Ground Water Board 331, 332t
Central Statistical Organization (CSO) 221
Centre for Science and Environment (CSE) 113, 209; calculations on carbon dioxide and methane produced by country 82–4, 83f, 86f, 87f; methodology for calculating emissions for global warming 85; State of India's Environment report 209, 214; study of emissions varying according to income 218, 221, 223t, 224, 226–7
Ceres 260
CFCs 84
Chakravarty, S. 9, 150, 154n, 181, 221
Chaudhary, J. 236–7
Chauhan, C. 111, 266, 279
Chellam, R. 213

chill unit calculation models 54
China: agreement with US at Copenhagen Summit 377; Arctic ice melt and strategic equation between US and 381; CBDRRC principle and views on emission reduction targets 125; CDM projects 256, 258; comparison of authors for IPCC ARs from India and 68t; cooperation with India over climate change 90, 153, 189, 192; electricity prices 290; food sector carbon dioxide emissions 160, 161f; GHG emissions 173, 190, 199, 251, 376; green technology 193, 245, 249; high-speed trains in 299; Indian media coverage on emissions in US and 277–8; international pressure over emission reductions 251–2, 376; as a key developing country in climate change debate 157–8; perspective on India's climate change strategy 188–91; position on UNFCCC 90, 91, 92, 94, 180, 375; proposal to define entitlement to carbon space 148–9; renewable energy industries 378–9; share of carbon space 142; size of 157; technology transfers through CDM 258; voluntary undertakings on GHG emissions 176, 252
Chipko movement 211, 212, 213
Chu, S. 276
Chung, C.E. 34, 35
Church, J.A. 43
city climate adaption plans 308–9
city form and links to public transport 307
Clean Development Mechanism (CDM) 249–50; business associations building awareness of 259; Chinese projects 256, 258; emissions reductions from 258, 261–3, 261f; forestry projects under 213, 348; inclusion in Kyoto Protocol 108, 210, 375; Indian projects 256–8, 258f; India's response to 210; investment in Indian and Brazilian sugar and cement industries study 261–3, 262f; for low risk technology 363; share of total projects by region 257f
clean energy technology 191, 193, 200
Climate Analysis Indicators Tool 221
Climate Change Co-operation Accord 189
climate change, defining 29
climate change impact in India xix–xx, 5–7; in 20th century 32–4; in 21st century 35–8; aerosols 34–5; development and challenges 158–60; imaginative strategies on 87–8; media coverage of 272–3, 278–9, 280–1, 285t; programmes for vulnerability to 159, 159f, 160f; vulnerability of poor to 184, 304, 305; on water resources 328–9; see also apple

388 *Index*

cultivation in Himachal Pradesh; sea level rise and impact on Tamil Nadu coast study
climate change studies evolution in India 69–70
climate diplomacy 374–7, 378, 381
Climate Modelling Forum 153, 198
climate models 29–30, 30f, 35–8, 73–4
climate negotiations: *see* international climate negotiations and India's role
Climate Technology Centre and Network (CTCN) 363
CNDP 296
co-benefits: informing NAPCC 16–18, 20, 21, 200, 203, 353; privileging of mitigation actions with 313; sustainable development to promote 203, 204, 205
coal: clean technologies for 360–1; climate diplomacy and effect on world trade 378; comparisons with solar energy 297; and justification of RE subsidies 297; opposition to increasing use of 185, 215; in power generation mix 190, 235, 294t, 355f; projected use over next decade 298; supplies of domestic 295
coastal protection measures 48; *see also* sea level rise and impact on Tamil Nadu coast study
Coch, N.K. 45
Cogan, D.G. 260
common but differentiated responsibilities and respective capabilities (CBDRRC) 11, 118–30; Article 3.1 of UNFCCC 102, 118, 119, 121, 123–4, 126n, 130–1, 138, 139, 144; conflation with 'basis in equity' 131, 139, 140; to counter developed countries avoidance of responsibility 172–3; dissecting meaning of 118–23; 'ignorance challenge' 122, 148–9; in Kyoto Protocol 108, 118, 123–4; legal status 123; per capita cumulative emissions and reflection of 139; in post-2012 climate negotiations 124–5
common but differentiated responsibility (CBDR): in carbon budget approach 140; case for Indian government to internally implement 219; change to wording in IPCC First Assessment Report 106; and issues of historical responsibility 138–9, 148–9; principle followed in Indian print media 278; Rio Principle 7 121, 122, 126n
'common concern' treaties 119–20
Confederation of Indian Industries (CII) 247, 249, 251, 252, 259
consumption patterns 304, 369, 371
contract and converge approach (C&C) 133, 136, 148

contract and differentiated convergence (CDC) 133, 152t
Convention on Biological Diversity 119, 123
Copenhagen Accord: CBDRRC principle highlighted in 118; and financial assistance for developing countries 165, 166–7, 175, 242, 245; goal of containing temperature increase 165, 377; international consultation and analysis 166, 241, 243; last minute compromise 104, 111, 177; MEF statements paving way for 175; voluntary undertakings on GHG emissions 20, 176–7, 252, 290, 293
Copenhagen Summit: agreement between US and China 377; background to climate diplomacy at 376; controversy in run up to 67; emergence of power structure in climate diplomacy 376–7; Indian parliamentary debates on 233–45; India's non-negotiables for 110, 111, 238–9; media portrayal of India as a problem case in run up to 10–11; peaking emissions 240–1, 244–5; print media coverage of 271m270, 272, 275, 278, 286t; Ramesh addresses Indian parliament on India's position on non-negotiables 238–9; smaller countries 165, 177, 377; two track process of negotiations 10–11, 175, 369–70
corporate responses to climate change 15–16, 254–65; and corporate governance 260; drivers for 260–3; operational practices 255–8; political activities 259–60; *see also* private sector and climate change
Council for Scientific and Industrial Research (CSIR) 69, 359
Crawford, A. 381
Crawford, J. 120
Crook, D. 120
CSD 210
cumulative emissions: correlation between per capita cumulative emissions and per capita cumulative GDP 140, 141f; developments in science and 11, 136–7; entitlements on an equity basis vis-à-vis availability of carbon space 140–4; equity-based allocations of carbon space 138–40; India's 144–5, 198; mitigation and carbon budget approach 137–8, 140, 143, 144, 152t, 153
cyclonic disturbances in India 33, 43, 248

Dadhich, P.K. 257
Daly, H. 290
dams 211, 212, 213, 214, 330
Dangerous Anthropogenic Interference (DAI) 74, 77n, 130, 131, 144, 187, 353
Das, S 23n, 48, 252

Das, S. and S. 252
Dasgupta, A. 248
Dasgupta, C. 96n, 111, 112
Dasgupta, S. 44, 270
Dash, S.K. 32, 33
de Vries 304
Dechezlepretre, A. 258
deforestation rates 81–2, 85, 209, 341; *see also* UN Collaborative Initiative on Reducing Emissions from Deforestation and forest Degradation (UN-REDD)
den Elzen, M. 147, 151, 298
Dengue 38
Department of Economics and Statistics 51, 60
Desai, N. 112, 204, 383n, 384n
development: commonalities of developing countries 185–6; debate over path of domestic 227; and environmental challenges 158–60; to eradicate poverty 111, 112, 157, 165, 168, 185, 187, 290; protecting economic growth in international climate negotiations 181, 184–5, 186–8, 193, 202–3, 209–10; strategies to protect against climate change in India 86–7
development in energy sector and integration with domestic policy on climate change 16–20; 'co-benefits' framework 2, 16–18, 20, 21, 200, 203, 353; electricity sector 293–9; energy development linkage 289–93; transport sector 299–300; *see also* urbanization and climate change in India
displacement of peoples 304, 308, 348, 380
Diwan, R. 346
Dixit, A. 337
domestic politics on climate change in India 13–16, 197–207; 'co-benefits' approach to climate mitigation 2, 200, 203; debate on allocating responsibility for accumulation of GHG emissions 198; framing mitigation of climate change 199–200; growth-first realist perspective 202–3, 205; issue of gross internal inequalities in per capita emissions of GHGs 198–9; move to low carbon strategy 111, 249–51; strategic narratives on climate change 200–5, 201t, 202t; sustainable development internationalists 204–5; sustainable development realists 203–4, 205; view that cannot avoid responsibility of growing GHG emissions 186, 198, 248, 376
Dovers, S.R. 324
drought 273, 328, 329; migration caused by 303, 304, 309; proofing 160f, 309; resistant crops 319, 322

D'Souza, M. 172
Dubash, N.K. 3, 4, 7, 8, 10, 17, 21, 22, 22n, 199, 206n, 210, 211
Dutt, B.C. 267
Dworkin, R. 119
Dyson, T. 304, 305

ECO 93, 94
economic growth in India, protection of 181, 184–5, 186–8, 193, 202–3, 209–10
The Economic Times 268, 269f, 279, 280
The Economist 10, 219
education 159, 307; delivery 312; rural 160f, 305
Ehrlich, P.R. 323
El Niño 32
electricity 293–9; access to 190, 199, 227, 289, 295; balancing climate and development objectives 297–9, 298f; consumption per capita 291f; conventional supply options 295–6; elasticity of electricity to GDP 293–4, 293f; generation by source 294, 294t; prices 290; rationing 290; renewables and energy efficiency 296–7
Emanuel, K.A. 43
emissions intensity of the economy index 290, 292f, 293
Emissions Trading Scheme 189
energy: agenda for climate change and 360–2; air conditioning use 305; biomass 191, 224, 236, 256–7, 258f, 289, 294t, 355f; BLUE scenario 354, 354f, 355f; coal *see* coal consumption in India 2007–2050 190; consumption per capita 159; electricity *see* electricity emissions intensity of the economy index 290, 292f, 293; energy efficiency 296–7, 378–9; gas 296, 378; hydro-power 295; and links with development 289–93; markets 21, 22, 378; move to low carbon strategy 111, 249–51; nuclear 211, 212, 213, 295–6, 354; oil 299, 377–8; opportunities for India to lead way in sustainable 371–2; pilot programme distributing CFLs 371; production and consumption patterns and use of 370–1; R&D in India 360–1; ratio of urban to rural energy consumption 305–6, 306f; renewable *see* renewable energy rural poor and limited access to modern services 224, 227, 228n; security 190, 377, 380; solar technology *see* solar technology state as 'early adopter' of technology 363; and transport sector 299–300; urbanization and channels of increased consumption 305–8; wind 256–7, 296–7, 354, 379

390 Index

Energy Conservation Building Code 309, 310
Enkvist, P.-A. 260, 261
environmental challenges and development 158–60
environmental colonialism, example of 81–8
Environmental Kuznets Curve (EKC) 162–4, 163f, 163t, 164t, 165t
environmental movement and climate change in India 14, 208–17; engagement with mitigation questions 210–11; environmentalism of the poor 211–12; Indian environmentalism 211–14; initial disinterest in 208–9; and issues of equity-based engagement 209–10; multi-dimensional nature of 214–15; social justice concerns 211, 213; wildlife conservationists 213
environmental refugees 304, 380
ENVIS 43
equity: carbon budget approach to emissions 137–8, 140, 143, 144, 152t, 153; CBDRRC conflation with 'basis in equity' 131, 139, 140; contract and converge approach (C&C) 133, 136, 148; contract and differentiated convergence (CDC) 133, 152t; entitlements on an equity basis vis-à-vis availability of carbon space 140–4; environmental movement and equity-based engagement 209–10; equity-based allocations of carbon space 138–40, 147–50, 151, 182, 198; equity-based proposals and implications for India 151–3, 152t, 153t; intranational 150–1, 198–9 see also GHG emissions by class in Indiakey negotiating issue for India 180, 181, 233; media coverage of burden-sharing and 275–7, 279–80, 286t; moral issues in equity proposals 150–1; and need to end two-track approach to energy use 369–70, 371; problems with principle of per capita emissions 181–2; protecting economic growth behind arguments of 209–10; pursuing 'no-lose' mitigation strategies 151; relationship between international climate politics and equity scholars 153–4
Ethiopia 183
European Commission 379, 383n
European Community (EC) 91, 92–3, 93–5, 107; see also European Union (EU)
European perspective on India's climate position 180–3
European Union (EU): committed to strong global agreement on emission cuts 377–8; corporate responses to climate change 254; Emissions Trading Scheme 189; on historical responsibility 276; power in

climate diplomacy 376; and relationship with US on climate change 175; support for Kyoto Protocol 103; see also European Community (EC)
executive process in India 231–2
Expert Group for Low Carbon Economy xx, 11, 16, 182
Eyckmans, J. 122

FAO 317, 318, 321, 323, 324, 329, 341
FE-EVI Report 260, 261
Federation of Indian Chambers of Commerce and Industry (FICCI) 15, 206n, 259, 260
Fernandes 280
finance: for climate change technology 175, 245, 352, 362, 363; Copenhagen Accord and issues of 165, 166–7, 175, 242, 245; issues in making of UNFCCC 91, 92, 187; US lack of domestic support for assisting developing countries 191
Financial Express 256, 268, 269f, 272
First World Climate Conference 1979 101
Fisher, B.S. 353
Five Year Plans: 11th 314n, 330; 12th xx, 16, 111
floods 248, 328, 329; coastal 43, 44, 48, 308; control 160f, 338t; in Himalayan region 235, 323; Mumbai 248, 307
Florini, A. 22
Food and Agricultural Organisation 341
food sector emissions 160, 161f
food security 51, 380; contribution of small farms to 322; production technologies for 319–21
foreign policy in India on climate change 112–15; changing policy 109–10, 114–16, 176–7, 251–2; domestic consensus weakening on 114, 115, 198, 202; lack of parliamentary discussion on 232; not considered a domestic concern 197; reasons for continuity 113
Forest Act 1927 344, 345
Forest Rights Act 2006 345, 346, 347
Forest Survey of India 343, 344
forests 19, 210, 212, 214, 215; attempts at enclosure 345; background to chaos of forest records in India 344–6; British timber extraction 344–5; 'carbon forestry' projects in South America 347; CDM and carbon-trading dilemmas 210, 343, 348; CDM projects 213, 348; and climate change 341–3; decline in Amazonian 209, 273; defining 343–4; deforestation rates 81–2, 85, 209, 341; democratic government of 215, 346, 347, 349–50; difficulties in establishing extent of Indian 343–4; GHG emissions from deforestation 341; Joint Forest

Management (JFM) 346, 347, 349; problems with implementing incentives model in Indian context 346–7; REDD in context of political economy of 347–8; REDD incentives model to protect 342–3; water security 337
fossil fuels: carbon dioxide emissions in India from 255f; for economic growth in developing countries 131, 188n, 215; in energy mix 289; Indian dependence on 235, 255, 257, 289, 294
Fowler, H. 75, 76
frames for climate change 3
France 86f, 91, 224, 360f
Frankel, J. 149
Friedman, H. 320
Fuente, A. 305
Funk, C.C. 319, 321
future trends in climate debate 20–2, 177–8, 369–72, 381–2

G8 171, 172, 174, 175, 248
G8+5 104, 109, 174, 175, 178
G20 104, 174
G22 172, 174
G77: BASIC as a sub-group 184; benefits to India from alliance 190; divisions within 375, 376; India's role in climate negotiations 107, 180, 183, 185, 188; negotiations in creation of UNFCCC 91, 92, 93, 94, 180, 375; in post-2012 climate negotiations 185
Gabcikovo-Nagymaros 119
Gandhi, I. 112
Gandhi, M. 126n, 188, 213
Ganesan, M.R. 280
Garg, K.C. 267
gas 296, 378
gases in earth's atmosphere 31
GDP: agriculture share in 320; carbon dioxide emissions per $1000 255f; correlation between per capita cumulative emissions and per capita cumulative 140, 141f; EKC turning points in respect of 164, 165t; elasticity of electricity to 293–4, 293f; GERD as a percentage of 359, 360f; India's expenditure on programmes to address climate change as a percentage of 159, 159f; an insufficient measure of development 290; and links with GHG emissions 187
Geevan, C. P. 279
geopolitics of climate change 21–2, 174–5, 373–4; climate change with direct security implications for India 380–1; climate diplomacy 374–7, 378, 381; geopolitics of mitigation actions 377–9; intersection of climate science and security analysis

379–81; longer term impact of 382; medium term impact of 381–2; need for an effective climate agreement 382
German Advisory Council on Global Change (WBGU) 41, 42f, 148, 152t, 189
Germany 90–1, 189, 236
GHG emission reductions: see burden-sharing in emission reductions
GHG emissions: 2030 projections 109, 134f, 135f, 153, 198, 224, 225f, 225t, 298; 2050 projections 134f, 135f, 171, 173, 353, 354; from agriculture 317, 318; CDM projects and reductions in 258, 261–3, 261f; Centre for Science and Environment (CSE) calculations 82–4, 83f, 86f, 87f; of China 173, 190, 199, 251, 376; climate sceptic view of 238; concept of peaking 240–1, 244–5; from deforestation 341; development linked with 187, 289–90; emissions intensity of the economy index comparing countries 290, 292f, 293; global 2004–5 173; household 220–1; India and increases in 109, 173, 198; India as a major emitter of 172, 186, 198, 248, 376; in Indian industry 255; Indian media coverage on emissions in US and China 277–8; international pressure on China and India over reductions 251–2; intranational rates of 150–1, 198–9 see also GHG emissions by class in India IPCC AR4 recommendations on 171–2; and links with GDP growth 187; and need to act across all countries 173; per capita see GHG per capita emissionspower plant 293; reductions through energy efficiency 296; sectoral emission targets 166; stabilization levels 131; stocks and flows of 9, 11, 176, 198; in transport sector 162, 162f, 299; US 84, 86f, 189, 190, 198, 199, 376; voluntary undertakings on 20, 109, 110, 111, 176–7, 252, 290, 293; World Resources Institute (WTI) Report calculations 81–2, 84, 87f; WRI-CAIT 2007 data 190; see also cumulative emissions
GHG emissions by class in India 218–29, 235; access to modern energy services 224, 227, 228n; comparing richest and poorest and levels of 224, 226, 227; context of studies 218–20; CSE studies 218, 221, 223t, 224, 226–7; and debate over development 227; future projections 224–6, 225f, 225t; Hiding Behind the Poor 218–20, 222t, 224, 226, 227; methods of measuring emissions 220–1; Parikh study on 219, 220, 221–3, 222t, 223f, 224, 227; political choices in

392 *Index*

comparing 226–7; results of studies 221–4; rural and urban emissions 221, 223, 223f, 224
GHG inventory in India 69, 73
GHG per capita emissions: and arguments for exemption from mitigation commitments for developing countries 102, 153; burden-sharing based on 148–9; France willing to limit 91; global 190, 199; and historical responsibility 170, 172; by income 223t; of India 190, 198–9, 214, 224, 225f, 318; Indian UNFCCC draft convention on 90; principle of 9; and principle of equity 89–90; problems with principle of 181–2; promoted by India 153, 172, 173, 181, 209
Ghosh, P. 110
Ghosh, S. 348
Ghotke, N. 322
glaciers xix–xx, 33, 33–4, 338t, 383n; Himalayan glaciers controversy 5–6, 33, 74–6, 273–4; parliamentary debate on 234–5
Global Commons Institute (GCI) 148
Global Environment Facility 363
Global Warming in an Unequal World 9; action in India for 87–8; Centre for Science and Environment (CSE) calculations 82–4, 83f, 86f, 87f; lack of third world research 85–6; sharing of global common sinks 85; World Resources Institute (WTI) Report calculations 81–2, 84, 87f
GNI per capita in India 289
Golait, R. 320
Gopalakrishnan, A. 350n
Gopalakrishnan, S. 296
Gore, A. 238
Gosseries, A. 122
Goswami, A.G. 280
Goswami, B.N. 33
Government of India 22n, 198, 200, 203, 204, 247, 297, 301n, 320, 353, 359, 360
Green Business Centre (GBC) 251
Green India Mission xx, 182, 335–6
Greenhouse Development Rights (GDR) approach 132–3, 149–50, 152t, 153
Greenland 34, 42
Greenpeace 22n, 199, 347
Greenpeace India study *(Hiding Behind the Poor)* 218–20
GRIHA (Green Rating for Integrated Habitat Assessment) 306
Grubb, M. 4, 7, 22n, 122
Grübler, A. 356
Grundmann, R. 6
Guha, R. 14, 211, 212

Gunawardena, M. 44
Gundimeda, H. 210
Gupta, J. 4
Gupta, S. 210

Hague Declaration 1989 118, 121
Haigler, E. 17
Halarnkar, S. 279
Halden, P. 379
Hannah, L.J. 208
Hansen, J. 41
Haribar Polyfibres 212
Hasnain, S.I. 75
HBF 324
health 35, 380
heat waves in India 32, 35, 38
Herendeen, R. 220, 221
Hezri, A.A. 324
Hiding Behind the Poor 218–20, 222t, 224, 226, 227
Himalayan glaciers xix–xx; IPCC Report controversy 5–6, 33, 74–6; media coverage of misreporting on 273–4
The Hindu 268, 269f, 271
The Hindu Business Line 268, 269f, 270, 277
Hindustan Times 268, 269f, 274, 275, 279
Hoffert, M.I. 354
Höhne, N. 133, 134f, 135f, 148, 151, 152, 154n
home ownership and transport demand 313
Hulme, M. 3
Hultman, N.E. 257, 261
Human Development Index (HDI) 158f, 168n, 290, 291f
Huq, S. 34, 183–5
Hurrell, A. 101
Hwang 307
hydro-power 295

IAASTD 319, 320
IATP 321
'ignorance challenge' 122, 148–9
INCCA (National Network for Climate Assessment) xx–xxi, 69, 76, 275, 318, 322
Indian Constitution 74th Amendment 312
Indian Council for Agricultural Research (ICAR) 320, 359
The Indian Express 268, 269f, 271
Indian Meteorological Department (IMD) 32
Indian Network for Climate Change Assessment (INCCA) 69
Indian Ocean 32, 33
Indonesia 176, 183, 376, 378
INECC 211
Input-Output (I-O) tables to measure emissions 220

Index 393

Integrated Assessment Models 132
intellectual property rights 167, 242, 359, 362, 363
Inter-Academy Council (IAC) 67, 75
Intergovernmental Negotiating Committee (INC) 89, 93, 94, 102, 106–7, 112
Intergovernmental Panel on Climate Change (IPCC) 5–6, 63–77; 1st Assessment Report 7, 8, 64, 68t, 71–2t, 73, 102, 106; 2nd Assessment Report 64, 68t, 69, 71–2t, 102; 3rd Assessment Report 64, 68t, 71–2t, 103, 131, 171, 184; 4th Assessment Report *see* Intergovernmental Panel on Climate Change (IPCC) Fourth Assessment Report5th Assessment Report 64, 68t, 70, 71–2t, 74; author selection 65–6, 67, 68t, 70, 71–2t; awarded Nobel Peace Prize 66; Bureau 64, 64f, 70, 76; definition of climate change 69; guidelines for accessing grey literature 67; independent review 2010 67; India's participation in 67–74, 68t, 76, 106; monsoon variability and modelling extreme events 73–4; process 63–7; recent criticism of 67; review procedure 65, 65f, 66, 76; rice field methane emissions 66, 70, 73; setting up 29, 101–2, 374; structure 64f; timeline of key events 105–6t
Intergovernmental Panel on Climate Change (IPCC) Fourth Assessment Report 29–30; authors 68t, 70; burden-sharing mitigation in WG III 132; carbon dioxide 29–30, 35, 353; changes needed for emission reduction goals 353; climate change as unequivocal 103, 171, 248; climate prediction models 29–30, 30f, 35, 36f; deforestation estimated emissions 341; developing countries' emissions 172; glacier controversy 5, 33, 74–6; media coverage of errors in 270, 273, 274; recommendations on mitigation trajectories 171–2; reviews of 66; SLR estimates by 2100 30, 31f, 34, 41; stabilization levels for GHGs 131; sustainable agriculture 319, 322
international climate negotiations and India's role xxi, 10–11, 104–12, 180–1; background to 101–4; Bangladesh's perspective on 183–5; China's perspective on 188–91; cooperation between China and India 90, 153, 189, 192; Europe's perspective on 180–3; future of 20–3, 177–8, 369–72, 381–2; India's foreign policy behaviour on 112–14; India's perspective for future 164–8; India's position in light of developments in science of climate change 172–3; as a key

developing country in debate 157–8; as a major emitter and need to act responsibly on world stage 172, 186, 198, 248, 376; moving towards a new position for India 176–7; Philippines perspective on 185–8; post 2012 negotiations 104, 108, 124–5, 171, 181, 185, 243, 376; as a proactive player on global stage 251–2; protecting India's economic growth 181, 184–5, 186–8, 193, 202–3, 209–10; shifting geopolitics 174–5; 'strategic partnership' with US 114, 175, 191; timeline of key events in climate change negotiations 105–6t; US perspective on 192–4; voluntary undertakings on GHG emissions 20, 109, 110, 111, 176–7, 252, 290, 293
International Commission for Snow and Ice 75
International Court of Justice (ICJ) 119, 120, 126n
International Energy Association (IAE) 22, 190; Energy Technology Perspectives Report 354, 355f
irrigation 32, 211, 330, 330f, 331f, 332, 338t
island states 91, 92, 102, 107, 174, 175, 176
ITC 247–8, 249, 348
Ivins, E.R. 41

Jain 275
Jaitley, A. 240, 240–2
Jamasb, T. 357
Jamieson, D. 148
Japan: corporate responses to climate change 254; EKC turning point 165t; GHC emissions 84, 86f; oil imports 299; position at Kyoto 157, 254; position at UNFCCC negotiations 91, 92, 93, 107; power in climate diplomacy 376; recycling 160; references to CBDRRC principle 125; research 359, 360t
Jawaharlal Nehru National Solar Mission (JNNSM): *see* National Solar Mission
Jayaraman, T. 22n, 172, 198
Jebraj, P. 277, 278
Jiahua 150, 152
Jiang, L. 218, 224
Jindal, K.K. 57
Jodha, N.S. 321
Jogi, R.L. 320, 322
Joint Forest Management (JFM) 346, 347, 349
Joshua, A. 276
Joyner 266
Joyner, C.C. 123

Kalsi, S.R. 44, 46f

394 Index

Kanagaratnam, P. 41
Kanitkar, T. 145n, 148, 149, 152t, 172, 182, 198
Kant, P. 210
Karanth, K.U. 213
Kent, J. 219
Khor, M. 20, 104, 177, 364
Kim, M.K. and K.M. 35
Kitoh, A. 35, 37f
Knox-Hayes, J. 257
Köhler, J. 357
Kolli, R.K. 73
Korea 183, 360t
Kothari, A. 214
Krey, M. 258
Krishnan, N.R. 277, 278
Kulkarni, A.V. 33
Kulkarni, N.R. 320, 331, 333, 333f
Kyoto Protocol: CBDRRC principle 108, 118, 123–4; developed countries effort to replace 104, 110–11, 124, 178, 189–90, 243; emission targets 95, 102–3, 108, 375–6; formal adoption of 103; inclusion of CDM 108, 210, 375; India's commitment to 233, 243; India's role and contribution to negotiations 107–8, 180–1; 'joint implementation' (JI) 108, 116n; post 2012 negotiations 104, 108, 124–5, 171, 181, 185, 243, 376; technology transfer obligations 175, 177; US rejection of 103, 124, 157, 192, 375, 383n

Lal, M. 74, 322
Landsea, C.W. 43
Lang, C. 320, 349
Lau, K.M. 35
Lee, K.N. 212
LEED (Leadership in Energy and Environmental Design) 306
Leggett, J. 254
legislative process in India 230–1
Lele, S. 8, 212, 213, 214, 323
Leontief, W. 220
Lewis, J. 257
Li Chin, L. 324
life expectancy in India 159
lifestyles: and sustainability 160–4; unsustainable 168; valuing disposability over durability 371
Lobell, D.B. 319, 321
local government 312–13
Lohmann, L. 8
Lokare, S.M. 320
Lovejoy, T. 208
low-carbon growth 13, 176, 188, 193, 300; barriers to 362; business response to 247–8, 249–50, 252; drivers for

investment in technologies 261–3; in Europe 375, 376; Expert Group to report on xx, 11, 16, 182; global support for 182–3; resistance to EU aim for all countries to adopt 181; role of gas in India 296; strategy for 11, 249–50; trade offs with poverty 200; US attitude to technologies for 191
Lucas, P. 147, 151
Lutken, S.E. 258

Maas, A. 379, 383n
Maharashtra State Energy Distribution Corporation 371
Mahtab, S. 235–6
'mainstreaming' climate change 21, 369–72
Major Economies Forum (MEF) 104, 109–10, 174–5, 178
Malaria 38
Malone, E. 3
Mandal, T. 237–8
mangroves 44
Manmohan Singh Convergence Principle 133
Marrakesh Accords 103, 108
Marshall, C. 32
Mathur, J. 213
Matthews, H.D. 136, 137, 145n
Matthews, R. 209
Maurin, F. 296
McGranahan, G. 45
McKinsey & Company 248, 255, 257, 260, 300n
Meadows, D. 8, 112
Meattle, K. 272
media 1, 232
media coverage on climate change, study of 16, 266–75; burden-sharing and equity issues 275–7, 278, 279–80, 286t; climate change impacts coverage 272–3, 278–9, 280–1, 285t; climate scepticism 274–5, 285t; domestic policies versus politics 275–80, 286t; following principle of CBDR 278; frequency of news coverage 270, 271f; literature on 267–8; methodology 268–70; nationalism in Indian media 280; news content 271–2, 272f, 285t; pinning blame on USA and China 277–8; science of climate change 272–5, 273f, 274f; view that emerging economies are catching up on emissions 277, 277f, 278
Mehra, M. 200
Meinshausen, M. 137
methane 31; CSE report calculating production by country 82–4, 86f, 87f; emission from rice fields 66, 70, 73, 243–4; lack of third world research on production of 85–6; sinks for 82–4, 138;

WRI report calculating production by country 81–2, 84, 87f
Mexico 157, 174, 176, 183, 251; CDM projects 258
Meyer, M. 268
Michaelowa, A. 149, 257, 258
migration as a result of climate change 305, 380
Ministry of Environment and Forests (MoEF) 63, 65, 67, 69, 70, 74, 76, 224, 293, 329, 343, 349
Ministry of Urban Development 307, 311
Mint 268, 269f, 275, 279–80, 286t
Mitra, A,P. 69, 73
MNRE 297
Modi, A. 210
Moench, M. 332, 337
Moltmann, S. 133, 134f
monsoon rainfall xix, 32–3; aerosols impact on 34–5; impact of changed patterns and strategic responses 338t; IPCC climate models to predict changes in Indian 35, 36f; littoral drift of east coast and patterns of 43; predicted patterns in 329; research on variability and modelling extreme events 73–4
Montreal Protocol 1987 8, 102, 123
Morris, H. 122
MoWR 328, 336
MRV (measuring, reporting and verification) accountability 109, 111, 166, 190, 191, 192, 242
Mukherji. R. 9
Muller, B. 149, 150
Mumbai floods 248, 307
Murthy, N.S. 218, 222t
Myers, N. 219

Nakicenovic, N. 132
Nanjangud Industrial Area (NIA) 371
Narain, S. 88n, 113, 148, 206n, 209, 212
Narlikar, A. 114
National Action Plan on Climate Change (NAPCC): 'co-benefits' framework informing 16–18, 20, 21, 200, 203, 353; criticism in parliamentary debate 235–6; Green India Mission xx, 182, 335–6; increasing contribution of renewable energy 297; launch 17, 109; National Mission for Enhanced Energy Efficiency xx, 200, 235; National Mission for Sustainable Agriculture (NMSA) 317, 318–19, 321, 324, 353, 361t; National Mission on Sustainable Habitat (NMSH) 251, 306, 310, 311, 313, 335, 361t; National Solar Mission xx, 182, 198, 237, 271, 297, 298, 353, 357, 361t; National Water Mission 19, 328, 335,

336–7; omissions 321; response to climate change 364; science and technology-related aspects of missions 361, 361t; target to reduce emissions intensity 188
National Communication (NATCOM) 69
National Disaster Management Agency (NDMA) 309
National Geographic's Greendex 162
National Green Mission xx, 182, 335–6
National Mission for Enhanced Energy Efficiency xx, 200, 235
National Mission for Sustainable Agriculture (NMSA) 317, 318–19, 321, 324, 353, 361t
National Mission on Sustainable Habitat (NMSH) 251, 306, 310, 311, 313, 335, 361t
National Network for Climate Assessment (INCCA) 69, 76, 275, 318, 322
National Planning Commission 16, 111, 168n, 182, 275, 331, 337
National Rainfed Areas Authority (NRAA) 322
National Sample Survey Organization (NSSO) 221, 222
National Solar Mission xx, 182, 198, 237, 271, 297, 353, 357, 361t
National Water Mission 19, 328, 335, 336–7
Nationally Appropriate Mitigation Actions (NAMAs) 111, 166, 169n, 190, 298, 300
natural disasters 248
Nature Conservancy 342
Naylor, R.L. 35
NCEUS 320
Nellemann, C. 320
Nelson, G.C. 319, 321
Nemet, C.F. 357, 358f
Nepal 32, 86f
New Scientist 75
Newell, P. 4
Newman, P. 307
Newsham, G. 306
NFFPFW 210
Nicholls, R. 44
Nigam, S. 37
Nivola, S. 312
Non-Aligned Movement (NAM) 185
non-governmental organisations 107, 113, 199, 203, 256, 342
Noordwijk Declaration 1989 121
Norway 91, 164, 165t, 183
nuclear energy 211, 212, 213, 295–6, 354

Obama, B. 244, 377
Oberthur, S. 102, 107

396 *Index*

OECD countries 91, 92–3, 94, 103, 259, 289, 304, 376
oil 299, 377–8
Olausson, U. 266, 267, 270, 280
ONGC 247, 248
OPEC countries 107, 180, 374
Oppenheimer, M. 41
Ostrom, E. 4
Ott, M.E. 102, 107

Pacala, S. 354
Pachauri, R. 64, 274
Pachauri. S. 218, 221, 224, 305
Pacific Ocean 32
Painter, J. 266, 272, 274
Palanivel, S. 320
Pan, J. 148, 152t, 189
Panagariya, A. 203, 206n
Panda, M. 37
paper industry 257
Parikh and Parikh 181
Parikh, J. 108, 218, 219, 220, 221–3, 222t, 223f, 224, 225f, 227, 228n
Parikh, K. 279
parliamentary debates on climate change 14–15, 230–45; Bali Action Plan (BAP) 234; criticism of NAPCC 235–6; dismissal as political rather than scientific 237–8; excerpts from debates post Copenhagen 239–45; excerpts from debates pre Copenhagen 233–9; need for innovative approaches 236–7; Ramesh addresses Indian parliament on India's position on non-negotiables 238–9; Sikkim glaciers 234–5; support for historic responsibility arguments 233–4
Parry, M. 209
Parsai, G. 270
Partap, U. and T. 60
particulates 32, 34, 35
patent applications 359, 362
Paterson, M. 101, 107
Patil, S. 231
Patwardhan, A. 74
peak warming response 137
peaking emissions 240–1, 244–5
Pearce, F. 75
Peoples Science Movement 176
Perform Achieve and Trade (PAT) mechanism xx
Perkins, R. 257
Pettenger, M. 3
Philippines 94; perspective on climate strategy of India 185–8
Piketty, T. 226
Pimentel, D. and M. 321
'pledge and review' agreement 9, 104; proposal for UNFCCC 91, 92–3, 96

Plio-Pleistocene records 41, 42f
Poffenberger, M. 210
politics of climate change 4, 275–80
polluters and pollutees 212
Pope, C.A. 35
population 157, 190, 304
positive feedback 31
poverty: balance between climate protection and alleviation of 188; need for development to eradicate 111, 112, 157, 165, 168, 185, 187, 290; poverty-based emission rights 133, 150, 153; in rural communities 168n, 199, 320, 321; statistics 158, 168–9n, 190, 199, 228n; sustainable development to benefit poor 200; and vulnerability to adverse impacts of climate change 184, 304, 305
Prime Minister's Council on Climate Change (PMCCC) 16, 109, 182, 271, 318
Prins, G. 219
private sector and climate change 15, 246–53; business response to climate change 247–8, 252; policy framework 249–52; relationship between business and government 246–7; small-and-medium scale enterprises 15; *see also* corporate responses to climate change
Probable Maximum Storm Surge 44, 46f
product life-cycle (PLC) 356
production patterns 369, 370–1
property tax 312
Pulver, S. 259, 261
Purohit, P. 257

Raghunandan, D. 22n, 175, 176, 177, 198, 204, 266
Rahmstorf, S. 34
Rai, Shri Prem Das 234
railways 299, 311, 312
Raina, S. 5, 75, 76, 319, 323
rainfall: agriculture and adaptation to low 322; change in patterns and links to increase in vector borne diseases 38; decrease in Kerala 37; impact of changed patterns and strategic responses 338t; in India in 20th century 32–3; IPCC climate models to predict 35–8, 36f, 37f; river runoff 329, 338t; trends affecting apple growing 51, 57, 61; *see also* monsoon rainfall
Raj, N. 75
Rajamani, L. 3, 4, 20, 21, 22n, 114, 123, 124, 125, 126n, 127n, 198, 205
Rajan, M.G. 106, 107
Rajendran, K. 32–3, 35, 37f
Rajesh, M.B. 233–4
Ramachandran, N. 110, 227

Ramanathan, V. 34, 35
Ramarao, P. 359
Ramdas, S. 322
Ramesh, J. 74, 110, 111, 182, 234, 238–9,
    239, 240–2, 243–5, 251, 266, 271, 275,
    277, 278
Rao, N. 153, 210, 295
Ravindranath, N.H. 64, 68t, 210
Rayner, S. 219
recycling 160–2, 161f; in Nanjangud
    Industrial Area (NIA) 371
REDD: *see* UN Collaborative Initiative on
    Reducing Emissions from Deforestation
    and forest Degradation (UN-REDD)
Reddy, A.K.N. 209, 214, 290
Redgwell, C. 120, 123
renewable energy: co-benefits of 261, 299;
    and energy efficiency 296–7; growth in
    257; incentives for 237, 263; India's
    co-operation with China on 189; need for
    collaborative response in shift to 369–71;
    share in power generation mix 296;
    targets for 188, 297; technologies 300,
    354, 362, 378–9
research: and development in India 358–61;
    evolution of climate change studies in
    India 69–70; global expense on climate
    change R&D 360f; lack of third world
    research on emissions 85–6
resource-sharing frame 148–9, 150–1, 152t,
    153
responsibility, historical 138–9, 148–9, 153,
    165, 170, 172, 233–4, 276–7; Brazilian
    Proposal and 138, 149
Reuters 277, 278
Reva 247
Revi, A. 304, 305, 314
rice fields methane emissions 66, 70, 73,
    243–4
Rignot, E. 41
Rio Declaration 123; Principle 7 121, 122,
    126n
Rio Earth Summit 1992 8, 113, 121, 374–5;
    signing of UNFCCC 102
Risk and Vulnerability Atlas 309–10
Rittel, H. 311
rivers: conflict over 209, 212, 379, 380,
    383n; flooding 329, 338t, 380; Ganges
    and Brahmaputra river systems 303, 380;
    runoff 329, 338t; water sharing 209, 379,
    383n
Robert, E.R. 57
Rowan, J.S. 44
Roychowdhury, A. 209
Rupa Kumar, K. 32, 73
rural communities: disparity in rural-urban
    emissions 221, 223, 223f, 224; household
    emissions 224; housing 289; limited

access to modern energy 224, 227, 228n;
    migration to urban areas 305; non-farm
    employment 320; poverty in 168n, 199,
    320, 321; ratio of urban to rural energy
    consumption 305–6, 306f; and
    Rurbanism 314; share of transport
    consumption 307; use of biomass energy
    236; water supply 332, 334
Rurbanism 314
Russia 10, 103, 255f, 360f, 376, 378, 381

Saluja, M.V. 221, 228
SANDRP 211
Sant, G. 293, 297
Saran 112
Saran, S. 2, 275
Sarin, M. 346, 347
Sathirathai, S. 44
Saudi Arabia 91, 378
Schiermeier, Q. 6
Schneider, M. 257
Schneider, S.H. 74
Schokkaert, E. 122
Science 329
science and technology in India 358–62
science of climate change xx–xxi, 5–7,
    170–2, 173; cumulative emissions and
    development of 11, 136–7; Himalayan
    glaciers controversy 5–6, 33, 74–6,
    273–4; Indian scientists' participation in
    IPCC 67–74, 68t, 76, 106; India's
    position in light of developments in
    172–3; media coverage of 272–5, 273f,
    274f
Scientific Committee on Antarctic Research
    (SCAR) 41
sea level rise: estimates on 30, 31f, 34, 41–2;
    impact of 174, 328 *see also* sea level
    rise and impact on Tamil Nadu coast
    studyin India in 20th century 33–4; IPCC
    Report on 30, 31f, 34, 41; and maritime
    and border security 380; vulnerability to
    xix
sea level rise and impact on Tamil Nadu
    coast study 6–7, 42–8; adverse impact on
    wetlands and ecosystems 43, 48;
    background 41–2; calculating height of
    storm surges 44; data and methods 43–5;
    economic costs of 6–7, 43–4, 45, 47t;
    recommendations 48–9; results 45–7;
    storm surges 43, 44–5, 46f, 46t;
    vulnerability of coast to SLR 42–3
sea surface temperature 32, 32–3
Seal, V. 15
Second National Communication on Climate
    Change 259
Second World Climate Conference 1990 118,
    121, 374

398 *Index*

security, climate change a threat to 373–4, 380
Sekar, T. 267
Selin, H. 4
Semenov, S. 74
Sen, A. 226, 290, 320
Sethi, N. 110, 348
SEWA Bharat 307
Shah, A. 247
Shah, M. 322
Shah, T. 330, 332
Shankar, D. 34
Shapiro, M. 347
Sharma, A. 209
Sharma, S. 64
Shaw, J. 41
Shekhar, M.S. 33
Shiva, V. 213
Shourie, A. 1, 204
Shreshta 32
Shulkla, P.R. 213, 315n
Singer, P. 148, 151
Singh 296
Singh, A. 247
Singh, M. 109
Sinha, D. 371
sinks for methane and carbon dioxide 82–4, 85, 138
size of India 157
Slack, E. 312
Smith, J. 319
Smith, K.R. 17
Snidal, D. 21
snowfall 33, 55, 59–60, 60f
social accounting matrix (SAM) 221
Socolow, R. 354, 354f
solar technology 20, 236, 237, 295, 297, 354, 379; National Solar Mission xx, 182, 198, 237, 271, 297, 298, 353, 357, 361t
Somashekhar, B.S. 210
Sonwalkar, P. 268
soot 34, 35
South Africa 114, 168n, 174, 255f, 290, 292f, 360f
South Asian Association for Regional Cooperation (SAARC) xxi
South Commission 8
springs 335, 335f, 336f, 338t
Sreekumar, N. 295
Srinivasan, J. 31, 73
Standing Committees 231–2
Stapleton, S. 332
State Forest Department 343, 345, 346, 347, 348
State of India's Environment 209, 214
steel industry 255, 257
Stern Review 44, 104, 188n, 248

Stone, C. 123
storm surges: estimating 44, 46f; SLR and risk to Tamil Nadu coast 43, 44–5, 46f, 46t
Subramanian, A. 1, 151
sugar industry 259–60, 261–3, 262f
Sugiura, T. 51
sulphate aerosols 34
Suneja 275
sustainable development 8, 151, 182, 189, 251; Business Council for Sustainable Development 246–7, 259; 'co-benefits' of 200; global collaborative response to 369–71; perspectives on 201, 203–5; using CDMs for 251
Suzlon 193, 247
Swaminathan, M.S. 320
Swart, R. 132
Sweden 91, 165t, 359

Taiwan 307
Takahashi, K. 35
Tamil Nadu coast study: *see* sea level rise and impact on Tamil Nadu coast study
Tanaka, J. 221
Tänzler, D. 379
Tata Group 246–7, 248
Tata Nano car 219
technology 19, 352–65; business response to climate change 247–8, 249, 258; in context of Indian national policy on climate change 352–3; financing climate change 175, 245, 352, 362, 363; GHG mitigation costs in developing countries 167; global expense on R&D 360f; green technology in China 193, 245, 249; Indian agenda for climate change and energy 360–2; intellectual property rights 167, 242, 359, 362, 363; lack of capacity problem 362; market entry and early adoption 363; in multilateral process 362–4; need for global collaborative efforts on 370–1; process of technological change 356–8, 357f, 358f; public-private partnerships 359; and science in India 358–62; significance in climate change 353–6; to support climate change mitigation and action in developing countries 167; in transport sector 354, 355f; US-Indian relationships on 193, 194
Technology Executive Committee (TEC) 363
technology life-cycle (TLC) 356
technology transfers: Article 4 of UNFCCC on 95, 106, 187, 242, 362; barriers to 362; Cancun Agreements and progress on 363–4; challenging conventional view of 352; need to temper existing IPRs on 167, 362, 363–4; obligations under Kyoto

Protocol 175, 177; through CDM 258; UNFCCC negotiations over 91, 92, 187; view that India does not require 245

temperature: calculation of cumulative emissions and impact on 136–7; climate sceptics view of rise in 237–8; impact of aerosols on 34; impact on apple cultivation 56–7, 59–60, 61; impact on water resources and strategic response 338t; increases and impact on agriculture 35, 37–8, 329; increases and links to increase in vector borne diseases 38; in India 37; IPCC Report on increases in 29–30, 30f, 35

TERI 64, 75, 108, 144t, 161f, 162f, 164n, 165t, 210, 257, 306

Thakkar, H. 329, 330, 331

Thakur, N. 15

The Times of India 15, 268, 269f, 273, 275

TISS-DSF model 142, 143, 143t, 144t

TNN 110, 271, 275

transport sector: 'Avoid-Shift-Improve' paradigm 299–300; city form and links to public transport 307; emissions from passenger 162, 162f; energy 299–300; energy consumption by 307; home ownership and transport demand 313; increasing use of public transport 308t, 311–12; subsidization of 235–6; Tata Nano car 219; technology in 354, 355f

tsunami 2004 43

Tucker, M. 254

UN Collaborative Initiative on Reducing Emissions from Deforestation and forest Degradation (UN-REDD) 19; 'carbon trading' model of financial incentives 348; in context of political economy of forests 347–8; creating incentives to protect forests 342–3, 349–50; high degree of support for 343, 348; incentives model in context of Indian forests 346–7; possible safeguards to address issues with 348–9; REDD-plus 343, 347–8, 378; removal of 'Cochabamba People's Agreement' from negotiating text 348–9

UN Framework Convention on Climate Change: Article 2 74, 77n, 130, 131, 144, 187, 353; Article 3.1 102, 118, 119, 121, 123–4, 126n, 130–1, 138, 139, 144; Article 4.2 95, 102; Article 4.5 187, 362; Article 4.7 95, 106, 187, 242; Conference of Parties 1 (Berlin Mandate) 102, 107, 108, 118, 180; Conference of Parties 3 102; Conference of Parties 7 (Marrakesh Accords) 103, 108; Conference of Parties 8 103, 108, 259; Conference of Parties 11 103; Conference of Parties 13 see Bali

Action Plan (BAP)Conference of Parties 15 see Copenhagen Accord; Copenhagen SummitConference of Parties 16 see Cancun Agreementscore principles 102; current deadlock between North and South 95–6; defining climate change 69; 'equity' debate 131; India's role and objectives in negotiations 107, 108–9, 172–3, 180–1; Kyoto Protocol to see Kyoto Protocoltimeline of key events 105–6t

UN Framework Convention on Climate Change, creation of 89–97; breakthrough in negotiations at May meeting 1992 94–5; Britain's position 91, 94; call for developing countries to accept a binding mitigation commitment 90–1, 94–5, 96, 107; Canada's position 93; China's position 90, 91, 92, 94, 180, 375; coalition diplomacy 92–3; 'common but differentiated responsibility' 121, 375; EC position 91, 92–3, 93–5, 107; financial and technological support issues 91, 92, 187; France's position 90–1; G-77 91, 92, 93, 94, 180, 375; geopolitics of climate diplomacy 374–5; Germany's position 90–1; impasse in negotiations 93–4; India's 'non-paper' draft framework convention 89–90; India's role and contribution to 89–90, 91, 106–7, 112–13; initial differences between and within groups 89–92; Japan's position 91, 92, 93, 107; Norway's position 91; 'pledge and review' agreement 91, 92–3, 96; Sweden's position 91; US-EC text on commitments of developed countries 94–5; US position 89, 91, 93–5, 107, 119, 121, 375; window of opportunity for multilateralism 375

UN General Assembly 101, 102, 105t, 106, 119, 126n; Article 48 of the Articles on State Responsibility 119

UNEP 120, 177, 298

UNEP/GPA 44, 258, 374

UNEP-IISD 320, 321

UNEP/Risoe 256, 257, 258, 264n

United Kingdom 91, 94, 360f

United States of America: agreement with China at Copenhagen Summit 377; in agreement with EC regarding creation of UNFCCC 94–5, 175; Arctic ice melt and strategic equation between China and 381; cap-and-trade legislation 193–4; corporate responses to climate change 254; electricity prices 290; GHG emissions 84, 86f, 162, 162f, 189, 190, 198, 199, 376; Indian media coverage on emissions in China and 277–8; lack of

400 *Index*

domestic support for technology transfers 191; LEED buildings in 306–7; perspective on India's climate change strategy 192–4; position on creation of UNFCCC 89, 91, 93–5, 107, 119, 121, 375; proposal to replace Kyoto treaty 104, 110–11, 178; references to CBDRRC principle in submissions to FCCC 124–5; rejection of Kyoto Protocol 103, 124, 157, 192, 373, 383n; relationship with India on technology 193, 194; shift in attitudes since Cancun 192–3; strategic partnership with India 114, 175, 191; use of MEF statements at Copenhagen 175

University of East Anglia Climate Research Unit 67

Unnikrishnan, A.S. 34

urbanization and climate change in India 303–16; action on mitigation 310–13; building codes and regulations 310; buildings' energy consumption 306–7; challenges of 303–4; city climate adaption plans 308–9; decentralization and service delivery 312–13; effects of climate change on urbanization 304–5; effects of urbanization on climate change 305–8; existing models as unsustainable 313; home ownership and transport demand 313; increased use of appliances 305–6; need for multi-level institutional co-ordination 309–10; parking issues 315n; public transport use 308t, 311–12; and *Rurbanism* 314; and urban sprawl 312, 313; water consumption 310; water supply energy consumption 308

USAID 323

V&A Programme 319, 322, 323
vanDeever, S. 4
Vanderheiden, S. 148
Vanthournout, H. 260, 261
vector borne diseases 38
Vedwan, N. 57
Vermeer, M. 34
Vienna Convention 1985 102, 123
Vijay Shankar, P.S. 320, 331, 333, 334, 334f
Visaria, L. 304, 305

Wang, Q. 322
wastewater treatment 308, 310, 311

water resource management in India 19, 328–40; changing patterns and impact on agriculture 329, 332; climate change as an opportunity for improved 337–9; conceptual framework for 333–5; debate over impact of climate change on 331–3; Green India Mission xx, 182, 335–6; groundwater assessments 331; 'groundwater irrigation' 330–1, 331f; impact of climate change 328–9; impact of impacts of climate change 332, 337, 338t; investment under NMSH 311; irrigation programmes 330, 330f; National Water Mission 19, 328, 335, 336–7; springs, management of 335, 335f, 336f, 338t; and water consumption 310; water resources 329–31

water security 331, 332, 337, 379–80; in Arab world and Central Asia 383n

water sharing 209, 379, 383n

water supply energy consumption 308

water vapour 31

WBGU (German Advisory Council on Global Change) 41, 42f, 148, 152t, 189

Webber, M. 311

Weiss, E.B. 123

Wild Life (Protection) Act 2005 344

wildlife conservation 213

Williamson, J. 8

wind energy 256–7, 296–7, 354, 379

Wodak, R. 268

Woods, N. 101

World Bank 22, 289, 295, 307

World Bank Indicators 289

World Resources Institute (WRI) 376; calculations on carbon dioxide and methane produced by country 81–2, 84, 87f; Climate Analysis Indicators Tool 221; issues of justice and morality in 82; WRI-CAIT 190, 289

World Trade Organisation 110, 194, 203, 251, 359

World Wide Fund for Nature (WWF) 74, 75, 213, 348

WRI-CAIT 190, 289

Yadav, B. 221, 228n
Yechury, S. 242
Yokozawa, M. 51

Zhang, Z. 190, 278